Torture and Impunity

Critical Human Rights

Series Editors

Steve J. Stern ✿ Scott Straus

Books in the series **Critical Human Rights** emphasize research that opens new ways to think about and understand human rights. The series values in particular empirically grounded and intellectually open research that eschews simplified accounts of human rights events and processes.

Torture, the application of extreme pain and isolation to destroy the integrity of the person, is a classic human rights issue. The method is physically brutal, but the point is often psychological—dread, degradation, and inner shattering. In this book Alfred W. McCoy reveals the conditions that give rise to torture and the mechanisms that permit impunity. He breaks new ground by analyzing psychological torture as such; by tracing the role of U.S. officials, the CIA, and scientists in its development from the 1950s to the present; and by probing its voyeuristic, erotic, and empowering impacts on perpetrators and observers. The result is a unique historical critique of torture and the culture of impunity that allowed such systematic abuse in the U.S. and abroad, from the Cold War through Abu Ghraib and Guantanamo.

Torture and Impunity
The U.S. Doctrine of Coercive Interrogation

Alfred W. McCoy

The University of Wisconsin Press

The University of Wisconsin Press
1930 Monroe Street, 3rd Floor
Madison, Wisconsin 53711-2059
uwpress.wisc.edu

3 Henrietta Street
London WCE 8LU, England
eurospanbookstore.com

Printed in the United States of America

Library of Congress Cataloging-in-Publication Data
McCoy, Alfred W.
Torture and impunity: the U.S. doctrine of coercive interrogation / Alfred W. McCoy.
    p. cm.—(Critical human rights)
    Includes bibliographical references and index.
    ISBN 978-0-299-28854-9 (pbk. : alk. paper)—ISBN 978-0-299-28853-2 (e-book)
    1. Torture—United States—History. 2. Torture—Government policy—United States. 3. Military interrogation—United States—History. 4. Impunity—United States. 5. United States. Central Intelligence Agency. I. Title. II. Series: Critical human rights.
HV8599.U6M34 2012
364.6'7—dc23
2011043916

For MARIA ELENA ANG and the many victims of torture, whose courageous testimony will one day end this inhumane practice.

Contents

Illustrations

Acknowledgments

This work is the culmination of a quarter-century of thinking about torture. Back in 1986, I happened upon this sordid topic, quite by accident, in the aftermath of the Philippine "people power" revolution. A television producer had hired me as a consultant for a miniseries to research the back story behind this world-historic event. My interviews with the colonels whose coup attempt had sparked this mass uprising were intended to be informative, even laudatory. But their remarks soon struck some discordant, even disconcerting notes. Subsequent research into the records of human rights groups revealed that almost all these supposed heroes had served as torturers in the dictatorship they later fought to overthrow.

How and why did these once-loyal servants of the state seek to become its master? This troubling paradox set me off on a fifteen-year search for answers that led to a conclusion stark in its simplicity yet complex in its implications. Torture, particularly the psychological variant practiced in the Philippines, was a mutually transformative experience, simultaneously impairing the victim and empowering the perpetrator.

In conducting this Philippine research, first published in 1999 as a book titled *Closer Than Brothers*, I accrued many debts that have carried forward into this current project. My host in Manila, Dr. Helen Mendoza, was an unfailing source of support, with contacts that opened doors across this vast city. The country's top journalists were well informed and enormously helpful, notably Melinda de Jesus, Marites Dañguilan-Vitug, and Sheila Coronel.

When this book was done, I tried to put this troubling topic behind me and move on to another subject—biography, photography, anything but torture. As it turned out, I may have been done with torture, but the torture issue was not yet done with me. At a conference on human rights violations at Capetown, South Africa, in 2000, our convener Leigh Payne asked me to turn the analytical lens away from the developing world and focus on America, particularly the U.S. government's tolerance of torture by its Cold War allies. So I drafted a paper that would become, in time, the seed for this book.

Since this was a controversial topic, I was nervous about my paper's reception before an audience of human rights experts gathered at historic Robben Island, the prison where Nelson Mandela had been held for eighteen years. When I finished this presentation about the CIA's global propagation of torture techniques during the Cold War, my Wisconsin colleague Steve Stern responded: "You mean to say these dictators in Latin America and elsewhere couldn't even figure out how to torture on their own?" The sharpness of this response from the leading historian of human rights abuse under General Pinochet gave me pause, making me realize both the significance of my argument and the need for its clarification. We are not, I replied, talking about the simple physical abuse that comes naturally to any military regime, but instead a sophisticated psychological doctrine developed by leading cognitive scientists and propagated globally by the world's most powerful covert agency. Two other Wisconsin colleagues present, Kesenija Bilbija and Jo Ellen Fair, joined in that discussion which lies, even now twelve years later, at the core of the inquiry that produced this book.

Yet I held back, reluctant to pursue this project. Any academic book takes a decade and I was unwilling to spend another living with and thinking about this depressing dimension of human society. After all, the Cold War was over and the CIA's role in propagating psychological torture was fast fading into the past.

Then came the terrorist attacks of September 11, 2001. In the months following 9/11, I was troubled to hear politicians and media commentators arguing that torture was necessary, even imperative for our nation's security, seemingly unaware of the lasting damage torture does to any modern society. Three years later, when CBS Television broadcast those famous photos from Abu Ghraib, I could see the telltale signs of the CIA's basic psychological torture techniques in every frame. With knowledge comes responsibility, and I felt compelled to resume my work on this troubling topic—to trace the connections between these recent events and the history I knew all too well from earlier research.

Once launched into this project, I received strong support from an ad hoc human rights coalition that sprang up across the country and around the world. In Boston, the editor of the *New England Journal of Public Policy*, Padraig O'Malley, accepted my first essay on the history of CIA torture research. In Hamburg, Dr. Till Tolkemitt of the publishing house Zweitausendeins solicited a short book manuscript, which his company published in German in

2005. In New York, editor Tom Englehardt commissioned an expanded form of that manuscript for his firm, Henry Holt, which published it under the title, *A Question of Torture*, in 2006.

Usually when an author publishes a book, it is question asked, question answered, move on. But not this time. Instead of providing definitive closure to my work on torture, that book opened me to larger questions. And it gave me a ticket to travel America and the world, gaining insights into a complex issue whose ramifications reached far beyond the borders of the United States. The politics of torture were being played out on a global not national stage. And impunity is a seemingly small process with an extraordinary power to twist societies worldwide into knotty legal and political contradictions. There was still much to learn.

Only weeks after my book's publication, film director Alex Gibney interviewed me for his documentary about torture by U.S. interrogators in Afghanistan, *Taxi to the Darkside*, asking probing questions that pushed beyond the limits of my book. A subsequent interview with director Rory Kennedy for her documentary *Ghosts of Abu Ghraib* was an intense encounter that stretched my thinking further.

As I traveled continuously for the next three years lecturing about torture across the country and around the world, dialogue with audiences and fellow speakers deepened my engagement with this issue. In Manila for a human rights conference hosted by Teresita Quintos-Deles in 2001, I was invited to Malacañan Palace for a dinner conversation with President Gloria Arroyo, who was still reeling from a massive coup attempt by unreconstructed military torturers. These conversations gave me a strong, visceral sense of the high costs of impunity for any society that has tolerated torture.

During a conference at Humbolt University in Berlin, I profited from a dialogue with Manfred Nowak, the UN Special Rapporteur on Torture, who had a unique international perspective on the Bush administration's policies. A second trip to Berlin for a conference sponsored by the Republic Attorneys' Association (RAV), arranged by its director Wolfgang Kaleck, revealed the deep, lasting imprint that human rights abuse leaves on any society. And it introduced me to activist Jennifer Harbury, whose loss of her husband to CIA-sponsored torture in Guatemala made her an eloquent witness. At the Centre for Investigative Journalism in London in 2006, I shared a podium with the Russian reporter Anna Politkovskaya, whose insights about the difficulties of exposing Russian human rights abuse were given added weight when she was gunned down outside her Moscow apartment three months later. Throughout these trips to Berlin, Capetown, London, and Manila, my wife Mary McCoy was present, distilling insights and deepening my understanding.

During travels to Australia, the writer Mark Aarons introduced me to the editor of *The Monthly* magazine, Sally Warhaft, who solicited two articles about David Hicks, the Australian detainee at Guantanamo, requiring my immersion in this illuminating facet of the torture controversy. While researching these essays, Bob Debus, then attorney general for New South Wales, expressed his country's growing disquiet over Canberra's handling of the Hicks case—insights sharpened by conversations with veteran journalist Marian Wilkinson, anthropologist Brian Fegan, radio host Phillip Adams, and documentary film director Curtis Levy.

Weekly travels across America for lectures at campuses from Boston to Seattle allowed ample opportunity for discussion and debate. At the University of California Santa Barbara, symposium conveners Elisabeth Weber and Richard Falk were thoughtful about the legal and humanistic dimensions of America's torture debate. A daylong reflection on the torture issue at Drew University allowed a productive dialogue with Jeremy Varon, a scholar of American political history at the New School. At Michigan State University, anthropologist Beth Drexler convened a dialogue with her students that drew us into a productive exchange about the comparative dynamics of impunity in Indonesia and America. A national teach-in on torture at Seton Hall University, organized by Professor Mark Denbeaux, allowed thought-provoking conversations with a diverse array of specialists—Craig Haney of the University of California Santa Cruz, Walter Pincus of the *Washington Post*, General Stephen Xenakis (ret.), and Leonard Rubenstein of Physicians for Human Rights. A lecture before public health professionals at University of Washington, arranged by Professor Amy Hagopian, allowed me to feel the strong sense of outrage over their government's use of torture felt by this important segment of the nation's caregivers. Several seminars at the University of California at Davis, organized by Almerindo Ojeda of the Center for the Study of Human Rights in the Americas, provided rich insight into the cognitive complexities of the torture experience.

Closer to home in Madison, the editor of *The Progressive* magazine, Matthew Rothschild, commissioned a timely essay on the "ticking bomb scenario" that drew me deeper into this dimension of the nation's torture debate. On several occasions, host Joy Cardin of Wisconsin Public Radio invited me to participate in on-air conversations, asking thoughtful questions in her measured manner. As research into the politics of torture continued, my associate Brett Reilly used his formidable skills to track down elusive sources.

When the time came to capture all this experience between two covers, my editor at the University of Wisconsin Press, Dr. Gwen Walker, encouraged the project. Once I began delivering chapters in the summer of 2011, she not only read the text with an unerring editorial eye, but she also challenged assumptions and interpretations, forcing me to sharpen my analysis at several key points. When the work was in press, Adam Mehring supervised the book's production with his usual care and tolerated my many revisions. Bringing this decade-long voyage of discovery full circle, Steve Stern, who had challenged my argument so sharply at Capetown back in 2000, read the book manuscript and graciously accepted it for his series on human rights at the University of Wisconsin Press. Though I am most grateful for all this help, I remain solely responsible for any errors or omissions.

Madison, Wisconsin
April 2012

Abbreviations

AMRSP	Association of Major Religious Superiors in the Philippines
APA	American Psychological Association
ARVN	Army of the Republic of Vietnam
BSCT	Behavioral Science Consultation Team (US)
CAT	Convention against Torture (UN)
CI	Special Group-Counter-Insurgency (US)
CIA	Central Intelligence Agency (US)
CICV	Combined Intelligence Center Vietnam (US)
CIO	Central Intelligence Organization (South Vietnam)
CORDS	Civil Operations and Rural Development Support (US program in South Vietnam)
CSRT	Combatant Status Review Tribunal (US)
CSU	Constabulary Security Unit (Philippines)
CT	Counter Terror (US program in South Vietnam)
CTC	Counterterrorism Center (CIA)
DIOCC	District Intelligence and Operations Coordination Center (South Vietnam)
DDEL	Dwight D. Eisenhower Library (US)
DRB	Defense Research Board (Canada)
EDSA	Epifanio de los Santos Avenue (Manila, Philippines)
HEF	Human Ecology Fund (US)
HRE	Human Resources Exploitation (US)
ICEX	Infrastructure Intelligence Coordination and Exploitation (US program in South Vietnam)
ICRC	International Committee of the Red Cross
IPA	International Police Academy (U.S. AID)
ISAFP	Intelligence Service, Armed Forces of the Philippines

JSOC	Joint Special Operations Command (US)
MAP	Military Assistance Program (US Army)
Metrocom	Metropolitan Command (Philippines Constabulary)
MI	Military Intelligence (US)
MISG	Military Intelligence and Security Group (Philippines)
MP	Military Police (US)
NAFP	New Armed Forces of the Philippines
NARA	National Archives and Research Administration (US)
NATO	North Atlantic Treaty Organization
NAWASA	National Water and Sewage Authority (Philippines)
NDS	National Directorate of Security (Afghanistan)
9/11	September 11, 2001, terrorist attacks on the United States
NPA	New People's Army (Philippines)
NSA	National Security Archive (US)
NSC	National Security Council (US)
NSF	National Science Foundation (US)
NUC	National Unification Commission (Philippines)
OMS	Office of Medical Services (CIA)
ONR	Office of Naval Research (US)
OPS	Office of Public Safety (U.S. AID)
PACC	Presidential Anti-Crime Commission (Philippines)
PIC	Provincial Interrogation Center (South Vietnam)
PMA	Philippine Military Academy
PRU	Provincial Reconnaissance Unit (US program in South Vietnam)
PSB	Psychological Strategy Board (US)
QC	Queen's Counsel (Australia)
RAM	Reform the Armed Forces Movement (Philippines)
SAP	Special Action Program (US)
SELDA	Samahan ng mga Ex-Detainee Laban sa Detensyon at para sa Amnestia (Philippines)
SERE	Survival, Evasion, Resistance, Escape (US)
SHAPE	Supreme Headquarters, Allied Powers Europe
TSD	Technical Services Division (CIA)
UCMJ	Uniform Code of Military Justice (US)
UN	United Nations
U.S. AID	U.S. Agency for International Development
VC	Viet Cong (Vietnam)
VCI	Viet Cong Infrastructure (Vietnam)

Torture and Impunity

Introduction

Torture occurs in small, secret places and yet has profound global implications. Every act of torture plays out on a narrow stage—not a battlefield with opposing armies arrayed before countless witnesses but a sequestered chamber, closed to the eyes of the world, where one individual accosts another in ways that are intrusively, destructively intimate. As rumors or reports of such transgressions inevitably leak and spread, these private acts become profoundly political. For nearly three centuries, peoples worldwide have reacted in fear and anger as states and empires used their enormous power to inflict unimaginable pain upon hapless individuals. Since the dawn of the Enlightenment in the eighteenth century, social reformers have worked to ban this ancient punishment, making torture synonymous with tyranny.

After two centuries of such struggle, the United Nations General Assembly voted unanimously in 1948 to adopt the Universal Declaration of Human Rights, which stated, unequivocally, in Article 3: "No one shall be subjected to torture or to cruel, inhuman or degrading treatment or punishment." A year later, the third Geneva Convention stated explicitly in Article 17: "No physical or mental torture, nor any other form of coercion, may be inflicted on prisoners of war to secure from them information of any kind whatever. Prisoners of war who refuse to answer may not be threatened, insulted, or exposed to unpleasant or disadvantageous treatment of any kind."

Over the next half century, governments around the globe enacted national, regional, and international agreements that banned torture in all its means and methods. Most important, in 1984 the UN approved the Convention against Torture by a unanimous vote that represented an absolute repudiation of such inhumanity. Four years later, President Ronald Reagan sent that convention to Congress, advising that its ratification "will clearly express United States opposition to torture, an abhorrent practice unfortunately still prevalent in the world today."[1] When Congress finally approved this UN Convention in 1994, the United States joined a hundred other nations in a comprehensive ban. By the dawn of the twenty-first century, humanity had agreed that torture was an illegal, immoral practice that stigmatized any ruler or regime that stooped to such barbarism.

Throughout the Cold War and the decade that followed, the United States was an outspoken defender of human rights. Evidence would occasionally come to light suggesting that the world's preeminent power might be guilty of tolerating torture by its allies. But it was only in America's response to the terrorist attacks of September 2001 that the nation's public image would really be tested, at home and abroad. In the aftermath of 9/11, the Bush administration defied international moral and legal standards by adopting torture as its prime weapon in the War on Terror and authorizing the Central Intelligence Agency (CIA) to use harsh psychological methods. In the weeks right after 9/11, senior officials made public statements that hinted at these practices with oblique metaphors about "gloves coming off" and working the "dark side." But there were no questions and no elaboration. Three years later, however, these secret orders for torture were exposed to public view when photographs of abuse leaked from Abu Ghraib prison in Iraq, showing prisoners stripped naked, sexually humiliated, blindfolded, and painfully shackled.

At first, the White House denied any responsibility, attributing these acts to a few "bad apples" among the military police. But, as investigators began tracing responsibility to the highest levels in Washington, the Bush administration became increasingly bold in its embrace of tortures that it euphemized as "enhanced interrogation." Asked if he had authorized a medieval form of torture called waterboarding, former president George W. Bush told the London *Times* in November 2010: "Damn right! We capture the guy, the chief operating officer of al-Qaida, who kills 3,000 people. We felt he had the information about another attack. . . . I believe that decision saved lives."[2] His former vice president, Dick Cheney, proclaimed himself "a staunch proponent of our enhanced interrogation program," calling it, in May 2009, "legal, essential, justified, successful, and the right thing to do."[3]

With the election of President Barack Obama, the problem of torture did not, as many had hoped, disappear, wiped away by new executive orders. Instead, it entered a particularly sordid phase called "impunity." Simply put, impunity is the failure to punish a wrongful act. But reaching that seemingly simple end in a nation of laws requires an enormously complex political process. In the United States, multiple actors have contributed to this failure by ignoring or facilitating torture: politicians and lawyers, scientists and scholars, media and the public. Once a state, such as the United States, willfully transgresses its own laws and principles to torture, it twists itself into a knot of contradictions from which there is no easy end or exit. As the Obama administration and its successors struggle over the disposition of detainees at Guantanamo, as revelations about tolerance of torture in Iraq mount, and as new exposés of detainee abuse emerge from Afghanistan and other covert battlegrounds, torture will remain one of the most vexing issues at the intersection of U.S. public debate and scholarly discussion.

For a half century, through evasion, euphemism, and denial, the American public and their academy failed to address the torture issue with an appropriate analytical engagement, producing a thin discourse. Then, for three years after the 9/11 attacks, prominent academics and media pundits popularized the idea that torture was a necessary and effective weapon in the War on Terror. After the Abu Ghraib scandal broke in mid-2004, there was a brief burst of more critical coverage in books, articles, and documentary films, much of it exploring the same rudimentary question: Who was responsible for the abuse we saw in those photos? More in-depth reportage focused on the question of efficacy, asking whether or not torture works and often answering ambiguously. Though this discussion was a necessary first step, its narrow focus ignored the deeper damage that torture does to a society, empowering perpetrators, coarsening the national culture, compromising the rule of law, and damaging its international legitimacy.

Whatever its analytical merits, this intense public debate over torture has, since 2004, produced a wealth of new documentation that now affords a closer analysis. During the decades that human rights groups like Amnesty International have struggled to ban the practice, medical understanding of torture's lasting impact upon its victims has grown significantly, particularly through studies into the lasting pain of psychological torture.[4] Moreover, the steady release of information about Bush's interrogation policy allows an inside look at decision making in his administration. In the years since the CBS television network broadcast those notorious Abu Ghraib photos back in 2004, fast-breaking events and ongoing revelations have superseded most published sources, including my own 2006 book on this topic. Yet, in the months that followed Obama's inauguration in 2009, critics became less vocal and discussion slowly faded. In this widening gap between mounting information and ill-informed public perception, between international opinion and U.S. policy, there is a vast and growing void that this book hopes to fill.

To explore these many complex issues, the chapters that follow are both independent and intertwined. As an historian, I find that examining events in chronological order reveals an underlying logic within the processes of change far beyond a mere succession of dates, intimating and imitating the force of time driving human developments. Thus, there is a chronological thread throughout the volume, moving from the CIA's experimentation with psychological torture during the 1950s, through its propagation of these techniques worldwide during the Cold War, then revival and normalization of the practice for the War on Terror under President Bush, and, finally, impunity for past perpetrators under President Obama. The first chapter provides a succinct overview of this progression, albeit from the perspective of the CIA's pursuit of psychological torture since the start of the Cold War. Each of the subsequent chapters offers a self-contained argument illuminating different facets in the history of torture as practiced by the U.S. and its allies. As they unfold sequentially, however, these chapters also tell a larger story, one that leads back at each successive stage, sometimes predictably, sometimes surprisingly, to renewed violations of civil liberties and human rights.

By reviewing the CIA's psychological interrogation techniques over the past sixty years, the opening chapter introduces the reader to Washington's tacit tolerance of torture, from early, secret experimentation under President Eisenhower through impunity under Obama. Though its effects are often sanitized in the language of science or the euphemisms of politics, interrogation aimed at manipulating the minds of its subjects can cause intense suffering and long-term damage. As documented by treatment specialists over the past forty years, the lasting effects of psychological torture include loss of volition, recurring depression, persistent fear or anxieties, and a wide array of physical ailments—crippling headaches, exhaustion, sleeplessness.

Unlike most physical forms of torture, however, psychological techniques leave no visible scars, what human rights lawyers call physical sequelae. As an elusive phenomenon, mental abuse resists prosecution and lends itself well to the politics of impunity. Psychological torture thus emerged as a persistent, albeit covert adjunct to U.S. foreign policy during Washington's rise to global power. Offering an overview of the processes that have led to this outcome, the first chapter traces a narrative arc that begins with the origins of a contradictory U.S. human rights policy during the Cold War and then follows this tangled history through the administrations of President George W. Bush, when Washington finally resolved this contradiction by the de facto legalization of torture, to President Barack Obama, who placed a bipartisan imprimatur on this policy through impunity.

Despite ratification of the UN's Universal Declaration in 1948 and the Geneva Conventions of 1949 with their explicit renunciations of torture, Washington soon mobilized its scientists for secret research to develop ingenious new torture techniques in contravention of those same international conventions. From 1950 to 1962, the CIA led a secret research effort, detailed in chapter 2, to crack the code of human consciousness, a veritable Manhattan Project of the mind, with costs that peaked at a billion dollars a year. Reacting to news of Soviet mind-control experiments, Washington's secret research moved through two distinct phases. First, CIA in-house exploration of exotic methods (drugs, hypnosis, electroshock) failed in their aim of controlling the subject or extracting coherent information. But somewhat later, more mundane behavioral methods were outsourced to leading cognitive scientists who succeeded in identifying innovative techniques foundational for the agency's emerging psychological paradigm. Through case studies of two eminent biomedical researchers—Dr. Donald O. Hebb (a titan of twentieth-century cognitive science) and Dr. Henry K. Beecher (the father of modern medical ethics)—this chapter explores the corrosive influence of this secret research upon American science.

After a decade of such mind-control research, in 1963 the CIA codified its findings in a secret instructional handbook, the "KUBARK Counterintelligence Interrogation" manual. Originally designed for interrogation of a few suspected Soviet spies, KUBARK's doctrine involved a mix of sensory deprivation drawn from Hebb's research and self-inflicted pain through stress positions adapted from KGB interrogation by other CIA-funded cognitive scientists. Leaving few visible marks on their victims, KUBARK's mental methods easily eluded detection and proved especially useful in secret counterguerrilla operations that could not win broad support from the American public.

Over the next thirty years, the CIA propagated these torture techniques among anticommunist allies across Asia and Latin America. Under its Phoenix program in South Vietnam, detailed in chapter 3, these methods soon metastasized into a lethal brutality, with more than forty prisons, thousands of mercenaries, computerized data banks, countless torture-interrogations, and forty-one thousand extrajudicial executions. As the Cold War shifted to Central America, the CIA taught Honduran military interrogators that they should, in the words of a 1983 training manual, "manipulate the subject's environment to create . . . intolerable situations to disrupt patterns of time, space, and sensory perception"—in short, a total assault on the sensory pathways to the existential platform of human identity. Although the Phoenix program failed in its objective of neutralizing the Viet Cong's clandestine infrastructure, the use of similar methods in Central America was encoded in CIA institutional memory and reemerged during the Iraq war nearly twenty years later, producing intriguing parallels between these conflicts.

Between the Phoenix program in South Vietnam during the 1960s and the CIA's Latin American adventures of the 1980s, another close Cold War ally, the Philippines, elaborated upon the agency's methods to develop an array of tortures, both psychological and physical. While the United States tried to conceal the tortures used against its enemies, the Philippine state deployed such abuse openly and emphatically against its own citizens. During the fourteen years of President Ferdinand Marcos's dictatorship, 1972–1986, his elite antisubversion squads expanded the agency's psychological paradigm into a Grand Guignol of sexualized torture and extrajudicial killings that made the country a virtual proscenium of terror. Through this case study of global propagation, chapter 4 explores the long-term damage to democracy when a nation's security forces engage in systematic torture.

Through interviews with both Filipino interrogators and their victims, this chapter also recreates the torture moment, revealing it as a transactional experience that simultaneously destroys the victim and empowers the perpetrator. Following a decade in the "safe houses" of the Marcos regime, the Filipino perpetrators were transformed from uniformed servants of the state into Nietzschean supermen who would be its master. After a half-dozen abortive coup attempts between 1986 and 1989, these military rebels went underground for three years of terror before emerging to win impunity for crimes ranging from torture to rebellion. Their superman self-image made these rebel colonels woefully incompetent as coup commanders. But this same inflated egotism, freed from regret or remorse, proved brilliantly effective in the arena of mass media and electoral politics, where they eventually won immunity from prosecution. These findings about the ways torture emboldened its Filipino perpetrators provide important insights for this book's final chapter about the United States, particularly the way that similarly empowered Republican torture advocates would extract impunity from a Democratic administration committed to human rights reform.

Building upon these insights from study of the CIA's methods in Central America, South Vietnam, and the Philippines, chapter 5 returns to the United States, exploring the enticing appeal of psychological torture for perpetrators, the powerful who command them, and the public that sustains and supports both. Starting from Susan Sontag's analysis of the Abu Ghraib photos as mirror of America's pornographic subculture, this chapter probes an unsettling psychological terrain that ranges from simulated torture demonstrations inside the White House to lurid practices inside CIA prisons.

In the aftermath of 9/11, Americans at all levels seemed enthralled by the power of the torturer. In top-secret CIA "black sites" from Thailand to Poland opened after 9/11, interrogators twisted the agency's psychological paradigm into a paroxysm of mental cruelty, inventing harsh techniques and waterboarding one detainee 183 times in a single month. While the White

House ordered torture and national security agencies inflicted abuse on thousands of detainees from Guantanamo to Baghdad to Kabul, ordinary U.S. citizens consumed countless torture simulations through film, television, and video games. In the public arena, screens large and small across America were filled with dramatizations portraying both the allure and the efficacy of torture. Significantly, after *Taxi to the Dark Side* won the Oscar for Best Documentary Feature in 2008 for its sobering depiction of torture inside a U.S. prison in Afghanistan, the Discovery Channel refused to air this measured description of detainee treatment, claiming its content was too disturbing.[5] Fictional, fetishized portrayals of torture were acceptable on both broadcast and cable television. But an informed depiction of torture's harsh reality was banned from at least one major cable network. Through the invisible tendrils that tie mass media to their government, the nation's news and entertainment industries thus normalized torture in the aftermath of 9/11, effectively indoctrinating Americans into a belief in the necessity, efficacy, and enticement of torture.

Looking back on this extraordinary chapter in America's political history, we might ask a counterfactual question: How much greater might the opposition of the American people to abuse have been if their vast, sophisticated media had confronted them with the realization that their own government was guilty of torture? Brought home by the release of the photos from Abu Ghraib prison, this revelation of a particularly degrading form of torture, perpetrated by Americans wearing their country's uniform, seemed for a time to threaten the nation's self-image as what the president called, in the wake of the 9/11 attacks, the world's "brightest beacon of freedom and opportunity." But the victims of this and other types of torture were doubly distanced from ordinary Americans: first by their status as citizens of other nations, and second through their rapid fictionalization in film and television. Indeed, the very sophistication of twenty-first-century media seemed to encourage identification not with the victim but with the perpetrator.

Shifting from representation to reality, chapter 6 explores Bush's policies of endless incarceration and enhanced interrogation through the legal biography of a single Guantanamo detainee, the Australian David Hicks, and his defense attorney, Major Michael Mori of the U.S. Marines. When the United States invaded Afghanistan in 2001, Hicks was guarding a Taliban tank in a parking lot. Captured and sold by an Afghan warlord, he was tortured by American soldiers before being transferred to Guantanamo, where he endured months of solitary confinement aimed at forcing him to confess to terrorist activities. As the first "unlawful combatant" put on trial before the controversial military commissions, Hicks is a figure of exceptional significance who, by his refusal to capitulate after 244 days of sensory deprivation, exposed the injustice

engrained in this new system of presidential justice. Through his tireless advocacy for his client, Major Mori exemplifies the ethics and independence of the
Judge Advocate General corps, whose officers fought, often at the cost of their
careers, the deep flaws within Bush's military commissions.

In the first months following 9/11, the Australian people agreed with their
conservative prime minister that Hicks was an outcast, unworthy of their
concern or protection. But, after he suffered five years of incarceration and
inconclusive litigation, a rising chorus of protest from the Australian public
forced Prime Minister John Howard to press Vice President Cheney for Hicks's
repatriation. Suddenly, a possible prison term of twenty years was cut to nine
months, and Hicks was homeward bound on an executive jet for a few months'
imprisonment in Adelaide, South Australia. By that time, however, the scandal
of his ill treatment had wounded Howard's government, until then one of the
longest serving in Australian history. Through a mix of economic and moral
issues, the prime minister suffered a stunning electoral defeat in late 2007.
Intensive media coverage and mass protests over his harsh treatment at Guantanamo made Hicks a genuine cause célèbre in his native Australia. But, absent
any coverage in the U.S. media, Americans remained blindingly ignorant of
Guantanamo's negative portrayal in the international press and the serious
damage it was doing to their country's reputation overseas.

Viewed in retrospect, this trial illustrates the way that Guantanamo has
become a latter-day Devil's Island, a palpable symbol of America's defiance
of international law that eroded the legitimacy of its global leadership, even
among the closest of allies. Despite the transparent weaknesses of this ad hoc
judicial system erected under Bush, the military commission survived and was
revived under Obama, becoming a problematic legacy of the War on Terror.

To conclude this volume's analysis of torture in America, chapter 7 explores
the politics of impunity, placing this recent process after Abu Ghraib in the
context of a half-dozen U.S. torture controversies reaching back over the span
of thirty years. From 1970 to 1997, recurring torture exposés by Congress and
the press failed to arouse sufficient public outrage or political pressure for major reforms. Even so, as the Cold War drew to a close, Washington felt the international stigma from its failure to ratify the UN Convention against Torture
and, under President Clinton in 1994, moved toward nominal compliance.

Through U.S. contingencies or "reservations" attached to that ratification,
the Clinton administration effectively split the UN Convention's ban on both
physical and psychological torture, affirming the rejection of physical abuse but
evading the prohibition of psychological methods. Building upon these reservations, which were soon codified in U.S. federal law, the Bush administration
authorized "enhanced" techniques after 9/11 that the International Red Cross

would later deem to be "torture." By parsing these federal codes in a series of lengthy memos, political appointees inside the Bush Justice Department not only authorized psychological abuse by CIA interrogators but also laid the legal foundations for a later impunity. And, just as Republicans were losing their majority control over Congress in 2006, this exculpation was ratified with the passage of the Military Commissions Act by bipartisan majorities in both the House and Senate. Assisting this deft bit of legal legerdemain, the Bush lawyers played upon the elusive character of psychological torture, which leaves no physical sequelae, making it resistant to any attempt at prosecution or prohibition.

Although President Obama announced dramatic reforms to U.S. interrogation policy on his second day in office, the accumulated weight of this exculpatory legislation, compounded by media thunder on the Republican right, pressed his administration toward compromise. At this intersection of law and politics, the United States moved, during Obama's first two years, through the three basic tactics that perpetrators have used to win impunity in societies worldwide. First, blame the supposed "bad apples." Second, invoke national security as justification for the abuse. Finally, appeal to national unity as a reason to forget this troubled past. But the Obama administration also experienced an uncommon fourth tactic found most visibly in Indonesia, Russia, and America—a political counterattack by perpetrators and their protectors who excoriate human rights reformers for weakening the nation's security by their criticism of state agencies.[6]

Battered by these attacks from the right, which were compounded by an indifferent commitment to its own principles, the Obama administration retreated from its original defense of human rights—permitting the CIA to practice rendition, continuing the controversial military commissions, and allowing Special Operations Command to operate secret prisons in Afghanistan. This process of impunity pushed Washington back toward the contradictory torture policy that it had adopted during the Cold War: that is, publicly advocating human rights while covertly outsourcing torture to allied governments.

In sum, there is a cumulative logic, revolving about a tension between concealment and exposure, that has been driving events at each stage in the history of U.S. human rights policy from the Cold War to the present, deepening impunity with each succeeding decade. Initially, impunity thrived mainly on secrecy. Classified research conducted in the 1950s led to lessons applied in covert operations overseas—two key factors that preserved a secrecy conducive to impunity. Another factor was the type of torture. Loath to engage in physical abuse that contradicted its advocacy of human rights, the United States developed forms of psychological coercion that permitted it to deny, perhaps even to itself, that it was involved in torture. Whether intentionally or just coincidentally, the CIA's psychological methods promoted impunity by the absence of contusions or other physical sequelae that would aid investigation and prosecution.

After 9/11, with its dramatic attacks on the Pentagon and the Twin Towers, America's public commitment to human rights was put to the test and failed. Building on the legal foundations laid by its more liberal predecessor, the conservative Bush administration parsed the black-letter texts of U.S. anti-torture laws, using their excessively narrow definition of psychological harm to provide the CIA and military intelligence with orders for harsh interrogation that soon crossed the line into torture. Congress, led by Republican majorities, failed to check this process and, despite some dissent, generally endorsed it. In the atmosphere of fear that prevailed after 9/11, prominent pundits and academics gained a media megaphone to call for torture of terror suspects, drowning out the few dissident voices.

In the final analysis, however, the American public was not sufficiently opposed to "enhanced interrogation" to insist on stopping it. During these same years after 9/11, the U.S. mass media regularly produced and the public eagerly consumed countless representations of torture whose overall effect was to normalize abusive practices that, pre-9/11, Americans might have forcefully disavowed. Thus, exposure alone has not done away with torture. The release of the photos from Abu Ghraib produced a shock to the American psyche, creating a short-lived potential to reverse the processes of impunity that had been decades in the making. But the American self-image soon recovered, and the public pressure for reform faded. Already accustomed to their leaders' argument that torture, or "enhanced interrogation," was necessary for national security, Americans, by now inured to abuse through its glamorized media representations, tried to move on as if nothing had happened. But something had. America's position in the world was changing. Amidst a decade of financial profligacy and military misadventure that spilled the nation's strength into desert sands, those photos of torture from Abu Ghraib and reports of abuse at Guantanamo did irreparable damage to America's moral authority as world leader.

Placing this history in a comparative perspective raises some disconcerting historical parallels. In the long wind-down of their global empires, both Britain and France used torture to contain anticolonial resistance, producing scandals that delegitimated their imperial rule. In Algeria from 1954 to 1962, the French resorted to systematic torture against nationalist guerrillas and thereby "normalized terror to forestall the collapse of the empire in an age of decolonization," exposing with "dazzling clarity the narcissistic and ideological cultural core of colonial rule."[7] Indeed, the French counterinsurgency that secured the city of Algiers in 1957 entailed systematic torture of thousands and more than three thousand summary executions, dumping the victims' bodies in the desert.[8] "You might say that the battle of Algiers was won through the use of torture," observed the British historian Sir Alistair Horne, "but that the war, the Algerian war, was lost."[9] Similarly, in its long imperial recessional, Great Britain also used torture—sporadically in Malaya, systematically in Aden and Kenya, and scandalously in Northern Ireland—finding in each case that exposé weakened the moral legitimacy of its cause.

If torture is the last gasp of a dying empire, not simply consequence but indeed cause of imperial retreat, then the United States may well be suffering a similar experience. By focusing its full might to break a hapless individual through torture, an empire, whether French or American, reveals the gross power imbalance otherwise concealed within daily exercise of dominion, turning once-compliant subjects into bitter opponents. Looking back on the occupation of Iraq a half century hence, future historians may well find that the Abu Ghraib scandal was emblematic, as both cause and consequence, of the decline of U.S. global power. From the perspective of informed opinion in Berlin, Brasilia, Cairo, Mumbai, Tokyo, and Beijing, America could not and cannot simultaneously claim moral leadership of the international community and the sovereign prerogative to torture in defiance of international law.

We cannot justify any state's descent into torture on grounds that terrorists are an exceptional threat that requires extralegal measures. The rules for a national government and its outlaws must be different. The state, in all its majesty, must uphold the law and the highest standards of the human community. The state, particularly one that aspires to world leadership, is not only an enforcer; it is an exemplar.

Faced with Washington's ingrained resistance to reform, history itself, the recording of a troubled past, can serve as an antidote to the oblivion that is the prime requisite of impunity. In this unequal struggle between state security's deep institutional memory and the public's media-induced amnesia, history has proven, by default, an effective medium for reconstructing the past and recovering its patterns. Like Penelope unraveling her weaving by night to delay the day of reckoning, state security seeks to tear at the threads of collective memory, making each exposé seem isolated, anecdotal, and, ultimately, insignificant. But, by weaving these threads together into the tapestry of collective conscious, history allows the public to discover a larger design, seeing torture as an instrument of state power, impunity as its necessary adjunct, and, in rare circumstances, the past as a path to prevention.

Yet, this history is by no means uncontested. Indeed, the past, as we will see in the chapters that follow, has many uses. For lawyers in service to the powerful, history provides pretext and precedent for extralegal action. In the end, when these deeds are done and victims' screams no longer echo, the powerful can reconfigure this history to serve as exculpation and even justification. For critics in the human rights community, by contrast, recovery of this past is essential for both prosecution and prevention of these crimes. And, for historians such as this writer, history's most elemental tool, chronology, provides a trail through clandestine bureaucracies cloaked in layers of secrecy—akin to the thread that guided Theseus through the Minotaur's labyrinth to slay the monster and liberate his victims.

Once the shock of revelation has faded, history, like film or television, can also serve to numb and normalize extralegal state action among the citizens of a nation. But, in an age of globalization, such revelations ramify uncontrollably, informing formal complaints before international bodies and emboldening other states to exercise their universal jurisdiction for crimes against humanity, thereby constraining the usual processes of impunity that once operated largely within national boundaries.

In an era of declining U.S. power, Americans no longer enjoy the political options of indifference and impunity. Under the doctrine of universal jurisdiction, European courts and international tribunals regularly prosecute foreign violators whose homelands have failed in their legal obligation to punish crimes against humanity, whether genocide or torture. Already, national leaders from Chile, Yugoslavia, and Liberia have been arrested for such crimes. In 2009, an Italian court convicted two dozen CIA agents in absentia for the kidnapping and rendition of an Egyptian national in Milan. In 2010, George Bush was forced to cancel a trip to Switzerland to avoid possible arrest on charges of torture. In these same years, the United States has used its diplomatic leverage to block similar indictments against Bush and his senior officials in Germany and Spain. But the day may yet come when the U.S. failure to investigate torture charges fully will allow a foreign court to indict a senior American official for crimes against humanity.

Apart from the still distant threat of international sanction, the United States has good reason to investigate and reform on its own. Over the past forty years, there have been a half-dozen major scandals over torture that produced dozens of congressional and executive investigations, usually yielding very modest reforms. In July 2011, while releasing an unusually detailed, hard-hitting report on crimes of torture committed by Bush-era officials, Human Rights Watch recommended: "An independent, nonpartisan commission, along the lines of the 9/11 Commission should be established to examine the actions of the executive branch, the CIA, the military, and Congress, with regard to Bush administration policies and practices that led to detainee abuse."[10]

Unless such a formal inquiry is convened to investigate this history of coercive interrogation and begin to break the cycle of secrecy, exposé, and impunity, we are likely in a few years to find ourselves once again facing another major torture scandal arising from some newly discovered dungeon in Asia, Africa, or the Middle East. When that happens, the world will not have forgotten those photos from Abu Ghraib. The damage to this country's international standing will likely be nothing short of devastating.

1

The CIA's Pursuit of
Psychological Torture

On April 28, 2004, American viewers were stunned when the CBS Television network broadcast those troubling photographs from Iraq's Abu Ghraib prison, showing hooded Iraqis stripped naked and American soldiers standing by, smiling. As the scandal grabbed headlines around the globe, U.S. Defense Secretary Donald Rumsfeld insisted that the abuses were "perpetrated by a small number of U.S. military," whom the conservative *New York Times* columnist William Safire branded "creeps."[1]

The iconic photo of a hooded Iraqi standing on a box with arms extended showed not just the sadism of a few "creeps" but also the two key trademarks of the coercive psychological interrogation developed by the Central Intelligence Agency (CIA). The hood was for sensory deprivation. The arms were extended for self-inflicted pain. Indeed, the same two techniques recur in most of the 1,600 still-classified photos that the U.S. Army's Criminal Investigation Command collected from the Abu Ghraib crime scene. While these methods leave no permanent marks on the body, they cause serious, lasting harm to the mind and emotions. They are, in short, forms of psychological torture.

Nor were these methods a recent innovation. Tracking the trail of these distinctive tortures through declassified documents, we find an extraordinary institutional continuity, from the Cold War past to counterterror present. From 1951 to 1962, the CIA led a secret effort to unlock the mysteries of the human mind, searching for methods that would make spies reveal their secrets, turn enemy agents into double agents, and persuade millions through a subtle psychological warfare. With costs that peaked at a billion dollars a year, this psywar project developed, as its most lasting legacy, a distinctive method of psychological torture.[2] For the next thirty years, the CIA disseminated these techniques among allied security agencies worldwide. After a decade-long hiatus following the collapse of the Soviet Union in 1991, Washington revived the agency's harsh methods for its war on Islamic terrorists, refining the psychological paradigm to exploit both cultural sensitivities and personal phobias. Over the past sixty years, the CIA's pursuit of psychological torture has passed through four basic phases—experimentation, propagation, perfection, and, most recently, impunity. Thus, this Cold War past is both prologue and precedent for Washington's recourse to torture in the Global War on Terror.

Through this long skein of historical continuity, there is one noteworthy element of discontinuity in U.S. torture policy. The CIA developed techniques, trained torturers, and exploited the intelligence throughout the Cold War. But, with a few transitory exceptions, the agency left the dirty work of actually running prisons and conducting interrogations to allied agencies in Asia, Latin America, and the Middle East. After the terrorist attacks of September 2001, however, the CIA created its own global gulag of so-called black sites, while U.S. military intelligence conducted interrogations at dozens of prisons in Afghanistan, Iraq, and Guantanamo Bay. Though a seemingly small distinction at an ethical level, this change would have profound implications, bringing the torture issue into U.S. domestic politics, entangling Washington in the labyrinthine process of impunity, and damaging America's international standing.

Experimentation

At the start of the Cold War in the late 1940s, communist states in Eastern Europe staged show trials that shocked the West with automaton-like confessions by Protestant pastors and a Catholic prelate.[3] This concern that the Soviets had somehow learned to manipulate human consciousness was one factor in Washington's decision to launch a massive, often misdirected mind-control effort that reflected the era's rudimentary knowledge of cognitive science.

Inside the CIA, moreover, covert operatives working in Germany like Richard Helms "realized that they were being defrauded by double agents" and needed some means to ferret out such betrayals. Consequently, as early as 1949 a team from the agency's Office of Security "experimented with drugs and hypnosis under a project called BLUEBIRD" whose aims were almost entirely defensive.[4] According to a later CIA memo for Senate investigators, this project began with the objective of "discovering means of conditioning personnel to prevent unauthorized extraction of information" and "establishing defensive means for preventing hostile control of Agency personnel." But the project soon found, through interrogations done overseas, that mind control had broader potential and the CIA added another goal: "the evaluation of offensive uses of unconventional interrogation techniques, including hypnosis and drugs."[5]

By 1951, the agency had shifted the aims of its top-secret program, renamed Project Artichoke, away from simply studying enemy techniques to creating its own capacity for the "development of any method by which we can get information from a person against his will and without his knowledge."[6] In April of that year, Allen Dulles, then CIA deputy director for covert operations, met with military intelligence chiefs to seek their assistance in launching Project Artichoke. Within weeks, the agency had acquired secret prisons in the Canal Zone, West Germany, and Japan, and was dispatching Artichoke teams overseas for interrogations with drugs, hypnosis, "psychological harassment," and "special interrogation techniques." The aim of all this activity was, according to an April 1952 agency review, to discover a method so powerful that "an individual under its influence will find it difficult to maintain a fabrication under questioning."[7]

Announcing his agency's battle against communist "brain warfare," CIA director Allen Dulles told Princeton University alumni in 1953 that the Soviet Union was using powerful combinations of drugs and electroshock for "the perversion of the minds of selected individuals who are subjected to such treatment [so] that they are deprived of the ability to state their own thoughts."[8] In launching an expanded mind-control effort dubbed MKUltra in April 1954, Richard Helms wrote his CIA director that this program would test chemicals that "could potentially aid in discrediting individuals, eliciting information, and implanting suggestions and other forms of mental control."[9]

Decades later in 1977, the *New York Times* conducted a major investigation into this "secret, 25-year, $25 million effort by the Central Intelligence Agency to learn how to control the human mind." The agency "was able to assemble an extensive network of non-government scientists" for experiments the agency's inspector general "considered to be professionally unethical and in some instances border on the illegal."[10] In this mobilization, the CIA employed a combination of financial incentives and collegial manipulation by a few leading researchers to effect a subtle redirection of the nascent cognitive science community.

This alliance between the intelligence and science would prove seminal. Through a seemingly erratic yet systematic process, the CIA and its contract researchers produced a distinctively American approach to psychological torture grounded in a scientific understanding of the sensory pathways to human consciousness. In centuries past, even the most brutal physical tortures had an inadvertent psychological component. The Inquisition's interrogations with scalding irons and painful *stappado* also played upon spiritual fears of eternal damnation. Medieval European cities confined victims in stocks or pillory that combined physical immobility with public humiliation. Waterboarding, though scientifically refined by CIA scientists after 9/11, dates back to the sixteenth century and was described in graphic detail in a 1541 French judicial handbook. Absolutist regimes practiced mock executions, notably when czarist police placed Fyodor Dostoevsky and his group of liberal reformers before a firing squad before sentencing them to years of imprisonment. After the Russian Revolution, communist regimes, as discussed in chapter 2, combined physical and mental methods to break prisoners psychologically, forcing them to make false confessions.

But these past approaches seem crude when compared to the CIA's scientific form of psychological torture. Through its collaboration with leading behavioral scientists, the agency developed a doctrine that was explicitly psychological and scientific—grounded in cognitive research, published in peer-reviewed journals, and refined by interrogators whose innovations were recorded in classified manuals and memoranda. Using this doctrine, the agency found that physical abuse was, at best, a distraction and that the senses were pathways to the mind that could, when properly manipulated, influence human behavior.

In retrospect, there seem to be two dominant threads, detailed in chapter 2, running through this tangled decade of CIA research that advanced fitfully, by trial and error, toward a coherent psychological doctrine: first, a largely in-house exploration of exotic techniques such as drugs, electroshock, and hypnosis; and, second, more mundane behavioral research outsourced to leading scientists at hospitals and universities. The experiments with drugs proved chimerical—a failure illustrated by a hidden chapter in the otherwise distinguished career of Dr. Henry K. Beecher of Harvard University. After the army's Medical Intelligence Branch sent him a captured Gestapo report in 1947 claiming that mescaline was effective for interrogation, Beecher spent the next decade in a quixotic quest for such a "truth serum," first visiting Germany for information about mescaline and later conducting LSD experiments on unwitting subjects at Massachusetts General Hospital.[11]

Although such drug research was pursued vigorously at CIA headquarters and at a half-dozen university research hospitals for a decade, this controversial agency experimentation led nowhere except to lawsuits. By contrast, conventional behavioral research at leading universities, supported by secret CIA funding, contributed to the development of a distinctly American form of psychological torture. This behavioral approach was given real impetus by an American-British-Canadian research effort that was launched in 1951 when Sir Henry T. Tizard, the senior scientist at Great Britain's Ministry of Defense, crossed the Atlantic for meetings in Montreal with representatives of Canada's Defense Research Board and the CIA to plan mobilization of allied scientists for mind warfare against the Soviet Union.[12] After this meeting, the Canadian Research Board gave Dr. Donald O. Hebb, a professor of psychology at McGill University, a "confidential" grant to explore "sensory isolation" as means for "intervention in the individual mind."[13]

All this research produced two findings foundational for the CIA's psychological paradigm. For his part, Dr. Hebb soon discovered the extraordinary power of sensory deprivation to induce virtual psychosis in just twenty-four to forty-eight hours. For two days, his paid student volunteers at McGill University simply sat in a comfortable cubicle deprived of sensory stimulation by goggles, gloves, and earmuffs—a seemingly benign procedure that induced extreme hallucinations similar to the effect of mescaline.[14] After Hebb started releasing his results in 1954, more than 230 related articles appeared in peer-reviewed journals during the next four years, confirming his findings about sensory deprivation and demonstrating the effectiveness of the CIA's manipulation of the cognitive science community.[15]

During the 1950s, as well, two researchers at Cornell Medical Center working for the CIA found, in a second significant contribution, that the KGB's most devastating torture technique involved not brutal beatings but simply enforced standing. When victims were forced to remain immobile for days at time, legs swelled, skin sometimes erupted in suppurating lesions, and hallucinations began—all incredibly painful. This procedure became integral to the CIA's psychological paradigm and is now called "stress positions."[16]

These two researchers, cardiologist Lawrence Hinkle and neurologist Harold Wolff, a close friend of CIA director Allen Dulles, also directed the Human Ecology Fund (HEF), which served as a covert conduit for agency funding and an exemplary mechanism for secretly steering the scientific community toward the CIA's research needs. As the agency's mind-control focused more on behavioral factors such as isolation and stress, the Fund contracted two unwitting social scientists, Alan Howard and Robert A. Scott, to do library research, which they later published as a journal article on stress and gastric disease. Simultaneously, the Fund made that research available to the agency, which "reverse engineered" the findings to understand how a subject under coercive interrogation might "reduce the 'imbalance' of discomfort or pain . . . by providing the interrogator with the requested information." In doing a similar library study on the seemingly obscure topic of bereavement, these two junior scholars reached a conclusion that would likely interest the CIA: "When social isolation is involuntary . . . the individual experiencing separation from others may become obsessed with the idea of death."[17]

Although the main goal of this mind-control research was for offense, either breaking or controlling enemy agents, there was a renewed interest in its defensive uses between 1953 and 1955, when American prisoners of war who had suffered communist "brainwashing" returned home from North Korea.[18] After a protracted military inquiry, President Dwight Eisenhower ordered, in August 1955, that every soldier at risk of capture be given "specific training and instruction designed to better equip him to . . . withstand all enemy efforts against him." Consequently, the Air Force developed its SERE (Survival, Evasion, Resistance, Escape) program to train its pilots to resist psychological torture, and the other branches of the military soon followed.[19]

As the Pentagon consulted psychologists and psychiatrists to diagnose past POW treatment in Korea, there thus developed two related strands in mind-control research—offensive (for CIA interrogation of communist agents) and defensive (for training American troops to resist enemy interrogators). The most famous of these defensive studies, by Air Force sociologist Albert D. Biderman, contained a chart of eight basic communist interrogation techniques, indicating that enforced standing was the most "excruciating," since the "immediate source of pain is not the interrogator but the victim himself," thereby turning the "individual against himself." Indicating how completely the two research strands for offense and defense merged into a single inquiry, Biderman's major publication, *The Manipulation of Human Behavior* (1961), collected studies funded by the Human Ecology Fund and another CIA conduit to explore not just resistance techniques but "interrogation . . . for the purposes of intelligence."[20]

After a decade of research, the CIA concluded that its exotic methods of mind control using drugs and electroshock were not effective. As John Gittinger, an agency psychologist, later told the Senate, by 1963 the CIA had recognized that "brainwashing was largely a process of isolating a human being, keeping him out of contact, putting him under long stress in relationship to interviewing and interrogation, . . . without having to resort to any kind of esoteric means."[21]

Consequently, in 1963, the CIA distilled this decade of secret mind-control research into its "KUBARK Counterintelligence Interrogation" manual, which detailed its doctrine for psychological torture. Citing "experiments conducted at McGill University," KUBARK—a CIA code name or cryptonym for itself—explained that sensory deprivation was effective because "the calculated provision of stimuli during interrogation tends to make the regressed subject view the interrogator as a father-figure . . . strengthening . . . the subject's tendencies toward compliance." This CIA manual also stated that Biderman's study of "lessons derived from the interrogation of American POW's by

Communist services" was "one of the most useful works consulted," adding that "few KUBARK [CIA] interrogators would fail to profit from reading it."[22]

The KUBARK manual was not a dead document filed away for future reference, but instead became the basis of a major agency training program that lasted about a decade. Calling it the CIA's "premier course" open only to the "best recruits," one former agent, Bill Wagner, attended the three-week interrogation program in 1970 at "The Farm," the agency's famed training center near Williamsburg, Virginia. Competition for admission was so strong among ambitious young agents that many secured slots by first volunteering for the role of "captives." For weeks, these volunteers, following the KUBARK program, "were deprived of sleep, kept doused with water in cold rooms, forced to sit or stand in uncomfortable positions for long periods, isolated from sunlight and social contacts, . . . and subjected to mock executions." Even for hardened agents, the psychological abuse was so devastating that at least 10 percent of the volunteers "dropped out" and many later refused to take the course when their turn came. By the time this controversial program was shut down during Congress's investigations of the agency in the mid-1970s, an entire generation of CIA agents and interrogators had been trained in psychological torture.[23]

If we can attribute any genius to these discoveries, then the CIA's development of this no-touch torture was the first real revolution in the cruel science of pain since the sixteenth century. Throughout two thousand years of Western judicial torture, the same problem had persisted—the strong defied pain, while the weak blurted out whatever was necessary to stop it. In the third century AD, when scourging witnesses with beatings and hot irons was a requisite of Roman law, the jurist Ulpian noted the "deceptive" nature of torture, writing: "For many persons have such strength of body and soul that they heed pain very little . . . while others are so susceptible to pain that they will tell any lie rather than suffer it."[24]

By contrast, the CIA's psychological paradigm fused two new methods, the sensory disorientation discovered by Hebb and the self-inflicted pain documented by Cornell researchers, in a combination that would, in theory, cause victims to feel responsible for their own suffering and feel subservient to their inquisitors. Refined over the next forty years, the CIA's method came to rely on a mix of sensory overload and sensory deprivation via the manipulation of seemingly banal factors—heat and cold, light and dark, noise and silence, feast and famine—all meant to attack the five essential sensory pathways into the human mind. In effect, the agency's psychological techniques could transmit intolerable pain directly to the brain through means that eliminated any need for physical abuse. Yet even though the methods for inflicting pain were now sophisticated and scientific, the basic human responses to such suffering remained pretty much as Ulpian had described them so many centuries ago, rendering all torture, whether physical or psychological, generally ineffective.

In its clandestine journey across continents and decades, this American form of psychological torture would prove elusive, innovative, enticing, and destructive. In a fundamental sense, the subtle intertwining of these facets into a distinctive doctrine lends some coherence to the broad term "psychological torture." Since these attributes have allowed the CIA's method to persist to the present and perhaps into the future, we need to review each one briefly.

Unlike its physical variant, psychological torture is *elusive*, lacking clear signs of abuse and greatly complicating any investigation, prosecution, or attempt at prohibition. With no visible marks to indicate the degree of severity, psychological torture is particularly vulnerable to the definitional challenges inherent to any finding of torture. After being trained in this doctrine by British intelligence, the Royal Ulster Constabulary applied these methods on IRA suspects at Belfast in 1971 by using the so-called five techniques: enforced wall standing, hooding, blaring music, sleep deprivation, and dietary manipulation. After articles in the British press stirred controversy, a parliamentary inquiry by Lord Parker of Waddington found that these psychological methods greatly complicated any determination of torture. "Where," Lord Parker asked, "does hardship and discomfort end and for instance humiliating treatment begin, and where does the latter end and torture begin?" The answer, he stated with uncommon prescience, turns on "words of definition," and thus "opinions will inevitably differ."[25]

Although a majority of Lord Parker's panel were thus willing to countenance the continued use of these five techniques with safeguards, the report's disturbing findings prompted Prime Minister Edward Heath to tell Parliament in March 1972: "The government . . . have decided that the techniques which the Committee examined will not be used in the future as an aid to interrogation."[26]

When Dublin sued London over this Belfast incident in 1977, the European Court of Human Rights found Britain guilty of "inhuman and degrading treatment" but not torture. Alone among this court's seventeen justices, Judge Demetrios I. Evrigenis of Greece, a nation then just emerging from its own landmark torture trials, criticized the majority's narrow definition of torture, pointing out that this ancient abuse is now "based on methods of inflicting suffering which have already been overtaken by the ingenuity of modern techniques . . . developed in multidisciplinary laboratories which claim to be scientific." Although there are now "new forms of suffering that have little in common with the physical pain caused by conventional torture," they can, the justice observed, produce "the disintegration of an individual's personality, the shattering of his mental and psychological equilibrium and the crushing of his will," whose sum "must have caused . . . extremely intense physical, mental and psychological suffering, inevitably covered by the strictest definition of torture."[27]

Similarly, when General Randall Schmidt investigated conditions at Guantanamo for the Pentagon in 2005, he found that the standards for physical "torture" were clear, but "anything else beyond that was fairly vague," adding that "something might be degrading but not necessarily torture. And . . . it may be humiliating, but it may not be torture." In reviewing the treatment of the camp's star prisoner, the general "felt that the cumulative effect of simultaneous applications of numerous authorized techniques had an abusive and degrading impact on the detainee"—a finding later rejected by the military's higher echelons.[28]

Perpetrators and their protectors have a strong stake in maintaining the elusive quality of this psychological paradigm by muddying definitions of torture or resisting them all together. At the annual convention of the American Psychological Association (APA) in August 2006, a time when Washington was defending its use of enhanced interrogation, the U.S. Army's surgeon general, Kevin Kiley, emphasized the imprecision of legal definitions for torture, asking, in an intimidating, almost mocking manner: "How loud does a scream have to be? How many angels can dance on the head of a pin?"[29] Indeed, definitions of terms such as "severe mental pain," "degrading," "cruel," and even "torture" have played a key role in both the defense and the prosecution of perpetrators, making these "words of definition" a central focus in the political struggle over torture at home and abroad.

Reflecting the scientific rigor that helped to create this distinctive doctrine, the CIA's psychological paradigm has also proven surprisingly supple, with each sustained application producing *innovation*. Such innovation is not accidental but is the result of scientific research and systematic application at each key stage in this doctrine's evolution over the past sixty years. During both the experimentation of the 1950s and the application of the doctrine in later decades, the U.S. intelligence community consulted cognitive scientists, usually psychologists, and frequently combined interrogation with close observation to refine techniques.

For both the perpetrators and the powerful who command them, psychological torture also offers an *enticing* sense of empowerment, allowing them to dominate their enemies through sanitized scientific methods without recourse to crude physical force. The language of science can make psychological torture seem like a series of carefully controlled procedures, sanctioned by rational experts who have the aura of authority that comes with knowledge and credentials. Psychological torture also avoids the unseemly physical brutality unpalatable to the American public. Even though a *New York Times* headline in 2009 warned that "Memos Spell Out Brutal C.I.A. Mode of Interrogation," the public seemed nonplussed by the release of Justice Department documents detailing, in clinical medico-legal language, the CIA's use of beatings, stress positions, and a form of simulated drowning called "waterboarding." Simultaneously, however, the White House refused to release photographs of similar interrogations, apparently aware of the power of these graphic images to arouse anger at home and abroad.[30]

Mental methods, moreover, share a multifaceted appeal with their physical counterparts, ranging from psychological compensation for insecurity to a masochistic sensuality. In 1956, cognitive scientists working for the CIA described torture's allure for the Soviet leadership in words with universal implications: "When feelings of insecurity develop within those holding power, they [the Soviet leaders] become increasingly suspicious and put great pressures upon the secret police to obtain arrests and confessions. At such times police officials are inclined to condone anything which produces a speedy 'confession,' and brutality may become widespread."[31] Even when the abuse is initially intended for only a few, it soon spread in two directions—wide proliferation beyond the selected targets and a rapid escalation up the scale of brutality. So strong is the allure of such abuse that the powerful, whether in the Kremlin or in the White House, often concoct rationales to preserve their prerogative of torture in defiance of strong evidence that it is both ineffective and entails high political costs.

There is, moreover, a performative dimension to such enticement. In the medieval age, when judicial torture was common, art frequently depicted such cruel treatment in almost anatomical detail. Similarly, in post-9/11 America, mass media complemented the state's revival of torture with enticing simulations in film and television. In such displays, the boundary between seduction and revulsion is surprisingly fluid. The photos from Abu Ghraib, with their gritty vision of actual torture by U.S. soldiers, repulsed the American public. But aestheticized portrayals of torture in film and television attracted mass audiences and built political support for use of harsh methods whose reality was shown in those same Abu Ghraib photos.

Although seemingly less brutal than physical techniques, psychological torture has proven emotionally *destructive*, inflicting deep trauma and lasting emotional scars. Indeed, the early experiments in sensory deprivation elicited the behavior one would expect of someone undergoing torture. As described in chapter 2, subjects in these experiments done back in the 1950s experienced hysteria, collapsed in uncontrollable sobbing, and pounded in desperation on the boxes that confined them. In 2007, a half-century after the CIA codified these methods, researchers published clear clinical evidence that psychological torture is just as traumatic as its physical variant. "Ill treatment during captivity, such as psychological manipulations . . . and forced stress positions," reported Dr. Metin Basoglu in the *Archives of General Psychiatry* after interviews with 279 Bosnian victims, "does not seem to be substantially different from physical torture in terms of the severity of mental suffering."[32] In a subsequent study of 432 survivors, Dr. Basoglu concluded that the "inhuman and degrading treatment" were the "major determinants of lasting psychological damage in detainees," indicating the need for a "broader definition" beyond "a rather stereotypical image of torture as involving only certain atrocious acts of physical violence."[33]

This quest for definitional precision by advocates on both sides of the torture debate has induced some firming of an inherently blurry boundary between physical and psychological methods. Muddling such distinctions, many techniques deemed "psychological" have a physical component. On a spectrum from greater to lesser physical contact, psychological torture includes blocking breath with water, forcing ingestion of drugs, making a victim assume an intolerable posture, staging mock executions, imposing an excess of audio and visual stimuli or uncomfortable temperatures, manipulating diet, and enforcing sensory deprivation by confinement in a darkened or deadened space. Complicating the issue further, perpetrators often mix methods; for example, after 2001, the CIA's black sites stiffened sensory deprivation with an expressly physical technique called "wall slamming."

Nonetheless, this distinction between mental and physical methods remains elemental to the practice of torture, its prohibition, and the treatment of its victims. The UN Convention against Torture states, in Article 1, that "torture means any act by which severe pain or suffering, whether physical or mental, is intentionally inflicted on a person for such purposes as obtaining from him or a third person information or a confession." Leading treatment specialists such as Dr. Basoglu employ this physical/mental binary in categorizing the dozens of torture techniques used by security forces worldwide. On the opposite side of such praxis, U.S. security agencies have, for the past sixty years, worked closely with psychologists in refining techniques distinct from the more physical methods of their Third World allies. Clearly, in the realm of thermal techniques, there is a definable difference between confining a victim in a room with temperatures beyond the narrow range humans find tolerable (primarily a mental method) and scourging the victim's flesh with red-hot metal (a physical method used by Roman and medieval inquisitors).

Ultimately, from a U.S. perspective, this physical/mental distinction rests in the realm of legal evidence between methods that leave no trace and those that produce actionable physical sequelae, which can be photographed for forensic examination to determine, with surprising precision, the degree of abuse. At the outset of the Cold War, the CIA focused on psychological techniques in a scientific quest for mind-control methods far more potent than mere physical violence. After their codification in the 1960s, American officials, who had little occasion to employ these psychological methods themselves, transmitted this doctrine to authoritarian allies in Asia and Latin America who actually ran the prisons and dirtied their hands, often commingling physical and psychological methods. After 9/11, when U.S. agents started interrogating terror suspects inside their own prisons, the risks of media exposé and legal action mounted. In a mute dialogue with the federal anti-torture laws enacted in the 1990s prohibiting physical abuse, U.S. intelligence has generally favored psychological methods that did not cross the line into the physical and thus the criminal.

In effect, the law's logic has inclined U.S. interrogation doctrine toward undetectable methods that leave invisible scars in the mind, not visible contusions on the body. If the term "no-touch torture" encompasses many psychological methods, then the term "no-trace torture" is perhaps a more accurate description of techniques that the CIA and U.S. military intelligence have employed since 9/11. In the long history of torture reaching back millennia, this U.S. interrogation doctrine, with its emphasis on undetectable psychological methods, represents a significant departure from past practices.

Propagation

After codification in the 1963 KUBARK manual, the CIA spent the next thirty years propagating these torture techniques within the U.S. intelligence community and among anticommunist allies across Asia and Latin America. During the Vietnam War, the CIA, as detailed in chapter 3, applied these techniques in South Vietnam under the Phoenix program with methods that became brutally physical, producing more than forty thousand extrajudicial executions. Moreover, from 1966 to 1991, the U.S. Army's military intelligence ran "Project X" to teach counterinsurgency lessons learned in South Vietnam to armies across Latin America via Spanish-language manuals, interrogation curricula, courses at the School of the Americas, and field training programs.[34] There is also evidence, discussed in chapter 4, that U.S. advisers transmitted these techniques to the Philippines, which offers a telling example of the corrosive impact of torture upon a country's officer corps.

During the 1980s, as intensified counterinsurgency in Central America prompted a "resurgence of interest in teaching interrogation," the CIA launched its Human Resources Exploitation (HRE) program, which, the agency's inspector general later reported, was "designed to train foreign liaison services on interrogation techniques."[35] In its *Human Resources Exploitation Training Manual—1983*, prepared for the Honduran military, the CIA reiterated the two basic methods found in its 1963 KUBARK handbook, sensory disorientation and self-inflicted pain, now refined with harsh techniques learned through twenty years of intervening experience. Most fundamentally, agency instructors taught Honduran interrogators to assault the sensory pathways to human consciousness by disrupting the subject's "patterns of time, space, and sensory perception." Since "the torture situation is a . . . contest between the subject and his tormentor," the interrogator must make the subject "very much aware that the 'questioner' controls his ultimate disposition." Moreover, the manual made a strong case for imposing self-inflicted pain, saying that the "pain which is being inflicted upon him from outside himself may actually intensify his will to resist. On the other hand, pain which he feels he is inflicting upon himself is more likely to sap his resistance."[36]

In 1984–85, however, pressures built for reform as Congress uncovered CIA cooperation with Central American security forces that had "killed, imprisoned and tortured thousands of suspected enemies." Simultaneously, the agency's own inspector general "investigated allegations of misconduct by two Agency officers who were involved in interrogations and the death of one individual." In the aftermath, the CIA dispatched officials to its overseas stations "to ensure Agency personnel understood its policy on interrogations, debriefings, and human rights issues."[37]

In the midst of this crisis, the agency also made changes to its *Human Resources* manual, some cosmetic and some quite substantial. Indeed, the sum of these revisions makes it clear that the CIA had concluded that these psychological techniques, which would be revived after 9/11, were torture. The original text drafted in 1983 had contained explicit instructions for Honduran soldiers in harsh methods ("While we do not stress the use of coercive techniques, we do want to make you aware of them and the proper way to use them."). But, in 1984, this text was edited with penciled excisions, some transparently cosmetic, to render such offensive passages innocuous ("While we ~~do not stress~~ *deplore* the use of coercive techniques, we do want to make you aware of them ~~and the proper way to use them~~ *so that you may avoid them.*").[38]

Yet, CIA headquarters also made a number of substantive changes to this manual, stating, explicitly and repeatedly, that many of the agency's standard psychological methods constituted "torture," while others could easily lead to abuse—and banning both types for that reason. Originally, the manual stated: "The questioner should be careful to manipulate the subject's environment to disrupt patterns." But now a penciled correction warned: "However if successful it causes serious psychological damage and therefore is a form of torture." Originally, the manual had advised: "If the debility-dependency-dread state is unduly prolonged, the subject may sink into a defensive apathy from which it is hard to arouse him." But now a handwritten caution was added: "This illustrates why this coercive technique may produce torture." The earlier text had summarized the tactical lessons of sensory deprivation experiments, saying: "Deprivation of sensory stimuli induces stress and anxiety. The more complete the deprivation, the more rapidly and deeply the subject is affected." This instruction was now rewritten to become a caution: "*Extreme* deprivation of sensory stimuli induces *unbearable* stress and anxiety *and is a form of torture. Its use constitutes a serious impropriety and violates policy.* ~~The more complete the deprivation, the more rapidly and deeply the subject is affected.~~"

In a concluding section, the CIA instructor had originally told his Honduran students: "As I said at the beginning . . . , the purpose of all coercive techniques is to induce regression. . . . There are a few non-coercive techniques which can be used to produce regression . . . : A. Persistent manipulation of time. B. Retarding and advancing clocks. C. Serving meals at odd times. D. Disrupting sleep schedules. E. Disorientation regarding day and night." But now a penciled insert warned: "It is illegal and against policy to use them to produce regression. Following is a list of these non-coercive techniques which require great care because of their susceptibility to abuse."[39]

Significantly, the original techniques described in this 1983 Central American program seem quite similar to those outlined twenty years *earlier* in the CIA's Kubark manual and those that would be used twenty years *later* at Abu Ghraib and Guantanamo Bay—despite the agency's intervening repudiation of these same psychological techniques as "torture." Offering visual confirmation of this continuity, the detainees at Guantanamo's Camp X-Ray in 2002 wore prison suits with goggles, gloves, and ear muffs that bear a striking resemblance to equipment Dr. Hebb used to test sensory deprivation on student volunteers at McGill University in 1952.

When the Cold War came to a close in 1990, Washington rescinded its torture training and resumed its advocacy of human rights. After that earlier controversy over its human rights abuse in Central America, the CIA had already ended all interrogation training for foreign counterparts by 1986.[40] In a similar, somewhat later process inside the Defense Department, the assistant secretary for intelligence oversight advised Secretary Dick Cheney, in a March 1992 memo, that seven counterinsurgency and interrogation manuals, compiled during the 1980s for Project X, contained "material . . . not to be consistent with U.S. policy." Interviews with army personnel who had used these

U.S. military police at Camp X-Ray, Guantanamo, observe the prisoners during in-processing to this temporary detention facility on January 11, 2002. (Shane T. McCoy, U.S. Navy)

manuals revealed they believed incorrectly that U.S. regulations on "legal and proper" interrogation "did not apply to the training of foreign personnel." As a corrective, the Defense Department tried to retrieve the training documents from Latin American governments and ordered that all so recovered, except for a file copy, "should be destroyed"—an experience that may have contributed to Cheney's knowledge of these dark arts.[41] Indeed, one investigator later reported that Secretary Cheney and his staff counsel, David Addington, "saved the only known copies of abusive interrogation technique manuals taught at the School of the Americas."[42]

Most important, the Clinton administration ratified the UN Convention against Torture (CAT) in 1994, seemingly resolving the tension between Washington's anti-torture principles and its torture practices. Yet, when President Bill Clinton sent this convention to Congress for ratification, he included exculpatory language, drafted by the State Department under President Ronald Reagan, with an extended diplomatic "reservation" focused on just one word in the convention's twenty-six printed pages.[43] That word was "mental."

This reservation opened large loopholes in the UN's language that would later allow the CIA's use of psychological torture after September 2001. Under Article 3, the UN Convention defined "torture" as "any act by which severe pain or suffering, whether physical or mental, is *intentionally inflicted* on a person for such purposes as obtaining . . . information."[44] Instead of the UN's broader use of the phrase "intentionally inflicted," this U.S. definition, as analyzed in chapter 7, stated that, "in order to constitute torture, an act must be *specifically intended* to inflict severe physical or mental pain."[45] This emphasis on the perpetrator's "specific intention" was reinforced by a limitation of "mental pain" to just four techniques, discussed below, and a stricture that such mental suffering must be caused by "procedures *calculated* to disrupt profoundly the senses." If any pain inflicted through the CIA's techniques was not "calculated" and "specifically intended"—and intention was now situated subjectively in the mind of the torturer, not objectively in the nature of his actions—then, under this U.S. law, torture was not torture.[46]

Rather than the UN Convention's broad language about "severe pain or suffering," this U.S. reservation also narrowed the standard for psychological torture by requiring that "prolonged mental harm" be caused by just four specific acts: "(1) the intentional infliction or threatened infliction of severe physical pain or suffering; (2) the administration or application, or threatened administration or application, of mind altering substances or other procedures calculated to disrupt profoundly the senses or the personality; (3) the threat of imminent death; or (4) the threat that another person will imminently be subjected to death, severe physical pain or suffering, or the administration . . .

of mind altering substances."[47] This language also offered what seemed a broad ban on "other procedures calculated to disrupt profoundly the senses or the personality." But the insertion of qualifiers requiring "*prolonged* mental harm" caused by "procedures calculated to disrupt *profoundly* the senses" complicated any finding of criminality, effectively eviscerating this broad ban. By specifically barring just these four techniques and using ambiguous language about anything else, this U.S. definition of mental pain effectively preserved the CIA's right to use coercive psychological techniques—including sensory deprivation and self-inflicted pain. Significantly, the definitions in this diplomatic reservation were reproduced verbatim when the Clinton administration enacted complementary domestic legislation, first in Section 2340 of the Federal Code and later in the War Crimes Act of 1996.[48]

Through this legal legerdemain, Washington effectively split the UN Convention down the middle, banning physical torture but exempting the CIA's psychological methods from any legal prohibition. In a clear violation of the Convention even as ratified by Congress, Clinton also issued a presidential directive, dated June 21, 1995, authorizing the CIA to ship terror suspects to allies, such as Egypt, notorious for their use of torture. Although Clinton and his aides later insisted that they had sought assurances of humane treatment from Egypt, former CIA operative Michael Scheuer has called these claims, under oath, "a lie." For seven years following the start of the Clinton administration's covert campaign against Al Qaeda in 1995, the CIA avoided direct involvement in torture by sending some seventy terror suspects to Middle East allies notorious for their willingness to employ brutal, physical tortures.[49]

This practice, called "extraordinary rendition," is explicitly banned under the UN Convention's Article 3. Only a year after ratifying the UN Convention against Torture, Clinton thus violated one of its key clauses, indicating that Washington would continue to favor covert operations over compliance with international law. By failing to repudiate the CIA's use of torture, while adopting a UN convention that condemned its practice, the United States left this contradiction buried like a political land mine, ready to detonate with exceptional force just ten years later in the Abu Ghraib prison scandal.

Perfection

Right after his address to a shaken nation on September 11, 2001, President George W. Bush gave his staff secret orders for torture, saying: "I don't care what the international lawyers say, we are going to kick some ass."[50] In that same spirit, Bush issued a secret, fourteen-page directive on September 17 ordering the CIA to conduct a relentless, worldwide pursuit of Al Qaeda and authorizing the agency to "detain terrorists" and "to set up detention facilities outside the United States." Following months of recondite legal research, mid-level administration attorneys translated their president's potentially unlawful orders into U.S. policy through three controversial, neoconservative legal findings: (1) the president is above the law; (2) torture is a legally acceptable exercise of presidential power; and (3) the U.S. Navy base at Guantanamo Bay is not U.S. territory.[51]

After discussions among these neoconservative lawyers concluded that the Geneva Conventions did not apply to Al Qaeda, White House counsel Antonio Gonzales advised the president, in a memo dated January 25, 2002, that 9/11 created an extraordinary need for executive action. "This new paradigm," he wrote, "renders obsolete Geneva's strict limitations on questioning of enemy prisoners and renders quaint some of its provisions requiring that captured enemy be afforded such things as commissary privileges."[52] Consequently, two weeks later the president ordered that "none of the provisions of Geneva apply to our conflict with al Qaeda in Afghanistan or elsewhere throughout the world," thereby making "minimum standards for humane treatment" operative only if "military necessity" permits.[53] Over the next seven years, these faceless, midlevel attorneys, almost all conservative political appointees, would become the driving force in implementing a policy of harsh interrogation, breaking down legal restraints through meetings or memoranda and pushing interrogation toward torture.

In the first year of the War on Terror, the CIA became "a global military police," seizing more than three thousand suspects in over a hundred nations. Most were turned over to allied security services from Pakistan to Egypt. But the handful found to be Al Qaeda leaders, perhaps as few as fourteen among the three thousand, were held at the agency's own "black sites."[54] In a sharp break with past U.S. practice that outsourced torture to foreign security services, the White House now authorized the CIA to build its own network of prisons, planes, and allied agents so that it could seize suspects from sovereign states and incarcerate them inside this global gulag. Between 2002 and 2006, the agency operated two dozen jet aircraft that made thousands of secret flights ferrying detainees between the U.S. base at Guantanamo, some eight CIA black sites from Thailand to Poland, and allied prisons from Morocco to Uzbekistan. Moreover, the Bush administration gave the CIA primary control over Al Qaeda captives, ending the FBI's lead role in U.S. counterintelligence, which it had held since 1940, apparently because the agency, unlike the bureau, had an institutional history that allowed it to torture.[55]

In a rare public admission of the CIA's new role, the head of its Counter-terrorism Center, Cofer Black, told Congress about the agency's approach to interrogation on September 26, 2001, just two weeks after the terrorist attacks: "All I want to say is that there was 'before' 9/11 and 'after' 9/11. After 9/11 the gloves come off."[56]

Although systematic torture inside U.S. facilities, both military prisons and agency black sites, soon became the most distinctive feature of Bush's war on terror, rendition remained a bulwark of the CIA's ongoing campaign against Al Qaeda. Through sub rosa alliances with clandestine services world-wide, the CIA snatched terror suspects off streets in cities from Stockholm to Kuala Lumpur and flew them to nations long notorious for brutal physical torture—Morocco, Egypt, Syria, Jordan, and Pakistan.

To this roster of reliable partners, the agency now added some surprising new allies, Libya and Uzbekistan. After 9/11, Washington leased a massive air base in Uzbekistan just ninety miles from the Afghan border, and the CIA be-gan flying prisoners into the country for torture inside the prisons of President Islam Karimov. There terror suspects were commingled with the regime's six thousand political prisoners and subjected to scalding water, ripped fingernails, and brutal beatings. In July 2004, the British ambassador to Tashkent, Craig Murray, complained to London: "We receive intelligence obtained under tor-ture from the Uzbek intelligence services, via the US. . . . Tortured dupes are forced to sign confessions showing what the Uzbek government wants the US and UK to believe, that they and we are fighting the same war against terror."[57]

In the same period, 2002 to 2007, the CIA also shipped at least eight prisoners to Libya in full knowledge of "the country's reputation for torture." When Libyan intelligence asked for rendition of an Islamic activist named Abdel Hakim Belhaj, the agency assured Tripoli of its commitment "to devel-oping this relationship for the benefit of both our services." In March 2004, the CIA had the suspect seized at Kuala Lumpur, assigned two agents to tor-ture him in Bangkok, and then flew him home to Libya for six years of beat-ings and solitary confinement inside the worst of Colonel Qaddafi's prisons.[58]

Though the gloves were off inside CIA black sites, American interrogators still had to be taught how to hit. According to the CIA inspector general's 2004 report, the "Agency had discontinued virtually all involvement in in-terrogations after encountering difficult issues" in Central America and the Middle East during the 1980s, leaving "almost no foundation" for interroga-tion. Compounding the problem, the CIA "lacked adequate linguists" and "had very little hard knowledge" about Al Qaeda's leaders, denying the agency any metric for assessing the effectiveness of its interrogation techniques. In the ten years after the end of the Cold War, the only government unit with an institutional memory of harsh methods was the Pentagon's SERE program, which trained U.S. troops to withstand "sensory deprivation, sleep disruption, stress positions, waterboarding, and slapping." Starting in early 2002, several SERE psychologists, using Dr. Biderman's earlier research into communist techniques, advised both Defense and the CIA about ways to "reverse engineer" these training methods for effective interrogation of terror suspects. In Senate testimony, CIA director Michael Hayden admitted using waterboarding, while an assistant attorney general stated that the agency's procedure was "adapted from the SERE training program."[59] Similarly, a later British inquiry into abuse of detainees in southern Iraq during 2003–04 found that the notorious "five techniques," banned from all UK interrogations after the Parker inquiry in 1972, had remained a part of British SERE training, producing "an enduring problem . . . of such exercises spilling over into resistance interrogation training."[60]

Almost from the start, however, revival of the CIA's psychological paradigm through this prism proved problematic. As the Senate Armed Services Committee later pointed out, the SERE methods were derived, in part, from "coercive methods used by the Chinese Communist dictatorship to elicit *false confessions* from U.S. POWs during the Korean War," not to gather accurate, actionable intelligence (emphasis added).[61]

The problematic nature of this revamped SERE technique was soon evident in the work of two contract psychologists, James Mitchell and Bruce Jessen, who developed the CIA's new interrogation protocol. During the 1980s, both had served as staff psychologists supervising SERE training for the Air Force Survival School at Fairchild Air Base near Spokane, where Dr. Jessen was known for his aggressive performance as mock enemy interrogator. As chief psychologist there after 1985, Jessen prepared a paper detailing the many techniques that captors use to bend prisoners to their will, including: "Threats of death, physical pressures including torture which result in psychological disturbances or deterioration, inadequate diet and sanitary facilities with constant debilitation and illness, attacks on the mental health via isolation, reinforcement of anxieties, sleeplessness, stimulus deprivation or flooding, disorientation, loss of control both internal and external locus, direct and indirect attack on the PWs [prisoner of war's] standards of honor, faith in . . . country, religion, or political beliefs." Jessen's paper concluded that such harsh treatment was effective, saying: "Confronted with these conditions, the unprepared prisoner of war experiences unmanageable levels of fear and despair."[62]

After 9/11, the two psychologists reverse-engineered their SERE training to create a harsh interrogation protocol for leaders of the CIA's Counterterrorism Center, Cofer Black and Jose A. Rodriguez Jr. When the Al Qaeda leader

Abu Zubaydah was captured in March 2002, his interrogation at a CIA black site in Thailand became an important, even historic test for the relative efficacy of the agency's coercive techniques of psychological abuse versus the FBI's noncoercive method, which builds rapport through language skills and local knowledge.

The significance of this single interrogation, among the countless thousands conducted during the War on Terror, cannot be overstated. The CIA would twist events inside this Thai safe house into a spurious yet convincing justification for its harsh "enhanced interrogation" techniques, allowing their spread to agency and military prisons worldwide. President Bush would later cite this interrogation, in a 2006 television address, to justify his authorization of these "enhanced techniques." The first revelation about what "enhanced" might mean came a year later when retired CIA operative John Kiriakou told ABC News that Abu Zubaydah had "answered every question" with invaluable intelligence after being waterboarded just once for "probably 30, 35 seconds"—a sensational and spurious claim that reverberated incessantly in conservative media circles for two years until agency documents showed the detainee had been waterboarded not once but eighty-three times.[63] Vice President Cheney would point to this single interrogation, in speeches and memoirs, to defend the harsh methods. Echoing these arguments, Republican pundits and presidential candidates would insist, for the next decade, that such abuse was necessary for the nation's defense. Despite all these claims of efficacy, Abu Zubaydah's interrogation represents something akin to a scientific experiment that establishes not the success but the failure of the CIA's coercive psychological techniques—a topic we will examine, briefly below and more closely in chapter 7.

The first round of Abu Zubaydah's interrogation was conducted by an FBI team led by agent Ali Soufan, a Lebanese American counterterrorism specialist. Flying from Washington, Soufan landed at Bangkok with a decade of experience as an interrogator, fluency in Arabic, and an empathetic method of proven effectiveness—what he has called the "informed interrogation approach," which leverages "knowledge of the detainee's culture and mindset," together with all known biographical information. When Zubaydah gave his alias at the start of the interrogation, the FBI man replied in Arabic, "How about if I call you Hani?"—the nickname his mother had given him as a child. According to Soufan's Senate testimony, Zubaydah "looked at me in shock, said 'OK,' and we started talking." During the first hour of this noncoercive interview, the FBI gained "important actionable intelligence" and in the days that followed learned "the role of KSM [Khalid Shaikh Mohammed] as the mastermind of the 9/11 attacks"—critical information that was then unknown.[64]

At first, CIA director George Tenet seemed delighted and "congratulated" the interrogators. But when told they were FBI and not CIA, Tenet became "furious and angrily slammed his hand on the table." The CIA director retracted the commendation and dispatched a team from his own Counterterrorism Center led by the contract psychologist James Mitchell under orders "to take over." Arriving at the Thai safe house, Dr. Mitchell, who had never conducted an actual interrogation during his many years as a SERE trainer, told Soufan, a veteran FBI interrogator, "my method is more effective," adding that Abu Zubaydah would "become fully compliant without us having to do any work." When the FBI man seemed incredulous, Dr. Mitchell replied: "This is science."[65]

With Mitchell serving as both instructor and chief interrogator, the FBI men were removed and the CIA team started climbing the scale of coercive methods, moving from nudity to "low-level sleep deprivation (between 24 and 48 hours)." Frustrated, Soufan had "to sit and watch for days as nothing was gained through techniques that no reputable interrogator would even think of using." When day after day of these methods yielded "no information" and Washington demanded more results, the FBI men were allowed to resume their informed interrogation approach, again gaining important intelligence that "included the details of Jose Padilla, the so-called 'dirty bomber.'" But then Dr. Mitchell and his CIA team took control once more, moving to "the next stage in the force continuum" by placing Abu Zubaydah in "a confinement box." Convinced that the CIA's methods were becoming "borderline torture," Soufan filed a protest with his FBI director, Robert Mueller, and "was pulled out."[66]

Now in full control, the CIA psychologist Mitchell ordered the detainee "stripped, exposed to cold and blasted with rock music to prevent sleep." After Washington approved use of the harshest SERE methods, Zubaydah was "confined in a box, slammed into the wall and waterboarded 83 times." Although the detainee had, in the view of the U.S. Senate, already "given up his most valuable information without coercion," the agency later claimed that these extreme psychological methods were effective, and it would later use this harsh protocol on dozens of other prisoners, including Khalid Sheikh Mohammed.[67] After observing Dr. Mitchell's work closely, Ali Soufan summed up his coercive psychological methods in words that seem a paraphrase of the CIA's old *Human Resources Exploitation Training Manual—1983*: "The idea was the detainee has to look at the interrogator as if he is his God. He is the one who determines if his life is going to be better or worse."[68]

In response to a White House inquiry about the legality of such techniques, Assistant Attorney General Jay Bybee and his subordinate John Yoo,

a neoconservative law professor on leave from the University of California–
Berkeley, found grounds in an August 2002 memo for exculpating any CIA
interrogator who tortured but claimed his intention was information, not
pain. Moreover, by parsing the definition of torture in Section 2340 of the
Federal Code, they argued that "physical pain amounting to torture must be
equivalent in intensity to the pain accompanying serious physical injury such
as organ failure"—in effect, allowing abuse up to the point of death. "For
purely mental pain or suffering to amount to torture," the memo continued,
"it must result in significant psychological harm . . . lasting for months or even
years"—loose language reflecting both U.S. law's permissive standard and the
elusive character of psychological torture.[69] Such a definition, of course, also
extended almost indefinitely the period prosecutors must wait before bringing
charges of psychological torture.

Further up the chain of command, Condoleezza Rice, then the U.S. national security adviser, recalled how the "CIA sought policy approval from
the National Security Council (NSC) to begin an interrogation program for
high-level al-Qaida terrorists." Consequently, she convened a high-level NSC
working group in 2002–03 that received detailed descriptions of the proposed
methods from the CIA and approved all of the agency's requests for harsh
interrogation, even those that crossed the line, as defined by the international
standards, into torture.[70] Their recommendations were delivered to President
Bush, who told ABC News in April 2008: "Yes, I'm aware our national security
team met on this issue. And I approved."[71]

Through this tangled decision making, Bush allowed the CIA ten "enhanced" interrogation methods designed by "agency psychologists," including
waterboarding, that represented a marked intensification of the CIA's psychological paradigm. Among these ten techniques, three showed clear continuity from the agency's Cold War counterintelligence techniques—"cramped
confinement" in a dark box for sensory deprivation, the "stress positions"
originally copied from the Soviet KGB, and "wall standing," used by British intelligence at Belfast in 1971. In a secret memo dated August 2002, the
Justice Department approved the agency's use of these methods "in some sort
of escalating fashion, culminating with the waterboard."[72] Of the ninety-four
detainees in CIA custody by mid-2005, about twenty-eight would be subjected
to some combination of these "enhanced techniques."[73]

Six years later, after a close review of the agency's program, Senator Dianne
Feinstein (Democrat, California) stated: "As chairman of the Select Committee on Intelligence, I can say that . . . coercive and abusive treatment of detainees in U.S. custody was far more systematic and widespread than we thought.
Moreover, the abuse stemmed not from the isolated acts of a few bad apples

but from [the] fact that the line was blurred between what is permissible and impermissible conduct, putting U.S. personnel in an untenable position with their superiors and the law."[74]

During the CIA program's first year, from early 2002 to mid-2003, the absence of clear guidelines or close supervision over its prisons allowed what the agency itself later called "unauthorized, improvised, inhumane, and un-documented . . . interrogation techniques." Reflecting torture's inexorable es-calation in brutality, the CIA inspector general found a wide range of cruelly "improvised actions"—including, the use of "air conditioning/blanket depri-vation" to inflict extreme cold in July 2002; the staging of "mock executions" by brandishing or firing handguns in September and October; racking "an unloaded semi-automatic . . . once or twice" and revving a "power drill" close to a detainee's head in December; threatening, through an Arabic interpreter, to begin "sexually abusing female relatives in front of the detainee"; telling a high-level prisoner "we're going to kill your children"; and beating an Afghan detainee to death "with a large metal flashlight" in June 2003. When asked about abuse of detainees via temperature modification, one CIA interrogator replied with an empowered arrogance, "How cold is cold?" Even though the death threats were clear violations of U.S. anti-torture laws, both Section 2340 and the War Crimes Act, Bush's Justice Department decided, symbolically on September 11, 2003, not to prosecute any agency interrogators, with exception of that single contract operative who had killed an Afghan detainee.[75]

This first year of CIA operations was also a time for testing new interro-gation techniques. An MI-5 summary of forty-two CIA documents, released by a British court over Washington's strenuous objections in 2009, offers rare insight into the agency's methods during these first months of the war on terror. Inside a Pakistani prison, the detainee Binyam Mohamed was, in the words of this British report, subjected to a "series of interviews . . . conducted by the United States authorities prior to 17 May 2002 as part of a new strat-egy designed by an expert interviewer"—probably one of the agency's SERE psychologists. American interrogators employed a range of techniques, includ-ing shackling, "threats and inducements," and "fears of being removed from United States custody and 'disappearing.'" Significantly, MI-5 reported that, during the "interview process by the United States authorities, BM [Binyam Mohamed] had been intentionally subjected to continuous sleep deprivation. The effects of the sleep deprivation were carefully observed." Although MI-5 found that all this was "at the very least cruel, inhuman and degrading treat-ment by the United States authorities," certainly a very controversial conclu-sion, its most significant finding was that such treatment was "designed by an expert interviewer" and that the "effects of the sleep deprivation were carefully observed." If MI-5 is correct, then the CIA was apparently testing new methods inside its black sites—adding another instance of the scientific innovation that has long characterized the agency's psychological paradigm. Moreover, this British report corroborated an earlier finding by Physicians for Human Rights that such close observation may constitute "using the detainees as human subjects, a practice that approaches unlawful experimentation."[76]

After CIA headquarters issued clear "guidelines" in January 2003, this ad hoc improvisation slowly ended, and interrogation inside the secret prisons followed a graded roster of standard and enhanced techniques. As described in the classified *Background Paper on CIA's Combined Use of Interrogation Techniques* compiled in 2004, each detainee was transported to an agency black site while "deprived of sight and sound through the use of blindfolds, earmuffs, and hoods." Once inside, he was reduced to "a baseline dependent state" through "nudity, sleep deprivation (with shackling . . .), and dietary manipulation." For "more physical and psychological stress," CIA inquisitors used coercive measures such as "an insult slap or abdominal slap" and then "walling," that is, slamming the detainee's head against a cell wall. If these failed, then interrogators escalated to waterboarding, which the Bush Justice Department called "the most intense of CIA interrogation techniques."[77]

This medieval technique, called "Standard Gallic Torture" in a 1541 French judicial handbook, would now become what CIA director Porter Goss called, in 2005, a "professional interrogation technique."[78] Indeed, so seductive was this torture that both CIA field operatives and Langley officials violated the agency's own guidelines to increase both its intensity and its frequency. In 2004, the CIA inspector general reported that "the waterboard was used with far greater frequency" and "in a different manner" from that approved by the Justice Department. While SERE trainers had disrupted airflow by a brief, carefully supervised "application of a damp cloth over the air passages," actual agency interrogators "applied large volumes of water to a cloth that covered the detainee's mouth and nose."[79] To intensify the effect, the CIA, according to a later investigative report, built a special gurney with the perfect angle to flood the lungs with water, using saline solution to avoid death by "hyponatremia" from excessive ingestion of water, necessary since agency interrogators were allowed three "applications" every hour. Detainees were also fed special liquid diets to prevent suffocation during vomiting induced by waterboarding. Interrogators were encouraged, in the pursuit of technical perfection, to record their torture sessions in log books.[80] All of these procedures, grounded in sophisticated medical knowledge, suggest strongly that the CIA involved doctors or scientists at some stage in developing this extreme version of

As shown in this sixteenth-century judicial manual, interrogators practiced *torturae Gallicae ordinariae* (ordinary French torture) by pouring water on a cloth covering the victim's nose and mouth, a method quite similar to the CIA technique now called waterboarding. (from Jean Milles de Souvigny [Joannes Millacus], *Praxis Criminis Persequendi* [Paris, 1541])

waterboarding—a supposition that, if correct, indicates that the innovative character of the agency's interrogation paradigm had persisted.

Using these refined techniques, the Al Qaeda captive Abu Zubaydah was waterboarded "at least 83 times during August 2002" and Khalid Sheikh Mohammad 183 times in a single month, March 2003—excess that raises questions about the method's effectiveness and the rationality of the CIA interrogators.[81] Significantly, the agency's own investigators concluded that "there was no *a priori* reason to believe that applying the waterboard with the frequency and intensity with which it was used by the psychologist/interrogators was either efficacious or medically safe."[82]

Even though Justice Department lawyers cited SERE training to advise the CIA in August 2002 that waterboarding was not torture, their conclusions seem questionable.[83] After French paratroopers tortured him with this technique during the Battle of Algiers in 1957, the journalist Henri Alleg wrote a moving description in a book that turned France against the Algerian War. "I tried, by contracting my throat," he wrote, "to take in as little water as possible. . . . But I couldn't hold on for more than a few moments. I had the impression of drowning, and a terrible agony, that of death itself, took possession of me."[84]

Let us speculate about the deeper meaning of Alleg's words. Why would a small amount of water forced into his lungs create not just discomfort or even fear but "a terrible agony, that of death itself"? Instead of simply blocking breath with a hand or dry cloth, torturers from the French inquisition to the Khmer Rouge have learned, in their perverse genius, to turn pain into panic by either flooding the lungs with water or just covering the nose and mouth with a wet cloth. Why does the mind's sense of water in the cloth instantaneously trigger the extreme agony of impending death? In retrospect, Alleg's description of the trauma sparked by waterboarding seems to foreshadow the discovery, two decades later, of what would be called the "mammalian diving reflex." Among the many possible threats to human survival, the brain has a unique defense against drowning embedded into its control over the involuntary muscles that allows infants, but not adults, to survive complete immersion in cold water for up to sixty minutes, diverting blood to vital organs (heart, lungs, brain) and emerging, almost miraculously, alive and without any brain damage. As waterboarding blocks air to the lungs, the mind's survival mechanisms might somehow set off an instant reflexive panic from the ultimate fear—the fear of death itself.[85] Whatever the precise cause, waterboarding is clearly a form of torture, violating the prohibition on death threats under U.S. law and the infliction of pain in the UN anti-torture convention.

By finding such harsh methods legal under U.S. law, the Justice Department's August 2002 memos also allowed proliferation of these "enhanced techniques" from CIA black sites to the military prison at Guantanamo Bay and war zones across the Middle East. Within a month of that memo's circulation, military interrogators and psychologists from Guantanamo Bay, Cuba, would travel to Fort Bragg, North Carolina, to observe SERE training. On September 25, CIA general counsel John Rizzo visited Guantanamo to brief prison staff. A week later, the chief legal counsel at the agency's Counterterrorism Center, Jonathan Fredman, followed to share the CIA's success in using "aggressive techniques," persuading prison staff of the efficacy of such extreme measures.[86]

As this latter meeting opened, Major John Leso, a psychologist who led Guantanamo's Behavioral Science Consultation Team, observed that "force is risky, and may be ineffective" since the detainees "are used to seeing much more barbaric treatment." By contrast, he added, "psychological stressors are extremely effective (i.e., sleep deprivation, withholding food, isolation, loss of time)." When Guantanamo's chief of staff interjected, saying that "we can't do sleep deprivation," the prison's senior attorney, Lieutenant Colonel Diane E. Beaver, replied, "Yes, we can, with approval." Apparently mindful that such methods violated diplomatic conventions, she added that "we may need to curb the harsher operations while the ICRC [International Committee of the Red Cross] is around."

Summarizing the agency's legal position on harsh interrogation, CIA attorney Fredman interjected with words that mimed the Bybee memo: "The language of the statutes is written vaguely. . . . Severe physical pain described as anything causing permanent damage to major organs or body parts. Mental torture [is] described as anything leading to permanent, profound damage to the senses or personality." Then, he added coolly, "It is basically subject to perception. If the detainee dies you're doing it wrong." Significantly, he argued that the partial U.S. ratification of the UN Convention against Torture "gives us more license to use more controversial techniques." Although the CIA had found that "aggressive techniques have proven very helpful," he suggested that those "on the harshest end of the spectrum must be performed by a highly trained individual" to avoid deaths, since "the backlash of attention would be severely detrimental." Specifically, Fredman suggested it was "very effective to identify detainee phobias, and to use them (i.e., insects, snakes, claustrophobia)." Recommending waterboarding by "a well-trained individual," he said: "It can feel like you're drowning. The lymphatic system will react as if you're suffocating, but your body will not cease to function."[87]

From these extemporaneous remarks, Fredman was clearly aware of that language in Section 2340 of the U.S. code about "procedures calculated to disrupt profoundly the senses or personality." But he seemed to ad lib the addition of the word "permanent," perhaps influenced by Bybee's August 2002 memo arguing that the psychological harm inflicted by any act would have to last "for months or even years" if that act were to qualify as torture. More broadly, this meeting illustrates the enormous weight of words as legal analysis moved through the bureaucracy via such midlevel meetings and memoranda, simultaneously shaping policy at the highest levels in Washington and the quality of interrogation inside prison cells at the periphery of American power.

After requests from Guantanamo for permission to use these methods worked their way from these meetings up the chain of command, Defense Secretary Rumsfeld approved fifteen aggressive interrogation techniques in December 2002, suggesting use of harsh stress positions in a handwritten note: "I stand for 8–10 hours a day. Why is standing limited to 4 hours?"[88] Simultaneously, he appointed General Geoffrey Miller to command Guantanamo, with a wide latitude for interrogation that soon made this prison an ad hoc behavioral science laboratory. Under the general's command, military intelligence stiffened the psychological assault by exploring Arabs' "cultural sensitivity" to sexuality, gender identity, and fear of dogs. In another innovation, Miller also allowed so-called Behavioral Science Consultation Teams of military psychologists to probe each detainee for individual phobias. In addition to mining medical files, military psychologists, as the *New York Times* reported, advised interrogators how to exploit "a detainee's fears and longings to increase distress," noting one prisoner's "fear of the dark" and another's "longing for his mother."[89] Through this three-phase attack on sensory receptors, cultural identity, and individual psyche, Guantanamo perfected the CIA's psychological paradigm—creating an interrogation protocol that the International Red Cross called, after repeated visits, "a form of torture."[90] Sustained application of psychological methods had once again produced innovation.

These techniques then escalated virally, in part through the enticing quality of torture analyzed in chapter 5. By ordering harsh interrogation at Guantanamo, Secretary Rumsfeld, as the Senate Armed Services Committee later reported, "unleashed a virus which ultimately infected interrogation operations conducted by the U.S. military and coalition forces in both Afghanistan and Iraq."[91] Within weeks, intelligence officers at Bagram prison in Afghanistan were shown "a power point presentation listing the aggressive techniques that had been authorized by the Secretary"—encouraging a harsh climate that allowed guards to beat shackled detainees "with virtual impunity."[92] According to the *New York Times*, U.S. Special Operations forces operated five field interrogation centers across Iraq in 2004–05 where detainees were subjected to sensory deprivation, beating, burning, electric shock, and waterboarding. Among the thousand soldiers in these elite units, thirty-four were later convicted of abuse, and many more escaped prosecution only because records were officially "lost."[93] Similarly in 2003, British forces at Basra in southern Iraq revived the "five techniques" for mental torture banned by their government twenty years earlier and subjected prisoners to combinations of "wall postures, hooding, noise, deprivation of sleep, and deprivation of food and water," producing one fatality and 150 documented cases of detainee abuse.[94]

As violence erupted across Iraq in August 2003, General Miller arrived from Guantanamo with detailed instructions for his new protocol, prompting the U.S. commander for Iraq, General Ricardo Sanchez, to order harsh interrogation techniques at Abu Ghraib prison, including:

X. Isolation: Isolating the detainee from other detainees . . . [for] 30 days.

Y. Presence of Military Working Dogs: Exploits Arab fear of dogs while maintaining security during interrogations. . . .

AA. Yelling, Loud Music, and Light Control: Used to create fear, disorient detainee and prolong capture shock. . . .

CC. Stress Positions: Use of physical posturing (sitting, standing, kneeling, prone, etc.)[95]

Indeed, my own review of the 1,600 still-classified photos collected at Abu Ghraib by the army's Criminal Investigation Command reveals not random acts by putative "creeps," but just three psychological torture techniques repeated over and over: first, hooding for sensory deprivation; second, shackling and enforced standing for self-inflicted pain; and, third, those recent innovations, nudity, sexual humiliation, and dogs for exploitation of Arabs' cultural sensitivities. It is no accident that Private Lynndie England, one of the most notorious of the perpetrators at Abu Ghraib, was photographed leading an Iraqi detainee leashed like a dog.

Impunity

In response to widespread anger over revelations of detainee abuse at Abu Ghraib, the Bush White House fought back by defending CIA interrogation and endless detention as presidential prerogatives necessary for the War on Terror. But, in a sharp rebuke of the president's position, in June 2006 the Supreme Court ruled in *Hamdan v. Rumsfeld* that the military commissions, the special anti-terror tribunals Bush had convened at Guantanamo, were illegal because they did not meet the Geneva Conventions' requirement that detainees be tried with "all the judicial guarantees . . . recognized as indispensable by civilized peoples."[96]

In a dramatic bid to legalize his now-illegal policies, President Bush made a televised address to the nation three months later, on September 6, 2006, before families of the 9/11 victims assembled in the East Room of the White House. The president announced that he was transferring fourteen top Al Qaeda captives from the secret CIA prisons to Guantanamo Bay. As detailed in chapter 5, Bush defended his interrogation program with claims of counterterror successes reminiscent of scripts from the popular television show *24*. To allow the "CIA program" with its "alternative set of procedures" to go forward, Bush said he was sending legislation to Congress that would legalize these same presidential prerogatives.[97]

After negotiations inside Vice President Dick Cheney's Senate office on September 21, Republican partisans drafted legislation that sailed through Congress, without amendment, to become the Military Commissions Act 2006. Significantly, this law allowed CIA interrogators both legal immunity for past physical abuse and ample latitude for future psychological torture.[98] Buried in the legislation's thirty-six pages of dense print, this law defined "serious physical pain" as the "significant loss or impairment of the function of a bodily member, organ, or mental faculty"—a paraphrase of that iconic definition of physical torture as pain "equivalent in intensity to . . . organ failure" in the notorious August 2002 Bybee/Yoo torture memo, which, ironically, had already been repudiated by the Justice Department.[99]

Moreover, by using verbatim the narrow definition of "severe mental pain" from Section 2340 of the Federal Code enacted back in 1994, this 2006 legislation immunized CIA interrogators for both past and future use of these "enhanced" techniques. By focusing on the means rather than the end result, both Section 2340 and the Military Commissions Law limited the crime of inflicting "severe mental pain" to just four specific acts: first, infliction of extreme physical pain, actual or threatened; second, drug injection; third, death threats; fourth, threats to inflict any of these on a third party.[100] Beyond these four actions, all of the CIA's many psychological torture techniques were excluded from the definition of "severe mental pain" and became, by default, legal under U.S. law.

This legislation's permissive intent was confirmed nine months later when President Bush, as provided under the act, issued new guidelines for CIA interrogation that did restrain the range of temperature modification and restrict waterboarding. But the president's order remained classified, masking many of its provisions. And it still denied the International Red Cross access to agency prisons. Most important, under this law, Bush's concessions were a presidential prerogative and could be rescinded at any time to allow a resumption of waterboarding and other tortures.[101] Through this legislation and executive decree, Bush resolved an underlying contradiction between U.S. anti-torture principles and torture practices dating back to the Cold War. But he did so not by banning torture but, instead, by legitimating CIA psychological methods as a lawful instrument of American power.

In the transition from the Bush to Obama administrations, Washington thus made a bipartisan move back to the contradictory U.S. policy toward torture that had developed during the Cold War: that is, publicly advocating human rights, while covertly outsourcing torture to allied intelligence agencies. In retrospect, the real aberration of the Bush years lay not in torture policies per se but in the president's order that the CIA should operate its own prisons and American agents should dirty their hands with waterboarding and wall slamming. The advantage of the contradictory approach during the Cold War was that it insulated Washington from the taint of torture, even when it was widely practiced by U.S. allies.

During its first months in office, the Obama administration did introduce some significant reforms by closing the CIA's prisons, barring its coercive methods, and transferring the agency's lead role in counterterror interrogation back to the FBI. Simultaneously, Attorney General Eric Holder, who had been appalled by the detailed descriptions of abuse in a CIA inspector general's report, overruled the Bush-era exoneration of agency interrogators and appointed a special prosecutor to investigate possible crimes.

Over the next three years, however, the Obama administration moved, through relentless Republican demands for exoneration and its own tough stance on national security, to complete impunity for past perpetrators— quashing civil suits by torture victims, applying diplomatic pressure to slow foreign prosecutions, and curtailing Justice Department investigations. There were also clear signs of a shift to outsourcing interrogation, much as Washington had done during the Cold War. Starting in the last months of Bush's presidency, in mid-2008, U.S. intelligence captured a half-dozen Al Qaeda suspects and, instead of shipping them to CIA secret prisons, had them interrogated by allied agencies in the Middle East. Showing that this policy of outsourcing torture was again bipartisan, Obama's new CIA director, Leon Panetta, announced that his agency would continue to engage in the rendition of terror suspects to allies like Egypt, Jordan, or Pakistan, where the United States can, in theory at least, "rely on diplomatic assurances of good treatment."[102]

This reversion to the Cold War policy of relegating harsh interrogation to allies such as South Vietnam was now being repeated in both Iraq and Afghanistan. In the aftermath of the Abu Ghraib scandal, U.S. officials reacted to adverse publicity by transferring incarceration to local allies and studiously ignoring their human rights abuse. Afghan and Iraqi police, both created and trained by the United States, began torturing detainees systematically and simultaneously—a coincidence that hints at U.S. complicity.

Two months after the Abu Ghraib photos were broadcast in April 2004, the Coalition command in Iraq issued orders for its troops to overlook any detainee abuse by Iraqi forces.[103] Within a year, the BBC reported that Iraq's new police faced accusations of widespread torture inside their prisons.[104] Although the U.S. military received 1,365 reports about torture of detainees by Iraqi forces between 2004 and 2009, American officers either failed to investigate or refused to take action, even though the abuse was often extreme.[105]

Other NATO allies adopted a similar stance toward Iraqi tortures. In mid-2004, the Danish Defense Ministry received documentation that "prisoners in Iraqi prisons had been burned with cigarettes, had their molars crushed, and been beaten around their genitals," but deleted those passages from its reports to parliament, apparently from government concerns that such "information could harm Danish-Iraqi cooperation." To avoid their obligations under international law, Danish soldiers subsequently adopted a "systematic policy" of allowing Iraqi forces to make the "actual arrests" of some five hundred detainees. When the news of such complicity broke in early 2012, the Copenhagen press condemned this policy of "ordering soldiers to turn a blind eye to the likely mistreatment of detainees," and called for a full investigations "even if that means allowing . . . senior statesmen to be felled in the process"—an apparent reference to Anders Fogh Rasmussen, Denmark's prime minister during this period who later became NATO's secretary-general.[106]

Similarly, Washington's Afghan allies turned increasingly to torture after the Abu Ghraib scandal had prompted U.S. officials to transfer most incarceration and interrogation to local authorities. In 2009, a United Nations report stated that "Afghans are arbitrarily detained by police, prosecutors, judges and detention centre officials with alarming regularity." Two years later the UN found, after interviewing 324 detainees, that Afghan police and intelligence practiced "systematic torture" during interrogation of detainees who were beaten badly, hung by their hands, and had genitals twisted painfully. Of the 273 detainees held by Afghanistan's National Directorate of Security (NDS), nearly half were tortured to gain information via similar techniques at five separate facilities—indication, said the UN, that "torture is practiced systematically in a number of NDS detention facilities throughout Afghanistan." At the Kandahar lock-up, one NDS interrogator told a detainee before starting the torture: "You should confess what you have done in the past as Taliban; even stones confess here." At the NDS office in Kabul, where high-value detainees were confined, prisoners faced virtually a 100 percent chance of being tortured. Among the 117 detainees held by Afghan National Police, the UN found "credible evidence" that over a third were tortured to extract information. Both British and Canadian forces curtailed prisoner transfers to Afghan authorities after such reports of torture. But the U.S. military continued to turn over its detainees with few restrictions. Indeed, the *New York Times* commented that such widespread torture by these U.S. funded agencies "raises serious questions about potential complicity of American officials."[107]

Such abuse, deeply engrained in local security services, will likely continue long after the U.S. has withdrawn from Iraq and Afghanistan. This systemic brutality will, in all likelihood, complicate the process of nation building in both countries. But it may well persist, both from local institutional inertia and Washington's need for reliable partners in future rendition, interrogation, or counterterror operations.

Legacy of Torture

In retrospect, this recourse to CIA psychological torture under Bush corrupted U.S. intelligence and compromised America's international standing. CIA director George Tenet has claimed that these enhanced techniques were "extremely valuable in obtaining . . . critical threat information." But a careful review by the agency's inspector general found that "effectiveness . . . cannot be so easily measured," since there is no means to "determine . . . the totality of the intelligence the detainee actually possesses" or whether waterboarding, rather than simple "length of detention," was the "catalyst" for eventual compliance.[108]

Drawing on a decade of experience in U.S. counterterror operations, former FBI agent Ali Soufan told Congress in 2009 that it was "a mistake" to use enhanced interrogation techniques because they are "ineffective, slow and unreliable." In sharp contrast to the FBI's "informed interrogation approach," which produces reliable results within the bounds of law, the CIA's coercive method, Soufan said, "doesn't use the knowledge we have of the detainee's history, mindset, vulnerabilities, or culture." Instead, the CIA's technique "tries to subjugate the detainee into submission through humiliation and cruelty," seeking "to force the detainee to see the interrogator as the master who controls his pain." This fundamental flaw, Soufan testified, produced four major problems with the CIA's coercive doctrine. Since Al Qaeda terrorists were trained to resist the brutal torture "they would expect to receive if caught by dictatorships," CIA interrogators had to escalate to "harsher and harsher methods" until they reached their most extreme technique, waterboarding, which they had to use "again and again"—on Abu Zubaydah 83 times and on Khalid

Sheikh Mohammed 183 times. In effect, the CIA hit a "glass ceiling of harsh techniques," and detainees could "eventually call the interrogator's bluff." Second, Soufan testified, these coercive methods are unreliable because "there is no way to know whether the detainee is being truthful, or just speaking to either mitigate his discomfort or to deliberately provide false information," leading to "the disastrous case of Ibn al-Shaykh al-Libi who gave false information on Iraq, Al Qaeda, and WMD [weapons of mass destruction]." Third, he said, coercive methods are too slow. In contrast to the accurate intelligence that this agent got from Abu Zubaydah in just one hour with the FBI's "informed interrogation approach," the CIA's sleep deprivation required 180 hours while waterboarding Abu Zubaydah 183 times took weeks—far too long for any useful tactical intelligence. Finally, the agency's method ignored the requirement of U.S. courts for "due process," thereby making it impossible to successfully prosecute terror suspects after the interrogation was done. Consequently, this top FBI counterterror specialist concluded that "many of the claims made . . . about the success of the enhanced techniques are inaccurate."[109]

While the utility of the CIA's coercive method for gathering accurate intelligence is dubious at best, evidence has been building since 2004 that the Bush administration used torture to fabricate evidence of an alliance between the Iraqi dictator Saddam Hussein and Al Qaeda. After the CIA started interrogating the first Al Qaeda captive, Ibn al-Shaykh al-Libi, in early 2002, its director George Tenet testified before the Senate that Iraq had "provided unspecified chemical or biological weapons training for two al-Qa'ida associates." On the basis of such CIA intelligence, Secretary of State Colin Powell told the UN Security Council in February 2003 that "this detainee describes . . . Iraq offering chemical or biological weapons training for two al-Qaida associates."

A year later, in January 2004, however, al-Libi admitted to CIA investigators that he had "fabricated information while in U.S. custody" after being threatened with torture and forced to sleep on a cold floor. To get socks and a bed, he claimed full membership in Al Qaeda, although he was really only a minor employee, and rattled off all the names he knew. Following his transfer to Egyptian intelligence, al-Libi was asked about "al-Qaida's connections with Iraq"; he first "said he knew nothing." But, after seventeen hours in a "small box" and being "punched for 15 minutes," suddenly "he came up with a story that three al-Qai'ida members went to Iraq to learn about nuclear weapons." This story "pleased his interrogators, who directed that al-Libi be . . . given food."[110]

In May 2009, Secretary Powell's former military aide, Colonel Lawrence B. Wilkerson, charged that Vice President Cheney had ordered the torture of al-Libi to extract false intelligence about contacts between Saddam Hussein and Al Qaeda. "So furious was this effort," the colonel recalled, that, "even when the interrogation team had reported to Cheney's office that their detainee 'was compliant' (meaning the team recommended no more torture), the VP's office ordered them to continue the enhanced methods. . . . This ceased only after Ibn al-Shaykh al-Libi, under waterboarding in Egypt, 'revealed' such contacts."[111] With just socks, a wooden box, and a wet rag, the CIA and its allies easily fabricated intelligence about Iraq's nonexistent nuclear weapons that persuaded both the U.S. Senate and the UN Security Council—illustrating the extraordinary power of torture to force false confessions and compromise the intelligence process.

In the years since Secretary Powell shared the specious story about al-Libi with UN delegates, torture has, as discussed in chapter 6, done enormous damage to U.S. prestige among its closest allies. In 2006, the Council of Europe's secretary general became concerned by "press reports about prisoner transfers by the CIA" and called for "stronger supervision over the activities of national secret services" with closer controls "in respect of foreign services."[112] A few months later, Italy launched the trial of twenty-five CIA agents in absentia for the Milan kidnapping of a Muslim cleric who had been flown to Egypt for months of torture—an extraordinary rupture in covert relations.[113] Thus, the worldwide web of intelligence collaboration, central to CIA operations in Europe for more than half a century, was being ripped beyond repair.

As the traumatic events of 9/11 recede to allow a more sober perspective, this revival of CIA Cold War torture for the War on Terror seems, on multiple levels, a misguided decision. Just as the CIA's psychological protocol has become a distinctively American form of torture, so there is an alternative American approach that we might call "empathetic interrogation." During World War II, a Marine Corps interrogator, Major Sherwood F. Moran, a former missionary fluent in Japanese, used empathy to establish "intellectual and spiritual" rapport with Japanese prisoners, prompting the U.S. Navy to train a corps of Japanese-speaking interrogators who got quick, accurate order-of-battle intelligence from supposedly fanatical Japanese soldiers on islands across the Pacific.[114]

From 1940 to 2002, the FBI controlled all U.S. counterintelligence operations and used this empathetic method to successfully investigate threats to domestic security. After the bombings of U.S. embassies in East Africa in 1998, FBI teams used such empathy to gain some of the best U.S. intelligence on Al Qaeda and then to win convictions of the accused in federal courts. Right after 9/11, the FBI agent Ali Soufan employed this same method, which he calls the "informed interrogation approach," to question the captured Al Qaeda terrorist Abu Jandal, obtaining "a treasure trove of highly significant actionable intelligence" that included "Osama Bin Laden's terror network, structure, leadership, membership, security details, facilities, family, communication methods, travels, training, ammunitions, and weaponry." But, after President Bush transferred control of terrorism suspects from the FBI to the CIA in early 2002, experienced bureau interrogators from Cuba to Afghanistan would spend the next six years complaining bitterly to headquarters that the agency's extreme methods were blocking effective interrogation.[115]

No matter what position Washington might adopt toward CIA interrogation, the tangled history detailed in the chapters that follow has one clear lesson. As a powerfully symbolic state practice synonymous with brutal autocrats throughout the ages, torture—even of the few, even of just one—has raised profound questions about the quality of America's justice, the character of its civilization, and the legitimacy of its global leadership.

2

Science in Dachau's Shadow

I n August 2006, U.S. Army surgeon general Kevin Kiley, dressed in full combat uniform, appeared before the national convention of the American Psychological Association (APA) to defend the participation of psychologists in interrogation at Guantanamo. "Psychology," he declared, invoking a military maxim that many psychologists present may have found unsettling, "is an important weapons system."[1]

Indeed, for more than a half-century, psychology has served the U.S. intelligence community as a secret weapon in wars against its ideological enemies, first communism and then Islamic fundamentalism. Since the start of the Cold War, several generations of select psychologists have worked for U.S. intelligence agencies in the discovery and development of extreme interrogation methods that constitute nothing less than psychological torture. During the War on Terror, psychologists designed "enhanced" CIA interrogation methods, including the cruel technique called "waterboarding," and participated in military interrogations at Guantanamo Bay that International Red Cross condemned as "tantamount to torture."[2] In exchange for this service, the U.S. intelligence community has lavished rewards upon some members of the psychology profession, providing both generous funding for experimental researchers and employment for clinical specialists.

Psychology's service to U.S. national security has produced a variant of what the psychiatrist Robert Lifton has called, in his study of Nazi doctors, a "Faustian bargain." In this case, the price paid has been the American Psychological Association's collective silence, ethical "numbing," and, over time, historical amnesia.[3] Indeed, Lifton emphasizes that "the Nazis were not the only ones to involve doctors in evil"; in defense of this argument, he cites the Cold War "role of . . . American physicians and psychologists employed by the Central Intelligence Agency . . . for unethical medical and psychological experiments involving drugs and mind manipulation."[4]

During the early years of the Cold War, the CIA used this secret behavioral research to develop a new form of torture that relied on psychological rather than physical pain. The CIA's psychological paradigm fused two new techniques, sensory disorientation and self-inflicted pain, whose combination would cause victims to feel responsible for their own suffering and, in theory, capitulate more readily to their torturers. Refined through years of practice, the agency's psychological paradigm came to rely on a mix of sensory overload and sensory deprivation for a systematic attack on all human stimuli via seemingly banal, even benign procedures—manipulation of heat and cold, light and dark, noise and silence, isolation and then intense interrogation. The first clinical evidence of the severity of these methods appeared in 2007, when Dr. Metin Basoglu drew upon interviews with hundreds of torture victims to report, in the *Archives of General Psychiatry*, that psychological manipulation "does not seem to be substantially different from physical torture in terms of the severity of mental suffering."[5]

From the perspective of intelligence and interrogation, the development of a method that could inflict severe suffering via psychological rather than physical methods was a discovery of considerable import, a major advance in the cruel science of pain. If this breakthrough had conventional instead of covert uses, then the search for new forms of interrogation might have become another of those heroic, history-of-science narratives about a brilliant researcher working alone, besting rivals, and capturing the crown of discovery with all its recognition and reward. Just as the discovery of natural selection supposedly involved a race between Charles Darwin and Alfred Wallace or the development of the polio vaccine a rivalry between Jonas Salk and Albert Sabin, so the CIA's refinement of psychological torture can be reduced, in all its complexity, to a narrative of competing approaches by two titans of twentieth-century medical science—Donald O. Hebb's behavioral methods and Henry K. Beecher's drug experimentation.[6]

Their eminence should not be underestimated: Hebb is a towering figure in cognitive science, and his 1949 book *The Organization of Behavior* is regarded by some as second only to Darwin's *Origin of the Species* in scientific significance;[7] Beecher is remembered as a pioneer in American anesthesiology and, above all, modern clinical ethics.[8] Yet, for both researchers, there was a fortuitous convergence between the CIA's mind-control project and their own professional trajectories, providing funds for the human experimentation central to their research and rising reputations. Such support came with all the ethical compromises inherent in classified scientific work.

Though research into psychological torture was indeed a dark science, it was science nonetheless and has a significant history that commands close attention rather than willful amnesia or spurious denials. For probing this covert confluence between CIA research and cognitive science reveals not only the discovery of a virulent form of psychological torture that has persisted to the present but also the development of its potential antidote in the form of modern medical ethics. In one of history's ironies, this secret CIA research, with its harsh treatment of human subjects, also seemed to produce its own correction, making Dr. Beecher, in an ambiguous sense, the ultimate victor in this silent, scientific competition.

Dual Legacy of Dachau

At the dawn of the Cold War, the human mind became a covert battleground contested with new weapons of mass persuasion and individual interrogation. From 1950 to 1962, the CIA led a secret research effort to crack the code of human consciousness. After reviewing five thousand pages of documents and interviewing CIA veterans, the *New York Times* reported, in 1977, the existence of a "secret, 25-year, $25 million effort by the Central Intelligence Agency to learn how to control the human mind." Prompted by the behavior of defendants at communist show trials in Eastern Europe in 1948–49, the CIA's project was launched in the short-lived belief, which was later "proved unfounded," that the Soviets had developed sophisticated methods for brainwashing. But, by the early 1950s, the *Times* reported, "the C.I.A. quickly turned to an offensive use for behavior control," seeking to "crack the mental defenses of enemy agents—to be able to program them to carry out any mission even against their will and 'against such fundamental laws of nature as self-preservation.'"[9]

In 1950, after just a few months of such investigation, the CIA decided to "transfer the psychological part of the [research] program to an outside agency, where more adequate facilities . . . and volunteers could be utilized as subjects." One of the first of these new contracts was for $300,000, paid through the Navy, to a "Department of Psychology" at an unnamed university. Within two years, the Office of Naval Research (ONR), with an unknown portion of its grants from the CIA, would become an influential patron for experimental psychology by funding 117 contracts at fifty-eight universities.[10]

More broadly, as Christopher Simpson explains, "the Department of Defense and the Central Intelligence Agency helped bankroll substantially all of the post-World War II generation's research into techniques of persuasion, opinion measurement, [and] interrogation." At their peak, total costs for psychological research and operations reached a billion dollars a year.[11]

In understanding this Cold War mobilization of behavioral science, Lifton's study of the Nazi doctors offers a useful analogue. Soon after taking power, Nazi appeals to the ingrained conservatism of the medical profession persuaded 45 percent of German physicians to join the party, while a smaller number, about 350 doctors, later participated in "medical crimes" through a process of psychological "numbing." Just as Lifton asked how these German doctors could betray their Hippocratic oath, so we might ask how American psychologists dedicated to healing pain might instead choose to inflict it through medical experiments or interrogation.[12]

But the Nazi doctors are much more than metaphor or analogue in the history of CIA torture research. Just as the U.S. space program benefited from the work of Wernher von Braun's rocket scientists at Peenemünde and the Luftwaffe's murderous medical experiments at Dachau, so this CIA mind-control effort continued the research of the Nazi doctors, both their specific findings and their innovative use of human subjects. In 1942, the Luftwaffe did pioneering research into altitude sickness and hypothermia on some two hundred prisoners at the Dachau concentration camp, documenting their agonizing deaths in graphic films shown at the 1942 Nazi aviation medical conference. After the war, the U.S. Air Force, enticed by the scientific significance of this work, recruited thirty-four of these Nazi doctors who had eluded Nuremberg's net to establish its School of Aviation Medicine at Randolph Field, Texas—bringing the Reich's research esprit into the heart of U.S. military medicine.[13] In 1950, the U.S. Air Force effectively expunged these crimes from the historical record by publishing *German Aviation Medicine: World War II*, a hagiographic account of these Nazi doctors as heroic men who "showed great scientific understanding . . . and personal concern in aeromedical research."[14]

More broadly, the Nazi use of human subjects in defiance of long-standing clinical restraints had contradictory effects—cautioning medical science about the need for ethics that were embodied in the 1947 Nuremberg medical code, while simultaneously alerting the U.S. national security community to the potential yield from such inhumane treatment.[15] "The Nuremberg Code has remained official American policy ever since 1946," John Marks explained in his landmark study of CIA mind-control research, "but, even before the verdicts were in, special U.S. investigating teams were sifting through the experimental records at Dachau for information of military value."[16] In sum, medical science was repulsed by Dachau's inhumanity, but U.S. national security was intrigued.

Consequently, Washington's postwar defense research was soon infected by the Dachau model, whose methods it mimed across a broad spectrum of Cold War experiments on literally tens of thousands of unwitting human subjects for atomic, chemical, biological, and psychological warfare.[17] To cite just a few examples, atomic experiments exposed more than 200,000 U.S. servicemen to radiation and used 3,000 more as human subjects; a range of "psychoactive chemicals," particularly LSD, was tested on some 6,700 unwitting subjects, including 1,000 soldiers; virulent biological warfare agents were administered to some 2,300 Seventh-Day Adventist volunteers; and chemicals were tested on thousands of soldiers, including 1,366 who were exposed to CS riot-control gas.[18]

Behavioral scientists who collaborated with the CIA's mind-control research during the 1950s also drew from Dachau's poisoned well. Reflecting this era's ethical ethos, all the behavioral researchers cited in this chapter who had ties to secret research—Hebb, Beecher, Maitland Baldwin, Ewan Cameron, Stanley Milgram, Donald Wexler, Jack Mendelson, Herbert Leiderman, and Philip Solomon—conducted experiments whose success entailed infliction of psychological pain upon human subjects in violation of the Nuremberg Code of medical ethics.

Significantly, this secret mind-control research coincided, at midpoint in its development, with Washington's condemnation of communist "brainwashing" in North Korea, a form of psychological torture that forced captured American pilots to make false statements about U.S. war crimes. This coincidence soon produced two paths in U.S. mind-control research, offensive and defensive, that would intersect for the next half-century. Starting in 1951, the CIA launched allied scientists on a determined search for psychological methods that could be used against the enemy, either interrogating captives or turning their agents into double agents. Four years later, after extensive investigations into communist abuse of POWs in Korea, Washington ordered that all American military personnel subject to capture be trained to resist such psychological torture, producing a second, defensive element in U.S. mind-control research, easily repurposed later for offensive uses.

Not only did this Korean coincidence add a defensive dimension to cognitive research, but it also fostered a clear contradiction in U.S. human rights policy. Publicly at the UN and in other international forums, American representatives condemned torture, particularly the communists' use of psychological techniques. Simultaneously and secretly, however, U.S. government agencies were already engaged in classified research to find more effective methods of mind control—fostering a contradiction in American human rights policy that would persist for the next forty years.

Communist "Brainwashing"

During the last year of the Korean War, Washington was confronted with the issue of communist "brainwashing" and responded in the principled manner of a power that had participated in drafting the Geneva Conventions and the UN Universal Declaration of Human Rights. In October 1952, Radio Peking broadcast a brief report, generally ignored by the international press, that four captured U.S. Air Force pilots had confessed to knowledge of biological warfare in North Korea. But then, in February 1953, Radio Peking read a lengthy deposition by another POW, Marine Colonel Frank S. Schwable, detailing orders delivered "personally and verbally for security reasons . . . to test under field conditions various elements of bacteriological warfare and possibly to expand field tests at a later date into an element of regular combat operations."[19]

Within hours, the Allied Far East commander, General Mark Clark, publicly condemned the colonel's statement as a product of the "mind-annihilating methods of these Communists in extorting whatever words they want."[20] In Washington, CIA director Allen Dulles sent President Eisenhower a memo advising that "a quick search in the CIA shows little scientific evidence to support brainwashing. There is rather massive evidence in the form of case reports . . . which leads to the conclusion that it is not a difficult matter, given the time, to force almost anyone to make an inaccurate statement, provided that the time at which the statement is to be made can be controlled."[21]

Reflecting the seriousness of the matter, Defense Secretary Charles E. Wilson recommended that U.S. statements "explaining the techniques employed" by communists in coercing these confessions "provide the initial point for an effective counter propaganda campaign designed to create revulsion throughout the world concerning the Communist program." In Wilson's view, the communists were guilty of "a 'new' form of war crime, and a new refinement in atrocity techniques; namely, 'mind murder' or menticide."[22]

To make sure that the United States was not guilty of the same crimes, the secretary then drew upon the language of the Nuremberg medical code to issue guidelines for all Defense Department work involving "the use of human volunteers . . . in experimental research in the fields of atomic, biological and/or chemical warfare." These regulations noted that the "voluntary consent of the human subject is absolutely essential," and such subjects be used only for experiments likely "to yield fruitful results for the good of society, unprocurable by other methods or means of study."[23]

Simultaneously, the White House turned to medical experts for suggestions to counter the threat of communist "brainwashing." According to Dr.

Henry P. Laughlin, a consultant to the National Security Council and an officer of the American Psychiatric Association, Western scientists accustomed "to humane standards" are "totally unfamiliar with the methods as employed." Brainwashing requires, he added, "many months of time and effort on the part of the most skilled operators." Since "we possess high moral and ethical standards," Laughlin continued, "we cannot fight 'fire with fire.'" For the United States, he recommended, "the moral condemnation . . . of the inhuman methods of brain-washing constitutes a weapon of considerable strength." People will "view the process with loathing and thoroughly condemn the perpetrators of such inhuman methods."[24]

In May 1953, after repeated accusations about germ warfare were broadcast by Radio Peking, the Eisenhower administration made careful preparations for countercharges of communist brainwashing before the UN General Assembly.[25] In planning to assure maximum impact, the State Department suggested that affidavits from former POWs emphasize the "varying amounts of food given to them during those efforts, amount of sleep allowed, clothing allowance, description of type of shelter and bedding given, instances of lack or denial of medical attention, physical abuse."[26]

Consequently, just six weeks after North Korea released the U.S. airmen who had made the germ warfare charges, the alternate U.S. representative, Dr. Charles W. Mayo, son of the founder of the famed Mayo Clinic, told the UN General Assembly's Political Committee in September 1953 about the psychological torture inflicted on these American pilots, producing moving testimony that won worldwide press coverage.[27] Among the 107 captured pilots accused of bacteriological warfare, 40 had refused to sign confessions and 36 had agreed only after suffering "extreme and prolonged physical and mental torture." Six of these pilots had confessed "after interrogation and physical and mental torture in solitary confinement, lasting . . . nearly five months." To give UN delegates a sense of this harsh treatment, Dr. Mayo related, in starkly clinical detail, the tortures inflicted on an Air Force pilot, Lieutenant James L. Stanley:

He was stood at attention for five hours at a time; confined eight days in a doorless cell less than six feet long; held to the ground by two guards while a third kicked and slapped him; stood at attention 22 hours until he fell, then hit while lying down with the side of a hatchet and stood up for two more hours; interrogated three hours with a spotlight six inches from his face; ordered to confess while a pistol was held at the back of his head; placed under a roof drain all night during a rainstorm; left without food three days and without water eight days, tempted with promises of good treatment and letters from home; put before a firing squad and given a last chance; hung by hands and feet from the rafters of a house.[28]

Making a clear distinction between physical and mental methods, Dr. Mayo emphasized that the "the tortures used in these cases, although they include many brutal physical injuries, are not like the medieval tortures of the rack and the thumbscrew." The communists' tactics were, he emphasized, "subtler, more prolonged, and intended to be more terrible in their effect," designed to "disintegrate the mind of an intelligent victim." It was, he said, a "pattern of intimidation, deprivation of basic physical needs, isolation, and physical and mental torture." Prisoners were "bullied incessantly, deprived of sleep and browbeaten into mental anguish."[29]

Simultaneously, the Defense Department, after an internal debate, launched a parallel public relations campaign, releasing detailed descriptions of the brainwashing used to extract these false confessions. One film about the pilots who confessed was withheld after a staff analyst on the Psychological Strategy Board objected to its portrayal of brainwashing as a "mysterious technique." In fact, he argued, the method was quite clear and involved bringing "overwhelming pressure . . . on an individual without laying a hand on him by simply with-holding sleep or physical and mental relaxation . . . and the *threat* (not actual use other than provocative slapping . . .) of physical harm."[30]

After suppressing that film, the Pentagon released another, titled *POWs Who Did Not Confess*, for television and newsreels; this one featured five pilots "who refused to confess to germ warfare and other crimes," even though they were "starved, clubbed, pistol-whipped, tossed into dungeons and subjected to incessant Communist indoctrination."[31] Several days later, the *New York Times* published a statement submitted to the UN by one of the pilots who had confessed, Walker M. Mahurin, describing the isolation, cold, and protracted stress positions that had been used to extract his story about supposed biological warfare planning by the U.S. Air Force command.[32]

With the communist germ warfare propaganda effectively blunted before the UN,[33] the Eisenhower administration still faced some difficult policy choices—whether to prosecute the pilots who had confessed and what procedures to introduce to prevent future incidents. After much internal debate, the military services decided, in January 1954, not to prosecute the thirty-six pilots who had confessed to germ warfare, with the notable exception of Colonel Frank Schwable, the Marine pilot who had made the most detailed confession on Radio Peking.[34]

In an era of global war, the trial of this Marine colonel, a graduate of Annapolis with twenty-five years of distinguished service, became a major media event and proved seminal in shaping a new military code of conduct. For nearly two months, from February to April 1954, a tribunal of four general officers took testimony at Marine Corps headquarters in Arlington, Virginia, with heavy coverage by the national press.[35] Testifying as a psychiatric expert, Dr. Joost Meerloo said the Soviets had drawn upon Dr. Ivan Pavlov's work on the "conditioned reflex" to develop "brainwashing" to the point that any victim "will inevitably capitulate" and "identify himself completely with his interrogator."[36] At a press conference a few days later, President Eisenhower endorsed this view, suggesting that men like Colonel Schwable who were subject to such methods "must not be condemned too severely."[37]

In his own testimony, the colonel emphasized the role of psychological methods, saying: "I want to re-emphasize that I did not undergo physical torture." He added, "Perhaps I would have been more fortunate if I had [undergone actual physical torture], because people nowadays seem to understand that better. This was torture of a more subtle form." Instead of simple beatings, he was immobilized in stress positions for countless hours while subjected to isolation, extreme cold, and threats of indefinite incarceration.[38] In its verdict, the Marine tribunal recommended that "no disciplinary action be taken"—a precedent that the Air Force followed a year later when it reinstated, without discipline or demerit, four pilots who had given germ-warfare confessions.[39]

Yet the vexing problem of future guidelines for American POWs remained. In the run-up to the Schwable trial, the *New York Times* had editorialized that "our soldiers . . . must be taught to deal with this tactic of terror."[40] Indeed, in accepting the tribunal's verdict, Navy Secretary Robert Anderson wrote that "the efforts of a diabolical enemy to utilize . . . the distortion of the mental and moral . . . thinking and conduct of the prisoners of war" require that the Defense Department study these methods and develop a program of "training and indoctrination" to enable future captives to resist these "methods of physical and mental torture."[41]

Consequently, in August 1955, after deliberating for three months and seeking advice from sixty-seven experts, a Pentagon panel issued a code requiring resistance by all future POWs and recommending that every soldier liable to capture be given "specific training . . . to cope with all enemy efforts against him."[42] That same day, President Dwight Eisenhower issued such an executive order—leading the Air Force, within a year, to develop a rigorous training program (called SERE, for Survival, Evasion, Resistance, Escape) to prepare pilots for psychological torture.[43] As the military consulted psychologists and psychiatrists to diagnose past POW treatment in Korea and propose an antidote, there thus developed, starting in late 1955, two related strands in mind-control research—offensive, for CIA interrogation of enemy agents, and defensive, for training American pilots to resist enemy interrogators.[44]

Through these two years of diplomatic and military debate, from 1953 to

1955, Washington resolved that torture could extract false confessions from even the most disciplined soldier; torture was morally abhorrent; and revelations of such abuse by any nation would arouse international condemnation. Yet, in defiance these same principles, secret U.S. research into mind-control methods would continue undisturbed for another decade, ultimately producing a doctrine almost as harsh as the techniques that communist interrogators had used against American POWs in North Korea.

Two Pathways to Mind Control

While Washington was denouncing communist brainwashing, the CIA was already deeply involved in sustained research into similar methods of mind control. In contrast to the command-economy models for scientific mobilization used in the Soviet Union or the Third Reich, the CIA employed financial incentives and collegial manipulation to effect a subtle redirection of the cognitive science community, making its covert agenda a major focus of American behavioral research during the 1950s. As the *New York Times* reported in its investigation of this secret CIA effort "to control the human mind," the agency "was able to assemble an extensive network of non-government scientists and facilities—apparently without the knowledge of the institutions where the facilities were located." According to a report by the CIA inspector general compiled in 1957, the agency "had added difficulty in obtaining expert services" since some experiments "are considered to be professionally unethical and in some instances border on the illegal." Hence, as one member of the CIA's Technical Services Division told the *Times*, "secrecy has been used to protect the researchers from peer group pressure should it be known that they were working for the Agency."[45]

Apart from a few lead researchers who were knowing collaborators, most of those involved in this research—their colleagues, junior faculty, and graduate assistants—were probably unaware of the covert agenda and often pursued research remote from the agency's goals. Nonetheless, the CIA presided over a scientific research effort that made major advances: notably, elimination of exotic methods such as hypnosis and LSD and, above all, discovery of innovative behavioral techniques for interrogation. While the agency's in-house testing of exotic drugs such as LSD produced negative results, seemingly mundane CIA-funded behavioral experiments, outsourced to leading Canadian and U.S. universities, soon made significant contributions to the agency's doctrine of psychological torture.[46]

Our Man in Montreal

After a short-lived defensive reaction to Soviet mind-control efforts in 1948–49, the CIA's cognitive research quickly shifted from defense to offense.[47] By 1951, the agency was launched, in close collaboration with its British and Canadian allies, on a determined search for mind-control methods, both interrogation and mental reprogramming, that might prove effective against the enemy. That March, the agency initiated what it called, in a classified memo, a "top secret" research program into "all aspects of special interrogation" through "exchange of information and coordination of related programs."[48]

Consequently, in the words of a later Canadian inquiry by George Cooper, QC, "a high-level meeting took place at the Ritz Carlton Hotel in Montreal on June 1, 1951." Attending were Sir Henry T. Tizard, the influential senior scientist from the British Ministry of Defense; Dr. Omond Solandt, head of Canada's Defense Research Board (DRB); Dr. Donald O. Hebb, chief of the Board's Behavioral Research and chair of the psychology department at McGill University; and two Americans, Dr. Caryl Haskins and Commander R. J. Williams. These latter two were identified, in a "handwritten note" found in Research Board files, as "CIA."[49]

Indicative of the import of this meeting, Dr. Tizard's earlier trans-Atlantic voyage at the start of World War II had mobilized thousands of physicists to develop radar as a key weapon in the Allied defeat of the Axis powers.[50] And, indicative of the extent of CIA penetration of the U.S. scientific establishment, Dr. Haskins became, five years after this meeting, president of the influential Carnegie Institution of Washington, a position he held for fifteen years until his retirement in 1971.[51]

According to the Board's minutes of this Montreal mind-control summit, "Dr. Hebb suggested that an approach based upon the situation of sensory isolation might lead to some clues" to answering "the central problem" that interested this covert research coalition: "'confession,' 'menticide,' 'intervention in the individual mind,'—together with methods concerned in psychological coercion." Reflecting the CIA's ongoing effort, discussed earlier, to mentally reprogram enemy agents "to carry out any mission even against their will," Hebb suggested that, by "cutting off all sensory stimulation . . . the individual could be led into a situation whereby ideas, etc. might be implanted." In response, Sir Henry Tizard concurred, stating that these issues "had become a matter of concern in the U.K." On an historical note, he added that "the methods of psychological coercion . . . had been well developed by the inquisition."[52]

As consensus formed about "research methods and design," the group adopted Hebb's suggestion that "experimental isolation in various forms for the production of *sensory isolation*" might place subjects "in such a position psychologically that they would be susceptible to implantation of new or different ideas." Despite the Research Board's later claims to the contrary, its minutes indicate clearly that its primary concern in backing Hebb's brainwashing work was not defensive research to protect allied personnel but offensive operations against communist enemies. "With respect to . . . useful results," the Montreal principals agreed, "present methods of offence had moved over into the psychological field and that the whole area of change in public opinion and individual attitude was assuming rapidly increasing importance." Then, as an afterthought and an apparently secondary concern, the group noted: "In addition, the project itself would serve to open up this general area for research by those concerned with defense."[53]

The CIA's own minutes concur with the DRB's emphasis on offensive aims, recording that the Montreal group agreed there was "no conclusive evidence" that the Soviets had made anything akin to "revolutionary progress" and dismissed their interrogation as "remarkably similar . . . to the age-old methods." Behind closed doors, therefore, the defensive pretense evaporated, and these allied scientists decided to pursue control over human consciousness for offensive "cold war operations": ideological conversion and coercive interrogation.[54]

"Medical science," reads a February 1952 CIA memo that seems to echo this Montreal meeting, "particularly . . . psychiatry and psychotherapy, has developed various techniques by means of which some external control can be imposed on the mind/or will of an individual, such as drugs, hypnosis, electric shock and neurosurgery."[55] In a memo dated January 25, 1952, the agency summarized the overarching offensive aims of its mind control effort, now coordinated under Project Artichoke, as "the evaluation and development of any method by which we can get information from a person against his will and without his knowledge," allowing "control of an individual where he will do our bidding against his will and even against such fundamental laws of nature as self-preservation."[56]

Within just a few years, this allied scientific offensive would pursue classified research concealed inside public and private facilities of five major nations—including a British "intelligence research unit" at Maresfield, Sussex; an Anglo-American facility near Frankfurt for lethal experiments on captured Soviet-bloc "expendables"; CIA-funded psychology research at leading U.S. hospitals and universities; periodic allied conferences to exchange results; and, above all, classified Canadian studies of sensory deprivation at McGill University.[57] In marked contrast to the uniformly unsuccessful yield from the CIA's drug experiments, three among the hundreds of behavioral research projects outsourced to academics produced important results.

Three months after the Montreal meeting, in one of the most significant steps for the gestation of the CIA's psychological paradigm, Ottawa's Defense Research Board awarded Dr. Hebb a "secret" grant, under Contract DRB-X38. From 1951 to 1954, Hebb's team used these funds for experiments that discovered the devastating psychological impact of sensory deprivation. As Hebb explained in his classified 1952 report, these experiment were measuring "whether *slight* changes of attitude might be effected" by shorter periods of isolation intensified by "wearing (a) light-diffusing goggles, (b) earphones through which white noise may be constantly delivered . . . , and (c) cardboard tubes over his [the subject's] forearms so that his hands . . . cannot be used for tactual perception of the environment." In contrast to the modest impact initially anticipated, Hebb reported that "motivational disturbance appears great." Among twenty-two subjects, "four remarked spontaneously that being in the apparatus was a form of torture." Evidently encouraged, Hebb concluded that "the contract is opening up a field of study that is of both theoretical and practical significance."[58]

With a growing sense of this project's scientific import and concerned that his McGill colleague Dr. Ewan Cameron was "now undertaking some

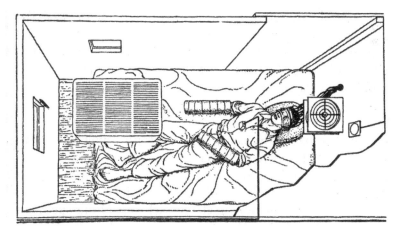

Isolation cubicle for student volunteers in Dr. Donald O. Hebb's experiments in sensory deprivation via goggles, hand tubes, and ear baffles, McGill University, 1952–54. (from "Cognitive and Physiological Effects of Perceptual Isolation," by Woodburn Heron, in *Sensory Deprivation*, edited by Philip Solomon et al., Harvard University Press, copyright © 1961 by the President and Fellows of Harvard College, copyright © renewed 1989 by Philip Solomon)

work with this method," Dr. Hebb pressed the Research Board for permission to publicize his results. But the Board resisted by insisting on secrecy and, if necessary, deceptive cover stories.[59] A year later, Hebb argued that a full presentation, albeit one masked by a cover story to conceal the project's real aim, in Dr. Cameron's psychiatry conference at McGill's Allen Memorial Institute "would be useful to me, for the furtherance of our work and for getting financed." After reminding the Board that "I *have* worked hard for you people, with no other pay than getting these experimental results," Hebb concluded his impassioned, ultimately unsuccessful appeal by sketching, at the bottom of his letter, a kneeling figure with arms raised in supplication.[60] While public disclosures were thus restricted, Hebb's 1952 annual report was distributed to all three branches of the U.S. military, along with "1 copy to Central Intelligence Agency (USA)."[61]

After three years of secret research, the story finally leaked to the *Toronto Star* in January 1954. In a background memo for his supervising cabinet minister, Dr. Solandt, the head of the Defense Research Board, explained that Hebb's work had "originated from a discussion among Sir Henry Tizard, representatives of the U.S. Central Intelligence Agency, Dr. Hebb . . . , and myself in June 1951." Hebb's subsequent research, he said, had "given some indication that significant changes in attitude can be brought about by use of propaganda under conditions of isolation." Simultaneous with this correspondence, the Research Board soon quieted the press with a cover story about Hebb doing research to relieve monotony among those monitoring radar screens.[62]

Even so, questions were raised in Canada's Parliament, and the Cabinet decided, on "questions of principle," that "the contract with Hebb at McGill be cancelled." In an internal memo to Dr. Solandt, a Defense official noted that "there continues to be interest from U.S. in this project, . . . Hebb has previously had several official U.S. visitations."[63] In his report for the Cabinet, Dr. Solandt, hinting at continuing CIA contacts, noted that Hebb's work had been of "appreciable interest to U.S. research agencies, representatives of which have by arrangement visited Hebb."[64]

While Canada was cutting Dr. Hebb loose, the CIA maintained regular contact. In September 1954, more than six thousand psychologists filled New York City's Statler Hotel for the annual convention of the American Psychological Association. There an anonymous CIA scientist met Hebb's close colleague, Dr. Edward C. Webster, later chair of psychology at McGill, for a detailed briefing on the sensory deprivation experiments.[65] According to another of Hebb's McGill colleagues, Dr. Peter M. Milner, at some point after the termination of their Canadian funding "the project . . . did receive money from a research foundation that was later revealed to be a front for the C.I.A."[66]

Two years later, the director of the U.S. National Institutes of Health, Dr. Robert H. Felix, demolished Hebb's carefully constructed cover story when he told Congress about a study by "Dr. Donald Hebb, Professor of Psychology, McGill University," that used sixty students "who stayed as long as they could on a bed in an air conditioned box." Asked if "this is a form of brainwashing," Dr. Felix replied: "You can break down anyone with this, I don't care what their background." After coverage in the *New York Times* in April 1956 prompted "brainwashing" headlines in the Montreal *Gazette*, Dr. Hebb insisted, inaccurately, on the "defensive" nature of his research, saying: "We were not trying to find bigger and better ways of torturing others, but to find out how to protect our own men."[67]

There is good reason to doubt the credence of Dr. Hebb's assertion that the prime aim of his research was defensive. As is evident in extant CIA memoranda and the Research Board minutes of the June 1951 Montreal meeting, his research was launched in a period, 1951–52, when the paramount objective of the agency and its Canadian allies was the development of mind-control methods for offensive operations—interrogation of communist captives, conversion of enemy agents into double agents, and imposition of alien beliefs on target assets. Three years after his research started, there was a renewed interest in the defensive uses of mind control when the release of American prisoners from North Korea allowed military debriefings about communist "brainwashing." But Hebb's secret research for Canada's Defense Research Board was terminated in August 1954—a full year before President Eisenhower's order that U.S. soldiers should be trained to resist interrogation would prompt new research into defensive methods.[68] In sum, almost all this work on defensive measures started in late 1955, well after Hebb had already completed his four years of offensive mind-control research for the CIA and the Defense Research Board.[69]

Just as Hebb insisted the aim of his research was defensive, so Canada's Research Board made similarly exculpatory statements that "the scientists . . . were extremely careful to limit the research techniques so that there was no possibility of damage to the subjects who volunteered."[70] Once again, there are grounds for a contrary view. Since his experiments discovered the driver in CIA psychological torture, it seems logical, almost undeniable, that Hebb's research subjected his student subjects to this same torture—a complaint, in fact, made by four of his original volunteers. So extreme was this sensory deprivation that Hebb's subjects had unanticipated hallucinations akin to those induced by mescaline. In his narrative poem "Listening to the Candle," one of these student subjects, Peter Dale Scott, later a professor at the University of California–Berkeley, described how he first noticed the vivid hallucinations.[71]

yet the very aimlessness
preconditioning my mind . . .
for blank lucrative hours
of sensory deprivation
as a paid volunteer
in the McGill experiment . . .
my ears sore from their earphones'
amniotic hum my eyes
under two bulging halves of ping pong balls
arms covered to the tips with cardboard tubes
those familiar hallucinations
I was the first to report
as for example the string
of cut-out paper men
emerging from a manhole
in the side of a snow-white hill
distinctly two-dimensional

Many of Hebb's subjects were McGill medical students. In an interview, one subject, a retired medical doctor who had no prior history of hysteria, described how he suffered a complete breakdown after participating in the experiment, collapsing on the floor during lecture in a paroxysm of weeping so uncontrollable and so protracted that the professor was forced to clear the classroom.[72] Although repeating the Research Board's claim that Hebb had "the highest regard for the welfare of the volunteer students," Cooper's inquiry did note "an unconfirmed report that one student developed a form of mental illness following the experiment." But he dismissed the matter after hearing an unsubstantiated "suggestion . . . that the illness was incipient in any event, and would have resulted regardless of Dr. Hebb's experiments."[73]

In contrast to these exculpatory official statements on his behalf, Hebb himself admitted that he did not screen his subjects for instability and was not prepared for the extreme hallucinations. "For subjects," he recalled in a memoir written before his death in 1985, "we simply called the employment office at McGill and hired the student they sent us. Presently we found that . . . the subjects, some of them, were seeing things in the experimental conditions, and feeling things. One felt his head was disconnected from his body, another had two bodies." Hebb was also shocked at the devastating impact of his experiments: "It scared the hell out of us to see how completely dependent the mind is on a close connection with the ordinary sensory environment, and how disorganizing to be cut off from that support."[74]

The implications of Hebb's experiment for both cognitive science and CIA interrogation were, in retrospect, profound. As Hebb himself later put it, "the experiment did give support for my theory of behavior" first propounded, without experimental confirmation, in his landmark 1949 book, *The Organization of Behavior*, and got him "recognized abroad."[75] Within seven years of his team's first publications, more than 230 articles on sensory deprivation appeared in leading scientific journals, citing Hebb's work and contributing to his rising reputation.[76] In June 1958, the Office of Naval Research (ONR), a major CIA conduit, funded a symposium on sensory deprivation at the Harvard Medical School, featuring Hebb and some of the other leading cognitive scientists of his generation. Their papers confirmed the significance of his discovery and further explored the devastating impact of sensory deprivation on the human mind.[77]

Several follow-up experiments into sensory deprivation by Hebb's junior colleagues also risked inflicting dangerous trauma on their human subjects. At the U.S. National Institute of Mental Health in 1955, Dr. Maitland Baldwin, a neurosurgeon who had studied with Hebb at McGill, confined an Army volunteer in a specially constructed sensory deprivation box. After forty hours inside, the man began "an hour of crying loudly and sobbing in a most heart-rending fashion" before kicking his way out. This dramatic denouement persuaded Dr. Baldwin that "the isolation technique could break any man, no matter how intelligent or strong-willed," and anything more than six days of sensory deprivation would "almost certainly cause irreparable damage." At the prompting of Morse Allen, chief of the CIA's Artichoke Project, Dr. Baldwin agreed to push the experiment further into "terminal type" tests if the agency would provide expendable human subjects—a proposal that a CIA medical officer rejected as "immoral and inhuman."[78]

When another of Hebb's former researchers, Dr. John Zubek, proposed building a similar coffin-box for long-term experiments in sensory deprivation at the University of Manitoba in 1960, the chair of the psychiatry department objected. "The immobilization can be expected to result in an increased incidence of psychotic ideation—hallucinations, delusions, disorientation, etc.," warned Dr. George C. Sisler. "The possibility of individuals predisposed to psychotic illness having some continuing reaction is thereby increased." Nonetheless, Zubek, as chair of psychology at Manitoba, conducted such extreme experiments for the next fifteen years with grants totaling $275,000 from Canada's Defense Research Board and $90,000 from the U.S. National Institute of Mental Health. When that funding ended in 1974 amid controversy over Britain's use of sensory deprivation to torture detainees in Belfast, Dr. Zubek

drowned himself in Winnipeg's Red River. One of his human subjects, Gordon Winocur, then an undergraduate and later a psychology professor at the University of Toronto, recalled his ninety minutes inside that coffin, saying: "It was horrible, really uncomfortable. If you have any latent claustrophobia, it's going to come out."[79]

Through a similar experiment in 1957, a team of four Harvard University psychiatrists, funded by the Office of Naval Research, a frequent CIA front, confined seventeen paid volunteers "in a tank-type respirator" arranged "to inhibit movement and tactile contact." After seventeen hours, one subject, a twenty-five-year-old dental student, "began to punch and shake the respirator," his "eyes full of tears, and his voice shaking." Four volunteers terminated because of "anxiety and panic," and all suffered "degrees of anxiety."[80] We have no way of knowing whether such trauma did lasting damage, for none of these researchers—Hebb, Baldwin, Zubek, or the Harvard psychiatrists—reported any follow-up treatment.

Just a few months later, another CIA contractor, Dr. Lawrence Hinkle, of the Cornell University Medical Center, conducted a comprehensive review of "interrogation . . . for the purposes of intelligence," finding Hebb's isolation "the ideal way of 'breaking down' a prisoner, because . . . it seems to create precisely the state that the interrogator desires: malleability and the desire to talk, with the added advantage that one can delude himself that he is using no force or coercion."[81]

Finally, in 1963, the CIA synthesized this decade of mind-control research in its "KUBARK Counterintelligence Interrogation" manual, which emphasized the implications of Hebb's work for effective interrogation. Citing "experiments conducted at McGill University," this report explained that sensory deprivation was effective because "the calculated provision of stimuli during interrogation tends to make the regressed subject view the interrogator as a father-figure . . . strengthening . . . the subject's tendencies toward compliance."[82]

The compilation of this report, combined with the CIA inspector general's discovery of legal problems in the mind-control research, produced a radical reduction in funding from the agency and other national security sources, creating a crisis in the ranks of Canadian psychology. "Departments of psychology in Canadian universities are now about to starve to death for lack of research support," reported Dr. C. R. Myers, of the country's Defense Research Board, in 1964. Noting the critical role of U.S. defense funds in sustaining this field, Dr. Myers concluded: "There appears to be no other scientific discipline in Canada that is so dependent for research support on U.S. sources."[83]

The CIA and Canada

Controversy over mind-control experiments at McGill flared anew in the mid-1980s when nine victims of CIA-funded research at the campus's Allen Memorial Institute filed a civil damages suit against the agency in Washington, DC, producing important revelations about this research. With annual CIA payments of $20,000 from 1957 to 1963, the head of Allen Memorial Institute at McGill, Dr. Ewan Cameron, had used approximately a hundred patients, many admitted to his clinic with moderate problems, as involuntary subjects to test a three-stage method for "brainwashing" or "depatterning"—first, a drug-induced coma spiked with LSD for up to eighty-six days; next, extreme electroshock treatment three times daily for thirty days; and, finally, a football helmet clamped to the head with a looped tape repeating, up to a half-million times, messages like "my mother hates me."[84]

Despite the devastating abuse and lasting psychological damage, the Canadian political establishment quickly closed ranks behind Washington—with Cooper's investigative report dismissing the agency's role as a "side issue" or "red herring"; medical deans finding Cameron's research ethical by the standards of the day; Ottawa's Justice Department denying legal responsibility; the Canadian Psychiatric Association, unlike its American counterpart, refusing any apology; and Prime Minister Brian Mulroney's government offering each victim a nugatory $20,000 "nuisance" payment even though Ottawa had provided most of Dr. Cameron's research funding ($495,000 versus the CIA's $64,000).[85] After years of denials from Ottawa and Langley, the litigation led the CIA director and the former chief of Canada's Defense Research Board to finally admit the truth—admissions that, in conjunction with CIA documents extracted in the trial's discovery phase, cast considerable light on the dark side of Ottawa's Cold War relations with the CIA.

Throughout the litigation, Dr. Solandt spoke frankly about Ottawa's close cooperation with the CIA during his tenure as head of the Defense Research Board from 1946 to 1957. "During the 1950's," Solandt stated in a sworn affidavit, "the United States Central Intelligence Agency had a resident representative at the United States Embassy in Ottawa who was publicly introduced as such . . . and was free to attend Defense Research Board . . . meetings where defense research programs were discussed."[86] In an interview with the *Toronto Star*, Solandt revealed his Board's secret protocol with the CIA: "If they wanted classified research they came to the board and if we thought it was suitable we paid for it and then passed it on to the U.S. We never knowingly let the U.S. place a contract with any agency in Canada."[87] After similar communications with Dr. Solandt, Cooper reported that this protocol allowed Canadian researchers like Hebb to work for the CIA or Pentagon without being paid by Washington. In lieu of direct payments, there was a "rough quid pro quo in that, when Canada requested the U.S. to do certain work in exchange, the work would be done south of the border." In defense of Ottawa's "open policy with the CIA," Dr. Solandt told the press that "we got five times the information from them that they received from us."[88]

Despite later denials by McGill colleagues that Dr. Hebb had any U.S. contacts, this lawsuit documented his close, continuing relationship with the CIA.[89] According to the plaintiffs' attorney Joseph L. Rauh Jr., in pretrial discovery "the CIA formally admitted in court papers . . . its close ties with Dr. Hebb"—specifically, that Hebb received an agency briefing in 1963 and was issued "a special CIA security clearance" on April 10, 1964, a decade after Canada had terminated its participation in the collaborative mind-control research.[90]

Ottawa's denials ended only when the CIA finally admitted its culpability after eight years of litigation. As Prime Minister Mulroney's conservative, pro-American government became "an active and hostile opponent" of this lawsuit by its own citizens, the plaintiffs' attorney, Joseph Rauh, a long-time Washington insider, noted with growing dismay that Ottawa's nominally "independent study" was chaired by George Cooper, "a former M.P. who maintained close ties with the Tory machine." Cooper's staff, he said, accepted assessments on key points "from the lips of the CIA's lawyers," and consequently Cooper's 1986 report was "a complete whitewash."[91] Providing some corroboration of Rauh's critique, Cooper's report described Dr. Cameron as "a good man . . . trying to do the best he could for his patients" and even speculated that he "did not know of CIA involvement" in his funding.[92]

Ironically, Cooper's exculpation of the CIA was rendered risible just two years later when the agency itself paid the Canadian victims damages of $750,000, the maximum allowable under U.S. law. After evaluating the evidence, CIA director William Webster ordered the settlement, saying: "Sometimes you see the right thing to do, and you do it."[93] As for Dr. Cameron's treatment of his patients, the eminent psychiatrist Robert Lifton stated, in an affidavit for the plaintiffs, that his depatterning experiments had "deviated from standard and customary psychiatric therapies in use during the 1950s" and instead "represent a mechanized extension of . . . 'brainwashing' methods."[94] As for Cooper's speculation about Cameron's ignorance of the CIA's role, other sources show that the McGill psychiatrist was a close personal friend of spymaster Allen Dulles from their days at the Nuremberg tribunal for Nazi war criminals. Years later, when Dulles was the agency's director, Cameron met with him in Washington to arrange covert CIA funding for his

McGill experiments.[95] Indeed, his Nuremberg experience and exposure there to the Nazi medical experiments might explain why Cameron later conducted his own research with a cruelty that no one, including Cooper, can explain.[96]

Although acknowledging that Hebb was "a very fine scientist" and "Canada's foremost psychologist," Cooper's report nonetheless implied that his work had contributed to the dark art of interrogation, saying: "By 'softening up' a prisoner through the use of sensory isolation techniques, a captor is indeed able to bring about a state of mind in which the prisoner is receptive to the implantation of ideas contrary to previously held beliefs."[97] In view of his discovery of the key principle in the CIA's new psychological paradigm and his long collaboration with the agency's research, it seems appropriate to regard Dr. Hebb as the "progenitor of psychological torture."[98] Today, however, his colleagues prefer to regard him as a moral paragon and annually offer the Donald O. Hebb Award in behavioral and cognitive sciences to honor "an individual whose influence has been exerted through leadership as a theorist or spokesperson for the discipline."[99]

Dr. Milgram's Obedience Experiments

As Lifton reminds us in his study of Nazi doctors, we must view the ethical compromises of individual practitioners in the wider context of their profession's response to state pressures. Indeed, other leading scientists contributed to the CIA's evolving psychological paradigm—notably, the distinguished Cornell neurologist Harold Wolff and the cardiologist Lawrence Hinkle, who, while working under a CIA contract to test "useful secret drugs (and various brain damaging procedures)," identified self-inflicted pain as the most effective Soviet interrogation technique. Their report led to a second, central facet in the agency's emerging psychological paradigm.[100] Apart from their own research, Hinkle and Wolff mobilized nearly a hundred scientists through their CIA-funded foundation. And these were just some of the hundreds more—senior and junior, known and unknown, ignorant and informed—who participated in the CIA's mind-control research.

In retrospect, Stanley Milgram seems like another of the many researchers whose work was unwittingly co-opted into this larger mind-control project. In the early stages of his career, Milgram benefited from the patronage of behavioral scientists connected to the national security apparatus. After the head of group psychology at the Office of Naval Research (ONR), a key CIA conduit for covert funding, reviewed Milgram's proposal for conducting what he called obedience experiments, the National Science Foundation (NSF) awarded him a substantial grant of $24,700—a surprisingly generous award for a junior researcher when compared to the $40,000 over four years given to Hebb and the $64,000 over seven years awarded to Cameron, both senior scholars. In later years, as the CIA completed its mind-control research and the field of cognitive science shed the agency's pervasive influence, Milgram never received another NSF grant—even though he later proposed a project that made similar use of a mechanical device to test human behavior.[101]

Like others linked to this mind-control project, Milgram showed an apparent disregard for his human subjects. But, whereas the others sought to understand the mind of the subject, Milgram wanted to understand the mentality of the inquisitor. After using innocuous advertisements in the local newspaper to recruit forty "ordinary" residents of New Haven, Connecticut, Milgram then manipulated them, through deceptive instructions, to participate in the torture of a fake "victim" with simulated electric shocks. At Yale's Interaction Laboratory, a uniformed experimenter seated the subjects before a machine labeled "Shock Generator Type ZLB" and ordered them to activate thirty switches that supposedly provided shocks ranging from 15 to 450 volts. At 75 volts, the victim, who was an actor, gave a "little grunt." At 315 volts, the victim gave a "violent scream." At 330 volts, the victim "was not heard from."

The test induced what Dr. Milgram called "extreme levels of nervous tension" in some subjects, marked by "sweating, trembling, and stuttering." One poised businessman was, Milgram said, reduced in just twenty minutes to "a twitching, stuttering wreck, who was rapidly approaching a point of nervous collapse." With the exception of some exit interviews for the camera, he then dismissed his subjects, without any real counseling, to bear the unsettling knowledge that they were, like the Gestapo, moral monsters who could inflict suffering upon their fellow humans. Indeed, one subject, a military veteran named William Menold, recalled feeling like "an emotional wreck," a "basket case," because of the realization "that somebody could get me to do that stuff." Privately, Milgram himself viewed the experiment as "ethically questionable," since "it is not nice to lure people into the laboratory and snare them into a situation that is stressful and unpleasant to them."[102] In this sense, Milgram clearly violated the first principle of the 1947 Nuremberg Code requiring that subjects "be able to exercise free power of choice, without . . . force, fraud, deceit."[103]

All this research led Milgram to conclude that anyone, when instructed by a credible authority figure, can torture, and a majority will do so to the point of death. This research was driven, as a close colleague explained, "by deep personal concerns about how readily the Nazis had killed Jews during the Holocaust." But Milgram's torture experiments do not address this historical issue as directly or, arguably, as effectively as Christopher Browning did in his more revealing archival study, *Ordinary Men*—and Browning did so without inflicting trauma on anyone.[104] In this sense, Milgram failed to abide by Article 2 of the Nuremberg Code, which stipulates: "The experiment should be such as to yield fruitful results for the good of society, unprocurable by other methods or means of study."[105]

Yet Milgram was a skilled publicist, filming the experiment for a documentary titled *Obedience* (1962), whose allure overshadowed the ethical reservations of his contemporaries. While his motivations may have been admirable, Milgram also provided the intelligence community, in this Cold War context, with useful information as it began global propagation of its new psychological torture paradigm: that anyone could be trained to torture.[106]

In retrospect, Milgram's work might be best studied as another Faustian quest for knowledge and power that led, during a dark decade in the history of behavioral science, to ethical compromises in the treatment of human subjects. And, in ways that Milgram apparently did not anticipate, his experiments revealed how science could be used to sanction torture, wrapping this ancient barbarism in the patina of high modernism. Attired in a standard white lab coat, Milgram's experimenter used the authority of science to inflict untold emotional pain on compliant human subjects, just as the product of this wider mind-control research, modern psychological methods, could be used to torture without the crude physical abuse that might provoke public revulsion.

The Nazi Doctor's Apprentice

While Hebb and his followers pursued the behavioral approach, the CIA also funded extensive research into the use of dangerous drugs for mind control. In September 1951, just three months after the CIA's secret Montreal meeting, Dr. Henry K. Beecher, the Dorr Professor of Anesthesiology at Harvard University, crossed the Atlantic in a determined search for drugs that would prize open the human mind for more effective interrogation. For the next decade, Beecher would pursue this secret military research at home and abroad, testing powerful psychotropic drugs, mescaline and LSD, on unwitting human subjects and drinking deep from Dachau's poisoned well.

Our earliest indication of Beecher's interest in interrogation is a letter, dated February 7, 1947, from Dr. Arthur R. Turner, chief of the U.S. Army's Medical Intelligence Branch, that reads: "Inclosed for your retention is a brochure, dealing with the Dachau Concentration Camp, which has just arrived. I . . . thought it might be of interest to you." This brochure, by the German aviation medical research unit, detailed thirty mescaline experiments performed on Dachau inmates by SS-Hauptsturmfuhrer Dr. Kurt Ploetner. The experiments aimed "to eliminate the will of the person examined . . . by the Gestapo." In enticing words that promised to unlock the mind for interrogation, the report concluded: "If the Messkalin had an effect on the mental state of the P.E.'s, the examining person succeeded in every case in drawing even the most intimate secrets from the P.E. when the questions were cleverly put."[107]

In an apparent effort to encourage Beecher's research in this area, the U.S. Army's surgeon general later sent him other reports on the Mauthausen concentration camp and LSD research at the Swiss Sandoz Company.[108] To assist the Army's Medical Research Board in its search for drugs that might serve as "truth sera" in interrogation, Beecher reported, in June 1950, that he had consulted colleagues about the "considerable problem here in the use of healthy young volunteers" to test "synthetic agents in the mescaline group." And he soon found that at Massachusetts General Hospital "we have an almost ideal set-up here in Boston for study of this problem."[109]

Though we cannot be certain that SS-Hauptsturmfuhrer Ploetner's report inspired his quest, in September 1951 Dr. Beecher set off on a scientific odyssey, criss-crossing Europe to search for research "on the subject of the 'ego-depressant' drugs, usually called truth serum in the newspapers," paying particular attention to the Gestapo's drug of choice, mescaline. As he explained to the U.S. Army' surgeon general, this search was an extension of the military's "orderly examination of the merits of various drugs" for use "as part of a broad attack on the central nervous system"—offensively "on prisoners (civil and military)," defensively "to know if by the use of such agents a man of integrity and discretion can be altered without his knowledge."[110] In other words, Beecher was pursuing the same offensive uses of mind control that the CIA had discussed three months earlier at its June 1951 Montreal meeting.

Reflecting the Anglo-American cooperation forged at Montreal, Dr. Beecher had access to dozens of top scientists at the first stop in his European odyssey. At the Ministry of Defense in London, Dr. B. A. R. Gater gave him a "bibliography on several drugs considered as promising," with eight citations for mescaline and fourteen for LSD. At Stratford-upon-Avon, Sir Frederick Bartlett, professor of experimental psychology at Cambridge University, agreed that "that data are probably more readily obtainable with drugs than without and hence of special value if many men are to be interrogated." By stages, however, Dr. Beecher's hunt for appropriate collaborators led him full circle back to the Nazi war criminals he had encountered in reading Dr. Ploetner's report on Gestapo drug tests at Dachau.[111]

Crossing the English Channel to Supreme Headquarters, Allied Powers Europe (SHAPE) at Marley-le-Roi, in France, Beecher learned, in discussions with U.S. officers, that he could best expand his secret drug research by going beyond the medical corps to military intelligence, since "the Central Intelligence Agency has representatives . . . on the Joint Intelligence Committee."[112] Indeed, at Heidelberg, Germany, Dr. Beecher was sharply reminded of the immorality of his research, from a medical perspective, when the Chief U.S. Surgeon for Europe, General Guy B. Denit, advised him "that as a physician under the Geneva Convention he [Denit] could have nothing officially to do with the use of drugs for the purposes in mind and turned me over to G-II." Consequently, U.S. Army G-II, or military intelligence, transferred Dr. Beecher from the moral realm of military medicine to "Oberursel, to the European Command Interrogation Center," the dark center of the Allied interrogation effort.[113]

Outside Frankfurt, site of the CIA's German headquarters, the rolling Taunus Hills concealed two of the most secret U.S. intelligence facilities. Oberursel, the former home of the Luftwaffe's famed "Durchgangslage Luft" interrogation center, had now become Camp King, the site of the European Command Interrogation Center. There, after 1948, a staff of ex-Gestapo soldiers and former Nazi doctors, including the notorious deputy Reich health leader Kurt Blome, were employed in inhumane interrogations of Soviet defectors and double agents. Nearby in the town of Kronberg, the CIA used Haus Waldhof, a former country estate, as a safe house for drug testing, brutal torture, and lethal experiments on Soviet bloc prisoners deemed expendable. In 1952, for example, the head the CIA's Project Artichoke, Morse Allen—assisted by Dr. Samuel V. Thompson, a Navy psychiatrist, and Professor G. Richard Wendt, a University of Rochester psychologist—would use this site to test dangerous combinations of drugs such as Benzedrin and Pentothal-Natrium on Russian captives, under a research protocol specifying that "disposal of the body is not a problem."[114]

At Oberursel, Dr. Beecher discussed possible drug uses for interrogation with six staffers, including a Major Hart, head of a "brutal interrogation team" known as the "rough boys," and Captain Malcolm Hilty, the chief interrogator. All agreed: "It would be desirable for me to return, perhaps in a year, when we know better the signs and symptoms of the newer derivatives of mescaline and lysergic acid [LSD], to interrogate especially high level escapees from Russian interrogation." In the interim, they recommended that Dr. Beecher work with a Dr. Schreiber, Camp King's former staff doctor, whom Beecher described as "a physician and former German general who is now on his way to the States, will be at the School of Aviation Medicine. . . . Schreiber is intelligent and helpful."[115]

Who was Dr. Schreiber, this "intelligent and helpful" partner for Professor Beecher's secret drug research? He was, in fact, General Walter Schreiber, former medical chief for the Wehrmacht command who had presided over Nazi "concentration camp . . . experiments on inmates that usually resulted in a slow and agonizing death." After Camp King commended Schreiber's "high efficiency," the Pentagon sent him to Texas where he joined other Nazi doctors at the School of Aviation Medicine, albeit only until May 1952 when complaints about his war crimes forced a sudden departure for Argentina.[116]

Moving on to Berlin, Dr. Beecher met with a military intelligence officer and "Mr. Peter Sichel, C.I.A.," the agency's station chief, to discuss acquisition of human subjects for his plans "to interrogate as many high-level escapees as possible as to the presence of significant signs and symptoms [of drugs] during periods of interrogation." All agreed that "the best sources of material for me are high level refugees and ranking political figures of the Eastern Zone who may defect." When Dr. Beecher's report on his voyage into this intelligence netherworld reached the Pentagon in October 1951, it was, at his recommendation, stamped "TOP SECRET" and not declassified until 1977, a few months after his death.[117]

In August 1952, Dr. Beecher, now discarding Dr. Ploetner's preference for mescaline, returned to Europe, where he now focused solely, almost obsessively, on the threat and promise of LSD 25. In the year between his visits, Beecher had joined the U.S. intelligence community's interrogation project with a "top secret" security clearance and a Pentagon grant to study the "Response of Normal Men to Lysergic Acid Derivatives."[118] Just as Dr. Ploetner's paper had once heralded the promise of mescaline, so a report from the Sandoz Company that had developed the drug, provided by the Pentagon, hinted that this new chemical compound might open the human mind for interrogation. "LSD 25," read the Sandoz statement, "can bring thoughts from the subconscious into the conscious, can increase associative activity and, by removing inhibitions, can also improve the ekphoric ability." But Sandoz had also warned that the new drug produced "a peculiar personality disturbance similar to 'split personality'" and induced a "tendency to pathological reactions (hysterical attacks, trances, epileptic fits)."[119] Evidently intrigued, Beecher wrote the company's chief pharmacologist in Basel, Switzerland, Dr. Ernst Rothlin, to arrange a meeting, explaining that "we have been doing some work in main with . . . LSD 25, which was kindly furnished us by your company."[120]

Subsequently, Dr. Beecher returned from his second European sojourn warning about LSD's effect of "severe imbalance, hysteria" on, say, "a battleship's crew." In a secret report to the U.S. Army's surgeon general, he advised that this drug should be studied "(1) as aids to obtain suppressed information . . . (2) as threats to security when used by an enemy agent . . . (3) as tools of biological warfare." Above all, he urged research into the use "of these agents as offensive weapons," since "the water supply of a large city could probably be disastrously and undetectably (until too late) contaminated." Determined that "the United States . . . not get behind in this field for want of an organized plan of attack," he now planned to intensify dosages on subjects in his Boston LSD experiments, saying: "We need to know the effects of larger doses, of prolonged administration of small doses and so on." Fortunately for Beecher's plans, a professor he had met in Europe "has promised to send me for study the new L.A.E. (a mono ethyl amide of lysergic acid). This is said to be more excitant to normal individuals than is L.S.D. 25."[121]

Over the next two years, Dr. Beecher carried out these LSD tests on unwitting human subjects because he believed, from his unclassified experimentation, that their ignorance of the procedure was essential for serious pharmacological research—creating, for Beecher, a productive confluence of his covert and conventional work.[122] In his final report to the Pentagon on these tests, Beecher noted that, after administering LSD doses "as unknowns," four among his nine human subjects given the stronger LAE variant of the drug became "mildly hostile and paranoid; another experienced acute panic."[123]

In this decade of secret drug testing, Dr. Beecher thus sacrificed his subjects to the cause of national security. During his European travels in 1951–52, he had sought expendable subjects for secret interrogation experiments. Back home at Harvard, Beecher, though aware of the drug's painful effects from the Sandoz report, still tested powerful LSD and LAE doses that inflicted the trauma of "paranoid" reaction and "acute panic" on his unwitting, uninformed human subjects—a "psychosis in miniature" that, he said coolly in his published report, "offers interesting possibilities." In sum, knowing the serious trauma these drugs would cause, Beecher placed unwitting subjects at risk by giving them dangerous doses dictated by the needs of his secret research—all in violation of the Nuremberg Code. Yet, he also maintained a perfect cover, minimizing public knowledge of his military research by publishing only one LSD study as third author—and even that was packaged innocuously as the last in a series of drug tests. Throughout these long years of his secret drug research on unwitting human subjects, he sat on influential biomedical bodies, such as the National Research Council, setting the U.S. national research agenda.[124]

During the period of his classified drug research, which clearly violated the principles of the Nuremberg Code, Dr. Beecher was, not surprisingly, quite vocal in his opposition to the federal government's attempt to impose the Code's ethical restraints on clinical researchers. In a 1959 article for the *Journal of the American Medical Association*, Beecher offered an extended critique of the Nuremberg Code, arguing that a "rigid interpretation" of its first rule for "the voluntary consent of the human subject" would "effectively cripple, if not eliminate, most research in the field of mental disease" and bar the use of placebos, which he called, not surprisingly given his own prominence in this area, "essential to progress in which judgment is involved in decision." Beecher was equally critical of Nuremberg's second rule, requiring that experiments be "not random and unnecessary in nature," and dismissed it with the flat assertion that "most of the epoch-making discoveries in science have been unexpected." Magisterially waving away the import of the Nuremberg Code, he concluded that "the problems of human experimentation do not lend themselves to a series of rigid rules."[125]

Two years later, Dr. Beecher applied these criticisms, forcefully and effectively, when the U.S. Army's surgeon general tried to impose its version of the Nuremberg Code on new university research contracts. On behalf of the Harvard Medical School, Beecher drafted new clauses that set aside the "rigid rules" he so disdained in favor of loose guidelines to be interpreted by the "virtuous investigator." In July 1962, a Harvard University delegation won Pentagon approval for this less restrictive approach.[126]

Modern Medical Ethics

The past as described in this chapter, particularly its more public aspects, has some important lessons for the contemporary debate over professional ethics within the American Psychological Association that erupted in the aftermath of 9/11 attacks. By the early 1960s, as the CIA's secret drug research wound down and lucrative defense contracts thus dwindled, Dr. Beecher seems to have been freed from conflicts that might have dulled his conscience about the ethics of medical research.[127] Whether his change of heart was a sweeping epiphany or simple opportunism, we cannot say. But after years of fighting federal restraints on clinical research and years more of conducting dangerous drug experiments on unwitting subjects, he suddenly became, with the end of his classified Pentagon drug research, an impassioned advocate for ethical standards.

In 1965, Beecher first voiced his new concerns in a lecture to journalists titled "Ethics and the Explosion of Human Experimentation," which contained his only hint of a mea culpa. "Lest I seem to stand aside from these matters," he said, without providing any details of his secret drug testing on unwitting subjects, "I am obliged to say that in years gone by work in my laboratory could have been criticized."[128]

A year later, Dr. Beecher published his famous essay, "Ethics and Clinical Research," in *The New England Journal of Medicine*, citing twenty-two instances of medical research whose human subjects "never had the risk satisfactorily explained to them" and thus suffered "grave consequences . . . as a direct result of experiments." After reviewing these cases where clinical researchers had sacrificed their subjects to advance science, Beecher concluded that the "ethical approach to experimentation" had two clear requisites: first, a genuine effort to obtain fully "informed consent" for "moral, sociologic and legal reasons"; second, "the presence of an intelligent, informed, conscientious, compassionate, responsible investigator," by which he presumably meant the principal investigator or lead scientist. He warned that unethical practices "will do great harm to medicine unless soon corrected" and questioned whether "data obtained unethically should be published even with stern editorial comment."[129]

With his reputation as an ethical paragon growing, Dr. Beecher did not elaborate further on his opaque mea culpa. Moreover, he began voicing a stern moral opposition to counterculture LSD experimentation that seems, in light of his earlier classified research with the same drug, stunningly hypocritical. When controversy erupted over utopian LSD experimentation at Harvard in the late 1960s, Dr. Beecher played the moralist, roundly condemning one of Timothy Leary's colleagues, Dr. Walter N. Pahnke, for using the drug to ease the pain of the terminally ill. "There is an abundance of evidence," intoned Dr. Beecher, "that LSD can produce, has produced lasting, serious damage to young people."[130]

Initially controversial, Dr. Beecher's 1966 article on clinical ethics soon made his name synonymous with "informed consent" and ethical treatment of human subjects—a moral legacy commemorated today with the annual award of the Henry K. Beecher Prize in Medical Ethics at Harvard Medical School.[131] The award's 1993 recipient, Yale bioethics professor Jay Katz, praised Dr. Beecher lavishly for "the moral passion that punctuated his every word" in that landmark 1966 essay.[132] Typical of this laudatory treatment, a 2001 article in the *Bulletin of the World Health Organization* describes how Dr. Beecher drew upon his "deep Christian faith" to produce "the most influential single paper ever written about experimentation involving human subjects" and thereby "played a significant role" in bringing about the enactment of strict federal regulations that precluded future abuse of human subjects.[133]

Apart from Beecher's own oblique references to his lab's ethical lapses, the literature seems ignorant of his darker side. Even aggressive exposés of government abuses have hailed him as a hero of medical ethics, while investigations of the CIA's scandalous drug experiments make but cursory references to his earlier LSD research.[134] Today, every academic researcher in America and Canada lives under Dr. Beecher's long shadow, forced to submit all research proposals to institutional review boards that would certainly ban the experiments once done by Hebb, Cameron, Milgram, and, ironically, Beecher himself.

Legacy of a Dark Decade

Although these researchers were all long dead by September 2001, the legacy of their ethical compromises apparently lived on through institutional ties between the U.S. military and the American Psychological Association (APA). Reflecting the long involvement of its members in military research and CIA behavioral experiments, the APA provided important political cover for the aggressive interrogation adopted by the Bush administration after 9/11.

When controversy erupted inside the profession in 2005 over the role of military psychologists who had participated in Behavioral Science Consultation Teams at Guantanamo, the APA insisted that its members were not barred from "national security endeavors." In response to the ensuing crisis over ethics, the APA formed a special task force, stacked with serving military psychologists, which stated, pro forma, that "psychologists do not engage in, direct, support, facilitate, or offer training in torture or other cruel, inhuman, or degrading treatment." But the report of this APA task force, released in June 2005, still hesitated to bar members from military interrogations outright, saying, simply and vaguely, that they should be "mindful of factors unique to these roles . . . that require special ethical consideration." And the task force refused to recommend that members be bound by "international standards of human rights."[135]

In the ensuing debate, sparked by a succession of protests at the APA's national conventions, the association's leadership sought compromise rather than ethical clarity, producing a bitter, five-year battle inside a major professional organization with some 150,000 members. After both the American Psychiatric Association and the American Medical Association barred their members from directly participating in interrogations in mid-2006, pressure by critics within the APA gained momentum. Following years of divisive debate that peaked in protests at the organization's 2008 Boston meeting, the membership passed a resolution stating that, at Guantanamo Bay, "torture took place in the context of interrogations under the direction and supervision of Behavioral Science Consultation Teams (BSCTs) that included psychologists." The members therefore resolved that, henceforth, psychologists may not work in settings where "persons are held outside of, or in violation of, either International Law . . . or the U.S. Constitution (where appropriate), unless they are working directly for the persons being detained or for an independent third party working to protect human rights."[136] Finally, in 2010, the APA's executive board agreed to amend its professional standards to require that psychologists working in organizations "in conflict with this Ethics Code" must "take reasonable steps to resolve the conflict," mindful that "under no circumstances may this standard be used to justify or defend violating human rights."[137]

What can we learn from stories of ethical compromises by these titans of modern science, Donald Hebb and Henry Beecher? Clearly, both men were important researchers responsible for lasting contributions to cognitive science and the betterment of humankind. But, in the shadows of the national security state, both also made ethical compromises and conducted secret research that did harm to their human subjects, contributing to the development of a form of psychological torture that has inflicted untold suffering on countless victims worldwide.

Yet, in the fullness of time, their moral lapses and those of their colleagues did prove, in a limited sense, self-correcting, as the scientific community and the wider society struggled over the ethics of secret research. Beecher's story is particularly telling because it also speaks to the larger problem of impunity, whether for those who torture or those who inflict harm upon unwitting human subjects. Nothing in the medical or legal systems prevented Beecher's research. Whatever regulations or oversight existed at the time were insufficient to expose it. Even if his LSD experiments on unwitting human subjects had been exposed in his lifetime, he would have suffered, at worst, some sort of professional rebuke—an insufficient deterrent to others similarly tempted.

Whatever the cause of Beecher's own eventual change of heart, whether an ethical epiphany or the end of secret research funds, it had to come from within him. And an effective medical/legal system cannot rely on individual epiphanies to correct such proclivities to inflict harm upon the helpless, whether prisoners or human subjects. Recognizing the limits of such ethical restraints, the federal government and its grant recipients, universities and hospitals, responded quickly to Beecher's 1966 critique by requiring that experiments on human subjects pass some sort of institutional review.

But creating ethical regulations and enforcing their sanctions are clearly two different matters. At this writing in 2012, complaints against military psychologists for alleged ethical lapses at Guantanamo and at CIA prisons have yet to produce any individual sanctions by state licensing boards in New York, Ohio, and Texas.[138] While institutional review boards enforce standards for research in universities and hospitals and the APA sets broad norms for the psychology profession, ethical misconduct in U.S. facilities overseas falls, by default, to state licensing boards, which are loath to oversight federal agencies. Faced with such a gap in institutional oversight, peer pressure for ethical compliance can serve as a partial corrective. In filing these complaints, whatever their outcomes, psychologists have implicitly affirmed a shared commitment to high ethical standards. While prominent professionals, whether general officers or leading psychologists, can often achieve virtual impunity for harming their human subjects, such excesses do produce a reaction within collegial ranks, potentially raising the barrier against similar lapses in the future.

Through a fitful, flawed process, the press exposed the excesses of mind-control research, officials like CIA director William Webster made amends, researchers like Henry Beecher proposed ethical standards, and scientists struggled, in succeeding decades, to enforce those professional codes for treatment of human subjects. Slowly, society and its scientific community have worked to reduce the harm that powerful institutions can do to innocent individuals. It was not a perfect outcome. But it was progress.

3

Torture in the Crucible
of Counterinsurgency

After the attacks on September 11, 2001, the White House made torture its secret weapon in the War on Terror. Although Washington mobilized its regular military forces for conventional attacks on Afghanistan and Iraq, the main challenge in this new kind of warfare was a covert campaign against "nonstate actors," terrorists who moved easily, elusively, across the Muslim world from Morocco to Manila in "ad hoc networks that dissolve as soon as the mission is accomplished." With its countless Cold War victories, overthrowing enemies on four continents by coups and covert operations, the Central Intelligence Agency had an aura of invincibility and soon became Washington's chosen instrument it its battle against Al Qaeda. But, in truth, the agency's reputation for clandestine derring-do was inflated, and its qualifications for this new mission were slender indeed.[1]

Though the CIA was often successful when deployed against states or state agencies, the agency remained, at base, a centralized Washington bureaucracy, usually lacking the local knowledge, languages, or street smarts needed for effective intelligence gathering on nonstate actors. In its half-century history before September 2001, the CIA had fought only one covert war comparable to its new anti-terror mission against Al Qaeda, and the results of these operations during the Vietnam War were decidedly mixed. Desperate for intelligence about its invisible enemy in that conflict, an underground movement called the Viet Cong, the agency soon descended into systematic torture of suspected communists, with dismal results. Yet forty years later when the CIA launched a second, similar campaign against another nonstate actor, in this case Islamic terrorists, it soon found it had few, if any, assets inside Al Qaeda or militant Muslim circles, leading the agency to revive the torture techniques it had once used in South Vietnam.

With surprising speed, Washington's recourse to torture in Afghanistan and Iraq soon replicated the same patterns first seen during its "dirty war" in Vietnam—rapid proliferation of torture into a generalized brutality, descent into extrajudicial killings, anger among the local population, and alienation of the American people from the war effort.[2] Despite these troubling parallels, Vietnam was nonetheless a seminal experience for the CIA, expanding it from an elite espionage agency into a sprawling counterinsurgency bureaucracy engaged in incarceration, interrogation, and assassination on a mass scale.

These changes in the agency's mission came suddenly. Only four years after the CIA compiled its 1963 interrogation manual for use against a few Soviet counterintelligence targets, its agents were operating forty interrogation centers in South Vietnam that killed more than twenty thousand suspects and tortured countless thousands more. Similarly, just a few months after the CIA used its harsh techniques on a few "high-value" Al Qaeda suspects, the practice spread to the interrogation of hundreds of Afghans and thousands of Iraqis. In both cases, not only did torture spread, but the level of abuse escalated relentlessly beyond the scientific patina of the agency's psychological methods to become pervasively, perversely brutal. In sum, the development of CIA techniques at the height of the Cold War created a covert interrogation capacity that the White House could deploy at times of crisis, whether in South Vietnam in 1968 or in Iraq in 2003. Across the span of four decades, there was, therefore, a marked continuity in U.S. torture techniques and in the agency's recourse to assassination as its ultimate weapon in these covert wars.

Office of Public Safety

The CIA's involvement in South Vietnam was part of a global counterinsurgency effort. From 1962 to 1974, the CIA worked through the Office of Public Safety (OPS), a division of the U.S. Agency for International Development (U.S. AID), which sent American police advisers to developing nations around the globe.[3] Established by President John F. Kennedy in 1962, OPS grew, in just six years, into a global anticommunist operation with an annual budget of $35 million and more than four hundred U.S. police advisers assigned worldwide. By 1971, the program had trained more than a million policemen in forty-seven nations, including eighty-five thousand in South Vietnam and one hundred thousand in Brazil.[4] Concealed in the midst of this larger effort, CIA interrogation training soon proved controversial as allied police agencies throughout the Third World became synonymous with human rights abuse— particularly in South Vietnam, Brazil, Uruguay, Iran, and the Philippines.

To launch this aggressive Cold War effort in the early 1960s, the Kennedy administration formed the interagency Special Group-Counter Insurgency (CI), whose influential officials could cut across bureaucratic boundaries to get the job done. These influentials included General Maxwell Taylor, chairman of the Joint Chiefs of Staff; McGeorge Bundy, the national security adviser; John McCone, director of the CIA; and U. Alexis Johnson, Undersecretary of State.[5] According to a 1962 National Security Action Memorandum, "the President desires that careful consideration be given to intensifying civil police programs in lieu of military assistance where such action will yield more fruitful results in terms of our internal security objective."[6] Although "the police program is even more important than Special Forces in our global C-I [counterinsurgency] effort," argued staff member Robert W. Komer, a CIA veteran, in an April 1962 memo, finding a "congenial home" for this multiagency initiative proved difficult.[7] This effort effected a major reorganization of the Civil Police Division within the U.S. foreign aid bureaucracy, which had been training foreign constabularies since 1955 "to destroy the effectiveness of the Communist apparatus in free world countries vulnerable to Communist subversion."[8]

In sum, the problem was how to expand U.S. AID's conventional police training so that it could function as cover for a more aggressive CIA counterinsurgency among Third World allies. The solution, apparently, was to expand the public safety program within U.S. AID while simultaneously placing it under the control of CIA officers—notably the program's head, Byron Engle.[9] After serving with the Kansas City police from 1939 to 1946 and starting their police training program, Engle joined the U.S. occupation of postwar Japan, where he founded that country's first police academy, and later worked for the CIA as a police adviser in Turkey—experiences that catapulted him to command of the U.S. Civil Police Division by the late 1950s.[10] During his decade as chief of OPS after 1962, Engle recruited agency personnel for the program and worked closely with its intelligence mission.[11]

The hybrid nature of OPS gave CIA field operatives an ideal cover for the dissemination of the agency's new interrogation techniques. In South Vietnam, for example, Public Safety trained national police in what the U.S. chief adviser called "stringent wartime measures designed to assist in defeating the enemy." At the provincial level, Vietnamese National Police Field Forces, trained by OPS, worked with CIA mercenaries in apprehending suspected communists for interrogation.[12] In Latin America, the agency used Public Safety to recruit local police for training at a clandestine center in Washington, International Police Services, which operated behind the cover provided by U.S. AID's International Police Academy (IPA). In its audit of OPS in 1976, the General Accounting Office reported that "there were allegations that the academy . . . taught or encouraged use of torture," but its investigation did not support a formal finding of that nature.[13]

Elsewhere in this worldwide effort, the CIA worked with public safety advisers in Brazil and Uruguay to provide local police with training and interrogation equipment. Through its field offices in Panama and Buenos Aires, the agency's Technical Services Division (TSD), the unit responsible for this psychological research, shipped polygraph and electroshock machines in diplomatic pouches to Public Safety offices across Latin America.[14] Although it was a global program, Public Safety's operations were, as the Vietnam War heated up in the 1960s, increasingly concentrated in South Vietnam.

The Rise of Phoenix

From the start of the U.S. advisory effort in South Vietnam in 1961, the military concentrated on conventional combat, leaving unconventional "dirty war" operations against the communist underground to the CIA. For nearly fifteen years, the agency waged a covert campaign against the communist infrastructure that culminated in its most controversial operation, the Phoenix program. After experimenting with police training, psychological warfare, and rural reconstruction, the CIA settled on a program of systematic torture and extrajudicial executions that killed, by its own count, more than twenty thousand suspected communist cadre.

The first Public Safety advisers sent to South Vietnam tried to transform the country's National Police into an effective counterinsurgency force. But, by 1963, the apparent failure of this effort created pressures for an aggressive approach. Arriving at Saigon in December of that year, the new CIA chief of station, Peer DeSilva, was shocked to enter a village and see the local chief and his family impaled on sharpened stakes, executed by the Viet Cong. "To make sure this horrible sight would remain with the villages," he wrote in his memoirs, "one of the terror squad used his machete to disembowel the woman, spilling the fetus on the ground." He soon decided that "the Vietcong were monstrous in their application of torture and murder to achieve the *political* and *psychological* impact they wanted." Impressed nonetheless by the enemy's "implacable use of terror" to control the countryside, DeSilva organized small counterterror teams, dressed in peasants' black tunics, "to bring danger and death to the Vietcong functionaries themselves, especially in the areas where they felt secure."[15] This vision of an effective counterterror that could destroy the invisible guerrilla apparatus would lead the CIA, by degrees, to the development of extreme methods housed, after 1967, in the Phoenix program.

The CIA thus embarked on a project of both expanding and centralizing South Vietnam's scattered intelligence operations, which all fell under its local counterpart agency, Saigon's Central Intelligence Organization (CIO). Four CIA advisers gave the South Vietnamese hands-on training by interrogating the hundreds of prisoners at the CIO's National Interrogation Center. After a year under DeSilva's leadership, each of the forty-plus provinces in South Vietnam formed a Province Intelligence Coordination Committee and built its own concrete prison compound. In these same years, the CIA sent many experts, "most of whom had worked on Russian defectors," from its Technical Services Division to train South Vietnamese interrogators. In place of the "old French methods" of crude physical torture practiced by the Saigon police, the Vietnamese, in the words of one CIA instructor, "had to be re-taught with more sophisticated techniques," including the agency's new psychological paradigm. At the provincial centers, however, crude physical methods continued to prevail, including electrical shock, beatings, and rape.[16]

As the CIA brought this covert war to the countryside in 1965, its senior field operative, William Colby, launched the Counter Terror (CT) program. "CIA representatives," wrote agency analyst Victor Marchetti, "recruited, organized, supplied, and directly paid CT teams, whose function was to use . . . techniques of terror—assassination, abuses, kidnappings and intimidation— against the Viet Cong leadership." A year later, the CIA "became wary of adverse publicity surrounding the use of the word 'terror' and changed the name of the CT teams to the Provincial Reconnaissance Units (PRUs)." Colby also supervised construction of the Provincial Interrogation Centers (PIC), where a CIA employee "directed each center's operations," particularly "the torture tactics against suspected Vietcong, such torture usually carried out by Vietnamese nationals."[17] By 1965–66, the CIA had thus developed a nationwide intelligence-collection system that reached from the National Interrogation Center in Saigon down to the country's rice roots via the PIC operations and the PRU counterterror campaigns.

Since conventional combat was failing to defeat the enemy, the U.S. mission moved toward a centralized pacification effort, later called Phoenix, to correct a major contradiction in its alliance with South Vietnam's weak government. The National Police, despite doubling its strength to 120,000 officers between 1966 and 1972, suffered poor leadership and "pervasive corruption" that blunted its effectiveness against the Viet Cong's resilient underground. And the South Vietnamese army, as one of its officers explained, felt that "this unarmed enemy was not their proper adversary." With Saigon's police unable and its army unwilling to engage in effective counterinsurgency, the CIA felt the need for a new kind of clandestine operation to attack this invisible communist apparatus that threatened to defeat the U.S. war effort.[18]

After two years of escalating military intervention, the U.S. command sensed, by mid-1966, that it had failed in its key mission of destroying the enemy's underground, which it called the "Viet Cong infrastructure," or VCI. Realizing the limitations of conventional combat, Washington and its Saigon mission reviewed numerous smaller programs whose fusion might forge an expanded, effective pacification effort.[19]

In the Mekong Delta's IV Corps, for example, the chief of U.S. Army intelligence, General Joseph McChristian, finding himself in conflict with the CIA, allied with the head of the National Police, General Nguyen Ngoc Loan, to launch Operation Cong Tac IV in mid-1966 with the aim of gathering "intelligence on the identification and location of Viet Cong." As this program expanded, General Loan, in turn, delegated supervision to his CIA-trained branch chief, Colonel Dang Van Minh, who proposed to transform it into an agile program he called *Phung Hoang*, or Phoenix, reflecting his view that VC cadre were "to be monitored, not killed."[20]

In the far north inside I Corps, by contrast, the U.S. Marines and the CIA collaborated effectively in pacification. To help the Marines cut casualties from entrenched Viet Cong units, the regional CIA paramilitary chief, Robert Wall, developed a localized counterguerrilla net, the District Intelligence and Operations Coordination Center (DIOCC), that became "the model on which Phoenix facilities were later built throughout Vietnam."[21]

After a long, fitful gestation, a new approach to counterinsurgency began to crystallize in November 1966 when Nelson H. Brickham, a senior CIA analyst generally credited with "the organizational reforms that paved the way for Phoenix," briefed the U.S. commander, General William Westmoreland, on his proposal for an "Attack against the Viet Cong Infrastructure." Viewing the Viet Cong as a "mafia" that controlled the countryside through terror, Brickham proposed a multifaceted assault on the communist underground through a mix of penetration, arrest, and assassination by an array of nonmilitary forces—including the National Police Special Branch, the CIA's Provincial Reconnaissance Units, and Vietnamese regional militia. "Without an infrastructure," Brickham said of the communists, "there is only a headless body. Destroy the infrastructure, you destroy the insurgency."[22]

The program expanded in 1967 when Washington established a centralized pacification bureaucracy, called Civil Operations and Rural Development Support, or CORDS. Under this umbrella, the CIA drew all the scattered U.S. counterinsurgency operations—Public Safety police training, military intelligence, the CIO, and its own interrogation units—into the central CORDS bureaucracy and then used this apparatus as cover for the covert assassination campaign that later became the Phoenix program. With limitless funding and unrestrained powers, Phoenix represented an application of the most advanced U.S. interrogation techniques to the task of destroying the Viet Cong's revolutionary underground.

Reflecting these new priorities, in May 1967 President Lyndon Johnson dispatched Robert Komer, a tough CIA bureaucratic in-fighter known as the "blowtorch," to head CORDS and to serve as his handpicked pacification czar—arming him with the honorary rank of ambassador and a formal delegation of presidential authority as the "single manager" over an "unprecedented melding of civil and military responsibilities" for "the other war."[23]

To coordinate with this new bureaucracy, the CIA's Saigon station chief assigned Brickham to draft "a general plan for pacification," and he, in turn, sent Komer his "Personal Observations" for an intensified attack on the Viet Cong. "The war is a run on a treadmill," Brickham warned, "as long as existing and totally inadequate process and facilities for detention and neutralization of captured VC remains unchanged." In most rural districts, a refugee officer "kicks bags of rice off of his helicopter and then disappears"; a Public Safety officer assigned to open a detention camp "looks around for fifteen minutes and disappears, never to be seen again"; and a Popular Forces company receives "an occasional visit by a so-called adviser." Instead of focusing on the battle for the countryside, most agencies, Vietnamese and American, devoted themselves to "private wars" against bureaucratic rivals in Saigon. ARVN, for example, "will have nothing but contempt for Police Intelligence," while combat units "ignore [the VC] 'infrastructure' and go around looking for big main force enemy which they never or rarely find." This Babel of autonomous information systems—Police Special Branch, the PICs, and military intelligence—meant that "no effective attack has yet been devised for . . . degradation of VC infrastructure."[24]

To correct these "numerous grave weaknesses," Brickham recommended a "centrally designed and controlled reporting and information system" using "automated data processing systems which have a greatly expanded capacity for storing, manipulating and reproducing information." With a management model borrowed from the Ford Motor Company, he proposed the formation of a centralized pacification committee in Saigon, with Komer as chair and a "board of directors" drawn from all U.S. intelligence organizations.[25]

Ambassador Komer found the proposal persuasive. In June 1967, his CORDS office convened a whirlwind round of meetings among top American and Vietnamese officials to build support for a fundamental reorganization of allied intelligence. Under the rubric of the ICEX program, bureaucratic shorthand for "Infrastructure Intelligence Coordination and Exploitation," he proposed nothing less than an all-out attack on the Viet Cong. At one of these early briefings in Saigon, CORDS explained that, until now, the Vietnamese National Police had compiled most of the intelligence on the Viet Cong's eighty thousand members, but much of this data had been "buried in files, and little effort has been directed toward properly exploiting this information." To facilitate "the identification and destruction of the infrastructure," ICEX, a direct predecessor of the Phoenix program, would operate at four closely coordinated levels from Saigon down to the rural districts where the VC presence was strong. Although this ICEX structure was still new, there were soon, CORDS reported, some promising signs—notably, the identification of "9,000 VC personalities," the insertion of "21,000 additional names . . . in the base data," and the recent capture of 160 VC cadre inside Saigon.[26]

Within days, both the U.S. embassy and the military command endorsed "the proposed concept for mounting a stepped-up, coordinated attack on the VC infrastructure." In internal memos, CORDS reported that the U.S. military had committed 126 additional officers to "a joint civil-military management structure." By centralizing all existing intelligence operations under ICEX, this new effort would, CORDS promised, produce a "timely exploration of operational intelligence" for a "more sharply focused attack."[27]

From the outset, however, the Saigon regime's bureaucratic inertia, corruption, and incapacity threatened the program's success. Most fundamentally, the country's judicial system proved problematic. As ICEX generated a tide of arrests, CORDS soon discovered what it called "the total inadequacy of physical facilities . . . for either processing, holding or imprisoning civil detainees."[28] Since the country's forty-four civil and military prisons were filled beyond capacity, most detainees rounded up in these early sweeps were soon released. In general, CORDS concluded, "any individual possessing a sufficient amount of cash can purchase his freedom at any level of the penal system in Vietnam."[29]

More critically, the ICEX program, as CORDS noted in an internal memo, "cannot succeed without acceptance and energetic support by the Director General of National Police," the all-powerful General Nguyen Ngoc Loan. As the trusted ally of Premier Nguyen Cao Ky and the head of every major Saigon security agency, General Loan was the dominant force in Saigon's security effort. When CORDS presented the ICEX program to Loan, he "turned it down flat," in part because he thought it would promote his rival, Nguyen Van Thieu, and in part because, as Brickham put it, he "looked upon it as an infringement of their sovereignty."[30] It was not until November 1967 that General Loan's "earlier misgivings" were overcome after assurances that "that police intelligence sources and operations need not be revealed, and that police participation . . . will be to their advantage." By late 1967, however, it was still not clear whether Saigon officials would "really be willing to go all out and apprehend, try, and imprison, or destroy identified and identifiable VC infrastructure."[31]

In December, the prime minister's office finally backed the ICEX program by issuing a "Directive on the Neutralization of the VCI," instructing all relevant South Vietnamese agencies to "take full note of the importance of the matter." By ordering that the "committees in charge of VCI are called Phung Hoang Committees," the Saigon government gave the program both its distinctive name, Phung Hoang or Phoenix, and its basic organizational character as a collaborative Vietnamese-American pacification effort.[32] Six months later, in July 1968, President Nguyen Van Thieu issued a supplementary directive establishing Phoenix in its final form as "a program, not an organization, to bring about collaboration . . . among all government agencies which could contribute to the identification and neutralization of the VCI." Within a year, as Vietnamese took control, U.S. officials withdrew from "direct responsibility for the program," though they remained involved as advisers to the Vietnamese Special Police and coordinators for intelligence gathering "on the American side."[33]

In Saigon, the fully evolved Phoenix program used sophisticated computer information banks, located at the U.S. Combined Intelligence Center Vietnam (CICV), to centralize all data on the Viet Cong infrastructure, identifying key communist cadre for interrogation or elimination. Starting in mid-1968, Ambassador Komer pushed a program to issue "tamperproof identification cards to every Vietnamese man and woman over the age of 15"—training hundreds of "little Vietnamese girls at the technique of collating and filing fingerprints" inside national police headquarters in Saigon. In the countryside, Phoenix made use of this intelligence through specially trained counterguerrilla teams, the PRUs, attached to one of the CIA's forty-plus Provincial Interrogation Centers. Imitating the clandestine cell structure of the Viet Cong units, each PRU was a six-man team that, through a pyramid structure, was part of a provincial unit of 146 men. By 1970, such programs would make CORDS into a massive bureaucracy of 5,500 American advisers and 550,000 Vietnamese officials, with its funding for pacification tripling from $586 million in 1966 to $1.5 billion by 1970.[34]

After three years of operations, from 1967 to 1969, the CIA transferred Phoenix operations to the U.S. Army's military intelligence, and the U.S. command, in turn, ceded control to the Vietnamese police. Upon arrival in Saigon in November 1969, the new CIA station chief, Ted Shackley, decided that "the pacification programs had come of age . . . [and] that the agency contribution was no longer required"; he launched a six-month phase-out that would "free up CIA resources to improve the quality of the intelligence product, to penetrate the Vietcong." In this transition, the CIA conducted an internal review of Phoenix that summarized the program's fitful three-year progress. In effect, the situation in the countryside could be described as a "race" between the Viet Cong, now reduced to sixty-three thousand members, and the Saigon government, which was still slow "in developing its tools for this new nature of the war, Phoenix and the National Police." Despite promising growth since its inception in mid-1967, Phoenix was still troubled by "its poor press image, highlighted by charges that it was a program of assassination." Indeed, through what the mission called an "intensive effort at computer mechanization," the program had developed "a successive hardening of the quota system . . . to obtain maximum incentive toward elimination of higher level VCI," raising the monthly total of those "captured, rallied, killed" from 1,200 in 1968 to 1,800 in 1969. By October 1970, Phoenix accounted for "82.9 percent of VCI killed or captured" by all allied forces, both U.S. and South Vietnamese. Simultaneously, a "series of actions were launched to . . . make more effective the overall Phoenix program": notably, the creation of "operations centers . . . at the national, regional, provincial, and district level"; an acceptance among Saigon officials that it was, in fact, their program; and, in May 1970, a decision by the Saigon government to place the entire program under the Directorate General of National Police.[35]

The sum of these changes was, the CIA reported, a significant increase in the Saigon government's presence in the countryside. Long the "stepchild" of the Saigon government, the National Police was finally moving well beyond its "colonial tradition" as a highly bureaucratic capital security force "in the best French tradition." Starting in 1969, the National Police shifted its focus from capital to countryside, placing 50 percent of its forces at the district level and establishing 1,800 village police stations. This latter move had produced promising results by permitting direct reporting "through Police channels to Phoenix." From a low of 16,890 officers in 1963, the National Police had grown rapidly, through transfer of 25,000 military personnel, to a projected strength of 122,000 by late 1971. Centralization of Saigon's effort under the National Police had, moreover, facilitated the ongoing U.S. advisory support for Phoenix by CORDS, Public Safety, military intelligence, and the CIA. Through its lead role in rural pacification, the National Police was overcoming its low status as an organization "behind the power curve in this military society" and was "slowly rising (albeit from the cellar) in public . . . esteem."[36]

Simultaneously, the CIA reported that the detention system had shown a marked improvement in operation and capacity. Instead of the wholesale corruption evident in 1967, legal handling of captured VCI had improved "to provide a greater component of justice in the proceedings." Between 1966 and

1970, some 193,000 prisoners, including 100,725 "communist criminals," had been released from correction centers after serving their sentences. But there was still little effort "on a consistent basis in Vietnam to rehabilitate detainees." Nonetheless, the sum of these changes allowed the Saigon government, in October 1969, to launch the "Phoenix Public Information program" in an attempt to "surface Phoenix publicly, under the rationale of protecting the people from terrorism."[37]

Even so, the program preserved much of the covert and coercive facets ingrained in its institutional DNA. In 1970, the first year of Vietnamese control, the number of assassinations by Phoenix operatives reached an all-time peak of 8,191. Vietnamese police officers selected for training in advanced interrogation techniques at the International Police Academy in Washington, a front for covert CIA torture training, readily accepted such brutality as essential for national security. After devoting four pages of his fourteen-page thesis to a history of European torture, Luu Van Huu of the National Police summarized lessons learned: "We have 4 sorts of torture: use of force as such; threats; physical suffering, imposed indirectly; and mental or psychological torture."[38] Similarly, in his 1971 paper for the IPA, Le Van An of Vietnam's National Police defended torture, saying: "Despite the fact that brutal interrogation is strongly criticized by moralists, its importance must not be denied if we want to have order and security in daily life."[39]

Despite CIA rhetoric that gave Phoenix a sanitized, technical patina, the program soon devolved into an exercise in brutality that produced many casualties and few verifiable results. For all its management gloss, the program's strategy remained grounded in DeSilva's original vision of counterterror. After a PRU brought in suspected communists, PIC interrogators, often under CIA supervision, tortured these prisoners and summarily executed many without trial. Often, these PRUs degenerated into petty protection rackets, extracting bribes from accused communists and exterminating suspects identified by unsubstantiated gossip. "So many thousands of arrested VCI have been let go again promptly," recalled Ambassador Komer, "as to raise questions as to why they were apprehended in the first place or whether they bribed their way out."[40] Although early recruits were often well motivated, the PRUs began to attract social outcasts, including convicted criminals, who embraced their basic task of murder by tattooing themselves "Sat Cong" (Kill Communists). According to a 1970 report in the *New York Times*, each PRU "consists of a dozen or more South Vietnamese mercenaries, originally recruited and paid handsomely by the CIA," who were usually "local hoodlums, soldiers of fortune, draft-dodgers, defectors."[41] Even Komer admitted that that the PRUs "were more inclined to knock these guys off than to bother to bring them in."[42]

In their memoirs, former CIA operatives confirmed this dismal assessment of Phoenix's operations. During a tour of the program's provincial interrogation centers near Saigon in 1969, a CIA regional chief, Orrin DeForest, was "disgusted" to find them "irretrievable, just a horrible mess . . . commonly considered the sites of the worst tortures—in particular the water treatment, where they forced water down prisoners' throats until their stomachs swelled up, or the torture in which they applied electric shock to the genitals and nipples."[43] Assigned to this same region as CIA chief for Gia Dinh Province in 1968, Ralph W. McGehee found himself in "the middle of an insane war" that defied rationality and mocked the statistical indices of progress amassed by the vast CORDS counterinsurgency program. "The CORDS meetings," he recalled, "the killings by the CIA's assassination teams—the Provincial Reconnaissance Units—and the absurd intelligence-collection activities progressed as in a Greek tragedy."[44]

As he left Saigon in 1970, the Phoenix program's founder, Robert Komer, described it as "a small, poorly managed, and largely ineffective effort." Indeed, one Pentagon contract study of Phoenix's operations found that, in 1970–71, only 3 percent of the Viet Cong "killed, captured, or rallied were full or probationary Party members above the district level." More than half the supposed Viet Cong captured or killed "were not even Party members."[45] CIA veteran McGehee was even blunter, stating: "The truth is that never in the history of our work in Vietnam did we get one clear-cut, high-ranking Viet Cong agent."[46] Not surprisingly, a pacification effort based on this problematic program failed either to crush the Viet Cong or to win the support of Vietnamese villagers, contributing to the ultimate U.S. defeat in the Vietnam War.[47]

Though sharply critical, such American assessments still failed, then and now, to contemplate the most obvious reason for the failure of the formidable Phoenix intelligence apparatus: enemy counterintelligence. Just as British and Soviet security flipped German spy rings in their midst during World War II, so Vietnam's communist apparatus, which honeycombed the Saigon regime and penetrated the CIA's cross-border operations in the early 1960s, may have compromised Phoenix with false intelligence and clogged its killing machine with innocent victims.[48]

Investigating Phoenix

The character of CIA pacification in Vietnam was first exposed to the American public, albeit obliquely, in 1969 during the investigation of Colonel Robert B. Rheault, a West Point graduate and Special Forces commander, for the summary execution of a suspected Viet Cong spy named Thai Khac Chuyen. After the Green Berets captured a roll of film revealing that their Vietnamese operative was a double agent working for the enemy, they used sodium pentathol ("truth serum") and lie-detector tests, possibly with CIA assistance, for an interrogation that supposedly confirmed his treason. Thinking that the agency had ordered his "elimination," the Special Forces unit at Nha Trang drugged Chuyen with morphine, shot him with a .22 caliber pistol, and dumped his body at sea. Furious, the U.S. commander in Vietnam, General Creighton Abrams, ordered a "no-holds-barred" investigation that culminated in murder charges against Colonel Rheault, the alleged trigger man Captain Robert F. Marasco, and five other Green Beret officers. But the CIA, at the behest of the Nixon White House, refused to allow its agents to testify, ultimately forcing the Army to back down and dismiss charges against Colonel Rheault and his co-accused. In its analysis of the case, the *New York Times* argued that the killing was a product of confused intelligence operations that had been the impetus, two years earlier, for the formation of the CIA's Phoenix program to train Vietnamese assets "in the fine art of silent killing." Indeed, two years later, Captain Marasco admitted that he had shot the double agent on "very, very clear orders from the CIA" and claimed there had been "hundreds" of similar summary executions in South Vietnam. Despite the case's dismissal, the investigation alerted the U.S. Congress and the public to the covert war against the Viet Cong, one that apparently included summary executions of "suspected" VC agents.[49]

After nearly four years of these murky operations, Congress finally exposed the Phoenix program in 1970. Testifying before the Senate Foreign Relations Committee, William Colby, a career CIA officer and chief of pacification in Vietnam, admitted that in 1969 alone Phoenix had killed 6,187 members of the 75,000-strong Viet Cong infrastructure. Although conceding there had been some "illegal killings," Colby rejected a suggestion by Senator J. William Fulbright (Democrat, Arkansas) that Phoenix was "a program for the assassination of civilian leaders."[50]

In the wake of this press exposé, the Operations Subcommittee of the U.S. House of Representatives conducted the first wide-ranging congressional probe of CIA pacification operations and found that Phoenix had killed 9,820 Viet Cong suspects in the past fourteen months. "I am shocked and dismayed," said Representative Ogden R. Reid (Republican, New York). "Assassination and terror by the Viet Cong or Hanoi should not, and must not, call forth the same methods by Saigon, let alone the United States, directly or indirectly."[51]

Several days later, Colby told the House committee that Phoenix had killed

20,587 Viet Cong suspects since 1968. The Saigon government provided additional figures, attributing 40,994 Viet Cong kills to the Phoenix program.[52] When Representative Reid charged that Phoenix was responsible for "indiscriminate killings," Colby defended his program as "an essential part of the war effort" that was "designed to protect the Vietnamese people from terrorism."[53]

In these same hearings, K. Barton Osborn, a military intelligence veteran who had worked with the CIA's Phoenix program in 1967–68, described "the insertion of the six-inch dowel into the ear canal of one of my detainee's ears and the tapping through the brain until he died; and the starving to death of a Vietnamese woman who was suspected of being part of the local [Viet Cong] political education cadre." He also recalled "the use of electronic gear such as sealed telephones attached to the ... women's vagina and the men's testicles ... [to] shock them into submission." During his eighteen months with the Phoenix program, not a single VC suspect had survived CIA interrogation. All these "extralegal, illegal, and covert" procedures were, Osborn testified, found in the Defense Collection Intelligence Manual issued to him during his intelligence training at Fort Holabird, Maryland. Adding to this lethal aura, by 1972 the Phoenix total for enemy "neutralization" had risen to 81,740 Viet Cong eliminated and 26,369 prisoners killed.[54]

To discredit such damaging testimony, the U.S. Army Intelligence Command conducted a thorough investigation of Osborn's charges. The results were released in a declassified summary by William Colby during his 1973 confirmation hearings for the post of CIA director. Although the Army's classified report nitpicked many of his secondary details, it did not challenge Osborn's overall sense of Phoenix's systematic brutality—an assessment confirmed by both eye-witness accounts and official studies.[55]

In early 1968, for example, two CORDS evaluators, John G. Lybrand and L. Craig Johnstone, had conducted an official review of the program in II Corps (Central Vietnam), finding that: "The truncheon and electric shock method of interrogation were in widespread use, with almost all [U.S.] advisers admitting to have witnessed instances of the use of these methods." As their Saigon counterparts started these cruel interrogations, the study found that: "Most advisers claimed they did not personally take part in [tortures] but 'turned their backs on them.'" Similarly, an American who advised PRU irregulars in Binh Thuan Province during 1968–69, Richard Welcome, indicated that Americans allowed their Saigon allies in Phoenix wide latitude: "Prisoners were abused. Were they tortured? It depends on what you call torture. Electricity was used by the Vietnamese, water was used, occasionally some of the prisoners got beat up. Were any of them put on the rack, eyes gouged out, bones broken? No, I never saw any evidence of that at all." Even

Colby himself, the program's founder, admitted that "various of the things that Mr. Osborn alleges might have happened." In the wink-nudge approach that Phoenix advisers adopted to abuses by their Saigon allies, Colby added that "Phoenix . . . was not to be a program of assassination and we issued instructions . . . that not only were Americans not to participate . . . but they were to make their objections known. . . . I did receive some reports of this nature . . . and took them up with the government of South Vietnam. . . . I knew there were people killed, there is no question about it, . . . but I certainly reject the idea that it was a systematic program of assassination." Reviewing this evidence, one recent conservative history of Phoenix concluded that "the large majority of South Vietnamese interrogators tortured some or all of the Communist prisoners in their care" and "a smaller number tortured villagers suspected of collaborating with the Communists."[56]

Lessons for Latin America

In retrospect, Phoenix proved a seminal experience for the U.S. intelligence community, combining both physical and psychological techniques in extreme methods that would serve as a model for later U.S. counterinsurgency training in Latin America. In the midst of this shift in covert battlegrounds, the year 1975 became doubly significant, marking not only the defeat of the United States in Vietnam but also the dissolution of the Office of Public Safety, a long-time cover for CIA torture training.

Amid these troubled transitions, the CIA, in collaboration with the Defense Department, intensified its efforts in Latin America, where Washington was determined, in the aftermath of its defeat in Vietnam, to hold the line against global communism. Denied access to the region's police after the abolition of OPS in 1975, the CIA would now work primarily through U.S. military advisers to train allied armies. Absent other documentation, we can track the paper trail of this bureaucratic shift through once-secret Pentagon memos about "Project X," the U.S. Army's program for transmitting Vietnam's lessons to South America. From 1965 to 1990, the agency and military intelligence instructed several generations of Latin American officers in counterinsurgency and interrogation through field training, courses at the School of the Americas in Panama, and detailed manuals. Through an internal review done in 1991, the Pentagon found six manuals totaling 1,100 pages that contained numerous passages explaining harsh methods; the Pentagon estimated that "as many as a thousand copies" had been distributed by its Southern Command to trainee officers in Latin America.[57]

In 1965–66, Army intelligence launched "Project X" as a program designed "to develop an exportable foreign intelligence package to provide counterinsurgency techniques learned in Vietnam to Latin American countries," according to a confidential Pentagon memo.[58] A Pentagon counterintelligence staffer, Linda Matthews, reported that, in 1967–68, the team of Army officers drafting one of the project's training manuals, "Intelligence for Stability Operations," was in contact with "a resident instruction course . . . in the Phoenix program" at the Army Intelligence School and that "some offending material from the Phoenix program may have found its way into the Project X materials."[59]

One of these manuals, in the Pentagon's words, "provided training regarding use of sodiopentathol compound in interrogation, abduction of adversary family members to influence the adversary, prioritization of adversary personalities for abduction, exile, physical beatings and execution"—in short, all the trademark Phoenix techniques.[60] For the next quarter century, the U.S. Army would transmit these extreme tactics, by both direct training and instructional manuals, to the armies of ten Latin American nations. By the mid-1980s, counterguerrilla operations in Colombia and Central America would thus bear an eerie but explicable resemblance to those in South Vietnam.

Eventually, Project X developed a complete counterinsurgency curriculum based on seven training manuals, all in Spanish, that addressed key tactical problems, notably *Handling of Sources, Interrogation, Combat Intelligence*, and *Terrorism and the Urban Guerrilla*. Among these seven handbooks, at least five contained violent counterterror tactics far beyond anything in the CIA's 1963 KUBARK manual. For example, the agency's handbook *Handling of Sources* refers, in the words of a Pentagon content analysis, "to motivation by fear, payment of bounties for enemy dead, beatings, false imprisonment, executions and the use of truth serum."[61]

Upon closer reading, the 1989 edition of *Handling of Sources* also offers chilling lessons about control of assets in counterinsurgency by applying past examples from the Philippines and Malaysia to current Latin American operations. By appealing to "mercenary motivations" or using "fear as a weapon," the counterintelligence agent can, the manual suggests, recruit an "employee" for infiltration into a guerrilla zone, taking care to psychologically manipulate the employee's every emotion and thus "maintain the necessary control." To establish his asset's credibility as a "guerrilla recruit," the manual says, the agent "could cause the arrest or detention of the employee's parents, imprison the employee or give him a beating." And, if regular scrutiny of the employee's reports reveals "possible deception," the manual suggests that the agent begin with "friendly character interrogations," checking all answers against an operational archive and preparing a "new Declaration of Personal History." If this friendly approach fails to produce a breakthrough, this manual adds, the agent should escalate to the "mental test," waking the employee from a deep sleep for questioning, and then to the "mechanical test," using an injection of sodiopentathol ("truth serum"). If the employee turns out to be an "information trafficker" or a guerrilla "penetration agent," then our operative should "initiate termination proceedings" on "bad terms" through means "which are only limited by the agent's imagination." Although "threats of physical violence or true physical abuse" should, if possible, be avoided, the agent can effect an erring employee's "removal by means of imprisonment" after setting him up "to commit an illegal act." Or, in the ultimate twist, the agent can send "him in a specially dangerous mission for which he has been inadequately prepared . . . [and] pass information to guerrilla security elements"—thus, saving his government the cost of a bullet.[62] Apart from these cold-blooded tactics of kidnap, murder, beatings, and betrayal, the manual evidences, throughout its 144 single-spaced pages, a studied amorality apparently hardened on the anvil of the Vietnam conflict.

For more than twenty years, Project X was energetic, even determined, in its dissemination of these ruthless techniques. From 1966 to 1976, the U.S. Army's School of the Americas, then based in Panama, taught these methods to hundreds of Latin American officers at its military intelligence course. After a four-year hiatus caused by President Jimmy Carter's human rights concerns, the U.S. Army's Southern Command resumed the training at the School in 1982 and, five years later, elaborated its lesson plans through these Spanish-language manuals for distribution to trainees in Colombia, Peru, Ecuador, El Salvador, and Guatemala.[63] Between 1989 and 1991, moreover, the School of the Americas, now relocated to Georgia, issued 693 copies of these handbooks as texts in intelligence courses for students from ten Latin American nations.[64]

Human Resources Manual

Though the U.S. intelligence community operated in this way across the continent, our detailed knowledge of the actual torture training in Latin America comes from a single surviving document, the *Human Resources Exploitation Manual—1983*, which the CIA used to train Honduran soldiers. In contrast to the Army's Project X handbooks, with their violent Phoenix-style methods of kidnapping and murder, this CIA manual emphasizes psychological techniques defined in the original KUBARK interrogation program—a reason, perhaps, that this document survived the Pentagon's later destruction of almost all

Project X handbooks. After completing a training session for Honduran military interrogators in early 1983, an anonymous CIA instructor evidently combined his field experience with the agency's psychological doctrine to produce, in this document, a relatively complete statement of its interrogation methods.[65]

At the outset of the Honduran training session, this anonymous instructor emphasizes that he will explain two types of "psychological techniques," the coercive and the noncoercive. While the CIA does not emphasize the use of coercive methods, the agent tells his students, "we do want to make you aware of them and the proper way to use them."[66] In his review of noncoercive techniques, the agent explains that they "are based on the principle of generating pressure inside the subject without application of outside force. This is accomplished by manipulating the victim psychologically until resistance is broken and an urge to yield is fortified."[67]

To establish control at the start, the CIA instructor said, the questioner should "manipulate the subject's environment, to create unpleasant or intolerable situations, to disrupt patterns of time, space, and sensory perception. The subject is very much aware that the 'questioner' controls his ultimate disposition."[68] Among many possible techniques, the subject can be arrested at a time selected to "achieve surprise and the maximum amount of mental discomfort," particularly early morning when "most subjects experience intense feelings of shock, insecurity, and psychological stress."[69] Once in custody, a subject should be immediately placed in "isolation, both physical and psychological," then "completely stripped and told to take a shower" while blindfolded before a guard and "provided with ill-fitting clothing (familiar clothing reinforces identity and thus the capacity for resistance)."[70] If the subject proves resistant, then an interrogator can employ a "few non-coercive techniques which can be used to induce regression," such as "persistent manipulation of time" or "disrupting sleep schedules."[71]

Although the manual's overall approach is psychological, the CIA trainer points out that coercion still plays an important role in effective interrogation. "The purpose of all coercive techniques," he explains, "is to induce psychological regression in the subject by bringing a superior outside force to bear on his will to resist." As this coercion is applied, the subject suffers "a loss of autonomy, a reversion to an earlier behavioral level."[72]

There are, the manual states, three basic coercive techniques—debility, disorientation, and dread. "For centuries," the CIA trainer stated, "'questioners' have employed various methods of inducing physical weakness . . . [on the] assumption that lowering the subject's physiological resistance will lower his psychological capacity for resistance."[73] While disorientation can "destroy his capacity to resist," sustained dread also "induces regression."[74]

But even within the CIA's psychological paradigm, there are times when threats of physical pain are necessary. "Threat is basically a means for establishing a bargaining position by inducing fear in the subject," the trainer explains, adding: "A threat should never be made unless it is part of the plan and the 'questioner' has the approval to carry out the threat."[75] Yet, even when using threats of physical harm, the trainer emphasizes the primacy of the psychological over the physical, saying: "The threat of coercion usually weakens or destroys resistance more effectively than coercion itself. For example, the threat to inflict pain can trigger fears more damaging than the immediate sensation of pain."[76] Indeed, pain inflicted on the victim "from outside himself may actually . . . intensify his will to resist," but pain that "he feels he is inflicting upon himself is more likely to sap his resistance."[77]

Comparing this 1983 Honduran handbook with the CIA's original 1963 KUBARK manual reveals, in ten key passages, that the later document copies almost verbatim the language of the earlier manual in both conceptual design and technical detail. After outlining psychological techniques to induce "regression" in the subject, both documents emphasize elimination of "sensory stimuli" through "solitary confinement to induce sensory disorientation." In their emphasis on the use of self-inflicted pain, both texts warn that pain inflicted externally, by an interrogator, can actually strengthen a subject's resistance. Having articulated these two central elements, both documents then itemize the particular methods whose sum will effect a devastating psychological assault on individual identity—disorienting arrest, isolation, manipulation of time, threats of physical pain or drug injection, and careful staging of the interrogation room. Between 1963 and 1983, enemies, continents, and interrogators might have changed, but the two essential elements of this interrogation method remained constant—sensory disorientation and self-inflicted pain.

The Global War on Terror

Under the pressure of the occupation of Iraq in 2003, these brutal interrogation policies were revived and quickly proliferated to involve thousands of ordinary Iraqis. In August, Baghdad suffered a wave of terror bombings that rocked the Jordanian Embassy, causing nineteen deaths, and blasted UN headquarters, leaving twenty-three dead. One U.S. military study soon found that the lethal roadside bombings were "the result of painstaking surveillance and reconnaissance" by rebel sympathizers inside both the Iraqi police and the secure U.S. Green Zone in downtown Baghdad. In striking contrast to the insurgents, the U.S. command realized, in this study's words, that its own "human intelligence is poor or lacking . . . due to the dearth of competence and expertise." As the number of American casualties surged and violence spread, U.S. headquarters in Baghdad ordered sweeps of civilian neighborhoods that rounded up suspects and filled military prisons, whose populations soon swelled from 3,500 to 18,000. "The gloves are coming off gentlemen regarding these detainees," a captain e-mailed his military intelligence (MI) comrades in mid-August. "Casualties are mounting and we need to start gathering info to help protect our fellow soldiers from any further attacks."[78]

In the midst of this crisis, the CIA's coercive interrogation techniques reached Baghdad's Abu Ghraib prison by two routes—indirectly from Afghanistan and directly through transmission from the military prison at Guantanamo Bay, Cuba. As the insurgency erupted in August, Defense Secretary Donald Rumsfeld ordered his "special-access program" operatives into Iraq, inserting them into military prisons with authority to conduct harsh interrogation beyond what was allowed by U.S. Army regulations.[79]

That summer, at a Pentagon briefing about the growing insurgency, Secretary Rumsfeld "complained loudly" about poor intelligence from Iraq, contrasting it with the yield from his new "extreme" interrogation practices at Guantanamo. Voicing "anger and frustration" over restraints imposed on U.S. interrogators in Iraq by the Geneva Conventions, Rumsfeld gave oral orders for his Guantanamo commander, General Geoffrey Miller, to "Gitmoize" intelligence collection in Baghdad. Consequently, in early September 2003, the general, who had spent the past nine months developing Guantanamo's harsh regimen, inspected Iraqi prisons with "a team of personnel experienced in strategic interrogation." Afterward, he observed, in a classified report for army headquarters at Baghdad, that "it is essential that the guard force be actively engaged in setting the conditions for successful exploitation of internees." General Miller also urged a radical restructuring of detainee policy to make Iraq's prisons the front line for information warfare, saying: "Detention operations must act as an enabler for . . . the expeditious collection of intelligence." In expansive, almost visionary rhetoric, Miller wrote that his program would allow Abu Ghraib to "drive the rapid exploitation of internees to answer . . . theater and national level counter terrorism requirements," thus meeting the "needs of the global war on terrorism." If implemented immediately, his plan would, he said, produce "a significant improvement in actionable intelligence . . . within thirty days."[80]

Elaborating on his plan to "Gitmoize" Abu Ghraib, General Miller added, "We're going to select the MPs [Military Police] who can do this, and they're going to work specifically with the interrogation team." During his visit to Abu Ghraib prison, the general turned over an interrogation manual and a compact disk (CD) with what he called "training information" to facilitate integration of the MPs into his new procedure. In one of his internal reports that September, Miller also advised that "teams, comprised of operational behavioral psychologists and psychiatrists, are essential in developing integrated interrogation strategies and assessing interrogation intelligence."[81]

Indeed, on September 14, just five days after General Miller's departure, the U.S. commander for Iraq, Lieutenant General Ricardo S. Sanchez, signed a detailed memo authorizing, in the words of a later inquiry, "a dozen interrogation techniques beyond [Army] Field Manual 34–52—[and] five beyond those applied at Guantanamo."[82] In his instructions, Sanchez explained that his "Interrogation and Counter-Resistance Policy" was "modeled on the one . . . for interrogations conducted at Guantanamo Bay, but modified for applicability to a theater of war in which the Geneva Conventions apply." In this memo, which remained in effect until modified in October and continued to influence conditions for months thereafter, the general ordered sophisticated psychological torture:

T. Dietary Manipulation: Changing the diet of a detainee . . .

U. Environmental Manipulation: Altering the environment to create moderate discomfort (e.g., adjusting temperatures or introducing an unpleasant smell) . . .

V. Sleep Adjustment: Adjusting the sleeping times of the detainee (e.g., reversing the sleeping cycles from night to day) . . .

X. Isolation: Isolating the detainee from other detainees . . .

Y. Presence of Military Working Dogs: Exploits Arab fear of dogs while maintaining security during interrogations . . .

Z. Sleep Management: Detainee provided minimum 4 hours of sleep per 24 hour period, not to exceed 72 continuous hours.

AA. Yelling, Loud Music, and Light Control: Used to create fear, disorient detainee and prolong capture shock . . .

CC. Stress Positions: Use of physical posturing (sitting, standing, kneeling, prone, etc.)

So extreme was the sum of these methods that military lawyers objected, and, a month later, Sanchez rescinded some of the "harshest techniques." Nonetheless, the force of these memos was soon felt at remote Army outposts and inside Abu Ghraib prison. "On 15 Oct 2003," one prisoner told investigators, "they started punishing me in all sorts of ways . . . and they cuffed me high for 7 or 8 hours. And that caused a rupture to my right hand. . . . And in the following days, they also put a bag over my head, and of course, this whole time I was without clothes and without anything to sleep on." That September as well, the 82nd Airborne Division started torturing Iraqi captives with "beatings, exposure to extremes of heat and cold, . . . and sleep deprivation."

Of particular note, the *New York Times* reported that the soldiers had learned these "stress techniques" in Afghanistan by observing "Central Intelligence Agency operatives interrogating prisoners."[83]

Significantly, General Sanchez, though trained as an ordinary combat commander, had issued orders for a multifaceted assault on the human psyche. The synergy of these specific interrogation techniques was a systematic attack on all human stimuli, psychological and biological, quite similar to the CIA's 1963 KUBARK manual and its 1983 Honduran handbook. Indeed, a close comparison of Sanchez's memo with the CIA's 1983 manual reveals six key points of similarity, both in broad principles and in particular methods. In their lists of specific techniques, all three documents try to create an environment that elevates the interrogator by making him, as Sanchez put it, "appear to be the one who controls all aspects of the interrogation" while simultaneously breaking down the detainee by "significantly increasing the fear level." This sequence of psychological techniques indicates that the CIA's methods had, in both design and detail, spread to become the conceptual foundation for standard U.S. interrogation doctrine, even within the regular military.[84]

In another mode of transmitting these extreme techniques, veteran army interrogators from the 519th Military Intelligence Battalion, led by Captain Carolyn A. Wood, arrived at Abu Ghraib from the CIA's Bagram prison, near Kabul, in July 2003. As the insurgency intensified, these interrogators were working to introduce harsh methods to Abu Ghraib—including some that had already produced several Afghan fatalities. From October to December 2003, moreover, a six-person team traveled from Cuba to Iraq, bringing the "lessons learned" at Guantanamo Bay, notably the use of military dogs. One team member, Staff Sergeant James Vincent Lucas, later testified that the team introduced Abu Ghraib interrogators to Guantanamo's aggressive, innovative techniques, including "short chaining" and "clothing removal." Apparently building upon these procedures, military police in the security blocks at Abu Ghraib began to soften up detainees for CIA and MI interrogation. One of the MPs later convicted of abuse, Private Ivan L. Frederick, recalled that an interrogator gave him lists of prisoners whom he wanted dog handlers to visit; guards then used the animals to "intimidate inmates." Significantly, cell blocks 1-A and 1-B, the sites of the notorious Abu Ghraib photographs, had been informally removed from the MP's authority and were now controlled by two intelligence officers who reported directly to General Sanchez's headquarters in Baghdad—Colonel Thomas M. Pappas and Lieutenant Colonel Steve Jordan.[85]

Then, on November 19, 2003, General Sanchez issued orders removing all of Abu Ghraib prison from the MPs and assigning it, along with the top-secret facility near Baghdad airport known as Camp Cropper, to the 205th Military Intelligence Brigade under Colonel Pappas—a division of authority that army investigators later called "not doctrinally sound," since it exacerbated an already "ambiguous command relationship." In the months of most intense abuse in late 2003, General Sanchez summoned Colonel Pappas for periodic grillings and pressed him hard to deliver more intelligence.[86]

Under Colonel Pappas, MPs at Abu Ghraib were responsible for an initial phase of intensive disorientation to prepare detainees for later interrogation by the CIA, military intelligence, and private contractors, producing what the Army's investigation later called "numerous incidents of sadistic, blatant, and wanton criminal abuses . . . on several detainees." In the words of Major General Antonio Taguba's inquiry, this abuse involved "punching, slapping, and kicking detainees" and "keeping them naked for several days at a time." In the uncontrolled escalation that often accompanies psychological torture, harsh treatment soon moved beyond sleep and sensory deprivation to sexual humiliation marked by "photographing naked male and female detainees; forcibly arranging detainees in various sexually explicit positions . . . ; forcing groups of male detainees to masturbate while being photographed." Dismissing the idea of such behavior as simply aberrant, General Taguba's inquiry found that "Military Intelligence (MI) interrogators and Other U.S. Government Agency's (OGA) [CIA] actively requested that MP guards set physical and mental conditions for favorable interrogation."[87]

In making this latter charge, General Taguba cited a revealing statement by one of the MPs later accused of abuse, Sabrina Harman, who was, she said, ordered to stop prisoners from sleeping; to this end, one prisoner was famously photographed on a box with wires attached to his hands and feet. "MI wanted them to talk," she said, implicating two of her fellow MPs: "It is Graner and Frederick's job to do things for MI and OGA [CIA] to get these people to talk."[88]

As part of General Taguba's investigation, the MI chief at Abu Ghraib, Colonel Pappas, drew up a memo titled "Interrogation and Counter-Resistance Policy" in January 2004 outlining his procedures in cell blocks 1-A and 1-B. Significantly, his orders required MI interrogators, in cooperation with physicians and MPs, to apply a method whose larger design seems derived from the CIA's trademark fusion of sensory deprivation and self-inflicted pain. "Typically," Pappas wrote, MI interrogators gave MP guards "a copy of the interrogation plan and a written note as to how to execute [it]. . . . The doctor and psychiatrist also look at the files to see what the interrogation plan recommends." This policy, Pappas contended, followed innovations at Guantanamo Bay, where teams of psychologists and psychiatrists helped tailor harsh techniques to break individual prisoners. At Abu Ghraib, Colonel Pappas's interrogators used seven sensory-disorientation techniques to soften up prisoners, including:

1. dietary manipulation—minimum bread and water, monitored by medics;
2. environmental manipulation—i.e. reducing A.C. [air conditioning] in summer, lower[ing] heat in winter;
3. sleep management—for 72-hour time period maximum, monitored by medics;
4. sensory deprivation—for 72-hour time period maximum, monitored by medics;
5. isolation—for longer than 30 days;
6. stress positions; and
7. presence of working dogs.[89]

Then, in the second phase of Colonel Pappas's program, trained MI and CIA operatives administered the requisite mix of interrogation and self-inflicted pain—a process that evidently took place outside the frame of the now-famous photographs. Under the 205th Military Intelligence Battalion, forced nudity became a standard interrogation procedure to humiliate and break prisoners at Abu Ghraib as investigators sought answers to seven key questions—notably, "who and where are the mid-level Ba'athists," "which organizations or groups . . . will conduct high payoff attacks," "what organizations are Ba'athist surrogates," and "who are the saboteurs against infrastructure?" Amid this harsh regimen, there were, moreover, increasing incidents of capricious cruelty. In November 2003, for example, five Iraqi generals suspected of instigating a small prison riot were manacled, blindfolded, and beaten by guards "until they were covered in blood." Although the prison's Detainee Assessment Branch filed at least twenty reports of serious abuse with General Sanchez, his headquarters did not intervene. Significantly, General Taguba later found that Colonel Pappas and his deputy, Lieutenant Colonel Steven L. Jordan, chief of the Joint Interrogation and Debriefing Center, were "directly or indirectly responsible" for prisoner abuse at Abu Ghraib.[90]

In contrast to General Taguba's dispassionate descriptions, a February 2004 Red Cross report offered explicit, even chilling details of U.S. interrogation techniques. By late 2003, the International Committee of the Red Cross (ICRC) had made twenty-nine visits to U.S. detention facilities across Iraq, exercising its right to arrive unannounced for unrestricted inspections. While conditions for most detainees were, the Red Cross found, satisfactory, those "under supervision of Military Intelligence were at high risk of being subjected to a variety of harsh treatments ranging from insults, threats and humiliation to both physical and psychological coercion, which in some cases was tantamount to torture." Some coalition military intelligence officers told the ICRC that "between 70 percent and 90 percent" of detainees in Iraq, totaling more than forty-one thousand individuals by mid-2004, "had been arrested by mistake." During their visits to Abu Ghraib's military intelligence section, several U.S. officers told the ICRC that "it was part of the military intelligence process to hold a person . . . naked in a completely dark and empty cell for a prolonged period [and] to use inhumane and degrading treatment, including physical and psychological coercion." In words that could have been lifted almost verbatim from past CIA interrogation manuals, the ICRC detailed the forms of "ill treatment" that U.S. military intelligence used "in a systematic way to . . . extract information" from Iraqi detainees, including:

Hooding, used to prevent people from seeing and to disorient them, and also to prevent them from breathing freely . . . ;
Beatings with hard objects (including pistols and rifles) . . . ;
Threats (of ill-treatment, reprisals against family members, imminent execution . . .);
Being stripped naked for several days while held in solitary confinement . . . ;
Being paraded naked outside their cells in front of other persons . . . ;
Being attached repeatedly over several days, for several hours each time, with handcuffs to the bars of their cells door in humiliating (i.e. naked or in underwear) and/or uncomfortable position causing physical pain;
Being forced to remain for prolonged periods in stress positions such as squatting or standing with or without the arms lifted.[91]

During a visit to Abu Ghraib in October 2003, at the height of General Sanchez's extreme regimen, the ICRC discovered detainees "completely naked in totally empty concrete cells and in total darkness, allegedly for several days." The Red Cross medical staff determined that prisoners so treated were suffering from "memory problems, verbal expression difficulties, incoherent speech, acute anxiety reactions, . . . and suicidal tendencies." In sum, the ICRC concluded that U.S. military intelligence was engaged in practices that "are prohibited under International Humanitarian Law."[92]

In the aftermath of the Abu Ghraib scandal, the national press pursued stories confirming that the abuse shown in those photos was not, as the Defense Department would have it, the work of a few bad apples but was in fact widespread. In September 2005, for example, the *New York Times* reported allegations by Captain Ian Fishback, a West Point graduate, that the 82nd Airborne Division had engaged in routine torture of Iraqi captives that included "beatings, exposure to extremes of hot and cold, stacking in human pyramids and sleep deprivation." Indicating the covert source of such methods, soldiers had, he said, "learned the stress techniques from watching Central Intelligence Agency operatives interrogating prisoners" in Afghanistan.[93]

Similarly, in April 2006, the *Times* reported that a special military intelligence unit called Task Force 6–26, operating from a secret base near Baghdad in 2003–04, had used a mix of elaborate psychological and crude physical tortures in its search for Al Qaeda leaders, becoming capriciously cruel in its treatment of detainees.[94] A later Pentagon inquiry found that Special Operations forces had, during a four-month period in 2004, subjected Iraqi detainees to an extreme form of psychological torture involving starvation, stress positions, extreme cold, blaring music, and confinement in cells so small that prisoners could neither stand nor sit.[95]

As protests rose against the occupation at Basra in the south, British forces there revived the long-banned "five techniques" used at Belfast back in the 1970s, subjecting prisoners to hooding, stress positions, sleep deprivation, close-quarter shouting, and beatings.[96] When we reflect on these incidents in Abu Ghraib prison and beyond, it seems that torture was systematic, not aberrant, and that its widespread proliferation was symptomatic of both command decisions and a crisis in the ranks over a failing pacification effort.

In the wake of the Abu Ghraib controversy, the U.S. military shifted incarceration duties to its Iraqi allies, producing another analogy with South Vietnam, where all prisons, even those funded by the CIA, were under Saigon's nominal control. This more recent move coincided with a major change in U.S. counterinsurgency strategy that, starting in April 2004, emphasized the formation of sectarian militia and police squads to secure local communities. In the two-year hiatus before the formation of a competent Iraqi officer corps, General David Petraeus, commander of the Multi-National Security Transition Command in Iraq, incorporated local militias, such as the two-thousand-strong Wolf Brigade, into the national police with authority to incarcerate and interrogate.[97]

Two months later, in June, the U.S. command issued Fragmentary Order (FRAGO) 242, directing coalition troops not to investigate detainee abuse by Iraqi forces. When coalition troops encountered any Iraqi security forces abusing Iraqis, "only an initial report will be made. . . . No further investigation will be required unless directed by HQ."[98] Within a year, the BBC reported that Iraq's new police faced accusations of "systematic abuse and torture of people in detention." One survivor among a group of ten Sunnis arrested by Shi'a police commandoes in Baghdad told reporters: "The police started to beat us, tied our hands and blindfolded us. We were left from 5:30 that evening inside a kind of container that had no air vents. After one hour, we lost consciousness and some people began to die, the others were dead by one o'clock in the morning."[99]

After the group WikiLeaks provided a vast cache of classified documents, the Bureau of Investigative Journalism in Britain surveyed four hundred thousand military logs and determined that, among the 180,000 people detained in Iraqi prisons between 2004 and 2009, the U.S. military received 1,365 reports of torture. In these reports about Iraqi prison conditions, coalition soldiers described "men and women blindfolded, beaten with cables, their genitals electrocuted, fingernails ripped out, sodomised with bottles and hoses." On at least two occasions, U.S. soldiers were ordered to take no action since only Iraqis were involved in the abuse. There were, moreover, seventy-six reports of alleged abuse by Iraqi personnel moving through the U.S. chain of command, indicating that Americans had knowledge of the problem. Nonetheless, after six inspections of Iraqi prisons in 2005–06, a coalition military spokesman stated: "The facilities were, by our standards, overcrowded, but the people being held at those facilities were being properly taken care of. . . . So no abuse, no evidence of torture in those facilities."[100] Judging from this disparity between internal knowledge and public statements, U.S. officials delegated the gritty task of mass incarceration to Iraqis after Abu Ghraib and then turned a blind eye to the tortures their allies used to extract intelligence for counterinsurgency.

Conclusion

If an analogy between Vietnam and Iraq has any relevance beyond a few obvious similarities such as the use of torture, then other aspects of the Phoenix program should prove predictive of future revelations about the underside of the Iraq war. Though it is difficult to document, torture's dual psychopathology of fear and empowerment makes it possible that harsh mass incarceration was adopted in Iraq not just to extract information but to pacify a recalcitrant population with something akin to the counterterror used in South Vietnam. For hints of these and related revelations to come, we can look beyond the specifics of the Phoenix torture techniques for other aspects of a counterterror campaign that may have been operating sub rosa in Iraq.

Apart from torture per se, CIA black lists, death squads, and deep-penetration agents were other key facets of Vietnam's Phoenix program that might have been deployed in the cities and villages of Iraq, beyond the ken of a press cosseted inside Baghdad's Green Zone. To cite but one telling example, it took decades for the most serious of Vietnam-era atrocities to emerge. It was not until 2003 that a Toledo newspaper published a Pulitzer prize–winning account of a systematic counterterror campaign by the 101st Airborne's so-called Tiger Force that murdered hundreds of unarmed civilians back in 1967 with the full approval of the unit's command.[101]

To date, just a few hints of similar covert operations have escaped the strict press controls that the Bush administration imposed on combat operations in Iraq. The first revelations about the CIA's use of Iraq mercenaries emerged when the *Denver Post* won a court order breaking the national-security seal on pretrial hearings for soldiers charged with the murder of Major General Abed Hamed Mowhoush, the former Iraqi air defense chief. According to court records, General Mowhoush had walked into Forward Base "Tiger" at Al Qaim, in the Iraqi desert, on November 10, 2003, asking to see U.S. officers about the release of his son. At first, the general cooperated, telling interrogators he was "commander of the al Quds Golden Division," a network of Saddam loyalists supplying the insurgents. When tough tactics backfired and the general grew silent, soldiers turned him over to a CIA operative named "Brian" and his four-man squad of "Scorpions," Iraqi mercenaries the agency was using for counterguerrilla operations—just as the Phoenix program had once used the PRUs in South Vietnam. After a severe beating and subsequent abuse, the general expired, and his body was transferred to Abu Ghraib, where, with severe contusions about the face, it was famously photographed.[102]

Subsequent research indicates that the scope of the CIA's Scorpion operation was larger and more lurid than it appeared from these first, fragmentary revelations. A year after the *Denver Post* exposé, the *Washington Post* reported that the CIA, acting on a presidential order signed in early 2002, had formed the Scorpions for an elaborate destabilization operation before the Iraq invasion. Later, after Baghdad's fall, the agency used them to penetrate the insurgency, doing what one agent called "the dirty work." At some point in this process, the CIA began using the Scorpions to snatch informants from dangerous areas outside the Green Zone. Reporter Michael Isikoff, after interviewing the agency official who ran the program, revealed that about eighty Scorpions had been trained in Nevada and were used for sabotage operations in western Iraq before the U.S. invaded in March 2003. During the actual invasion, however, they were preempted by another CIA squad of Kurdish paramilitary that "conducted a deadly series of drive-by shootings and ambushes of Iraqi military and Baath Party security officials. These were in effect targeted assassinations against identified regime figures."[103]

More broadly, the veteran *Washington Post* reporter Bob Woodward revealed, in late 2008, that much of the success of President Bush's troop surge in suppressing the Iraqi resistance was the result not of boots on the ground but of bullets in the head. Starting in May 2006, American intelligence agencies launched a series of Special Action Programs (SAPs) using "the most highly classified techniques and information in the U.S. government" in a successful effort "to locate, target and kill key individuals in extremist groups such as al Qaeda, the Sunni insurgency and renegade Shia militias." Under the leadership of General Stanley McChrystal, the Joint Special Operations Command (JSOC) used "every tool available simultaneously, from signals intercepts to human intelligence," for "lightning quick" strikes. One intelligence officer said the techniques were so effective that they gave him "orgasms." President Bush called them "awesome." In a television interview, Woodward said, "I would somewhat compare it to the Manhattan Project in World War II," adding that cutting Iraq's violence in half within a matter of months "isn't going to happen with the bunch of joint security stations or the surge."[104]

These assassinations were part of a broader authority that Defense Secretary Donald Rumsfeld gave JSOC in early 2004 to "kill or capture al-Qaeda terrorists" in twenty countries across the Middle East. Indeed, this authorization produced dozens of far-flung lethal operations, including an AC-130 air strike on Somalia in January 2007, a special forces raid in Pakistan's tribal areas that killed twenty in September 2008, and a CIA-directed assault in Syria in October 2008 that left eight dead. Throughout 2008, as well, Predator drones operated inside Pakistan with lethal efficiency, killing nine of the twenty top-priority Al Qaeda targets identified by the U.S. intelligence community and starting a sustained campaign of aerial assassinations.[105]

At this rather preliminary point in our knowledge about the Global War on Terror, it seems that the CIA revived at least three key attributes of its Vietnam-era Phoenix program to prosecute its clandestine war in Iraq—torture, assassination, and native mercenaries. In the future, we can expect more such revelations whose sum will portray the full scope of the covert operations in Iraq and allow us to evaluate the similarities and differences, the continuities and discontinuities, that link the Iraq war and the earlier U.S. efforts in South Vietnam.

4

 Theater State of Terror

The Philippines offers eloquent testimony about the transactional nature of psychological torture. From 1972 to 1986, torture served as a key instrument in President Ferdinand Marcos's martial-law rule, creating a cohort of junior officers whose careers were shaped by years of coercive interrogation and extrajudicial killing. As abuse proliferated, these Filipino interrogators combined psychological theatricality with physical brutality to induce terror not just among their many victims but in an entire society. Through their involvement in thousands of torture sessions over the span of fourteen years, these officers and their victims reveal the transactional dynamics of such torture, which simultaneously devastates its victims while empowering the perpetrators.

These colonels and their engrained violence are emblematic of an authoritarian age. By 1985, military juntas held power in more than half of the hundred-plus nations that constituted the developing world. With ruthlessness and idealism, these martial regimes often attempted a social transformation through systematic violence. The more extreme used terror to wage civil war on their enemies, whether ideological, ethnic, or religious. When their time had passed and these regimes collapsed in the 1980s, the politicized, brutalized armed forces they left behind were often a barrier to democratization—clinging to power, resisting reforms, and struggling to prevent any accounting for the past.

Under Marcos's martial-law regime, the Philippine military played such a role, spawning numerous factions that became deeply politicized and defiant of civil authority. But none could rival the violent extremes of the Reform the Armed Forces Movement, or RAM. Led by a clique of middle-ranking officers, this group plotted a coup d'état against the Marcos dictatorship in 1986 and, failing to take power, launched five more attempts against his successor, Corazon Aquino. In their repeated failures, these colonels reveal much about the mentality of the military officers who served as instruments of state terror in this authoritarian age. Within the Philippines itself, RAM represented, above all, a breakdown in military socialization. Most of its members were regular officers who had graduated from the Philippine Military Academy (PMA) during the 1970s. There, for four years, they were drilled in obedience and indoctrinated into a belief in civilian supremacy over the military.

Unlike earlier generations, however, these future rebels graduated into a martial-law military and then spent their formative years as junior officers fighting a civil war in Mindanao or interrogating dissidents in Manila. As torture and extrajudicial killings became more frequent, they came to personify Marcos's capricious violence and became veritable superstars in his theater state of terror. For these young officers, torture also proved transformative, freeing them from their socialization in subordination learned at the military academy and inspiring a will to power—no longer self-effacing servants of the state but empowered political actors who would be its master. With egos inflated as lords of life and death, pain and suffering, they emerged from the regime's safe houses onto the national stage with the aura of "Nietzschean supermen," protean creator/destroyers whose awesome violence would sweep away all that stood between them and the crown of power.

In their leap from interrogation to coup d'état, these rebel colonels highlight our need to study the torturers instead of focusing solely on their victims. These military rebels illustrate how torture can inspire a sense of empowerment in the perpetrator—an unsettling topic largely ignored in the literature on human rights and human psychology. To understand the impact of authoritarian rule and its use of coercion on the military, we need to examine how the torturers' experience of torture informed and even inspired a political vision that troubled many of these democratic transitions.

The Phenomenology of Torture

We are only just beginning to understand torture. As authoritarian regimes and their systematic brutality proliferated in the mid-twentieth century, the international community reacted with treaties to outlaw the abuse and therapy to treat its victims.[1] At the close of its first worldwide Campaign for the Abolition of Torture in 1972, Amnesty International realized the limitations of its lawyerly practice of documentation and appealed to the medical profession for support. A group of Danish doctors responded with research among victims that discovered a pernicious, often incapacitating form of posttraumatic stress disorder. "When you've been tortured," explained Dr. Inge Genefke, "the private hell stays with you through your life if it's not treated." But the victims did respond surprisingly well to therapy. In 1982, these therapists founded Copenhagen's Rehabilitation and Research Centre for Torture Victims (RCT) and then built a global network of ninety-nine centers that treated forty-eight thousand victims in 1992 alone. Together, Amnesty and the RCT played a catalytic role in turning world opinion against torture, culminating in the adoption of the UN Convention against Torture in 1984 and the World Conference on Human Rights in 1993, when 183 nations condemned torture as "one of the most atrocious violations against human dignity."[2]

Through this global effort, therapists have discovered that torture is a uniquely debilitating experience that does lasting psychological harm to its victims. As research expanded after the Cold War, therapists reported that survivors suffer "sleep disturbances with frequent nightmares, affective symptoms (chronic anxiety, depression), cognitive impairment (memory defects, loss of concentration) and changes in identity." Such suffering is persistent, often permanent. In the early 1990s, Polish psychiatrists interviewed victims tortured more than forty years earlier and found "symptoms of mental disorder were present in almost all."[3]

This medical research has also explored the role of power in the process of torture. Victims "experience depersonalization, fear of annihilation, and the destruction of their body image," reported a team of Argentinean therapists. "Essential to torture," Amnesty explained in a 1984 report, "is the sense that the interrogator controls everything, even life itself."[4] Similarly, a Philippine therapist found that torture's trauma arises "from the experience of extreme powerlessness" and can be treated by "reempowering the survivor." If torture leaves the victim feeling weak, even crippled, might it not have an opposite impact upon perpetrators—in effect, inducing an emotion of empowerment?[5]

Insights from the treatment of Chilean victims tortured under General Augusto Pinochet's regime offer a point of entry into this problem. Otto Doerr-Zegers, a psychotherapist, found that victims suffer "a mistrust bordering on paranoia, and a loss of interest that greatly surpasses anything observed in anxiety disorders." The subject "does not only react to torture with a tiredness of days, weeks, or months, but *remains a tired human being*, relatively uninterested and unable to concentrate." These findings led him to a strategic question: "What in torture makes possible a change of such nature that it appears similar to psychotic processes and to disorders of organic origin?"[6]

The answer, Doerr-Zegers argues, lies in the "phenomenology of the torture situation," involving (1) an asymmetry of power; (2) the anonymity of the torturer to the victim; (3) the "double bind" of either enduring or betraying others; (4) the systematic "falsehood" of trumped-up charges, artificial lighting, cunning deceptions, and "mock executions"; (5) confinement in distinctive spaces signifying "displacement, trapping, narrowness and destruction"; and (6) a temporality "characterized by some unpredictability and much circularity, having no end." Thus, much of the pain from torture is psychological, not physical, and is based upon denying its victims any power over their lives. In sum, the torturer strives "through insult and disqualification, by means of threats . . . to break all the victim's possible existential platforms." Through this asymmetry, the torturer eventually achieves "complete power" and reduces the victim to "a condition of total or near total defenselessness."[7]

There are, within torture's phenomenology, elements that evoke theatrical parallels. In a sense, Doerr-Zegers seems to be saying that torture, as done in Chile, was a kind of total theater, a constructed unreality of lies and inversion, with a plot that ended inexorably with the victim's self-betrayal and destruction. In the theater, there is, of course, an asymmetry of power between the actors, who know the plot, and the audience, which does not. Working from a well-rehearsed script, the torturers are actors who force the victim to become an audience of one in the drama of his or her own degradation. To make their artifice of false charges, fabricated news, and mock executions convincing, inquisitors become inspired thespians. The torture chamber itself often has the theatricality of a set, with special lighting, sound effects, props, and backdrop, all designed with a perverse sort of stagecraft to evoke an aura of fear. Both cell and stage construct their own temporality: the drama collapses and expands time to carry the audience forward toward denouement, while the prison distorts time to disorient and then entrap the victim in a mind maze that leads inexorably to self-betrayal.

Significantly, both torturers and victims use the language of theater to describe their experiences. A Greek victim, referring to his prison and its torturer, said, "KESA was a kind of theatre of the absurd with Kainich as producer." Two Argentine victims described a sadistically effective interrogator succinctly, saying, "He turned torture into an act of theater." Elaine Scarry notes that "in the torturers' idiom the room in which brutality occurs was called the 'production room' in the Philippines, the 'cinema room' in South Vietnam, and the 'blue lit stage' in Chile." On such a stage, torture became what she called "the production of a fantastic illusion of power, . . . a grotesque piece of compensatory drama."[8]

From 1965 to 1990, as discussed in the previous chapter, the U.S. Army transmitted extreme counterinsurgency tactics and interrogation methods, derived in part from the CIA's Phoenix program in South Vietnam, to the armies of ten Latin American nations through direct training and delivery of Spanish-language manuals.[9] These techniques are so similar to Philippine practices, detailed below, that we must ask whether this was just coincidence or instead evidence of similar U.S. torture training on both sides of the Pacific. In 1978, a human rights newsletter reported that the Marcos regime's leading torturer, Lieutenant Colonel Rolando Abadilla, was studying at the U.S. Command and General Staff College, Fort Leavenworth. A year later, another group claimed that his understudy, Lieutenant Rodolfo Aguinaldo, was going to the United States "for six months to one year for additional training under the Central Intelligence Agency."[10] Were these officers given training in either tactical interrogation or torture?

Definitive answers must await further release of classified documents. At present, we have to content ourselves with comparison. Though the CIA may have taught torturers on both sides of the Pacific, the methods of the Filipino interrogators, particularly the theatricality of the future RAM officers, seems closer to the spirit of the U.S. manuals than the physical tortures practiced elsewhere. Whether they read these texts or received similar training, Marcos's torturers elaborated such psychological methods into a heightened theatricality that often featured sexualized torture.

The preference of Marcos's inquisitors for the psychological and the theatrical had important political consequences for the Philippines. By breaking their superiors through mental manipulation, these officers gained a sense of their society's plasticity, fostering an illusion that they could break and remake the social order at will. Through their years of torturing priests and professors for Marcos, these officers learned the daring to attack Marcos himself.

The torture cell was a play within a larger play. Inside the safe house, Filipino interrogators acted out their script before the victim, their audience of one. If the plot, through twists and turns, ended with the victims' death, then the interrogators discarded the mangled remains in a public place—a plaza, roadside, or field—to be seen by passers-by. Such displays, called "salvaging" in Filipino-English, was the larger play that made the road or plaza, indeed all public spaces, a proscenium of terror.[11] Seeing the marks on the victim's body or simply hearing of them, Filipinos could read, in an instant, the entire script of the smaller play that had been acted out inside the cell.

"In this liturgy of punishment," said Michel Foucault of eighteenth-century Europe, "it is the prince—or at least those to whom he has delegated his force—who seizes upon the body of the condemned man and displays it marked, beaten, broken. The ceremony of punishment, then, is an exercise of 'terror.'"[12] In the modern world, however, torture not only dignifies the prince but also empowers his servant, the perpetrator. "We are God. We are the law," Argentinean torturers told their victims. "In this place where you are now,"

Filipino torturers told a priest, "we are the judge." One Greek torturer asked his victim, a senior navy officer, "Do you know who I am? I am Antonopoulos, before whom all Greece trembles." For the torturer, Elaine Scarry concludes, "His blindness, his willed amorality, *is* his power." Such men who shed civility and embrace cruelty arouse fear and fascination. They become powerful and perversely charismatic, striking a disturbing chord in our consciousness.[13]

Origins of Terror

The rise of RAM rebels, with their vision of violence, is but one manifestation of martial law's impact upon the Philippine military. With communist insurgency spreading in the countryside and terrorism roiling the capital, President Marcos, weighing his words with a lawyer's care, issued Proclamation 1081 on September 22, 1972, imposing a state of martial law: "By virtue of the power vested upon me by . . . the Constitution . . . do hereby command the Armed Forces of the Philippines . . . to enforce obedience to all laws and decrees, orders and regulations promulgated by me personally."[14]

The armed forces were no longer the servant of the state but the bastion of Marcos's martial-law regime. Backed by his generals, the president wiped out warlord armies, closed Congress, and confiscated corporations. Marcos involved the military in every aspect of authoritarian rule—censorship, repression, and governance. Officers became corporate managers, civil servants, local officials, and judges.[15]

Charged with suppressing dissent, the armed forces were brutal and brutalized. Among the authoritarian regimes of the 1970s, the Marcos government was exceptionally lethal. Argentina's junta (1976–83) established an unequaled record of 8,960 "documented" dead and an estimated 30,000 "missing." The Marcos regime's tally of 3,257 killed is far lower, but it still exceeds the 2,115 extrajudicial deaths under General Pinochet in Chile (1973–90) and the 266 dead and missing during the Brazilian junta's most lethal period (1964–79). Under Marcos, moreover, military murder was the apex of a pyramid of terror—3,257 killed, 35,000 tortured, and 70,000 incarcerated.[16]

The administration of repression had a profound impact upon the military. Inserted into every aspect of Philippine life through its new roles, legal and extralegal, the military became politicized in the most fundamental sense. To sustain these multiple missions, the armed forces budget increased by 500 percent in the first four years of martial law, and its strength doubled to 113,000 troops. U.S. military aid also doubled to $45 million annually, providing ample weaponry for an expanded Marcos military.[17]

The armed forces thus strengthened the president's authoritarian capacities. But, over the longer term, these changes also created an opening for a coup d'état. After a decade of dictatorship, Marcos had so politicized the military that its hierarchy split into rival factions and its middle-ranking regular officers nurtured rising resentments. Sensing their anger, Marcos's defense minister, Juan Ponce Enrile, began courting this latter echelon for a coup against Marcos. His ambitions and their grievances merged over time to become the Reform the Armed Forces Movement, or RAM.

By the mid-1980s, RAM would grow into a movement of some three hundred regular officers drawn, with few exceptions, from just eleven PMA classes—1965 through 1975. Within this larger pool of 861 academy alumni, only eight officers, largely from just one class, 1971, would exercise overall control. That a small group of junior officers could lead a sustained revolt against the entire military hierarchy reflects deep changes within the culture of the officer corps.

As catalyst in the many coups d'état of the late 1980s, the Philippine Military Academy's Class '71 is an apt case for the study of the breakdown of military socialization. Not only did this class provide the leaders for most of the country's many coup attempts, but about 15 percent of its classmates participated in the massive 1989 coup that nearly seized power.[18] These officers were, in every sense, the nation's military elite. Most had been outstanding cadets—regimental officers, top athletes, and leading scholars. They were natural leaders, men who, in the normal course of events, would have risen to the highest echelons of command. How can we explain their careers marked instead by torture, terror, and coups?

Like others in the long gray line, Class '71 went through the military

Table 1. Leaders of the Reform the Armed Forces (RAM) Core Group, 1985

Name	PMA Class	Murder Alleged	Torture Alleged	Coup d'état
Rodolfo Aguinaldo	1972	x	x	1986, 1987, 1989
Victor Batac	1971	x	x	1986, 1987, 1989
Hernani Figueroa	1966	—	x	1986, 1987, 1989
Eduardo Kapunan	1971	x	x	1986, 1987, 1989
Gregorio Honasan	1971	x	x	1986, 1987, 1989
Oscar Legaspi	1971	x	x	1986, 1987, 1989
Rex Robles	1965	—	—	1986, 1987
Felix Turingan	1965	—	—	1986, 1987, 1989

Source: *The Final Report of the Fact-Finding Commission (pursuant to R.A. No. 6382)*, Table VI-6, Appendix J; Alfred W. McCoy, *Closer Than Brothers*, chapters 6–8.

academy's usual four-year cycle from "dumbguard" to "immaculate," or from neophyte to command. The class yearbook's narrative of their progression by the "class historian," Victor Batac, the future strategist of RAM's revolt, is unexceptional, even bland.[19]

Looking back, however, we can discern secondary factors at the academy—excessive hazing and group dynamics—that later allowed torture to act on this class with such a corrosive effect. When Class '71 became upperclassmen, the practice of hazing first-year "plebes," suppressed for nearly a decade, was revived with an extraordinary physical brutality. After new cadets arrived in April 1969, one plebe was admitted to the hospital bleeding; he died nine days later. Four days after his burial, another hospitalized plebe wrote the *Manila Times* charging that his classmate had "died of over-exhaustion due to hazing" and that others had been hospitalized with "broken ribs and stomach trouble." At the later court-martial, plebes testified that they had been awakened by blows; left their rooms via a gauntlet of upperclassmen who pummeled their stomachs; and were ordered to squat while being beaten bloody about the face and torso. Among many possible suspects, five upperclassman, including a member of Class '71, were later implicated.[20] Through later interviews with military torturers, Dr. June Lopez found that the "physical and psychological abuse" of hazing at the academy gave the cadets "some sort of invisible badge of honor" that "instills camaraderie and brotherhood." She concluded with a provocative question: "If they can subject their own selves to abuse, what is there to stop them from inflicting the same, if not greater, violence on a perceived enemy?"[21]

Instead of the more diffuse leadership of other classes, Class '71 had a distinctive group dynamic with a dominant personality who became the class's single, preeminent leader. Every year for four years, his classmates elected Gregorio "Gringo" Honasan II, the future leader of the RAM revolt, class president. In his senior year, the tactical officers selected him cadet first captain, or "baron." Honasan also exercised moral authority as chairman of the Honor Committee and twice captured the school title as "best debater." In addition to five varsity letters in sports ranging from boxing to basketball, he earned the grade of "sharpshooter" with the M-1 rifle and took a gold medal at the National Wrestling Tournament. His yearbook biography celebrated these achievements in almost reverential tones: "Gringo!—Comfortably warm and constantly dynamic; enough determination and perseverance in achieving his goals, coupled with characteristic humility and compassion for the less fortunate."[22]

Only eighteen months after graduation, Class '71 became the defenders of dictatorship. Instead of garrison duty or conventional combat that would mold them into uniformed servants of the state, these young officers, in this second formative phase of their military socialization, were thrust into civil war and charged with surveillance of civilian society.

Their experience in Mindanao bonded and brutalized these young officers of Class '71. After Marcos imposed martial law, in 1972, Muslims in western Mindanao launched a secessionist revolt, and the military mounted a five-year campaign that threw recent PMA graduates into a vicious conflict. For three years after graduation, Lieutenant Gringo Honasan served in Mindanao, where he earned a reputation as a fearless, sometimes ruthless fighter, winning at least one Gold Cross medal for "heroism."[23] According to one member of a military tribunal, Honasan "participated in the revenge killing of a Muslim leader, who had allegedly killed his classmate." But he ultimately evaded prosecution "because of his links to the defense secretary." Service in this bloody war also strengthened bonds among the class. When Honasan was wounded during combat in 1973, Lieutenant Eduardo "Red" Kapunan defied his superior and flew his helicopter through enemy fire to rescue his classmate, making the two "bosom friends."[24]

After one or more combat tours, many classmates rotated to Manila for staff assignments involving surveillance and interrogation. These special duties trained the future RAM leaders for political warfare, giving them the skill and experience that would later inspire their attack on the state. Among the eighty-five graduates of Class '71, five reportedly practiced torture, six were allegedly murderers, fifteen were involved in two or more coups, and most saw combat in counterinsurgency (see Table 2). Instead of defending their society from foreign invasion, these young lieutenants were forced to treat fellow citizens as the enemy, fighting ordinary civilians in a brutal counterguerrilla war and, as society's jailers, degrading their social superiors—priests, professors, politicians, and senior officers.

During the late 1980s, Class '71 became leaders of a military revolt against civil authority. Not only did these coups define them, but the class itself defined the role of the coup d'état in Philippine politics. Apart from providing the leadership for five major coups, these eighty-five graduates supplied fifteen of the seventy-seven officers involved in two or more coups—by far the highest for any single class.[25]

Why did one PMA class play such an influential role in so many coups? Why did so many members of this class rebel against their military socialization? Lacking their own admissions, we must look to events for evidence. Some older academy alumni were involved in torture, and a number of younger classes joined these coups, but only Class '71 exhibited this coincidence of torture experience and coup leadership. Under martial law, almost all members of Class '71 who later became RAM's core leadership had experiences of torture,

Table 2. Members of PMA Class of '71 Active in Two or More Coups d'État

Name	Coup d'état	Torture Alleged	Role in 1989 Coup
Jerry Albano	1986, 1987, 1989	—	combat
Victor Batac	1986, 1987, 1989	x	leader
Franklin Brawner	1987, 1989	—	combat
Ruben Cabagnot	1986, 1987	x	—
Neon Ebuen	1986, 1987, 1989	—	leader
Tiburcio Fusilero	1986, 1987, 1989	—	leader
Rafael Galvez	1986, 1989	—	combat
Gregorio Honasan	1986, 1987, 1989	x	plotter
Eduardo Kapunan	1986, 1987, 1989	x	leader
Oscar Legaspi	1986, 1987, 1989	x	combat
Marcelino Malajancan	1986, 1987, 1989	—	leader
Eduardo Matillano	1986, 1987, 1989	—	combat
Reynaldo Rivera	1987, 1989	—	combat
Ceferino Sarmenta	1987, 1989	—	combat
Diosdado Tabamo	1987, 1989	—	combat

Source: The Final Report of the Fact-Finding Commission (pursuant to R.A. No. 6382),
Table VI-6, Appendix J; AlfredW. McCoy, *Closer Than Brothers*, chapters 6–8.

interrogation, espionage, or civil war. When RAM tried to capture the state, each of its coup attempts would evince elements that can be traced, through close analysis, to these experiences.

Ethos of Torture

Under Marcos's martial-law dictatorship, torture became an instrument of state power. A 1975 report by Amnesty International concluded, in a statement that angered Marcos, that the Philippines "has been transformed from a country with a remarkable constitutional tradition to a system where star chamber methods have been used on a wide scale to literally torture evidence into existence." In response, the palace announced in November 1976 that some seven hundred military personnel had been disciplined "for maltreating prisoners held under martial law."[26]

Despite this gesture, torture continued. In 1981, Amnesty returned to discover a Philippine gulag of "safe houses" where "members of the Armed Forces . . . had been responsible for acts of unusual brutality." The Philippine Medical Action Group found that 102 of the 120 political prisoners held at the National Penitentiary had been severely tortured—forty-eight subjected to Russian roulette, nineteen electrocuted, seventeen "fed feces," five sexually abused, and four buried alive. After Marcos fell from power, in 1986, an organization of ex-detainees, SELDA, estimated that thirty-five thousand political prisoners had "suffered some form of torture."[27]

Why such extraordinary brutality? Even at its peak, the Marcos state, reflecting the underlying poverty of Philippine society, lacked the information infrastructure for blanket repression. With only fifty-five thousand troops in 1971, the armed forces constituted only 0.1 percent of the country's population—by far the lowest ratio in Asia. Although the military grew to 153,000 troops by 1978, it was still poorly financed and lacked efficient communications.[28] By 1984, a severe fiscal crisis restricted surveillance agents to only five liters of petrol per day and the distribution of photographs for wanted dissidents to a single province.

By contrast, the Argentine military, operating in an advanced, urbanized society, attempted the systematic eradication of all dissidents. In the words of the governor of Buenos Aires, General Iberico Saint-Jean, "first we kill all the subversives, then we will kill their collaborators, . . . then . . . those who remain indifferent, and finally we will kill the timid." By the late 1970s, the junta was operating a network of 340 secret camps to fight a systematic "dirty war" that left an estimated thirty thousand *desparacidos*, victims who disappeared without trace or remains.[29]

Instead of a machinery that crushed all resistance, the Marcos regime used the spectacle of violence for civil control, becoming a virtual theater state of terror. In the first three years of martial law, the military incarcerated some fifty thousand people. But, faced with a rising insurgency, the regime soon abandoned this costly enterprise. Moreover, as a lawyer rather than a career officer, Marcos maintained a facade of legality, speaking with pride of his "constitutional authoritarianism." Responding to President Jimmy Carter's pressure for human rights reform, Marcos had, by 1977, emptied his prisons, leaving only 563 political prisoners.[30]

The regime bridged this growing gap between the fiction of legality and the reality of repression with extrajudicial executions. As arrests and imprisonment declined, the number of so-called salvagings climbed. Military murders rose from only 3 in 1975 to 538 in 1984, with most coming after 1981, when Marcos inaugurated his nominally democratic "New Republic." In striking contrast to the situation in Argentina, only 737 Filipinos "disappeared" between 1975 and 1985. But nearly four times that number, some 2,520, equivalent to 77 percent of all victims, were "salvaged"—that is, tortured, executed, and displayed.[31] Indeed, this practice had such a disturbing resonance within the country's collective consciousness that the Filipino-English dialect coined the neologism "salvaging" to capture this aura of terror.[32]

Marcos's rule thus rested upon a theatrical terror. His officers were not impersonal cogs in a military machine. They were actors who personified the violent capacities of the state. If the president had written a script of terror for his New Society, then these young officers, the future RAM leaders, were his players. When the president ordered the military to enforce authoritarian rule, it was the lower echelons that became the instrument of his will.[33]

As chief of Constabulary, Marcos's cousin and close ally, General Fidel Ramos, commanded the main civil control units and their notorious torturers—the 5th Constabulary Security Unit (CSU) and the Military Intelligence and Security Group (MISG).[34] Officers in these elite units were the embodiment of an otherwise invisible terror. As Marcos's favored instrument, the MISG "produced some of the most fearsome and brutal cops in memory." Its commander for twelve years, Colonel Rolando Abadilla (PMA '65), in the words of his obituary, "towered over other heavies in that closed, tight-knit, psychotic club of martial-law enforcers—next only to Gen. Ver . . . in the dictator's trust and confidence."[35] Only his former understudy, Lieutenant Rodolfo Aguinaldo of the 5th CSU, could rival his psychopathic interrogations. There was an intense competition among ambitious officers to capture top subversives and extract intelligence. Success was the pass to a military fast track with cash, cars, and promotion.

As the military mobilized for war on its own society, these elite commands could call upon the intelligence section of every unit, from infantry battalions near Manila to Constabulary companies on remote islands.[36] Military units in this state of civil war made arrests without warrant and confined suspects in extralegal "safe houses" for a "tactical interrogation" that often involved torture. Armed with a blanket ASSO (Arrest Search and Seizure Order) or PCO (Presidential Commitment Order), military personnel raided homes on the basis of mere suspicion and took suspects to unknown locations for limitless interrogation. In effect, martial law abrogated due process and allowed the military to operate with a "*de facto* or *de jure* immunity" to civil prosecution, producing what Amnesty called "gross and systematic violations of human rights."[37]

The existence of this gulag served as a warning to all who might resist. As officers assumed extraordinary powers, civilians were reluctant to defy them, aware that they were subject to arbitrary, indefinite detention. Even officers who never tortured participated, albeit indirectly, in the aura of power that invested everyone in uniform. "Except for . . . Marcos's immediate political cronies," wrote the political scientist Felipe Miranda, "the military intimidated civilian politicians and government officials practically everywhere."[38]

Some officers enjoyed their new power over civilians. "We in the military were mud before martial law," an officer told an American researcher in 1975. "Now the people come to the military tribunal seeking justice."[39] We know from the detainees themselves that officers did not torture before the declaration of martial law in 1972. One long-term prisoner, Leoncio Co, noted that the PMA-trained officers who arrested him in 1969 were "very understanding" and even advised him "do not incriminate yourself." After martial law, however, attitudes were "very different"—a change epitomized when Co witnessed a recent PMA graduate, Lieutenant Rodolfo Aguinaldo, torturing a woman with such severity that she "nearly lost her mind."[40]

Significantly, in the victims' transcripts, it is usually lieutenants, not majors or colonels, who appear as the actual torturers. After graduating into a martial-law military, the lieutenants of Class '71 were assigned to arrest, interrogate, and, ultimately, torture civilian dissidents. Later, as they rose through the ranks, they would take command of the regime's safe houses and detention centers.

The Plot of Torture

Only the collective weight of torture transcripts can convey the actual work of these junior officers during this formative phase of their careers. By letting the victims speak to us of their pain, we can gain some sense of its reality. Their recollections reveal distinctive patterns in the torturers' methods that may have informed their later conduct as coup leaders.

In the victims' statements, the names of the future RAM leaders recur. They did not operate as dispassionate technicians, raising the level of pain to extract information. Thespians all, they assumed the inquisitor's role, using a theatrical torture to heighten the victim's pain and disorientation. Many practiced a pose of latent threat that could, if provoked, unleash unlimited violence. Some appeared as creators/destroyers whose psychological and physical powers could bend any prisoner to their will. A few played the omnipotent by sending detainees off for torture by minions.

Many of these sessions share a similar plot. The torturer begins with a few questions, meets resistance, and then applies coercion, physical and psychological, to elicit cooperation. Within this common script, each inquisitor seems to extemporize around a guiding metaphor that becomes embedded in the victim's recollection. One officer crafted his script around imagery of production; another constructed a near conceit of social inversion.

A rural priest tortured by a future RAM leader offered the most acute insight into their methods. Arrested for subversion in October 1982, Father

Edgardo Kangleon, Social Action Director of the Western Samar Diocese, was subjected to two months of constant interrogation before breaking down. In his confession, he admitted to being a communist agent and named his fellow clergy as subversives—charges that the regime seized upon to harass the Church.[41] Throughout his long confinement, the priest suffered only limited physical abuse and was instead psychologically terrorized by his chief interrogator, Lieutenant Colonel Hernani Figueroa (PMA '66), RAM's later chairman. Only a week after his release, Fr. Kangleon composed a twenty-five page memoir that describes the aura of terror that surrounded Marcos's interrogators and the theatricality of their tortures. In his account, the cell becomes studio, the inquisitors actors, and the detainee an audience for a psychological drama crueler than physical pain.

After each long day as a prisoner in a military compound with no release in sight, Fr. Kangleon found darkness a time of fear. "For a detainee, the day's ending signals the possibility of facing the nightmare called tactical interrogation," he explained. "Hence, I, fully aware of the secrets the night hides in these portions of the earth, literally sweated it out night after night. Till finally and so unexpectedly, my turn came. And, God, there was nothing more excruciating than to be confronted by that final leap into eternity!"[42] On his fifty-first night of detention, Fr. Kangleon was brought before the chief interrogator, Lieutenant Colonel Figueroa, a name synonymous with terror on Samar Island. Significantly, the colonel's methods echoed techniques outlined in the CIA's *Human Resources Exploitation Training Manual—1983*, then being used to train Honduran officers on the other side of the Pacific. As prescribed in this manual, which was discussed in chapter three, the Filipino colonel entered Fr. Kangleon's cell with bulging files and maintained a controlling calm, like an actor striding to center stage with a prop signifying his omniscience:[43]

The entry of the dreaded chief intelligence officer, who came in with a thick pile of documents, dashed to the ground the last bit of my hopes to get out their [*sic*] "unscathed." His initial declaration: "Father, the general has decided that we start interrogating you tonight" was enough to unleash that fear that was building up inside me for these past two months. I felt cold sweat, sweat broke all over my body and I thought I was going to faint.

For several hours, predator and prey fenced around verbally, one sizing up the other. Questions were posed and answers of innocence were given. Suddenly the "chairman" changed his approach. He said that since I would not answer his questions without my lawyer's presence, it would suffice if I would just give my biodata. And readily I fall for it. . . . I had fallen into a trap. I was already talking. Hastily, I tried to correct it by sticking to innocent or safe answers.

Sensing that I had caught up to what he was up to and, irritated with the futility of that encounter, Ltc. Figueroa finally said: "Since you refused to cooperate, Father, we will be forced to use other means. We cannot allow ourselves to be taken for fools."

The colonel projects an image of absolute control. He enters carrying files symbolic of knowledge and power. He starts by probing like a "predator" for an opening to establish dominance. When his priestly "prey" resists, Figueroa announces, with a calm that evokes enormous strength, that the priest will be tortured for arousing his "irritation." The colonel seeks not just information but subordination to his will.

At the colonel's command, the priest was taken to the nearby offices of the Military Intelligence Group. There, blindfolded, Fr. Kangleon discovers a metaphor central to our understanding of the RAM officers:

Inside I was made to sit on a stool. I felt a small table being placed in front of me. Then, I heard voices—new voices! Three or four of these voices—the more commanding ones—took their places around me. And with actors in their places, the most crucial stage of my detention started to unfold.

"Now, Father, you are going to answer our questions!"

"In court, ha? Now you are detained you are invoking the legal processes of this system. . . . In this place where you are now, we are the judge. And you are going to tell us what we want you to tell us."

"As the NPA [New People's Army] utilizes terrorism, we are also willing to use counter-terror. . . . Every time you preached against us, I wished at that time to just shoot you there at the altar."

"What's the name of that sister you used to visit at the Sacred Heart College? She is your girlfriend, *ano*? You are fucking her? How does it feel? . . .

"For me, he is not a priest. Yes, your kind is not worthy of a respect of a priest."

"OK, take off his shirt. Oh, look at that body. You look sexy. Even the women here think you are macho. You are a homosexual, *ano*?"

"Let's see if you are that macho after one of my punches." A short jab below my ribs.

"Hey, don't lean on the table. Place your arms beside you. That's it." Another jab.

"You, take that stool away from him." I stood up. A blow landed behind my ears. I started to plead that they stop what they are doing to me. I started to cower. More blows. . . .

"You better answer our questions or else you will get more of this." With that, a short blow landed in my solar plexus.

I was already quaking with fear. The psychological and physical aspect . . . of my interrogation had finally taken its toll. I finally broke down. "Yes. Go call Ltc. Figueroa. I am now willing to cooperate."[44]

As Fr. Kangleon implies by calling the interrogators "actors," his torture is a theater of humiliation far more painful than simple physical brutality. After blindfolding, stripping, and insulting the priest, the soldiers communicate their dominion by beating him, almost playfully, and forcing him to assist in his own degradation. He is beyond the help of courts and the law.

As their interrogation proceeds, the torture becomes a drama of social inversion. In this Catholic nation, the simple honorific "Father" is a title of great respect, perhaps more prestigious than any military rank except general. After proclaiming themselves "judge," these soldiers strip the priest of his office and his cloth, signifying their superiority. When he resists, they begin with sexual abuse of a celibate clergyman, commenting on his bared body and accusing him of both homosexuality and fornication with a nun. Less courageous but more intelligent than most, the priest sees the inevitable. Inside this cell, he is no longer a priest, honored and protected. Naked and blind, he is theirs. He surrenders to the colonel's power. He calls out the name of his tormentor as his savior.

The colonel required a complete capitulation. After confessing his Communist Party membership, Fr. Kangleon was flown to Manila for a press conference, where he denied being tortured and denounced fellow clergy as communists—a sensational exposé that provided the regime with a pretext for repression against the Church. Abandoning his mission to the poor of Samar, Fr. Kangleon became a military chaplain and was issued a pistol, symbolically joining the ranks of his torturers. Then, on New Year's Day 1984, the priest was injured in a traffic accident and taken to a Manila hospital, where he remained in a coma for three days. There, under mysterious circumstances that prompted several bishops to call for an investigation, Fr. Kangleon died on January 4.[45]

The Torturers

While Lieutenant Colonel Figueroa delegated the torture, Lieutenant Rodolfo Aguinaldo (PMA '72), another future RAM leader, immersed himself in the violence, both physical and psychological. A review of human rights under the Marcos regime rated Aguinaldo as its "top torturer," finding him "implicated in the torture of at least 27 detainees." A 1980 report by Task Force Detainees (TFD) described Aguinaldo as a "persistent and systematic torturer" whose "legendary maniacal torture sessions . . . left many detainees permanently injured."[46]

From his victims, Task Force Detainees compiled a portrait of Aguinaldo's transformation. After graduating second in PMA's Class of 1972 just months before martial law was imposed, he was assigned to the 5th Constabulary Security Unit (CSU), where his interrogations were soon distinguished by their relentless determination, physical violence, and psychological cruelty. Beyond simple physical pain, he had a unique ability to engage his victims emotionally, using his sexuality and aggression to probe for personal weakness. "One of his tactics is seducing wives and sisters of political detainees," noted a TFD report. "He relishes the ensuing misunderstandings and splits between couples and families."[47]

In its first Philippine mission, in 1975, Amnesty identified Aguinaldo as "among the most persistent and systematic torturers at 5 CSU . . . who appeared to have treated prisoners with outrageous cruelty." His methods involved "prolonged beating with fists, kicks and karate blows, . . . the pounding of heads against walls . . . , the burning of genitals and pubic hair with the flame of a cigarette lighter." From interviews with detainees, Amnesty detailed one case of particularly brutal torture:

Mrs. Jean Cacayorin-Tayag . . . was transferred to 5 CSU where she was kept sleepless for eight days and nights, made to stand to several hours naked before a full-blast air conditioner and was slapped hard. . . . Lieutenant R—[odolfo] A—[guinaldo], her main tormentor, told her that "whether you like it or not," he would take her away from her husband, who was also being interrogated. She said: "He told me he would hurt me where it would hurt most." She was forced to undergo "unwanted caresses." He had threatened to ruin her moral reputation and to spread gossip about an affair. He had threatened her husband and her child.[48]

Over the next nine years, Aguinaldo's many victims reported his obsession with male genitals. Confined at Fort Bonifacio in 1974–75, Fr. Luis Jalandoni saw men returning from Aguinaldo's sessions with genitalia badly burned. Sometimes the lieutenant inserted a match into the head of the penis and struck. Sometimes he singed the pubic hair. In 1982, Aguinaldo grew frustrated when strangulation, beating, and electrocution failed to extract information from a twenty-five-year-old male prisoner named Marco Palo. "Sonofabitch," the lieutenant shouted at his subordinates. "Make him undress completely and electrocute his balls!"[49] A lay missionary recalled torture sessions by Aguinaldo and Lieutenant Vic Batac with a string of sensory fragments: "electric treatment (penis), water cure, karate kick, strangulation, Russian roulette, asked to masturbate at count of 10 penis did not erect—hit by .45 cal. pistol."[50]

Aguinaldo used a mix of physical and psychological means to humiliate his social superiors, whether journalists, professors, artists, or activists.[51] "On two occasions . . . between 2:00 to 3:00 a.m.," the political science professor Temario Rivera wrote in a later deposition, "I was roused from sleep and interrogated by then Lt. Rodolfo Aguinaldo. During these sessions, he repeatedly punched me in the chest and abdomen. While interrogating me, he would time and again point a .45 caliber pistol in my face and pull the trigger."[52] After his unit took Juan Villegas, a philosophy professor, to a safe house, Aguinaldo administered a dramatized torture: "Villegas was . . . told that he would be taken to a cemetery where he would be killed and buried," read a human rights report. "He was taken by car, presumably to the cemetery, and made to alight. . . . The next morning he was again interrogated by Lt. Aguinaldo who pointed a cocked .45 cal. [pistol] at his head."[53]

Aguinaldo played a leading role in the torture of Satur Ocampo, former business editor of the *Manila Times* and later chief negotiator for the NPA guerrillas. Arrested in January 1976, Ocampo suffered a two-day torture session at Camp Olivas, outside Manila, with a plot that seems driven by a theme of inversion: junior officers humiliate a media executive, feces becomes food, genitals carry pain:

The torturers took Ocampo to the first floor, stripped him naked, poured cola drinks all over his body and forced him to stand up almost throughout the torture period up to the wee hours of the morning. The electrically charged spoon was repeatedly pressed on several parts of his body like the knees, thighs, genitals, groin, abdomen, ears, nipples, shoulders, neck, chin, face and nose. . . .

Besides this punishment on his body, Ocampo was spat upon by his torturers. His mouth was forced open and he was fed human excreta. Lighted cigarettes were pressed on his nipples, on the corner of his mouth and his toes.

Throughout the torture the jeerers would chorus whenever the electric shock was applied to Ocampo's genitals: "We'll make you impotent for the rest of your life!" . . .

Only when the torturers became physically exhausted did they stop the punishment. Identified among them were Lt. Rodolfo Aguinaldo of the 5th CSU and Lt. Amado Espino Jr. of CSU and Major [Benjamin] Libarnes of the 1st PC Zone who was present during the torture session.[54]

After this group assault led by Major Libarnes (PMA '67) failed, Ocampo was transferred to Fort Bonifaco in Manila for a one-on-one encounter with Lieutenant Aguinaldo—a revealing psychological duel between a communist leader and Marcos's top torturer. On day one, the lieutenant, unlike others who concealed their identity, removed Ocampo's blindfold and pointed to his own face with forefingers forming pistols, saying, "Look at me. Look at my eyes." Without any questions, Aguinaldo then beat Ocampo and left, promising, "I'll come back tomorrow."

For the next six days, the interrogations followed a pattern. Aguinaldo would try to draw his victim out with tantalizing confessions from a comrade.

When Ocampo remained silent, Aguinaldo muttered something like "*matigas ka masyado*" (you are very hardheaded) and then erupted with dramatically athletic blows crashing down on his victim's immobile body, which was manacled to a steel bed. Determined to "show defiance," Ocampo "sort of psychologized myself [so] that I don't feel anything. So I kept on staring at him and he kept beating me, so I think it made him unsteady because I wasn't breaking down, I wasn't shouting." Ocampo added, "That enraged him more. . . . He kept cursing me." With a final karate kick to his victim's body, Aguinaldo would leave. On the seventh day of this routine, he disappeared.

After a month's absence, Aguinaldo reappeared, saying, "Oh, now let's find out how thick [tough] you are." Unlocking the manacles, he led his victim to the window and, pointing to the Makati skyline, asked, "What place is that?" Ocampo, understanding Aguinaldo's need for conquest, answered, "That's Manila Bay." The lieutenant laughed, "Ha, ha, ha. You're mad. Sorry you are disoriented." Then, he walked out of the cell and out of his victim's life for the next sixteen years. With insight heightened by his need to survive, Ocampo understood that Aguinaldo's drive for dominance dwarfed any need for actual information. The aim of all torture was, he concluded after a decade in prison, "to terrorize the victims into submission or to break their will."[55]

With his relentless ambition, Lieutenant Aguinaldo scored a major intelligence coup in 1977, capturing the Communist Party's founder and ideologue, Jose Maria Sison. Following a lead that Sison was hiding on the Ilocos Coast, Aguinaldo won funding from his superior, General Ramos, for a six-week surveillance mission that finally nabbed the country's number one communist on a provincial highway. After the arrest, Aguinaldo was promoted to captain and given command of his own antisubversion unit, with a motorpool of fast cars and an armory of sophisticated weapons.[56]

Another member of the 5th CSU, Lieutenant Vic Batac (PMA '71), later known as "the brains of RAM," emerges from his victims' affidavits as a persistent torturer. While Aguinaldo assaulted his victims with a relentless energy, Batac grew too obese for such activity and instead posed as the all-powerful inquisitor, ordering violence and theatrical torture to break his victims.[57]

In 1974, only three years after his graduation, Batac participated in the torture of a senior officer ordinarily due the deference of rank. "I was picked up at my residence in Makati at about 9 p.m. on 25 May 1974 by 5th CSU . . . intelligence led by 1st Lt. Batac," recalled Navy Captain Danilo Vizmanos, then recently retired after a senior posting as inspector general for the armed forces. "They had no arrest warrant." After being blindfolded and driven to a safe house, Vizmanos "heard the metallic click of an automatic pistol being loaded" and then felt "the muzzle pressed at the back of my head . . . for at least one minute [that] seemed like an eternity." Under "threat of liquidation," he was "ordered to identify certain names." When he refused to cooperate, the captain was locked in "a tomblike cell made of concrete with a solid steel door" for sixty days of solitary confinement. During his 808 days of detention, Vizmanos noted that the future "RAM officers who participated in my arrest, detention, & torture were Lt. Batac, Lt. Aguinaldo, Lt. Bibit."[58] For young lieutenants, trained to obey superiors without question, these acts—breaking into a senior officer's home, hauling him off without warrant, subjecting him to death threats and detention—represented a serious rupture in their military socialization, manifest in their later leadership of the RAM revolt.

Among Lieutenant Batac's many victims, it is a journalism student, Maria Elena Ang, who has provided the most detailed description of his methods. In her account, Batac's unit crafted a metaphor of inverted social production: assaulting her organs of sexual reproduction, while calling their water torture the "NAWASA session" after the national waterworks and dubbing electrical shocks the "Meralco treatment" after the city's power utility.[59]

On the morning of August 5, 1976, I was on my way to Lourdes Church in Quezon City when unidentified military authorities pounced on me . . . and dumped me into the car. . . . It was about a five-minute trip from my place of arrest to the secret headquarters of ISAFP [Intelligence Service, Armed Forces of the Philippines]. . . . Immediately, I was subjected to a most degrading, inhuman and humiliating experience I would never want to relive again. But the memories keep coming back. Up to now in detention, I still have recurrent nightmares.

I remember that while being restrained in a high-backed chair, several men about 10 to 20, swelled the ranks of those already in the room. Immediately, they swamped me with a battery of questions and psywar tactics. They threatened to kill me, get my relatives and friends and torture them in front of me. They kept telling me nobody saw them taking me in.

Failing to answer one of their questions, I immediately received a slap in the face and a blow in the thighs.

By this time, I was able to remove my blindfold and identify two of the officers in the room as Atty. Lazaro Castillo of the National Intelligence Security Authority and Lt. Victor Batac of the 5th CSU or Constabulary Security Unit. . . .

Then, several agents began clamoring that I be given what they called the MERALCO treatment. . . . An agent then forcibly removed my blouse and bra and unzipped my fly. Another brought in a hand-cranked electric generator used in military telephone. . . .

Two exposed wires were then tied around the little fingers of my right hand foot. Atty. Castillo, with a sneer on his face, started cranking the generator and fired another barrage of questions. Suddenly, the current shot painfully through my body. I could do nothing but scream and plead and scream but he only turned the crank until I was screaming continuously. . . . The electric shock session lasted for nearly two hours and was repeated in the evening. . . .

After the electric shock session, the military authorities still were not satisfied. . . . This time I was stripped naked and forced to lie on a short table.

At this instance, Major Arsenio Esguerra of the 5th MIG ISAFP entered the room and signaled the start of the water cure, which they laughingly called the NAWASA session. . . . This time, besides four men restraining my hands and feet, another formed my hair into a bun and pulled my head down so that it kept hanging on the air until I felt that the water was racing through my brains. I passed out twice but they kept pouring water until I thought I would die.

Beside pouring water, several agents mashed my breasts while another contented himself by inserting his fingers in my vagina after failing to make me masturbate.

Alone among the RAM leaders, Batac has been forced to respond to allegations of torture. While he was speaking at the University of Wisconsin–Madison in October 1986, the local Amnesty chapter confronted him with the 5th CSU's record of torture. "Yes," he answered, "we were aware of abuses in the unit." Admitting that comrades "may have been guilty," Batac explained that torture arose from "individual initiatives to get information in a short time." Although he denied any role in Maria Ang's torture, claiming that he was asleep at the time, Batac still insisted on the state's sovereign right to do "anything necessary" to protect itself.[60]

Despite his denials, Maria Elena Ang insisted that the lieutenant directed her torture. "Batac ordered me stripped naked and tied to a chair," she stated in a 1989 interview. As soldiers gave her electrical shocks with a crank radio, "Batac . . . sat there, leaning back in his chair with his feet on the table facing me with a smirk on his face. At one point I can recall him saying 'give her the NAWASA treatment.' And they filled me up with water." As she drowned in water and vomit, Batac was "leaning back with arms behind his head with that smirk on his face."[61]

The future RAM leaders may also have engaged in salvaging. After interviewing members of the Human Rights Commission in April 1986, a correspondent for *The Australian* newspaper reported that Colonel Honasan "has been linked with several salvagings in the late 1970s," including one particularly brutal killing in 1983. "Unconfirmed reports strenuously denied by Colonel Honasan," wrote this reporter, "say he played a role in the brutal slaying of a dissident, Dr. Johnny Escandor, whose body was found dumped outside military headquarters in Manila, the brain removed from his skull and his underpants stuffed in the cavity."[62]

The coterie at the heart of RAM also tortured together. During the first nine days after his arrest in 1983, the activist Randall Echanis was blindfolded, with his hands handcuffed behind his back, and subjected to round-the-clock interrogation by Honasan, his classmate "Red" Kapunan, and Aguinaldo. When the prisoner asked Kapunan to unlock his handcuffs, the RAM leader answered coolly, "Sorry about that, we just don't have the key here." The prisoner remained painfully handcuffed for the next nine days. After Echanis proved uncooperative, Kapunan spoke in a tone of threat, saying, "Think about it well because you have just a few days. I won't be able to do anything if the others take over, so you decide." Transferred to RAM's provincial stronghold in Cagayan, Echanis found himself in a cellblock with nine detainees who had been tortured by Major Rodolfo Aguinaldo, including a couple "whom he had beaten with a baseball bat including the wife."[63]

Group torture encouraged lasting bonds. From victims' questionnaires collected for litigation, it seems that torturers operated as stable teams inside the regime's elite antisubversion units. At the 5th CSU, Aguinaldo (PMA '72) worked regularly with his classmate Billy Bibit and with Vic Batac ('71), forming close ties that would later help them cohere in RAM. To cite but one example of their daily routine, after a victim was stripped naked and handcuffed, "Lt. Rodolfo Aguinaldo and Lt. Bibit alternately punched him in the ribs"—a syncopated, rhythmic brutality that may have bonded these torturers. Similarly, at the rival MISG, its commander, Rolando Abadilla (PMA '65), and two close comrades, Robert Ortega and Panfilo Lacson (PMA '71), tortured together for more than a decade, forming a close-knit faction that would oppose RAM and then rise together within the police after Marcos's downfall.[64]

What is the impact of torture upon the torturer? Since the literature has largely ignored this question, we can only speculate. If officers such as Hernani Figueroa were involved in a single incidence of torture, then we could accept it as an aberration with minimal impact upon the officer corps. But, when torture becomes duty and officers spend years in a daily routine of terror, the experience becomes a significant aspect of their socialization. For a young lieutenant to degrade and dominate society's leaders—priests, professors, and senior officers—may well induce a sense of mastery, even omnipotence.

The move from mastery over social superiors to dominion over society seems, within the mindset of a military torturer, the next step. Once officers have crossed a threshold by transgressing against social superiors, then it takes but a short leap of the imagination for them to turn their guns upon the state. After subjugating strong-willed activists and politicians through limitless violence, the RAM officers may have emerged from the safe houses feeling like supermen capable of seizing the state.

As lead actors in Marcos's theater of terror, the RAM leaders discarded

the military habit of subordination and adopted a flamboyance that seemed
to express an expansion of individual will. When I visited Colonel Honasan
at the Defense Ministry between coup attempts in July 1986, his security office had taken on the air of Q's laboratory in a James Bond film. In place of
standard-issue weapons, officers toyed with cross bows, Israeli assault rifles,
and automatic pistols. Rather than the regulation dress uniform for headquarters duty, the RAM boys marched about the air-conditioned corridors in
jungle camouflage outfits with quick-draw holsters holding exotic weapons.
Instead of short military haircuts, the RAM boys grew flamboyant manes,
beards, and mustaches. It was as if they had erupted out of cadet uniforms,
with their statement of constrained power, into a costume of lethal masculin-
ity, expressive of a volatile capacity for destruction and an untrammeled will.

Colonel Honasan, RAM's overall leader, cultivated an image of threat. A
tank of a half-dozen piranhas greeted visitors to his office. Plastered to his office door was his personal statement: "My Wife Yes, My Dog Maybe, But My
Gun Never." He entertained special guests with a jar of dried ears slashed from
the corpses of Muslim rebels in Mindanao. He encouraged journalists to write
about his exploits: his habit of sky diving with his pet python, Tiffany, around
his neck; quick-draw shooting practice; black-belt competition in both karate
and Filipino *arnis* cane fencing. His hair was a leonine mane, his uniform
consisted of custom-tailored jungle fatigues, and his military name patch read
just "GRINGO."[65]

Instead of rejecting its experiences in the safe houses, RAM invested violence with a romantic power. On day one of the people power uprising in 1986,
Lieutenant Colonel Red Kapunan (PMA '71) told the journalist Sheila Coronel a story of "combing the country in search of a hired assassin reportedly
out to kill the defense minister. Kapunan found the assassin and later had him
killed." At a party for RAM leaders after Marcos's downfall, several women
journalists were stunned when Lieutenant Colonel Tiburcio Fusilero ('71) tried
to impress them with a story. "After a few drinks, Fusilero was not that drunk,"
recalled Sheila Coronel. "He . . . said he was given a list of forty people to kill
and only two got away." Another journalist present, Jo-Ann Maglipon, wrote
that "reformist T. F. admits typing out a two-page hit list of Marcos enemies
upon the declaration of martial law in 1972. He noted, with neither pride nor
regret, that . . . only one got away; his were professional and clean hit jobs."
When Maglipon asked T. F. if he would kill again, Fusilero replied coolly, "Yes,
it is my duty to obey."[66]

Through their charm and charisma, the aura of violence around this Class
'71 coterie seduced other officers, making this violent machismo the model
for RAM's members. Among Colonel Honasan's many followers, few could

surpass the devotion of Navy Captain Rex Robles (PMA '65), the group's political theorist. Observing Robles at a party after Marcos's fall, a journalist wrote: "The moment Greg [Honasan] arrived . . . Rex turned into a screaming, hysterical fan."[67]

Captain Robles reflected on RAM's theory of political actions in a July 1986 interview, revealing a romanticized belief in the power of violence and an inflated view of himself as its master. Without prompting, he offered blood and terror in reply to my mundane questions about chronology and policy. Short, balding, and desk-bound for two decades, he mimed the language and mannerisms of robust RAM leaders like Honasan and Kapunan—combat veterans, torturers, and coup commanders. Reflecting the infectious nature of RAM's empowered aura, Robles had broken free from his military socialization to embrace a vision of empowering violence:

Question: These discussions [of a coup against Marcos] were taking place from about August [1985] onwards?

Robles: One time I remember was in November [1985], when our discussion ran until 2:00 in the morning about the crown of power. It's like when Napoleon said, "there was a crown that was lying in the street and all I had to do was bend over and pick it up with a sword."

I told them, it doesn't end there. You put the crown on your head, and you hold on to this sword, and anybody who even tries or even thinks of getting that crown from your head, you have to be ready to cut his head off. . . .

You have to kill a lot of people to do this. Are we prepared to shed a lot of blood? That's my belief. That is why I am so afraid of this stuff. You have to kill. You have to have the stomach to kill cold bloodedly a lot of people. Because power does not stay on the head of people by itself. It has to be actively maintained—and by blood, especially blood—until people realize that you are serious about it. And they will fall back and say, "Hey, this guy means business. We have to follow him." Unless you do that, I don't think you are going to be very successful. You need to do that. . . .

When do you stop killing? One of the questions I asked was, "Are we prepared to give ruthless examples?" For instance, if a general misbehaves in Region I, we move over and hit him. Execute him in public. So that people will be interested, "this guy means business."[68]

For Captain Robles, power is amoral, a prize to be won by any means and held at all cost. In its pursuit and possession, he and his comrades believed in the transformative power of unrestrained violence. Once they had captured the crown, the RAM colonels planned to rule by terror. Mass slaughters and ritual executions done with a theatrical flair, would, they believed, captivate the mass and strengthen the hold of their junta.

While the bookish Captain Robles theorized about violence in the abstract, many RAM leaders had lived his fantasy of blood and terror. Through service in the safe houses of the Marcos regime, they were freed from the restraints of military socialization. Torture taught them to embrace violence as both ideology and strategy. It inspired their will to power. Stepping out of the safe houses onto the national stage, they would launch a half-dozen coups with tactics informed by torture. Just as their abuse of helpless victims inside cells and safe houses had been theater writ small, so their coups would become theater writ large, with all Manila as its stage. But torture also gave them an inflated sense of the political efficacy of violence, culminating in a vision of their last coup as a cleansing cataclysm of mass slaughter. Not only did torture inspire their many coups; it would preordain every one to failure.

Political Lessons of Torture

During the late 1980s, the Philippines suffered more coup attempts than any other country in the world. For nearly five years, coup threats dominated the country's politics, blocking major social reforms and slowing the nation's economic recovery. In this troubled transition to democracy after fourteen years of dictatorship, several active military cliques rebelled against the restoration of civil authority. Among the nine attempted coups d'état between 1986 and 1990, five were serious, and these were all led by that small group of regular officers who called themselves the Reform the Armed Forces Movement, or RAM. One of these attempts featured a lurid mix of torture and terror, another culminated in a massacre of civilian bystanders, and a third was a massive assault that nearly seized power.

At a meeting with Defense Minister Enrile in January 1986, the RAM colonels formulated their plan for a coup against Marcos that was flawed by an extreme overconfidence. They agreed that the president would engage in systematic fraud to defeat the opposition candidate, Cory Aquino, in the February presidential elections, creating a crisis of legitimacy and an opening for a coup. Accordingly, at "H-hour," midnight on February 22, 1986, Colonel Honasan's twenty-man commando team would somehow slip past nine thousand palace guards by crossing the Pasig River on rubber rafts, capture the president, and hold him hostage. Once the commandos had secured the president and his first lady, two thousand rebel troops would surround the palace in the predawn darkness to prevent a counterattack, assuring the RAM rebels a sudden, decisive victory.[69]

Their plan also contained a fundamental contradiction between, first, a commando raid to seize the palace with twenty men (requiring absolute secrecy) and, second, a mass uprising by two thousand rebel soldiers (a number so large that secrecy was humanly impossible).[70] As details of the coup plans inevitably leaked to the CIA and then to the palace, Marcos reinforced Colonel Honasan's landing spot on the banks of the Pasig River with two full Marine battalions.[71] Marcos's loyal military chief, General Fabian Ver, mined the river with enough explosives to vaporize any commandos who tried to cross.[72]

But, in a last-minute patrol on the eve of his coup attempt, Colonel Honasan spotted the Marines guarding his landing spot on the palace grounds.

Col. Gregorio "Gringo" Honasan in a 1986 studio photograph, projecting a lethal image of threat reflected in his leadership of six coup attempts against the Philippine government. (Jaime Zobel de Ayala)

Realizing that the secrecy of their coup attempt had been "blown," Honasan and Enrile chose to join forces with Constabulary chief Fidel Ramos and launch an open mutiny against Marcos. Reflecting its spontaneity, this move, too, was badly planned and saved from certain defeat only by events so unpredictable that many Catholic faithful regarded them as a miracle.[73]

The mass uprising that followed was a drama in four acts over four days—February 22 to February 26. Its stage was Epifanio de los Santos Avenue, or EDSA, the eight-lane highway that rings Manila and runs between Camp Crame, General Ramos's Constabulary headquarters, and Camp Aguinaldo, the site of Enrile's Defense Ministry.

On Day One—Saturday, February 22, 1986—Enrile and Ramos declared their revolt against Marcos at an afternoon press conference as the small contingents of forces loyal to them occupied Manila's two main military cantonments, Camp Aguinaldo and Camp Crame. The situation was, to say the least, desperate.

Then at 9:00 p.m., the hand of God, in the person of Manila's Cardinal Jaime Sin, intervened, speaking to the city's faithful over the Church-owned Radio Veritas: "I call the people to come out from their houses and to protect our friends, the soldiers."[74] As phones rang across the city, a crowd of some fifty thousand people gathered within hours at the gates of Camp Aguinaldo. Simultaneously, rebel officers were working the telephones, calling military comrades and classmates to neutralize Marcos's crushing superiority. In these critical hours, General Ramos won the support of his subordinate, General Prospero Olivas, commander of the Metrocom antiriot squads. That night, as Marcos called repeatedly with direct orders to clear the crowds from the camp gates, General Olivas gave his assent but then failed to issue any commands.[75] Through luck and personal contacts, Day One had ended in a stalemate.

Day Two, Sunday, February 23, saw the unexpected triumph of "people power." At 3:02 a.m., General Ver assembled some twenty general officers and their aides at Fort Bonifacio to plan an attack that assigned the assault to Marines commanded by General Artemio Tadiar.[76] Since most of his Marines were tied down defending the palace, it would take eight hours to extract them from their current positions and form up for an advance.[77]

At 2:15 p.m., the Marines finally drove up the EDSA highway in a cavalcade that included seven tanks, ten armored transports, and three thousand troops. As the tanks approached Camp Aguinaldo, they were stopped in their steel tracks by the crowds, which had grown to more than a half-million by midafternoon. The Marine commandant radioed the palace for instructions and was ordered: "Ram through the crowds, regardless of casualties." But in front of the Marines were thousands of people kneeling, led by a phalanx of nuns in white habits reciting the rosary. Suddenly, the tank engines roared, and the steel treads lunged forward one meter. But the nuns did not budge. People power had stopped the tanks.[78] This was the turning point. Although neither realized it, both Marcos and Enrile had both lost their bid for power to Cory Aquino, the opposition presidential candidate and the moral leader of these masses.

Day Three, on Monday, February 24, was the time of battle. At dawn, Marcos's riot troops cleared a path through the thin crowds at the back of Camp Aguinaldo, allowing a cavalcade of six armored vehicles and twenty-eight trucks carrying a brigade of Marines to enter the cantonment. By 8:30 am, the Marines were arrayed on the high ground in Camp Aguinaldo, a position that allowed them to shell the rebels concentrated inside Camp Crame directly across the EDSA highway with a lethal arsenal—three 105 mm howitzers, six recoilless rifles, six rocket launchers, twenty-eight mortars, sixty machine guns, and nearly a thousand M-16 rifles.

The rebel forces prepared to die. At 9:00 a.m., the palace gave the "kill order" to the commander of these Marines, Colonel Braulio Balbas. But this tough, battle-hardened colonel hesitated, uncertain that Marcos would ultimately "back me . . . for the killing of these innocent civilians." So Colonel Balbas quietly refused, telling the palace command, "We are still positioning the cannons," and "we need maps for the coordinates."[79]

At 2:00 p.m., Cory Aquino emerged from hiding and visited the people power barricades on EDSA, where she led the crowds in singing "Our Father"—signaling that sovereignty was now embodied in this crowd and that it had, with its voices, chosen her as the nation's legitimate leader.

Day Four, Tuesday, February 25, was denouement. That morning, Cory Aquino was sworn in as president by a Supreme Court justice. In the final hours of the drama, Marcos telephoned his old patron Ronald Reagan and instead got a return call from Senator Paul Laxalt (Republican, Nevada), who told him to "cut and cut cleanly." That same evening, Marcos and his entourage were flown by U.S. helicopters to Clark Field, en route to exile in Hawaii.[80]

After Marcos fled, his successor, Cory Aquino, faced a succession of military coups that troubled the country's transition to democratic rule for the next five years. Transformed by their experiences of torture and terror under Marcos, the RAM boys could not accept the restoration of civilian rule and launched four coups against President Aquino. With egos inflated by a sense of power, RAM's supermen failed to plan their coup attempts carefully, and each one collapsed through the same sort of strategic blunders so evident in their planning for the February 1986 uprising.

After two abortive coups that collapsed within a day in 1986 and 1987, Colonel Honasan forged plans, inspired by the Indonesian army's slaughter of a million civilians in 1965, for a cleansing maelstrom of mass violence. "Honasan said the problem of the EDSA and subsequent revolutions was that they had been achieved . . . with few casualties," a U.S. Embassy attaché reported after dining with Honasan in February 1989. "He said the Filipino people needed a national catharsis of great proportions, so they would wake up and be disciplined." A revolution with "half a million casualties," could, Honasan felt, make the people "frightened" enough to accept fundamental change.[81]

In December 1989, RAM launched a massive coup that came quite close to capturing the palace. In contrast to their poor planning in 1987, the rebels had secured all the elements for victory: a coherent strike force, superior firepower, and control of the air. But the RAM leaders again made poor strategic and tactical decisions that reflected, at base, the narcissism of their extraordinary empowerment. Although Honasan had sufficient forces to capture the capital, he diverted them to secondary targets and symbolic actions that doomed him to defeat.

Honasan unleashed his attack at midnight on December 1, 1989, with seeming precision and a superior force of Marines and Rangers supported by tanks, artillery, and aircraft. Since the capital had been stripped of troops as a preemptive measure after his earlier 1987 coup, Armed Forces Headquarters held only a small contingents of light infantry, giving the rebels an overwhelming advantage. As planned, the coup forces struck decisively at their initial objectives—Villamor Air Base, Sangley Point Naval Station, and Fort Bonifacio—which proved to be of secondary and indecisive import.[82]

In this first wave of attacks, Lieutenant Colonel Red Kapunan (PMA '71) and his classmate Lieutenant Colonel Vic Batac led rebel Marines and three armored vehicles in seizing TV Channel 4 in Quezon City. At 4:00 a.m., Kapunan set up a command post inside a studio penthouse to broadcast twelve videocassettes with messages to the city from his leader Honasan. But the station manager, before slipping out, had disconnected a critical mechanism, blocking any transmission and forcing the rebels to reinforce the station against attacks. For a full twenty-four hours, the most critical period in any coup, the rebel command wasted valuable time and resources—aircraft, armored vehicles, and an infantry battalion—in holding a television studio while trying, without success, to broadcast Honasan's image. Had these forces been used to attack Camp Aguinaldo or Malacañan Palace, the decisive objective, the coup's outcome might well have been different.[83]

By the end of Day One, the tide began to turn against the rebels. After rebel T-28 propeller aircraft bombed the palace at 6:25 a.m. and continued to strike at the government forces throughout the day, the Aquino administration appealed to Washington. At 2:04 p.m., two U.S. Air Force Phantom jets from Clark Air Base made a low pass over Manila, threatening retaliation for any more rebel air strikes. Simultaneously, government aircraft bombed rebel-held airfields, blocking further attacks.[84]

Over the next two days, the coup slowly collapsed as its commanders refused orders, troops delayed striking at key objectives, and the government rallied loyal forces that soon countered the rebels' superior strength. Just before dawn on Day Three, the coup died when two thousand defenders inside Camp Aguinaldo turned back an attack by a thousand rebel Marines with firepower that soon forced their surrender.[85]

In a violent coda to the coup, rebel Scout Rangers occupied the tall towers in the Makati financial district for five days until December 7, when negotiations allowed them to march back to their barracks.[86] During this standoff, most RAM leaders escaped into a rebel underground, where they remained for the next three years, plotting relentlessly and launching one more coup attempt, an abortive regional revolt that provided further proof of their dismal leadership.

Impunity

After six coup attempts in five years, the RAM colonels were further from power than ever before. They had launched more coups with less success than any army on four continents. They had exhausted almost every option within the tactical canon of the coup d'état—commando raid on the palace, assault on the capital, urban terrorism, and rural revolt. All had failed.

By the end of 1990, one option remained—surrender. Facing criminal charges for capital crimes of murder, rebellion, and torture, the RAM colonels, like their peers elsewhere in the Third World, were determined to lay down their arms in a way that would ensure their immunity against any future prosecution. Over the next five years, through a mix of violence, bluff, and bravado, they not only won an absolute amnesty but also placed their leader in the Philippine Senate, the country's most powerful legislative body. Like their counterparts in Argentina and Chile, the Philippine military achieved "impunity" for its many crimes and coups.[87]

As a recent phenomenon, impunity is a little-understood process with far-reaching ramifications. After military dictatorships collapsed and fledgling democracies rose around the globe in the 1980s, euphoria was soon tempered by the realization that uniformed criminals were manipulating their weak states to escape punishment. During the VI International Symposium on Torture at

Buenos Aires in 1993, delegates defined impunity as "the fact that, even in countries where dictatorship has given way to democratic rule, many torturers and other violators of human rights go unpunished." In some countries, impunity comes by new amnesty laws; in others, indirectly through a political and legal stalemate that stalls either investigation or prosecution.[88] Expanding upon this narrow definition, torture therapists have reported that impunity prevents the full rehabilitation of their patients and contaminates the whole of society. In 1992, the Philippine psychologist Elisabeth Marcelino surveyed a hundred ex-detainees and found that half suffered "stress symptoms, one of which is fear of recapture or reprisals from the agents of the state who were responsible for their torture."[89] Thus, at the VII International Symposium on Torture at Capetown in 1995, delegates noted the "enormous emotional power" of impunity as societies are torn between "a long-term vision of reconstruction" and "a natural desire for justice."[90]

At a fundamental level, such struggle for impunity often entails a debate over remembering and forgetting. Atavistic elements, usually within the military, urge forgetting in the guise of national reconciliation, while their victims demand an accounting. "The same powers that resorted to State terrorism are actively are promoting collective oblivion," wrote two Argentinean psychiatrists in 1996, "the usual way that the winners tell the story."[91] They argued that, since the "social body has been deeply wounded" by years of repression, collective trauma, unless confronted through remembrance and redress, will be "transmitted from generation to generation."[92]

In this battle between justice and impunity, the sites of contestation are many—the courts, the ballot box, commemorations, and collective memory. By threatening the stability of a fragile democracy, recalcitrant officers and their commanders can engage in a protracted political campaign that often forces civilian authorities to abandon inquires and concede amnesty. While the advocates of forgetting usually maneuver in silence, they also, at times, compete openly to shape the public representation of the past. Denied justice in local courts, the victims launch their own oppositional politics, which often entails remembrance at home and litigation abroad. In this struggle, mass media are often heavily contested as partisans seek to persuade the public of their viewpoint through cinema, television, and the press.

More than any other nation, the Philippines provides an example of extreme impunity. The tumultuous decade after the dictator's downfall reveals much about this troubling phenomenon, both its political dynamics and its long-term consequences. In the Philippines, impunity has left what one scholar has called the "entrenched legacy of martial law"—a lingering collective malaise that subtly but directly shaped and distorted the nation's political process.[93]

Seeking to placate a restive military, President Aquino, whose term in office extended from 1986 through 1992, abandoned the prosecution of human rights violators and embraced a militant anticommunism. Similarly, her successor, Fidel Ramos (1992–98), offered a blanket amnesty and symbolic concessions that, on the surface, completed the military's transition from a body enjoying the privileges of dictatorship to one that accepted the constraints of democracy. Of greater significance, Ramos provided the substance of law and the stuff of politics that perfected the process of impunity. As chief of Constabulary for all of the fourteen years of the Marcos dictatorship, Ramos remained legally responsible for the brutal, systematic tortures carried out by the special intelligence units under his command. As president, Ramos therefore bestowed the imprimatur of a lasting legality upon an impunity that had been, under Aquino, a short-term compromise. Moreover, he effected the reintegration of former torturers into society and their elevation to positions of authority—a central element of impunity. Working less visibly, this president also encouraged RAM's entry into electoral politics by supporting Colonel Gringo Honasan's 1995 Senate candidacy.

After his inauguration in July 1992, President Ramos established the National Unification Commission (NUC) to negotiate the surrender of all rebel forces, RAM included.[94] As a sign of good will, he then ordered the military courts to suspend prosecution of rebel officers for the duration of the negotiations.[95] When Honasan and a handful of other surviving RAM leaders finally surfaced from their rebel underground that December, President Ramos hailed them as "prodigal sons who had returned to the fold."[96]

In an elaborate ceremony at the University of the Philippines Law School, Defense Secretary Renato de Villa led a delegation of military officers in full-dress uniforms glittering with braid and medals. Honasan's rebels all wore maroon polo shirts emblazoned in bold gold with the RAM slogan, "Our Dreams Shall Never Die."[97] Both sides signed the preliminary peace accord, which stipulated an "immediate and complete cessation of hostilities" and the suspension of "court martial proceedings." Secretary de Villa promised to release all rebels still detained in military stockades. Both parties agreed to meet in January to begin negotiations for a final agreement.[98]

As the talks wound their torturous way through a first year and into a second, RAM officers appeared at countless public meetings and media interviews, courting public support for an amnesty to cover past crimes and an acceptance of their future role as political leaders. Throughout the three years

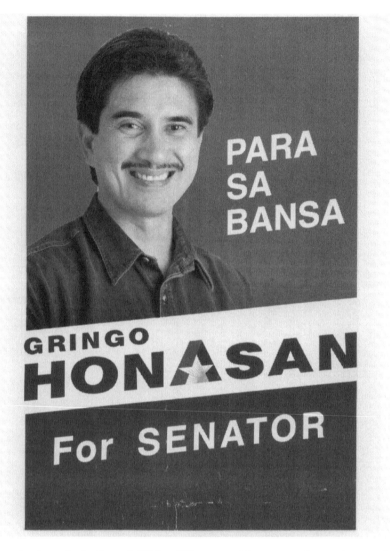

Surrendered coup leader Gregorio "Gringo" Honasan evoking an aura of avuncular warmth in his successful 1995 campaign for a seat in the Philippine Senate.

of stop-start negotiations, RAM first refused to discuss its hidden arsenal of light antitank weapons (LAW) and then retained enough of these missiles to destroy the military's entire tank force—making the group a credible threat to resume revolt should talks fail.[99] Through a mix of public charm and periodic threat, the rebels began to win a de facto impunity for their capital crimes.

In the country's rightward drift, mass media and its cultural production

of collective memory recast the past, transforming these human rights violators into heroes. In RAM's makeover from military rebels to social reformers,
the Filipino cinema played a transformative role. With their appealing mix of
idealism and violence, these colonels were ready-made material for the Filipino "action film" and its long romance with the gunman as an instrument
of social justice. In August 1993, not long after RAM's surrender, Regal Films
released *Aguinaldo: The True-to-Life Story of Gov. Rodolfo Aguinaldo of Cagayan*
on fifty-seven screens in metropolitan Manila, launching this epic as one of
the year's major box office successes.[100] Reinventing his life for the wide screen,
Aguinaldo was transformed from the nation's most notorious torturer into the
cinematic "Agui"—a heroic figure who is repulsed by torture and animated by
a quiet courage that makes him a moral center between the violence of communist revolution and the oppression of the country's ruling elite.

A year later, as campaigning for the 1995 legislative elections began, Gringo
Honasan's long-awaited movie opened on sixty-seven screens across the Manila area. Although the film was titled *Colonel Billy Bibit—RAM!*, Honasan's
portrayal was the film's focal point.[101] This script lacked the rich symbolism of
the Aguinaldo film, but its reinvention of the past was even bolder. Once denounced as "monsters" and hunted as outlaws, the RAM cinematic characters
became idealists fighting for social justice against the corrupt government of
Cory Aquino.

These films were the first sign of RAM's bid for political office as both en-
trée to power and capstone to its quest for impunity. Ultimately, these military
rebels would field ten candidates in the 1995 elections—four for congress, one
for governor in Mindanao, and five more for local offices.[102] As the campaign
shifted into high gear after the New Year, Honasan announced his race for the
Senate and soon won a "guest slot" on the slate of the People's Reform Party
(RFP), led by the gadfly oppositionist Miriam Defensor Santiago.[103]

Honasan's first campaign rally was an extraordinary event, even in a nation with a century-long history of flamboyant elections. When Miriam Santiago led her senatorial slate to a major rally at Bacolod City in March, Honasan's speech avoided serious issues, and his delivery was lackluster. But, as he
stepped down from the platform and moved toward his car, the crowd of thirty
thousand erupted in a sexualized frenzy.[104] According to the *Manila Chronicle*,
"Honasan was swamped with 'love notes' or short personal messages from
residents here, mostly young women," and his "battle-tested security personnel . . . were helpless before the hordes of people that flocked the candidate.
It took the leader of seven failed coup attempts a full 20 minutes to reach
his waiting vehicle from the stage because of the enormity of the crowd that
wanted to kiss or just hold him."[105]

How can we explain the intensity of this response? With looks, manner, and gesture eliding with his reputation for power, cruelty, and violence, Honasan may have projected a seductively lethal aura. Whatever the appeal, thousands lost control in his presence and yielded to collective ecstasy, shouting and screaming. Though large and frenzied, these campaign crowds apparently were not representative. On election day, women rejected Honasan in overwhelming numbers, producing a marked gender gap, with 10 percent more men than women voting for him.[106] Although the other RAM candidates fared badly in the May voting, Honasan won a Senate seat easily with a lock on ninth place. His long-time patron Juan Ponce Enrile also won just enough votes to join the "magic twelve," making two of the country's twenty-four senators principals in RAM's revolt and ensuring the group's exoneration, which soon followed in October.[107]

Simultaneous with RAM's political ascent, the Ramos administration reintegrated Marcos-era human rights violators into the apex of the country's security apparatus—ensuring them protection, legitimacy, and undue political influence. Soon after his inauguration in July 1992, Ramos formed the Presidential Anti-Crime Commission (PACC) to curb the country's crime wave and filled its ranks with officers who had served in Marcos's elite antisubversion squads. The former commander of Constabulary's notorious Metrocom Military Intelligence and Security Group (MISG), Rolando Abadilla, now became senior adviser to the PACC.[108]

In his twelve years at the helm of Marcos's notorious security group, Abadilla and his band of "MISG boys" had evoked what one Manila reporter called "countless images of pain—blocks of ice, droplets of ice water, clothes, hangars, barbed wire, steel drums, light bulbs, car batteries."[109] Adding to the continuity from the Marcos era, several of these former "MISG boys" joined this empowered strike force, notably Abadilla's former deputy, Panfilo Lacson, who took command of the PACC's Task Force Habagat. These appointments soon produced a surge in lurid police violence, marked by torture and extrajudicial killings, that dominated Manila's press for much of Ramos's term.[110]

Conclusion

Through the compromises necessitated by impunity, the Philippines, beneath the surface of a restored democracy, suffered the lingering legacies of the Marcos era—a collective trauma, a pervasive brutality, and an ingrained institutional habit of torture. The lasting trauma that Marcos's torturers had inflicted on thousands of Filipino victims is amply documented in decades of litigation and thousands of depositions. But, if we are to grasp the transactional nature of this experience, we must look beyond the victims' suffering to ask what impact torture had upon the torturers. When Marcos, as commander-in-chief, declared martial law, regular officers had little choice but to obey and enforce his authoritarian rule. Once his regime opened a gulag of safe houses for routine torture, the young lieutenants of Class '71 were the echelon assigned to this duty, and they experienced its impact. These prisons became sites of a transactional torture, more psychological than physical, that damaged the victims and empowered the perpetrators.

Through the theatrics of psychological torture, RAM's leaders gained a sense of themselves as supermen, emboldened to shed their subordination and to rebel against the civilian authority they had sworn to serve. Not only did they launch a succession of coups, but these attempts were remarkable for their consistent failure. With few exceptions, military coups d'état in the Third World were usually singular in number and often succeeded in seizing power. To fail, as RAM did, six times in a row should be something of a record. Why such an extraordinary record of failure?

Much of the explanation may lie with the mentality of RAM's leaders. Enamored of their own aura, the colonels of Class '71 failed to plan adequately for these coup attempts. Overestimating the power of violence after years of torture and terror, they expected the capital to be awed by the majesty of their blazing rifles, thundering bombs, and rumbling tanks. Even when possessed of superior force in December 1989, Colonel Honasan and his aides were so absorbed in a narcissistic projection of their power that they dallied in a television studio and failed to attack the objectives that would give them victory. By the time they resumed the fight, the hour for a successful attack on the presidential palace had passed. The crown of power thus slipped from the grasp of these would-be Nietzschean supermen.

Yet, this extreme self-confidence, freed from reflection or remorse, served the RAM colonels well in their struggle for impunity after surrender. Their self-adulation segued easily into cinema, producing images of heroic service and sacrifice. In press and television interviews, they focused solely on the government's failings, not their own crimes of torture and rebellion. Throughout this struggle, they proved relentless in their demand for exoneration. Slowly, though political maneuver and media manipulation, their crimes were excused, the trauma of their torture and coups was erased, and their demand for impunity was won.

In their success and in their failure, the RAM colonels and their distinctive psyche dominated Philippine politics for nearly a decade, complicating the country's transition to democracy and achieving an impunity that left the trauma of authoritarian rule unresolved—much as their military counterparts were doing elsewhere in Asia and Latin America. Nor was this experience limited to these peripheries of global power. As we will see in the closing chapter, impunity is a universal political process. Just as these Filipino torturers were so successful in winning immunity for their crimes of treason, rebellion, and murder, so American perpetrators would engage in similar media manipulations to escape any sanction for human rights violations during the War on Terror.

5

The Seduction of
Psychological Torture

Just four weeks after the CBS television network broadcast those sixteen photos showing the torture of prisoners by U.S. soldiers at Abu Ghraib prison in April 2004,[1] Susan Sontag published a subtle yet sensational cover story in the *New York Times Magazine*. She simply asked us to look again at that iconic image we all thought we knew so well— the one that shows a hooded Iraqi standing on a box, electrical wires hanging from his outstretched arms. By expanding the photo's frame just a fraction of an inch, Sontag captured a casually dressed American soldier in the right foreground, nonchalantly adjusting the setting on his digital camera—a perspective that revealed both the fact of torture and the fascination it holds for many.

Except for the bare legs, the hooded Iraqi in that photo is fully clothed, the features hidden, the form indistinguishable in the ample folds of his robe. In stark contrast, other photos in the sequence have, as Sontag remarked, an explicitly sexual theme. In fact, she argued, referring to the notorious prison guard Private Lynndie England, "most of the pictures seem part of a larger confluence of torture and pornography: a young woman leading a naked man around on a leash is classic dominatrix imagery. And you wonder how much of the sexual tortures inflicted on the inmates of Abu Ghraib was inspired by the vast repertory of pornographic imagery available on the Internet—and which ordinary people, by sending out Webcasts of themselves, try to emulate." In the midst of this critique of Americans and their culture, Sontag noted in passing, without any evidence or elaboration, that these "torture photographs are interleaved with pornographic images of American soldiers having sex with one another."[2]

Where? Where were those sensational "pornographic images of American soldiers having sex with one another"? Not in the pages of the *New York Times*. Not anywhere on the Internet that a Google search could find. Something

Hooded Iraqi detainee standing on box, electrical wires hanging from his arms, while a U.S. soldier adjusts his digital camera, Abu Ghraib prison, Iraq, 2003. (U.S. Army Criminal Investigation Command)

was missing. Sontag had shown us what we thought were the worst of the photos—Iraqis naked, forced fellatio, piles of nude male bodies. But, as bold as that essay might have been, Sontag was holding back. There was something important, something she had apparently seen but was not going to share—not the photos, or any description beyond those few words.

After nearly two years with little publication of any more leaked images, an Australian television network grabbed headlines around the globe in February 2006 by releasing more and much grittier Abu Ghraib photos.[3] A few days later, a compact disc (CD) arrived in my University of Wisconsin campus mailbox via air courier from that same television studio in Sydney, Australia. The first document on the disc was a report, with attached spreadsheets, from the U.S. Army's Criminal Investigation Command indicating that "a computer forensic examination" had recovered some 1,600 photos from two perpetrators of abuse at Abu Ghraib, identified as Private Lynndie England and Corporal Charles Graner.[4] The sequencing and time dates of the thousand-plus photos on that Army computer log indicate that Corporal Graner and Private England had interleaved off-duty autoerotic photography of their intimacy with on-duty, on-camera sexual humiliation of Iraqi prisoners, often stripped naked.

To view these photos, I selected my computer's "slide show" function and clicked, starting a sequence of dozens of photos of sexual intimacy and sexualized torture until I came to "0032.jpg"—the one Sontag had published in the *New York Times*—showing that hooded Iraqi on a box while the unknown U.S. soldier adjusted his digital camera. Surveying those hundreds of photos, one depraved, disturbing image after another, took me into some dark, unfamiliar recess of human consciousness that one U.S. senator who saw these same photos compared to Dante's "rings of hell"—revealing acts far more cruel than anything CBS had shown and far more perverse than the simple autoeroticism that Sontag had written about.

In seeking some explanation for torture's adoption as a formal prerogative of American power in the decade since 9/11, we are confronted with a mystifying contradiction. On the one hand, the United States has long joined the international community in enacting conventions, declarations, and laws that make torture and inhumane treatment illegal. And the American people have proved, over the past half-century, deeply humanitarian in their support for disaster relief and development aid abroad and equally humane at home in their charity, philanthropy, and social policy. Yet, in defiance of law, reason, and morality, Washington, in the aftermath of the 9/11 terrorist attacks, embraced torture as state policy and refused, for eight years, to repudiate the practice. And the American people generally supported this decision. How, we might ask, did a humane people come to support inhumane treatment of detainees?

To probe this contradiction, Sontag offers an interesting, important observation about the ways that American popular culture informed the behavior of the Abu Ghraib perpetrators and, by implication, influenced the public response to their photographs. "What formerly was segregated as pornography," she observed with unerring prescience, "as the exercise of extreme sadomasochistic longings—as in Pier Paolo Pasolini's last, near-unwatchable film, *Salò* (1975), depicting orgies of torture in the Fascist redoubt in northern Italy at the end of the Mussolini era—is now being normalized, by some, as high-spirited play or venting." Sontag decried the "culture of shamelessness" evident in this homemade pornography exported to the theater of war, with Iraqi prisoners forced to play a role in the sadomasochistic fantasies of their captors. Yet how many of the "ordinary people" who made webcasts of themselves having sex might be titillated by the sexualized torture of Iraqi prisoners? Did such vicarious erotica induce U.S. leaders to order torture? She declined to ask.

Despite her sedulously cultivated self-image as a cultural iconoclast who could stare with sang-froid into the most horrific image, Nazi death camps or Southern lynchings, it seems she had finally found, in this her last major essay, some recess of the human mind too dark, too disturbing for even Susan Sontag. Musing on the "increasing acceptance of brutality in American life,"

Sontag did ask whether a new video game featuring torture—say, "Interrogating the Terrorists"—might not be too far in the future. Indeed, the next several years would see a rash of such games, together with countless depictions of torture in film and on television.[5]

Building upon Sontag's observations about the relation between torture and popular culture, we can examine, through the study of visible media artifacts, the acceptance of such abuse within the American popular imagination in the aftermath of 9/11. Focusing on the *normalization* of torture via film, television, and video games will lead us back to the political arena, where, by 2008, popular culture would effect a radical redefinition of the terms for the nation's public debate over human rights.

Indeed, the arguments for the use of torture after 9/11 reside squarely in this realm of the country's collective imagination. At the outset of America's decade-long debate over torture in 2001–02, its proponents' main justification was the so-called ticking bomb scenario, a hypothetical elaboration of an exercise in academic philosophy so remote from reality that it is tantamount to fantasy.[6] In the years that followed, television networks and Hollywood studios would—through the invisible tendrils that tie modern media to the state—produce an amazing array of dramas depicting torture as always effective and often eroticized. Most importantly, a new Fox Television show titled *24* was aired only weeks after the events of 9/11, introducing a powerfully persuasive icon into the American political lexicon—the fictional secret agent Jack Bauer, who tortured regularly, repeatedly, and successfully to stop terrorist attacks on Los Angeles, attacks that often involved ticking bombs.

With such depictions filling screens large and small across America, the boundary between fiction and reality, always tenuous in this country, became blurred as these dramatizations dominated the political debate over torture. Just as the media propagated the ticking-bomb hypothetical without critical examination, so U.S. officials, quick to distance themselves from the ugly reality of Abu Ghraib, eagerly identified with the attractive hero of the popular TV show *24*, who tortured in almost every episode.

By the 2008 presidential campaign, these two iconic arguments, the hypothetical ticking bomb and the fictional federal agent, served as the main metaphors in the country's political discourse over torture. Within the loose rubric of campaign rhetoric, political leaders like Bill Clinton invoked the ticking-time-bomb scenario to advocate the creation of formal presidential torture warrants in case of such a critical event. Simultaneously, the invocation of Jack Bauer's name served as political code for an informal policy of allowing CIA agents, acting on their own outside the law, to use torture for extreme emergencies. In sum, the world's preeminent power grounded its most controversial policy decision of the early twenty-first century not on research or rational analysis but in fiction and fantasy.

The CBS broadcast of just sixteen snapshots from Abu Ghraib, even though sanitized with blackouts over bared male genitalia, shocked the sensibilities of humankind, provoking emotional protests around the globe. To minimize the damage to the United States, the Bush administration sought to suppress further leaks from the Army's archive of 1,600 photos. Simultaneously, the American people recoiled. As Sontag noted just weeks after the photos' release, "Some Americans are already saying they have seen enough." Averting their gaze from the repulsive images of Abu Ghraib, most Americans would turn instead to the airbrushed images of torture so prevalent in their mass media. And yet, wrote Sontag, "The photographs are us." The acts of torture captured in these photos were the predictable, even likely outcome of "the policies prosecuted by this administration and the hierarchies deployed to carry them out"—policies and hierarchies that would soon be sanctioned, at least implicitly, by the American electorate in the upcoming November 2004 presidential elections.[7]

Is there, for some, an inherently seductive quality to the tortures revealed in those photos from Abu Ghraib? If so, that same quality may be at work in the willingness of so many Americans to accept the enticing depictions of torture in their popular culture. To enjoy commercial success, which they certainly did, these creative works in film and television must strike some receptive chord in their audiences. Among the many possible explanations for torture's acceptance, we should admit the possibility that U.S. mass media made torture seem tolerable, normal, and even appealing for a significant segment of Americans.

From both public policy and its dramatic portrayals after 9/11, there is ample evidence for torture's seductive quality, namely its ability to empower, exact retribution, and establish a hierarchy of superior and inferior. Beneath the public declarations of security and intelligence, there were acts of retribution and re-empowerment—restoring the order of ruler and ruled and salving the wounds from 9/11 at a time when world leaders were wracked by fear. With egos inflated as masters of pain and pleasure, perpetrators and the powerful who commanded them became forceful proponents of abuse, striding across the American political landscape, rather like those fictional "Nietzschean supermen" in Pasolini's film *Salò* whose sexually charged power over life and death enraptured and brutalized everyone in this sadomasochistic spectacle, torturer and spectator alike.[8]

As news of these abusive practices spread inevitably among the American public through rumor, press report, and media display, ordinary citizens reacted with a tangled mix of fear and fascination, passivity and anger that soon made torture a major focus of political debate. In the decade after the 9/11 terrorist attacks, the discussion and representation of torture in the U.S. media thus served to normalize the practice, whether by glamorizing or by rationalizing it. What is normal began to acquire an air of legitimacy. And that sense of legitimacy would lead first to public tolerance of torture and later to impunity for the perpetrators and their political leaders.

Historical Antecedents

The aestheticization of torture is by no means unique to post-9/11 America. In both its medieval and its modern incarnations, the closeted, often secretive infliction of intolerable pain has been mimed by public displays in artistic works that serve to legitimate and even popularize the practice. Many of these depictions, in both high art and low, not only normalize but also eroticize inhumane practices by rendering the human form under torture as exaggeratedly healthy, vigorous, and beautiful, its sufferings at once sensual, exquisite, and sublime. From the perspective of representation, there is certain continuity from medieval depictions of the aestheticized abuse of Christ and his martyrs through present-day projections of eroticized torture in film and television.

In the decades before and after 9/11, public engagement with torture occurred mainly through the ubiquitous media of film, television, and video games—popular art forms whose national dissemination served to bind a heterogeneous American culture into a shared social experience. In medieval Europe, the growing use of torture in civil and canonical courts was paralleled by a proliferation of religious art with almost anatomical displays of physical scourging, producing images that permeated the main socially binding experience of that era, attending church. After a Catholic council abolished trial by ordeal in 1215, European secular courts revived Roman law, with its reliance upon torture to obtain confessions in pretrial interrogations—an approach that persisted for the next five centuries.[9] With the parallel rise of the Inquisition, Church interrogators also used torture for both confession and punishment, a procedure that was formalized under Pope Innocent IV in 1252. By the fourteenth century, the Italian Inquisition had routinized the physical scourging of heretics through use of the *strappado* to suspend victims with ropes and weights in five degrees of escalating duration and severity.[10]

The impact of judicial torture upon medieval culture went far beyond the courts, coinciding with a subtle shift in theological emphasis from the life of Jesus to the death of Christ. This change was reflected in artistic representations of his body being scourged and crucified. From the slender details of Christ's agonies in the Gospels, medieval artists, in the words of the art historian Mitchell B. Merback, "approximated these grisly violations with the unerring eye of a forensic pathologist," creating an artistic convention of the pain inflicted on Christ's battered body that mimed and may have legitimated the increasingly gruesome legal spectacles of torture and public execution.[11]

Later, in the sixteenth and seventeenth centuries, Europe's early-modern states elaborated upon this judicial spectacle of torture and the artistic display of suffering. "Military torture was prodigious," wrote Alec Mellor of these absolutist regimes, "religious torture was regularized; and judicial torture was enriched daily by new varieties."[12]

In the religious realm, the Counter Reformation fought challenges to Church authority by establishing the Roman Inquisition in 1542 while pursuing bloody military campaigns against Muslims and Protestants. In this age of royal and religious patronage of the arts, there were, as the art historian Stephen Eisenman argues, close parallels between state policy and artistic practice. One of Michelangelo's frescos in the Sistine Chapel (1511) depicts the *Execution of Haman* with "finely articulated musculature of the body" that "signals ecstasy as much as torment"; next door, in the Sala Regia, *The Massacre of the Huguenots* (1572) by the artist Giorgio Vasari details the bloody slaughter of these thirty thousand "leering blasphemers" as "the triumph of Catholicism over heresy." In that same spirit, Vasari covered the great Sala di Cosimo I at the Palazzo Vecchio in Florence with a fresco (1560) showing Saturn using a ponderous metal scythe to castrate his father Uranus, who lies prone and passive while a naked goddess nearby fondles her breasts in orgasmic pleasure. As the Counter Reformation embraced the Baroque aesthetic, this "cult of sacred and eroticized violence" spread widely. Indeed, "the combined erotic and sanguinary desires of noble and religious patrons" took form, for example, in Jusepe di Ribera's painting of *Martyrdom of St. Bartholomew* (1644), which shows the saint's torturer as "a divine instrument in the miracle of salvation."[13]

But, in the eighteenth century, the Enlightenment slowly eclipsed the twinned practice of judicial scourging and artistic depiction of torture as "eroticized chastisement."[14] Amid growing doubts among jurists about the accuracy of testimony obtained through torture, evaluation of evidence on its merits replaced coerced confessions in the secular courts. Following his coronation, in 1740, Frederick II of Prussia banned torture after writing a dissertation that criticized it "as cruel as it is useless." Meanwhile, his friend Voltaire famously condemned torture, sparking a movement for its abolition that spread across Enlightenment Europe during the early nineteenth century.[15] The arts followed the state's retreat from torture, a trend exemplified by Édouard Manet's painting of *The Mocking of Christ* (1865), which shows a "pasty skinned, knobby-kneed Frenchman" surrounded by motley inquisitors—expressing thereby a modern sensibility that torture degrades both perpetrator and victim.[16]

Torture as U.S. Policy

At the dawn of the twenty-first century, these resonances between art and politics revived to again legitimate the use of torture as state policy. Reflecting the far greater penetration of mass media within modern society and popular consciousness, there was soon a convergence of U.S. statecraft and a dramatization of torture that served, over time, to erase the boundaries between fact and fiction. When Washington made abusive interrogation its official practice after the attacks of September 2001, the U.S. news media featured pundits advocating torture as necessary for national security. From this media chatter emerged the iconic ticking time bomb scenario, a hypothesis so remote from reality that it took the country's political discourse into the realm of fantasy.

Hollywood soon followed with film and television portrayals of torture as imperative, effective, and enticing. With all the cinematic artifice that made his actions seem unassailable, Jack Bauer, the hero of Fox Television's hit show *24*, acted out brutal interrogations and argued with fictional presidents about torture. Actual military interrogators from Baghdad to Guantanamo would use his methods on real terror suspects. President George W. Bush mimed Jack's mannerisms in White House speeches. Torture advocates cited this fictional hero as justification in presidential debates.

For a generation that grew up with the assumption of American supremacy, 9/11 had struck a serious blow. In both realms, political and fictional, torture signified a reassertion of that wounded power. In a blurring of representation and reality, the ticking bomb fantasy and a fictional secret agent would become powerfully persuasive media icons in the U.S. debate over torture.

Instead of the covert, concealed practice of decades past, the Bush administration adopted harsh interrogation as formal state policy and performed it in the tough-talking vernacular of the spy genre. Right after his public address to a shaken nation on September 11, 2001, President Bush gave his White House staff secret orders for torture, saying: "I don't care what the international lawyers say, we are going to kick some ass."[17]

In a televised interview on *Meet the Press* just five days after the September 11 attacks Vice President Dick Cheney communicated a mix of fear, anger, and bravado. Explaining the fearful nature of the terrorist threat, Cheney explained that "we begin every day reading the intelligence reports . . . on the plotting by al-Qaeda members . . . and contemplating the possibility of an attack against the U.S. with far deadlier weapons than anything we've seen to date." Addressing the people of Afghanistan, he warned that, "if you provide sanctuary to terrorists, you face the full wrath of the United States of America." To defeat these enemies, he insisted, the United States had to use extreme methods. "We'll have to work sort of the dark side," he said. "We've got to spend time in the shadows in the intelligence world. A lot of what needs to be done here will have to be done quietly, without any discussion, using sources and methods available to our intelligence agencies. . . . So it's going to be vital for us to use any means at our disposal."[18] Ten days later, Cofer Black, the head of the CIA's Counterterrorism Center, summed up the agency's approach to interrogation before Congress, saying: "After 9/11 the gloves come off."[19]

In the seven years of torture that followed the 9/11 attacks, the parameters of these techniques were elaborated in interrogation manuals, legal memoranda, and staff meetings that communicated authorization from the White House down the chain of command to field interrogators at Abu Ghraib and Guantanamo and in CIA prisons from Thailand to Poland. Within the executive branch, Condoleezza Rice, then national security adviser, later recalled that, "in the spring of 2002, the CIA sought policy approval from the National Security Counsel (NSC) to begin an interrogation program for high-level al-Qaida terrorists." Consequently, she "convened a series of meetings of NSC principals in 2002 and 2003 to discuss various issues . . . relating to detainees."[20]

These principals—including Vice President Cheney, Attorney General John Ashcroft, Secretary of State Colin Powell, and CIA director George Tenet—met dozens of times inside the White House Situation Room. According to ABC News, "some of the interrogation sessions were almost choreographed—down to the number of times CIA agents could use a specific tactic." After watching agency employees pantomime what Rice called "certain physical and psychological interrogation techniques," these leaders repeatedly authorized extreme psychological techniques stiffened by hitting, wall slamming, and waterboarding. During one of these meetings, Attorney General Ashcroft asked aloud: "Why are we talking about this in the White House? History will not judge this kindly." Nonetheless, this national security team apparently authorized every CIA request for torture. Even after the Abu Ghraib photos sparked worldwide protests, these principals met again inside the White House in mid-2004 to approve the use of CIA torture techniques on still more terror suspects. Despite growing concern about the damage that Abu Ghraib was doing to America's reputation, Condoleezza Rice coolly commanded agency officials, reportedly saying: "This is your baby. Go do it."[21]

Under this expansive executive interpretation of U.S. law, Defense Secretary Rumsfeld approved aggressive techniques at Guantanamo in late 2002,[22] and appointed General Geoffrey Miller to command this military prison, with authority to translate these guidelines into a harsh interrogation regime.[23] In both formal policy and informal practice, the directives for tough treatment produced the sexualized tortures that would eventually come to light at Abu Ghraib and elsewhere.

Reflecting the notion circulating among neoconservatives in the Bush administration that "Arabs are particularly vulnerable to sexual humiliation," Guantanamo's command began to probe such sensitivities, using female interrogators to humiliate Muslim males.[24] According to a sergeant who served under General Miller, female soldiers regularly removed their shirts, and one wiped red ink on a detainee's face, saying she was menstruating, leaving him to "cry like a baby." Singled out for sexualized humiliation, the alleged hijacker Mohamed al-Kahtani was subjected to a "special interrogation plan" that combined rigorous sensory deprivation with psychological tactics called "ego down," "futility," and "gender coercion via some domination." During forty-eight days of interrogation, intensified by acute sleep deprivation, al-Kahtani was "told his mother and sister were whores"; mocked for "homosexual tendencies and that other detainees knew"; "forced to dance with a male interrogator"; "forced to wear a bra and a thong . . . on his head"; "led around by a leash tied to chains"; "forced to stand naked in front of a female interrogator"; and held down while a female interrogator "straddled" his groin.[25]

In September 2003, General Miller flew to Baghdad and delivered his Guantanamo regimen to military intelligence officers inside Abu Ghraib prison. Within days, the U.S. commander for Iraq, General Ricardo Sanchez, authorized a wide range of extreme interrogation techniques at Abu Ghraib that signaled a tolerance for twisted behavior.[26] Four months later, U.S. Army criminal investigators, alerted to possible violations of military regulations, conducted an investigation and compiled a single compact disc with 1,600 images that documented the illegal treatment and sexualized degradation of detainees—the same images I watched on "slide show" function after that CD landed in my university mailbox via courier from Sydney.

In the first file, marked "CG CD Marks 1," the opening photo, labeled "0001.jpg," showed a woman sucking hard on an erect penis. In the photo "0002.jpg," the same woman, smiling and with her eyes closed, is shown holding the pink head of an erect circumcised penis. The photo labeled "0005.jpg" shows the same female mid-coitus, with her face blurred. Then, in "0009.jpg," that woman, now recognizable as Private Lynndie England, stares directly into the camera, lifting her shirt to expose her breasts. Photo "00027.jpg" shows a male soldier, Corporal Charles Graner, kissing the same woman's left breast and holding her right breast. And, toward the end, "0055.jpg" shows an Iraqi woman in a prison cell lifting her shirt to expose her breasts.

In the file "CG CD Marks 3," there are eight photos of U.S. soldiers in a prison corridor with two leashed German shepherds. The first photo, "0001.jpg," shows soldiers leading a dog, fangs open, toward an Iraqi prisoner, completely naked, his hands behind his head, penis exposed.

File "CG CD Marks 4" opened with a half-dozen photos of Iraqi prisoners shackled in contorted positions. The photo labeled "0008.jpg" shows an Iraqi male prisoner chained to a bed frame with woman's underwear on his face, unclothed, his penis exposed. In photo "0020.jpg," Private Lynndie England leads an Iraqi male who is crawling, completely naked, on the floor, leashed like a dog. In photo "0024.jpg," U.S. soldiers force three Iraqi male prisoners to lie down in the corridor, their naked bodies touching one another, their hands intertwined. Then, in photo "0034.jpg," Corporal Charles Graner is seen in a pile of four hooded, semiclothed Iraqis, punching one in the back of the head with a gloved fist. Photo "0038.jpg" shows an Iraqi who is hooded and naked sitting on another naked prisoner while Private Lynndie England points to his penis, smiling and with her thumbs up.

Though repulsive, these photos are nonetheless revealing—not just about the private lives of ordinary Americans, *pace* Susan Sontag, but about torture as U.S. public policy. In particular, they reveal a great deal about the performative dimensions of a distinctively American form of psychological torture that was refined, under the exigencies of the War on Terror, to exploit cultural and, above all, sexual sensitivities. There are just a few egregious incidents of physical abuse, but almost all these photos show techniques that courts would consider psychological or psychosexual abuse.

Torture Advocacy by Professors and Pundits

Throughout these years of escalating brutality after 9/11, the Bush administration's covert embrace of these aggressive methods drew political sustenance from the public advocacy of torture by pundits and professors, both liberal and conservative. Instead of ignoring these views as irresponsible, illegal, or even dangerous, mainstream media became a megaphone for torture advocates, further normalizing practices once viewed as antithetical to American society. Combined with a steady stream of enticing media treatments of torture in film and television, discussed below, this punditry created strong support for torture among a significant sector of the American public.

In November 2001, just three months after the attacks of 9/11, the columnist Jonathan Alter wrote in *Newsweek*: "In this autumn of anger, even a liberal can find his thoughts turning to . . . torture." Alter advocated psychological torture or the transfer of suspects to "our less squeamish allies."[27] When a panelist on PBS's *McLaughlin Group* asked fellow commentators where they would send Al Qaeda suspects for torture, Rich Lowry, the editor of the *National Review*, bellowed, "The Turks!" And host John McLaughlin shouted out, "The Filipinos!"[28]

Adding academic gravitas to this media swagger, Harvard Law professor Alan M. Dershowitz mounted a sustained campaign for the legalization of torture to deal with the threat of what he branded the "ticking-bomb" scenario. Of course, he conceded, in a November 2001 op-ed for the *Los Angeles Times*, torture shocks the conscience. "But what if it were limited to the rare 'ticking bomb' case—the situation in which a captured terrorist who knows of an imminent large-scale threat refuses to disclose it? Would torturing one guilty terrorist to prevent the deaths of a thousand innocent civilians shock the conscience of all decent people?" The solution, he said, was the creation of a "torture warrant" that would allow limited, court-controlled torture.[29] In a January 2002 interview on CBS Television's popular *60 Minutes* news program, Dershowitz argued that torture was inevitable: "If you've got the ticking-bomb case, the case of the terrorist who knew precisely where and when the bomb would go off, and it was the only way of saving five hundred or a thousand lives, every democratic society would, have, and will use torture."[30]

After the Abu Ghraib scandal broke, in mid-2004, Harvard Law School faculty members, including Dershowitz, circulated a petition signed by 481 prominent professors of law and political science at 110 top universities nationwide calling for serious consideration of "a coercive interrogation policy . . . made within the strict confines of a democratic process." In effect, many of the country's leading academics were asking Americans to set aside two centuries of Enlightenment principles and to think seriously about legalizing torture.[31]

Simultaneously, a joint project by faculty at two Harvard schools, the Law School and the Kennedy School of Government, drew up a code for coercive interrogation, complete with rules, oversight, and accountability. Their final recommendations, drafted by law professor Philip B. Heyman, went to Congress, where, in early 2005, they attracted support from the ranking Democrat on the House Intelligence Committee, Representative Jane Harman. "If you're serious about trying to get information in advance of an attack," she told a

New York Times reporter, "interrogation has to be one of the main tools. I'm O.K. with it not being pretty." But furious opposition from human rights groups and concerns about civil liberties in Congress killed this attempt at legalizing torture.[32]

The Ticking Time Bomb

Despite this political defeat, the pro-pain pundits scored an extraordinary triumph in the realm of public opinion, persuading many Americans that Professor Dershowitz's ticking-bomb scenario justified torture as a necessary evil in an age of terror. Upon closer examination, public support for the Bush administration's embrace of torture was grounded not on rock-hard intelligence about terrorist threats or torture's efficacy but, instead, on a wispy mix of philosophical supposition and political scenario whose sum was fantasy.

More than thirty years earlier in 1973, the philosopher Michael Walzer had written about the ancient philosophical problem of "dirty hands" for an obscure academic journal, *Philosophy and Public Affairs.* He speculated about the morality of a politician "asked to authorize the torture of a captured rebel leader who knows the locality of a number of bombs hidden in apartment buildings around the city, set to go off within the next *twenty-four hours.*" Even though he believes torture is "wrong, indeed abominable," this politician orders the terrorist tortured, "convinced that he must do so for the sake of the people who might otherwise die in the explosions."[33]

In all likelihood, Walzer's abstract ruminations would have remained unnoticed on page 167 of an unread journal if not for the efforts of his academic acolyte, Professor Dershowitz. In newspaper op-eds and television appearances after 9/11, Dershowitz transformed this fragmentary philosophical speculation into a full-blown case for torture. In his scenario, torture might become necessary when, as Dershowitz put it, "a captured terrorist . . . refuses to divulge information about the imminent use of weapons of mass destruction, such as a nuclear, chemical or biological device, that are capable of killing and injuring thousands of civilians."[34]

From this hypothetical, Professor Dershowitz segued to the realm of reality, offering an argument that did not ask whether torture was being used or whether it ever should be used but that instead began with an implicit acceptance of its use. "If torture is, in fact, being used and/or would, in fact, be used in an actual ticking bomb terrorist case, would it be *normatively* better or worse to have such torture regulated by some kind of warrant?"—which, he tells us, will authorize interrogators to shove steel needles under Arab fingernails.

After this sleight-of-hand shift from the hypothetical to the real, Dershowitz concludes that his putative torture warrants "would reduce the incidence of abuses," since high officials, operating on the record, would never authorize "methods of the kind shown in the Abu Ghraib photographs."[35]

Yet, few asked whether this imagined scenario had some basis in history or common sense. In the real world, the probability that a terrorist might fall into police custody after concealing a ticking nuclear bomb in Times Square was so slender that this scenario seems a rather fanciful foundation for U.S. national security policy. When examined a bit more closely, this hypothetical seems an improbable, even impossible, five-stage sequence of variables that runs something like this. First, the FBI or CIA captures a terrorist. Second, the agency captures him at the precise moment between the timer's first tick and the bomb's burst. Third, the interrogators somehow have enough detailed foreknowledge of this particular plot to know they must interrogate that very person and do it now, right now. Fourth, these same officers have sufficiently accurate intelligence to know all about this specific terrorist and his ticking bomb—except for the few critical details that only torture can divulge. Finally, even if we accept the unlikely supposition that the stars might someday align in this particular sequence to place such a terrorist in police hands only minutes before his ticking bomb is due to detonate, this scenario still rests on a critical, unexamined assumption: that torture is the most effective method to extract intelligence from this or any hardened terrorist.

Most fundamentally, this extraordinary string of coincidences probably never has and never will occur. Visiting Israel to test this torture-stops-ticking-bomb thesis, the *New York Times* reporter Joseph Lelyveld was "repeatedly told that coercive interrogation had effectively thwarted . . . would-be suicide bombers." But nobody could cite a single "specific case." Instead of hundreds of cases, his Israeli sources finally named just one, that of a Hamas organizer broken under torture and, coincidentally, "the same one that the Israeli Justice Ministry cited in a letter to Human Rights Watch a couple of months earlier."[36]

With reality so uncooperative, torture advocates spun two sorts of scenarios, the fictional and the fabulous. Usually, they stuck to the hypothetical "Times Square bomber." But sometimes they twisted historical fact into a fable, a facsimile of this implausible scenario, claiming, for example, that the brutal torture of Abdul Hakim Murad at Manila in 1995 had stopped a plot to blow up a dozen trans-Pacific aircraft and kill four thousand innocent passengers. In defense of his argument for "torture warrants" to deal with a ticking-bomb case, Professor Dershowitz cited the "lifesaving information" that Manila police beat out of Murad to argue that torture can sometimes "prevent harm to civilians."[37]

But, in reality, Murad's torture did nothing of the sort. As the *Washington Post* has reported, Manila police officers got all their important information from Murad at the moment of his arrest, when they seized his laptop with full details of the entire bomb plot. Most of the supposed information gained from the sixty-seven days of incessant beatings, spiced by techniques like cigarettes to the genitals, was, as one Filipino officer testified in a New York court, police fabrications that Murad parroted to end the pain.[38]

In another real-world case, an alleged member of Al Qaeda's original 9/11 hijacking crew, Zacarias Moussaoui, sat in a Minneapolis cell in the weeks before the attacks under desultory investigation as a possible "suicide hijacker" because the FBI did not have precise foreknowledge of the terrorist plot. In pressing for a search warrant *before* 9/11, the Bureau's Minneapolis field supervisor even warned he was "trying to keep someone from taking a plane and crashing into the World Trade Center." But FBI headquarters in Washington replied that there was no evidence Moussaoui was a terrorist—providing us with yet another reminder of how difficult it is to grasp the significance of even such a stunningly accurate inference in the absence of foreknowledge. "A maximum U.S. effort to investigate Moussaoui conceivably could have unearthed his connections to [Ramzi] Binalshibh," wrote the 9/11 Commission in a flight beyond the hypothetical into the counterfactual. "Those connections might have brought investigators to the core of the 9/11 plot . . . , though it was not an easy trail to find."[39]

But, just as FBI and CIA headquarters failed to realize Moussaoui's significance in the weeks before the 9/11 attack on the Twin Towers and the Pentagon, so FBI or CIA agents might detain some future terrorists while still remaining ignorant of their intentions. "The CIA and NSA may be sleek and omniscient in the movies," reads the 2005 report of the president's Commission on Intelligence Capabilities, "but in real life they and other intelligence agencies are vast government bureaucracies."[40]

Even had Moussaoui been tortured, he might have confessed in rambling, half-crazed rhetoric to a nonexistent plot, as he actually did at his trial four years later, when he said: "I am guilty of a broad conspiracy to use a weapon of mass destruction to destroy the White House." Had he actually spoken in this megalomaniac manner when arrested in August 2001, would his FBI interrogators have attributed some significance to these ravings? Testing has found that professional interrogators perform within the 45 to 60 percent range in sorting truth from lies, little better than flipping a coin. Thus, as intelligence data move through three basic stages—acquisition/interrogation, analysis, and action—the possibility of human error is infinite and, without the divine gift of foresight, the chances that even accurate intelligence will be ignored are high. "After the event," Roberta Wohlstetter wrote in her classic study of that other great U.S. intelligence failure, Pearl Harbor, "a signal is always crystal clear; we can now see what disaster it was signaling since the disaster has occurred. But before the event it is obscure and pregnant with conflicting meanings."[41]

In the real world, the impossibility of perfect prescience makes this plea to torture the few an opening to torture of the many. Once we agree to torture that nonexistent terrorist with his hypothetical ticking bomb, then we admit a possibility, even an imperative, for torturing hundreds who might have ticking bombs or thousands who just might have some knowledge about those bombs. "You can't know whether a person knows where the bomb is," explained Georgetown University law professor David Cole, "or even if they're telling the truth. Because of this, you end up going down a slippery slope and sanctioning torture in general."[42]

Writing to the *Washington Post* in 2007, two top U.S. generals drew upon their years of command experience to warn of such a slippery slope. "As has happened with every other nation that has tried to engage in a little bit of torture," the generals wrote, "the abuse spread like wildfire, and every captured prisoner became the key to defusing a potential ticking time bomb. Our soldiers in Iraq confront real 'ticking time bomb' situations every day, in the form of improvised explosive devices, and any degree of 'flexibility' about torture at the top drops down the chain of command like a stone—the rare exception fast becoming the rule."[43]

Despite claims by CIA director Porter Goss that tough interrogation of Al Qaeda suspects led to "documented successes," the agency, in statements both on the record and off, could not claim anything akin to stopping a ticking bomb after years of torture. And there is ample precedent for such failure. "We recognize that espionage is always chancy at best," the president's Commission on Intelligence Capabilities reminded us. "50 years of pounding away at the Soviet Union resulted in only a handful of truly important human sources."[44]

Looking back on four years of using torture to fight the War on Terror, Jack Cloonan, a veteran FBI counterintelligence officer, felt that Washington had already replicated this dismal Cold War result. "Have we gotten enough information out of [Guantanamo Bay] or anywhere else to justify the negative?" Cloonan said in a 2005 interview. "There's a certain naiveté in thinking that any schmuck taken off the battlefield on any given day—or taken off a street somewhere and flown half way around the world and being held incommunicado with no rights and no charges—will know where Bin Laden is or what's going to be planned in Iraq or Afghanistan."[45]

Media as Pro-Torture Propaganda

As this "ticking-bomb" scenario began to fade from political discourse, the Bush administration's harsh interrogation policy drew political sustenance from the rapid proliferation of torture scenes in film and television. While violence had long been a staple of Hollywood films, the sudden emergence of torture as a major multimedia theme was a distinct post-9/11 phenomenon. U.S. television networks began broadcasting hundreds of hours of popular television dramas that portrayed torture as effective, even exciting; video games with elaborate torture scenarios proliferated; and major Hollywood films featured graphic torture scenes. Surveying the most popular of these displays indicates, moreover, that there was a progressive coarsening of representation, with ever more explicit violence paralleling the administration's increasingly overt embrace of torture. From all this media display, fictional agent Jack Bauer emerged as a potent symbol whose mere name could sway mass audiences toward tolerance for torture.

By the time President Bush left office in January 2009, screens large and small across America were saturated with torture simulations, serving as ad hoc propaganda for torture's efficacy often made more enticing by its eroticized representation. Through such pervasive media display, torture was, for many Americans, transformed from an unthinkable barbarism synonymous with fascist or communist regimes into a weapon necessary for U.S. national security.

While studying the effect of media upon individual behavior is difficult and positing any precise correlation between national broadcasts and public opinion is doubly so, the temporal sequence of media display and public support for torture is undeniable. Moreover, the migration of the ticking-bomb scenario and the Jack Bauer character from mass media to political debate establishes a clear connection. Over time, the repeated display in video games, television dramas, and feature films served to normalize torture, changing an inhumane criminal act into a credible policy option. By simultaneously showing torture's efficacy for interrogation and often eroticizing the experience, mass media may well have desensitized ordinary Americans to the inhumanity of abuse, ultimately allowing a rather muted public reaction to the Abu Ghraib photos.

According to the Parents Television Council, torture scenes on U.S. network broadcasts shot upward from just 20 per annum in the five years before 9/11 to more than 150 annually in the four years thereafter. Instead of the deviant drug dealers or the evil Nazis who did the torturing in the older shows, most post-9/11 perpetrators were upright U.S. officials defending America from terrorists or other malefactors.[46]

Television's first sustained engagement with harsh interrogation methods may have laid the groundwork for its treatment of torture following 9/11. For 261 shows over twelve seasons, from 1992 to 2005, Detective Andy Sipowicz, the everyman hero of ABC Television's top-rated series *NYPD Blue*, put his badge and his pension on the line by deciding to "tune up" this week's suspect with threatened or actual beatings. Although the "suits" from the district attorney's office moved in and out of the plot, regularly telling the detectives that threats and violence were morally and legally wrong, Sipowicz's approach was always vindicated, extracting timely information to solve yet another horrible crime. Looking at and learning from Andy Sipowicz, many Americans, or at least the twenty million who watched weekly, might well have believed that the "tune-up" was regrettably necessary for effective interrogation.[47]

If *NYPD Blue* exhibited a certain ambiguity about the morality of abuse, Fox Television's hit show *24* was an unrestrained advertisement for torture. First aired in October 2001, just weeks after the 9/11 attacks, *24* soon became the informal signature program of President Bush's War on Terror. By the end of his presidency in early 2009, the show had broadcast 192 episodes over the span of six seasons, each attracting between 8 and 14 million viewers. Significantly, *24* was also tops in torture, with sixty-seven such scenes during its first five seasons. By its last broadcast at the end of season eight in May 2010, the show's iconic hero, Jack Bauer, had become synonymous with torture, inspiring copycat television shows worldwide—*Sleeper Cell*, *The Unit*, and *Burn Notice* in America; *Spooks* in England; and *Time Bomb* in India.[48]

Each week, as a large clock ticked menacingly, Jack Bauer, the counterintelligence unit's lead agent played by the ruggedly masculine Kiefer Sutherland, used torture to save Los Angeles or the nation from the threat of terrorists armed with horrific weapons of mass destruction, often a nuclear bomb. With the clock displayed after each commercial break and the hero discovering a time bomb an average of twelve times each season, the show served as dramatic reification of the "ticking-bomb scenario" and its argument for torture's necessity in post-9/11 America.[49]

Some liberals such as the show's fictional president might waver, but Jack's torture was always stunningly effective, producing timely, accurate intelligence. In episode six of season five, broadcast on January 31, 2006, for example, Russian separatists acquire dozens of nerve gas canisters for terrorist attacks that could kill millions. At the last moment, Jack Bauer, in the presence of the president, interrogates the White House chief of staff, Walt Cummings, a traitor who knows the location of these lethal weapons. As the camera closes in, Jack poises the glinting steel point of his hunting knife above the traitor's moist eyeball, an enticing orb inviting penetration—much as Salvador Dali and Luis Buñuel did famously with a straight razor in their surrealist short film *Un Chien Andalou* (1929).

Jack: I don't know what this man has told you, but we need to find this nerve gas now, and I mean immediately—before it is too late.
President Logan: It's already too late.
Jack: What do you mean?
President Logan: Apparently it's on its way out of the country. . . .
Jack: Where is it? [He keeps hitting Walt.]
President Logan: He told me he doesn't know!
Jack: He's lying to you, sir.
Walt: The man I had inside has gone dark. I don't know.
[Jack pulls out a knife and holds it near Walt's eyes. President Logan grimaces.]
Jack: I'm done talking with you. . . . The first thing I'm going to do is take out your right eye, and then . . . take out your left, and then I'm going to . . . keep cutting you until you give me the information that I need. Do you understand me? So, for the last time, where is the nerve gas?
Walt: I don't know.
[Jack moves the knife closer to his eye. . . .]
Walt: Stop! Stop! Stop! I'll tell you. I'll tell you. It's on a freighter leaving the port at Longbridge at 2:30.[50]

In the 2006 season of the FOX Television show *24*, the heroic counterterrorist agent Jack Bauer tortures a traitorous White House chief of staff in the presence of the president to learn where terrorists are holding nerve gas canisters that can kill countless thousands of Americans.

Setting aside the rule of law embodied by the chief executive, Jack tortures the White House chief of staff in the president's presence and, once again, demonstrates both the success and the sensuality of torture. In the next season's heavily publicized opening episode, broadcast in January 2007, Jack is back from eighteen months of being abused inside a Chinese prison, returning home "a broken yet honorable man." In a scene of suffused sexuality, he strips off his shirt before two male colleagues to show the stigmata of torture's tracks down his torso, shaven and sculpted in the conventions of homoerotic pornography. Instead of appearing like a real-life torture survivor—shaking with trauma, emaciated, and disfigured by scabrous lesions—Jack shows the viewer his muscled torso and smooth alabaster skin, making his torture experience, as both perpetrator and now victim, seem alluring. Though nearly broken by torture, Jack is soon back on the trail of the ruthless Abu Fayed when, in episode four, the utterly unthinkable finally happens—the terrorists detonate a nuclear bomb and a mushroom cloud rises above Los Angeles.[51] Audiences responded to this approach, lifting the show to its peak of 14 million viewers and helping it win an Emmy award for best dramatic series.[52]

At the confluence of film and reality common to American culture, the show's interrogation scenarios represented torture as effective and enticing, thereby affirming for millions of loyal viewers, from active-duty soldiers to Supreme Court justices, that torture was a necessary weapon in the War on Terror. "Jack Bauer saved Los Angeles. . . . He saved hundreds of thousands of lives," U.S. Supreme Court Justice Antonin Scalia told a 2007 legal seminar in Ottawa. "Are you going to convict Jack Bauer?" he asked. "Is any jury going to convict Jack Bauer? I don't think so."[53] Similarly, Diane Beaver, who served as Staff Judge Advocate on Guantanamo's Joint Task Force in 2002–04, when it adopted harsh methods, told an interviewer that the show 24 had inspired many of the eighteen controversial interrogation techniques used on detainees, including waterboarding, sexual humiliation, and the terrorizing of prisoners with dogs. Jack Bauer, she said, "gave people lots of ideas," adding: "We saw [24] on cable [and] it was hugely popular."[54]

While those sympathetic to torture saw the show as a mirror of reality, others criticized it as a dangerous fantasy that damaged U.S. foreign policy. Concerned about the show's effect on the country's junior officers, West Point's dean of students, General Patrick Finnegan, accompanied three military and FBI interrogators on an unrewarding visit to the offices of 24's producers in Los Angeles, telling them the show was "hurting efforts to train recruits in effective interrogation techniques and is damaging the image of the U.S. around the world." Finnegan added, "I'd like them to stop," suggesting in vain that "they should do a show where torture backfires."[55]

In case the televised version of 24 left any doubt about its advocacy of torture, the video-game version allowed millions of consumers not merely to watch but to simulate torture—reinforcing the players' identification with the perpetrators, rather than the victims. Released in early 2006 on Play Station 2 by Sony Computer Entertainment, 24: The Game programmed a torture scenario into the buttons that move the chief character, Jack Bauer. "Torture is no longer . . . confined to an ambiguous moral and legal territory," observed the media analyst Mark Sample, "it has instead been incorporated deep within the structure of the game, normalizing what would otherwise be an affront to human dignity."[56]

But, in the world of video games, brutalization had just begun. In the 2008 edition of World of Warcraft, which sold a record 2.8 million copies on the first day of its release, the player uses a "Neural Needler" that "inflicts incredible pain to target" and thereby extracts accurate information from a bound sorcerer.[57] In another gratuitous game devoid of any exculpatory narrative, the "free and increasingly popular" Torture Game 2, which appeared on Internet portals in 2008, features "ragdoll physics [that] lend a sickeningly hypnotic charm to . . . every touch of your cruel hand, every cut of the chainsaw" as the player dismembers a bleeding humanoid.[58] By 2009, interactive torture scenarios were integral to a wide range of popular video games—Bethesda's Brink, The Punisher, Red Faction: Guerrilla, Killzone 2, and Grand Theft Auto: Vice City, to name just a few.[59]

The temper of these times also made torture a significant theme in a surprising number of feature films with leading stars, including George Clooney in Syriana (2005), Matt Damon in The Good Shepherd (2006), and Daniel Craig in Casino Royale (2006). Admittedly, liberal Hollywood later produced a few films critical of torture—notably Rendition (2007), a box-office bust that grossed a lackluster $27 million worldwide even though it featured major stars, including Jake Gyllenhaal, Reese Witherspoon, and Meryl Streep.[60]

With a script that was little more than a frame for sadistic, utterly gratuitous torture scenes, Hostel (2005) became a surprising box office hit, earning an impressive $81 million worldwide on a meager investment of $4.5 million.[61] At the opposite pole of movie making, the big-budget studio version of Casino Royale (2006) revitalized the fading James Bond franchise with a script whose chief innovation was an extended genital torture scene. This film depicts a brutal homoerotic sadism, expanding upon the original novel's portrayal of what its author, Ian Fleming, called a "sexual twilight where pain turned to pleasure and where hatred and fear of the torturers turned to masochistic fascination."[62]

In past Bond films, the hero's genitals were threatened with a certain decorum, notably in the famed Goldfinger (1964) scene. Still cool and confident,

Still image of the villain Auric Goldfinger torturing Agent 007, played by Sean Connery, who maintains a cool demeanor while a powerful laser beam slices through a steel table as it moves slowly toward his groin, in the 1964 film *Goldfinger*, the third in the popular James Bond series. (MPTV Images)

Agent 007 is manacled to a metal table, fully clothed while a laser beam moves slowly between his legs, burning a smoking groove in the steel sheet—until it suddenly stops just short of his crotch as Bond cleverly deceives the villainous Goldfinger. In *Casino Royale* (2006), by contrast, secret agent 007 is lashed to a chair completely naked. His shaved, muscled torso writhes in eroticized pain while an empowered terrorist pounds at his genitals with a knotted rope. Instead of succeeding in a clever escape from an impossible situation, as was mandatory in past Bond films, our contemporary 007, played by the muscular Daniel Craig, is entombed in a concrete dungeon, illuminated in the dramatic down lights of inescapable isolation, passive before the power of sexual torture. Just as the villain prepares to castrate Bond for his refusal to talk, another terrorist breaks in and, angry over the villain's failures, executes him and frees 007.

In an otherwise lackluster film that minimizes the stunning scenery and outlandish stunts of past Bond movies, this scene of sexual torture is the film's focal point—serving as the story's dramatic climax and infusing the script with the visual conventions of sadomasochistic pornography. As *Casino Royale* became a

A scene from the 2006 film *Casino Royale* showing agent James Bond (007), played by Daniel Craig, stripped naked, bound, and beaten about the genitals by the villain Le Chiffre.

box office smash with $594 million in total sales, the highest grossing among the twenty-one Bond films, millions of Americans witnessed a wide-screen spectacle of torture as subliminally erotic and devastatingly effective—a weapon so potent it can break the will of the world's most audacious secret agent.[63]

Even in a nominally religious film, *The Passion of the Christ* (2004), director Mel Gibson reverted to the medieval focus on the physicality and sensuality of Christ's torture on the road to Golgotha. Drawing on just eleven sparse words about Christ's flogging in the gospels—three words in Matthew 27:26 ("after flogging Jesus") and eight more in John 19:1 ("Then Pilate took Jesus and had him flogged")—Gibson creates an elaborate torture sequence that occupies 8 of the film's 125 minutes. After Roman soldiers lead him into a stone courtyard, Christ drops his robe to reveal a lean, shaven, blemish-free torso. Before a crowd of a hundred spectators, three burly soldiers select rods and cat-o'-nine-tails from a rack of torture implements. They then scourge Christ by beating his back into a mass of oozing lesions, laughing with satisfied, sadistic pleasure as they wipe his spattered blood from their faces. Periodically, the camera, reprising a technique from Leni Riefenstahl's *Triumph of the Will* (1935), frames the faces of both torturers and spectators, allowing viewers to insert themselves into the cinema as imagined participants in this gruesome spectacle.[64] Again, the hero/victim seems a compliant participant in his own torture, reacting

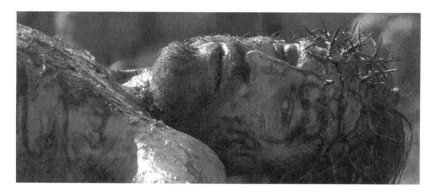

After being beaten by Roman soldiers in a long scene lasting eight minutes in the film *The Passion of the Christ* (2004), Jesus falls to the ground, his torso a mass of bleeding lesions.

with a suffused masochistic silence that transforms a vulgar inhumanity into the aestheticized mutuality of sadomasochistic bondage.

Just as grisly medieval canvasses depicting Christ's suffering normalized that era's gory rituals of punishment and public execution, so this film's blood-soaked scourging of the Messiah contributed to a torture-saturated media that may have prepared the American public for acceptance of the Abu Ghraib photos. On February 25, 2004, Gibson's gruesome film was released on 4,643 movie screens across America, and, by the end of March, it was the country's highest grossing R-rated film, eventually earning $611 million. Whether coming to the cinema as ordinary moviegoers or as pious Christians, tens of millions of Americans now saw torture normalized as a central facet in the life and death of their savior.[65]

Four weeks later on April 28, Americans offered a mixed reaction to a CBS television broadcast of those iconic images of prisoner abuse at Abu Ghraib, with some angered and others unmoved. Indeed, two months after the release of these photos, an ABC News/*Washington Post* poll found that 35 percent of Americans still felt that torture was acceptable in some circumstances.[66] Accustomed to the slick portrayals of torture in popular culture, many Americans no doubt reeled when confronted with the ugly reality of those prison photos. But style and presentation are very powerful media features, and the images of torture at Abu Ghraib looked undeniably different from its dramatization in *NYPD Blue*, *24*, and major feature films that had, in all likelihood, laid the cultural groundwork for a defense of torture. Moreover, the Bush administration soon responded in ways that reassured the American public. Officials portrayed the repellent torture of Abu Ghraib as an aberration, and a dozen official investigations reiterated that view—reassurances that reverberated throughout the national press for weeks on end. In this way, White House officials sought to isolate Abu Ghraib and inoculate themselves, their agencies, and the American public from its effects. They also worked to suppress any further leaks of any more images, successfully keeping all but a handful of those 1,600 Abu Ghraib photos securely classified—under both Bush and Obama.[67]

President Plays Jack Bauer

After the Abu Ghraib scandal broke in April 2004, America's tacit consensus for torture weakened as criticism rose at home and abroad. In the years of fitful debate that followed, media representation of torture, particularly by the fictional Jack Bauer character in Fox's *24*, became the dominant referent for embattled defenders of Bush's harsh methods.

Only weeks after CBS broadcast those sixteen Abu Ghraib photos, the Pentagon held a closed-door slide show for Congress, with hundreds more of the now-classified photos flashing by. Legislators emerged grim and shaken. "I saw cruel, sadistic torture," said Senator Bill Frist (Republican, Tennessee), the Majority Leader. Across the partisan divide, Senator Richard J. Durbin (Democrat, Illinois) said: "It felt like you were descending into one of the rings of hell, and sadly it was our own creation." On May 10, after the Senate unanimously condemned this abuse, President Bush obliquely acknowledged the problem, stating that there would be "a full accounting for the cruel and disgraceful abuse of Iraqi detainees."[68]

Apart from criticism in Congress and the press, the Bush administration faced its sharpest challenge in the courts. In June 2006, the U.S. Supreme Court ruled, in *Hamdan v. Rumsfeld*, that Bush's military commissions at Guantanamo were illegal because they violated the Geneva Conventions. Three months later on September 6, the White House staged a theatrical response that transformed a stinging Supreme Court rebuke into a stunning political victory.

Before an applauding audience of 9/11 families assembled in the East Room, President Bush announced the transfer of fourteen top Al Qaeda captives from secret CIA prisons to Guantanamo Bay. He then segued to an inspired defense of his interrogation policy. Speaking with clipped diction and secret-agent argot evocative of the Jack Bauer character in *24*, Bush told a national television audience a tale of covert action derring-do, spiced with transparent euphemisms for torture. After "they risked their lives to capture some of the most brutal terrorists on Earth," he said, courageous American agents found it "necessary to move these individuals to an environment where they can be held secretly, questioned by experts . . . outside the United States, in a separate program operated by the Central Intelligence Agency." There, Bush added, the agents "worked day and night . . . to find out what the terrorists know so we can stop new attacks."

Through these untiring efforts, said the president, these CIA operatives scored a major breakthrough by capturing "a trusted associate of Osama Bin Laden" named Abu Zubaydah—the same name that recurs repeatedly in these exculpatory accounts. But, once in custody, Zubaydah proved "defiant and evasive." Knowing that "captured terrorists have . . . intelligence that cannot be found any other place," the CIA, with White House approval, applied an "alternative set of procedures" and extracted timely information that "helped in the planning and . . . execution of the operation that captured Khalid Shaikh Mohammed."

Once in custody, "KSM was questioned by the CIA using these procedures," said Bush, producing timely intelligence that stopped a remarkable succession of ticking bombs—including "anthrax for attacks against the United States," "a planned strike on U.S. Marines at Camp Lemonier in Djibouti [with] an explosive laden water tanker," "a planned attack on the U.S. consulate in Karachi using car bombs and motorcycle bombs," "a plot to hijack passenger planes and fly them into Heathrow or the Canary Wharf in London," and "planned attacks on buildings inside the United States [with] explosives . . . to prevent the people trapped above from escaping." Beyond these specific attacks, he said, "information from terrorists in CIA custody has played a role in . . . providing everything from initial leads to photo identifications, to precise locations of where terrorists were hiding," thus taking "potential mass murderers off the streets before they were able to kill."

After all these broad hints that the CIA was engaged in torture, Bush, in a deft rhetorical twist, announced to the American people and the world: "The United States does not torture. It's against our laws, and it's against our values. I have not authorized it—and I will not authorize it." Even the "alternative set of procedures" the CIA used against Abu Zubaydah was, he insisted, reviewed by the Justice Department "to comply with our laws, our Constitution, and our treaty obligations." Although security prevented him from describing "the specific methods used," Bush assured his audience that "the procedures were tough, and they were safe, and lawful, and necessary."

To allow continuation of this critical "CIA program" with its "alternative set of procedures"—two code phrases for torture—Bush announced that he was sending legislation to Congress that would protect agency interrogators from the threat of prosecution. Amid a vigorous round of applause from the

9/11 families, Bush urged prompt passage of this bill to protect "intelligence personnel involved in capturing and questioning terrorists [who] could now be at risk of prosecution under the War Crimes Act—simply for doing their jobs in a thorough and professional way."[69]

Emulating the dialogue of the spy thriller *24*, President Bush thus made a public appeal for the president's prerogative to torture that was striking for its subtle juxtaposition of competing claims. By invoking the language of this television show and its rich visual subtexts, Bush could hint to conservatives in his audience that the CIA had used "tough" measures tantamount to torture. Bush also used his privileged access to top-secret intelligence with telling effect, offering what was shown, three years later, to be a tendentious, even specious account of the CIA's use of "alternative procedures" on Abu Zubaydah, a contradiction analyzed in chapter 7. Simultaneously, his denial of any torture assured international allies that the administration still respected human rights. With this bravura performance, Bush soon worked his will upon Congress. Just four weeks later, both houses passed, without any amendment, his omnibus anti-terrorist bill called the Military Commissions Act 2006 that prevented, just as he had directed, any prosecution of CIA interrogators for past actions and permits some future president to order torture.

Torture in the 2008 Elections

With his intuitive feel for American popular culture, President Bush used his East Room performance to make Jack Bauer the dominant metaphor for discussion of torture in the 2008 presidential campaign. In the first years of the War on Terror, the U.S. torture debate had been dominated by the hypothetical "ticking-bomb" scenario, with advocates asking audiences whether torture should be used in the rare instance when a terrorist had set the timer on a nuclear bomb in Times Square. But, by the time Bush made his East Room address, in September 2006, agent Jack Bauer was torturing anyone, friend or foe, who threatened America multiple times in every televised episode. Evading any discussion of the dismal reality inside Abu Ghraib or CIA black sites, politicians preferred to identify with this television hero and repeatedly invoked his scripted scenarios to justify tolerance for "enhanced interrogation."

As the 2008 presidential campaign started, political leaders, both Republicans and Democrats, had come to accept the reality of these hypotheticals, sometimes fusing them in a generalized argument for abuse, sometimes using them to advocate specific approaches toward torture. Within the narrowly circumscribed rhetoric of the party primaries, the ticking-bomb scenario often supported an argument for formal presidential torture warrants, while Jack Bauer signaled an informal tolerance of torture by CIA agents acting outside the law.

Following their president's lead, Bush administration officials were quick to adopt the Jack Bauer image as justification for their policy of harsh interrogation. In his 2006 book *War by Other Means*, John Yoo, a former member of Bush's Justice Department, merged the two hypotheticals, asking: "What if, as the popular Fox television program *24* recently portrayed, a high-level terrorist leader is caught who knows the location of a nuclear weapon in an American city?"[70] Similarly, Michael Chertoff, the secretary of homeland security, found Jack Bauer an inspiring figure. "This is what we do every day," said Chertoff referring to the television show *24*, "that is what we do in the government, that's what we do in private life when we evaluate risks."[71]

During the first months of the 2008 presidential campaign, there was a muted debate among the candidates over torture, with Republicans outdoing themselves to defend Bush and Democrats adopting a somewhat critical stance. An early Republican primary debate in May 2007 became what the *Los Angeles Times* called "a Jack Bauer impersonation contest." When presented with the ticking-time-bomb scenario, Mitt Romney replied: "You said the person's going to be in Guantanamo. I'm glad they're at Guantanamo. . . . Some people have said we ought to close Guantanamo. My view is, we ought to double Guantanamo." And he added, using Bush's euphemism for torture: "Enhanced interrogation techniques have to be used." Similarly, Representative Tom Tancredo (Republican, Colorado) said: "We're wondering about whether water-boarding would be a—a bad thing to do? I'm looking for Jack Bauer at that time, let me tell you." Both comments were greeted with applause and laughter from the audience. Asked the same question, former New York mayor Rudolf Guiliani replied: "I would tell the [interrogators] to use every method. . . . It shouldn't be torture, but every method they can think of." And, the moderator asked, what about waterboarding? "I would—and I would—well," said Guiliani, "I'd say every method they could think of." Only Senator John McCain, who had been tortured as a POW in North Vietnam, dissented, reminding viewers that "it's not about the terrorists, it's about us. It's about what kind of country we are."[72]

While most prominent Democrats avoided the issue, former president Bill Clinton, chief adviser to the presidential campaign of his wife, Hillary Rodham Clinton, tried to stake out a centrist position for his party by coopting the two fictions used by torture advocates. "If they really believe that that scenario is likely to occur," Clinton told National Public Radio in September 2006, referring the to the "ticking-bomb" hypothetical, "then let them come forward with an alternative proposal, which allows the intelligence services of the country to come to the president for a finding which then could be reviewable even on a post-facto basis by the Foreign Intelligence Surveillance Court. In other words, we have a system of laws here where nobody should be above the law, and you don't need blanket advance approval."[73]

That same month on NBC's *Meet the Press*, Bill Clinton again invoked the ticking-bomb hypothetical to argue for creation of a presidential torture warrant. "Every one of us can imagine the following scenario," said Clinton. "We get lucky, we get the number three guy in al-Qaeda, and we know there's a big bomb going off in America in three days, and we know this guy knows where it is, know we have the right and the responsibility to beat it out of him. They could set up a law where the president could make a finding or could guarantee a pardon . . . post-facto to the intelligence court just like we do now with the wiretaps."[74]

In marked contrast to her husband's ambiguous bumbling on this issue, Hillary Clinton herself flatly rejected these fanciful scenarios as a justification for torture. "As a matter of policy, it cannot be American policy period," she said on NBC's *Meet the Press* in September 2007. "Now, there are a lot of other things that we need to be doing that I wish we were: better intelligence, making . . . our country better respected around the world, working to have more allies. But these hypotheticals are very dangerous, because they open a great big hole in what should be an attitude that our country and our president takes toward the appropriate treatment of everyone. And I think it's dangerous to go down this path."[75]

Confronted with his wife's very public rejection of his position, Bill Clinton quickly jettisoned the ticking-bomb hypothetical and embraced the other iconic argument for torture, Jack Bauer. Within hours, Clinton abandoned his recommendation for presidential torture warrants, telling the New York *Daily News* that individual agents should, like the fictional hero, defy the law on their own to torture suspects when necessary. "If you're the Jack Bauer person," said Clinton, speaking of this television character as if he were real, "you'll do whatever you do and you should be prepared to take the consequences. . . . If you have any kind of a formal exception, people just drive a truck through it, and they'll say, 'Well, I thought it was covered by the exception.' . . . When Bauer goes out there on his own and is prepared to live with the consequences, it always seems to work better."[76]

Six months later, as Hillary Clinton faced off against Barack Obama in the April 2008 Pennsylvania primary, the CNN cable network hosted a "Compassion Forum" on faith and politics. Dr. David Gushee, president of Evangelicals for Human Rights, asked whether there was any "justification for policies on the part of our nation that permit physical and mental cruelty toward those who are in our custody." In his response, Obama went beyond any other candidate, including Hillary Clinton, to offer unqualified opposition not only to direct U.S. use of torture but also to indirect involvement through rendition. "We have to be clear and unequivocal. We do not torture, period. . . . Our government does not torture," he said, adding: "That will be my position as president. That includes, by the way, renditions. We don't farm out torture. We don't subcontract torture." In defense of this position, Obama offered a sustained critique of torture, starting with a pragmatic question of efficacy:

Torture does not end up yielding good information—most intelligence officers agree with that. I met with . . . a distinguished group of former generals who . . . talk in forums about how this degrades the discipline and the ethos of our military. It is very hard for us when kids, you know, 19, 20, 21, 22 are in Iraq having . . . to restrain themselves and operate within the law. And then to find out that our own government is not abiding by these same laws that we are asking them to defend? That is not acceptable.

Interrupted by frequent bursts of applause, Obama then moved to matters of principle, saying we must "send a message to the world that we will lead not just with our military might but we are going to lead with our values and our ideals. That we are not a nation that gives away our civil liberties simply because we're scared." Then, with the moving rhetoric that would soon win the election, Obama concluded: "Fear is a bad counsel and I want to operate out of hope and out of faith."[77]

But, in the transition from Bush to Obama after the 2008 presidential elections, the dynamics of partisan wrangling over CIA interrogation produced a bipartisan move toward impunity for past abuse. In this slide toward impunity, the Republicans deployed Jack Bauer in ways that pushed the Obama White House to compromise its commitment to human rights.

Only days after an attempted suicide bombing on a Northwest Airlines flight near Detroit in December 2009, Liz Cheney, the former vice president's daughter, launched a new patriotic group, "Keep America Safe." Using the distinctive split-screen visuals of the television show 24, the group's website released a video titled "100 Hours" that mocked Obama's response to this terrorist threat, juxtaposing video clips of federal officers surrounding the aircraft at Detroit, the president playing golf in Hawaii, and White House officials insisting that the "system worked." Amid the pulsating sound track and the flashing clock graphics from 24, the video closed with a question: "How long did it take you to realize the system failed?"[78] Simultaneously, the group's online manifesto blasted Obama, saying: "He should inform Attorney General Holder that he will no longer allow the Justice Department . . . to investigate or prosecute CIA officials who kept us safe after 9/11, or disbar or otherwise punish the lawyers who provided the legal framework for programs that saved American lives."[79]

Within weeks, the administration capitulated. In February 2010, as detailed in chapter 7, Obama's Justice Department exonerated two former White House lawyers, Jay Bybee and John Yoo, for writing memos permissive of torture under President Bush, removing any possibility of future prosecution or disbarment.[80]

Illustrating the power of these media metaphors to undercut the administration's opposition to torture, Obama's second nominee for CIA director, General David Petraeus, cited the ticking bomb scenario at his June 2011 confirmation hearings. When the Senate Intelligence Committee asked for his views about "enhanced interrogation techniques widely considered to be torture," the general said the legal methods in the Army Field Manual had generally proven effective. But, he added, the CIA should be allowed to consider the use of enhanced techniques if confronted with a ticking bomb scenario. "I would submit . . . that there may be consideration of a special case," he said, when "you have the individual in your hands who you know has placed a nuclear device under the Empire State Building. It goes off in thirty minutes. He has the codes to turn it off." For such a "special case," Petraeus urged formation of a policy that would spare CIA field officers from being forced to consider torture "under an extraordinary sense of pressure in such a situation."[81]

In written answers to further questions, the general elaborated saying, "the 'ticking time bomb' scenario does pose a unique set of challenges that must be discussed at length before such a situation arises. We may face situations where large numbers of U.S. citizens face an imminent threat. In such time-constrained scenario, policy makers may have not had the luxury to allow interrogators to take the time to establish the type of relationship that will provide valuable intelligence."[82]

Just as his predecessor Leon Panetta had used the confirmation hearing to claim the CIA's right to rendition, so General Petraeus took the next step down this slippery slope, seeking a pretext for the agency's authority to torture on its own. Although the general stated unequivocally that the CIA should be allowed to torture in defiance of law and treaty, his invocation of the iconic ticking bomb scenario seemed to insulate him from any criticism. The Senate lavished praise upon Petraeus before confirming his nomination as CIA director unanimously.[83]

Torture in the 2012 Campaign

By the time the Republican race for the 2012 presidential nomination moved into high gear, torture had become, through this decade of media discussion, fully normalized—no longer a crime that shocked the conscience and violated international law, but a routine policy option whose adoption or rejection was a matter of personal preference. At the Republican foreign policy debate in South Carolina, the leading candidates advocated waterboarding in a matter-of-fact manner, stripped of artifice or euphemism or allusion. Asked "whether waterboarding constitutes torture or is an enhanced technique," candidate Herman Cain said it was not torture and promised to revive the practice if elected. Similarly, Representative Michele Bachmann (Republican, Minnesota) called waterboarding "very effective" and condemned President Obama for "allowing the A.C.L.U. to run the C.I.A."

Straining to best his opponents in pleasing the Republican Party's right wing, front-runner Mitt Romney insisted that anyone bearing arms for Al Qaeda "is fair game for the United States of America." Excoriating Obama for thinking "America's just another nation," Romney insisted "America is an exceptional nation" and promised "to conduct foreign policy . . . with American strength." In case conservatives thought he was ducking the question, Romney later confirmed his view that waterboarding was not torture and promised to use "enhanced interrogation techniques . . . against terrorists." In this jarring juxtaposition, Romney seemed to say that America's exceptional moral stature allowed it the prerogative of torture.[84]

Two minor candidates, both trailing badly in the polls, dissented during this debate. The libertarian Representative Ron Paul (Republican, Texas) insisted that "waterboarding is torture and . . . it's illegal under international law and under our law. It's also immoral. And it's also very impractical. There's no evidence that you really get reliable evidence." He added: "I think it's uncivilized . . . and has no practical advantages and is really un-American to accept on principle that we will torture people that we capture." Former U.S. ambassador Jon Huntsman drew upon his international experience to argue: "We diminish our standing in the world and the values that we project which include liberty, democracy, human rights, and open markets when we torture. We should not torture. Waterboarding is torture."[85]

Asked about this advocacy of waterboarding by the Republican candidates, President Obama told a press conference: "They're wrong. Waterboarding is torture. It's contrary to America's traditions. It's contrary to our ideals. That's not who we are. That's not how we operate. We don't need it in order to prosecute the war on terrorism. And we did the right thing by ending that practice." In a reprise of his position during the 2008 campaign, he added: "If we want to lead around the world, part of our leadership is setting a good example. And anybody who has actually read about and understands the practice of waterboarding would say that that is torture. And that's not something we do—period."[86]

With a certain sadness, Senator John McCain, the Republican Party's candidate in 2008, said "waterboarding is torture," and pronounced himself "very disappointed" by statements to the contrary in his party's debates. More forcefully, the *New York Times* called Romney's refusal to renounce waterboarding "disturbing," saying he joined the ranks of those who "will defend the United States by promising to extract information from captives using pain and simulating death, degrading the nation's reputation."[87] After a decade of the War on Terror, torture had been transformed from a covert executive action, shrouded in secrecy, to a policy option openly debated by the nation's leaders.

Amidst this ongoing Republican primary campaign, the U.S. Senate adopted, by a crushing 93 to 7 bipartisan majority, a draft of the 2012 defense appropriation with draconian provisions far beyond anything the Bush administration had proposed—including, indefinite detention without trial for all suspected of terrorism including U.S. citizens, military justice for all terrorist suspects, and their mandatory detention at Guantanamo.[88] An impassioned debate, resonant with inflections from the ticking bomb scenario and the television show *24*, arose over a Republican amendment proposing a secret interrogation protocol that would override President Obama's executive order limiting all agencies to techniques in the Army Field Manual.

While admitting "the horrible abuses that happened at Abu Ghraib prison . . . tarnished America's reputation," Senator Kelly Ayotte (Republican, New Hampshire) complained that "terrorists can go online and . . . know exactly which techniques they will be subject to if captured," making the Army Manual "the equivalent of interrogation CliffsNotes to terrorists." Then in a rhetorical bow to Jack Bauer, the senator pleaded for measures "to *prevent nuclear attacks* and protect our country." To this end, she proposed Amendment 1068 for development of a harsh "classified annex . . . that would allow members of the intelligence community . . . to utilize interrogation techniques . . . designed to interrogate the worst terrorists who are likely to have valuable information about future attacks." Talking tough in support of this secret protocol, Senator Joseph Lieberman (Independent, Connecticut) said he wanted any terrorist captured "to be terrified about what is going to happen to them while in American custody." He added: "I want the terror they inflict on others to be felt by them."[89]

Calling this amendment "dangerous," the chair of the Senate Intelligence

Committee, Dianne Feinstein (Democrat, California), replied that the "systematic and widespread" abuse of detainees at Abu Ghraib and elsewhere had come "from the fact the line was blurred between what was permissible and impermissible conduct." In 2009, she added, the interagency High Value Detainee Interrogation Group, comprised of CIA and Defense, "unanimously asserted that it had all the guidance and tools it needed to conduct effective interrogations."[90] After arousing strong opposition from both peace activists and a coalition of twenty-six retired generals, this amendment died quietly when the Senate ruled it "non-germane" on procedural grounds.[91]

Even with the secret interrogation protocol removed, the final form of the Senate's National Defense Authorization Act for 2012 was extreme. As supporter Senator Lindsey Graham (Republican, South Carolina) explained, the bill will "basically say in law for the first time that the homeland is part of the battlefield" and suspects can be imprisoned without charge or trial, "American citizen or not." By effectively barring the FBI from counterterror investigations, the bill also aroused strong opposition from bureau director Robert Mueller, Defense Secretary Leon Panetta, and CIA director David Petraeus.[92]

Although a House-Senate conference committee moderated the text, the defense appropriation's final language still allowed indefinite detention of U.S. citizens suspected of terrorist affiliations without charges or trial. And the stipulation for military custody of all non-American terror suspects had been moderated by granting the president authority to waive the requirement. Mollified by these changes, President Obama withdrew his threatened veto and signed the bill into law in December 2011. Simultaneously, the president issued a signing statement criticizing the requirement for military custody as "ill conceived." Calling Obama's reversal "a complete political cave-in," the *New York Times* condemned the law's "terrible new measures" that required military trial for suspected terrorists, even U.S. citizens, allowed the president authority "to throw American citizens into prison for life without charges or trial," and made "it impossible to shut the prison at Guantanamo Bay." In sum, this law would, the paper said, "do more harm to the country's international reputation." Apparently such strong criticism had an impact. Two months later, in February 2012, the administration issued a broad waiver in any case when military custody might impede investigation, effectively assuring civilian trials for most terror suspects. Other objectionable provisions, however, remained.[93]

After ten full years of ticking bomb scenarios and televised torture scenes, the nation's political discourse had shifted sharply in directions that made mainstream conservatives vocal advocates of torture and the Congress willing to circumscribe the nation's civil liberties. The last U.S. troops had left Iraq and the War on Terror had wound down, but these media metaphors remained imbedded in American political consciousness, shaping political debate and public policy. A full decade after the 9/11 attacks, fiction and fantasy continued to frame key facets of U.S. national security policy.

Conclusion

So what meaning can we retrieve from America's interweaving of state practice and media representations of torture? Driven by impulses and desires from within the dark, still unexplored recesses of the human mind, many find torture so alluring, so compelling that there is no such thing as a little bit of torture. Whether wracked by fears or enticed by empowerment, the most senior officials of the Bush administration chose time and again to parse the law and press ahead with interrogation methods that were nothing other than torture in the eyes of the international community, whether the International Red Cross or close allies like the United Kingdom.

Once such extreme methods became state policy, much of the press abjured its role as the critical fourth estate and instead became a megaphone for persuading the American people to accept this illegal policy as an exigency of war. And the American people, on the whole, allowed themselves to be persuaded. During the first months of the War on Terror, mass media, both newspapers and television, publicized Professor Dershowitz's "ticking-time-bomb" scenario without subjecting it to any serious critical examination. Reporters for the *Washington Post* and the *New York Times* did provide detailed reports from Israel and the Philippines controverting the only evidence that advocates of this scenario could offer. But the lengthy texts of these articles lacked the impact of the succinct hypotheticals aired repeatedly on television and editorial pages. While the views of Dershowitz and fellow torture advocates appeared on mass media seen by millions, dissenters usually published their critiques in academic journals read by dozens.[94] Reverberating endlessly in the media echo chamber, the "ticking-bomb" scenario gained credence and shaped U.S. public debate over torture even though its sole basis was a hypothetical exercise in philosophy published thirty years earlier in an obscure academic journal.

Very quickly, however, argument of any description, no matter how flawed, gave way to the raw emotive visuals of torture scenarios in film, television, and video games. As mass media filled screens large and small with such simulations, Fox's *24* introduced the character Jack Bauer as an American cultural icon for the age of terror. Through a complex emotional layering of split-screen visuals, ticking clock, pulsating music, and eroticized torture moments, the show's phenomenal impact soon made the mere mention of his name a complete and convincing argument for abuse. Across the political spectrum, Bill Clinton praised him, President Bush imitated him, and Justice Scalia cited him. Through this mix of fiction and fantasy masquerading as logic and evidence, the American people set aside law, constitution, and UN convention to accept torture, shrouded in the euphemism of "enhanced interrogation," as necessary for their national security.

These eight years of multimedia torture displays—lurid, stimulating, even seductive—may have coarsened the country's popular culture, with unpredictable consequences for its political process in years to come. Will such spectacular defiance of law and morality introduce a corrosive cynicism into the country's political process, eroding the already strained civility among rival parties and their leaders? The impact will likely be too subtle, too elusive for polling or other standard tools of political analysis. Absent conventional means or metric to measure the impact of the arts upon politics, we might best turn to the stage.

In April 2009, just as the Obama administration was releasing those graphic Bush-era torture memos, New York playwright Christopher Durang, whose forte was close examination of American culture, staged a two-hour drawing room comedy, *Why Torture Is Wrong and the People Who Love Them*. Amidst zany repartee and absurdist humor, the play was a seriously satirical look at the percolation of twisted values into an ordinary suburban household. When daughter marries a maybe Middle Eastern terrorist after a one-night stand, Dad does what any right-thinking conservative would do and tortures the new son-in-law in his upstairs Abu Ghraib den, severing three fingers and an ear in a paroxysm of patriotic zeal. "John Yoo from the Justice Department wrote a torture memo saying that it isn't torture unless it causes organ failure," says Dad, justifying dismemberment in defense of the nation. "I myself feel that the play is a catharsis, a comic catharsis, for the last eight years," Durang told the *New York Times*. "What's particularly strange and unusual, though, is the play running when all of a sudden all these torture memos are released and discussed."[95]

The play lurches to an expected ending, as daughter stops the action and suggests reversing all that has happened because, she says, the torture troubles her. "Someone said to me that the play's ending captures our desire to undo the last eight years," explained its artistic director. "I do think Chris [Durang] was tapping into a longing in this country that is very deep to redo things, to say, 'Torture is not who we are.'" Despite its controversial subject and sharp criticism of senior Bush aides, this play struck a responsive chord, winning positive reviews, an extended New York run, a Pulitzer Prize nomination, and road productions in Philadelphia, Washington, DC, and cities across America.[96]

Meanwhile, the Bush administration, seconded by Obama, succeeded in helping most of the American public file Abu Ghraib away in some remote corner of the national psyche. Yet, those images of torture will survive indefinitely in the global media, greatly damaging America's international image and diminishing its capacity for world leadership. Those photos of ordinary U.S. soldiers reveling in an orgy of torture are unstoppable, etched in computer hard drives and human memory for years to come. Indeed, Susan Sontag makes that telling point in her essay when she reminds us that "in our digital hall of mirrors, the pictures aren't going to go away" and will, over time, inflict "damage—to our reputation, our image, our success as the lone superpower."[97]

6

 The Outcast of Camp
Echo

On or about January 11, 2002, a small, slender, twenty-six-year-old Australian named David Hicks, recently captured fighting alongside the Taliban in Afghanistan, was one of the first detainees flown to Guantanamo Bay, Cuba, for incarceration at Camp X-Ray. As a high-school dropout, former drug addict, sometime car thief, mercenary soldier in Kosovo, Taliban fighter against America, graduate of four terrorist-training courses, and unconvincing convert to radical Islam, Hicks seemed to many Americans and Australians alike the despicable face of global terror.[1]

As the first of seven hundred detainees began to arrive at Guantanamo, U.S. Defense Secretary Donald Rumsfeld branded them "the most dangerous, best trained, vicious killers on the face of the earth."[2] Australia's prime minister, John Howard, seconded that view, saying of Hicks: "He knowingly joined the Taliban and Al Qaeda. I don't have any sympathy for any Australian who's done that."[3] On January 14, Canberra's attorney general, Daryl Williams, dismissed concerns over the conditions of Hicks's confinement, calling the detainees "about as dangerous as a person can be in modern times."[4] In his reply to a father's desperate plea for Australia to "arrange contact between David and his family," the attorney general delivered a cool brush-off, saying this was "ultimately a matter for the United States."[5] While the United Kingdom would soon recoil from the harsh conditions at Guantanamo and demand repatriation of all nine of its nationals confined there, Prime Minister Howard led his countrymen in washing their hands of Australia's two Guantanamo detainees, Hicks and a later arrival, Mamdouh Habib.

From the start, a handful of American and Australian civil libertarians realized the dangers of the Guantanamo legal regime. Only days after Hicks reached the camp, attorney Michael Ratner, chair of New York's Center for

Constitutional Rights, decided he had to defend the Australian—no matter how unpalatable his record might be—because his status as an "unlawful combatant" threatened the rule of law at home and abroad. "When it became known that I was representing him," Ratner recalled, "I got the worst hate mail I have ever received. I got letters asking me why I didn't just let the Taliban come to my house and eat my children."[6] Similarly, when Hicks's trial started before Guantanamo's controversial military commission, the Melbourne lawyer Lex Lasry, an Australian observer, warned: "This is much less about David Hicks than it is about . . . Australia's own moral authority . . . if it continues to condone this process as 'fair or just.'"[7]

Though they were just two among seven hundred detainees, these Australians soon achieved extraordinary significance for both advocates and opponents of the U.S. anti-terror regime. Mamdouh Habib's years of brutal torture would, when reported by the *New York Times* in 2005, become a chilling cautionary tale about the capricious use of rendition and torture as secret weapons in the War on Terror.[8] For his part, Hicks was eventually singled out for the most extreme form of sensory deprivation: eight months of total isolation in a windowless cell at Camp Echo, an isolated cluster of wooden buildings used by the CIA and the U.S. military for the intensive interrogation of up to two dozen high-value detainees.[9] Among hundreds of prisoners, Hicks was picked as the first to stand trial, on White House orders, in a test of its new military commissions, a hybrid system of presidential courts that would prove enormously controversial.

But, most important, Hicks was one of the few to resist Guantanamo's devastating mix of interrogation and isolation and to persevere, without compromise, in a habeas corpus action that would later become the landmark Supreme Court case *Rasul v. Bush*. Starting only weeks after detainees arrived at Guantanamo, Michael Ratner fought the case on behalf of Hicks and two British detainees, Asif Iqbal and Shafiq Rasul, through the lower courts, challenging President Bush's right to hold these prisoners indefinitely as "enemy combatants" without civil or human rights—an argument that the U.S. Supreme Court would affirm, two years later, in a stinging rebuke to the president's policy.[10]

Stripped of all rights as an "unlawful combatant," isolated inside a concrete cell, abandoned by his homeland, and pushed to the brink of suicide, David Hicks somehow managed, despite his utter powerlessness, to defy the world's most powerful person, George W. Bush.[11] His tenacious, possibly courageous resistance to months of psychological torture denied the White House a potent conviction that would have legitimated its regime of inhumane interrogation and extralegal incarceration. Whatever Hicks might have been before he reached Guantanamo, his five-year passage down this latter-day Via Dolorosa of brutal beatings, endless solitary confinement, and mock trials transformed him into an unlikely yet potent symbol for the sanctity of human rights. For what was being done to this outcast, stripped of diplomatic protection and reduced to a hapless human subject in Bush's anti-terror regime, could also be done to others.

Indeed, in April 2004, as Hicks, forgotten by Canberra and his countrymen, was entering his tenth month of solitary confinement and sensory deprivation at Guantanamo, the world got its first glimpse of detainee treatment when CBS Television broadcast those disturbing photographs from Abu Ghraib prison of Iraqis naked and hooded. Although Secretary Rumsfeld assured Congress that this abuse was "perpetrated by a small number of U.S. military," these photos revealed the innovative psychological torture techniques that had metastasized inside the U.S. intelligence community since the 9/11 attacks and that were being used, albeit less spectacularly, on Guantanamo detainees like David Hicks.

Just as the significance of Hicks's seemingly bizarre treatment becomes clear when seen through the lens of CIA torture techniques, so the painful experiences of these two Australian detainees provide a unique way to penetrate the opacity of hundreds of faceless Guantanamo "terrorists" and thereby grasp the human cost of the secret U.S. prisons that Amnesty International has called the "gulag of our time."[12] Perhaps most important, a close study of the incarceration of this seemingly inconsequential individual, David Hicks, allows us to calculate the incalculable damage that Abu Ghraib and Guantanamo have done to America's moral authority as world leader.

Guantanamo Bay

In the months following the 9/11 attacks, the Bush administration began building a global gulag for torture at Abu Ghraib, Guantanamo, and at least eight CIA "black sites" worldwide. After the president signed a classified order soon after 9/11 that gave the agency "new powers" to detain captives on its own, Washington negotiated supporting agreements for secret prisons in Thailand, Afghanistan, Eastern Europe, and Diego Garcia Island. When harsh physical techniques were needed, the CIA, continuing a practice used against Al Qaeda suspects since the mid-1990s, engaged in "extraordinary rendition" by flying detainees to allied nations notorious for torture: Morocco, Egypt, Jordan, Syria, and Uzbekistan. Inside the long-established U.S. Navy base at Guantanamo, the CIA also operated an austere cluster of huts concealed inside "Camp Echo," the Pentagon's interrogation center where Hicks would later spend eight months. Knitting this far-flung prison network together, the agency shuttled its captives around the globe in a fleet of two dozen jets operated by front companies, which made some 2,600 rendition-related flights between 2001 and 2005.[13]

Complementing these covert operations, the Bush administration also drafted formal regulations, starting in November 2001, that stripped detainees of Geneva Convention protections and allowed both indefinite incarceration and prosecution before special military commissions. In drafting these provisions and their complementary court procedures, administration attorneys avoided anything but the most cursory consultation with the country's leading specialists in military law, the senior officers of the Judge Advocate General (JAG) corps.[14]

As the administration prepared for the incarceration of terror suspects at Guantanamo, John Yoo, a senior Justice Department lawyer, prepared a memo arguing that this U.S. Navy base was not on American territory and was thus beyond the writ of U.S. courts.[15] Simultaneously, Secretary Rumsfeld crafted conditions for confinement that, in the view of Hicks's civilian attorney, Joshua Dratel, made Guantanamo a "physical and legal island" where Washington could do whatever it wanted.[16] As Major Michael Mori, the military lawyer later assigned to defend Hicks, explained, Rumsfeld exercised "overall control of the prosecution arm, he . . . approves charges against individuals, he . . . creates rules and regulations as well."[17] In a series of controversial orders, the defense secretary denied detainees protection under the Geneva Conventions, convened military commissions that mocked U.S. standards of justice, and issued secret instructions for inhumane interrogation. But, above all, by authorizing extreme techniques beyond those allowed by the Army Field Manual and assigning a handpicked general to carry out his commands, Rumsfeld transformed Guantanamo into an ad hoc behavioral science laboratory. Its inmates became involuntary human subjects for experiments that refined the CIA's psychological torture paradigm.

When the first Afghan captives started arriving at Guantanamo on January 11, 2002, Rumsfeld accepted the advice of his neoconservative staff attorneys and denied these detainees legal status as prisoners of war, saying: "Unlawful combatants do not have any rights under the Geneva Convention." He added: "We have indicated that we do plan to, for the most part, treat them in a manner that is reasonably consistent with the Geneva Conventions, to the extent they are appropriate."[18] Although U.S. Admiral John Stufflebeem branded the Guantanamo detainees, whose numbers soon reached seven hundred, "the worst of the worst," a study by Seton Hall Law School later found that 86 percent of prisoners on the Pentagon's inventory were arrested not by U.S. forces but by Afghan and Pakistani mercenaries eager for the $5,000 bounty on each captive. Leaflets airdropped across Afghanistan were inviting people to "inform the intelligence service and get the big prize."[19] While there were, no doubt, about forty or fifty hardened Al Qaeda members at Guantanamo, most prisoners were hapless tribesmen or poor peasants brought in by bounty hunters: not the worst of the worst, but the least of the least.

In October 2002, after just ten months of Guantanamo's operation as the chief U.S. prison for the War on Terror, the Pentagon removed General Rick Baccus as commander after complaints from military interrogators that he "coddled" detainees by restraining abusive guards. Appointed in November with Pentagon orders to get tough and get information, General Geoffrey D. Miller would hold the post for a critical year, developing new doctrines for harsh interrogation that would spread to Iraq.[20]

To facilitate this work, Guantanamo interrogators asked the Southern Command chief, General James T. Hill, for more latitude in interrogating potential assets, such as the camp's most valuable prisoner, Mohamed al-Kahtani, a twenty-six-year-old Saudi dubbed "the twentieth hijacker." In support of their request, General Hill sent the Pentagon a memo from Guantanamo's Joint Task Force 170 that recommended, first, "stress positions (like standing) for a maximum of four hours"; second, "isolation facility for up to 30 days"; third, "deprivation of light and auditory stimuli"; fourth, hooding; fifth, "use of 20-hour interrogations"; and, finally, "wet towel and dripping water to induce the misperception of suffocation."[21] In sum, these orders refined the two foundational techniques for psychological torture developed by the CIA during the Cold War—sensory deprivation and self-inflicted pain, with an additional level called waterboarding.

When these requests reached the Pentagon in November 2002, senior military lawyers warned that the proposed techniques violated U.S. law and diplomatic conventions. The head of the Army's International Law Division wrote a memo arguing that the proposed use of stress positions, deprivation of light and auditory stimuli, and exploitation of personal phobias "crosses the line of 'humane' treatment," would 'likely be considered maltreatment" under the Uniform Code of Military Justice (UCMJ), and "may violate the torture statute." This senior Army attorney found Guantanamo's request for tough techniques "legally insufficient" and recommended additional review. Senior attorneys for the Air Force, the Marines, and the Criminal Investigative Task Force reached similar conclusions. But Rumsfeld's chief counsel, a neoconservative lawyer named William J. Haynes II, wrote a one-page memo endorsing all but three of the eighteen techniques that Guantanamo had requested, including "stress positions, removal of clothing, use of phobias (such as fear of dogs), and deprivation of light and auditory stimuli."[22]

Consequently, in early December, Defense Secretary Rumsfeld "approved" sixteen techniques beyond the seventeen already allowed in the U.S. Army's standard FM 34–52 interrogation manual, written in the early 1990s to comply with the Geneva Conventions. By authorizing a multifaceted attack on sensory receptors, Rumsfeld's orders had a devastating impact on their first target, al-Kahtani, who, for fifty days from November 2002 to January 2003, was subjected to twenty-hour interrogation sessions spiked by novel psychological pressures. After guards filled al-Kahtani's bladder full with more than three bags of intravenous fluid, they denied him a toilet break until he answered questions. When his replies proved unsatisfactory, interrogators made him urinate in his pants. Playing upon Arab attitudes toward dogs, the Guantanamo guards, in their entry for December 20, 2002, wrote: "Began teaching the detainee lessons such as stay, come, and bark to elevate his social status up to that of a dog. Detainee became very agitated."[23]

These procedures and the legal opinions that permitted them were the work of a wider circle of neoconservative lawyers inside the Bush administration, many of them networked through the Federalist Society—Alberto Gonzales, counsel to the president; John Yoo, a political appointee in the Justice Department; William Haynes, chief counsel to Secretary Rumsfeld; and, above all, David Addington, chief of staff to Vice President Cheney. Their ascent was the culmination of a conservative revolt against the liberal effort to restrain executive authority during the Vietnam War. The epicenter of this movement was the Federalist Society, founded in 1982 to fight, in the words of its website, an "orthodox liberal ideology which advocates a centralized and uniform society" by creating "a conservative and libertarian intellectual network that extends to all levels of the legal community," including, by 2006, three U.S. Supreme Court justices. Inspired by a neoconservative doctrine of overarching presidential power called "the New Paradigm," these administration attorneys argued that, in wartime, the president should suspend all domestic laws or international treaties to defend the nation, thus correcting restraints imposed upon executive power by Congress during the Vietnam era.[24]

Not only did their advice set aside the Geneva Conventions of 1948, which requires "civilized" justice for captives, but these neoconservative lawyers also ignored the U.S. Uniform Code of Military Justice, which was drafted in 1950 to meet this international standard. For a half-century, these two foundational texts guided generations of military lawyers in the Judge Advocate General (JAG) corps within the four branches of the U.S. military. Just as the neoconservative lawyers revived the sovereign prerogatives of the Tudor-Stuart monarchs to order torture, so these JAGs were heirs to two great revolutions against such unchecked state power. In the seventeenth century, the English Civil War against Stuart absolutism brought appointment of the British army's first Judge Advocate General, codification of habeas corpus, and abolition of torture. Closer to home, the eighteenth-century American Revolution barred the use of coerced or tortured testimony under the Fifth Amendment to the U.S. Constitution. More immediately, these neoconservative lawyers were political appointees loyal to a party and a president; while the JAG attorneys were military professionals sworn to "defend the Constitution of the United States against all enemies, foreign and domestic."

At every major turn in America's torture debate under Bush, events evolved, directly or indirectly, through a bitter struggle between these military attorneys and the neoconservative lawyers inside the administration. While mid-ranking JAG defense attorneys fought Bush's military commissions at Guantanamo, the military's top JAG commanders would speak out with stunning effectiveness, sparking opposition to Bush's policies in both Congress and the courts.

Indeed, inside the Pentagon the most vocal opposition to Rumsfeld's orders for harsh treatment at Guantanamo came from the Navy's general counsel, Alberto J. Mora. Learning of the abusive techniques from his investigators at Guantanamo, Mora objected strenuously, stating that interrogations authorized by the secretary "could rise to the level of torture." Insisting that the Pentagon's senior attorney, William Haynes, consider the deeper legal implications of these techniques, Mora, an old-school conservative who equated torture with communism, asked: "What did 'deprivation of light and auditory stimuli' mean? Could a detainee be locked in a completely dark cell? And for how long? A month? Longer?" But Haynes, a forceful leader of the neoconservative coterie, insisted that "some U.S. officials believe the techniques were necessary to obtain information from . . . Guantanamo detainees."[25]

In mid-January 2003, Mora finally threw down the gauntlet, threatening to sign a formal legal finding that these techniques "constituted, at a minimum, cruel and unusual treatment and, at worst, torture." Within days, Rumsfeld retreated and ordered an internal review by a working group that soon produced a draft document with a narrow definition of torture and a broad interpretation of executive power.[26]

Rejecting these arguments, senior military lawyers advocated strict adherence to U.S. law and international treaties. In February 2003, the deputy JAG for the Air Force, Major General Jack Rives, warned that the "more extreme interrogation techniques, on their face, amount to violations of domestic criminal law and the UCMJ" and placed "interrogators . . . at risk of criminal accusations" at home and abroad. Should information about "the more extreme interrogation techniques become public," it will attract press coverage that, he said, "could have a negative impact on international, and perhaps even domestic, support for the war on terrorism."[27]

All these warnings by senior JAG lawyers were informed by decades of military experience. All would prove unerringly prescient. All were ignored. On March 8, 2003, Secretary Rumsfeld staged a final meeting of the working group, thanking the members for their service and mouthing soothing platitudes about "the need to ensure that Group's recommendations were consistent with U.S. law and values." As it turned out, however, Mora and his military allies had been deceived. Adopting a clever "two-track" policy, the defense secretary publicly abjured abuse while issuing top-secret orders for torture at Guantanamo. In April, therefore, Rumsfeld restored the wide latitude for Guantanamo interrogators, albeit with a few new restrictions, sanctioning seven methods beyond the seventeen in the Army's field manual, including "environmental manipulation," "reversing sleep cycles from night to day," and isolation for up to thirty days. Through back channels, General Miller was briefed about these new guidelines, and his military intelligence units at Guantanamo soon adopted a "72-point matrix for stress and duress" using "heat or cold; withholding food; hooding for days at a time; naked isolation in cold, dark cells for more than 30 days, and . . . 'stress positions' designed to subject detainees to rising levels of pain."[28]

When blatant violation of the Geneva Conventions thus became Pentagon policy, a delegation of very senior, very anonymous "uniformed military lawyers" came to New York for an unofficial call on Scott Horton, then head of the City Bar Association's Human Rights Committee. Speaking off the record, these JAG officers expressed grave concern that new Pentagon procedures, detailed in classified memos, were barring military lawyers from their usual "watchdog role in the interrogation facilities" and would soon "lead to the abuse of detainees held in the Global War on Terror." They urged Horton's committee "to challenge the Bush administration about its standards for detentions and interrogation."[29] Suddenly, mysteriously, these same classified memos began leaking out of the Pentagon into the press, first in a trickle and then in a torrent that broke through the Bush White House's obsessive concern with secrecy. Within just months, Joshua Dratel, the New York attorney who later joined the Hicks defense team, had collected enough of these leaked documents to compile a ponderous thousand-page volume for Cambridge University Press that he published under the title *The Torture Papers: The Road to Abu Ghraib*.

The Torture of David Hicks

David Hicks was one of the first to learn the real meaning of Rumsfeld's orders for "deprivation of light and auditory stimuli." By the time he started to feel the full effect of these enhanced psychological methods in July 2003, Hicks had already suffered nineteen months of extreme treatment. After a Northern Alliance warlord sold him to U.S. Special Forces for $1,000 in mid-December 2001, Hicks was packed into the brig of the USS *Bataan* in the Arabian Sea. From there Hicks was twice flown, shackled and blindfolded, to a nearby land base for seven-hour torture sessions marked by kicking, beatings with rifle butts, punching about the head and torso, and death threats at gunpoint—all by Americans. During his later transport from base to base around Afghanistan, he was made "to run in leg shackles that regularly ripped skin off my ankles" and was handcuffed for up to fifteen hours so tightly that his arms were numbed. For the daylong military flight across the Atlantic to Guantanamo in January 2002, Hicks endured the standard sensory-deprivation package of drugs, earmuffs, blackened goggles, and chains.[30]

Throughout his first seventeen months in the general prison population at Guantanamo's Camp X-Ray and Camp Delta, Hicks was, according to court affidavits, subjected to regular sleep deprivation; threatened with rendition to Egypt for torture; given injections of unknown substances; fed a reduced diet that stripped pounds from his small frame; and offered enticements to cooperate, including promises of prostitutes and even eventual repatriation to Australia.[31] Two of his fellow detainees, Rasul and Iqbal, felt that Hicks was singled out for "very aggressive" treatment, with constant cell changes to deny him human support and almost daily interrogations that slowly made him "more willing to cooperate"—apparently convincing authorities to pick Hicks as the first detainee to be tried by the new military commission.[32] In a later affidavit, Hicks himself stated, "I felt like I was being intentionally isolated to break my will to resist my upcoming trial."[33]

During these endless interrogations, inquisitors became "furious" when Hicks contradicted their narrative. Displaying a photo of a detainee's face beaten into a mass of lesions, the interrogators threatened, "If you don't co-operate, we will send you to Egypt. You can find out if he's dead and experience how it happened." Slowly, Hicks later recalled, "I became too exhausted to argue. I allowed the interrogators to frame my words and say anything they wanted." After eighteen months of exhausting incarceration, daily beatings, and the endless screams of crazed prisoners broken by this harsh treatment, Hicks swapped assurance of immediate repatriation to Australia for his signature on a confession full of what he called "the most outrageous assertions."[34]

Following a few months of similar abuse, the "American Taliban" John Walker Lindh, Hicks's alleged comrade-in-arms from Afghanistan, capitulated in July 2002. To avoid a life sentence, Lindh pled guilty to aiding "terrorists who reject our values of freedom," retracted all "charges that he was mistreated while in military custody," and promised to cooperate "fully, truthfully and completely" with intelligence officers.[35]

Yet, even Hicks's first nineteen months of harsh treatment could not have prepared him sufficiently for what would happen next: an extreme application, almost unprecedented in its severity, of the CIA's established sensory-deprivation torture technique, involving eight full months of strict solitary confinement. On July 3, 2003, President Bush personally approved the prosecution of six detainees before the military commissions—two British nationals, two Yemenis, a Sudanese, and one Australian, David Hicks. Six days later, to await the start of his case before the military commission, Hicks was transferred to Guantanamo's Camp Echo—an "off-limits" cluster of a dozen wooden houses, each with a "steel cage, a restroom, and a table for interviews." Here he was isolated inside a windowless, one-step wide cell designed to deny its occupant all cognitive stimulus. As the other Australian detainee, Mamdouh Habib, put it, "Echo was a place where the Americans sent you mad."[36]

During the next 244 days, without sunlight, watched around the clock by taciturn guards, Hicks found his human contacts restricted to weekly visits by the Muslim chaplain and far less frequent conferences with his civilian and military attorneys. The chaplain, an austere West Point graduate named James Yee, limited his conversation to questions of Islamic doctrine and recitation of Arabic prayers. For his infrequent meetings with his attorneys, Hicks was moved just a few feet from his cell into an adjacent interview area where he was shackled, by steel chains about his hands and waist, to a bolt in the floor.[37] Family letters that passed military censors had all expressions of love or support blacked out—evidence of a carefully calibrated psychological strategy of crushing Hicks's will and forcing him to capitulate.[38] Instead of the normal cycle of daylight and darkness, the ceiling lights in this windowless cage glared twenty-four hours a day. Guards manipulated temperatures, setting the air conditioning to freezing while Hicks, barefoot in thin clothing, shivered uncontrollably. "The oppressive atmosphere is crushing, suffocating," Hicks wrote in a prison diary, "it eats at the mind, destroying it."[39]

Under these extreme conditions, Hicks lost thirty pounds from an already lean frame. He read a recondite thousand-page Islamic legal commentary, one of the few books allowed, seven times. Denied any sense of time, he experienced "extreme mood swings" almost hourly. He began to contemplate committing suicide by smashing his skull against the walls of his cell or cutting his wrists. Yet, he somehow survived and, through some inner reserve, refused to capitulate. By the time Hicks gained access to civilian counsel, in early 2004, his American attorney, Joshua Dratel, found him at the brink of despair—drawn so deeply inward that he was obsessed with the minutiae of his surroundings, almost unable to comprehend the reality of his trial and the larger issues at stake.[40]

The apparent aim of such sensory deprivation, one of the longest on record since the CIA adopted this torture technique fifty-odd years before, was to force a guilty plea and an end to Hicks's habeas corpus petition in the U.S. courts. After the confession of the "American Taliban" Lindh, identified as "Detainee 001" on the Pentagon's roster, Guantanamo's jailers had apparently moved down the list to the next poster boy for their tough anti-terror regime by breaking "Detainee 002," David Hicks. Indeed, his first American attorney, Michael Ratner, was convinced that Hicks was picked as the first to be tried by the military commissions because his jailers "thought they could make a deal" with a prisoner weakened by months of solitary confinement.[41]

Under similar, albeit less severe treatment, Hicks's fellow habeas corpus litigants, Rasul and Iqbal, made confessions. After three months of solitary confinement—broken only by twelve-hour interrogations with painful short-shackling, freezing air conditioning, strobe lights, and blasting music—the two English nationals confessed to everything and identified themselves, falsely, as faces in a crowd of forty jihadists seated before Osama Bin Laden in a pre-9/11 video. But the British government, under pressure from angry protests and a petition by some two hundred members of Parliament, soon intervened, pressing Washington for repatriation of all nine of its nationals. Consequently, in September 2003, a British MI-5 agent arrived at Guantanamo with irrefutable evidence that Rasul had been working in a British electronics shop at the same time he confessed to being in Afghanistan with Bin Laden.[42] In two batches, March 2004 and January 2005, all nine British detainees were flown to London and released within twenty-four hours, leaving Hicks the last litigant standing.[43]

In convincing testimony to the power of such sensory manipulation, an FBI agent at Guantanamo wrote headquarters in November 2002 that one detainee "subjected to intense isolation for over three months . . . in a cell that was always flooded with light . . . was evidencing behavior consistent with extreme psychological trauma (talking to non-existent people, reporting hearing voices, crouching in a corner of the cell covered with a sheet for hours on end)." In another case, an FBI agent observed: "The detainee was almost unconscious on the floor, with a pile of hair next to him. He had apparently been literally pulling his own hair out throughout the night."[44]

Other official investigations, U.S. and international, found that Guantanamo's interrogation methods constituted at best abuse and at worst torture. After repeated visits to the base between January 2002 and June 2004, a period that coincided with Hicks's protracted isolation inside Camp Echo, the International Red Cross concluded: "The construction of such a system, whose stated purpose is production of intelligence, cannot be considered other than an intentional system of cruel, unusual and degrading treatment and a form of torture."[45]

The Trial

Beyond these harsh interrogation methods, however, the most important of Secretary Rumsfeld's innovations at Guantanamo was a compromised form of military justice called the military commissions. Under the authority of the president's November 2001 order, Rumsfeld, as the original "appointing authority," issued Military Commission Order No. 1, establishing a new judicial system with its own ad hoc "Commission Law" that operated outside the Uniform Code of Military Justice. As Michael Ratner argued in his February 2002 petition on behalf of Hicks, this order "vests the President with complete discretion to identify the individuals that fall within its scope" and "expressly bars review by any court" anywhere in the world. In short, these military commissions represented unchecked presidential power. Significantly, Order No. 1 stated explicitly that all the rules enumerated therein did not create any enforceable rights—a legal Catch-22 that would allow Rumsfeld's handpicked presiding officers, who acted as both judges and jury, to make and break regulations almost at will. Of equal import, the commissions, unlike regular courts, were allowed to consider any evidence that "would have probative value to a reasonable person," in effect abandoning conventional rules of evidence to allow even testimony derived from torture or hearsay.[46]

The weakness of this ad hoc legal system became evident when the convening authority indicted just a handful among the hundreds of detainees at Guantanamo and then selected Hicks to be the first to stand trial before the military commissions. The conspiracy charges against Hicks and his co-accused were so ill defined that there were no clear criteria for guilt, allowing the presiding officer enormous discretion over evidence and sentencing.

Not only were the rules flawed, but Rumsfeld's commissioners were serving officers bereft of legal expertise and biased by combat experience against the Taliban. In this ad hoc tribunal, rules of evidence were "absent." Weighing up all these factors, in September 2004 the Australian Law Council's observer at Guantanamo, Lex Lasry, QC, concluded that "a fair trial for David Hicks is virtually impossible" and that any trial might well end with "a substantial miscarriage of justice."[47]

After watching court officers use port-a-potties on a dusty hillside and fumble for precedents as the commission prepared for its first trials in August 2004, a legal observer from Human Rights First felt "it would be crazy" to do just what they were doing, "to start building a new legal system from scratch."[48] Yet, there was a certain genius to this madness. Just as England's Tudor-Stuart monarchs had circumvented the common-law ban on torture by convening a royal court called the Star Chamber that was later closed by the Habeas Corpus Act of 1640, so President Bush evaded the U.S. Constitution's protections by creating these military commissions at Guantanamo, answerable only to himself as commander in chief.

As Hicks's legal team assembled at Guantanamo in early 2004, it was troubled by serious problems, some from the commission system, some of its own making—including inadequate staffing, primitive research resources, and unresolved conflicts between the civilian and military defense attorneys. When he joined Major Mori in February as the team's lead civilian counsel, Joshua Dratel highlighted the need for cooperation, saying: "I have more experience in the area of terrorism and the whole Al Qaeda terrorist type of prosecutions—he's got much more experience in dealing with the whole military system. It's complementary."[49]

As it turned out, such complementation was complicated by a clash of personalities and cultures—military versus civilian, Australian versus American. Major Mori was a military careerist with just one client. Joshua Dratel, though working pro bono, was a New York litigator with a fast-track career. Dratel was a Harvard Law School graduate. Mori had attended Western New England Law School at the antipodes of the same state and the U.S. legal profession. Dratel had a good grasp of courtroom procedure and anti-terrorist law from his defense of an Al Qaeda suspect in the 1998 East Africa bombings. Mori was a military lawyer who knew little of the international law central to his client's case.[50]

Then there were the cultural conflicts. At first Major Mori was put off by Hicks's thick Aussie accent and laconic ways, but he soon bonded with him as a fellow dropout. As a college rugby player, Mori had toured Australia and New Zealand for three weeks, developing a fondness for Australians and their culture.[51] Dratel, by contrast, was a high-octane trial lawyer who sometimes seemed impatient with the low-key manner of his Aussie colleagues, producing conflicts that simmered and eventually erupted in sharp exchanges. When an

Adelaide solicitor, Stephen Kenny, a respected attorney who represented Hicks in Australia, pressed his colleagues to make an issue of the abusive treatment, Dratel supported Kenny's sacking in early 2005, saying, "I don't see just the stamping of the feet and the complaining as being a very productive strategy."[52] As the first hearings approached with only weeks to prepare, the Hicks team was heading into trial before a hostile court with one well-briefed star backed by a limited staff and an under-researched case.

Before the Hicks trial could start, however, ongoing legal battles in the U.S. civilian courts intervened. In June 2004, only weeks after the Abu Ghraib exposé, the habeas corpus case filed by Michael Ratner two years earlier on behalf of Hicks, Habib, and other detainees finally reached the U.S. Supreme Court. In its landmark decision *Rasul v. Bush*, the Supreme Court affirmed the right of "enemy combatants" held at Guantanamo to due process under the law, flatly rejecting the White House's insistence on unchecked, unlimited detention. Suddenly, the Pentagon's plans to hold hundreds of detainees at Guantanamo without any judicial oversight were thrown into disarray, and the Bush administration was faced with a possible mass transfer of six hundred cases to the U.S. federal courts.[53]

To block that unpalatable possibility, the Pentagon convened, in just nine days, another ad hoc military court at Guantanamo—the Combatant Status Review Tribunal (CSRT)—and over the next six months pushed all the detainees through hasty hearings. On August 17, the CSRT reviewed the evidence against Hicks, without allowing him to see or challenge the charges, and found grounds to consider him an "unlawful combatant."[54] Though the White House thus claimed full compliance with the Supreme Court, this ad hoc military tribunal had denied detainees legal representation and made their military jailers both judge and jury.

A week later, on August 23, 2004, Hicks, after thirty months' imprisonment, finally had his first day in court. The day's emotional peak came at the start, when Hicks entered the courtroom and embraced his father, Terry, who had flown from Australia to Cuba for a few moments with his son. At a press briefing later that day, the elder Hicks expressed concern about the mental damage his son might have suffered from months of solitary confinement, adding pointedly that David had asked him "if family members were still on his side."[55]

After a formal reading of President Bush's order that Hicks was eligible for trial, the court then heard defense objections to the five-man panel on the grounds that, as serving officers, they lacked both legal experience and impartiality. In a dramatic challenge to the court of the sort that usually happens only in film or television, Dratel stripped away any illusion of the court's impartiality by exposing "a close personal relationship" between its presiding officer, Colonel Peter E. Brownback III, and the Pentagon's newly designated "appointing authority," Major General John D. Altenburg Jr. (ret.) With Major Mori largely silent at his side, Dratel fired a succession of sharp questions that forced Colonel Brownback to admit that he had given the "roast" at the general's retirement and attended his son's wedding, clear signs of bias that the appointing authority, none other than General Altenberg himself, had reviewed and found irrelevant. "How would you answer people who might say that you were chosen for this post not for your qualifications but for your close relationship with Mr. Altenburg?" Dratel pointedly asked the colonel. Stunned by this revelation, the legal observer from Human Rights First called this "a huge conflict . . . in some ways like the prosecutor in a criminal case and the lead juror being best of friends."[56]

At the close of these contentious proceedings, the presiding officer asked Hicks how he would plead to the charges: first, of conspiring with Osama Bin Laden to engage in "murder by an unprivileged belligerent . . . and terrorism"; second, "attempted murder"; and, third, "aiding the enemy." In a clear voice, Hicks replied, "Sir, to all charges, not guilty."[57]

Though Dratel was often brilliant during the verbal dueling, the Hicks legal team was still raw. While Dratel slashed away at the court, Major Mori sat taciturn throughout, an ill-advised strategy for building rapport with the uniformed officers on the military panel. Visually, the defense table presented poorly before the court—an emaciated, listless defendant sitting between the massive Major Mori and the energetic Dratel. Reflecting this improvised teamwork, Dratel's tactical victories in August would prove a strategic miscalculation in November.

During these same hearings that August, the commission also heard arguments for another of the six accused, Salim Ahmed Hamdan, who shared star billing in the opening trials with Hicks. Like the Australian, Hamdan was more foot soldier than general in Al Qaeda's army. As an unemployed Yemeni national, Hamdan had gone to work in Afghanistan as a chauffeur for Osama Bin Laden. Appearing for the Yemeni, Lieutenant Commander Charles Swift of the U.S. Navy launched a parallel challenge to the panel's impartiality, asking its chairman, Colonel Brownback, "Did you think these commissions were lawful when you were appointed?" After a long pause, the colonel admitted that he was not certain if they were, in fact, lawful.[58]

When the Hicks case resumed on November 1 after a two-month hiatus, the appointing authority, General Altenburg, responded to Dratel's protests by removing two members of the five-man panel. Though this ruling seemed at first glance a win for the defense, in reality it was at best a Pyrrhic victory. As an observer from Human Rights First explained, "in reducing the size of the panels for Hicks and Hamdan . . . Altenburg effectively halved the prosecutor's burden of proof." Instead of persuading four out of five panelists of Hicks's guilt, now, thanks to his own attorney, prosecutors faced a far easier task of convincing just two out of three judges. And, as Dratel himself had observed, the reduction in the panel's size would allow his main antagonist, the presiding officer Colonel Brownback, "to dominate the legal issues and legal questions and legal decisions."[59]

These renewed proceedings seemed even less viable to the Australian legal observer, Lex Lasry, QC. In the intervening weeks, several panel members had been dismissed, the release of some prosecution witnesses from Guantanamo had denied the defense any opportunity to challenge their evidence, and the court's slipshod procedures had left sixty-four major defense motions unanswered. In an arbitrary move showing the presiding officer's unchecked authority, the court summarily dismissed, without any legal basis, defense moves to call six leading international lawyers, including the Pentagon's own law-of-war expert.[60]

But in the long hiatus between hearings, the Hicks defense team had polished its act to show some deft teamwork. Opening for the defense on November 2, Joshua Dratel argued, with his customary skill, that the commission was "fundamentally flawed because it only authorized military commission trials for non-citizens," a violation of the Geneva Convention. After Dratel finished scoring points about the legality of the court, Major Mori rose to argue that their client Hicks, though captured as a combatant, should have been tried as a civilian, with full legal rights under the Fourth Geneva Convention. When the presiding officer, Colonel Brownback, insisted that Hicks was being properly tried under the Third Convention, the major, now well briefed on international law by Melbourne University law professor Tim McCormack, held his own. As Mori chipped away at the presiding officer's arguments, Colonel Brownback said bitingly, "I'm looking at Third Convention, Article 3, *Sunshine*." As an observer from Human Rights First noted, "Brownback's patronizing use of the nickname 'Sunshine' for Major Mori seemed to evince surprising disrespect for counsel."[61]

Six days later, on November 8, Lieutenant Commander Swift, who was now facing a similarly reduced three-man panel, was midway through a challenge to the court's new composition when a soldier entered silently and handed Colonel Brownback a note. Blandly, the colonel announced, without explanation: "We are going to take an indefinite recess." As the panel hurried out the door, the news rippled across the courtroom—"the federal court stopped the commissions."[62]

U.S. Courts Intercede

Indeed, a thousand miles to the north, in Washington, D.C., U.S. Judge James Robertson had handed down the first ruling in what would later become the defining Supreme Court case on detainee issues, *Hamdan v. Rumsfeld*. In another skirmish between the military JAGs and the Bush White House, the suit had been filed on behalf of Guantanamo defendant Salim Hamdan by his civil-military legal team, Lieutenant Commander Swift and Professor Neal Katyal of Georgetown University Law School. Ruling that "the president is not a tribunal," the judge found that Bush had no right to suspend the Geneva Conventions. Significantly, his ruling stated that the military commissions were "fatally flawed" because they were "contrary to or inconsistent" with the UCMJ, and thus all hearings at Guantanamo were to be suspended until they met the standards of a conventional court-martial. Significantly, the judge found defendant Hamdan's months of psychologically stressful solitary confinement at Camp Echo unacceptable and ordered his return to the general prison population at Camp Delta.[63]

As this sharply worded decision indicates, opposition to Bush's detainee policies was reaching a critical mass in the courts, Congress, and the press. In January 2005, U.S. District Judge Joyce Hens Green heard petitions from fifty detainees and affirmed the right of the federal courts to issue habeas corpus writs for Guantanamo prisoners. The judge found, in reviewing allegations by the Australian Mamdouh Habib about his abuse in Egypt, that evidence presented before the military commissions might well have been tainted by torture.[64] The judge noted Habib's claim that he had suffered "routine beatings to the point of unconsciousness," had been "locked in a room that would gradually be filled with water to a level just below his chin as he stood for hours on the tips of his toes," and had been "suspended from a wall with his feet resting on the side of a large electrified cylindrical drum"—thereby "extracting confessions that," said the defendant, "can be proven false."[65] After the *Washington Post* published a moving expose of Habib's agony and Canberra finally requested his repatriation, he was quickly released, without charges or explanation. After three years of detention and months of cruel tortures, Habib finally rejoined his family in Sydney, leaving David Hicks the sole Australian still confined at Guantanamo.[66]

Although the U.S. Court of Appeals reversed Judge Robertson's decision in July 2005, by that time New York's leading law firms had made Guantanamo Bay their preferred pro bono destination. As powerhouse corporate lawyers shuttled to Cuba to meet detainee clients and papered the federal courts with habeas corpus petitions, Guantanamo's isolation, once the military's most powerful psychological weapon, was shattered.[67] And, with *Hamdan v. Rumsfeld* moving up the docket of the U.S. Supreme Court amid anticipation of a definitive review of the military commissions, all proceedings against Hicks and the other detainees were suspended. It would, in fact, be two years before David Hicks would have another appearance before the commission—a delay that would effectively transfer his case from the halls of justice into the court of public opinion.

By mid-2005, the U.S. Congress, the courts, and the national press began to join the chorus of criticism about conditions at Guantanamo Bay. "Shut it down. Just shut it down," wrote the *New York Times* columnist Thomas L. Friedman with uncommon boldness. "Just shut it down and then plow it under. It has become worse than an embarrassment. I am convinced that more Americans are dying and will die if we keep the Gitmo prison open than if we shut it down."[68]

The controversy moved to Congress, where the Senate Judiciary Committee heard Lieutenant Commander Swift recall the first meeting his client, Salim Ahmed Hamdan. The Yemeni detainee had "already been in solitary confinement for . . . 45 days . . . in a windowless room" and was showing signs of "extreme mental stress." Backed by documents, Swift showed that due process before Guantanamo's commissions was being bent to a predetermined outcome. In a ringing reminder of the issues at stake, this JAG lawyer added that any court, whether military or civil, "says as much about the society that holds the trial as it does about the individual before it."[69]

Little more than a month later, in August 2005, the Pentagon's military lawyers leaked several damning e-mails about the commissions to the Australian Broadcasting Corporation's Washington correspondent, Leah Sales, that confirmed Commander Swift's criticisms.[70] A year earlier, as the military commissions were preparing for trial, one prosecutor, Captain John Carr, had complained that their office was about to "prosecute fairly low-level accused in a process that appears to be rigged." In a similar message, another JAG prosecutor, Major Robert Preston, stated that proceeding to trial with such weak evidence, particularly in the case against David Hicks, would be "a severe threat to the reputation of the military justice system and even a fraud on the American people." But their superior, Colonel Frederick L. Borch, had dismissed these complaints as "monstrous lies," and so no corrective action was taken.[71] To protest what they regarded as the rigging of court procedure, three career JAG prosecutors—Carr, Preston, and Captain Carrie Wolf—requested reassignment to other duties.[72]

As U.S. courts and military lawyers mobilized to stop detainee abuse at Guantanamo, Australia's prime minister, John Howard, who had been re-elected in October 2004 with an increased parliamentary majority, announced with seeming relief that "we have just received written advice from the [U.S.] Defense Department that after a very thorough investigation the allegations of Hicks and Habib about mistreatments whilst they were in American custody, no evidence has been found."[73]

With Canberra unwilling to defend its own, all action in the Hicks case shifted to the United Kingdom, where, in a far less hostile political climate, he could claim citizenship through his mother and the protection of a government committed to the rule of law. The British attorney general, Lord Goldsmith, had already spoken on the record against Guantanamo a year earlier, saying the military commissions there could not provide a fair trial by international standards. Moreover, Lord Steyn, the Lord Appeal in Ordinary, had damned the commissions as "a pre-ordained arbitrary rush to judgment by an irregular tribunal which makes a mockery of justice."[74] Although the High Court in London ruled definitively for Hicks in December 2005, the British government retracted his citizenship that same day.[75]

Amid this rising controversy over conditions at Guantanamo, the White House deployed the recently enacted Detainee Treatment Act in a bid to quash judicial oversight of its actions. On January 3, 2006, the Justice Department notified federal judges that it would seek the immediate dismissal of all 160 habeas corpus cases filed on behalf of Guantanamo detainees.[76] A week later, the U.S. solicitor general, citing this new law, advised the Supreme Court that it no longer had jurisdiction over Guantanamo and asked the justices to dismiss the potentially landmark "unlawful combatant" case, *Hamdan v. Rumsfeld*—a petition the Court set aside when it heard oral arguments, the first step toward a final ruling.[77]

At the very moment when the White House seemed to have the torture scandal under control—by manipulating Congress, silencing the courts, and disarming the national press—the international community intervened in an unprecedented manner. In February 2006, the UN Human Rights Commission released a report branding U.S. treatment of Guantanamo's prisoners "torture." Then, in a historic challenge, UN Secretary General Kofi Anan issued a dramatic call for the United States to close Guantanamo.[78] But, within hours, Secretary Rumsfeld shot back, insisting, in a public address before the Council on Foreign Relations in New York that the detainees are "being handled honorably," even though they are "terrorists, bad people, people if they went back out on the field would try to kill Americans."[79]

"The existence of Guantanamo remains unacceptable," announced Britain's attorney general, Lord Goldsmith, arguing that its closure "would help remove what has become a symbol to many . . . of injustice." Its military tribunals, he explained, failed to offer "sufficient guarantees of fair trial," a fundamental principle "on which there can be no compromise." In this ringing defense of the law's sanctity, he seemed to echo the House of Lords, which, the previous December, had affirmed the "bedrock moral principle" within the thousand-year tradition of British common law that torture is "an unqualified evil" and blocked deportations of a dozen Muslims convicted on "evidence . . . procured by torture inflicted by foreign officials."[80]

On similar moral grounds, Germany, the European Parliament, and the United Nations called for Guantanamo's closure. After detailed presentations by a U.S. delegation in early May 2006, the UN Committee on Torture, composed of ten human-rights experts from across the globe, found detention "for protracted periods at Guantanamo Bay without sufficient legal safeguards" unlawful under the laws of armed conflict and directed that Washington "should cease to detain any person at Guantánamo Bay and close this detention facility."[81]

Then, in June 2006, all these political tensions culminated in a dramatic denouement before the U.S. Supreme Court. In hearing a government appeal from Judge Robertson's decision in *Hamdan v. Rumsfeld*, the justices reminded the president that he is not above the law. Writing for the majority in a five-to-three decision, Justice John Paul Stevens ruled that the United States was bound by the Geneva Conventions that barred, under common Article 3, all "humiliating and degrading treatment" of detainees and required their prosecution with "all the judicial guarantees which are recognized as indispensable by civilized peoples."[82] Explaining the import of this decision to the Senate Judiciary Committee, Yale Law School's dean, Harold Koh, testified that Guantanamo represented a "five year misadventure of creating military commissions that plainly fall short of minimum global standards of fair trial."[83]

By mid-2006, Australia thus remained one of the few foreign nations that still accepted the legality of Guantanamo's endless detention and drumhead tribunals. In late March, right after a visit from the Australian consul, Hicks was—in clear violation of the Third Geneva Convention—moved back into solitary confinement at Camp Five, where he remained for months, isolated twenty-three hours a day inside a cement room with a solid steel door. Four powerful light bulbs kept the room bright twenty-four hours a day, and guards barred detainees from covering their eyes in any way. Ducts delivered blasts of cold air that made Hicks shiver constantly. Apart from a small window with opaque glass that emitted a faint glow during the day, he was again being denied human contact or sunlight, suffering the severe distress of sensory deprivation.[84] The other Australian detainee Mamdouh Habib, who spent seven months there, called Camp 5 "a terrible place—freezing cold, with constant loud music and noise, and glaring lights."[85] In the five years since Hicks's arrival at Guantanamo, Canberra had yet to protest such inhumane treatment.

Indeed, two months after that steel door slammed shut on Hicks, Australia's ambassador to Washington meekly concluded a formal agreement with the Pentagon's Office of Military Commissions, winning a promise of his repatriation once the trial was completed by agreeing to honor whatever terms the tribunal might impose.[86] For the plenipotentiary of a major nation to treat with a third-tier functionary of another state—the legal adviser to the appointing authority of the Pentagon's Office of Military Commissions—and thereby legitimate the illegal incarceration of one of its citizens was, in the view of Hicks's attorney Joshua Dratel, an inexplicable "surrender of Australia's national sovereignty."[87]

Release from Guantanamo

After five years of watching their countryman suffer imprisonment without trial, Australians were increasingly critical, and Prime Minister John Howard, after four successive victories, was in serious danger of being defeated in the upcoming Australian elections planned for late 2007. During the five years Hicks had been incarcerated, popular sentiment had shifted dramatically, from revulsion to concern. A spontaneous support movement had sprung up across this continent sparked by opposition to the harsh confinement and the lack of due process. Apart from growing anger among civil libertarians and human rights activists, Hicks's case also inspired a burst of creativity by Australia's artists. In 2004, the SBS national network broadcast a sympathetic documentary, *The President versus David Hicks*, which followed the father, Terry Hicks, on a lonely pilgrimage, locking himself in cages on city streets around the world to highlight the plight of his son. Two years later, Nigel Jamieson's dance/drama *Honour Bound*, an emotionally wrenching portrayal of Hicks as a wayward youth consigned to endless detention at Guantanamo, enjoyed a strong run at the Sydney Opera House.

Perhaps most important, between sessions at Guantanamo Bay Hicks's military counsel, Major Michael Mori, made a succession of well-publicized speaking tours of Australia. At the start of one such trip, in August 2006, the major walked off a trans-Pacific flight into a matinee of *Honour Bound* at the Sydney Opera House, taking the stage at the end of the performance to a round of thunderous applause. As a woman interviewer shot questions personal and professional, Major Mori answered with the disarming charm that had made this American military lawyer a folk hero to many in Australia. As a ready smile softened his centurion's chin and angular nose, Mori told, with wry self-deprecation, about dropping out of college at eighteen and serving a tour as an ordinary Marine recruit, learning the discipline he had long lacked. After law school and steady promotions to chief prosecutor in Hawaii, he was led by his sense of justice to transfer to the Pentagon, where he served as defense counsel for Guantanamo's newly formed military commissions. By late 2003, the major had become a military lawyer with just one client, David Hicks, and found himself working not in a conventional court-martial but in "show trials set up for political purposes." That experience soon forced him into a new, sometimes uncomfortable role as a critic "challenging the entire system because it was unfair."

When the microphone opened to the audience, questions came quickly. Many queries seemed acidly critical of America. But the major finessed them deftly, treating every speaker with deference and expressing strong opposition to the military commissions at Guantanamo. For four years, he said, Hicks had been locked in a U.S. political deadlock, and he would remain there "until the Australian Government asks them to send him home." Throughout his hour on the Opera House stage, the major courted his audience with references to cricket and rugby, drawing laughs with a wry remark about his client's history of drug addiction and terrorist training, saying: "Let's be frank. David made what even he would admit were some bad life choices."

As this dialogue drew to a close, one middle-aged woman seemed to sum up the surge of emotions the major had aroused in this audience: "You represent the America I always believed in, an America that seemed lost since September 11." The applause resounded, drowning out the obvious paradox of pacifists and peace activists enamored of a man whose bearing and uniform made him every inch a U.S. Marine.

That Sunday evening at the Opera House was just the start of the major's triumphal weeklong sweep across Australia, speaking before audiences that can only be called adoring, even adulatory. On Monday, while dining with Bob Debus, the New South Wales attorney general, and chatting with Sydney's Catholic primate, George Cardinal Pell, Mori was also appearing, via videotape, on ABC Television's popular interview program *Enough Rope*, telling its host, Andrew Denton, that Prime Minister Howard was seriously misinformed about his client. Hicks had, the major said, been tortured and was not guilty of anything akin to "serious offenses." Denton asked if the major had not "killed his career" by his passionate criticism of the powers that be in Canberra and Washington, D.C. Mori replied that he was just following "the core values that the Marine Corps have taught me of justice and judgment and integrity."

On Tuesday, the vice president of the New South Wales Law Society introduced him to a standing-room-only crowd of four hundred lawyers on Sydney's Philip Street, saying, in words that reflected the electric atmosphere the Marine seemed to stir among Australians, "I expected this lectern to be awash with underwear."[88]

Thursday saw the major in Canberra for meetings with members of parliament, both government and opposition. Although Attorney General Philip Ruddock was pointedly absent, he had already capitulated to the major's charisma by announcing he would seek Hicks's return if substantive new charges were not laid quickly. That evening, Mori won over the capacity crowd of five hundred at Australian National University, with audience members emerging to describe him as "a hero, a role model, and someone who should run for U.S. president."[89]

On Friday, the major flew down to Hobart, where, the *Mercury* reported, an "adoring crowd" of 720 packed a University of Tasmania lecture hall and responded to his criticisms of Canberra's handling of the Hicks case with "a thunderous standing ovation lasting about five minutes."[90]

Crossing to Adelaide over the weekend, Mori told five hundred protesters at a candlelight vigil that the Bush administration's new law creating military commissions was "unfair" and that, unless Canberra acted, "David will be stuck in Guantanamo for another two years." In darkness broken by flickering candles, the crowd marched to the local office of Foreign Minister Alexander Downer to present a petition with fifty thousand signatures calling for Hicks's release.[91]

Many in that Adelaide crowd were members of the activist group GetUp!, whose campaign in support of Hicks already counted 150,000 members across Australia.[92] With a mix of persistence and wry wit, these agitators mounted placards critical of the government's inaction on trucks and began circulating through Prime Minister Howard's own suburban electoral district in northern Sydney.[93] By appealing to Australia's strong sense of "fair go" for all accused, the campaign mobilized nationwide rallies for Hicks in December 2006, the fifth anniversary of his incarceration. Polls found that 71 percent of all Australians felt it was time to bring him home.[94]

This shift in public opinion was matched by a rising chorus of criticism from the country's elites. In a rare act of ecumenical solidarity, the Catholic cardinal George Pell joined the Anglican archbishop of Sydney in publicly condemning Hicks's lengthy incarceration. From Canberra, the opposition's shadow attorney general, Nicola Roxon, stated that "the Government's handling of Hicks amounted to the complete abandonment of an Australian citizen."[95] The former chief justice of the High Court, Sir Gerard Brennan, stated that Australia was "morally impoverished" by its complicity in the U.S. treatment of Hicks.[96] In November, the Law Council of Australia called the military commissions "grossly unfair" for allowing admission of evidence against Hicks that had been "obtained by unacceptable methods of interrogation."[97] Ten days later, the attorneys general for all of Australia's states "vented their anger" at their federal counterpart for failing to win a fair trial for Hicks.[98]

Even in the face of such rising criticism, the Howard government remained steadfast in support of the Bush administration. During a visit to Washington that October, Australia's attorney general, Philip Ruddock, declared that the "United States has made it clear that torture is not permissible." He then contradicted that assertion unwittingly by stating that "I don't regard sleep deprivation as torture."[99] Several days later, Prime Minister Howard defended those remarks, adding that, in the case of David Hicks, "allegations of torture have not been established."[100]

But by January 2007, as public support for Hicks grew, Prime Minister Howard's poll numbers sagged, and the date of Australia's next elections approached, Canberra's ambassador to Washington met Bush administration officials to press hard for progress before the military tribunal. Within days, the Pentagon's chief counsel, William Haynes, called Guantanamo's lead prosecutor, Colonel Morris Davis, to demand an acceleration of the case against Hicks. The prosecutor was both angered and confused by this pressure, later recalling: "We had no convening authority, we had no manual for military commissions, we had no regulations for trial by military commission. So, the major pieces were not in place and I'm having the DoD general counsel calling me up, the day after there was a meeting with the Australian ambassador, asking, 'how quickly I could charge David Hicks.'"[101]

A month later, when Vice President Cheney visited Australia to discuss Iraq, Prime Minister Howard, facing the threat of losing his office, took the opportunity to insist that Hicks be tried "with no further delay." Just five days later, Hicks was indicted under new terrorism charges, and the convening authority of the military commissions, Susan J. Crawford, a civilian and a loyal Cheney protégé, offered a tempting plea bargain without consulting her chief prosecutor, Colonel Davis. Instead of the twenty years in prison previously discussed, Crawford dangled a tempting nine-month sentence if Hicks would plead guilty and sign a statement that he had "never been illegally treated."[102]

After more than two years without a court hearing, David Hicks suddenly appeared before the military commissions on March 26, 2007, with his attorney, Major Mori, at his side. With the original charges of murder and conspiracy now dropped, Hicks stated that he would plead guilty to the only remaining accusation—providing material aid to terrorism. In the lengthy plea agreement signed that day, Hicks acknowledged that "I am an alien un-lawful enemy combatant" and stated that "I have never been illegally treated." Significantly, Hicks had to promise, in the agreement's most detailed clause, that "I will not communicate with the media in any way . . . for a period of one (1) year. I agree that this includes any direct or indirect communication made by me, my family members, my assigns, or any other third party made on my behalf."[103]

As the first and only detainee convicted at Guantanamo, Hicks had ad-mitted high crimes of terrorism and was then sentenced to just nine months' imprisonment in his native Australia—less time than he would serve for, say, petty theft or drunk driving. At a press conference after the sentencing, the chief prosecutor, Colonel Davis, admitted that he was shocked by the decision, saying, "I wasn't considering anything that didn't have two digits"—meaning at least ten years' imprisonment. Why this curious imbalance between crime and punishment? "What an amazing coincidence," remarked the Australian observer at Guantanamo, Lex Lasry, "with the election in Australia by the end of the year, he gets nine months and he is gagged for twelve months from talking about it."[104]

Even so, Prime Minister Howard, Bush's loyal ally, lost those elections badly in November 2007 after four straight electoral victories with growing majorities.[105] For months before the balloting, the activist group GetUp! ran a "Postcards to the PM" campaign that generated 10,143 protest letters from the prime minister's own electoral district, about 12 percent of all voters there. Simultaneously, the group's "Bring David Hicks Back Home" billboard truck was circulating on those same Sydney streets.[106] At the heart of the city's busi-ness district in March, Amnesty International set up a replica of the tiny isola-tion cell at Guantanamo's Camp Six, where Hicks had been confined for the past four months, from which passers-by emerged to describe the experience as "traumatizing."[107] Not only was Howard's party defeated, but also he suf-fered the ultimate humiliation within the Westminster parliamentary system of losing his own safe seat—in part because human rights advocates took the Hicks case into his electorate, where the opposition candidate's key swing bal-lots came from activist Green Party voters.[108]

Meanwhile back in Guantanamo, at midnight on May 18, 2007, an ar-mored van pulled up to a Gulfstream jet. Two rows of sentries formed a cordon between the van and aircraft. Armed U.S. soldiers marched Hicks, shackled hand and foot, through that cordon and handed him over to two Austra-lian prison guards. After sitting silent and listless during the twenty-four hour flight home, Hicks was confined in an Adelaide prison for the required nine

Uniting Church congregation in Sydney, Australia, protests the incarceration of David Hicks in the U.S. military prison at Guantanamo Bay, March 2007. (*The Daily Telegraph*)

months, emerging a few weeks after Prime Minister Howard left office. Waiting outside the gates was a small crowd of supporters with banners reading "This Could Have Been Your Son."[109] His lawyer later read a statement on his behalf to reporters, who had kept a round-the-clock vigil: "I had hoped to be able to speak to the media but I am just not strong enough at the moment."[110]

Within eighteen months, however, Hicks had moved to Sydney, got work in a landscaping nursery, and married. At the ceremony, in suburban Sydney, the bride, a doctoral student at Sydney University, glowed in a white veil, while Hicks was elegant in a black coat and white silk cravat. Major Mori was spotted in the crowd.[111] Though still suffering memory lapses, anxiety attacks, torturous nightmares, and speech defects from six years' incarceration, much of it in solitary, Hicks found his voice and won a book contract from Random House. Working alone for two years, he wrote a four-hundred-page memoir with taut narrative and clear prose that belied his formal status as a high school dropout. Appearing at the Sydney Writers' Festival to promote the book in May 2011, Hicks and his father received a "standing ovation" from the crowd of nearly a thousand supporters. A long line of adoring readers formed for autographed copies of *Guantanamo: My Journey*.[112]

Former Guantanamo detainee David Hicks (*left*) at book signing with his father Terry Hicks (*center*), Sydney Writers' Festival, May 2011, where he received a standing ovation from the nine hundred people in the audience. (*The Australian*)

Conclusion

In retrospect, the case of David Hicks challenges the logic underlying the Guantanamo legal regime. For more than five years, the military commissions failed to present any evidence that he was guilty of the original charges of murder and terrorism. Indeed, prosecutors close to the case felt that the attempt to prosecute Hicks raised serious questions about the quality of justice before the commissions. After five years and four months of incarceration, the court was ultimately forced to offer Hicks a light nine-month sentence that mocked the gravity of those original capital charges. And the role of Prime Minister Howard and Vice President Cheney in negotiating the final plea bargain indicates that Hicks's prosecution was, from beginning to end, a political show trial, badly scripted and badly acted.

Beyond Hicks, the military commissions proved a misguided attempt at creating a new system of presidential justice. After two centuries of U.S. civil courts and a half-century of military justice, the Bush administration tried to create a third, hybrid system without allowing sufficient time to develop rules of evidence, precedents, and procedures. After eight years of operation, the commissions managed to complete only four trials by mid-2010, with four convictions and a dismissal—a pathetic record of justice delayed and denied. Salim Hamdan was convicted in August 2008 and sent home to Yemen, where he was soon released. Another Yemeni, Ali Hamza Ahmad Suliman al Bahlul, was sentenced to life imprisonment in November of that year. Charges against the teen-age captive Mohamed Jawad were dismissed in July 2009. And a Sudanese captured in Afghanistan, Ibrahim Ahmed Mahmoud al-Qosi, was convicted a year later. When Khalid Sheikh Mohammed and four other top terrorists were arraigned at Guantanamo in May 2012, the Navy's former top JAG expressed strong doubts that the military commissions would, despite reforms under Obama, "ever get credibility back."[113]

This was a dismal record of judicial efficiency by any standard but particularly for a lavishly funded court with a legion of judges, prosecutors, translators, intelligence officers, and prison guards. The JAG defense lawyers who fought this compromised court were punished for their probity, with Major Mori denied promotion for three years and Lieutenant Commander Swift forced into early retirement.[114]

Whenever the sovereign, whether Charles I or Bush the younger, creates a court beholden to his executive authority, the result is a legal proceeding that, as one British law lord put it, makes "a mockery of justice." As for Hicks himself, his behavior in the four years since his release seems closer to that of a law-abiding citizen than anything akin to the "worst of the worst," much less "about as dangerous as a person can be in modern times."

Then there is the question, posed at the outset of this chapter, about using Hicks as a touchstone to assay the damage that Guantanamo, as a latter-day Devil's Island, might have done to America's international standing. If the treatment of this one detainee could spark such outrage in a close ally like Australia, then we can only imagine the feelings that Guantanamo aroused in far less sympathetic Muslim nations. To gain a sense of such damage to U.S. prestige circa 2006, we can multiply all the anger and agitation over this single Australian by the seven hundred detainees at Guantanamo, the more than twenty-five thousand prisoners in U.S. custody in Iraq, and the eighty thousand detainees held worldwide under the Global War on Terror.

7

Psychological Torture
and Public Forgetting

After eight years of the War on Terror under the leadership of George W. Bush, the United States was trapped
in the painful politics of impunity. Despite dozens of official inquiries in the
years since the Abu Ghraib photos first exposed the abuse in April 2004, the
ignominy of torture has continued to spread like a virus, infecting all who
touch it. By embracing a specific methodology of torture, covertly developed
by the CIA over decades and graphically revealed in those Iraqi prison photos,
Washington has condemned the nation to a recurring pattern of exposé and
cover-up that has damaged its image at home and abroad. At every stage in the
country's recent move toward impunity—Dick Cheney's unapologetic claims
for torture's efficacy and President Barack Obama's halting retreat from promises to end the abuse—Washington is returning step by step to a contradictory
policy that made torture America's secret weapon throughout the Cold War.

This is by no means the first time that a major political controversy over
U.S. torture has become mired in impunity, thereby failing to punish past
abuse or prevent future recurrence. Indeed, repeatedly over the past forty
years, the elusive character of the authorized tortures and their covert application have combined to defeat the country's usual processes of political reform
through press exposé, public protest, and congressional action—allowing the
practice to persist to the present and perhaps into the future.

Concealed from both Congress and the public, the CIA has spent the
past half-century developing sophisticated forms of torture meant to defy
investigation, prosecution, or prohibition—and so far has been remarkably
successful on all those counts. After co-opting leading cognitive scientists to
develop these techniques during the Cold War, the CIA then collaborated with
U.S. AID police advisers and military instructors in the dissemination of these
techniques among allies across the globe. Whenever Congress or the press

has exposed the agency's role in the development or propagation of torture techniques, the CIA, like state security services worldwide, has proven adept at avoiding any legal sanction. Whether in Manila or Santiago or Washington, the perpetrators and the powerful who command them can play upon the levers of state power to avoid prosecution through a political process called "impunity."

After each torture controversy quiets and the need again arises for such skills, security agencies can reach into their deep institutional memory to recover harsh practices supposedly erased by past reforms. Ironically, when the CIA revived its torture techniques in September 2001 after a decade-long hiatus, the memory of these methods resided in a military survival-training program meant to inure U.S. soldiers against such abuse by enemy interrogators.

In contrast to the bureaucratic influence and deep institutional memory of the U.S. intelligence community, the fluid human rights coalitions that form at each controversy necessarily focus on the present crisis, without the resources to probe for underlying continuities of law, policy, and doctrine that are the genesis of the problem. In this unequal struggle, the critics' main weapons—congressional investigation and media exposé—have proven blunt instruments, capable of stirring controversy but incapable of cutting through the complexities of law and bureaucracy to the core of the problem.

Over the past forty years, ad hoc civil society coalitions of Congress, the press, and the public have made repeated attempts to check the CIA's use of torture. Each time, they failed to pierce the veil shrouding the paradigm's elusive character and its covert application. Sometimes these exposés have been sensational, sometimes ephemeral. But all have proved unequal to the task of ending the ethos of impunity that surrounds CIA interrogation. By the time the next torture exposé erupts, these civil society groups are often a professional generation beyond the last scandal and start afresh, unaware of the continuity, the deep institutional roots underlying the current controversy.

The character of torture practiced by U.S. agencies further complicates the problem. Torture by the United States is perpetrated—and perpetuated—through a variety of mechanisms, facilitated by the difficulties of detecting the distinctive set of psychological interrogation techniques developed by the CIA and its affiliates. Leaving its most permanent scars on the psyche rather than the body, these techniques are like disappearing ink, their visible trail rapidly fading. This invisibility made it easier for Cold War behavioral scientists to tease out the possibilities of such methods and for the CIA to propagate them among allies in its wars against communism and terrorism. In times of crisis, this same invisibility has lent itself well to the rationalization, normalization, and even legalization of torture. Even when such torture is discovered, this invisibility has also enabled its perpetrators and their protectors to escape prosecution.

Impunity begins at the site of torture. These detention centers are closed to independent observers who might witness, document, or challenge. Responsibility for oversight falls instead to handpicked "experts," usually psychologists working for the federal government, who endorse harsh methods and assure interrogators that they will cause no serious or lasting damage. Such assurances shield perpetrators from charges of intentional abuse, a criterion in all U.S. definitions of torture. Officials at these facilities, aware that they are on dangerous ground, seek approval of their methods from higher authority. At the highest level, Department of Justice lawyers painstakingly dissect torture laws to seek justification for the methods used or contemplated. Unlike most crimes, torture is defined not merely ontologically—did it happen or not— but by the degree of the victim's suffering. What, for example, is "severe" pain? What procedures are "profoundly" disruptive? Legal advisers seeking to give interrogators wide latitude for abuse are assiduous in exploiting all ambiguities inherent in the language of torture, indeed, of language itself. Mindful of both domestic and international laws, these lawyers mine key documents for loopholes—arguing, for example, that the Geneva Conventions do not apply to suspected terrorists because terrorist groups are not states and that the Constitution of the United States grants the president authority to permit torture.

Occasionally, an investigative reporter probes. Or an inside source shares damning knowledge. In the rare instances when torture is discovered, responsible agencies destroy evidence and shift operations to new facilities. The president, forced to respond to the revelations, offers pro forma apologies and blames a few individuals who acted on their own. Politicians and pundits, as if sensing the larger scope of the problem, engage in a rhetorical campaign, rationalizing harsh interrogation on grounds of national security, minimizing the suffering of victims, and portraying opponents of such severe methods as weak. Congress undertakes an investigation but rarely probes to any depth, skirting classified matters and stopping at sketchy allegations. The bipartisan nature of U.S. torture policy implicates leaders of both parties, a mutual responsibility that mutes criticism. Rather than pressing for the prosecution of those who authorized torture or insisting on better oversight to prevent future violations, Congress accepts government promises to reform. To the extent that the American media report these events, they quickly lose interest, curtailing coverage to chase the next scandal, sometime serious, often frivolous. The American public soon forgets. This cycle of exposé and forgetting has been repeated, with some variation, six times over the past forty years.

In such circumstances, history can serve as an antidote to the public forgetting that is prime requisite for such impunity. By reconstructing this past and recovering its patterns, history allows the public to discover a larger design, seeing torture as an ineffective instrument for national security, impunity as the means for its persistence, and, on occasion, the past as prologue to prevention.

The Phoenix Program in Vietnam

The first of these defeats for reformers came in the aftermath of stunning revelations about the CIA's involvement in the Phoenix program, a covert effort to destroy the communist underground in South Vietnam with torture and extrajudicial executions. The character of these secret operations first emerged obliquely in 1969 during the investigation of Colonel Robert B. Rheault, a Special Forces commander accused, along with six of his subordinates, of assassinating a suspected Viet Cong spy. Although the charges were eventually dismissed, this investigation alerted the U.S. Congress and the public to the CIA's covert war against the Viet Cong, which included summary executions of "suspected" VC agents.[1]

After nearly four years of these classified operations, Congress and the press finally exposed the Phoenix program in 1970, when William Colby, chief of CIA pacification operations in Vietnam, told the Senate Foreign Relations Committee that, in 1969 alone, Phoenix had killed 6,187 members of the 75,000-strong Viet Cong underground.[2] A year later, Colby stated before a House committee that the program had killed 20,587 Viet Cong suspects since 1968. The Saigon government provided additional figures, attributing a total of 40,994 Viet Cong kills to the Phoenix program.[3] Despite these chilling statistics, both the Pentagon and the CIA insisted that Phoenix was a legitimate pacification program. Indeed, Colby flatly rejected any suggestion that Phoenix was "a systematic program of assassination."[4] Other witnesses gave detailed testimony about the brutality of these operations. But Congress took no action, and the controversy, amid the pressures of an ongoing war, soon faded.

While the Phoenix program was heavily debated and congressional findings remained inconclusive, discovery of the notorious "tiger cages" exposed the cruelty of America's Saigon ally. In July 1970, the head of the U.S. AID's police training program for South Vietnam was leading two U.S. congressmen on a tour of Con Son prison island when a young legislative aide, the future senator Tom Harkin (Democrat, Iowa), broke away to photograph cramped, sealed concrete cells covered with steel walkways. The five hundred prisoners confined below were bruised and mutilated from beatings, denied sunlight or exercise, living in the stench of their own filth, and pleading for water. Harkin's photographs of these horrific conditions, published in a July 1970 edition of *Life* magazine, served as visible icons of undeniable abuse and shocked the American people.[5]

As the Vietnam War wound down to defeat, public opinion, disturbed by reports of the harsh CIA tactics, created a momentary climate for reform. In December 1974, a *New York Times* investigative reporter, Seymour Hersh, revealed that the agency's "Operation Chaos" had conducted illegal mail intercepts and phone tapping against antiwar activists. In response to these revelations, President Gerald Ford appointed Vice President Nelson Rockefeller to investigate, and both houses of Congress formed special inquiries. Instead of stonewalling Congress as his predecessor had done, William Colby, by now CIA director, skillfully restrained these inquiries by feeding investigators just enough information to convince them that they were uncovering the whole truth.[6]

The Rockefeller Commission found that the CIA, in monitoring U.S. citizens, had done things that "should be criticized" but did not recommend any sanctions, since the agency claimed to have reformed itself. Alone among these inquiries, the U.S. Senate Select Committee to Study Intelligence Activities, led by Senator Frank Church (Democrat, Idaho), held hearings that probed aggressively in certain areas, notably assassination and destabilization operations. But a later history of the agency found that the Senate's inquiries into the CIA's drug experiments and subsequent torture training programs did not go beyond the anecdotal and superficial.[7]

Though these Senate hearings inspired four well-documented books on the CIA's mind-control experiments, there was no internal investigation or criminal prosecution of culpable officials. "I thought in 1978 when our books were appearing, when we were doing media work all over the world," recalled Alan Scheflin, author of *The Mind Manipulators*, "that we would finally get the story out, the vaults would be cleansed, the victims would learn their identities, the story would become part of history, and the people who had been injured could seek recompense. Instead, what happened was the great void."[8] Trying to explain why the CIA's "accomplices in torture" had escaped examination, author A. J. Langguth concluded: "Senator Frank Church tried to force some admissions but his witnesses sidestepped his staff's sketchy allegations. Given the willingness of Congress to accept the CIA's alibis about national security, I don't think any other public hearing would fare better."[9]

To correct the Senate's "fragmentary picture . . . of the extent to which the agency was engaged in behavior control research," in 1977, the *New York Times* published a major investigation into what it called a "secret, 25-year, $25 million effort by the Central Intelligence Agency to learn how to control the human mind." From 1948 to 1973, the agency had worked through distinguished scientists to test drugs, hypnosis, and sensory deprivation on unwitting subjects in hospitals, prisons, and psychiatric clinics. Behind a cloak of secrecy, the agency "was able to assemble an extensive network of non-government scientists and facilities—apparently without the knowledge of the institutions where the facilities were located." According to a report by the CIA inspector general completed in 1957, the agency "had added difficulty in obtaining expert services" since some experiments "are considered to be professionally unethical and in some instances border on the illegal."[10] Although the *Times* report corrected the historical record, the drama of congressional investigation had already faded, and, in the end, this front-page exposé had little lasting impact.

Even after these revelations about the CIA's mind-control experiments and its Phoenix program, there was still a deep, almost inexplicable silence in America over the issue of torture. In 1977, for example, former CIA agent Frank Snepp published a best-selling memoir of his Vietnam experience recounting, in graphic detail, the months he spent torturing a captured North Vietnamese cadre, Nguyen Van Tai. Just as the fictional interrogator in George Orwell's *1984* broke the antihero Wilson by discovering his fear of rats, so CIA and Vietnamese interrogators found that this dedicated communist cadre had one "psychic physical flaw"—a deep fear of cold. For more than four years, the CIA, using its torture technique of sensory deprivation, kept Tai under the intense psychological pressure of solitary confinement, locked inside an all-white, windowless room with just one feature: "heavy duty air conditioners." These CIA textbook techniques finally seemed to work, and the dossier began to grow as Tai, enticed by Snepp's hints of release, began talking—although much of the information he gave was probably calculated disinformation. Just before Saigon fell, however, a "senior CIA official" suggested that Tai should be "disappeared," and, Snepp claims, Tai was "loaded onto an airplane and thrown out over the South China Sea." But did he actually die? In fact, as the CIA later reported, the South Vietnamese intelligence agents assigned to do the assassination were fleeing Saigon. In the chaos, Nguyen Van Tai survived, later serving in the National Assembly and receiving his country's highest wartime decoration.[11]

By his references to an "American specialist" in interrogation, the elaborate sensory deprivation, and the efforts to induce personality regression, Snepp provided unmistakable clues that the CIA had developed sophisticated torture techniques. But the press focused on his titillating tales of political intrigue and ignored these indications that the CIA was engaged in torture.[12] There was, moreover, an important lesson from this tale that eluded even Snepp. According to another CIA officer, Merle Pribbenow, even though the South Vietnamese tortured Tai with electric shock, "beat him with clubs, poured water down his nose while his mouth was gagged, . . . and kept him tied to a stool for days at a time without food or water," he admitted his identity but nothing more. Transferred to American control and confined in the white room, Tai told CIA interrogators like Snepp "things they already knew, or that were not sensitive, while staying vigilant to protect Public Security's deepest secrets: the identities of its spies, agents, and assassins." In 1999, Nguyen Van Tai published his memoirs, describing "how he resisted years of unrelenting interrogation by some of the CIA's most skilled, and South Vietnam's most brutal, interrogators." In short, Snepp may have thought he was getting real information from Tai with sophisticated psychological torture. But this victim manipulated everyone, Americans and South Vietnamese alike, to ensure his survival and the security of his organization.[13]

Torture Training in Latin America

Although the Phoenix program was the agency's largest interrogation effort, it was exposés of CIA operations in Latin America that prompted a Senate attempt to end U.S. torture training altogether. Ironically, this story broke in August 1970, when the *New York Times* reported that the Tupamaro urban guerrillas in Montevideo had kidnapped Dan A. Mitrione, an American police adviser for the Office of Public Safety (OPS). Early reports described Mitrione as an ordinary family man from Indiana who headed the public safety program in Uruguay that operated under the U.S. Agency for International Development (U.S. AID), promoting "responsible and humane police administration."[14] In fact, OPS was a collaborative effort by U.S. AID and its silent partner, the CIA, to train Third World police for counterinsurgency, including harsh interrogation.

Only days after Mitrione's emotional funeral in his hometown of Richmond, Indiana, a senior Uruguayan police official, Alejandro Otero, told the *Jornal do Brazil* that this American had used "violent techniques of torture and repression"—charges that the U.S. Embassy in Montevideo called "absolutely false."[15] Eight years later, however, a Cuban double agent, Manuel Hevia Cosculluela, who had joined the CIA and worked with Mitrione in Montevideo, published a book describing this American as a master torturer. Mitrione's motto, said Hevia, was "The right pain in the right place at the right time." At a 1970 seminar for Uruguayan police trainees, the American tortured four beggars to death with electric shocks to demonstrate his techniques. Over drinks at home, Mitrione gave Hevia a summary of his methods, which showed the influence of the CIA's psychological paradigm: "He said he considered interrogation to be a complex art. . . . The objective was to humiliate the victim, separating him from reality, making him feel defenseless. No questions, just blows and insults. Then silent blows." Significantly, the Cuban charged that Mitrione's deputy in the Montevideo Public Safety office was William Cantrell, a CIA agent.[16]

Just months before Mitrione's death in Uruguay, an unsettling convergence of U.S. police training in Brazil and evidence of police torture there finally raised questions before Congress. In May 1971, the Senate Foreign Relations Committee summoned the head of the U.S. Office of Public Safety for Brazil, Theodore D. Brown, who attempted to explain away this disturbing coincidence.[17] Four years later, however, congressional investigations led by Senator James Abourezk (Democrat, South Dakota) found widespread allegations that the OPS program was training torturers in the Latin American police.[18] Concerned about these persistent reports, Congress finally cut off all funds effective July 1975 for "training or advice to police, prisons, or other law enforcement," in effect abolishing the Office of Public Safety. Many of the ordinary U.S. AID public safety officers soon found themselves disavowed, discredited, and unemployed.[19]

Though these reforms were well intentioned, Congress had failed to probe for the source of this torture training. By the time the Senate started investigating the Office of Public Safety, focusing on failures in U.S. A.I.D.'s administration, the CIA had already stopped using that program as a cover and shifted its torture training to the U.S. Army's Military Assistance Program (MAP).[20] Denied access to Latin American police after the abolition of OPS in 1975, the CIA would henceforth work through U.S. military advisers to train allied armies in interrogation and pacification.

Controversy over Central America

During the last decade of the Cold War in the 1980s, media probes and congressional pressure led to some surprising revelations about the extent of CIA torture training in Latin America. While congressional inquiries in the 1970s had been inconclusive, these later investigations established unequivocally that the agency had taught military interrogators throughout the region, propagating the systematic tortures that were the hallmark of its dictatorships.[21]

In 1988, only two years after a CIA training program in Honduras had ended, James LeMoyne, a reporter for the *New York Times*, uncovered the extent of the agency's role in that country's brutal counterinsurgency, producing another cycle of public concern and official indifference. As civil warfare intensified in Honduras during the late 1970s, the CIA imported Argentine officers, veterans of that nation's "dirty war," to train local army interrogators and sent Honduran soldiers to the United States for instruction by its own experts. "I was taken to Texas with 24 others for six months between 1979 and 1980," Sergeant Florencio Caballero told LeMoyne. "There was an American Army captain there and men from the CIA." The sergeant knew the chief CIA instructor only as a "Mr. Bill" who had served in Vietnam. Sergeant Caballero said the American officers "taught me interrogation in order to end physical torture in Honduras. They taught us psychological methods—to study the fears and weaknesses of a prisoner. Make him stand up, don't let him sleep, keep him naked and isolated, put rats and cockroaches in his cell, give him bad food, serve him dead animals, throw cold water on him, change the temperature."[22]

After their training, these soldiers joined Battalion 316, a special Honduran army intelligence unit supported by the CIA and organized by Colonel Gustavo Alvarez Martinez, a "vitriolic anti communist . . . trained in Argentina" who commanded both the national police and a private death squad. One of those tortured by Sergeant Caballero's unit, a young Marxist named Ines Murillo, recalled her eighty days of torture in an interview with the *New York Times*. Following her capture in 1983, she was taken to a secret army safe house in the town of San Pedro Sula, where she was stripped naked and subjected to electrical shocks for thirty-five days. Then, she was moved to a second, secret prison near Tegucigalpa, where her questioners, following the CIA's more refined psychological methods, "gave her raw dead birds and rats for dinner, threw freezing water on her naked body every half hour for extended periods and made her stand for hours without sleep and without being allowed to urinate." Although CIA agents visited both prisons and interrogated the prisoners, it is not clear whether they knew about these abusive practices and tolerated them. Sergeant Caballero said that the "Americans didn't accept physical torture," but the CIA backed the rise of Colonel Alvarez to command the army even though another Honduran colonel had denounced him as a killer at a press conference in 1982. Indeed, U.S. ambassador John D. Negroponte told the *Times* that Colonel Alvarez was "a hard man but an effective officer" who was needed in a country where "Marxist guerrillas are organizing." Another U.S. official was blunt about the torture, saying: "The C.I.A. knew what was going on, and the Ambassador complained sometimes. But most of the time they'd look the other way."[23]

This *New York Times* exposé of the CIA's role in Honduras prompted a congressional inquiry that, though somewhat cursory, revealed for the first time the existence of the agency's torture training manuals. When the U.S. Senate's Select Committee on Intelligence, responsible for legislative oversight of the CIA, met in closed session to review the allegations in June 1988, its chair, Senator David Boren (Democrat, Oklahoma), stated that, in the course of the CIA's internal review, "several interrogation training manuals, including one used to train the Hondurans, had been uncovered." In Boren's view, the techniques in these manuals were "completely contrary to the principles and policies of the United States."[24]

In secret testimony before the committee, the CIA's deputy director for operations, Richard Stolz, confirmed the essential accuracy of the *New York Times* story, admitting that "[Sergeant] Caballero did indeed attend a CIA human resources exploitation or interrogation course [deletion] from February 8th to March 13th, 1983." This five-week course, held in Honduras, featured "two weeks of practical exercises which included the questioning of actual prisoners by the students."[25] The chief instructor, Senator Boren added, was "an experienced CIA trainer," and, some months later, one of his colleagues drew upon "this man's accumulated materials and compiled the manual," producing the *Human Resources Exploitation Training Manual—1983*. This CIA trainer, Stolz explained, had prepared "the course lesson plan . . . based on his own experience in the U.S. Army . . . and on various other material [deletion] acquired over the course of [deletion] career." But the basic techniques were, he said, "assembled back in March of 1964"—an apparent reference to the CIA's original KUBARK manual.[26]

Deftly evading any further discussion of past CIA research into interrogation, Stolz implied that the CIA had already reformed itself from within. He said that, three years earlier in 1985, senior agency officers had ordered revisions to the Honduras manual and related CIA training policy—actions, in fact, taken only after damaging press exposés about the CIA's counterinsurgency training in Central America, described in chapter 1, had forced the agency to modify its interrogation policy. The manual's new text, Stolz insisted, banned "interrogation which results in the use of force, mental or physical torture, demeaning indignities or exposure to inhumane treatment of any kind as an aid to interrogation."[27]

But Senator Alan Cranston (Democrat, California) pointed out that the manual stated explicitly that "there are times when you should use coercive methods." Nonetheless, Stolz argued that "we were not talking anything about the kind of coercive methods that was alleged" in the *Times* article. Instead, he explained, "we are talking about . . . sitting in a chair on a stool for a long period of time, some sensory deprivations, sounds . . . and some techniques that while it might appear harsh were certainly not anything like what was alleged in the article." Then Senator Bill Bradley (Democrat, New Jersey) launched into an aggressive cross-examination of this witness about the article's accuracy, revealing both the broad outlines of the CIA's psychological paradigm and the committee's ignorance of its sophisticated methods.[28]

> *Senator Bradley:* Denying sleep?
> *Mr. Stolz:* Yes, there was some denied sleep.
> *Senator Bradley:* Making them stand up?
> *Mr. Stolz:* Yes.
> *Senator Bradley:* So making him stand up, denying him sleep—keeping him naked?
> *Mr. Stolz:* No. Definitely not.
> *Senator Bradley:* Rats?
> *Mr. Stolz:* No rats.
> *Senator Bradley:* Where it says: the CIA taught us psychological methods, to study the fears and weaknesses of the prisoner, make him stand up, yes; don't let him sleep, yes. Keep him naked and isolated [?]
> *Mr. Stolz:* No.
> *Senator Bradley:* Isolated?
> *Mr. Stolz:* Well, yes—the answer is yes.
> *Senator Bradley:* Naked no. Isolated yes.
> *Mr. Stolz:* Right.
> *Senator Bradley:* Changed the temperature?
> *Mr. Stolz:* I don't know the answer to that. That's not impossible.

A moment later, apparently aware that he had stumbled on to something larger than a few training manuals, Senator Bradley demanded to know: "Who was in charge of all this? Prior to 1984?" Mr. Stolz's four-line reply is blacked out.[29] In his closing remarks, Stolz assured the senators that the CIA's inspector general would conduct a prompt review of these allegations—a review that, if ever completed, has not been released.[30]

Significantly, a fact sheet prepared for the committee showed that U.S. Army Special Forces had conducted at least seven "human resources exploitation" courses in Latin America between 1982 and 1987, confirming that the CIA had indeed shifted its interrogation training from police advisers to U.S. Army instructors after Congress abolished OPS in 1975.[31] Although the leading U.S. newspaper had published a detailed report of CIA torture training, Congress was, as this committee demonstrated, still unwilling to expose the agency's human rights violations, much less to press for prosecution. Under the national security pressures of the Cold War, CIA torture training had again eluded serious reform.

Beyond the Cold War

While Washington was tacitly tolerating torture by its Third World allies, several European civil society groups launched a global movement to check the spreading abuse of human rights that would, in coming decades, complicate this U.S. policy. Concerned about the proliferation of abuse by authoritarian regimes, the international community proposed treaties to ban the practice and therapy to treat its victims. In 1972, Amnesty International asked the medical profession to assist its campaign against torture.

In response, a group of Danish doctors examined Greek and Chilean refugees for "forensic medical evidence about the after effects of torture" and discovered that they suffered from persistent posttraumatic stress disorder. Of the two hundred victims treated, Danish doctors found that nearly 70 percent still had "mental symptoms at the time of examination" many years after their torture, including nightmares, depression, panic attacks, and low energy. But the victims could recover with the right therapy. By 1982, these discoveries inspired the founding of Copenhagen's Rehabilitation and Research Centre for Torture Victims, which, within a decade, had formed a global network of clinics and developed a regimen to treat forty-eight thousand victims annually.[32]

These efforts broadened medical understanding of both physical and psychological torture while building international support for its abolition. After years of such global grassroots agitation, the UN General Assembly finally adopted the Convention against Torture (CAT) in December 1984, defining this crime broadly, under Article 1, as "any act by which severe pain or suffering, whether physical or mental, is intentionally inflicted on a person for such purpose as obtaining from him or a third person information or a confession."[33] Approved by a unanimous vote of the UN General Assembly, the Convention created enormous international pressure for compliance. Consequently, President Ronald Reagan sent it to Congress in 1988 with a ringing endorsement invoking "our desire to bring an end to the abhorrent practice of torture." Simultaneously, however, the administration proposed a record number of reservations that would stall ratification in the Senate for the next six years.[34]

When the Cold War came to a close, Washington retracted its torture training and resumed its advocacy of human rights. In 1991, Congress passed the Torture Victim Protection Act to allow civil suits against any foreign perpetrators who enter U.S. jurisdiction.[35] A year later, Defense Secretary Dick Cheney, as noted in chapter 1, ordered the recall and destruction of interrogation manuals that the U.S. Army had used to train Latin American militaries in illegal methods. At the 1993 Vienna Human Rights conference, Washington revived its vigorous advocacy of a universal standard for human rights, opposing the exceptions for "regional peculiarities" favored by dictatorships such as China and Indonesia.[36]

After years of delay, in 1994 the Clinton administration finally ratified the UN Convention against Torture, which banned, in equal measure, both physical and psychological methods.[37] On the surface, the United States had seemingly resolved the contradiction between its anti-torture principles and its torture practices. Yet, when this liberal president sent the UN Convention to Congress for ratification, he included the exculpatory language, written into the original "reservation" six years earlier by the conservative Reagan adminis- tration, that exempted the United States from particular aspects of the Con- vention, widened the loopholes for torture, and introduced new ambiguities that would shield perpetrators from prosecution.[38]

The UN Convention described the victim's experience in the broadest pos- sible terms, as "severe pain or suffering, whether physical or mental," and the parties to the Convention made no attempt to identify the acts that could be expected to result in such effects. While the United States was content to leave severe *physical* pain or suffering undefined, it zeroed in anxiously on just one word in the UN document's twenty-six printed pages. That word was "mental."

In a significant departure from the UN Convention, this U.S. reservation stated that, "in order to constitute torture, an act must be *specifically intended* to inflict severe physical or mental pain."[39] By referring to acts "specifically in- tended," this diplomatic reservation narrowed the UN Convention's inclusive definition of torture as any act that "intentionally inflicted" pain. In effect, the U.S. language, in both the reservation and subsequent legislation, served to ex- pand the element of intent already present in the U.N. Convention and inserted a series of qualifiers so ambiguous as to encourage evasion and endless debate.

Unlike the UN Convention, the U.S. reservation went on to list just four acts that, if resulting in "prolonged mental harm," would be considered torture: "(1) the intentional infliction or threatened infliction of severe physical pain or suffering; (2) the administration or application, or threatened administration or application, of mind-altering substances or other procedures calculated to disrupt profoundly the senses or the personality; (3) the threat of imminent death; or (4) the threat that another person will imminently be subjected to death, severe physical pain or suffering, or the administration or application of mind-altering substances or other procedures calculated to disrupt profoundly the senses or personality."[40]

Through subtle changes in the UN's original language, these four specifica- tions both narrowed and muddled the U.S. requisites for a finding of mental torture. Instead of the UN's clear standard of "severe pain or suffering" for an act to constitute torture, the U.S. reservations required "*prolonged* mental *harm*." This was a quantum leap beyond mere "suffering" to a far higher standard of long-term "harm" to the mind, presumably by damaging basic cognitive functions. But what actually constituted "harm"? The U.S. law was silent. And how much time must pass before a victim's harm would be considered sufficiently "prolonged" to bring charges of torture? Again, the law was silent. Apart from the law's silence, there was neither a body of case law nor any published standard, medical or legal, that could answer these questions. Not only was the phrase ambiguous; it was ambiguous in ways that bought indefinite time for torturers and their protectors to avoid any accounting for their actions. The juxtaposition of "*prolonged* mental *harm*" with the phrase "disrupt *profoundly* the senses" effectively muddled the broader U.S. prohibition on "other procedures calculated to disrupt profoundly the senses or the personality." By barring these four specific acts and introducing an element of ambiguity into the ban on other procedures, the reservation opened large loopholes that could permit CIA's later use of psychological techniques such as sensory deprivation or self-inflicted pain.

Moreover, by reference to "intentional" infliction of pain and to procedures "calculated" to disrupt profoundly the senses or the personality, the U.S. reservation also reinforced the exculpatory element of intent. As we have seen in previous chapters, each of the techniques developed by the CIA over the decades, from sensory deprivation to self-inflicted pain to waterboarding, meets this standard in that it *profoundly* disrupts the sense or the personality. And each is *calculated* to do so, in that the agency developed these methods for this express purpose. Although the history of CIA experimentation and propagation reveals clear intent at the institutional level, an individual interrogator could claim ignorance of this history—a claim that can acquire greater potency when the interrogator has received assurances about legality of his methods from official experts, attorneys or psychologists.

These intricately constructed reservations thus served to redefine torture, at least for the United States, in ways that would offer sufficient latitude for the continuation of the psychological techniques the CIA had developed and propagated for the previous forty years. Moreover, the Clinton administration reproduced this exculpatory language verbatim in domestic legislation enacted to give legal force to the UN Convention—first in Section 2340 of the Federal Code and later in the U.S. War Crimes Act of 1996.[41] This legal legerdemain reduced the force of stipulations in the latter law that any American, civilian or military, who commits war crimes, including torture (as defined in Section 2340), "shall be fined under this title or imprisoned for life or any term of years, or both, and if death results to the victim, shall also be subject to the penalty of death."[42]

Ultimately, however, it was this little-known part of the law, Section 2340, that shaped future U.S. interrogation policy, opening loopholes sufficient for the CIA's use of psychological torture after September 2001. Adopting the reservation's language, this law defined torture, in convoluted syntax, as "an act committed by a person acting under the color of law *specifically intended* to inflict severe physical or mental pain or suffering (other than pain or suffering incidental to lawful sanctions) upon another person within his custody or physical control." Although court rulings about the meaning of "specifically intended" were "ambiguous" and "inconsistent," the Bush Justice Department could still find, in a 2004 memo, that "if an individual acted in *good faith* . . . it appears unlikely that he would have the specific intent necessary to violate sections 2340–2340A"—an interpretation that privileged the perpetrator who remains the best arbiter of his own "good faith."[43]

Copying verbatim from the U.S. diplomatic reservation, Section 2340 then listed the four specific acts that must cause "prolonged mental harm" to become torture, including "other procedures calculated to disrupt profoundly the senses."[44] Instead of the UN's phrase "intentionally inflicted," this U.S. law required that, for an act to constitute psychological torture, it must be "specifically *intended*" to inflict "prolonged mental harm" by "procedures *calculated* to disrupt profoundly the senses." If any pain inflicted through CIA techniques, no matter how severe, was not "calculated" or "intentional"—and intent here resided solely in the mind of the perpetrator—then torture was not torture.

By placing the burden of proof on the perpetrator's interpretation of his own intentions rather than on the objective consequences of his actions, the larger effect of Section 2340 and other U.S. laws was to offer ample grounds for exculpation. Indeed, just six years later, the Bush Justice Department would exploit all these ambiguities time and again, as we will see below, in documents such as its iconic August 2002 "torture memo" to rule the abuse of detainees permissible under U.S. law.

While Congress enacted legislation loaded with loopholes, the U.S. military moved decisively to make its interrogation doctrine clear, comprehensible, and fully compliant with the UN and Geneva Conventions. In September 1992, U.S. Army's Intelligence Center at Fort Huachuca issued a revised field manual, *FM 34–52: Intelligence Interrogation*, using its recent experience in the Gulf War to "move interrogation into the 21st century." Most important, the manual offered an inclusive definition of torture, absent all the qualifiers later found in Section 2340, that read: "Physical or mental torture and coercion revolve around eliminating the source's free will. . . . Torture is defined as the infliction of intense pain to body or mind to extract a confession or information, or for sadistic pleasure." Instead of Section 2340's limitation of torture to specific techniques, the Army manual offered broad guidelines: "Examples of physical torture include—Electric shock, Infliction of pain through chemicals or bondage . . . , Forcing an individual to stand, sit, or kneel in abnormal positions for prolonged period of time, Food Deprivation, Any form of beating." Similarly, "examples of mental torture include—Mock executions, Abnormal sleep deprivation, Chemically induced psychosis." In marked contrast to the latitude for mental abuse granted in Section 2340, the Army also warned that the "psychological techniques . . . in this manual should neither be confused with, nor construed to be synonymous with, unauthorized techniques such as brainwashing, physical or mental torture, or any other form of mental coercion." Indeed, the Army manual, unlike U.S. laws, omitted the perpetrator's intention as a requisite for torture, did not limit torture to particular techniques, and made "the infliction of intense pain" the sole criterion for transgression.[45]

Taking full cognizance of international law, the Army manual cited the Geneva Conventions on both combatants and civilians to declare, categorically, that "physical or mental torture and coercion revolve around eliminating the source's free will, and are expressly prohibited." The manual also stated that torture "yields unreliable results, may damage subsequent collection efforts, and can induce the source to say what he thinks the interrogator wants to hear." Not only is the yield low, but the consequences are grave. "Revelation of use of torture by US personnel will," the manual warns, "bring discredit upon the US and its armed forces while undermining domestic and international support for the war effort."[46]

The sum of these civil and military reforms produced a contradictory conclusion to the Cold War. Congress had ratified the UN anti-torture convention in ways that legitimated psychological torture under U.S. criminal law, while the Army was complying fully with the Geneva Conventions by making mental as well as physical torture a crime under the U.S. Uniform Code of Military Justice. By the late 1990s, Washington had buried these contradictions—U.S. civil law versus military justice, and U.S. criminal code versus UN convention—only to have them explode with such phenomenal force, just ten years later, in the Abu Ghraib controversy.

Civil Society Protests

Although civil society could not fully grasp these contradictions in the historical moment, the country's dwindling community of peace activists sensed something amiss. Throughout the 1990s, an informal alliance of press and

peace advocates engaged this ambiguity in a fitful manner as civil society struggled to correct excesses that remained from the Cold War. Public advocacy of
human rights and official secrecy over their violation collided most notably
in a long-running controversy about torture instruction at the School of the
Americas, the U.S. Army's training facility for Latin American officers, which
had operated in Panama since 1949.[47]

As part of Washington's withdrawal from the Canal Zone, the school
moved to Fort Benning, Georgia, in 1984, bringing the facility within striking distance of the U.S. peace movement. Activists pressed for the abolition
of this "School of Assassins" by staging an annual demonstration outside the
base each November, led by Catholic activists, Hollywood stars such as Martin
Sheen, and Washington liberals such as Representative Joseph P. Kennedy II.
Sharpening the criticism of U.S. relations with Latin American militaries, Jennifer Harbury, a Harvard-trained lawyer, demanded the truth about the disappearance of her husband, a Guatemalan rebel last seen being tortured inside
a military jail. Her quiet eloquence and long fast outside the White House
translated this complex issue into a single, comprehensible human loss.[48]

With its mix of celebrity and idealism, the peace movement served as the
catalyst for further disclosures about U.S. torture training. Representative
Robert Torricelli (Democrat, New Jersey) charged that Harbury's husband
had been murdered by a Guatemalan colonel in the CIA's employ, prompting an investigation by the president's Intelligence Oversight Board. In June
1996, the board reported that "the School of the Americas and U.S. Southern
Command had used improper instruction materials in training Latin American officers, including Guatemalans, from 1982 to 1991," with passages that
condoned "executions of guerrillas, extortion, physical abuse, coercion, and
false imprisonment."[49]

In these same years, the national press exposed the nature of this U.S.
torture training to public scrutiny. After interviewing Honduran veterans of
the CIA-trained Battalion 316, the *Baltimore Sun* published a three-part report
in June 1995 detailing the agency's brutal torture techniques. "The first thing
we would say is that we know your mother, your younger brother," said Jose
Barrera, recalling the methods the CIA had taught them. "And better you cooperate, because if you don't, we're going to bring them in and rape them and
torture them and kill them."[50]

Over the next two years, moreover, the *Baltimore Sun*'s freedom-of-
information requests forced both the CIA and the Pentagon to release manuals
compiled during the 1980s to train Latin American militaries in pacification
and interrogation. In September 1996, the *Washington Post* reported that six
manuals, totaling 1,100 pages, distributed to "Latin American military offi-

cers . . . from 1982 to 1991 advocated executions, torture, blackmail and other forms of coercion against insurgents." According to a Pentagon summary, intelligence agents were trained to employ "fear, payment of bounties for enemy dead, beatings, false imprisonment, executions and the use of truth serum."[51] Another text, titled *Handling of Sources*, suggested that intelligence operatives could deal with a difficult asset by causing "the arrest of the employee's parents, imprison the employee or give him a beating."[52]

A year later, when the CIA released related documents to avoid litigation, the national press published extracts from the agency's *Human Resources Exploitation Manual—1983*, describing it as an interrogation handbook the agency had distributed to at least five Latin American armies.[53] "While we do not stress the use of coercive techniques, we do want to make you aware of them and the proper way to use them," read the manual's introduction, in this way implicitly condoning these harsh methods. "The threat to inflict pain may trigger fears more damaging than the immediate sensation of pain," the text explained. "In fact, most people underestimate their capacity to withstand pain."[54] Advising against "direct physical brutality," the CIA text said that "the torture situation is an external conflict, a contest between the subject and his tormenter." By manipulating time, disrupting sleep, and enforcing rigid standing or sitting positions, the interrogator could drive the subject "deeper and deeper into himself, until he no longer is able to control his responses in an adult fashion." Significantly, in its coverage of this manual's release in January 1997, the *New York Times* reported that the CIA's office of public affairs had "acknowledged for the first time today the agency's prior teaching and subsequent repudiation of psychological torture."[55]

Although these press descriptions of the CIA's use of mental torture were chilling, the public reaction was muted. Citizens and civic groups remained silent. Very few editorials called for investigation. Congress did not react. Throughout three decades of intermittent exposé and public protest, the press and public had focused on sensational excesses such as assassination and physical abuse, leaving the more complex issue of psychological torture largely unexamined. In effect, this public debate complemented the Clinton administration's resolution of the torture question in the aftermath of the Cold War: purging the Phoenix-style physical abuse but preserving, through loopholes in U.S. anti-torture laws, the original CIA psychological paradigm. Through the combined failings of state and civil society, America entered the twenty-first century with these contradictions unresolved.

In their aura of triumph after the Cold War, Americans seemed to view the new world order with a certain self-congratulation, reaching out into troubled regions beyond the country's borders to support democratic transitions with funds for electoral reform, press freedom, and human rights. But Americans did not, perhaps could not, ask whether fighting the Cold War abroad might have damaged democracy at home and the nation's adherence to human rights abroad. Absent any searching examination or binding reforms to restrain U.S. intelligence agencies, the torture doctrines developed during the Cold War lay fallow through the peaceful 1990s, ready to be revived in any future crisis—as indeed they would be in the traumatic aftermath of 9/11.

War on Terror, War of Torture

In the months after the 9/11 terrorist attacks, Bush administration attorneys produced a series of recondite legal memos for the president that asserted his exemption from laws barring torture and offered an expansive view of executive power. In times of war, these neoconservative lawyers argued, the president should be able to set aside all domestic laws or international treaties to defend the nation, correcting what Vice President Cheney condemned as "the unwise compromises . . . over the last 30 to 35 years" that have eroded "the powers . . . of the president of the United States to do his job."[56] In effect, these White House legal advisers argued that "the unitary executive" was the preeminent branch of government, challenging the constitutional principle that the presidency is one of three coequal branches. John Yoo, a University of California law professor who had served in the Bush Justice Department, asserted that "the founders intended that wrongheaded or obsolete legislation and judicial decisions would be checked by presidential action."[57]

Drawing on these advisers, President Bush ordered, in February 2002, that the Geneva Conventions on treatment of prisoners of war would not apply to members of the terrorist group Al Qaeda on the grounds that it was not a "high contracting party," that is, a state, and that "the war against terrorism ushers in a new paradigm." While admitting that "our values as a nation . . . call for us to treat detainees humanely," the president's memo made clear that the United States acted on these values only through its good graces, not as a matter of legal necessity.[58]

The White House also permitted the CIA to open overseas prisons and approved "enhanced interrogation" methods designed by agency psychologists, including "waterboarding."[59] To develop these techniques, psychologists working for the CIA "reverse engineered" the military's SERE survival training, which remained the U.S. government's sole institutional memory of the early CIA interrogation research done during the 1950s. Military psychologists who had spent years doing SERE training for American soldiers were seconded to the CIA, where they flipped these defensive methods for offensive use on Al Qaeda captives. "They sought to render the detainees vulnerable—to break down all of their senses," one official told Jane Mayer of *The New Yorker*. "It takes a psychologist trained in this to understand these rupturing experiences." Inside CIA headquarters, officials felt a "high level of anxiety" about possible prosecution for methods they knew to be defined as torture under both U.S. and international law. The presence of Ph.D. psychologists was considered a "way for CIA officials to skirt measures such as the Convention against Torture."[60]

In response to White House inquiries about the legality of these techniques, Assistant Attorney General Jay Bybee and his subordinate John Yoo found grounds, in their now notorious August 2002 memo, for exculpating any CIA interrogator who tortured but later claimed that his intention was obtaining information, not inflicting pain. Using the loopholes encoded in Section 2340 of the federal code and the U.S. War Crimes Act, the authors added that, "if a defendant acts with the good faith belief that his actions will not cause such suffering, he has not acted with specific intent," and "good faith may be established by, among other things, the reliance on the advice of experts." Thus, it was necessary only to produce some "experts"—in this instance, "personnel with medical training"—who would assure the agents that the methods employed would not result in severe or prolonged mental harm.[61]

These Justice Department lawyers were not only aggressive in their advocacy of torture; they were also meticulous in laying the legal groundwork for a later impunity. In addition to his August 2002 memo, Bybee also wrote secret guidelines that approved all ten of the agency's proposed interrogation techniques, including: "(1) attention grasp; (2) walling, (3) facial hold, (4) facial slap (insult slap), (5) cramped confinement, (6) wall standing, (7) stress positions, (8) sleep deprivation, (9) insects placed in a confinement box, and (10) the waterboard." To immunize agents who used the last and most severe of these methods, Bybee cited a contract psychologist at a CIA "black site" in Thailand who felt, on the basis of his experience as a SERE instructor who had subjected ten thousand Air Force recruits to waterboarding, that its long-term psychological effects "are certainly minimal." Even though Bybee himself found that "the use of the waterboard constitutes a threat of imminent death," it could still be considered legal because, first, it did not cause "prolonged mental harm . . . lasting months or years," and, second, "those carrying out these procedures would not have the specific intent to inflict severe physical pain or suffering."[62] One CIA lawyer reportedly called Bybee's memos a "golden shield" against any future prosecution.[63]

Three years later, in May 2005, Deputy Assistant Attorney General Stephen Bradbury replicated this exculpatory logic in three detailed torture memos, citing the U.S. diplomatic "reservation" to the UN Convention and Section 2340 to argue that waterboarding was perfectly legal because the "technique is not physically painful" and "nothing suggests that the detainee would be expected to suffer any prolonged mental harm." Again, the administration lawyers mentioned reliance on experts. "Psychologists who monitor the detainee's mental condition" were on hand to assure interrogators that they were causing no severe or prolonged harm—thus providing the shield of ignorance required to act "in good faith" and with no "intent" to hurt anyone. As for sleep deprivation, physicians from the CIA's Office of Medical Services had assured Justice, Bradbury added, "that no 'profound' disruption would result." Even if such disruption did occur, the lawyers insisted, "we do not believe it tenable to conclude in such circumstances that the use of sleep deprivation could be said to be 'calculated' to cause such profound disruption," a finding they based on the definition of "calculate" in *Webster's Third Dictionary*.[64] After careful legal review at Justice and CIA, all these enhanced techniques were, Bradbury counseled confidently, "unlikely to be subject to judicial inquiry."[65]

Since he drafted these memos long after the worst abuse was over, Bradbury's apparent aim was to provide legal cover for Bush's lawyers as they began to leave office. Six months later, in November 2005, the CIA, in a complementary move to conceal evidence of earlier abuse, destroyed ninety-two videotapes of Al Qaeda detainees being interrogated inside the agency's Bangkok black site.[66] In effect, the Bush administration was laying the legal foundation for a later impunity.

Bradbury's memos also indicated that the CIA had stiffened its psychological methods significantly under Bush in a protocol that escalated to a paroxysm of waterboarding. Indeed, agency interrogators waterboarded Abu Zubaydah "at least 83 times during August 2002" and Khalid Sheikh Mohammad 183 times in March 2003.[67] Higher up the chain of command, Attorney General John Ashcroft approved "expanded use" of these techniques at meetings with George Tenet, director of the CIA, in July and September 2003, even when "informed that the waterboard had been used 119 times on an individual."[68]

After a parallel legal review inside the Pentagon in late 2002, Defense Secretary Donald Rumsfeld approved fifteen aggressive interrogation techniques for the military prison at Guantánamo, authorizing harsh stress positions in a handwritten note reading: "I stand for 8–10 hours a day. Why is standing limited to 4 hours?"[69] Simultaneously, Rumsfeld gave General Geoffrey Miller command of the new American military prison at Guantanamo with ample authority to transform it into an ad hoc psychology laboratory. There military interrogators strengthened the psychological assault, moving beyond an attack on the senses to exploit the individual psyche and the cultural identity of Arab detainees.[70] After General Miller visited Iraq in September 2003, the U.S. commander, General Ricardo Sanchez, ordered Guantanamo-style abuse at Abu Ghraib prison.[71]

The Defense Department, like other Bush administration agencies, was careful to ensure impunity for those who used its aggressive methods, even in the frenzied first months of the War on Terror. In developing its expansive protocol during 2002, the Pentagon relied on the senior counsel at CIA's Counterterrorism Center, Jonathan M. Fredman, who echoed the Bybee-Yoo memo of August 2002 to advise that the legal definition of torture was "written vaguely" and "is basically subject to perception" by the perpetrator. Hence, he argued that U.S. law had no real restraints on interrogation, saying bluntly: "If the detainee dies, you're doing it wrong."[72]

This legal advice was reflected in interviews the International Red Cross later conducted with prisoners: "Mr. Khaled Shaik Mohammed alleged that, in his third place of detention, one of his interrogators stated that the green-light had been received from Washington to give him a 'hard time' and that, although they would not let him die, he would be brought to the 'verge of death and back again.'" In retrospect, it seems unlikely, even counterintuitive, that interrogators would reduce the level of threat when their intent was to coerce information, *unless* they had been instructed by lawyers that such an explanation immunized them against later prosecution.

Photos from Abu Ghraib

This seemingly strong consensus for torture as state policy evaporated with surprising speed after the media exposed conditions at Abu Ghraib prison. By early 2004, the abuse of detainees was so widespread and systematic that routine internal investigations by both the Army and the CIA began uncovering instances of serious mistreatment. Then, on April 28, 2004, CBS television broadcast just 16 of the 1,600 photos that the Army's Criminal Investigation Command had gathered as evidence of abuse at Abu Ghraib prison. Appearing on camera, Brigadier General Mark Kimmit, spokesman for General Sanchez, blamed "leadership, supervision" for the failings of the prison's military police, pointing an accusing finger at just one officer, General Janis Karpinski, commander of Military Police in Iraq. In June, more than a year after burying the CIA inspector general's report on detainee abuse, Attorney General Ashcroft suddenly announced the indictment of a single agency contractor, David A. Passaro, for beating an Afghan detainee to death. Ashcroft branded the accused one of "a small group of individuals" who had betrayed America's most basic values.[73] Simultaneously, the Pentagon launched a series of inquiries and criminal investigations of abuse at Abu Ghraib.

Ultimately, however, the upshot of a dozen inquiries and several hundred military prosecutions was a reprimand for one female general officer, Janis Karpinski, and convictions of low-ranking soldiers like Private Lynndie England. These military inquiries were, in effect, the first step in a slow slide toward impunity. Even as they exercised extraordinary power over others, the perpetrators and the powerful who commanded them were assiduous in trying to cover their tracks—constructing complex legal justifications, destroying records of their abusive acts, and pulling upon the levers of state power to escape any culpability for their crimes. Public response to the CBS broadcast of the Abu Ghraib photos was, moreover, muted. With the Iraq war going badly and a burst of color-coded terror warnings fostering a sense of fear across America, the political climate was not conducive to such an exposé.

A week after the Abu Ghraib story broke, the CIA's inspector general reported that interrogators at the agency's black sites had used improvisations ranging from the cruel to the possibly criminal, including threats to sexually abuse one detainee's female relative and to kill another's family. Even though these death threats clearly violated U.S. law, both Section 2340 and the War Crimes Act, Bush's Justice Department had already decided, symbolically on September 11, 2003, not to prosecute the agency interrogators responsible for this abuse and "turned these matters over to the CIA for disposition."[74]

In the months that followed the CBS broadcast, the Abu Ghraib scandal intensified as the disturbing power of those photos unleashed a complex interplay among public and private institutions that drove the controversy relentlessly forward through two distinct phases. During the first, from June to November 2004, the White House slowly ground down critics with its formidable powers of persuasion, moving the country by degrees toward a blanket impunity for all major actors implicated in torture at the prison. But, in the second, more intense phase of debate that followed the November presidential elections, a civil society coalition of courts, Congress, human rights groups, and the press redoubled its efforts, scoring some surprising successes in slowing the country's march toward impunity.

Just hours before the CBS exposé aired, on April 28, 2004, the Supreme Court had assembled for oral arguments in a detainee rights case, a coincidence that soon had far-reaching consequences.[75] In the hearing for *Rumsfeld v. Padilla*, Justice Ruth Bader Ginsburg challenged the executive's claim to exemption from judicial oversight, asking, "So what is it that would be a check against torture?" When the deputy solicitor general, Paul D. Clement, tried to evade the question with a bland assurance that military violators would be prosecuted, the justice pressed harder, saying, "Suppose the executive says mild torture we think will help get this information." To quiet that concern, the deputy solicitor insisted that "our executive" would never tolerate torture, adding that in wartime "you have to trust the executive to make the kind of quintessential military judgments that are involved in things like that."[76] Within hours, the justices, like the rest of the nation, would see those photos of torture from Abu Ghraib broadcast by CBS television. In coming months, the Supreme Court would issue a series of landmark decisions requiring that executive treatment of detainees comply with international and domestic law.

Responding to this deepening scandal in May and June 2004, the Bush White House issued pro forma apologies while attributing events at Abu Ghraib to a few "bad apples." At a Pentagon press conference on May 4, Defense Secretary Rumsfeld stated that "what has been charged thus far is abuse, which I believe technically is different from torture." When pressed, the secretary said, "I'm not going to address the 'torture' word." A few days later, Rumsfeld insisted that the abuses were "perpetrated by a small number of U.S. military." On May 10, after the Senate unanimously condemned the violence against detainees, President Bush obliquely acknowledged the problem, stating that there would be "a full accounting for the cruel and disgraceful abuse of Iraqi detainees." Speaking to the U.S. Army War College on May 24, the president promised to demolish Abu Ghraib as "a symbol of disgraceful conduct by a few American troops who dishonored our country and dishonored our values" and replace it with "a modern, maximum security prison . . . as a fitting symbol of Iraq's new beginning." But the move was soon blocked by a U.S. Army judge who ordered the prison preserved as a "crime scene" for prosecution of accused MPs.[77]

Despite these efforts at damage control, a torrent of leaked executive documents showed that officials up and down the chain of command had condoned the brutality: from White House lawyers who defined torture narrowly to allow abuse, through Defense Secretary Rumsfeld who ordered the harsh measures, to senior military who pressed subordinates to obtain better intelligence, all the way down to field grade officers and ordinary soldiers who carried out these commands, often with a steely professionalism but occasionally with a psychopathic abandon. Instead of dissolving into a typical media frisson, the issue of torture and treatment of detainees became, for a time, the subject of a serious political debate. Throughout, the White House maneuvered with determination to preserve executive prerogatives of incarceration and interrogation. Concerned, by contrast, about the implications of these practices for the rule of law, the human rights coalition mounted a sustained campaign to end prisoner abuse. The result was an epic political struggle and a substantive public discussion over questions of executive powers, civil liberties, and international law.

All of these political forces were soon arrayed in a battle over the Detainee Treatment Act of 2005, the first congressional attempt to regulate interrogation. Dissatisfied with the Pentagon's refusal to punish senior officers responsible for Abu Ghraib, leading Republicans on the Senate Armed Services Committee who were all military veterans—Lindsey Graham (South Carolina), John McCain (Arizona), and John Warner (Virginia)—began lobbying colleagues for legislation to limit executive authority over detainee treatment. Speaking to the Senate on July 25, 2005, John McCain moved amendments to the massive $442 billion defense appropriation that would require registration of all foreign prisoners with the International Red Cross "to eliminate the problem of 'ghost detainees' we faced in Abu Ghraib prison"; "establish the Army Field Manual as the uniform standard for interrogation" of all prisoners, except those held by the CIA; and bar any cruel or unusual punishment. During the floor debate, Senator Jeff Sessions (Republican, Alabama) opposed the motion, saying the detainees were not prisoners of war; "they are terrorists." But Senator McCain insisted that the issue "is not about who *they* are. It's about who *we* are."[78]

In a strong statement of support for Senator McCain, eleven retired military leaders, including the former chief of the U.S. Central Command, General Joseph Hoar (USMC, ret.), urged passage of this legislation. "The abuse of prisoners," they declared, "hurts America's cause in the war on terror, endangers U.S. service members who might be captured by the enemy, and is anathema to the values Americans have held dear for generations." Despite a threatened White House veto and a fierce debate, the Senate voted, by a margin of ninety to nine, with forty-six Republicans in favor, to ban "cruel, inhuman or degrading treatment" of anyone in U.S. custody—a stunning repudiation of Bush's interrogation policy. Countering with a bid to amend the legislation, Vice President Cheney took the CIA director to meet with Senator McCain and urge an exemption for the agency in "clandestine counterterrorism operations conducted abroad." As the vice president began to extol all "the invaluable intelligence we were obtaining through the program of enhanced interrogation," Senator McCain, who had been tortured as a POW in Hanoi, "stormed out of the meeting." The senator refused to capitulate, leaving the battle lines clearly drawn.[79]

After the Senate passed McCain's torture ban, the administration tried to neutralize its impact by backing an amendment authored by Senator Lindsey Graham (Republican, South Carolina). To nullify a landmark Supreme Court ruling in *Rasul v. Bush* that gave Guantanamo prisoners the right to challenge their detention before U.S. courts, Graham's amendment stipulated that "the term 'United States,' when used in a geographic sense, does not include the United States Naval Station, Guantanamo Bay," effectively denying detainees any legal basis for access to the courts.[80] According to Cheney himself, national security adviser Stephen J. Hadley negotiated "enough flexibility in the language of the amendment to allow the CIA program to continue in a pared-down way."[81] In sum, McCain's bill more or less banned torture, but Graham's amendment weakened the enforcement of that prohibition.

On December 15, 2005, all these tensions seemed to dissolve in a dramatic Oval Office handshake between Senator McCain and President Bush, who announced that the landmark legislation made it "clear to the world that this government does not torture."[82] That White House photo op was a media mirage. Right after signing a defense bill that included the McCain amendment at his Texas ranch on December 30, President Bush issued a "signing statement" insisting that his powers as head of the "unitary executive branch" allowed him to do whatever was necessary to defend the country.[83]

On January 3, 2006, the Justice Department, citing this new law, notified federal judges that it would seek the dismissal of all 160 habeas corpus cases already filed for three hundred Guantanamo detainees. On January 12, the solicitor general told the Supreme Court it no longer had jurisdiction over Guantanamo and asked the justices to dismiss another potential landmark "unlawful combatant" case, *Hamdan v. Rumsfeld*. Recoiling from the prospect of an "Imperial Presidency" implicit in these moves, a *New York Times* editorial on January 15 called on Congress "to curtail Mr. Bush's expansion of power" and his "unilateral rewriting of more than 200 years of tradition and law."[84] Significantly, the McCain amendment and the consequent public controversy convinced the CIA to suspend "enhanced interrogation" for a few months, from January to May 2006.[85]

Slow Slide toward Impunity

Confronted by public anger over the abuse at Abu Ghraib, the White House was slowly winning the debate by defending harsh interrogation as an imperative for the War on Terror. But in June 2006, in a dramatic rebuke of the president's position, the U.S. Supreme Court ruled, in *Hamdan v. Rumsfeld*, that Bush's military commissions were illegal because they did not meet the requirement, under Common Article 3 of the Geneva Conventions, that Guantanamo detainees be tried with "all the judicial guarantees . . . recognized as indispensable by civilized peoples."[86]

Three months later on September 6, 2006, in a bid to legalize his policies in the aftermath of this adverse decision, President Bush announced that he was sending legislation to Congress authorizing the same presidential prerogatives that had been challenged by the Supreme Court. Under this legislation, Bush proposed to set aside the Geneva Convention's requirement, under Common Article 3, for humane treatment of captives, making a lesser standard retrospective all the way back to 1997 to protect CIA interrogators from prosecution under the War Crimes Act. Detainees at Guantanamo would be tried by the military commissions under new guidelines that allowed the admission of hearsay and coerced testimony, as well as the concealment of classified evidence from the accused. By this speech, Bush resolved the convenient contradiction, dating back to the Cold War, between U.S. anti-torture principles and its torture practices. He did so, however, not by banning all abuse but by legalizing psychological torture as a lawful instrument of American power.[87]

In the House, Republican leaders were determined to pass Bush's bill verbatim but were challenged by the military's senior legal officers. Appearing before a hostile Armed Services Committee on September 7, the four top Judge Advocates General defended the Geneva Conventions as the basis for detainee treatment. The most outspoken, General James C. Walker, drew upon his quarter-century of service as a Marine Corps JAG to blast Bush's proposed legislation, saying: "I'm not aware of any situation in the world where there is a system of jurisprudence that is recognized by civilized people where an individual can be tried and convicted without seeing the evidence against him."[88]

In response, the Bush administration marshaled its forces for a full-bore assault. Firing the first shot on September 13, the Pentagon's neoconservative counsel, William Haynes, tried to neutralize these top JAGs, summoning them for a closed-door meeting where he handed them a prepared statement supporting Bush's bill. Confronted with the very provisions they had fought for five years, the military lawyers balked at signing this virtual surrender. The Navy's top JAG, Rear Admiral Bruce MacDonald, said bluntly that he could not agree, since Geneva's Common Article 3 barring "outrages on personal dignity" should remain the standard for detainee trial and treatment. After hours of skirmishing, Haynes finally extracted their signatures on a revised letter, striking for its terseness, stating that the legislation did not contradict the Geneva Conventions: "We do not object to section 6 of the administration's proposal which would clarify the obligations of the United States." The next day, the White House trumpeted this narrowly circumscribed concession as a ringing endorsement. CIA director Michael Hayden proclaimed his support for the Bush bill to protect his interrogators. Finally, on September 14, Bush and Cheney marched together about the halls of Congress, press-ganging Republican leaders into the battle for their bill.[89]

In this fight, McCain and fellow dissenters on the Senate Armed Services Committee received reinforcement from an unlikely ally. After years of loyal service to the president, Colin Powell broke ranks to write McCain that any tampering with the Geneva Conventions would cost America "the moral basis of our fight against terrorism."[90] Simultaneously, twenty-five retired general officers, including six top JAGs, warned the senators that Bush's bill would introduce "a flexible, sliding scale that might allow certain coercive interrogation techniques," with the result that "we would be viewed by the rest of the world as having formally renounced the clear strictures of the Geneva Conventions."[91]

After tense, daylong negotiations inside Vice President Cheney's Senate office on September 21, 2006, Republican partisans drafted compromise legislation that sailed through Congress within a week to become the Military Commissions Act of 2006. Significantly, this act provided CIA interrogators both legal immunity for past abuse and ample latitude for future psychological torture.[92] In presiding over the drafting of this law, Cheney included clauses, buried deep inside the bill's thirty-eight pages of dense print, that defined "serious physical pain" as the "significant loss or impairment of the function of a bodily member, organ, or mental faculty"—a striking paraphrase of the definition of physical torture as pain "equivalent in intensity to . . . organ failure" in John Yoo's infamous August 2002 memo. Ironically, that memo had already been repudiated by Bush's own Justice Department.[93]

By using verbatim the narrow definition of "severe mental pain" that the United States had first adopted in its 1994 reservation to the UN Convention against Torture, this legislation also carried forward those earlier loopholes. This exculpatory language was repeated in Para. § 950v, Part 11, Sub Section A of the Military Commissions Act, which reads: "Severe Mental Pain or Suffering Defined: In this section, this term 'severe mental pain . . .' has the meaning given that term in Sect. 2340 (2) of Title 18 [of the federal code]."[94] And how, we might remind ourselves, does Section 2340 define torture? It defines "torture" in a way that makes its determination depend upon the perpetrator's stated intention, and it effectively limits mental torture to four specific acts done with sufficient severity to cause "prolonged mental harm": drug injection, death threats, threats against another, and extreme physical pain. Anything else, including waterboarding, does not constitute severe mental pain and is thus permissible under U.S. law. By opening such loopholes, this exclusionary language allowed the exculpation of interrogators who had used the dozens of CIA psychological torture techniques developed during the past five decades.

The new law's permissive intent was confirmed nine months later when President Bush, as provided in the act, finally issued new guidelines for CIA interrogation, restraining the range of temperature modulation and restricting waterboarding. This order also contained a vague ban on humiliating or degrading treatment "so serious that any reasonable person, considering the circumstances, would deem [it] beyond the bounds of human decency." But the president's order denied the International Red Cross access to CIA prisoners and remained classified, masking many of its provisions. Most important, Bush's concessions were, under the law, a presidential prerogative and could be rescinded at any time, clearing the way for a resumption of waterboarding and other forms of torture.[95]

Amid this attempt at preemptive impunity, historical analysis provided the most telling critique of the administration's interrogation policy. In 2008, the Senate Armed Services Committee investigated interrogation practices since 9/11 and concluded that the abuse "cannot simply be attributed to the actions of 'a few bad apples' acting on their own." Indeed, the Senate said pointedly, "senior officials in the United States government solicited information on how to use aggressive techniques, redefined the law to create the appearance of their legality, and authorized their use against detainees."[96] More specifically, the Senate discovered that the CIA's methods dated back to the 1950s and were based on "Chinese Communist techniques used during the Korean war to elicit false confessions" from American prisoners held in North Korea. This data had shaped the SERE training used, for a full half-century, to prepare U.S. servicemen for enemy interrogation in the event of capture. After 9/11, however, the CIA had reverse engineered this SERE training to create the "enhanced" techniques used at its black sites worldwide.[97]

After tracing the genesis of these methods, the Senate hearings also raised questions about their effectiveness. SERE training involved "stripping students of their clothing, placing them in stress positions, putting hoods over their heads, disrupting their sleep, treating them like animals, subjecting them to loud music and flashing lights, and exposing them to extreme temperatures. It can also include face and body slaps and . . . waterboarding." All of the CIA interrogation techniques derived from such SERE training were, the Senate said, designed to produce "despair," "instill fear," "instill humiliation," make it "more difficult to think clearly, concentrate, and make rational decisions." Significantly, the Army's general counsel had found that proposals for using these methods did not adequately explain "how these techniques will result in our forces gaining any useful information." Indeed, one senior Pentagon criminal investigator told the committee that SERE techniques were "developed to better prepare U.S. military personnel to resist interrogations and not as a means of obtaining reliable information."[98]

Although the Senate's report provided a sharp critique of the Bush administration's interrogation policy, the findings were quickly obscured by the drama of the 2008 presidential campaign. The candidates for the Republican presidential nomination endorsed Bush's policy. Barack Obama, seeking the Democratic nomination, criticized "enhanced interrogation" sharply. But, once the campaign moved beyond the primaries, the issues of interrogation and incarceration played an inconsequential role in the presidential race.

A year later, the *New York Times* did publish a detailed investigative report that identified the two psychologists who had used their experience as SERE trainers for the Air Force to develop the CIA's harsh interrogation protocol after 9/11. But the impact of this finding, which hinted faintly at a half-century history of CIA mind-control research, was blunted when the *New York Times* overlooked the agency's early mind-control work and, at least by implication, attributed this development to the work of just two contract psychologists.[99]

Impunity under Obama

The Obama administration offered a contradictory response to the torture problem, taking office with the promise of bold reforms to correct Bush's excesses but then backtracking through a political dynamic that led, within three years, to complete impunity for these crimes. Right after his inauguration in January 2009, President Obama honored his campaign promises by signing executive orders in an Oval Office ceremony—closing the CIA's prisons, barring its coercive methods by requiring agency compliance with the Army Field Manual, releasing classified documents about enhanced techniques, and stripping the agency of its lead role in counterterror interrogation. The president also ordered the closure of Guantanamo, but Congress later blocked this reform.[100] With this dramatic gesture, Obama seemed to signal his repudiation of Bush's policies and his own administration's strong commitment to human rights.

Within a few months, however, the dynamics of partisan wrangling over CIA interrogation produced a surprising bipartisan move toward impunity. "The Bush administration constructed a legal framework for torture," noted the ACLU's Jameel Jaffer in late 2009, "but the Obama administration is constructing a legal framework for impunity."[101] Indeed, by the midterm elections in 2010, Obama had retreated from his original commitment to human rights and instead adopted many of the controversial security policies identified with his predecessor—canceling the plan to try Khalid Sheikh Mohammed in a New York civilian court, continuing the endless detention of Guantanamo detainees, reviving the controversial military commissions, accepting the CIA's

use of extraordinary rendition, allowing Special Operations Command to operate secret prisons in Afghanistan and Iraq, and invoking sovereign immunity
to quash civil suits by torture victims.

No matter how twisted the politics, the process of impunity—whether
in Britain, France, Indonesia, the Philippines, or America—usually involves
at least one of three common tactics. First, blame the supposed "bad apples."
Second, invoke national security ("It protected us"). Next, appeal to national
unity ("We need to move forward together"). To these three, we must add two
more most visible in America—a political counterattack by perpetrators and
their protectors, who excoriate human rights reformers for somehow weakening the nation's security; and, finally, revision of the historical record to justify
the use of torture. In President Obama's first three years in office, the United
States moved, via a mix of bipartisanship and bitter political in-fighting,
through all five tactics to reach a state of impunity.[102]

The first tactic enjoyed an unwitting bipartisanship. For a year after the
2004 Abu Ghraib exposé, Defense Secretary Rumsfeld claimed that the abuse
was "perpetrated by a small number of U.S. military." Similarly, while announcing his refusal to release more torture photos in May 2009, President
Obama echoed Rumsfeld, asserting that the abuse shown in these images "was
carried out in the past by a small number of individuals."[103]

In early 2009, Republicans made good use of the second tactic when former vice president Cheney stated that the CIA's harsh methods had "prevented
the violent deaths of thousands, perhaps hundreds of thousands, of people."
Obama did not controvert this claim, opening his administration to escalating
Republican criticism.[104]

Then, on April 16, 2009, President Obama advanced the third tactic in
the process of impunity when he released four Bush-era memos detailing CIA
torture techniques while insisting, "Nothing will be gained by spending our
time and energy laying blame for the past."[105] During a visit to CIA headquarters four days later, Obama promised that there would be no prosecutions
of its employees. "We've made some mistakes," he admitted, but he urged
Americans to "acknowledge them and then move forward." In the furor surrounding the release of those memos, the Senate Judiciary Committee chair,
Patrick Leahy (Democrat, Vermont), called for an independent commission
on interrogation. Even the House Minority Leader John Boehner (Republican, Ohio) seemed open to the idea. But the White House press secretary
stated "the president determined the concept didn't seem altogether workable"
because such an inquiry "might just become a political back and forth." The
president's position was in such blatant defiance of international law that the
UN's chief official on torture, Manfred Nowak, reminded him that Washing-

ton was legally obliged to investigate any violations of the Convention against Torture.[106]

While these first three tactics appeared quickly, the fourth, involving heated neoconservative attacks on human rights reforms, arrived through the dynamics of partisan politics over the next two years. Determined to escape any accounting for past abuse, former Bush officials attacked each attempt at reform, producing a recurring political pattern: thunderous Republican media criticism, followed by tacit concession from the Obama administration. Moreover, Obama's initial commitment to civil liberties was compromised by a willingness to use the expanded executive powers left by his predecessor. Through this interweaving of external pressure and internal compromise, the Obama administration moved, over the next two years, to impunity for human rights violations committed under his predecessor, ultimately capitulating to intense political maneuvering by Republican torture advocates.

From the outset of the Obama administration, Republican legislators pressured his attorney general, Eric Holder, to avoid any investigations of Bush-era excesses, threatening an exposé of the Clinton administration's many renditions to Egypt, a nation notorious for brutal torture. During one telling exchange in May 2009, a Republican senator, as the *New York Times* put it, "suggested that if Bush administration lawyers were to be investigated, perhaps those from the Clinton administration should get similar treatment"—a clear threat to Holder himself, who had served as deputy attorney general under Clinton at a time when renditions were ongoing.[107]

Senator Lamar Alexander (Republican, Tennessee): My last question is, once we begin this process, where is the line drawn? . . . The *Washington Post* says the former director of the Central Intelligence Agency, George Tenet, said there were about seventy renditions carried about before Sept. 11, 2001; most of them during the Clinton years. Mr. Attorney General, you were the Deputy Attorney General from 1997–2001. Did you know about these renditions? Did you or anyone else at the Department of Justice approve them?

Attorney General Holder: I think the concern that we have with renditions is renditions to countries that would not treat suspects in a way that's consistent with the laws and treaties that we have signed. If there is a rendition taking a person to a place where that person might be tortured? That's the kind of rendition that I think is inappropriate. My memory of my time in the Clinton Administration, I don't believe that we did that—that we had renditions where people were taken to places where we had any reasonable belief that they were going to be tortured.

Senator Alexander: But I think you can see the line of my inquiry which is . . . where does that stop? . . . In your case, in the Clinton Administration, we don't know what the interrogations were then. Perhaps you do and perhaps the question would be whether you approved them. I prefer President Obama's approach. I think it's time to look forward and I hope he sticks to that point of view.[108]

Within weeks, congressional Republicans charged their Democrat colleagues with complicity in Bush-era interrogations policies, asserting that House Speaker Nancy Pelosi, among others, had been briefed fully by the CIA. In her own defense, the speaker said she was "briefed on interrogation techniques the administration was considering using in the future," adding that the techniques were supposed to be legal.[109]

Thunder on the Right

Over the coming months, thunder from the Republican right countered every attempt at an accounting for the past, pushing the Obama White House toward a compromised position on human rights. After the administration released the Bush torture memos in April 2009, former vice president Cheney and his daughter Liz launched a sustained media counterattack. In his memoirs, Cheney says he was "appalled that the new administration would even consider punishing honorable public servants," arguing that the release of those memos "revealed to the world, including our enemies, methods used to question detainees . . . about future attacks." Outraged, Cheney squared off against the president in a pair of "dueling speeches" on May 21, 2009.[110]

Standing before the original Constitution at the U.S. National Archives, President Obama said: "I know that we must never, ever, turn our back on its enduring principles for expedience sake. . . . From Europe to the Pacific, we've been the nation that has shut down torture chambers and replaced tyranny with the rule of law." Unfortunately, he continued, after 9/11, "we set those principles aside as luxuries that we could no longer afford" and, under the previous administration, "established an ad hoc legal approach for fighting terrorism that was neither effective nor sustainable—a framework that . . . failed to use our values as a compass." Though some "have argued that brutal methods like waterboarding were necessary to keep us safe," he said to an applauding audience, "I categorically reject the assertion that these are the most effective means of interrogation." These methods, he argued, "alienate us in the world. They serve as a recruitment tool for terrorists, and increase the will of our enemies to fight us." Guantanamo, he added, "created more terrorists around the world than it ever detained" and "set back the moral authority that is America's strongest currency in the world."[111]

Speaking at a conservative think tank that same day, Cheney proclaimed himself "a staunch proponent of our enhanced interrogation programs," calling them "legal, essential, justified, successful, and the right thing to do."[112] In twelve television appearances on four networks in just nine days, his daughter Liz vehemently defended her father's use of harsh methods. On the CNN cable news network, she berated Obama for attempting to "libel the brave men and women who conducted this program" and denounced him for "suggesting that perhaps we would even be prosecuting former members of the Bush administration."[113]

Despite these mounting pressures, Attorney General Holder "reacted with disgust when he read graphic accounts" of abuse in a classified CIA inspector general's report. In August 2009, therefore, he instructed a special prosecutor, John H. Durham, to investigate possible crimes by agency interrogators, sparking a counterattack from the Republican right.[114] Appearing on *Fox News Sunday*, Dick Cheney admitted authorizing coercive methods such as waterboarding and blasted the decision to investigate CIA interrogators as an "intensely partisan, politicized look back at the prior administration." Within weeks as pressure mounted, Justice reduced the investigation to two or three egregious cases of detainee abuse—still too many for seven former CIA directors, who issued an open letter in late September warning that the probe could chill agency enthusiasm in future for "aggressive intelligence work." While the special prosecutor quietly continued his long-term investigation, the Obama administration backed away from further public comments about CIA interrogators and focused instead on the Bush administration lawyers who had authorized such harsh methods.[115]

In December, only days after the abortive bomb attempt on a Northwest Airlines flight near Detroit, Liz Cheney joined forces with the neoconservative pundit William Kristol to form a hyperpatriotic group, Keep America Safe. The group's opening media salvo blasted Obama for failing to defend the nation from terrorists and portrayed impunity for CIA torturers as synonymous with national security:

He should immediately classify Abdulmutallab, the Christmas Day bomber, as an illegal enemy combatant, not a criminal defendant. He should inform Attorney General Holder that he will no longer allow the Justice Department . . . to investigate or prosecute CIA officials who kept us safe after 9/11, or disbar or otherwise punish the lawyers who provided the legal framework for programs that saved American lives. President Obama has weakened American security by treating terror as a law enforcement matter, refusing to use every tool at his disposal to prevent attacks.[116]

A few weeks later, former vice president Cheney identified the "tool" in question, telling ABC News that the CIA should have considered waterboarding the Detroit bomber. And he called Obama's order that the agency comply with the Army Field Manual on interrogation "a mistake."[117]

Within weeks, these pressures from the right proved effective. In February 2010, Obama's Justice Department reversed an earlier finding that Bush lawyers Jay Bybee and John Yoo were "guilty of professional misconduct" in writing those 2002 torture memos that gave the CIA the authority to abuse detainees. Beating a hasty retreat from that position, a senior Justice official, David Margolis, now found that Yoo and Bybee had acted from an "extreme, albeit sincerely held view of executive power," thereby exempting them from any threat of disbarment—just as the Cheneys had demanded. Indicating the political nature of this reversal, Margolis insisted that this exoneration "should not be viewed as an endorsement of the legal work that underlies those memoranda." Simultaneously, the head of Justice's own Office of Professional Responsibility dissented from this decision, condemning the "lack of thoroughness, objectivity and candor" in the Bybee-Yoo memos.[118] In a sharply worded statement, the ACLU insisted that there was "extensive evidence" to support the prosecution of the two lawyers, saying: "They should have provided bona fide legal advice, but instead they served as knowing facilitators of criminal conduct. . . . The core problem was not one of rogue interrogators but one of senior government officials who knowingly authorized the gravest crimes."[119]

Shifting from defense to offense, the Republican right redoubled its attacks, charging Obama officials with duplicity tantamount to treason and thereby pushing the nation down the last steps toward impunity. In March 2010, Liz Cheney's group, Keep America Safe, released a video that branded Obama Justice Department officials who had previously defended detainees as the "Al Qaeda Seven," denouncing them for "engaging in a worldwide smear campaign against the CIA, the U.S. military and the United States itself while we are at war."[120] Many conservative lawyers compared this attack to "McCarthyism." Nonetheless, the political right ramped up its rhetoric, blasting Attorney General Holder for failing to disclose his earlier court briefs questioning President Bush's claim that he could imprison a U.S. citizen without trial as an "enemy combatant." So chastened was the White House by these attacks that, in late March, Obama refused to make a recess appointment for his nominee to head the Office of Legal Counsel, Indiana law professor Dawn Johnsen, who had antagonized Republicans by earlier criticisms of "Bush's corruption of our American ideals."[121]

Ending a self-imposed silence to publicize his memoirs, former president Bush added his voice to the view that waterboarding had saved lives. When asked if he had authorized this torture technique, Bush told the London *Times* in late 2010: "Damn right! We capture the guy, the chief operating officer of al-Qaida, who kills 3,000 people. We felt he had the information about another attack. . . . I believe that decision saved lives." In his memoirs, Bush wrote that these "interrogations helped break up plots to attack American diplomatic facilities abroad, Heathrow airport and Canary Wharf in London"—claims that British leaders, who were in a position to know, emphatically denied. Prime Minister David Cameron insisted that waterboarding was indeed torture, adding, "if actually you're getting information from torture, it's very likely to be unreliable information."[122] But the U.S. media did not really report this critique, and Bush's claims for the effectiveness of enhanced interrogation generally went unchallenged in the United States.

Compromising Human Rights

Apart from these Republican pressures, Obama's own aggressive views on national security contributed to a marked continuity with many of his predecessor's most controversial policies. He not only retained many top Bush security officials but also authorized detention without trial for fifty terror suspects, continued CIA rendition, preserved the military commissions, and fought the courts to retain executive counterterror prerogatives.

Obama's original January 2009 ban on CIA coercive interrogation contained legal loopholes. The order was "carefully tailored" to bar only agency black sites, letting the military maintain secret prisons in Afghanistan. When CIA counsel protested that closing all its prisons, even holding cells, would "take us out of the rendition business," Obama quietly added a footnote defining a "detention facility" to allow any used "on a short-term, transitory basis." Moreover, a presidential task force recommended, in August, against any changes to the Army Field Manual, which had been revised under Bush to permit abusive techniques such as stress positions and sleep deprivation.[123]

There were also signs that the Obama administration was resuming the policy of outsourcing interrogation, much as Washington had done during the Cold War. Since mid-2008, U.S. intelligence had captured a half-dozen Al Qaeda suspects and, instead of shipping them to secret CIA prisons, had them interrogated by allied agencies in the Middle East. Showing that this policy was becoming bipartisan, Obama's new CIA director, Leon Panetta, announced, in February 2009, that the agency would continue to engage in the rendition of terror suspects to allies such as Egypt, Jordan, and Pakistan. "In renditions where we returned an individual to the jurisdiction of another country, and they exercised their rights to try that individual and to prosecute him under their laws, I think that is an appropriate use of rendition," he explained, contravening the UN Convention's strict conditions for this practice.[124]

Indeed, as the CIA expanded covert operations inside Somalia, renditions from neighboring East African nations that had started under Bush continued under Obama. In July 2009, for example, Kenyan police snatched an Al Qaeda suspect, Ahmed Abdullahi Hassan, from a Nairobi slum and delivered him to the city's airport, where he was bound and blindfolded for a CIA flight to Mogadishu. There he joined dozens of prisoners grabbed off the streets of Kenya inside "The Hole"—an underground prison with "filthy small cells" buried in the windowless basement of Somalia's National Security Agency. While Somali guards, paid with U.S. funds, ran the prison, CIA and military intelligence operatives had open access for extended interrogation. Since an estimated eighty-five people were similarly rendered to Mogadishu in 2007 alone, Obama's CIA was clearly continuing a major rendition program started under Bush. Two years later, in July 2011, a fragment of this secret program was revealed when a Somali terror suspect, Ahmed Abdulkadir Warsame, who had been captured in the Gulf of Aden and interrogated for two months on a U.S. Navy ship, was delivered to New York City for trial.[125]

To block civil suits by victims seeking redress for Bush-era abuse, Obama's Justice Department followed its predecessor by invoking a "state secrets" doctrine. Although Attorney General Holder set a somewhat stricter standard, in September 2010 his staff persuaded a federal appeals court to quash a civil suit by five torture victims—a decision later affirmed by the Supreme Court. The application of the state secrecy doctrine to this case seemed arbitrary, since the victims were suing not a government agency but a private corporation— a Boeing subsidiary that ran rendition flights for the CIA. And the abuse was particularly egregious. One detainee, a British resident named Binyam Mohamed, had been flown to Morocco for eighteen months of torture that included cutting his penis with a scalpel. He was then sent to the CIA's "salt pit" prison in Afghanistan for months of confinement in total darkness and finally flown to Guantanamo for five years' confinement.[126]

In March 2011, after Congress barred transfer of any terrorist trials to the United States, the president rescinded his two-year ban on military tribunals at Guantanamo and ordered indefinite detention of Al Qaeda suspects "if it is necessary to protect against a significant threat to the security of the United States." In a shallow bow to civil liberties, Obama's order did provide periodic review of the case against each detainee, but these assessments were to take place before a body convened by the defense secretary.[127] The National Association of Criminal Defense Lawyers condemned this decision, saying that "the commission rules still permit the government to introduce secret evidence, hearsay and statements obtained through coercion."[128] The president of Human Rights First added: "This is a step . . . toward institutionalizing a preventive-detention regime."[129]

Simultaneous with this shift, the Obama administration's treatment of Bradley Manning, an American soldier accused of leaking classified documents to the website WikiLeaks, evoked, said the *New York Times*, "creepy memories of how the Bush administration used to treat terror suspects." After he downloaded and released some half-million diplomatic and military messages while on active duty in Iraq, Private Manning was arrested and sent to the Marine Corps Brig at Quantico for solitary confinement from July 2010 to April 2011. Restricted to an hour of daily exercise in shackles, Manning was forced to sleep stripped of clothing at night and stand outside his cell completely naked for morning inspection.[130] Such conditions led the UN special rapporteur on torture, Juan Mendez, to express concern to the State Department in 2011, prompting a State Department spokesman, Philip J. Crowley, to tell an audience that the Army's treatment of Manning was "ridiculous and counterproductive and stupid."[131]

In a stinging critique, some 295 legal scholars wrote an open letter condemning the conditions of Manning's confinement as a violation of the U.S. Constitution, arguing that his treatment would, if continued, constitute torture under that catch-all clause in Section 2340 banning "procedures calculated to disrupt profoundly the senses or the personality." In response, President Obama tried to assure the press that the "terms of his confinement are appropriate and are meeting our basic standards."[132] To quiet the growing protests, in April 2011 the Pentagon transferred Manning to a military prison at Fort Leavenworth, where he was confined without the punitive treatment.[133]

Undeterred, the Obama administration continued its crackdown on leaks, prosecuting six federal employees for providing media with information about classified programs, including Bush's enhanced interrogation. After a long investigation, in January 2012 the Justice Department charged former CIA agent John Kiriakou with unauthorized disclosures about the agency's brutal interrogation of Abu Zubaydah. Back in 2007, Kiriakou became an instant media sensation with his story that a single, thirty-second waterboarding had transformed Abu Zubaydah overnight from a hardened Al Qaeda leader into a complaint source—a claim proven false two years later when documents showed Abu Zubaydah had in fact been waterboarded eighty-three times and Kiriakou admitted he had not actually witnessed the interrogation.[134]

During his five-year career trafficking in such half-truths to press, film productions, and the Senate, Kiriakou revealed the names of two CIA operatives involved in Abu Zubaydah's interrogation to several reporters. One journalist passed the information to a Guantanamo defense team, angering the CIA and sparking a full FBI investigation that placed these ACLU attorneys under enormous pressure. In announcing Kiriakou's indictment, Justice also exonerated the defense attorneys, finding no laws had been broken. Although "relieved" by this exoneration, the ACLU's director charged the crackdown on leaks had a "chilling effect on defense counsel, government whistle-blowers, and journalists." By contrast, CIA director Petraeus announced he "fully supported the investigation from the beginning," indicating that Obama was finally healing the breach with the agency caused by his earlier release of documents about its harsh interrogations.[135]

Last Steps to Impunity

The Obama administration's assassination of Osama Bin Laden, in May 2011, provided an unexpected political opening for torture advocates to press for a penultimate step to full impunity. Within hours of the news of Bin Laden's death, these Bush-era perpetrators formed a media chorus, repeating the refrain that their harsh methods were responsible for this success and demanding an end to the Justice Department investigations of CIA interrogators.

Almost immediately, former Justice official John Yoo called Bin Laden's killing "a vindication of the Bush administration's terrorism policies [that] shows that success comes from continuing those policies, not rejecting them as Obama has tried to do for the last two years." Citing speculative, inaccurate news stories that appeared the morning after Navy Seals shot Bin Laden, Yoo argued that Bush's harsh interrogation had provided the first clue, the name of Bin Laden's courier, by extracting it from Khalid Sheikh Mohammed, the Al Qaeda operations chief who had been waterboarded 183 times.[136] Almost immediately, however, other news outlets reported that Khalid had consistently misled CIA interrogators with fake names and erroneous information.[137] Although the press quickly debunked the claims by Bush-era officials, Yoo published an op-ed in the *Wall Street Journal* insisting that Obama "should end the criminal investigation of CIA agents and restart the interrogation program that helped lead us to Bin Laden."[138] Making similar assertions, Jose Rodriguez, chief of the CIA's Counterterrorism Center under Bush from 2002 to 2005, told the media that the use of enhanced interrogation on Khalid Sheikh Mohammed and others had produced key intelligence "about Bin Laden's courier . . . that eventually led to the location of [Bin Laden's] compound and the operation that led to his death."[139]

Appearing on Fox News after Bin Laden's killing, former defense secretary Donald Rumsfeld said: "I think that anyone who suggests that the enhanced techniques—let's be blunt—waterboarding, did not produce an enormous amount of valuable intelligence just isn't facing the truth."[140] Reiterating his belief in the efficacy of harsh methods, Dick Cheney told Fox News: "I would assume that the enhanced interrogation program that we put in place produced some of the results that led to Bin Laden's ultimate capture."[141] Five days later, Cheney elaborated, saying: "It was a good program. It was a legal program. It was not torture." In defense of the CIA interrogators, he added: "These men deserve to be decorated. They don't deserve to be prosecuted."[142]

Similarly, President Bush's former attorney general, Michael Mukasey, writing in the *Wall Street Journal*, argued that the intelligence that led to Bin Laden "began with a disclosure from Khalid Sheikh Mohammed (KSM), who broke like a dam under the pressure of harsh interrogation techniques that included waterboarding."[143] On a Sunday morning talk show, Liz Cheney recited her well-rehearsed talking points: "These are not torture. These are techniques that we know worked, that debate is over. It worked, it got the intelligence, it wasn't torture, it was legal." Now, she asked, without enhanced interrogation or detention at CIA black sites, how would the Obama administration be able to get new information vital for the nation's security?[144] No longer were torture advocates citing the ticking time bomb or other arguments about saving lives. Now they were justifying abuse on grounds that it helped achieve a military objective—an instrumental logic that, if accepted, would allow harsh methods for any major national security goal.

Breaking a long silence in response to Republican attacks, the White House refuted their claims. "This is a distraction from the broader picture," said National Security Council spokesman Tommy Vietor, "which is that this achievement [of Bin Laden's death] was the result of years of painstaking work by our intelligence community that drew from multiple sources." Pointedly, he added: "It's not fair to the scores of people who did this work over many years to suggest that this is somehow all the result of waterboarding eight years ago."[145]

After interviewing CIA director Panetta about Bin Laden's killing, Senator John McCain broke ranks with his Republican colleagues to dismiss these assertions of torture's success. "The first mention of Abu Ahmed al-Kuwaiti—the nickname of the al-Qaeda courier who ultimately led us to Bin Laden," wrote McCain in a *Washington Post* op-ed, "came from a detainee held in another country, who we believe was not tortured. None of the three detainees who were waterboarded provided [the courier] Abu Ahmed's real name, his whereabouts or an accurate description of his role in al-Qaeda."[146]

Even though conservative claims for torture's role in Bin Laden's death had no factual basis, the Obama administration quickly capitulated and, within weeks, completed the process of impunity. In June 2011, Attorney General Holder announced that his special prosecutor, John Durham, had examined 101 instances of "alleged CIA mistreatment" and found that any further investigation "is not warranted."[147] Although the prosecutor would continue to investigate two deaths in CIA custody, this finding ended any possible prosecution of agency officials for torture during the War on Terror. "I welcome the news," said CIA director Panetta. "We are now about to close this chapter of our agency's history." But an ACLU official, Jameel Jaffer, condemned the decision, saying senior Bush officials had approved CIA interrogation that "subjected prisoners to unimaginable cruelty and violated both international and domestic law."[148]

Dueling Narratives

With the threat of legal action eliminated just before the tenth anniversary of the 9/11 attacks, the debate over Bush-era torture became a struggle over the historical record—the final step in the process of impunity. Among all the hundreds if not thousands of torture incidents from Guantanamo to Manila during the seven years of Bush's War on Terror, dueling memoirs focused on a single interrogation: the first use of "enhanced techniques" in early 2002 on the Al Qaeda leader Abu Zubaydah at a CIA safe house in Thailand.

In a memoir published on August 30, 2011, former vice president Cheney offered an account that seemed to justify torture, telling a story strikingly similar to the one Bush had told in his 2006 East Room address. "Although defiant," Cheney wrote, "Zubaydah provided useful information very early on, disclosing, for example, that the mastermind behind 9/11 had been Khalid Sheikh Mohammed, or KSM." Cheney's narrative continues to build toward a dramatic conclusion of CIA success, without mentioning the presence of an FBI team during the interrogation. "But then he stopped answering questions, and the CIA, convinced he had information that could potentially save thousands of lives . . . developed a list of enhanced interrogation techniques that were based on the Survival, Evasion, Resistance, and Escape Program. . . . The techniques worked. Abu Zubaydah gave up information about Ramzi bin al Shibh, who . . . was captured after a shootout in Pakistan. . . . Information from Abu Zubaydah and bin al Shibh led in turn to the capture of KSM, who after being questioned with enhanced techniques became a fount of information."[149]

Offering a strikingly different version of these same events in a memoir published on September 12, 2011, former FBI counterterror agent Ali Soufan drew upon his own firsthand experience inside that same Thai safe house for an account that both controverted Cheney's story and criticized CIA torture. Although his book's first edition was eviscerated by 181 pages of CIA deletions that the publisher found "outrageous," Ali Soufan's 2009 testimony before Congress, combined with the visible extracts from his book, offer us an uncensored version of these events.

As soon as Abu Zubaydah was captured after a shootout in Pakistan, Ali Soufan flew to Bangkok to start the interrogation with a combined FBI-CIA team. Using the "knowledge we have of the detainee's history, mindset, vulnerabilities, or culture" for noncoercive questioning, Ali Soufan, a veteran FBI agent fluent in Arabic, quickly gained "important actionable intelligence," including "the role of KSM as the mastermind of the 9/11 attacks and lots of other information that remains classified." Angered by the FBI's success, CIA director George Tenet dispatched his own counterterrorism team from Washington, led by a contract psychologist, Dr. James Mitchell, with authorization to use tough techniques that stripped Zubaydah of his clothes and subjected him to "low-level sleep deprivation." After these harsh methods got "no information," the FBI men resumed their empathic approach for a second time, again gaining important intelligence that "included the details of Jose Padilla, the so-called 'dirty bomber.'"

But then CIA team took over once more and moved "further along the force continuum, introducing loud noise and then temperature manipulation," as well as forty-eight hours of sleep deprivation. But this tough approach "wasn't working and Abu Zubaydah wasn't revealing any information." So, for a third time, the FBI men "were once again brought back in to interrogate him." To soften the coercive climate, Ali Soufan gave Abu Zubaydah his clothes, "switched off the music and let him sleep." By now, after days of CIA coercive interrogation, "We found it harder to reengage him this time, because of how the [harsh] techniques had affected him, but eventually, we succeeded, and he re-engaged again," giving more details of the Padilla bomb plot.

When the CIA insisted on escalating to "the next stage in the force continuum" by squeezing Abu Zubaydah into "a confinement box," Ali Soufan felt this was "borderline torture." Realizing that Dr. Mitchell "was being given a blank check by the White House and CIA headquarters" for his brutal and demonstrably unproductive techniques, Ali Soufan "began to wonder whether the real intent of the people back in Washington was to collect intelligence." After calling the FBI's deputy director in Washington and explaining the CIA's abusive method, Ali Soufan received a message from his director Robert

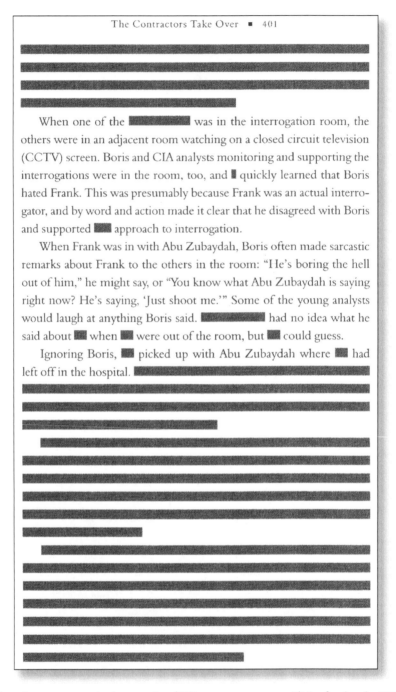

When one of the ███████████ was in the interrogation room, the others were in an adjacent room watching on a closed circuit television (CCTV) screen. Boris and CIA analysts monitoring and supporting the interrogations were in the room, too, and █ quickly learned that Boris hated Frank. This was presumably because Frank was an actual interrogator, and by word and action made it clear that he disagreed with Boris and supported ███ approach to interrogation.

When Frank was in with Abu Zubaydah, Boris often made sarcastic remarks about Frank to the others in the room: "He's boring the hell out of him," he might say, or "You know what Abu Zubaydah is saying right now? He's saying, 'Just shoot me.'" Some of the young analysts would laugh at anything Boris said. ██████████ had no idea what he said about ███ when ███ were out of the room, but ███ could guess.

Ignoring Boris, ███ picked up with Abu Zubaydah where ███ had left off in the hospital. ████████████████████████████████████

One of many passages in the memoirs of FBI counterterror agent Ali Soufan that the CIA blacked out to censor his criticism of the agency's unsuccessful use of "enhanced techniques"—that he called "borderline torture"—on the terrorist Abu Zubaydah. (from Ali H. Soufan, *The Black Banners* [New York: W.W. Norton, 2011])

Mueller saying, "We don't do that." Soufan quit the interrogation and flew back to New York.

After witnessing four successive cycles of failed CIA coercion and successful FBI empathy, Ali Soufan was bluntly dismissive of the yield from Dr. Mitchell's harsh methods: "We never get any actionable intelligence or any significant intelligence, comparatively to what we got before, when his techniques were going on." From this firsthand experience, Ali Soufan concluded that many CIA claims "about the success of the enhanced techniques are inaccurate." Since Abu Zubaydah was the first suspect subjected to enhanced interrogation techniques, "people in Washington rewrote the results to show that they passed the 'test case'"—propagating a blatant falsehood that allowed these abusive methods to proliferate. For the next six years, Ali Soufan, constrained by secrecy regulations, "had to remain silent as lie after lie was told about Abu Zubaydah and the success of the [enhanced] techniques."[150]

If we weigh the truth of these two accounts, Cheney's secondhand version completely omits the FBI presence, ignores the clear comparison between the two methods, and inaccurately attributes all the information gained from Abu Zubaydah to the CIA's "enhanced techniques." Although the facts seem to support Ali Soufan's view that psychological torture did not work, this fundamental yet fragile truth would again be obscured by a reconstruction of the past through CIA censorship and neoconservative casuistry. Indeed, in its 181 pages of excisions, the agency ruled that Abu Zubaydah's interrogation was still "classified," requiring that Ali Soufan's memoir delete his own presence at the questioning, change Dr. Mitchell's name to "Boris," and black out entire pages describing the Abu Zubaydah interrogation. In April 2012, Jose A. Rodriguez, the CIA Counterterrorism Center officer who supervised the torture of Abu Zubaydah, published his own memoirs under the provocative title *Hard Measures: How Aggressive C.I.A. Actions after 9/11 Saved American Lives*, calling FBI claims of success with noncoercive methods "bullshit." The book's website likened Rodriguez, unsurprisingly, to "a real-life Jack Bauer from television's 24." There has been no indication that this laudatory account has been subject to a single page of CIA censorship.[151]

International Impunity

Although the politics of impunity have protected Cheney, Rumsfeld, and other officials from both domestic prosecution and history's judgment, they have been targets of foreign indictments under universal jurisdiction for crimes against humanity. Indeed, their complete impunity required, in an era of globalization, a diplomatic dimension beyond the bounds of the nation-state. Since the adoption of the UN Convention against Torture, prosecution of crimes against humanity has gained numerous international venues—the UN, the European Court of Human Rights, and a half dozen European national courts that recognize the principle of universal jurisdiction.

Throughout the last years of Bush and the first years of Obama, Washington applied strong diplomatic pressure on Germany, Italy, and Spain to suspend prosecution of American officials responsible for illegal rendition of detainees. As early as 2007, the deputy chief of the U.S. mission in Berlin, John Konig, met with Germany's deputy national security adviser to warn that "issuance of international arrest warrants" for CIA officials involved in the case of Khalid El-Masri, a German citizen rendered to Afghanistan by the CIA, "would have a negative impact on our bilateral relationship"—pressures that served to slow legal action in Germany.[152]

Two years later, in 2009, the Obama administration worked to crush the threat of a Spanish indictment of six senior Bush-era officials for "creating a legal framework that allegedly permitted torture." At Washington in April, U.S. officials advised the Spanish foreign minister "that the prosecutions . . . would have an enormous impact on the bilateral relationship," and were delighted when Madrid's attorney general opposed proceeding with the charges.[153] Simultaneously, in Madrid, the U.S. Embassy learned that the presiding judge "has declined to process that case saying that before moving forward the USG should be asked if proceedings are underway in the U.S. He also offered to transfer the proceedings to the U.S." A month later, when Justice Baltasar Garzón accepted a second complaint into Bush-era torture, the Embassy noted that "the Chief Prosecutor for the National Court [Javier Zaragoza] tells us he will also fight Garzón's latest move." If Garzón resisted pressure to drop the case, the Embassy reported, "Zaragoza has a strategy to force his hand" by, first, charging Garzón with failing to investigate earlier reports of torture of Spanish citizens at Guantanamo. Should that not work, Zaragoza reported that "Garzon is already in hot water over his excessive zeal in . . . investigation into Spanish civil war atrocities, [and] there is now a criminal complaint against him in the Supreme Court, alleging abuse of authority." Despite Zaragoza's confidence, the Embassy did "not share his optimism that this problem will go away anytime soon" and recommended personal meetings on counterterrorism matters with the Spanish prosecutor during his upcoming visit to Washington.[154]

After Justice Garzón's first case was reassigned, the new presiding magistrate, Judge Eloy Velasco, adopted a much less aggressive stance. When Washington advised the Spanish court in March 2011 that "there exists no basis for the criminal prosecution of Yoo or Bybee," Judge Velasco simply transferred the case to the U.S. Department of Justice under a Mutual Legal Assistance Treaty. Although Garzón pursued the second torture case with his characteristic determination for nearly a year, finding that Spain had jurisdiction over these crimes against humanity, this case, too, was reassigned after his suspension in May 2010 for investigating atrocities from the Spanish civil war. The new judge resumed proceedings, hearing petitions in January 2011 that General Geoffrey Miller be subpoenaed, and the case continued thereafter, albeit at a more cautious pace.[155] Once again, U.S. diplomatic efforts blocked, at least momentarily, the threat of prosecution before a European court.

Despite these successes, Washington's diplomacy could slow but not stay the hand of international justice. In May 2009, a Milan court convicted twenty-two CIA agents and a U.S. Air Force colonel for the 2003 kidnapping of an Egyptian exile, Abu Omar, and his illegal rendition to Cairo for brutal tortures. One of those CIA agents convicted in absentia, Sabrina De Sousa, told ABC News that the U.S. "broke the law" with this rendition, "and we are paying for the mistakes right now, whoever authorized and approved this." The victim, Abu Omar, was eventually found innocent in Egypt and released to live quietly in Alexandria. "He was the wrong guy," said former CIA agent Robert Baer. "It was not worth putting the reputation of the United States on the line going after somebody like this."[156]

By late 2010, there were numerous official inquiries and legal cases against U.S. rendition in a half-dozen European nations. Apart from new cases in Germany, Italy, and Spain, there were ongoing investigations in Poland, Lithuania, Romania, Sweden, and Britain. Most significantly, Poland awarded a former CIA detainee, Abd al-Rahim al-Nashiri, formal "victim status," while the United Kingdom announced, in mid-2010, the opening of an official "Torture Inquiry" to investigate government complicity in the mistreatment of individuals.[157] Over the next two years, further inquiries in Britain and Denmark produced damaging revelations about the complicity of their defense forces in torture; while Polish investigations led to indictment of the country's former intelligence chief for helping the CIA set up a secret prison.[158] Some of these cases had the potential to release more sensitive details about U.S. rendition to CIA black sites that operated in Lithuania, Poland, and Romania during the Bush administration.

Showing the potential force of these foreign proceedings, in February 2011 former president George Bush canceled a trip to Switzerland after hearing that human rights groups were planning to present evidence of orders for torture, much of it drawn from his own memoirs.[159] Significantly, the Center for Constitutional Rights (CCR) in New York, the main author of the 2,500-page complaint, announced that "the Bush Torture Indictment would be waiting wherever he travels next," adding: "Torturers—even if they are former presidents of the United States—must be held to account and prosecuted. Impunity for Bush must end."[160]

In marked contrast to the dismissal of every complaint by torture victims in U.S. courts, these European proceedings have evinced a surprising openness to the evidence. After protracted litigation, British courts ruled that the former detainee Binyam Mohamed had been subjected to "cruel, inhuman and degrading treatment by the United States authorities" and, in February 2010, ordered release of suppressed information about CIA torture techniques—straining security relations with Washington.[161] In November the British government announced a payment of $80 million to settle lawsuits by fifteen former Guantanamo detainees, including Binyam Mohamed, whose civil suit had recently been dismissed by a U.S. appeals court. Confronted by a court order for the release of five hundred thousand confidential documents that left security services "paralyzed by paperwork," Prime Minister David Cameron approved the settlement and then went one step further, announcing an official inquiry into alleged collusion by MI-5 and MI-6 in the CIA's torture of terror suspects. In an unprecedented statement, the head of MI-6, Sir John Sawers, called torture "illegal and abhorrent under any circumstances, and we have nothing whatsoever to do with it."[162]

A year later, a British inquiry prompted by the 2003 death of an Iraqi detainee named Baha Mousa completed a three-year investigation of harsh interrogation by British forces in Basra, southern Iraq. In marked contrast to the dozen U.S. reports into Abu Ghraib which avoided naming or humanizing the Iraqi victims, the "driving force" behind the British inquiry was a grieving father, Colonel Daoud Mousa, a retired Iraqi police officer who wanted justice for his son, an innocent hotel worker beaten to death during interrogation. In its painstaking 1,400-page report compiled at a cost of $20 million, this inquiry found a pattern of "violent and cowardly assaults." British interrogators had revived the "five techniques" of mental torture, all banned after their use in Belfast back in 1972, involving hooding, stress positions, sleep deprivation, and noise barrage. Although low-ranking soldiers were the perpetrators, the inquiry blamed a "corporate failure" in the Defense Ministry, stating that senior officers bore "heavily responsibility" for failing to halt the excesses. Prime Minister Cameron condemned the "appalling abuse," and his defense minister called the report's conclusions "shocking and shameful."[163]

Continuing this relentless succession of revelations, Britain's Crown Prosecution announced, in January 2012, a criminal investigation into MI-6 collaboration with the CIA in the torture and rendition of former Libyan dissidents. Back in 2004, the two agencies had responded to a request from Colonel

Qaddafi's intelligence service for rendition of an Islamic dissident by seizing the suspect in Malaysia and shipping him back to Tripoli for years of torture. After the Libyan revolution toppled Qaddafi, that same dissident, Abdel Hakim Belhaj, emerged as the powerful chief of the new government's Military Council and retained British counsel to demand justice. So detailed and damaging were Belhaj's charges of British collusion with his years of torture that London was forced to scrap its limited administrative inquiry into MI-6 in favor of a full criminal investigation by the Metropolitan Police. This investigation would, the *New York Times* reported, "prolong the tensions between London and Washington" and place "major strains on intelligence links with the United States."[164]

Whether or not other cases before European courts produce similarly damaging revelations, their persistence indicated that the once strong sub rosa alliance between the CIA and European security services was attenuating. Bound by strict European and UN anti-torture protocols, not even the closest ally could any longer suppress human rights inquiries to preserve intelligence ties to the United States. With impunity protecting perpetrators at home, redress for torture, if it were to come anywhere, will increasingly be found in transnational venues remote from pressures for impunity. When Human Rights Watch called, in July 2011, for a U.S. inquiry into human rights violations by senior Bush officials, it recognized this sober reality, suggesting: "If the US government does not pursue credible criminal investigations, other countries should prosecute US officials involved in crimes against detainees in accordance with international law."[165]

Absent such an inquiry and the reforms it might bring, then the observations of the *New York Times* columnist Ross Douthat seem a prescient assessment of the War on Terror's long-term legacy. Writing in 2010 about Obama's retreat from human rights during his first three years in office, Douthat argued that "the basic post-9/11 architecture of executive power—expansive powers to detain, interrogate and assassinate, claimed for the duration of an open-ended war—looks destined to endure for presidencies to come."[166]

The Price of Impunity

For more than forty years, from 1970 to 2011, the usual U.S. processes of political reform through media exposé and congressional action were stymied by the forces of impunity following six separate exposés of CIA-sponsored torture—in South Vietnam (1970), Brazil (1974), Iran (1978), Honduras (1988), Latin America (1996–97), and Iraq and Afghanistan (2004–11). After each revelation, the public's shudder of revulsion quickly faded, allowing the agency to resume its dirty work in the shadows of executive power.

The history of torture in America indicates the complex interplay of social forces that fosters impunity in a democracy otherwise governed by the rule of law. As a powerful secret service whose charter permits executive operations outside the law, the CIA represents an implicit challenge to both due process and democracy, amplified by the agency's growing collaboration with the military in operations and intelligence. Compounding this problem, the presidency itself has an unrivalled ability, through executive agencies and partisan support, to shape public policy, even when it clearly violates both domestic law and international treaties. Over the past forty years, the capacity of reformers to restrain executive excess through public exposé has been checked repeatedly by the veil of state secrecy that shrouds CIA covert action. Whenever an ad hoc human rights coalition of activists, lawyers, media, courts, and Congress has discovered abuse akin to torture, the agency has hidden behind claims of state secrecy, adapting its covert operations to elude both law and legislative intent.

In the four decades since news of the Phoenix program broke in 1970, press exposés and public protests have done surprisingly little to change U.S. human rights policy. A key factor in this failure has been the intangible problem of public forgetting, a facet central to the process of impunity. Congressional investigators have often failed to link these disparate instances of CIA excess even when evidence of continuity should be clear, obscuring recurring patterns in U.S. policy.

The examples of such forgetting are legion. As they probed torture training in Central America during the mid-1980s, for example, Senator Bill Bradley and his colleagues seemed oblivious of congressional investigations, conducted just ten years before, into similar U.S. interrogation instruction elsewhere in Latin America. When the liberal Clinton administration dusted off the paperwork and sent the UN Convention against Torture to Congress for ratification in 1994, it seemed somehow unaware that the reservations written by the conservative Reagan government would subvert its aim of making U.S. policy compliant with international standards. After Senate hearings in mid-2008 discovered that the CIA had reverse engineered the military's SERE training to create "enhanced interrogation," the *New York Times* ignored a half-century of CIA mind-control research, carefully reported in its own columns, and attributed this development to two cash-hungry, contract psychologists—to just two scientific bad apples.[167]

In retrospect, this process of blaming a few rogue soldiers, scientists, or CIA contractors seems the first step toward impunity. Such blame assuages public concern about the need for reform and thus serves as a precondition for public forgetting. Meanwhile, the security agencies, with strong institutional continuity of personnel and procedures, can readily revive their abusive methods once the controversy has abated and the need again arises for these same questionable methods on yet another covert battleground. Without a legal process that assigns responsibility and holds higher-level officials accountable, exposés remain brief episodes easily eluded by political maneuvers, allowing policymakers to continue these illegal policies.

In a modern democracy, another major cause of impunity is the implication of government officials, both legislative and executive, in the illegality that necessarily accompanies torture. Since trifling with anti-torture laws and treaties has been bipartisan U.S. policy for two decades, senior legislators and executive officials are mutually implicated, reducing either political party's inclination to investigation or exposé. This shared complicity makes torture difficult to address through the usual rubric of partisan politics. As seen in the most recent torture revelations, Nancy Pelosi, the Democratic House Speaker during the last years of the Bush administration, appears, despite her dubious denial, to have been informed about the torture of suspects during the era of hyperpatriotism that followed 9/11. After the Democrats came to power under Obama, the involvement of past party leaders in rendition—Bill Clinton, Leon Panetta, and Eric Holder—militated against any investigation of Republican excesses under Bush. To start a searching, impartial inquiry would be a mutually self-destructive endeavor for long-time denizens of Washington, D.C. In a modern democracy, torture does not occur in a vacuum; it requires a shared, even a widely shared level of complicity that encourages impunity.

Against this general grain of public forgetting, historical memory, though heavily contested, remains the most salient antidote. Through the study of legislative history and judicial precedent, the legal profession has a built-in vehicle for memory, which is, of course, prone to partisanship. As demonstrated in the declassified interrogation memos from the Bush Justice Department, administration attorneys were single-minded in their appropriation of the past to serve present policy—searching U.S and European precedents for arguments and documenting their tendentious points with elaborate footnotes. Military lawyers, through a half-century of codified law and thirty-year careers with strong institutional memory, were the societal actors with the most consistent advocacy of human rights.

By contrast, civil society groups—whether human rights organizations, media outlets, or congressional committees—are staffed with succession of workers on ever-shifting assignments that, not surprisingly, often exhibit weak institutional memory. In the six years after the Abu Ghraib scandal broke in April 2004, the *New York Times* seemed averse to citing its own investigative reports from the 1970s, thus denying its coverage analysis of the continuity between the agency's past mind-control efforts and current interrogation policy. Compounding this problem, the failing business model for newspapers and newsweeklies has diminished their ability to serve as watchdogs. Struggling for survival, many of these periodicals have slashed staff and lack personnel for in-depth investigative reporting.[168]

Civil society groups did score some surprising gains in the aftermath of Abu Ghraib by limiting the Bush administration's embrace of torture as a presidential prerogative. But a tendency to overlook the continuity between Bush administration policy and past CIA involvement in torture hampered more strategic analysis by journalists, Congress, human rights groups, and dissident psychologists. Unmindful of this past, these groups often pursued short-lived exposés, worked for limited reforms, and left the ultimate source of torture buried inside the CIA, ready to re-emerge from the national security bureaucracy in some future foreign policy crisis, almost as if Abu Ghraib had never happened.

Beyond all these bureaucracies, civil and official, the American public has a notoriously short-term memory, readily absorbing the myriad details of current controversies yet unmindful of their historic antecedents. When the Abu Ghraib scandal broke, in April 2004, the American public evinced at best a vague understanding of past CIA excesses and the scale of its massive Cold War mind-control project. Yet, almost every adult American carried fragmentary memories of this past—LSD experiments, Phoenix program in Vietnam, murder of an American police adviser in Montevideo, School of the Americas, and CIA training manuals for Latin America. These fragments of memory could, and maybe should, have merged into a mosaic to reveal a clandestine agency probing the cruel underside of human consciousness. But few Americans were able to fit these pieces together and thus form the larger picture. There was, in sum, a studied avoidance of a deeply troubling topic akin to the collective forgetting that sometime shrouds this traumatic subject in postauthoritarian societies.

Though they write last and are little read, academic historians have the tools for critical analysis that can identify continuities in public policy from past to present and offer suggestions for correction. In the struggle to overcome the oblivion so central to impunity, historical narrative can appropriate other disciplines such as law and psychology, incorporating their strongest points, contextualizing their insights, and offering a comprehensive analysis. With the advent of the Internet, it is now possible for academics to avoid media gatekeepers and write directly for a wider public, offering an alternative source that might compensate for the challenges facing the press.

Clearly, there is a pressing need for a serious inquiry into the U.S. involvement in torture, following leads from the Senate's 2008 report. Whether by Congress, a presidential commission, or a coalition of civil society groups, such an investigation into both the ethics and the efficacy of torture might dispel the loose public consensus for abuse that developed under Bush and help bring reforms to make U.S. human rights policy compliant with international standards. Above all, such an inquiry could probe some pressing questions the nation needs answered. Who is correct, Ali Soufan or Bush-Cheney, about the supposed success of harsh methods in Abu Zubaydah's interrogation? Does torture actually produce accurate, timely intelligence? Or should we instead rely on well-briefed agents fluent in foreign languages conducting an informed, noncoercive interrogation? Do enhanced techniques really comply with U.S. law and treaty commitments? Should U.S. anti-torture laws be rewritten to meet international standards? Answers to these questions from a bipartisan inquiry akin to the 9/11 Commission might well build public support for binding reforms.

In the decades since the fall of the Berlin wall in 1989, the process of impunity has led Washington back to the contradiction that marked U.S. foreign policy during the Cold War: publicly advocating human rights before international forums such as the UN, while covertly outsourcing torture to allied security services. During these forty years of anti-communist struggle, Washington sent security suspects to allied prisons and harvested the intelligence from such harsh treatment. Since 2008, the U.S. has resumed this policy. In between, the real aberration of the Bush years lay not in its torture policies per se but in the president's order that the CIA operate its own prisons and that American agents dirty their hands with waterboarding and wall slamming.

The upshot of this protracted political struggle under both Bush and Obama has been not any abjuring of abuse but, instead, a return to indirect involvement in torture through rendition to allied security agencies. Throughout this post-9/11 decade of intense debate over torture between rival parties, federal agencies, television networks, legal coteries, and political leaders, the United States slowly reached, circa 2011, a hard-won political compromise. Pulled between the extremes of neoconservative torture advocates and liberal abolitionists, Washington healed the domestic breach over this contentious issue by defaulting, albeit quietly, to impunity at home and rendition abroad.

This political resolution, of course, falls far short of a firm commitment to international standards for human rights. Indeed, this is a compromise that does not bode well for the future of U.S. global leadership, should Washington persist in this policy. While America was debating the efficacy of torture, the international community was deepening its opposition to such abuse under the European Convention on Human Rights and the UN Convention against Torture. Setting aside long-standing ties to the United States, British commissions, Italian courts, the German press, Spanish magistrates, and the European Parliament have been aggressive in their investigations of excesses under the War on Terror. Spain's indictment of General Pinochet in 1998 for human rights violations, Italy's prosecution of two-dozen CIA agents for rendition in 2009, and Poland's indictment of its former intelligence chief in 2012 for facilitating CIA black sites are all harbingers of future pressures on U.S. policy. As the international rule of law strengthens in years to come, ever more rigorous enforcement of human rights and growing criticism of any violations will likely compel Washington to change its policies, at home and abroad.

Meanwhile, unchecked by any domestic or international sanction, the U.S. has slid down torture's slippery slope to find, just as the French found in Algeria, that extra-judicial execution lies in an abyss at the bottom. The systematic French torture of thousands during the Battle of Algiers in 1957 also generated over 3,000 "summary executions" as "an inseparable part" of this campaign, largely, as one French general put it, to ensure that "the machine of justice" not be "clogged with cases." Similarly, after the storm of controversy over Abu Ghraib, the Bush administration reacted by increasing its drone killings inside Pakistan from zero in 2005 to 286 three years later. Under Obama, aerial assassinations of suspected terrorists surged to 801 by 2010—bringing the U.S. total for drone deaths inside Pakistan, 2006 to 2012, to over 2,400. Simultaneously, the Obama administration took just one terror suspect into U.S. custody and did not add any new prisoners to Guantanamo. "Their policy is to take out high-value targets, versus capturing high-value targets," observed Senator Saxby Chambliss, ranking Republican member of the intelligence committee. Although Americans did not object to these assassinations, the drone program aroused bitter anger inside Pakistan and is likely, in the view of senior intelligence officials, to do long-term damage to U.S. national interests.[169]

Absent any searching inquiry or binding reforms, some future U.S. torture scandal might well arise from yet another iconic dungeon in a dismal, ever-lengthening historical procession from the "tiger cages" of South Vietnam to "the salt pit" in Afghanistan, Camp X-Ray at Guantanamo Bay, and "the hole" in Somalia. Next time, with those images from Abu Ghraib prison etched in human memory, the international community may well prove unforgiving. Next time, the damage to America's moral authority as world leader could prove deep and lasting.

Notes

Introduction

1. Ronald Reagan, "Message to the Senate Transmitting the Convention against Torture and Inhuman Treatment or Punishment," May 20, 1988, The American Presidency Project, University of California at Santa Barbara, http://www.presidency.ucsb.edu/ws/?pid=35858#ixzzSBSakULG, accessed July 15, 2011.

2. Haroon Siddique, "Waterboarding Is Torture, Downing Street Confirms," *The Guardian*, November 9, 2010, http://www.guardian.co.uk/world/2010/nov/09/george-bush-memoirs-waterboarding, accessed September 21, 2011.

3. Jon Karl and Karen Travers, "President Obama, Dick Cheney Face Off on National Security Issues," *ABC News*, May 21, 2009, http://abcnews.go.com/Politics/story?id=7643032&page=1, accessed July 4, 2011.

4. Metin Basoglu, Maria Livanou, and Cvetana Crnobaric, "Torture vs. Other Cruel, Inhuman, and Degrading Treatment: Is the Distinction Real or Apparent?" *Archives of General Psychiatry* 64, no. 3 (2007): 277–85; Metin Basoglu, "A Multivariate Contextual Analysis of Torture and Cruel, Inhuman, and Degrading Treatments: Implications for an Evidence-Based Definition of Torture," *American Journal of Orthopsychiatry* 79, no. 2 (2009): 135–45.

5. Amy Goodman, "Discovery Channel Accused of Political Censorship for Dropping Oscar-Nominated Doc on U.S. Torture," *Democracy Now!*, February 12, 2008, http://www.democracynow.org/2008/2/12/discovery_channel_accused_of_political_censorship, accessed July 16, 2011.

6. "Russia's Putin Criticizes Human Rights Groups," Reuters, May 26, 2004, http://nucnews.net/nucnews/2004nn/0405nn/040526nn.htm#561, accessed July 31, 2011; David Nowak, "Russian Treason Bill Could Hit Kremlin Critics," Associated Press, December 17, 2008, http://abclocal.go.com/wpvi/story?section=news/national_world&id=6559744; *New York Times*, December 20, 2008, http://www.nytimes.com/2008/12/21/world/europe/21russia.html, all accessed July 31, 2011.

7. Marnia Lazreg, *Torture and the Twilight of Empire: From Algiers to Baghdad* (Princeton: Princeton University Press, 2008), 3, 255–56.

8. Paul Aussaresses, *The Battle of the Casbah: Terrorism and Counter-Terrorism in Algeria 1955–1957* (New York: Enigma, 2002), 126–28, 162–63.

9. Interview with Sir Alistair Horne, *The Battle of Algiers: Remembering History* (produced by Kim Hendrickson, Criterion Collection, 2004).

10. Human Rights Watch, "United States: Investigate Bush, Other Top Officials for Torture," July 11, 2011, http://www.hrw.org/fr/news/2011/07/11/united-states -investigate-bush-other-top-officials-torture; Human Rights Watch, *Getting Away with Torture*, July 12, 2011, http://www.hrw.org/en/reports/2011/07/12/getting-away-torture, both accessed July 28, 2011.

Chapter 1. The CIA's Pursuit of Psychological Torture

Portions of this chapter were previously published in a volume edited by Marjorie Cohen, *The United States & Torture* (New York: New York University Press, 2011).

1. See U.S. Congress, Senate and House Armed Services Committees, *Testimony of Secretary of Defense Donald H. Rumsfeld*, May 7, 2004, http://www.defenselink.mil /speeches/speech.aspx?speechid=118, accessed August 25, 2009; *New York Times*, May 8, May 12, 2004.

2. Christopher Simpson, *Science of Coercion: Communication Research and Psychological Warfare, 1945–1960* (New York: Oxford University Press, 1994), 8–9.

3. Irving L. Janis, *Are the Cominform Countries Using Hypnotic Techniques to Elicit Confessions in Public Trials?* U.S. Air Force Project Rand Research Memorandum, RM-161, April 25, 1949 (Santa Monica: Rand Corporation), 1, 3, 6–7, 16–20; Walter Bowart, *Operation Mind Control* (New York: Dell, 1978), 67–71, 109–10.

4. Tim Weiner, *Legacy of Ashes: The History of the CIA* (New York: Random House, 2008), 72–74; Central Intelligence Agency, "Memorandum for the Record, Subject: Project Artichoke," January 31, 1975, National Security Archive, Washington, DC [hereafter, NSA], http://www.gwu.edu/~nsarchiv/NSAEBB/NSAEBB54/st02.pdf, accessed January 2, 2012.

5. U.S. Senate, 94th Congress, 2d Session, *Final Report of the Select Committee to Study Governmental Operations with Respect to Intelligence Activities. Book I* (Washington, DC: Government Printing Office, 1976), 387.

6. Ibid., 387–88; Patricia Greenfield, "CIA's Behavior Caper," *APA Monitor* (December 1977) 1, 10–11, http://www.cia-on-campus.org/social/behavior.html, accessed February 1, 2012.

7. Weiner, *Legacy of Ashes*, 72–74, 649.

8. Central Intelligence Agency, "Summary of Remarks by Mr. Allen W. Dulles at the National Alumni Conference of the Graduate Council of Princeton University, Hot Springs, VA," April 10, 1953, File: Artichoke Docs: 362–388, Box 5, CIA Behavior Control Experiments Collection, NSA.

9. U.S. Senate, 94th Congress, 2d Session, *Final Report of the Select Committee to Study Governmental Operations with Respect to Intelligence Activities. Book I*, 399.

10. *New York Times*, August 2, 1977.

11. John Marks, *The Search for the "Manchurian Candidate": The CIA and Mind Control* (New York: Times Books, 1979), 4–6; Technical Report no. 3331-45, "German Aviation Medical Research at the Dachau Concentration Camp," October 1945, U.S. Naval Technical Mission to Europe, H MS c64, Box 11, f. 75, Harvard Medical Library; letter from Arthur M. Turner, M.D., to Dr. Henry K. Beecher, February 7, 1947, Box 6, CIA Behavior Control Experiments Collection (John Marks Donation), NSA; letter from Henry K. Beecher to the Surgeon General, Department of the Army, October 21, 1951, Box 16, RG 319, U.S. National Archives and Research Administration; Project Title: Neuropsychiatry and Stress, Addendum. Beecher (MD 92), "Final Report, Response of Normal Men to Lysergic Acid Derivatives (Di- and Monoethylamide). Correlation of Personality and Drug Reactions," December 31, 1954, Box 6, CIA Behavior Control Experiments Collection (John Marks Donation), NSA.

12. Ronald W. Clark, *Tizard* (London: Methuen, 1965), 386–402. *Opinion of George Cooper, Q.C., Regarding Canadian Government Funding of the Allan Memorial Institute in the 1950's and 1960's* (Ottawa: Minister of Supply and Services Canada, Cat. No. J2-63, 1986), Meeting at Ritz Carleton Hotel, June 1, 1951; Handwritten Note titled "PA 2–1-[illegible]-38," Appendix 21.

13. *Opinion of George Cooper, Q.C.*, D. O. Hebb, W. Heron, and W. H. Bexton, "Annual Report, Contract DRB-38, Experimental Studies of Attitude," 1952, Appendix 22.

14. Woodburn Heron, "The Pathology of Boredom," *Scientific American* 196 (January 1957): 52–56.

15. For citations of these 230 articles, see, Philip Solomon et al., eds., *Sensory Deprivation: A Symposium Held at Harvard Medical School* (Cambridge, MA: Harvard University Press, 1961), 239–57.

16. Lawrence E. Hinkle Jr., "A Consideration of the Circumstances under Which Men May Be Interrogated, and the Effects That These May Have upon the Function of the Brain" (n.d., ca. 1958), 1, 5, 6, 11–14, 18, File: Hinkle, Box 7, CIA Behavior Control Experiments Collection (John Marks Donation), NSA; Lawrence E. Hinkle Jr. and Harold G. Wolff, "Communist Interrogation and Indoctrination of 'Enemies of the States': Analysis of Methods Used by the Communist State Police (A Special Report)," *Archives of Neurology and Psychiatry* 76 (1956): 115–74.

17. David H. Price, "Buying a Piece of Anthropology, Part II: The CIA and Our Tortured Past," *Anthropology Today* 23, no. 5 (2007): 17–22, http://homepages.stmartin.edu/fac_staff/dprice/Price-AT-HEF2.pdf, accessed August 5, 2011; Greenfield, "CIA's Behavior Caper."

18. *New York Times*, March 10, March 11, 1954; Edgar H. Schein, "Patterns of Reactions to Severe Chronic Stress in American Army Prisoners of War of the Chinese," 253–69, and Louis J. West, "United States Air Force Prisoners of the Chinese

Communists," 270–84, both in *Symposium No. 4. Methods of Forceful Indoctrination: Observations and Interviews* (New York: Group for the Advancement of Psychiatry, 1957).

19. Joseph Marguilies, *Guantanamo and the Abuse of Presidential Power* (New York: Simon and Schuster, 2006), 120–25; *New York Times*, August 23, 1954, August 14, August 18, 1955; Dwight D. Eisenhower, "Executive Order 10631—Code of Conduct for Members of the Armed Forces of the United States," August 17, 1955, American Presidency Project, University of California at Santa Barbara, http://www.presidency.ucsb .edu/ws/index.php?pid=59249#axzz1ZwwbuVnm, accessed October 4, 2011.

20. *New York Times*, August 20, September 15, September 17, December 14, 1955; Albert D. Biderman, "Communist Attempts to Elicit False Confessions from Air Force Prisoners of War," *Bulletin of the New York Academy of Medicine* 33, no. 9 (1957): 618–22; Albert D. Biderman and Herbert Zimmer, "Introduction," in Albert D. Biderman and Herbert Zimmer, eds., *The Manipulation of Human Behavior* (New York: John Wiley, 1961), 1, 10; Lawrence E. Hinkle Jr., "The Physiological State of the Interrogation Subject as It Affects Brain Function," in Biderman and Zimmer, *The Manipulation of Human Behavior*, 19–20, 43. Four of the seven essays in this volume were funded by two CIA conduits, the Office of Naval Research and the Society for the Investigation of Human Ecology, later known as the Human Ecology Fund.

21. U.S. Senate, 95th Congress, 1st Session, *Project MKUltra: The CIA's Program of Research in Behavioral Modification. Joint Hearing before the Select Committee on Intelligence and the Subcommittee on Health and Scientific Research of the Committee on Human Resources* (Washington, DC: Government Printing Office, 1977), 62.

22. "KUBARK Counterintelligence Interrogation" (July 1963), File: Kubark, Box 1: CIA Training Manuals, NSA, 87–90, 110–12; National Security Archive, "Prisoner Abuse: Patterns from the Past. Electronic Briefing Book No. 122" (Washington, DC, May 12, 2004), http://www.gwu.edu/%7Ensarchiv/NSAEBB/NSAEBB122/index.htm #kubark, accessed August 20, 2009.

23. Mark Bowden, "The Dark Art of Interrogation: A Survey of the Landscape of Persuasion," *The Atlantic Monthly* (October 2003), 72.

24. Edward Peters, *Torture* (Philadelphia: University of Pennsylvania Press, 1996), 1, 14–18, 25–33, 35.

25. "Directive to Army Not to Use Intensive Interrogation Methods on Terrorists," *The Times* (London), March 3, 1972; Lord Parker of Waddington, *Report of the Committee of Privy Counsellors Appointed to Consider Authorised Procedures for the Interrogation of Persons Suspected of Terrorism* (London: Stationery Office, Cmnd. 4901, 1972), 3–17.

26. *New York Times*, September 9, 2011; Sir William Gage, *The Baha Mousa Public Inquiry Report: Volume I* (London: Stationery Office, HC 1452-I, 2011), 9–10, http:// www.bahamousainquiry.org/f_report/vol%20i/volume%20i.pdf, accessed September 21, 2011.

27. "Ireland v. The United Kingdom," No. 5310/17, European Court of Human Rights, January 18, 1978, Separate Opinion of Judge Evrigenis, http://cmiskp.echr.coe

.int/tkp197/view.asp?item=1&portal=hbkm&action=html&highlight=5310/71&session id=26859787&skin=hudoc-en, accessed July 19, 2009; Amnesty International, *Torture in Greece: The First Torturers' Trial 1975* (London: Amnesty International, 1977).

28. U.S. Department of Defense, "Army Regulation 15-6: Final Report: Investigation into FBI Allegation of Detainee Abuse at Guantanamo Bay, Cuba Detention Facility" (April 1, 2005; amended June 9, 2005), 1, 20, http://www.defenselink.mil /news/Jul2005/d20050714report.pdf, accessed July 18, 2005; U.S. Senate Armed Services Committee, *Hearing on Guantanamo Bay Detainee Treatment* (July 13, 2005), 19, 20, 35, 55, http://humanrights.ucdavis.edu/projects/the-guantanamo-testimonials -project/testimonies/testimonies-of-the-defense-department/senate-armed-services -committee-hearing-on-guantanamo-bay-detainee-treatment, accessed October 4, 2011.

29. Arthur Levine, "Collective Unconscionable," *Washington Monthly* (January–February 2007), http://www.washingtonmonthly.com/features/2007/0701.levine .html, accessed May 28, 2007.

30. *New York Times*, April 17, April 19, April 21, May 14, 2009.

31. Hinkle and Wolff, "Communist Interrogation and Indoctrination of 'Enemies of the States,'" 135.

32. Metin Basoglu, Maria Livanou, and Cvetana Crnobaric, "Torture vs. Other Cruel, Inhuman, and Degrading Treatment: Is the Distinction Real or Apparent?" *Archives of General Psychiatry* 64, no. 3 (2007): 277–85.

33. Metin Basoglu, "A Multivariate Contextual Analysis of Torture and Cruel, Inhuman, and Degrading Treatments: Implications for an Evidence-Based Definition of Torture," *American Journal of Orthopsychiatry* 79, no. 2 (2009): 135–45.

34. See, Alfred W. McCoy, *A Question of Torture: CIA Interrogation, from the Cold War to the War on Terror* (New York: Metropolitan Books, 2006), chapter 3; *New York Times*, September 22, 1996.

35. Steven G. Bradbury, Office of the Principal Deputy Assistant Attorney General, Office of Legal Counsel, "Memorandum for John A. Rizzo, Senior Deputy Counsel, Central Intelligence Agency: Re: Application of United States Obligations under Article 16 of the Convention against Torture to Certain Techniques That May Be Used in the Interrogation of High Value al Qaeda Detainees," May 30, 2005, 32, http://www .justice.gov/olc/docs/memo-bradbury2005.pdf, accessed October 4, 2011; Central Intelligence Agency, Inspector General, "Special Review: Counterterrorism Detention and Interrogation Activities (September 2001–October 2003)," May 7, 2004, 9, http:// graphics8.nytimes.com/packages/pdf/politics/20090825-DETAIN/2004CIAIG.pdf, accessed October 4, 2011.

36. CIA, Inspector General, "Special Review: Counterterrorism Detention and Interrogation Activities," 10; Central Intelligence Agency, *Human Resources Exploitation Training Manual—1983*, Box 1, K–1, F–G, CIA Training Manuals, NSA; *New York Times*, January 29, 1997.

37. CIA, Inspector General, "Special Review: Counterterrorism Detention and Interrogation Activities," 9–10.

38. Central Intelligence Agency, *Human Resources Exploitation Training Manual—1983*, Introduction, http://www.gwu.edu/~nsarchiv/NSAEBB/NSAEBB27/02 -06.htm, accessed August 3, 2011; *New York Times*, January 29, 1997.

39. CIA, *Human Resources Exploitation Training Manual—1983*, K-2, K-3, K-7.

40. CIA, Inspector General, "Special Review: Counterterrorism Detention and Interrogation Activities," 10.

41. Werner E. Michel, Assistant to the Secretary of Defense (Intelligence Oversight), "Subject: Improper Material in Spanish-Language Intelligence Training Manuals," March 10, 1992 (Box 2, Intelligence Training Source Manuals, Folder: Untitled, NSA).

42. Mary Wheeler, "The 13 People Who Made Torture Possible," *Salon.com*, May 18, 2009, http://www.salon.com/news/feature/2009/05/18/torture/print.html, accessed July 6, 2011.

43. U.S. Senate, 101st Congress, 2d Session, Committee on Foreign Relations, *Convention against Torture: Hearing before the Committee on Foreign Relations* (Washington, DC: Government Printing Office, 1990), 1, 12–18, 34, 35, 40–43, 66–69, 70–71.

44. United Nations, *Convention against Torture and Other Cruel, Inhuman or Degrading Treatment or Punishment*, http://www.hrweb.org/legal/cat.html, accessed September 20, 2011.

45. United Nations, *Convention against Torture and Other Cruel Inhuman or Degrading Treatment or Punishment, Reservation Made by the United States of America*, http://www.unhchr.ch/tbs/doc.nsf/0/5d7ce66547377b1f802567fd0056b533?Open Document, accessed September 18, 2011.

46. Daniel Levin, Acting Assistant Attorney General, Office of Legal Counsel, "Legal Standards Applicable under 18 U.S.C. §§ 2340–2340A," December 30, 2004, http://www.justice.gov/olc/18usc23402340a2.htm, accessed September 19, 2011.

47. United Nations, *Convention against Torture and Other Cruel Inhuman or Degrading Treatment or Punishment, Reservation Made by the United States of America*.

48. U.S. Code, Section 2340, 18 USC§ 2340–2340A, http://codes.lp.findlaw.com /uscode/18/I/113C/2340, accessed September 20, 2011.

49. *New York Times*, March 6, 2005; Jane Mayer, "Outsourcing Torture: The Secret History of America's 'Extraordinary Rendition' Program," *The New Yorker*, February 14, 2005, 108–9; U.S. House of Representatives, 110th Congress, 1st Session, House Committee on Foreign Affairs, Subcommittee on International Organizations, Human Rights, and Oversight, Subcommittee on Europe, *Extraordinary Rendition in U.S. Counter Terrorism Policy: The Impact on Transatlantic Relations* (Washington, DC: Government Printing Office, 2007), 12; William J. Clinton, "Memorandum for the Vice President, Subject: U.S. Policy on Counterterrorsim (U)," June 21, 1992, http:// www.fas.org/irp/offdocs/pdd39.htm, accessed March 24, 2010.

50. Richard A. Clarke, *Against All Enemies: Inside America's War on Terror* (New York: Free Press, 2004), 24.

51. Weiner, *Legacy of Ashes*, 555–56, 772; U.S. Department of Justice, Office of Legal Counsel, "Memorandum for William J. Haynes, II, General Counsel, Department of

Defense," December 28, 2001, From: Patrick F. Philbin, Deputy Assistant Attorney General, and John C. Yoo, Deputy Assistant Attorney General, in Karen J. Greenberg and Joshua L. Dratel, eds., *The Torture Papers: The Road to Abu Ghraib* (New York: Cambridge University Press, 2005), 29, 37; Secretary of Defense, "Memorandum for Chairman of the Joint Chiefs of Staff, Subject: Status of Taliban and Al Qaeda," January 19, 2002, in Greenberg and Dratel, *The Torture Papers*, 80; Jay S. Bybee, Assistant Attorney General, Office of Legal Counsel, U.S. Department of Justice, "Memorandum for Alberto R. Gonzales, Counsel to the President, and William J. Haynes II, General Counsel of the Department of Defense," January 22, 2002, 37, http://www.washingtonpost.com/wp-srv/nation/documents/012202bybee.pdf, accessed June 28, 2004; *New York Times*, September 17, 2006.

52. Memorandum for the President, From: Alberto R. Gonzales, "Subject: Decision re. Application of the Geneva Convention on Prisoners of War to the Conflict with Al Qaeda and the Taliban," January 25, 2002, http://news.lp.findlaw.com/hdocs/docs/torture/gnzls12502mem2gwb.html, accessed, February 6, 2012.

53. U.S. Senate, Committee on Armed Services, 110th Congress, 2d Session, *Inquiry into the Treatment of Detainees in U.S. Custody* (Washington, DC: Government Printing Office, 2008), xiii; George W. Bush, The White House, Washington, For: The Vice President, "Subject: Humane Treatment of Taliban and al Qaeda Detainees," February 7, 2002, www.pegc.us/archive/White_House/bush_memo_20040207.doc, accessed October 4, 2011.

54. Weiner, *Legacy of Ashes*, 555–56, 560–61.

55. Stephen Grey, *Ghost Plane: The True Story of the CIA Torture Program* (New York: St. Martin's Press, 2006), 87, 181, 227, 269–308; *New York Times*, May 31, 2005; Mayer, "Outsourcing Torture: Annals of Justice," 110–12. Through investigations by the German and U.S. press, the location of CIA "black sites" has emerged slowly in the five years since their closure in 2006. We now know that CIA secret prisons were located inside Romania at a state security facility in downtown Bucharest, in Lithuania inside a converted horse stable, and in Poland at an intelligence facility near Szymany airbase where Khalid Sheikh Mohammed was waterboarded 183 times. See, Adam Goldman, "Inside Roumania's Secret CIA Prison," Associated Press, December 8, 2011, http://www.npr.org/templates/story/story.php?storyId=143325109; Matthew Cole and Brian Ross, "CIA Secret 'Torture' Prison Found at Fancy Horseback Riding Academy," *ABC News*, November 18, 2009, http://abcnews.go.com/Blotter/cia-secret-prison-found/story?id=9115978#.TuD1s2D-Jo4; John Goetz and Britta Sandberg, "New Evidence of Torture Prison in Poland," *Der Spiegel Online International*, April 27, 2009, http://www.spiegel.de/international/world/0,1518,621450,00.html, all accessed December 8, 2011.

56. U.S. Congress, 107th Congress 2d session, Cofer Black, Testimony to Senate Select Committee on Intelligence, Joint Inquiry into Intelligence Community Activities before and after the Terrorist Attacks of September 11, 2001, September 26, 2002, http://www.fas.org/irp/congress/2002_hr/092602black.html, accessed May 22, 2011.

57. Grey, *Ghost Plane*, 170–89.

58. *New York Times*, September 1, September 2, September 3, September 6, 2011, January 13, 2012; "Libya Rebel Leader 'Tortured by CIA' in Thailand," *Bangkok Post*, September 4, 2011, http://www.bangkokpost.com/lite/topstories/254917/libya-rebel -leader-tortured-by-cia-in-thailand, accessed October 4, 2011.

59. CIA, Inspector General, "Special Review: Counterterrorism Detention and In- terrogation Activities," 3, 83, 100; U.S. Senate, *Inquiry into the Treatment of Detainees in U.S. Custody*, xiv–xvi; *New York Times*, July 2, 2008.

60. *New York Times*, September 9, 2011; Sir William Gage, *The Baha Mousa Public Inquiry Report: Volume III* (London: Stationery Office, HC 1452-I, 2011), 1256–58, http://www.bahamousainquiry.org/f_report/vol%20iii/volume%20iii.pdf, accessed September 21, 2011.

61. U.S. Senate, *Inquiry into the Treatment of Detainees in U.S. Custody*, xiii, xx.

62. John Bruce Jessen, "Advances in Clinical Psychological Support of National Se- curity Affairs, Operational Problems in the Behavioral Sciences Course," Symposium: Advances in Clinical Psychological Support of National Security Affairs (n.d.), attached to Jason Leopold and Jeffrey Kaye, "CIA Psychologist's Notes Reveal True Purpose behind Bush's Torture Program," *Truthout*, March 22, 2011, http://www.truth-out.org /cia-psychologists-notes-reveal-bushs-torture-program68542, accessed June 29, 2011.

63. *New York Times*, April 27, 2009, January 25, 2012; Brian Ross, "CIA—Abu Zubaydah: Interview with John Kiriakou," *ABC News*, December 10. 2007, http:// abcnews.go.com/images/Blotter/brianross_kiriakou_transcript1_blotter071210.pdf, accessed January 26, 2012.

64. *New York Times*, August 26, 2011; U.S. Senate, Committee on the Judiciary, *What Went Wrong: Torture and the Office of Legal Counsel in the Bush Administration*, Testimony of Ali Soufan, May 13, 2009, http://judiciary.senate.gov/hearings/, accessed August 29, 2011; Ali H. Soufan, *The Black Banners: The Inside Story of 9/11 and the War against al-Qaeda* (New York: W.W. Norton, 2011), 377.

65. U.S. Senate, Committee on the Judiciary, *What Went Wrong*; Soufan, *The Black Banners*, 378, 395–96.

66. *New York Times*, August 26, 2011; U.S. Senate, Committee on the Judiciary, *What Went Wrong*; Soufan, *The Black Banners*, 397–98.

67. *New York Times*, August 12, 2009; U.S. Senate, *Inquiry into the Treatment of Detainees in U.S. Custody*, 19; U.S. Senate, Committee on the Judiciary, *What Went Wrong*.

68. Gordon Corera and Steve Swann, "Ex-FBI Interrogator 'Gagged' over 9/11 Backstory," *BBC News U.S. and Canada*, September 12, 2011, http://www.bbc.co.uk /news/world-us-canada-14891439, accessed September 14, 2011.

69. Jay Bybee, Office of the Assistant Attorney General, "Memorandum for Al- berto R. Gonzales, Counsel to the President, Re.: Standards of Conduct for Inter- rogation under 18 U.S.C. §§ 2340–2340A," August 1, 2002, 1, news.findlaw.com/wp /docs/doj/bybee80102mem.pdf, accessed October 4, 2011; U.S. Senate, *Inquiry into the Treatment of Detainees in U.S. Custody*, xv–xvi, xxi.

70. Jan Crawford Greenburg, Howard L. Rosenberg, and Ariane de Vogue,

"Sources: Top Bush Advisors Approved 'Enhanced Interrogation,'" *ABC News*, April 9, 2008, http://abcnews.go.com/thelaw/lawpolitics/Story?id=4583256&page=4, accessed December 24, 2008; CIA, Inspector General, "Special Review: Counterterrorism Detention and Interrogation Activities," 5, 24, 45, 101.

71. Jan Crawford Greenburg, Howard L. Rosenberg, and Ariane de Vogue, "Bush Aware of Advisers' Interrogation Talks," *ABC News*, April 11, 2008, http://abcnews.go.com/TheLaw/LawPolitics/story?id=4635175&page=1#.T7LOw47-LiZ, accessed December 24, 2008.

72. *New York Times*, November 9, 2005; CIA, Inspector General, "Special Review: Counterterrorism Detention and Interrogation Activities," 14–15, 20.

73. Steven G. Bradbury, "Memorandum for John A. Rizzo, Senior Deputy Counsel, Central Intelligence Agency," May 30, 2005, 5, http://media.luxmedia.com/aclu/olc_05302005_bradbury.pdf, accessed June 29, 2011.

74. National Defense Appropriations Act, NDAA Senate Debate: Detainee Provisions, December 1, 2011, 50–51, http://www.lawfareblog.com/wp-content/uploads/2011/12/Senate-NDAA-Debate-Dec-1-2011.pdf, accessed December 11, 2011.

75. CIA, Inspector General, "Special Review: Counterterrorism Detention and Interrogation Activities," 42–44, 69–79, 102–3.

76. Richard Norton-Taylor and Ian Cobain, "Top Judge: Binyam Mohamed Case Shows MI5 to Be Devious, Dishonest and Complicit in Torture," *The Guardian* (London), February 10, 2010, http://www.guardian.co.uk/world/2010/feb/10/binyam-mohamed-torture-mi5, accessed April 3, 2010; Stephen Soldz, "The Seven Paragraphs: Released Binyan Mohamed Abuse Evidence Poses Problems for Both British and U.S. Governments," http://www.opednews.com/articles/The-Seven-Paragraphs-Rele-by-Stephen-Soldz-100210-56.html, accessed February 10, 2010; *New York Times*, September 3, 2009, February 11, February 15, 2010; Physicians for Human Rights, *Aiding Torture: Health Professionals' Human Rights Violations Revealed in the May 2004 CIA Inspector General's Report* (August 2010), http://physiciansforhumanrights.org/library/documents/reports/aiding-torture.pdf, accessed April 3, 2010.

77. Steven G. Bradbury, Office of Legal Counsel, "Memorandum for John A. Rizzo, Senior Deputy General Counsel, Central Intelligence Agency, Re: Application of 18 U.S.C. §§ 2340–2340A to the Combined Use of Certain Techniques in the Interrogation of High Value al Qaeda Detainees," May 10, 2005, 53–56, http://media.luxmedia.com/aclu/olc_05102005_bradbury46pg.pdf, accessed June 29, 2011; CIA, Inspector General, "Special Review: Counterterrorism Detention and Interrogation Activities," 29–30, 103; *New York Times*, August 26, 2009.

78. Joannes Millacus, *Praxis Criminis Persequendi* (Paris: Prostant and Simonem Colinacum, 1541); *New York Times*, March 18, 2005.

79. Bradbury, Office of Legal Counsel, "Memorandum for John A. Rizzo, Senior Deputy General Counsel, Central Intelligence Agency," May 10, 2005, 43.

80. Mark Benjamin, "Waterboarding for Dummies," *Salon.com*, March 9, 2010, http://www.salon.com/news/feature/2010/03/09/waterboarding_for_dummies, accessed November 12, 2010; Bradbury, "Memorandum for John A. Rizzo," 43.

81. Bradbury, "Memorandum for John A. Rizzo," 37.

82. Ibid., 43.

83. Jay S. Bybee, Office of the Assistant Attorney General, "Memorandum for John Rizzo, Acting General Counsel of the Central Intelligence Agency. Interrogation of al Qaeda Operative," August 1, 2002, http://www.globalsecurity.org/intell/library/policy /national/olc_020801_bybee.htm, accessed October 4, 2011, 5–6, 11.

84. Henri Alleg, *The Question* (New York: G. Braziller, 1958), 61.

85. In a paper presented at the annual meeting of the American Lung Association in May 1977 at San Francisco, Dr. M. J. Nemiroff offered the first medical report on the diving reflex in humans, drawing on eleven cases from 1967 to 1976 to observe: "Survival is attributed to the diving reflex which redistributes blood flow from skin muscle and gut to the heart and brain." At this point in our limited knowledge of the human mind, the diving reflex seems the most likely cause for the profound psychological pain inflicted upon adults when a cloth moistened with cold water is placed over the nose and mouth. See M. J. Nemiroff, G. R. Saltz, and J. G. Weg, "Survival after Cold-Water Near-Drowning: The Protective Effect of the Diving Reflex," *American Review of Respiratory Disease* 115, no. 5 (1977): 145; Martin J. Nemiroff, MD, "Near Drowning," *Respiratory Care* 37, no. 6 (June 1992): 600–608; "40 Years of Great Lakes Research, Education, and Outreach," *Upwellings Online Edition* (December 2009), http://www.miseagrant. umich.edu/upwellings/issues/09dec/09dec-article1-1.html, accessed April 6, 2011.

86. U.S. Senate, Committee on Armed Services, 110th Congress, 2d Session, *Hearing to Receive Testimony on the Origins of Aggressive Interrogation Techniques: Part I of the Committee's Inquiry into the Treatment of Detainees in U.S. Custody (A.M. Session)* (Washington, DC: Government Printing Office, June 17, 2008), 5–7; U.S. Senate, *Inquiry into the Treatment of Detainees in U.S. Custody*, xvii.

87. U.S. Senate, Committee on Armed Services, "Counter Resistance Strategy Minutes," October 2, 2002, TAB 7, "The Origins of Aggressive Interrogation Techniques; Part I of the Committee's Inquiry into the Treatment of Detainees in U.S. Custody," http://www.scribd.com/doc/33064573/Guantanamo-Source-2, accessed August 2, 2011.

88. U.S. Senate, *Inquiry into the Treatment of Detainees in U.S. Custody*, xix; William J. Haynes II, General Counsel, Department of Defense, For: Secretary of Defense, "Subject: Counter-Resistance Techniques," November 27, 2002, http://www .gwu.edu/~nsarchiv/NSAEBB/NSAEBB127/02.12.02.pdf, accessed November 30, 2011.

89. *New York Times*, June 24, July 6, 2005; M. Gregg Bloche and Jonathan H. Marks, "Doctors and Interrogators at Guantanamo Bay," *New England Journal of Medicine* 353, no. 1 (July 7, 2005): 7; Jonathan H. Marks, "The Silence of the Doctors," *The Nation*, December 7, 2005.

90. *New York Times*, November 30, 2004.

91. U.S. Senate, *Hearing to Receive Testimony on the Origins of Aggressive Interrogation Techniques*, 7.

92. U.S. Senate, *Inquiry into the Treatment of Detainees in U.S. Custody*, xxii; *New York Times*, March 4, 2003, May 20, 2005.

93. *New York Times*, March 19, 2006.

94. *New York Times*, September 9, 2011; Gage, *The Baha Mousa Public Inquiry Report: Volume I*, 9–10.

95. Ricardo S. Sanchez, "Memorandum for: C2, Combined Joint Task Force Seven, Baghdad, Iraq 09335, Subject: CJTF-7 Interrogation and Counter-Resistance Policy," September 14, 2003; Ricardo S. Sanchez, "Memorandum for: C2, Combined Joint Task Force Seven, Baghdad, Iraq 09335, Subject: CJTF-7 Interrogation and Counter-Resistance Policy," October 12, 2003, http://www.aclu.org/SafeandFree/Safe andFree.cfm?ID=17851&c=206, accessed March 30, 2005.

96. U.S. Supreme Court, *Salim Ahmed Hamdan v. Donald H. Rumsfeld*, No. 05-184, Opinion of Stevens, J., June 29, 2006, 6, 69–73, http://www.law.cornell.edu /supct/html/05-184.ZO.html, accessed April 6, 2011; *New York Times*, March 27, June 30, 2006.

97. *New York Times*, September 7, September 8, 2006; The White House, Office of the Press Secretary, "President Discusses Creation of Military Commissions to Try Suspected Terrorists," September 6, 2006, http://georgewbush-whitehouse .archives.gov/news/releases/2006/09/20060906-3.html; "President Bush's Speech on Terrorism," *New York Times*, September 6, 2006, http://www.nytimes.com/2006/09/06 /washington/06bush_transcript.html?pagewanted=all, accessed August 4, 2011.

98. *New York Times*, September 22, September 23, September 26, September 27, September 28, September 29, September 30, 2006; U.S. House of Representatives, 109th Congress, 2d Session, *H.R. 6166: A Bill to Amend Title 10, United States Code, to Authorize Trial by Military Commission for Violations of the Law of War and for Other Purposes*, September 25, 2006, http://www.gpo.gov/fdsys/pkg/BILLS-109hr6166rfs /pdf/BILLS-109hr6166rfs.pdf, accessed February 12, 2012.

99. Bybee, "Memorandum for Alberto R. Gonzales Counsel to the President," August 1, 2002, 1; U.S. House of Representatives, *H.R. 6166: A Bill to Amend Title 10, United States Code*, 29, 35.

100. U.S. House of Representatives, *H.R. 6166: A Bill to Amend Title 10, United States Code*, 28.

101. *New York Times*, July 21, 2007; *Washington Post*, July 21, 2007.

102. *New York Times*, January 22, February 18, May 24, July 22, August 25, 2009.

103. Nick Davies, "Iraq War Logs: Secret Order That Let US Ignore Abuse," *The Guardian*, October 22, 2010, http://www.guardian.co.uk/world/2010/oct/22/iraq -detainee-abuse-torture-saddam, accessed July 28, 2010.

104. Richard Galpin, "Iraq Police Accused of Torture," *BBC News*, July 27, 2005, http://news.bbc.co.uk/2/hi/4718999.stm, accessed July, 28, 2011.

105. Rachel Oldroyd, "The Biggest Document Leak in History Exposes Real War," *Iraqi War Logs*, Bureau of Investigative Journalism, October 1, 2010, http://www.iraqwar logs.com/2010/10/21/the-leaked-us-files-and-what-they-mean/; Angus Stickler and Chris Woods, "US Troops Ordered Not to Investigate Iraqi Torture," *Iraqi War Logs*, Bureau of Investigative Journalism, October 22, 2010, http://www.iraqwarlogs.com/2010/10/22 /us-troops-ordered-not-to-investigate-iraqi-torture/, both accessed July 13, 2011.

106. Jennifer Buley, "Former Defence Minister to Be Questioned in Torture Trial," *Copenhagen Post*, January 2, 2012, http://www.cphpost.dk/news/international/former -defence-minister-be-questioned-torture-trial; "Editorial," *Copenhagen Post*, January 5, 2012, http://www.cphpost.dk/commentary/editorial/editorial-two-wrongs-don't-make -right-torture-allegations; Jeffrey Kaye, "Iraqi Torture Scandal Touches Highest Levels of NATO," *Truthout*, January 5, 2012, http://www.truth-out.org/iraqi-torture-scandal -touches-highest-levels-nato/1325794053, all accessed February 5, 2012.

107. *New York Times*, October 11, 2011; United Nations Assistance Mission in Afghanistan, UN Office of the High Commissioner for Human Rights, "Treatment of Conflict Related Detainees in Afghan Custody" (Kabul, October 2011), iii–iv, 1–2, 16–17, 18–40, http://unama.unmissions.org/Portals/UNAMA/Documents/October10 _%202011_UNAMA_Detention_Full-Report_ENG.pdf, accessed October 17, 2011.

108. CIA, Inspector General, "Special Review: Counterterrorism Detention and Interrogation Activities," 85–91, 100.

109. U.S. Senate, Committee on the Judiciary, Testimony of Ali Soufan, May 13, 2009.

110. U.S. Senate, 109th Congress, 2d Session, *Report of the Select Committee on Intelligence on Postwar Findings about Iraq's WMD Programs and Links to Terrorism and How They Compare with Prewar Assessments* (Washington, DC: Government Printing Office, 2006), 79–82, 106–8.

111. Colonel Lawrence B. Wilkerson, "The Truth about Richard Bruce Cheney," *Washington Note*, May 13, 2009, http://www.thewashingtonnote.com/archives/2009/05 /the_truth_about/, accessed July 28, 2011.

112. Council of Europe, Secretary General, "Report by the Secretary General under Article 52 ECHR on the Question of the Secret Detention and Transport of Detainees Suspected of Terrorist Acts, Notably by or at the Instigation of Foreign Agencies" (SG/ Inf [2006], February 28, 2006), 8, 10–11.

113. *New York Times*, December 1, December 24, 2005, July 6, 2006.

114. Stephen Budiansky, "Intelligence: Truth Extraction," *Atlantic Monthly* (June 2005), 32–35.

115. Mayer, "Outsourcing Torture: Annals of Justice," 110–12; U.S. Senate, Committee on the Judiciary, Testimony of Ali Soufan, May 13, 2009.

Chapter 2. Science in Dachau's Shadow

Portions of this chapter were previously published in an article titled "Science in Dachau's Shadow: Hebb, Beecher, and the Development of CIA Psychological Torture and Modern Medical Ethics," *Journal of the History of the Behavioral Sciences* 43, no. 4 (2007).

1. Arthur Levine, "Collective Unconscionable," *Washington Monthly* (January– February 2007), http://www.washingtonmonthly.com/features/2007/0701.levine. html, accessed May 28, 2007.

2. David Glenn, "A Policy on Torture Roils Psychologists Annual Meeting," *Chron-*

icle of Higher Education, September 7, 2007, A14–17; *New York Times,* November 30, 2004, November 9, 2005.

3. Robert Jay Lifton, *The Nazi Doctors: Medical Killing and the Psychology of Genocide* (New York: Basic Books, 1986), 418–19.

4. Ibid., xii; M. Gregg Bloche and Jonathan H. Marks, "Doctors and Interrogators at Guantanamo Bay," *New England Journal of Medicine* 353, no. 1 (July 7, 2005), http://www.nejm.org, accessed October 23, 2007.

5. Metin Basoglu, Maria Livanou, and Cvetana Crnobaric, "Torture vs. Other Cruel, Inhuman, and Degrading Treatment: Is the Distinction Real or Apparent?" *Archives of General Psychiatry* 64, no. 3 (2007): 277–85.

6. David M. Oshinsky, *Polio: An American Story* (New York: Oxford University Press, 2005), 4–7, 174–87; Ross A. Slotten, *The Heretic in Darwin's Court: The Life of Alfred Russel Wallace* (New York: Columbia University Press, 2004), 1–9; Michael Shotland and Richard Yeo, "Introduction," *Telling Lives in Science: Essays on Scientific Biography* (Cambridge: Cambridge University Press, 1996), 1–44; Thomas Söderqvist, "Existential Projects and Existential Choice in Science: Science Biography as an Edifying Genre," in Shortland and Yeo, *Telling Lives in Science,* 46; Hal Hellman, *Great Feuds in Science: Ten of the Liveliest Disputes Ever* (New York: John Wiley and Sons, 1998), xii–xv; Grove Wilson, *Great Men of Science: Their Lives and Discoveries* (New York: New Home Library, 1929).

7. R. E. Brown and P. M. Milner, "The Legacy of Donald O. Hebb: More Than the Hebb Synapse," *Nature Reviews/Neuroscience* 4 (2003): 1013–19.

8. C.E.W., "Henry K. Beecher, M.D.," *New England Journal of Medicine* 295, no. 13 (September 23, 11976): 730; Vincent J. Kopp, M.D., "Henry K. Beecher, M.D.: Contrarian (1904–1976)," *ASA Newsletter* 63, no. 9 (September 1999), http://www.asahq.org/Newsletters/1999/09_99/beecher0999.html, accessed June 5, 2007; Nicholas M. Greene, M.D., "Henry Knowles Beecher, 1904–1976," *Anesthesiology* 45, no. 4 (October 1976): 377–78.

9. *New York Times,* August 2, 1977.

10. Central Intelligence Agency, Project NM 001 056.0, May 1, 1952, File: Naval Research, Box 8, CIA Behavior Control Experiments Collection (John Marks Donation), National Security Archive, Washington, DC [hereafter, NSA]; H. E. Page, "The Role of Psychology in ONR," *American Psychologist* 9, no. 10 (1954): 621–22.

11. Christopher Simpson, *Science of Coercion: Communication Research and Psychological Warfare 1945–1960* (New York: Oxford University Press, 1994), 4, 9, 25–30, 127–32.

12. Lifton, *The Nazi Doctors,* 4, 16–17, 34–35, 37–39, 42–44, 269–78, 418–29.

13. Tom Bower, *The Paperclip Conspiracy: The Hunt for Nazi Scientists* (Boston: Little, Brown and Company, 1987), 3, 214–32; Philippine Coste, "Cette prison ou l'Amerique recyclait des savants Nazis," *L'Express,* no. 2898 (January 18, 2007), 60–65.

14. Linda Hunt, *Secret Agenda: The United States Government, Nazi Scientists, and Project Paperclip, 1945 to 1990* (New York: St. Martin's Press, 1991), 89–93, 287.

15. Telford Taylor, "Opening Statement for the Prosecution December 9, 1946," in

George J. Annas and Michael A. Grodin, eds., *The Nazi Doctors and the Nuremberg Code: Human Rights in Human Experimentation* (New York: Oxford University Press, 1992), 71–75, 77–78; Sharon Perley et al., "The Nuremberg Code: An International Overview," in Annas and Grodin, *The Nazi Doctors and the Nuremberg Code*, 149–68.

16. John Marks, *The Search for the "Manchurian Candidate": The CIA and Mind Control* (New York: Times Books, 1979), 9–11.

17. Jonathan D. Moreno, *Undue Risk: Secret State Experiments on Humans* (New York: W. H. Freeman, 2000), 119–55, 189–297; Andrew Goliszek, *In the Name of Science: A History of Secret Programs, Medical Research, and Human Experimentation* (New York: St. Martin's Press, 2003), 117–80; Eileen Welsome, *The Plutonium Files: America's Secret Medical Experiments in the Cold War* (New York: Delta, 1999), 189–236, 255–382; "Hidden History of U.S. Germ Testing," *BBC Radio 4*, http://news.bbc.co.uk/2/hi/programmes/file_on_4/4701196.stm, accessed June 4, 2007.

18. Ulf Schmidt, *Justice at Nuremberg: Leo Alexander and the Nazi Doctors' Trial* (New York: Palgrave Macmillan, 2004), 275–81; Moreno, *Undue Risk*, 250–51, 258–59; Hunt, *Secret Agenda*, 166–67, 172–73.

19. "Germ Warfare Charge," *Times of India*, October 22, 1952; *New York Times*, February 21, 1953, April 28, 1954.

20. "Gen. Clark Rips Renewal of Red Germ Charges," *Chicago Daily Tribune*, February 24, 1953; *New York Times*, February 24, 1953.

21. Memorandum, Allen Dulles to Undersecretary of State and Deputy Secretary of Defense, February 1953, Jackson, C. D.: Records, 1953–54, Box 2, "Brainwashing," Dwight D. Eisenhower Library [hereafter, DDEL]; *New York Times*, February 21, 1953.

22. Letter, Charles E. Wilson to Allen Dulles, George Morgan (Acting Director of PSB), Mr. Nash, February 19, 1953, White House Office, National Security Council Staff: Papers, 1953–61, Psychological Strategy Board (PSB) Central Files Series, Box 29, "PSB 702.5 (1) Brainwashing during Korean War," DDEL.

23. Secretary of Defense C. E. Wilson, Memorandum for the Secretary of the Army, Secretary of the Navy, Secretary of the Air Force, Subject: Use of Human Volunteers in Experimental Research, February 26, 1953, http://www2.gwu.edu/~nsarchiv/radiation/dir/mstreet/commeet/meet8/brief8/tab_k/br8k1a.txt, accessed April 6, 2011.

24. "Brainwashing: A Supplemental Report," Henry P. Laughlin, M.D. (Chairman, Public Information Committee, American Psychiatric Association), June 10, 1953, White House Office, National Security Council Staff: Papers, 1953–61, Psychological Strategy Board (PSB) Central Files Series, Box 29, "PSB 702.5 (1) Brainwashing during Korean War," DDEL.

25. Memorandum for the Record, "Forced Confessions," Charles R. Norberg (Acting Deputy Assistant Director, Office of Coordination), May 8, 1953, White House Office, National Security Council Staff: Papers, 1953–61, Psychological Strategy Board (PSB) Central Files Series, Box 29, "PSB 702.5 (1) Brainwashing during Korean War," DDEL.

26. Memorandum, Charles R. Norberg (Acting Deputy Assistant Director, Office of Coordination) to William Godel (Department of Defense), October 8, 1953, White

House Office, National Security Council Staff: Papers, 1953–61, Psychological Strategy Board (PSB) Central Files Series, Box 26, "PSB 383.6 [Prisoners of War] (File #2) (2)," DDEL.

27. "Historic P.O.W Exchange Ends," *Times of India*, September 7, 1953; "False Germ Warfare Confessions Wrung from Pilots," *Los Angeles Times*, October 27, 1953; *New York Times*, April 20, 1954.

28. Press Release No. 1786, "Statement by the Honorable Charles W. Mayo," U.S. Delegation to the General Assembly, October 26, 1953, White House Office, National Security Council Staff: Papers, 1953–61, Psychological Strategy Board (PSB) Central Files Series, Box 26, "PSB 383.6 [Prisoners of War] (File #2) (5)," DDEL; *New York Times*, October 27, October 30, 1953; "Russ Torture of U.S. Fliers in Korea Told," *Los Angeles Times*, October 27, 1953.

29. Press Release No. 1786, "Statement by the Honorable Charles W. Mayo."

30. Memorandum to Dr. Craig, From: Gordon E. Reckord, September 18, 1953, Psychological Strategy Board (PSB) Central Files Series, Box 29, PSB 702.5 (2), "Brainwashing during Korean War," DDEL.

31. "U.S. Discloses Brutal Torture of Five Pilots," *Los Angeles Times*, October 31, 1953.

32. *New York Times*, November 1, 1953.

33. *New York Times*, October 30, November 2, 1953, April 20, 1954.

34. *New York Times*, January 24, 1954.

35. *New York Times*, February 21, 1954.

36. *New York Times*, March 10, 1954; Robert Young, "Brainwashing Impact Told by U.S. Expert," *Chicago Daily Tribune*, March 4, 1954.

37. *New York Times*, March 11, 1954.

38. *New York Times*, March 12, 1954; "Armed Forces: The Dreadful Dilemma," *Time*, March 22, 1954, http://www.time.com/time/magazine/article/0,9171,819565,00 .html#ixzz1UN8EzNdB, accessed August 8, 2011.

39. *New York Times*, April 28, 1954, June 20, July 24, 1955.

40. *New York Times*, September 13, 1953, January 28, 1954.

41. *New York Times*, April 28, 1954.

42. "President Sets Up POW Code," *Los Angeles Times*, August 18, 1955.

43. *New York Times*, August 23, 1954, August 14, August 18, 1955; Dwight D. Eisenhower, "Executive Order 10631—Code of Conduct for Members of the Armed Forces of the United States," August 17, 1955, American Presidency Project, University of California at Santa Barbara, http://www.presidency.ucsb.edu/ws/index .php?pid=59249#axzz1b6pwMI4v, accessed October 17, 2011; Joseph Margulies, *Guantanamo and the Abuse of Presidential Power* (New York: Simon and Schuster, 2006), 120–25.

44. *New York Times*, August 20, September 15, September 17, December 14, 1955.

45. *New York Times*, August 2, 1977.

46. "Les victimes canadiennes d'un programme de la CIA veulent poursuivre Ottawa," *Le Devoir*, January 8, 2007, http://www.ledevoir.com/2007/01/08/126752

.html, accessed June 3, 2007; "Montreal Woman Tries to Launch Suit over Brain-washing," *CBC News/Canada*, January 10, 2007, http://www.cbc.ca/canada/montreal /story/2007/01/10/qc-cia20070110.html, accessed June 3, 2007.

47. *New York Times*, August 2, 1977

48. Central Intelligence Agency, Subject: Special Interrogation Program, March 19, 1951, CIA Behavior Control Experiments Collection (John Marks Donation), NSA (copy provided by Egmont Koch, producer, ARD-TV).

49. *Opinion of George Cooper, Q.C., Regarding Canadian Government Funding of the Allan Memorial Institute in the 1950's and 1960's* (Ottawa: Minister of Supply and Services Canada, Cat. No. J2-63,1986), 32–33, Meeting at Ritz Carleton Hotel, June 1, 1951, Handwritten Note titled "PA 2-1-[illegible]-38, Appendix 21."

50. David Zimmerman, *Top Secret Exchange: The Tizard Mission and the Scientific War* (Montreal: McGill-Queen's University Press, 1996), 3–5, 7, 19–20, 29, 49–50, 96–129, 147–48, 154–66, 190–204; Ronald W. Clark, *Tizard* (London: Methuen, 1965), 386–402; R. V. Jones, "Tizard's Task in the 'War Years' 1935–1952," *Biographical Memoirs of the Fellows of the Royal Society. Volume 7* (London: Royal Society, 1961), 338–41.

51. Maxine F. Singer, "Foreword," in James D. Ebert, ed., *This Our Golden Age: Selected Annual Essays of Caryl P. Haskins, President, Carnegie Institution of Washington 1956–1971* (Washington, DC: Carnegie Institution of Washington, 1996), ix–x.

52. *Opinion of George Cooper, Q.C.*, Meeting at Ritz Carleton Hotel, June 1, 1951, Appendix 21; *New York Times*, August 2, 1977.

53. *Opinion of George Cooper, Q.C.*, Meeting at Ritz Carleton Hotel, June 1, 1951, Appendix 21.

54. *Opinion of George Cooper, Q.C.*, 31–32; Marks, *The Search for the "Manchurian Candidate,"* 29–31. Central Intelligence Agency, Minutes of Meeting, June 6, 1951, File: Artichoke Docs. 59–155, Box 5; Central Intelligence Agency, Memorandum For: Assistant Director, SI, Subject: Progress on BLUEBIRD, July 9, 1951, File: Artichoke Docs. 59–155, Box 5, CIA Behavior Control Experiments Collection (John Marks Donation), NSA.

55. Central Intelligence Agency, Proposed Study on Special Interrogation Methods, February 14, 1952, CIA Behavior Control Experiments Collection (John Marks Donation), NSA.

56. *New York Times*, August 2, 1977.

57. Harvey M. Weinstein, *Psychiatry and the CIA: Victims of Mind Control* (Washington, DC: American Psychiatric Press, 1990), 274; James Meek, "Nobody Is Talking," *The Guardian*, February 18, 2005; Marks, *The Search for the "Manchurian Candidate,"* 32–33; Michael Ignatieff, "What Did the C.I.A. Do To His Father?" *New York Times Magazine*, April 1, 2001, 60.

58. *Opinion of George Cooper, Q.C.*, D. O. Hebb, W. Heron, and W. H. Bexton, "Annual Report, Contract DRB-X38, Experimental Studies of Attitude," 1952, Appendix 22.

59. *Opinion of George Cooper, Q.C.*, Letter from Dr. D. O. Hebb to N. W. Morton, December 15, 1952, Appendix 23.

60. *Opinion of George Cooper, Q.C.*, Letter from Dr. D. O. Hebb to N. W. Morton, November 2, 1953, Appendix 23; letter from Frederic Grunberg to George Cooper, QC, December 1985.

61. *Opinion of George Cooper, Q.C.*, "Proceedings of Fourth Symposium 1952 Was Distributed (Secret)," Memorandum from Ruth Hoyt, Human Resources Section, Defence Research Board, May 7, 1956, Appendix 22.

62. *Opinion of George Cooper, Q.C.*, Letter from D. O. Hebb to N. W. Morton, January 11, 1954, Letter from O. M. Solandt to The Minister, January 25, 1954, Appendix 23.

63. Arthur Blakely, "Life in a Cubicle I," *The Gazette* (Montreal), April 25, 1956; *Opinion of George Cooper, Q.C.*, Letter from D. M. Watters to Dr. O. M. Solandt, July 26, 1954, Appendix 23; Memorandum To: OMS 17/9, Answer: OMS 17/19, Appendix 23.

64. *Opinion of George Cooper, Q.C.*, Letter from Dr. O. M. Solandt to D. M. Watters, August 3, 1954, Appendix 24.

65. Central Intelligence Agency, Office Memorandum, To: Chief, Technical Branch, From: [Blacked-out], Subject: National Meetings of the American Psychological Association, September 30, 1954; Fillmore N. Sanford, "Summary Report of the 1954 Annual Meeting," *American Psychologist* 9, no. 11 (1954): 708. At this same APA meeting, the presidential address for the "Division of Experimental Psychology," on September 6, was by D. O. Hebb ("Drives and the C.N.S. [Central Nervous System]") (See American Psychological Association, "Program of the Sixty-Second Annual Meeting of the American Psychological Association," 295, 500, 501). This presidential address, evidently somewhat revised, was published a year later as D. O Hebb, "Drives and the C.N.S. (Conceptual Nervous System)," *Psychological Review* 62, no. 4 (1955): 243–54.

66. Letter from Peter N. Milner to The Editor, *McGill Tribune*, November 10, 1992 (copy provided by Mary Ellen Hebb).

67. *New York Times*, April 15, 1956; Brian Cahill, "'Isolation' Tests at McGill Hold Brain-Washing Clues," *The Gazette* (Montreal), April 17, 1956; "'Brainwashing' Defence Found," *The Gazette*, April 26, 1956.

68. *New York Times*, August 18, 1955; Eisenhower, "Executive Order 10631—Code of Conduct for Members of the Armed Forces of the United States," August 17, 1955.

69. Edgar H. Schein, "Patterns of Reactions to Severe Chronic Stress in American Army Prisoners of War of the Chinese," 253–69, and Louis J. West, "United States Air Force Prisoners of the Chinese Communists," 270–84, both in *Symposium No. 4. Methods of Forceful Indoctrination: Observations and Interviews* (New York: Group for the Advancement of Psychiatry, 1957). Indicating the rise in defensive research in 1955–56, well after Hebb's DRB contract was over in 1954, a bibliography of sixteen contemporary publications on the Korean brainwashing in West's essay lists two with no dates, two for 1954, three for 1955, and nine for 1956. (See West, "United States Air Force Prisoners of the Chinese Communists," 270–71.)

70. *Opinion of George Cooper, Q.C.*, Statement by Dr. G. S. Field, Acting Chairman of the Defence Research Board, n.d., Appendix 23.

71. Peter Dale Scott, *Listening to the Candle: A Poem on Impulse* (Toronto: McClelland and Stewart, 1992), 6–7; Peter Dale Scott, personal communication, Melbourne, Australia, August 10, 2006.

72. Personal communications, retired medical doctors and McGill medical school graduates, March 13, 2006, September 30, October 1, 2007.

73. *Opinion of George Cooper, Q.C.*, 35–36.

74. D. O. Hebb, "This Is How It Was," Canadian Psychological Association, ca. 1980 (copy provided by Mary Ellen Hebb).

75. D. O. Hebb, *The Organization of Behavior: A Neuropsychological Theory* (New York: John Wiley and Sons, 1949); Hebb, "This Is How It Was."

76. Philip Solomon et al., eds., *Sensory Deprivation: A Symposium Held at Harvard Medical School* (Cambridge, MA: Harvard University Press, 1961), 239–57; Stephen E. Glickman, "Hebb, Donald Olding," in Alan E. Kazdin, ed., *Encyclopedia of Psychology* (New York: Oxford University Press, 2000), 105–6; D. O. Hebb, *Essay on Mind* (Hillsdale, NJ: Lawrence Erlbaum Associates, 1980), 96–97.

77. Woodburn Heron and D. O. Hebb, "Cognitive and Physiological Effect of Perceptual Isolation," in Solomon, *Sensory Deprivation*, v–xvi, 1–2, 6–33, 239–57; Solomon, *Sensory Deprivation*, v–xvi, 1–2, 239–57.

78. Marks, *The Search for the "Manchurian Candidate,"* 23–25, 32–33, 106, 137–38, 201–2; Richard E. Brown, "Alfred McCoy, Hebb, the CIA and Torture," *Journal of the History of the Behavioral Sciences* 43, no. 2 (2007): 209.

79. Cecil Rosner, "Isolation: A Canadian Professor's Research into Sensory Deprivation and Its Connection to Disturbing New Methods of Interrogation," *Canada's History* (August–September 2010), 29–37.

80. Donald Wexler, Jack Mendelson, Herbert Leiderman, and Philip Solomon, "Sensory Deprivation: A Technique for Studying Psychiatric Aspects of Stress," *A.M.A. Archives of Neurology and Psychiatry* 79, no. 1 (1958): 225–33.

81. Lawrence E. Hinkle Jr., "A Consideration of the Circumstances under Which Men May Be Interrogated, and the Effects That These May Have upon the Function of the Brain" (n.d., ca. 1958), 1, 5, 6, 11–14, 18, File: Hinkle, Box 7, CIA Behavior Control Experiments Collection (John Marks Donation), NSA.

82. "KUBARK Counterintelligence Interrogation" (July 1963), File: Kubark, Box 1: CIA Training Manuals, NSA, 87–90.

83. Rosner, "Isolation," 34.

84. Elizabeth Nickson, "My Mother, the CIA and LSD," *The Observer* (London), October 16, 1994, 48–52; Weinstein, *Psychiatry and the CIA*, 110–20, 140–41; Gordon Thomas, *Journey into Madness: Medical Torture and the Mind Controllers* (London: Bantam Press, 1988), 114, 166–70, 176–77; Marks, *The Search for the "Manchurian Candidate,"* 132–41; D. Ewan Cameron et al., "The Depatterning Treatment of Schizophrenia," *Comprehensive Psychiatry* 3, no. 3 (1962): 65–76.

85. *Opinion of George Cooper, Q.C.*, 2–5, 41–44, 85–86, 96, 103–12, 117–22, 125–27; David Vienneau, "Ottawa Knew of Brain-Washing: Ex-Civil Servant," *Toronto Star*, April 16, 1986; Joseph L. Rauh Jr. and James C. Turner, "Anatomy of a Public Interest

Case against the CIA," *Hamline Journal of Public Law and Policy* 11, no. 2 (1990): 316, 325–330, 352–54; Weinstein, *Psychiatry and the CIA*, 278–81.

86. Rauh and Turner, "Anatomy of a Public Interest Case against the CIA," 335.

87. David Vienneau, "No Secrets Hidden from CIA, Former Official Says," *Toronto Star*, April 14, 1986.

88. *Opinion of George Cooper, Q.C.*, 97–99; Vienneau, "No Secrets Hidden from CIA."

89. David Vienneau, "Colleague Says McGill Doctor Probably Unaware of CIA Role," *Toronto Star*, April 17, 1986; letter from Peter N. Milner to The Editor, *McGill Tribune*, November 10, 1992 (copy provided by Mary Ellen Hebb).

90. Rauh and Turner, "Anatomy of a Public Interest Case against the CIA," 335 (footnote 33), 336–37; Vienneau, "Ottawa Knew of Brain-Washing."

91. Rauh and Turner, "Anatomy of a Public Interest Case against the CIA," 307, 352–53.

92. *Opinion of George Cooper, Q.C.*, 70, 96, 104–12.

93. Rauh and Turner, "Anatomy of a Public Interest Case against the CIA," 360–62.

94. Ibid., 333.

95. Weinstein, *Psychiatry and the CIA*, 92–95; Thomas, *Journey into Madness*, 102–3, 152–63.

96. *Opinion of George Cooper, Q.C.*, 110–11.

97. Ibid., 35–36.

98. Alfred W. McCoy, *A Question of Torture, CIA Interrogation from the Cold War to the War on Terror* (New York: Metropolitan Books, 2006), 33.

99. Canadian Society for Brain, Behaviour, and Cognitive Science (BBCS), "The Donald O. Hebb Distinguished Contribution Award," http://www.csbbcs.org/hebbrec11.html, accessed July 8, 2011.

100. Marks, *The Search for the "Manchurian Candidate*,*"* 147–63; Weinstein, *Psychiatry and the CIA*, 133–35; Thomas, *Journey into Madness*, 168; Lawrence E. Hinkle Jr. and Harold G. Wolff, "Communist Interrogation and Indoctrination of 'Enemies of the States': Analysis of Methods Used by the Communist State Police (A Special Report)," *Archives of Neurology and Psychiatry* 76 (1956): 116–17, 128–30, 134–35; David H. Price, "Buying a Piece of Anthropology, Part II: The CIA and Our Tortured Past," *Anthropology Today* 23, no. 5 (2007): 17–18, http://homepages.stmartin.edu/fac_staff/dprice/Price-AT-HEF2.pdf, accessed August 5, 2011.

101. Thomas Blass, *The Man Who Shocked the World: The Life and Legacy of Stanley Milgram* (New York: Basic Books, 2004), 65–72, 235–42; Vienneau, "Ottawa Knew of Brain-Washing."

102. Stanley Milgram, *Obedience to Authority: An Experimental View* (New York: Harper and Row, 1974), 1–43; Blass, *The Man Who Shocked the World*, 76, 114–16; Stanley Milgram, "Group Pressure and Action against a Person," *Journal of Abnormal and Social Psychology* 9, no. 2 (1964): 137–43; Arthur G. Miller, *The Obedience Experiments: A Case Study of Controversy in Social Science* (New York: Praeger Publishers, 1986).

103. "The Nuremberg Code," in Annas and Grodin, *The Nazi Doctors and the Nuremberg Code*, 2.

104. Philip Zimbardo, "When Good People Do Evil," *Yale Alumni Magazine* 70, no. 3 (January/February 2007): 42; Christopher R. Browning, *Ordinary Men: Reserve Police Battalion 101 and the Final Solution in Poland* (New York: HarperCollins, 1998), 159–89; Miller, *The Obedience Experiments*, 179–220.

105. "The Nuremberg Code," in Annas and Grodin, *The Nazi Doctors and the Nuremberg Code*, 2.

106. Milgram, "Group Pressure and Action against a Person."

107. In an interview with ARD-TV on March 3, 2007, the archivist at the Dachau KZ Memorial, Albert Knoll, "confirmed that the only papers from the medical experiments, which survived a burning action of the SS a couple of days before the U.S. Army freed the camp, had been seized, sent to the U.S. and analyzed by Beecher and his fellow experts." Hence, it is a facsimile of Dr. Beecher's copy of this Gestapo research report that today is on display at Dachau. (E-mails from Egmont Koch, producer, ARD-TV, Hamburg, Germany, March 13, 2007, May 29, 2007.) Marks, *The Search for the "Manchurian Candidate,"* 4–6; Technical Report no. 3331-45, "German Aviation Medical Research at the Dachau Concentration Camp," October 1945, U.S. Naval Technical Mission to Europe, H MS c64, Box 11, f. 75, Harvard Medical Library; letter from Arthur M. Turner, M.D., to Dr. Henry K. Beecher, February 7, 1947, Box 6, CIA Behavior Control Experiments Collection (John Marks Donation), NSA.

108. Letter from Arthur M. Turner to Dr. Henry K. Beecher, March 24, 1947, Box 6, CIA Behavior Control Experiments Collection (John Marks Donation), NSA; letter from Henry K. Beecher to Colonel William S. Stone, August 29, 1950, Box 6, CIA Behavior Control Experiments Collection (John Marks Donation), NSA.

109. Letter from Henry K. Beecher to Colonel William S. Stone, June 15, 1950, Box 6, CIA Behavior Control Experiments Collection (John Marks Donation), NSA.

110. Letter from Henry K. Beecher to the Surgeon General, Department of the Army, October 21, 1951, Box 16, RG 319, National Archives and Research Administration (copy provided by Egmont Koch, producer, ARD-TV).

111. Beecher to the Surgeon General, October 21, 1951.

112. Ibid.

113. Ibid.

114. Arnold M. Silver, "Questions, Questions, Questions: Memories of Oberursel," *Intelligence and National Security* 8, no. 2 (1993): 199–213; Randy Pruitt, "Camp King: A Casern with a Past," *Stars and Stripes* (European edition), January 18, 1993, 18–19; Egmont R. Koch and Michael Wech, *Deckname Artischocke* (Munich: Random House, 2003), 50, 89–121, 269; Bower, *The Paperclip Conspiracy*, 254–56.

115. Beecher to the Surgeon General, October 21, 1951.

116. Bower, *The Paperclip Conspiracy*, 255–58; U.S. Army, "SCHREIBER, Dr. Walter P., December 15, 1949," in Koch and Wech, *Deckname Artischocke*, 94; *New York Times*, August 28, 1946, October 27, 1948, February 13, 1952.

117. Beecher to the Surgeon General, October 21, 1951.

118. Letter from Major Arthur R. Lund to Whom It May Concern, May 26, 1951; Project Title: Neuropsychiatry and Stress, December 31, 1954, Box 6, CIA Behavior Control Experiments Collection (John Marks Donation), NSA.

119. From: Prof. Ernst Rothlin, Chief Pharmacologist, Sandoz Co., Basel, Switzerland, "d-Lysergic Acid Diethylamide (LSD 25)," n.d., Box 6, CIA Behavior Control Experiments Collection (John Marks Donation), NSA.

120. Letter from Henry K. Beecher to Dr. E. Rothlin, August 4, 1952; letter from Henry K. Beecher to Colonel William S. Stone, August 29, 1950, Box 6, CIA Behavior Control Experiments Collection (John Marks Donation), NSA.

121. From Henry K. Beecher, M.D., Consultant, Subject: Information from Europe Related to the Ego-Depressants, 6 August to 29 August 1952, September 4, 1952, CIA Behavior Control Experiments Collection (John Marks Donation), NSA (copy provided by Egmont Koch, producer, ARD-TV).

122. Henry K. Beecher, "Experimental Pharmacology and Measurement of the Subjective Response," *Science* 116, no. 3007 (August 15, 1952): 157–58; letter from Henry K. Beecher to *Science* 117, no. 3033 (February 13, 1953): 166–67.

123. "Project Title: Neuropsychiatry and Stress," Addendum. Beecher (MD 92). Final Report, "Response of Normal Men to Lysergic Acid Derivatives (Di- and Mono-ethylamide). Correlation of Personality and Drug Reactions," December 31, 1954, Box 6, CIA Behavior Control Experiments Collection (John Marks Donation), NSA.

124. Henry K. Beecher, *Measurement of Subjective Responses: Quantitative Effects of Drugs* (New York: Oxford University Press, 1959), 287, 309–11; J. M. von Felsinger, L. Lasagna, and H. K. Beecher, "Drug-Induced Mood Changes in Man: 2. Personality and Reactions to Drugs," *Journal of the American Medical Association* 157, no. 13 (March 26, 1955): 1113–19; J. M. von Felsinger, L. Lasagna, and H. K. Beecher, "The Response of Normal Men to Lysergic Acid Derivatives (Di- and Mono-Ethyl Amides)," *Journal of Clinical and Experimental Psychopathology and Quarterly Review of Psychiatry and Neurology* 17, no. 4 (1956): 414–28. Letter from Henry K. Beecher to Colonel William S. Stone, May 31, 1950; letter from Henry K. Beecher to Chauncey D. Leake, June 13, 1955; letter from Chauncey D. Leake to Henry K. Beecher, June 7, 1955, Box 6, CIA Behavior Control Experiments Collection (John Marks Donation), NSA.

125. Henry K. Beecher, "Experimentation in Man," *Journal of the American Medical Association* 169, no. 5 (January 31, 1959): 110, 120–22.

126. Moreno, *Undue Risk*, 243–45.

127. Goliszek, *In the Name of Science*, 179–80.

128. Moreno, *Undue Risk*, 241–42.

129. Henry K. Beecher, "Ethics and Clinical Research," *New England Journal of Medicine* 274, no. 24 (June 16, 1966): 1354–60.

130. Henry K. Beecher, "Response to the Ingersoll Lecture by a Physician," *Harvard Theological Review* 62, no. 1 (1969): 21–26; Martin A. Lee and Bruce Shlain, *Acid Dreams: The Complete Social History of LSD: The CIA, the Sixties, and Beyond* (New York: Grove Press, 1985), 74–76.

131. "Faculty and Staff—Dr. Henry Knowles Beecher, 1904–1976," Countway

Medical Library, Harvard University, http://.222.countway.harvard.edu/archives/iotm /iotm_2002-01.shtm, accessed February 16, 2007.

132. Jay Katz, "'Ethics and Clinical Research' Revisited: A Tribute to Henry K. Beecher," *Hastings Center Report* 23, no. 5 (1993): 31–39.

133. Jon Harkness, Susan E. Lederer, and Daniel Wikler, "Laying Ethical Foundations for Clinical Research," *Bulletin of the World Health Organization* 79, no. 4 (2001): 365–66.

134. Ibid., 365; Daniel J. Rothman, *Strangers at the Bedside: A History of How Law and Bioethics Transformed Medical Decision Making* (New York: Basic Books, 1991), 2–3, 70–84, 251; Moreno, *Undue Risk*, 239–42; Marks, *The Search for the "Manchurian Candidate,"* 67n, 72n; Lee and Shlain, *Acid Dreams*, 86.

135. *New York Times*, June 24, June 27, July 6, 2005; American Psychological Association, "Report of the American Psychological Association Presidential Task Force on Psychological Ethics and National Security" (June 2005), 1, 5, 8–9, http://www.apa .org/releases/PENSTaskForceReportFinal.pdf, accessed July 7, 2005.

136. American Psychological Association, "Overview of APA's Ongoing Efforts to Implement the Petition Resolution," September 10, 2009, http://www.apa.org/news /press/statements/implementation-steps.pdf, accessed June 2, 2011.

137. American Psychological Association, "Amending the Ethics Code," *Monitor on Psychology*, 41, no. 4 (April 2010), http://www.apa.org/monitor/2010/04/ethics .aspx, accessed June 2, 2011.

138. *New York Times*, April 27, 2011; New York Office of the Professions—Central Administration, Dr. Stephen Reisner, Licensing Complaint—John Francis Leso, NY License # 013492, Center for Justice and Accountability, http://www.cja.org/article .php?id=885, accessed August 8, 2011.

Chapter 3. Torture in the Crucible of Counterinsurgency

Portions of this chapter were previously published in a volume edited by Marilyn B. Young and Lloyd C. Gardner, *Iraq and the Lessons of Vietnam: Or, How Not to Learn from the Past* (New York: New Press, 2007).

1. Ron Baer, *See No Evil: The True Story of a Ground Soldier in the CIA's War on Terrorism* (New York: Three Rivers Press, 2002), 268–69.

2. *The 9/11 Commission Report: Final Report of the National Commission on Terrorist Attacks upon the United States* (New York: W. W. Norton, 2004), 90–93.

3. *New York Times*, February 16, 1986.

4. Michael T. Klare, *War without End: American Planning for the Next Vietnams* (New York: Alfred A. Knopf, 1972), 245, 241, 247, 250; Thomas David Lobe, "U.S. Police Assistance for the Third World" (doctoral dissertation, University of Michigan, 1975), 82.

5. Lobe, "U.S. Police Assistance for the Third World," 42–44.

6. Ibid., 46.

7. Robert Komer, Memorandum to McGeorge Bundy and General Taylor, "Should Police Programs Be Transferred to the DOD?" Secret (Declassified), April 18, 1962, http://www.thememoryhole.org/phoenix/, accessed May 8, 2006.

8. "Memorandum of Discussion at the 229th Meeting of the National Security Council, Tuesday, December 21, 1954," U.S. Department of State, *Foreign Relations of the United States, 1952–1954, National Security Affairs* (Washington, DC: Government Printing Office, 1954), 832–44; "Supplemental Progress Report on Actions Taken Pursuant to NSC Action 1290-d," September 6, 1956, U.S. State Department, *Foreign Relations of the United States, 1955–57, Volume X, Foreign Aid and Economic Defense Policy* (Washington, DC: Government Printing Office, 1956), 107–17.

9. A. J. Langguth, *Hidden Terrors* (New York: Pantheon, 1978), 47–52, 124–26, 300.

10. "History of the Kansas City Regional Police Academy," Kansas City Police Academy, http://www.kcmo.org/police/TrainingEducation/AboutUs/index.htm; Reg Davis and Harry James, *The Public Safety Story: An Informal Recollection of Events and Individuals Leading to the Formation of the A.I.D. Office of Public Safety* (Santee: The Public Safety Newsletter, 2001), 3–9, http://pdf.usaid.gov/pdf_docs/PCAAB135.pdf, both accessed November 2, 2011.

11. Lobe, "U.S. Police Assistance for the Third World," 56–57, 60–61, 72.

12. Klare, *War without End*, 245, 241, 247, 250, 260–65.

13. U.S. General Accounting Office, *Stopping U.S. Assistance to Foreign Police and Prisons* (Washington, DC: U.S. General Accounting Office, 1976), 14.

14. Langguth, *Hidden Terrors*, 125–28, 138–40, 251–52.

15. Klare, *War without End*, 261–64; Douglas Valentine, *The Phoenix Program* (New York: William Morrow, 1990), 59–60.

16. Valentine, *The Phoenix Program*, 63, 77–85. On page 84, Valentine identifies the CIA officers who trained the Vietnamese Special Branch as "experts from the CIA's Support Services Branch." In other accounts, this unit is identified as Technical Services Division (Langguth, *Hidden Terrors*, 138–40).

17. Victor Marchetti and John D. Marks, *The CIA and the Cult of Intelligence* (New York: Alfred A. Knopf, 1974), 245–46.

18. Andrew F. Krepinevich Jr., *The Army and Vietnam* (Baltimore: Johns Hopkins University Press, 1986), 227–28.

19. Valentine, *The Phoenix Program*, 112–15.

20. Ibid., 86–87, 119–22.

21. Ibid., 124–26.

22. Mark Moyar, *Phoenix and the Birds of Prey: The CIA's Secret Campaign to Destroy the Viet Cong* (Annapolis: Naval Institute Press, 1997), 51–52; Valentine, *The Phoenix Program*, 100–103, 118–20.

23. The White House, National Security Action Memorandum No 362, Subject: Responsibility for U.S. Role in Pacification (Revolutionary Development), May 9, 1967, Lyndon Baines Johnson Presidential Library, http://www.lbjlib.utexas.edu/johnson/archives.hom/nsams/nsam362.asp, accessed December 19, 2011; Robert

Komer, Interview II, August 18, 1970, 20–35, Oral History Interviews, Lyndon Baines Johnson Presidential Library.

24. Valentine, *The Phoenix Program*, 130–33; Nelson H. Brickham, Memorandum For: Ambassador R. W. Komer, Subject: Personal Observations, May 26, 1967, http:// www.thememoryhole.org/phoenix/, accessed May 8, 2006.

25. Brickham, Memorandum For: Ambassador R. W. Komer.

26. ICEX Briefing, n.d., http://www.thememoryhole.org/phoenix/icex_briefing. pdf, accessed May 8, 2006; Valentine, *The Phoenix Program*, 133–34; L. Wade Lathram, MACCORDS, Memorandum For: Ambassador R. W. Komer, Subject: Action Program for Attack on VC Infrastructure, 1967–1968, July 27, 1967, http://www .thememoryhole.org/phoenix/action_program.pdf, accessed May 8, 2006.

27. Lathram, MACCORDS, Memorandum For: Ambassador R.W. Komer.

28. Ibid.

29. John G. Lybrand, MACCORDS, Evaluation Report: Processing of Viet Cong Suspects, December 11, 1967, http://www.thememoryhole.org/phoenix/evaluation -report.pdf, accessed May 8, 2006.

30. Lathram, MACCORDS, Memorandum For: Ambassador R. W. Komer; Valentine, *The Phoenix Program*, 141, 145–46.

31. Paul E. Suplizio, Subj: Attack on VC Infrastructure, a Progress Report, To: CINCPAC, November 1967, http://www.thememoryhole.org/phoenix/macv-dtg-06 -09102.pdf, accessed May 8, 2006.

32. Republic of Vietnam, Office of the Prime Minister, Directive of the Prime Minister on the Neutralization of VCI, December 20, 1967, http://www.thememoryhole .org/phoenix/directive-pm.pdf, accessed May 8, 2006.

33. Central Intelligence Agency, Internal Security in South Vietnam—Phoenix, December 12, 1970, http://www.thememoryhole.org/phoenix/internal-security.pdf, accessed May 8, 2006.

34. Ian McNeill, *The Team: Australian Army Advisers in Vietnam 1962–1972* (St. Lucia: University of Queensland Press, 1984), 385–411; Central Intelligence Agency, Internal Security in South Vietnam—Phoenix; R. W. Komer, *Organization and Management of the "New Model" Pacification Program—1966–1969* (Santa Monica: Rand Corporation, May 7, 1970), 166, 187, 220.

35. Valentine, *The Phoenix Program*, 253–56, 276–79; Central Intelligence Agency, Internal Security in South Vietnam—Phoenix.

36. Central Intelligence Agency, Internal Security in South Vietnam—Phoenix.

37. Ibid.

38. U.S. Senate, 93rd Congress, 2d Session, *Congressional Record*, 1974, vol. 120, pt. 25, 33474.

39. Ibid., 33475; Valentine, *The Phoenix Program*, 365.

40. Komer, *Organization and Management of the "New Model" Pacification Program*, 159.

41. *New York Times*, February 18, 1970; Valentine, *The Phoenix Program*, 107.

42. Komer, *Organization and Management of the "New Model" Pacification Program*, 164.

43. Orrin DeForest and David Chanoff, *Slow Burn: The Rise and Bitter Fall of American Intelligence in Vietnam* (New York: Simon and Schuster, 1990), 54–57.

44. Ralph W. McGehee, *Deadly Deceits: My 25 Years in the CIA* (New York: Sheridan Square Publications, 1983), 142–44.

45. Krepinevich, *The Army and Vietnam*, 228–29.

46. McGehee, *Deadly Deceits*, 156.

47. Valentine, *The Phoenix Program*, 320–26; Dale Andradé, "Pacification," in Stanley Kutler, ed., *Encyclopedia of the Vietnam War* (New York: Charles Scribner's Sons, 1996), 417–23.

48. J.C. Masterman, *The Double-Cross System: The Incredible True Story of How Nazi Spies Were Turned into Double Agents* (New York: Lyons Press, 2000); John Loftus, *The Belarus Secret* (New York: Knopf, 1982); Tim Weiner, *Legacy of Ashes: The History of the CIA* (New York: Random House, 2008), 245–47, 697; Richard H. Schultz, Jr., *The Secret War against Hanoi: Kennedy's and Johnson's Use of Spies, Saboteurs, and Covert Warriors in North Vietnam* (New York: HarperCollins, 1999), 8–39.

49. *New York Times*, August 6, August 7, August 9, August 12, August 14, August 15, August 16, August 17, August 20, August 29, September 26, September 27, September 28, September 30, October 1, November 8, 1969, April 4, 1971; James Olsfen, ed., *Dictionary of the Vietnam War* (New York: Peter Bedrick Books, 1987), 389–90.

50. *New York Times*, February 18, 1970.

51. *New York Times*, July 16, 1971.

52. *New York Times*, July 20, August 2, 1971; Marchetti and Marks, *The CIA and the Cult of Intelligence*, 246.

53. *New York Times*, July 20, August 2, 1971; U.S. House of Representatives, 92d Congress, 1st Session, Subcommittee of the Committee on Government Operations, Hearings on August 2, 1971, *U.S. Assistance Programs in Vietnam* (Washington, DC: Government Printing Office, 1971), 349.

54. U.S. House of Representatives, *U.S. Assistance Programs in Vietnam*, 319–21, 327, 349; U.S. Senate, 93d Congress, 1st Session, Committee on Armed Services, Hearings on July 2, 20, 25, 1973, *Nomination of William E. Colby to Be Head of Central Intelligence* (Washington, DC: Government Printing Office, 1973), 101–17; Andradé, "Pacification," 423.

55. In its report, the U.S. Army Intelligence Command faulted K. Barton Osborn for refusing "to identify specific persons . . . on two occasions"—an understandable discretion when dealing with a CIA assassination program. In a personal comment that casts doubts upon his own credibility, William Colby added in a statement to Congress about Osborn: "The Phoenix program was essentially instituted in the summer of 1968 and began to work during the fall. . . . Mr. Osborn served in Vietnam from September 1967, to December 1968. In other words, his service essentially was before the Phoenix program really got rolling in any degree."

If we examine Colby's comment objectively, Osborn's Vietnam service overlapped with Phoenix from June to December 1968, a period of at least six months and fully half the standard military tour of duty in Vietnam—in short, a substantial period of service. (U.S. Senate, Committee on Armed Services, *Nomination of William E. Colby*, 116–117.)

56. Moyar, *Phoenix and the Birds of Prey*, 89–99; U.S. Senate, Committee on Armed Services, *Nomination of William E. Colby*, 116–17.

57. U.S. Department of Defense, Subject: USSOUTHCOM CI Training-Supplemental Information (U), July 31, 1991; U.S. Department of the Army, U.S. Army Intelligence Center and Fort Huachuca, Memorandum for Deputy Chief of Staff for Intelligence, Subject: History of Project X, [Sgd.] William J. Teeter, September 12, 1991, both in File: Project X, Consortium News, Arlington, Virginia.

58. U.S. Department of Defense, Office of the Assistant Secretary of Defense Command, Control, Communications and Intelligence, Memorandum for the Record, Subject: USSOUTHCOM CI Training-Supplemental Information (U), July 31, 1991, File: Project X, Consortium News, Arlington, Virginia; U.S. Department of Defense, Assistant to the Secretary of Defense, Memorandum for Secretary of Defense, Subject: Interim Report on Improper Material in USSOUTHCOM Training Manuals (U)-Information Memorandum, October 4, 1991, File: Project X, Consortium News, Arlington, Virginia.

59. U.S. Department of Army, Office of the Deputy Chief of Staff for Intelligence, Robert W. Singleton, Memorandum Thru the General Counsel, ATTN: PWC, Subject: History of Project X, November 4, 1991, File: Project X, Consortium News, Arlington, Virginia; Robert Parry, *Lost History: Contras, Cocaine and Other Crimes* (Arlington: Media Consortium 1997), 48–49.

60. U.S. Department of Defense, Office of the Assistant Secretary of Defense Command, Control, Communications and Intelligence, Point Paper Concerning USSOUTHCOM Proposed Counterintelligence (CI) Training to Foreign Governments, July 30, 1991, File: Project X, Consortium News, Arlington, Virginia.

61. U.S. Department of Defense, Assistant to the Secretary of Defense, Report of Investigation: Improper Material in Spanish-Language Intelligence Training Manuals, March 10, 1992, Intelligence Training Course Manuals, Folder: Handling of Sources, National Security Archive, Washington, DC [hereafter, NSA].

62. U.S. Army Intelligence Center and School, Study Manual: Handling of Sources—1989 (Secret. Not Releasable to Foreign Nationals; Declassified by Authority of the Secretary of the Army, September 19, 1996), Box 2: Intelligence Training Course Manuals, Folder: Handling of Sources, NSA, 5–6, 24–25, 42–44, 65–66, 110–12, 116–33.

63. U.S. Department of Defense, Point Paper Concerning USSOUTHCOM Proposed Counterintelligence (CI) Training to Foreign Governments, July 30, 1991; U.S. Department of Defense, Subject: USSOUTHCOM CI TrainingSupplemental Information, July 31, 1991; U.S. Department of Defense, Subject: Interim Report on Improper Material in USSOUTHCOM Training Manuals (U)-Information Memo-

randum, October 4, 1991, all in File: Project X, Consortium News, Arlington, Virginia. *New York Times*, September 22, 1996.

64. U.S. Department of Defense, Subject: Interim Report on Improper Material in USSOUTHCOM Training Manuals (U)-Information Memorandum, October 4, 1991.

65. U.S. Senate, Select Committee on Intelligence, "Transcript of Proceedings before the Select Committee on Intelligence: Honduran Interrogation Manual Hearing," June 16, 1988 (Box 1, CIA Training Manuals, Folder: Interrogation Manual Hearings, NSA), 14–15.

66. CIA, "Human Resource Exploitation Training Manual 1983," June 8, 1988 (Box 1 CIA Training Manuals, Folder: Resources Exploitation Training Manual, NSA), I-D.

67. Ibid., K-1.B.

68. Ibid., K-1.F-G.

69. Ibid., F-1.A.

70. Ibid., F-5.E, F-14.F, F-15.H.

71. Ibid., L-17.

72. Ibid., L-1, L-2.

73. Ibid., L-3.

74. Ibid., L-3, L-4.

75. Ibid., L-12.

76. Ibid., L-11.D.

77. Ibid., L-12.E.

78. Seymour Hersh, "The Gray Zone," *The New Yorker*, May 10, 2004, 40–42; Seymour M. Hersh, *Chain of Command: The Road from 9/11 to Abu Ghraib* (New York: HarperCollins, 2004), 57–59; Leon Worden, "SCV Newsmaker of the Week: Brig. Gen. Janis Karpinski," *Signal Newspaper* (Santa Clarita), July 4, 2004; Mark Danner, *Torture and Truth: America, Abu Ghraib, and the War on Terror* (New York: New York Review of Books, 2004), 33.

79. Hersh, *Chain of Command*, 16–17, 47–50, 59–60.

80. M. G. Antonio M. Taguba, Article 15–6 Investigation of the 800th Military Police Brigade, February 26, 2004, 7, 8, 15, http://www.cbsnews.com/htdocs/pdf/tagubareport.pdf, accessed May 10, 2004; *New York Times*, May 24, May 26, June 22, 2004, March 30, May 30, 2005; Human Rights Watch, *The Road to Abu Ghraib* (June 8, 2004), 32–33, http://www.hrw.org/en/reports/2004/06/08/road-abu-ghraib, accessed August 26, 2004; Hersh, *Chain of Command*, 30–31; Scott Horton, "Betr: Strafanzeige gegen den US-Verteidigungsminister Donald Rumsfeld, u.a.," An den: Herrn Generalbundesanwalt, Beim Bundesgerichtshof, Karlsruhe, January 29, 2005, para. 16, http://www.rav.de/StAR_290105_Horton.htm, accessed April 14, 2005; Jane Mayer, "The Experiment," *The New Yorker* (July 11–18, 2005), 63.

81. Worden, "Brig. Gen. Janis Karpinski"; Mayer, "The Experiment," 63; *New York Times*, May 24, May 26, June 22, 2004, March 30, May 30, 2005.

82. James R. Schlesinger et al., "Final Report of the Independent Panel to Review DoD Detention Operations," August 2004, 9, htttp://news.findlaw.com/cnn

/docs/dod/abughraibrpt.pdf, accessed August 26, 2004; *ABC News, Nightline*, "Broken Chain of Command," May 12, 2005.

83. Ricardo S. Sanchez, Memorandum for: C2, Combined Joint Task Force Seven, Baghdad, Iraq 09335, Subject: CJTF-7 Interrogation and Counter-Resistance Policy, September 14, 2003; Ricardo S. Sanchez, Memorandum for: C2, Combined Joint Task Force Seven, Baghdad, Iraq 09335, Subject: CJTF-7 Interrogation and Counter-Resistance Policy, October 12, 2003, http://www.aclu.org/SafeandFree/Safe andFree.cfm?ID=17851&c=206, accessed March 30, 2005; Translation of Sworn Statement by [name blacked out], 1430/21 JAN 04, in Danner, *Torture and Truth*, 247–48; *New York Times*, September 24, 2005.

84. CIA, "Human Resource Exploitation Training Manual—1983," June 8, 1988 (Box 1 CIA Training Manuals, Folder: Resources Exploitation Training Manual," NSA), E-33, I-D, I-5, I-22, L-3, 1–12; "KUBARK Counterintelligence Interrogation" (July 1963), File: Kubark, Box 1: CIA Training Manuals (NSA), 47; Sanchez, Memorandum for: C2, Combined Joint Task Force Seven, Baghdad, Iraq 09335, Subject: CJTF-7 Interrogation and Counter-Resistance Policy, September 14, 2003.

85. Taguba, Article 15–6 Investigation of the 800th Military Police Brigade, February 26, 2004, 7, 8, 15; *New York Times*, May 24, May 26, June 22, 2004, March 30, May 30, 2005; Human Rights Watch, *The Road to Abu Ghraib*, 32–33; Worden, "Brig. Gen. Janis Karpinski."

86. Taguba, Article 15–6 Investigation of the 800th Military Police Brigade, 38; Worden, "Brig. Gen. Janis Karpinski"; *New York Times*, May 19, 2004.

87. Taguba, Article 15–6 Investigation of the 800th Military Police Brigade, 16, 18; *New York Times*, May 19, 2004.

88. Taguba, Article 15–6, Investigation of the 800th Military Police Brigade, 18; Hersh, *Chain of Command*, 29–30.

89. M. Gregg Bloche and Jonathan H. Marks, "When Doctors Go to War," *New England Journal of Medicine* 352 (January 6, 2005), 4; Joint Interrogation and Debriefing Center, Abu Ghurayb, Iraq, 16, 23, http://www.publicintegrity.org/docs/Abu Ghraib/Tag29.pdf, accessed March 29, 2005.

90. Joint Interrogation and Debriefing Center, Abu Ghurayb, Iraq, 16, 23, 32–33, 40; *New York Times*, June 4, June 8, June 9, June 14, 2004.

91. Report of the International Committee of the Red Cross (ICRC) on the Treatment by the Coalition Forces of Prisoners of War and Other Protected Persons by the Geneva Conventions in Iraq during Arrest, Internment and Interrogation, February 2004, 3–4, 6, 8, 11, 12, http://www.redress.btinternet .co.uk/icrc_iraq.pdf; Craig Gordon, "25 Prisoners Have Died in US Custody," *Newsday*, May 5, 2004 http://www.newsday.com/news/printedition/stories/ny -ustorto53787580may05,0,7916261.story?coll=ny-news-print; Tom Squitieri and Dave Moniz, "3rd of Detainees Who Died Were Assaulted," *USA Today*, May 31, 2004, http://www.usatoday.com/news/world/iraq/2004-05-31-prison-abuse_x.htm, all accessed May 12, 2004.

92. Report of the International Committee of the Red Cross, February 2004, 13, 15, 17–18.

93. Tara McKelvey, "Brass Tacks," *The Nation*, December 26, 2006, 17; *New York Times*, September 24, 2005.

94. *New York Times*, March 19, 2006.

95. BG Richard P. Formica, "Article 15–6 Investigation of CJSOTF-AP and 5th SF Group Detention Operations" (June 7, 2006), 9–10, http://action.aclu.org/torture foia/released/061906/FormicaReport.pdf. accessed February 15, 2012; *New York Times*, June 17, 2006.

96. *New York Times*, September 9, 2011; Sir William Gage, *The Baha Mousa Public Inquiry Report: Volume I* (London: Stationery Office, HC 1452-I, 2011), 9–10, http://www.bahamousainquiry.org/f_report/vol%20i/volume%20i.pdf, accessed September 21, 2011.

97. Gareth Porter, "Torture Orders Were Part of U.S. Sectarian War Strategy," *Antiwar.com*, November 2, 2010, http://original.antiwar.com/porter/2010/11/01/torture-orders-were-part-of/, accessed July 28, 2011.

98. Nick Davies, "Iraq War Logs: Secret Order That Let U.S. Ignore Abuse," *The Guardian*, October 22, 2010, http://www.guardian.co.uk/world/2010/oct/22/iraq-detainee-abuse-torture-saddam, accessed July 28, 2010.

99. Richard Galpin, "Iraq Police Accused of Torture," *BBC News*, July 27, 2005, http://news.bbc.co.uk/2/hi/4718999.stm, accessed July 28, 2011.

100. Rachel Oldroyd, "The Biggest Document Leak in History Exposes Real War," *Iraqi War Logs*, Bureau of Investigative Journalism, October 1, 2010, http://www.iraqwarlogs.com/2010/10/21/the-leaked-us-files-and-what-they-mean/; Angus Stickler and Chris Woods, "U.S. Troops Ordered Not to Investigate Iraqi Torture," *Iraqi War Logs*, Bureau of Investigative Journalism, October 22, 2010, http://www.iraqwarlogs.com/2010/10/22/us-troops-ordered-not-to-investigate-iraqi-torture/, both accessed July 13, 2011.

101. Michael D. Sallah and Mitch Weiss, "Buried Secrets, Brutal Truths—Tiger Force," *Toledo Blade*, October 22–26, 2003, http://www.toledoblade.com/apps/pbcs.dll/article?AID=/20031022/SRTIGERFORCE/110190169, accessed July 28, 2011; Michael D. Sallah and Mitch Weiss, *Tiger Force: A True Story of Men and War* (New York: Little, Brown, 2006), 3–30, 62–73, 169–92, 307–22.

102. *New York Times*, May 31, 2004; Human Rights Watch, *The Road to Abu Ghraib*, 28–29; Hersh, *Chain of Command*, 44–45; Miles Moffeit, "Brutal Interrogation in Iraq," *Denver Post*, May 19, 2004, http://www.denverpost.com/search/ci_0002157003, accessed June 21, 2006; Arthur Kane and Miles Moffeit, "Carson GI Eyed in Jail Death," *Denver Post*, May 28, 2004, http://www.denverpost.com/ci_0002177070, accessed June 21, 2006; *Washington Post*, August 3, 2005.

103. *Washington Post*, August 3, 2005; Michael Isikoff and David Corn, *Hubris: The Inside Story of Spin, Scandal, and the Selling of the Iraq War* (New York: Crown, 2006), 155–56, 167, 211–12.

104. Bob Woodward, *The War Within: A Secret White House History, 2006–2008* (New York: Simon and Schuster, 2008), 380; "Secret Killing Program Is Key in Iraq, Woodward Says," *CNN.com*, September 9, 2008, http://www.cnn.com/2008/WORLD/meast/09/09/iraq.secret/index.html?iref=newssearch, accessed October 4, 2008.

105. *New York Times*, November 10, 2008, April 16, 2009.

Chapter 4. Theater State of Terror

Portions of this chapter were previously published in volume edited by Elliott V. Converse, III, *Forging the Sword: Educating and Training Cadets and Junior Officers in the Modern World* (Chicago: Imprint Publications, Volume 5, US Air Force Academy Military History Symposium Series, 1999).

1. Marcelo Suarez-Orozco, "A Grammar of Terror: Pyschocultural Responses to State Terrorism in Dirty War and Post-Dirty War Argentina," in Carolyn Nordstrom and JoAnn Martin, eds., *The Paths to Domination, Resistance, and Terror* (Berkeley: University of California Press, 1992), 230, 237.

2. *New York Times*, July 9, 1996; William Rees-Mogg, "The Torture Industry," in Rehabilitation and Research Centre for Torture Victims, *Annual Report 1995* (Copenhagen: Rehabilitation and Research Centre for Torture Victims, 1996), 5–6; Inge Genefke, "Some Steps towards a World with Less Torture," in Rehabilitation and Research Centre for Torture Victims, *Annual Report 1995*, 15–16; Rehabilitation and Research Centre for Torture Victims, *Annual Report 1995*, 21–23, 32–34; Keith Carmichael et al., "The Need for REDRESS," *Torture* 6, no. 1 (1996): 7; Erik Holst, "International Efforts on the Rehabilitation of Torture Victims," in June C. Pagaduan Lopez and Elisabeth Protacio Marcelino, eds., *Torture Survivors and Caregivers: Proceedings of the International Workshop on Therapy and Research Issues* (Quezon City: University of the Philippines Press, 1995), 8–14, 190–91; Helena Cook, "The Role of Amnesty International in the Fight against Torture," in Antonio Cassese, ed., *The International Fight against Torture* (Baden-Baden: Nomos Verlagsgesellschaft, 1991), 172–86.

3. Metin Basoglu et al., "Psychological Effects of Torture: A Comparison of Tortured with Nontortured Political Activists in Turkey," *American Journal of Psychiatry* 151, no. 1 (1994): 76–81; Finn Somnier, Peter Vesti, Marianne Kastrup, and Inge Kemp Genefke, "Psycho-Social Consequences of Torture: Current Knowledge and Evidence," in Metin Basoglu, ed., *Torture and Its Consequences: Current Treatment Approaches* (Cambridge: Cambridge University Press, 1992), 56–71; Janusz Heitzman and Krzysztof Ruthkowski, "Mental Disorders in Persecuted and Tortured Victims of the Totalitarian System in Poland," *Torture* 6, no. 1 (1996): 19–22; Dimocritos Sarantidis et al., "Long-Term Effects of Torture of Victims during the Period of Dictatorship in Greece," *Torture* 6, no. 1 (1996): 16–18; Amnesty International, *Report on Torture* (London: Duckworth, 1975), 44.

4. Amnesty International, *Torture in the Eighties* (London: Martin Robinson, 1984), 19; Carlos Madariaga, M.D., "Torture Prevention as a Public Health Problem," *Torture*

6, no. 4 (1996): 86–89; Diana Kordon, Lucila Edelman, et al., "Torture in Argentina," in Basoglu, *Torture and Its Consequences*, 433–51.

5. June C. Pagaduan Lopez, "The History of the Study of Psycho-Social Trauma (PST)," in Pagaduan Lopez and Protacio Marcelino, *Torture Survivors and Caregivers*, 82–82; Ellen Sherwood, "The Power Relationship between Captor and Captive," *Psychiatric Annals* 16, no. 11 (November 1986): 653–55.

6. Otto Doerr-Zegers, Lawrence Hartmann, Elizabeth Lira, and Eugenia Weinstein, "Torture: Psychiatric Sequeli and Phenomenology," *Psychiatry* 55, no. 2 (May 1992): 178–79; Lawrence Hartmann et al., "Psychopathology of Torture Victims," *Torture* 3, no. 2 (1993): 36–38.

7. Doerr-Zegers, "Torture," 179–83. Similarly, a group of six Argentinean psychotherapists found from treating survivors that "torture targets the individual's identity," which they defined as "a complex of representations of self . . . that produces the feeling of oneness and allows one to maintain internal coherence in time." (Kordon, "Torture in Argentina," in Basoglu, *Torture and Its Consequences*, 433–35).

8. Amnesty International, *Torture in Greece: The First Torturers' Trial 1975* (London: Amnesty International, 1977), 32; Marguerite Feitlowitz, *A Lexicon of Terror: Argentina and the Legacies of Torture* (New York: Oxford University Press, 1998), 10–11; Elaine Scarry, *The Body in Pain: The Making and Unmaking of the World* (New York: Oxford University Press, 1985), 28, 47, 53, 54, 56.

9. Christopher Simpson, *Science of Coercion: Communication Research and Psychological Warfare 1945–1960* (New York: Oxford University Press, 1994), 4–5, 72–73, 114–15; Gary Cohn, Ginger Thompson, and Mark Matthews, "Torture Was Taught by CIA," *Baltimore Sun*, January 27, 1997, http://articles.baltimoresun.com/1997 -01-27/news/1997027049_1_training-manual-torture-methods-counterintelligence -interrogation, accessed July 21, 2011; *Washington Post*, January 28, 1997; *New York Times*, January 29, 1997.

10. "Torturer in U.S. for Training," *Tanod* (Manila) 1, no. 3 (September 1978), 3; Task Force Detainees, *Pumipiglas: Political Detention and Military Atrocities in the Philippines* (Manila: Task Force Detainees of the Philippines, Association of Major Religious Superiors in the Philippines, 1980), 106–7.

11. The Philippine military apparently coined the neologism "salvaging" to describe its torture operations in the mid-1970s, and it was soon adopted by the country's human rights groups. (See Task Force Detainees, *Political Detainees of the Philippines, Book 3* [Manila: Association of Major Orders of Religious Superiors, March 1978], 41–44.) In a lead editorial on the "summary killings and disappearances" of the Marcos era, the *Philippine Daily Inquirer* (June 29, 1996) commented, "we call this 'salvaging,' demonstrating our talent to reinvent the English language."

12. Michel Foucault, *Discipline and Punish: The Birth of the Prison* (New York: Vintage, 1979), 49.

13. Frank Graziano, *Divine Violence: Spectacle, Psychosexuality, and Radical Christianity in the Argentine "Dirty War"* (Boulder: Westview Press, 1992), 203; Amnesty International, *Torture in Greece*, 28, 35–42; Scarry, *Body in Pain*, 56–57; Michael Taussig,

Shamanism, Colonialism, and the Wild Man: A Study in Terror and Healing (Chicago: University of Chicago Press, 1987), 83, 133; Feitlowitz, *Lexicon of Terror*, 3–4.

14. Ferdinand E. Marcos, *Notes on the New Society of the Philippines* (Manila: Marcos Foundation, 1973), 2–3; Amnesty International, *Report of an Amnesty International Mission to the Republic of the Philippines 11–28 November 1981* (London: Amnesty International, 1982), 56–57.

15. Republic of the Philippines, *The Final Report of the Fact-Finding Commission (pursuant to R.A. No. 6832)* (Manila: Bookmark, 1990), 43–50; Rigoberto D. Tiglao, "The Consolidation of the Dictatorship," in Aurora Javate-De Dios et al., eds., *Dictatorship and Revolution: Roots of People's Power* (Manila: Conspectus, 1988), 53.

16. Patricia Weiss Fagen, "Repression and State Security," in Juan E. Corradi, Patricia Weiss Fagen, and Manuel Antonio Garretón, eds., *Fear at the Edge: State Terror and Resistance in Latin America* (Berkeley: University of California Press, 1992), 49–55, 58–60; Neil J. Kritz, ed., *Transitional Justice: How Emerging Democracies Reckon with Former Regimes. Volume III: Laws, Rulings, and Reports* (Washington, DC: U.S. Institute for Peace, 1995), 146–47; Joan Dassin, ed., *Torture in Brazil* (New York: Vintage Books, 1986), 204–5, 235–38; *New York Times*, November 10, 1986; Kritz, *Transitional Justice. Volume II*, 431; Lawrence Weschler, *A Miracle, a Universe: Settling Accounts with Torturers* (New York: Pantheon, 1990), 53.

17. Philippines, *Final Report*, 52; Tiglao, "Consolidation of the Dictatorship," 55.

18. Philippines, *Final Report*, Appendix J.

19. Jose G. Ayap, *The 1971 Sword* (Baguio City: Cadet Corps Armed Forces of the Philippines, 1971).

20. *Baguio Midland Courier*, April 6, April 20, 1969, March 1, 1970; *Manila Times*, April 19, April 20, April 26, 1969.

21. June Pagaduan Lopez, M.D., Lan Mercado Carreon, et al., *Human Rights Violations: What Perpetuates the Perpetrator* (Quezon City: Psychosocial Trauma Program, Center for Integrative and Development Studies, University of the Philippines, 1995), 9, 17–18.

22. Ayap, *1971 Sword*; *Philippine Daily Inquirer*, October 7, 1994.

23. While Honasan's 1995 campaign literature claimed that he had won three Gold Cross medals, the register of the Armed Forces of the Philippines listed just one, for "leading his men in a fire fight against numerically superior rebels . . . [t]hough hit in the right thigh" at Lebak, Cotabato, in June 1973. (See Colonel Sinforoso L. Duque, *Soldier Heroes: A Handbook on the Winners of the Major Medals Awarded by the Philippine Constabulary and Armed Forces since 1902* [Manila: National Media Production Center, 1981], 91; "Tungkol Kay Gringo B. Honasan," *Para Sa Bansa Gringo Honasan Sa Senado* [Quezon City: Benny J. Brizuela, 1995.])

24. Viberto Selochan, "Professionalization and Politicization of the Armed Forces of the Philippines" (doctoral dissertation, Australian National University, 1990), 188; Sheila Coronel, "RAM: From Reform to Revolution," in Philippine Center for Investigative Journalism, *Kudeta: The Challenge to Philippine Democracy* (Manila: Philippine Center for Investigative Journalism, 1990), 60; *Mr. and Ms.*, February 27–March 5,

1987, 6; Fortunato U. Abat, *The Day We Nearly Lost Mindanao: The CEMCOM Story* (San Juan: FCA, 1993), 105; *PC Journal,* July 1986.

25. Philippines, *Final Report,* Appendix J, Table VI-6, 442–43.

26. Amnesty International, *Report of Amnesty International Mission to the Republic of the Philippines 22 November–5 December 1975* (London: Amnesty International, 1976), 13, 57, 72–73, 85.

27. Amnesty, *Philippines 1981,* 2, 8; *Philippine Graphic,* January 18, 1993; *New York Times,* November 10, 1986; Amnesty International, *Philippines: The Killing Goes On* (New York: Amnesty International, 1992), 14.

28. Carolina G. Hernandez, "The Extent of Civilian Control of the Military in the Philippines: 1946–1976" (doctoral dissertation, State University of New York at Buffalo, 1979), 216; Selochan, "Professionalization," 57, 68, 216.

29. Suarez-Orozco, "A Grammar of Terror," 235–36; Martin Edward Anderson, *Dossier Secreto: Argentina's Desaparecidos and the Myth of the "Dirty War"* (Boulder: Westview Press, 1993), 2, 5, 205–19; *Nunca Mas: The Report of the Argentine National Commission on the Disappeared* (New York: Farrar, Straus and Giroux, 1986), 209, 233; Feitlowitz, *Lexicon of Terror,* 8, 25, 45, 165–68, 172–74.

30. Task Force Detainees, *Pumipiglas* (1980), 44–45; Association of Major Religious Superiors in the Philippines, *Political Detainees in the Philippines Book Two* (Manila: Association of Major Religious Superiors in the Philippines, March 31, 1977), 1; Amnesty International, *Human Rights Violations in the Philippines* (New York: Amnesty International USA, 1982), 1.

31. Lawyers Committee for International Human Rights, *The Philippines: A Country in Crisis* (New York: Lawyers Committee, 1983), 32–49; Amnesty, *Philippines 1981,* 62; Ma. Serena I. Diokno, "Unity and Struggle," in De Dios, *Dictatorship and Revolution,* 146–47; Rev. La Verne D. Mercade and Sister Mariani Dimaranan, *Philippines: Testimonies on Human Rights Violations* (Manila: World Council of Churches, 1986), 89, 136; Richard J. Kessler, *Rebellion and Repression in the Philippines* (New Haven: Yale University Press, 1989), 137.

32. See note 11 above for an explanation of the term "salvaging."

33. Harold W. Maynard, "A Comparison of Military Elite Role Perceptions in Indonesia and the Philippines" (doctoral dissertation, American University, 1976), 461.

34. Gemma Nemenzo Almendral, "The Fall of the Regime," in De Dios, *Dictatorship and Revolution,* 200; Tiglao, "Consolidation of the Dictatorship," 54.

35. Amnesty, *Philippines 1981,* 21–23; *Philippine Free Press,* June 29, 1996; Task Force Detainees, *Pumipiglas* (1980), 64.

36. Amnesty, *Human Rights Violations,* 12–17.

37. Amnesty, *Philippines 1981,* 1–12, 22–23; Satur C. Ocampo, "Leaving the Pain Behind," *PST Quarterly* 1, no. 2 (July–September 1996), 13; Amnesty International, *Philippines: Unlawful Killings by Military and Paramilitary Forces* (New York: Amnesty International, 1988), 5–6.

38. Felipe Miranda, *The Politicization of the Military* (Quezon City: University of the Philippines Press, 1992), 12.

39. Maynard, "Comparison of Military Elite," 462.

40. Leoncio Co, University of the Philippines, Interdisciplinary Forum on Political Detainees, April 16, 1986.

41. Alfred W. McCoy, *Priests on Trial* (Melbourne: Penguin Books, 1984), 212–15.

42. Fr. Edgardo Kangleon, "A Moment of Uncertainty" (ms., December 8, 1982), 7, enclosed in letter To: Dear Papa/Mama/Rey, September 30, 1983 (copy furnished by Fr. Niall O'Brien, St. Columban's Mission Society, Bacolod City). Excerpts from this letter were published in Promotion of Church People's Rights, *That We May Remember* (Quezon City: PCPR, May 1989), 168–73.

43. Fr. Kangleon, "Moment of Uncertainty," 11–12.

44. Ibid., 13–16.

45. Promotion of Church People's Rights, *That We May Remember*, 172–73.

46. *Philippine Daily Inquirer*, July 23, 1993; Task Force Detainees, *Pumipiglas* (1980), 103.

47. Task Force Detainees, *Pumipiglas* (1980), 103–7.

48. Amnesty, *Report of 1975*, 21, 28.

49. Telephone interview with Luis Jalandoni, Utrecht, Netherlands, February 18, 1988; Task Force Detainees, *Pumipiglas: Political Detention and Military Atrocities in the Philippines, 1981-1982* (Manila: Task Force Detainees of the Philippines, Association of Major Religious Superiors in the Philippines, 1986), 59–64.

50. Eliseo C. Tellez, Jr., Proof of Claim Form for Torture Victims, December 8, 1992, Samahan ng mga Ex-Detainee Laban sa Detensyon at para sa Amnestia [hereafter, SELDA], Manila. Other affidavits and reports citing Lieutenant Aguinaldo's abuse of genitals were filed by Alfonso Abrazado (n.d.), Roberto Verzola y Sevilla (n.d.), Monico Atienza y Montenegro (n.d.), and Oliver G. Teves (July 13, 1993).

51. *Philippine Daily Inquirer*, July 23, 1993. Aguinaldo's victims included the journalists Satur Ocampo, Pete Lacaba, Julius Fortuna, and Oliver Teves; the University of the Philippines professors Roger Posadas and Temario Rivera; the photographer Anacleto Ocampo; the artist Nestor Buyayong; and the activists Allan Jazmines and Nilo Tayag.

52. Dr. Temario C. Rivera, "Details of Torture Inflicted on Temario C. Rivera" (ms., courtesy of the author, August 1996).

53. Association of Major Religious Superiors in the Philippines, *Political Detainees in the Philippines, Book Two* (Manila: Association of Major Religious Superiors in the Philippines, March 31, 1977), 8.

54. Association of Major Religious Superiors in the Philippines, *Political Detainees in the Philippines, Book Two*, 15.

55. Interview with Satur Ocampo, Quezon City, August 27, 1996; Ocampo, "Leaving the Pain Behind," 13.

56. Task Force Detainees, *Pumipiglas* (1980), 106–7.

57. Coronel, "RAM," 65. An early report about Batac stated: "Other officers of the 5th CSU who have been implicated in torture accounts of political detainees and

against whom no public investigation has been made: Capt. (now Major) Cecilio Penilla, Capt. Virgilio Saldajeno, Lt. Rodolfo Aguinaldo, Lt. Victor Batac, Lt. Robert Delfin, Lt. Cesar Alvarez." (See Task Force Detainees, *Political Detainees of the Philippines, Book 3*.) Other details of Batac's treatment of prisoners are found in interviews with Jose Ma. Sison, Alan Jazmines, and "Gene," University of the Philippines, Interdisciplinary Forum on Political Detainees, April 16, 1986.

58. Danilo P. Vizmanos, Proof of Claim Form for Torture Victims, *In Re. Estate of Ferdinand E. Marcos Human Rights Litigation*, MDL No. 840—Class Action (May 5, 1993); *Honolulu Star-Bulletin*, September 11, 1992; *Bulletin Today*, August 15, 1976.

59. Association of Major Religious Superiors in the Philippines, *Political Detainees in the Philippines, Book Two*, 8–9; *Daily Cardinal* (Madison, WI), October 16, 1986.

60. *Daily Cardinal*, October 17, 1986; *Capital Times* (Madison, WI), October 17, 1986.

61. Interview with Maria Elena Ang, Sydney, Australia, May 9, 1989.

62. *The Australian* (Sydney), April 26–27, 1986.

63. Interview with Randall Echanis, University of the Philippines, Interdisciplinary Forum on Political Detainees, n.d.

64. For references to Lieutenants Bibit, Batac, and Aguinaldo working together as torturers, see Domingo Luneta (November 22, 1992), Marcelio M. Talam Jr. (November 4, 1992), Ma. Paz Castronuevo Talam (November 3, 1992), Eliseo C. Tellez Jr. (December 8, 1992), Oliver G. Teves (July 13, 1993), Proof of Claim Form for Torture Victims, SELDA, Manila; and Monica Atienza y Montenegro (date of arrest: October 4, 1974; Present Confinement: 5th Constabulary Security Unit, Camp Crame), SELDA. For references to Rolando Abadilla and his two MISG comrades, Robert Ortega and Panfilo Lacson, see, Romeo I. Chan (March 11, 1993), Damaso de la Cruz (October 27, 1992), Proof of Claim Form for Torture Victims, SELDA, Manila.

65. *Malaya*, August 29, 1987.

66. Coronel, "RAM," *Kudeta*, 60; interview with Sheila Coronel, Manila, January 5, 1988; Neni Sta. Romana-Cruz, "Reformists Night Out: In Uniform but into Fun," *Mr. & Ms.*, March 21–27, 1986, 19–20; Jo-Ann Q. Maglipon, *Primed: Selected Stories 1972–1992* (Manila: Anvil, 1993), 228.

67. *Mr. & Ms.*, March 21–27, 1986; interview with Navy Captain Rex Robles, Manila, July 25, 1986; interviews with RAM leaders, Manila, July 1986.

68. Interview with Robles.

69. Philippines, *Final Report*, 125.

70. De Dios, *Dictatorship and Revolution*, 742.

71. Philippines, *Final Report*, 127; De Dios, *Dictatorship and Revolution*, 742; interview with General Artemio Tadiar, Fort Bonifacio, August 31, 1986; interview with Colonel Eduardo "Red" Kapunan, Manila, July 6, 1986.

72. Interview with General Tadiar, Fort Bonifacio; Angela Stuart Santiago, *Duet for EDSA: 1986 Chronology of a Revolution* (Manila: Foundation for Worldwide People Power, 1995), 13–14; Arturo C. Aruiza, *Ferdinand E. Marcos: Malacañang to Makiki* (Quezon City: ACAruiza Enterprises, 1991), 40.

73. Interview with Lieutenant Colonel Marcelino "Jake" Malajacan, Manila, August 29, 1986; interview with Colonel Gregorio "Gringo" Honasan, July 24, 1986; interview with Jaime Cardinal Sin, Manila, July 21, 1986; Antonio B. Lambino, S.J., "Theological Reflection on the Filipino Exodus," in Pedro S. de Achutegui, S.J., ed., *The "Miracle" of the Philippine Revolution: Interdisciplinary Reflections* (Manila: Loyola School of Theology, Ateneo de Manila University, 1986), 14–15; Lewis M. Simons, *Worth Dying For* (New York: William Morrow, 1987), 272.

74. Interview with Jaime Cardinal Sin, July 21, 1986.

75. General Prospero Olivas, "Narration of Activities of CG PCM/DIR, MPF, 22–28 Feb 86."

76. Brigadier General Isidoro de Guzman, Subject: Command Actions during the Crisis, To: Chief of Staff, NAFP [New Armed Forces of the Philippines], February 28, 1986.

77. Interview with General Tadiar, Fort Bonifacio.

78. Interview Tadiar; Aguirre, *People's Revolution*, 36; *Mr. & Ms.*, March 21–27, 1986; Santiago, *Duet for EDSA: Chronology*, 72–78.

79. Interview with Colonel Braulio Balbas, Fort Bonifacio, Manila, July 25, 1986; interview with General Tadiar, Fort Bonifacio. Colonel Braulio B. Balbas Jr., Subject: Participation Report, To: Chief of Staff, NAFP, March 1, 1986, 3–6.

80. Simons, *Worth Dying For*, 298.

81. Philippines, *Final Report*, 98; Criselda Yabes, *The Boys from the Barracks: The Philippine Military after EDSA* (Manila: Anvil, 1991), 140.

82. Philippines, *Final Report*, 261–64, 291, 292–93.

83. Philippines, *Final Report*, 261–64, 303–8; *Philippine Daily Inquirer*, December 17, 1989; Criselda Yabes, "Seven Days in December," *Kudeta*, 94.

84. Philippines, *Final Report*, 229–31, 495–96.

85. *Manila Chronicle*, December 4, December 10, 1989; *Philippine Daily Inquirer*, December 4, December 12, 1989; Philippines, *Final Report*, 228, 319–20.

86. Philippines, *Final Report*, 276–84.

87. June Pagaduan Lopez, M.D., "Mainstreaming Is Prevention," *PST Quarterly* 1, no. 1 (April–June 1996): 2.

88. Rehabilitation and Research Centre for Torture Victims, "Impunity," *Annual Report 1995* (Copenhagen: Rehabilitation and Research Centre for Torture Victims, 1996), 6.

89. Elisabeth Marcelino, "The Philippine Experience: Rehabilitation of Survivors of Torture and Political Violence under a Continuing Stress Situation," *Torture* 2, no. 1 (1992): 19–21.

90. Leslie London, M.D., "Conference Review. The VII International Symposium. 'Caring for Survivors of Torture: Challenges for the Medical and Health Professions,'" *Torture* 6, no. 3 (1996): 69.

91. Lucila Edelman and Diana Kordon, "Incidence of Social Belonging, Personal Identity, and Historical Memory in Different Approaches to Psychological Therapy," *Torture* 6, no. 1 (1996): 4–5.

92. Dr. Diana R. Kordon and Dr. Lucila I. Edelman, "Psychological Effects of Political Repression-II," in Diana R. Kordon, Lucila I. Edelman, et al., eds., *Psychological Effects of Political Repression* (Buenos Aires: Sudamericana/Planeta, 1988), 174; Dr. Diana R. Kordon and Dr. Lucila I. Edelman, "Violation of Human Rights: Text or Context in Couple and Family Analysis," in Kordon, Edelman, et al., *Psychological Effects of Political Repression*, 92.

93. Maria Serena I. Diokno, "Peace and Human Rights: The Past Lives On," in Lorna Kalaw-Tirol, ed., *Duet for EDSA: 1996 Looking Back, Looking Forward* (Manila: Foundation for Worldwide People Power, Inc., 1995), 92.

94. Republic of the Philippines, Office of the President, Executive Order No. 19, Fidel V. Ramos, September 1, 1992.

95. *Daily Globe*, September 10, 1992.

96. *Philippine Daily Inquirer*, December 29, 1992.

97. *Philippine Star*, December 24, 1992.

98. Republic of the Philippines, National Unification Commission, Press Statement, December 23, 1992; *Daily Globe*, December 27, 1992.

99. *Manila Bulletin*, February 7, 1993; Republic of the Philippines, National Unification Commission, "Principles for Characterization of Offenses for Confidence-Building and Amnesty," March 11, 1993; *Malaya*, May 10, 1993; *Philippine Star*, July 16, 1993; *Philippine Daily Inquirer*, May 28, July 2, 1993, October 5, 1996.

100. *Manila Bulletin*, August 19, 1993.

101. *Manila Bulletin*, September 22, September 24, 1994; *Malaya*, September 24, 1994.

102. *Philippine Daily Inquirer*, May 11, 1995.

103. *Philippine Daily Inquirer*, January 4, February 22, 1995.

104. *Manila Chronicle*, March 13, March 15, 1995; *Malaya,* March 14, 1995.

105. *Manila Chronicle*, March 14, 1995.

106. *Philippine Daily Inquirer*, May 16, 1995.

107. *Philippine Daily Inquirer*, May 25, October 14, 1995.

108. Joker Arroyo, "Military Justice Is No Justice at All," *Philippine Daily Inquirer*, June 20, 1996; *Philippine Graphic*, July 1, 1996; *Philippine Free Press*, June 29, 1996.

109. *Philippine Graphic*, July 1, 1996; *Philippine Free Press*, June 29, 1996.

110. "Curriculum Vitae of P/Supt Panfilo M. Lacson," File: Panfilo Lacson, Library, *Philippine Daily Inquirer* (Makati); Satur C. Ocampo, "The Boys from MISG," Philippine News and Features, June 22, 1996; *Philippine Graphic*, July 1, 1996; *Philippine Daily Inquirer*, May 28, November 16, 1999; *Manila Times*, November 20, 1999.

Chapter 5. The Seduction of Psychological Torture

1. "Abuse at Abu Ghraib," *CBS News, 60 Minutes*, http://www.cbsnews.com /stories/2004/05/05/60II/main615781.shtml?tag=currentVideoInfo;videoMetaInfo, accessed February 21, 2010.

2. Susan Sontag, "Regarding the Torture of Others," *New York Times Magazine,* May 23, 2004, 25–29, 42.

3. "New Abu Ghraib Abuse Photos Broadcast in Australia," Associated Press, February 15, 2006, *The Independent,* http://www.independent.co.uk/news/world/middle -east/new-abu-ghraib-abuse-photos-broadcast-in-australia-466680.html, accessed February 3, 2010.

4. SA David A. England, Computer Crime Coordinator, 10th MP Bn (CID), 3d MP Group (CID), Baghdad, Iraq, "Agent's Investigation Report," January 2004. A spreadsheet on this same CD labeled "CG CD5.xls" lists 1,640 images. In mid-2004, the *Washington Post* apparently obtained a copy of a similar CD but published very few of these photos. (See Sherry Ricchiardi, "Missed Signals," *American Journalism Review* [August–September 2004], http://www.ajr.org/Article.asp?id=3716, accessed February 21, 2010.) After this CD arrived at my University of Wisconsin–Madison office from Sydney in February 2006, *Salon.com* received similar material, which it summarized by quoting a report by Special Agent James E. Seigmund: "A review of all the computer media submitted to this office revealed a total of 1,325 images of suspected detainee abuse, 93 video files of suspected detainee abuse, 660 images of adult pornography, 546 images of suspected dead Iraqi detainees, 29 images of soldiers in simulated sexual acts, 20 images of a soldier with a Swastika drawn between his eyes, 37 images of Military Working dogs being used in abuse of detainees and 125 images of questionable acts." Of these thousand plus photos, *Salon.com* released just eighteen on its website. (See Mark Benjamin, "Salon Exclusive: The Abu Ghraib Files," *Salon.com,* February 16, 2006, http://www.salon.com/news/feature/2006/02/16/abu_ ghraib/, accessed February 22, 2010.)

5. Sontag, "Regarding the Torture of Others," 25–29, 42.

6. Michael Walzer, "Political Action: The Problem of Dirty Hands," *Philosophy and Public Affairs* 2, no. 2 (1973): 167; Alfred W. McCoy, "The Myth of the Ticking Time Bomb," *The Progressive* (October 2006), 20–24.

7. Sontag, "Regarding the Torture of Others," 25–29, 42.

8. Gideon Bachman, "Pasolini and the Marquis de Sade," *Sight and Sound* 45, no. 1 (Winter 1976), in *Salò or the 120 Days of Sodom* (Criterion Collection, DVD, No. 17d, 2008), 69–71.

9. John Langbein, *Torture and the Law of Proof: Europe and England in the Ancien Regime* (Chicago: University of Chicago Press, 1977), 7; Edward Peters, *Torture* (Philadelphia: University of Pennsylvania Press, 1996), 40–62.

10. Peters, *Torture,* 62–67; Malise Ruthven, *Torture: The Grand Conspiracy* (London: Weidenfeld and Nicolson, 1979), 57–59.

11. Mitchell B. Merback, *The Thief, the Cross and the Wheel: Pain and the Spectacle of Punishment in Medieval and Renaissance Europe* (Chicago: University of Chicago Press, 1999), 69–70, 129–57, 199–217; James Carroll, "The Bush Crusade," *The Nation,* September 20, 2004, 17.

12. Alec Mellor, *La Torture: Son histoire, son abolition, sa réapparition au XXe siecle*

(Paris: Horizons Litterraires, 1949), 105–15; Merback, *The Thief, the Cross and the Wheel*, 158–70.

13. Stephen F. Eisenman, *The Abu Ghraib Effect* (London: Reaktion Books, 2007), 60–69.

14. Ibid., 73.

15. Langbein, *Torture and the Law of Proof*, 10–12, 60–69; Ruthven, *Torture*, 12–15; John H. Langbein, "The Legal History of Torture," in Sanford Levinson, ed., *Torture: A Collection* (New York: Oxford University Press, 2004), 93–100; Peter Gay, *Voltaire's Politics: The Poet as Realist* (New York: Vintage, 1965), 275; Marcello Maestro, *Voltaire and Beccaria as Reformers of Criminal Law* (New York: Columbia University Press, 1942), 86–88.

16. Eisenman, *The Abu Ghraib Effect*, 88.

17. Richard A. Clarke, *Against All Enemies: Inside America's War on Terror* (New York: Free Press, 2004), 24.

18. *Meet the Press, NBC News*, September 16, 2001, http://stacks.msnbc.com /news/629714.asp, accessed June 21, 2011; Jane Mayer, *The Dark Side* (New York: Anchor Books, 2009), 9–10.

19. U.S. Congress, 107th Congress, 2d session, Cofer Black, Testimony to Senate Select Committee on Intelligence, Joint Inquiry into Intelligence Community Activities before and after the Terrorist Attacks of September 11, 2001, September 26, 2002, http://www.fas.org/irp/congress/2002_hr/092602black.html, accessed May 22, 2011.

20. U.S. Senate, Committee on Armed Services, 110th Congress, 2d Session, *Inquiry into the Treatment of Detainees in U.S. Custody* (Washington, DC: Government Printing Office, 2008), xv, xx–xxi, 16–17, http://www.democrats.com/senate-armed -services-committee-report-on-torture, accessed July, 21, 2009.

21. Jan Crawford Greenburg, Howard L. Rosenberg, and Ariane de Vogue, "Sources: Top Bush Advisors Approved 'Enhanced Interrogation,'" *ABC News*, April 9, 2008, http://abcnews.go.com/thelaw/lawpolitics/Story?id=4583256&page=4, accessed December 24, 2008; *Washington Post*, February 25, 2005.

22. U.S. Senate, *Inquiry into the Treatment of Detainees in U.S. Custody*, xix; William J. Haynes II, General Counsel, Department of Defense, For: Secretary of Defense, "Subject: Counter-Resistance Techniques," November 27, 2002, http://www .washingtonpost.com/wp-srv/nation/documents/dodmemos.pdf, accessed June 28, 2004.

23. M. Gregg Bloche and Jonathan H. Marks, "Doctors and Interrogators at Guantanamo Bay," *New England Journal of Medicine* 353, no. 1 (July 7, 2005): 7; Jonathan H. Marks, "The Silence of the Doctors," *The Nation*, December 7, 2005, http://www .thenation.com/doc/20051226/marks, accessed July 19, 2009.

24. Seymour M. Hersh, *Chain of Command: The Road from 9/11 to Abu Ghraib* (New York: HarperCollins, 2004), 38–39.

25. *New York Times*, July 13, July 14, July 15, 2005; U.S. Department of Defense, "Army Regulation 15–6: Final Report: Investigation into FBI Allegation of Detainee Abuse at Guantanamo Bay, Cuba Detention Facility" (April 1, 2005, amended

June 9, 2005), 12, 14–21, http://www.defenselink.mil/news/Jul2005/d20050714report.pdf, accessed July 18, 2005; Senate Armed Services Committee, *Hearing on Guantanamo Bay Detainee Treatment* (July 13, 2005), 13–17, http://humanrights.ucdavis.edu/projects/the-guantanamo-testimonials-project/testimonies/testimonies-of-the-defense-department/senate-armed-services-committee-hearing-on-guantanamo-bay-detainee-treatment, accessed October 4, 2011; Human Rights Watch, *The Road to Abu Ghraib* (Human Rights Watch, June 2004), 13, http://www.hrw.org/en/reports/2004/06/08/road-abu-ghraib, accessed July, 21, 2009; Peter James Spielmann, "Abuse of Iraqi Prisoners 'Was Sport,'" *Chicago Sun-Times*, January 28, 2005, http://www.docstoc.com/docs/26771935/Abuse-of-Iraqi-prisoners-was-sport, accessed, May 22, 2011; *Washington Post*, February 10, 2005.

26. Ricardo S. Sanchez, "Memorandum for: C2, Combined Joint Task Force Seven, Baghdad, Iraq 09335, Subject: CJTF-7 Interrogation and Counter-Resistance Policy," September 14, 2003; Ricardo S. Sanchez, "Memorandum for: C2, Combined Joint Task Force Seven, Baghdad, Iraq 09335, Subject: CJTF-7 Interrogation and Counter-Resistance Policy," October 12, 2003, http://www.aclu.org/SafeandFree/SafeandFree.cfm?ID=17851&c=206, accessed March 30, 2005.

27. Jonathan Alter, "Time to Think about Torture," *Newsweek*, November 5, 2001, 45.

28. Steve Randall, "Pro-Pain Pundits," *Extra!* (January–February 2002), http://fair.org/extra/0201/pro-pain.html, accessed December 22, 2002.

29. Alan M. Dershowitz, "Is There a Torturous Road to Justice?" *Los Angeles Times*, November 8, 2001, http://articles.latimes.com/2001/nov/08/local/me-1494, accessed June 17, 2011.

30. *CBS News, 60 Minutes* (co-host, Mike Wallace; executive producer, Don Hewitt), January 20, 2002; *Los Angeles Times*, November 8, 2001; Alan M. Dershowitz, *Why Terrorism Works: Understanding the Threat, Responding to the Challenge* (New Haven: Yale University Press, 2002), 136–39.

31. "Harvard Law Professors Urge Congress to Review Interrogation Policy and Hold Executive Branch Accountable," http://www.iraq-letter.com, posted June 14, 2004.

32. Joseph Lelyveld, "Interrogating Ourselves," *New York Times Magazine*, June 12, 2005, 43, http://www.nytimes.com/2005/06/12/magazine/12TORTURE.html?pagewanted=all, accessed June 17, 2011.

33. Walzer, "Political Action: The Problem of Dirty Hands,'" 160–80.

34. Alan Dershowitz, "Tortured Reasoning," in Sanford Levinson, ed., *Torture: A Collection* (New York: Oxford University Press, 2004), 259.

35. Ibid., 266–67, 274, 276–77.

36. Lelyveld, "Interrogating Ourselves."

37. *CBS News, 60 Minutes* (co-host, Mike Wallace; executive producer, Don Hewitt), January 20, 2002; *Los Angeles Times*, November 8, 2001; Dershowitz, *Why Terrorism Works*, 136–39.

38. Marites Dañguilan Vitug and Glenda M. Gloria, *Under the Crescent Moon: Rebellion in Mindanao* (Quezon City: Ateneo Center for Social Policy and Public Af-

fairs, 2000), 222–24, 229–30, 232; Matthew Brzezinski, "Bust and Boom," *Washington Post Magazine*, December 30, 2001, 9, http://www.prisonplanet.com/bust_and_boom .html, accessed June 17, 2011.

39. *The 9/11 Commission Report: Final Report of the National Commission on Terrorist Attacks upon the United States* (New York: W. W. Norton, 2004), 273–76.

40. Office of the President of the United States, *The Commission on the Intelligence Capabilities of the United States Regarding Weapons of Mass Destruction* (Washington, DC, March 31, 2005), 5–6.

41. *New York Times*, April 21, April 23, April 27, 2005; Aldert Vrij, *Detecting Lies and Deceit: The Psychology of Lying and the Implications for Professional Practice* (New York: John Wiley and Sons, 2000), 74–76, 96–97, 159–60; Gisli H. Gudjonsson, *The Psychology of Interrogations, Confessions, and Testimony* (New York: John Wiley and Sons, 1996), 183–85; Roberta Wohlstetter, *Pearl Harbor: Warning and Decision* (Stanford: Stanford University Press, 1962), 387.

42. Eyal Press, "In Torture We Trust?" *The Nation*, March 31, 2003, 11–15; Richard H. Weisberg, "Loose Professionalism, or Why Lawyers Take the Lead on Torture," in Levinson, *Torture: A Collection*, 304.

43. Charles C. Krulak and Joseph P. Hoar, "It's Our Cage, Too: Torture Betrays Us and Breeds New Enemies," *Washington Post*, May 17, 2007, http://www.washington post.com/wp-dyn/content/article/2007/05/16/AR2007051602395.html, accessed November 21, 2011.

44. *New York Times*, March 18, 2005; Office of the President of the United States, *The Commission on the Intelligence Capabilities of the United States Regarding Weapons of Mass Destruction*, 15–16.

45. Jason Vest, "Pray and Tell," *The American Prospect* 16, no. 7 (July 2005): 50.

46. *Los Angeles Times*, February 13, 2007, http://articles.latimes.com/2007/feb/13 /entertainment/et-torture13, accessed February 15, 2010; Jesse Holcomb, "Tortured Logic: Do Shows Like *24* Help Make Torture Acceptable?" *Sojourners Magazine* 36, no. 6 (June 1, 2007), http://www.sojo.net/index.cfm?action=magazine.article&issue =sojo706&article=07064b, accessed February 15, 2010.

47. Associated Press, "'NYPD Blue' Signs off after 12 Seasons," MSNBC.com, March 2, 2005, http://msnbc.msn.com/id/7052431/print/1/displaymode/1098/, accessed June 13, 2005; *The Star-Ledger* (Newark, NJ), February 27, 2005, http://www .stwing.upenn.edu/~sepingwal/farewell11.html, accessed June 13, 2005; *Clarkson Integrator* (Potsdam, NY), February 28, 2005, http://www.clarksonintergratror.com /global_user_elements/printpage.cfm?storyid=878822, accessed June 13, 2005; *USA Today*, February 28, 2005, http://www.usatoday.com/life/television/reviews/2005-02 -28-nypd-blue_x.htm, accessed June 21, 2005.

48. *New York Times*, May 25, 2010; Neal Justin, "Clock Is Ticking on '24' but Impact Remains," *Wisconsin State Journal*, May 24, 2010; *Los Angeles Times*, February 13, 2007, http://articles.latimes.com/2007/feb/13/entertainment/et-torture13, accessed February 15, 2010.

49. Dahlia Lithwick, "The Fiction behind Torture Policy," *Newsweek*, July 26, 2008, http://www.newsweek.com/2008/07/25/the-fiction-behind-torture-policy.html, accessed June 21, 2011.

50. *24*, 5X06—12:00 PM–01:00 PM. Original airdate (FOX) January 30, 2006, written by David Fury, directed by Jon Cassar. Transcript provided by KAT for TWIZ TV.COM, http://www.twiztv.com/scripts/24/season5/24-506.htm, accessed February 19, 2010.

51. Wiki *24*, Season 6, http://24.wikia.com/wiki/Season_6; Wiki *24*, Season Six, Day 6: 9:00 am–10:00 am, http://24.wikia.com/wiki/Day_6:_9:00am-10:00am, both accessed December 11. 2011.

52. Justin, "Clock Is Ticking on '24' but Impact Remains."

53. "*24*" (TV Series) *Wikipedia*, http://en.wikipedia.org/wiki/24_(TV_series), accessed September 4, 2009; Colin Freeze, "What Would Jack Bauer Do?" *Globe and Mail* (Toronto), June 16, 2007, http://license.icopyright.net/user/viewFreeUse .act?fuid=NzI2NDYxOA%3D%3D, accessed February 26, 2010.

54. Philippe Sands, *Torture Team: Rumsfeld's Memo and the Betrayal of American Values* (New York: Macmillan, 2009), 62.

55. Tom Reagan, "Does '24' Encourage U.S. Interrogators to 'Torture' Detainees?" *Christian Science Monitor*, February 12, 2007.

56. Mark L. Sample, "Virtual Torture: Video Games and the War on Terror," *Game Studies* 8, no. 2 (December 2008), http://74.125.95.132/search?q=cache:MsjUcyujRsEJ: gamestudies.org/0802/articles/sample+video+games+%22torture%22&hl=en&gl=us& strip=1, accessed March 1, 2010.

57. Clive Thompson, "Why We Need More Torture in Videogames," *Wired* (December 15, 2008), http://www.wired.com/gaming/virtualworlds/commentary /games/2008/12/gamesfrontiers_1215, accessed March 1, 2010; Daniel Terdiman, "'WoW: Wrath of Lich King' Sets Sales Record, *cnet news*, http://news.cnet.com/8301 -13772_3-10103951-52.html, accessed March 1, 2010.

58. Winda Benedetti, "Should You Take 'Torture' Seriously?" MSNBC, http://www .msnbc.msn.com/id/25337373/ns/technology_and_science-games/, accessed March 1, 2010.

59. AJ Glasser, "Torture in Video Games," *Kotaku*, September 10, 2009, http:// kotaku.com/5353873/torture-in-video-games?utm_source=feedburner&utm_ medium=feed&utm_campaign=Feed%3A+kotaku%2Ffull+%28Kotaku%29, accessed March 2, 2010.

60. "Rendition (Film)," *Wikipedia*, http://en.wikipedia.org/wiki/Rendition_(film), accessed March 2, 2010.

61. "Hostel (Film)," *Wikipedia*, http://en.wikipedia.org/wiki/Hostel_(film), accessed September 4, 2009.

62. Eisenman, *The Abu Ghraib Effect*, 92–93.

63. "Casino Royale (2006 Film)," *Wikipedia*, http://en.wikipedia.org/wiki/Casino _Royale_(2006_film), accessed September 4, 2009; Chuck Kleinhans, "Imagining Torture," *Jump Cut: A Review of Contemporary Media* 51 (Spring 2009), http://www

.ejumpcut.org/currentissue/, accessed September 4, 2009; Eisenman, *The Abu Ghraib Effect*, 31–32.

64. "The Passion of the Christ," directed by Mel Gibson, Newmarket Films (2004); *The Passion of the Christ*, Part 6 of 12 (Full Movie), http://www.youtube.com/watch ?v=gMnKpB6trUs&feature=related, accessed February 20, 2010; *The New Oxford Annotated Bible* (New York: Oxford University Press, 1994), 43, 154.

65. Wikipedia, "The Passion of the Christ," http://en.wikipedia.org/wiki/The_Passion_of_the_Christ, accessed February 20, 2010. For figures on the film's early earnings see Peter A. Maresco, "Mel Gibson's *The Passion of the Christ*: Market Segmentation, Mass Marketing and Promotion, and the Internet," *Journal of Religion and Popular Culture* 8 (Fall 2004), http://www.usask.ca/relst/jrpc/art8-melgibsonmarketing.html, accessed February 20, 2010; *Killer Movies*, http://www.killermovies.com/p/passion/, accessed March 29, 2005.

66. Michael Ignatieff, "Mirage in the Desert," *New York Times Magazine*, June 27, 2004, 14.

67. *Washington Post*, May 13, 2009.

68. *NewsHour with Jim Lehrer*, PBS, May 4, 2004, http://www.pbs.org/newshour/bb/military/jan-june 04/abuse1_05_04.html, accessed June 14, 2004; *New York Times*, May 11, May 15, May 25, 2004; "President Outlines Steps to Help Iraq Achieve Democracy and Freedom," May 24, 2004, http://www.whitehouse.gov/news/release/2004/05/print/20040424-10.html, accessed June 14, 2004; *Washington Post*, May 13, June 22, 2004; *New York Times*, May 8, May 12, 2004.

69. *New York Times*, September 7 and 8, 2006; The White House, Office of the Press Secretary, "President Discusses Creation of Military Commissions to Try Suspected Terrorists," September 6, 2006, http://www.whitehouse.gov/news/releases/2006/09/print/20060906-3.html, accessed September 8, 2006.

70. John Yoo, *War by Other Means: An Insider's Account of the War on Terror* (New York: Atlantic Monthly Press, 2006), 172.

71. Ibid., 74.

72. Rosa Brooks, "The GOP Torture Enthusiasts," *Los Angeles Times*, May 18, 2007, http://www.latimes.com/news/opinion/commentary/la-oe-brooks18may18,0,732795.column, accessed September 9, 2011.

73. "Former President Bill Clinton Discusses Vision for U.S. Torture Policy and the Importance of Engagement in Iran," *Morning Edition*, National Public Radio, September 20, 2006, http://www.npr.org/about/press/060920.clinton.html, accessed May 9, 2011.

74. *Meet the Press* transcript for September 30, 2007, NBC, http://www.msnbc.msn.com/id/21065954/ns/meet_the_press/t/meet-press-transcript-sept/#.T15d46urV4I, accessed August 31, 2011.

75. Ibid.

76. "Torture Like Jack Bauer's Would Be OK, Bill Clinton Says," *Daily News* (New York), October 1, 2007.

77. CNN Live Event/Special, Democratic Candidates Compassion Forum,

April 13, 2008, Transcript, http://transcripts.cnn.com/TRANSCRIPTS/0804/13/se.01 .html, accessed May 29, 2011.

78. Keep America Safe, *100 Hours*, January 8, 2010, http://www.youtube.com /watch?v=am6f5EdHUpU, accessed May 23, 2011.

79. *New York Times*, January 15, 2010; Statement by Liz Cheney in Response to President Obama's National Security Remarks, Keep America Safe, January 6, 2010, http://www.facebook.com/note.php?note_id=243193612065, accessed January 23, 2010.

80. *New York Times*, February 20, 2010.

81. U.S. Senate, Select Intelligence Committee Holds Confirmation Hearing on the Nomination of General David H. Petraeus to be CIA Director, June 23, 2011, *CQ Congressional Transcripts* (copy provided by office of Senator Dianne Feinstein, November 21, 2011); "Petraeus Tells Senators He Wanted CIA Job," *CNN Politics*, June 23, 2011, http://articles.cnn.com/2011-06-23/politics/petraeus.cia_1_petraeus-cia-job-senate -intelligence-committee?_s=PM:POLITICS, accessed November 20, 2011.

82. U.S. Senate, Select Committee on Intelligence, Nomination of General David Petraeus to Be Director of the Central Intelligence Agency, Questions for the Record, n.d., http://intelligence.senate.gov/110623/responses.pdf, accessed November 21, 2011.

83. Eli Lake, "Panetta Backs Rendition, but Not Torture," *Washington Times*, February 9, 2009, http://www.washingtontimes.com/news/2009/feb/06/panetta -supports-rendition-but-not-torture/, accessed July 12, 2011; *Washington Post*, June 30, 2011.

84. "CBS News/NJ Debate Transcript, Part 1," November 13, 2011, http://www .cbsnews.com/8301-505103_162-57323734/cbs-news-nj-debate-transcript-part-1/?page Num=9&tag=contentMain;contentBody, accessed November 16, 2011.

85. Ibid.

86. News Conference by President Obama, J.W. Marriott Ihilani Resort and Spa, Kapolei, Hawaii, The White House, November 13, 2011, http://www.whitehouse.gov /photos-and-video/video/2011/11/13/president-obama-holds-press-conference-apec -summit#transcript, accessed November 20, 2011.

87. *New York Times*, November 15, 2011.

88. David Cole, "Gitmo Forever? Congress's Dangerous New Bill," *New York Review of Books*, December 8, 2011, http://www.nybooks.com/blogs/nyrblog/2011/dec/08 /gitmo-forever-dangerous-new-bill/; ACLU, "Senators Demand the Military Lock Up of American Citizens in a 'Battlefield' They Define as Being Right Outside Your Window," http://www.aclu.org/blog/national-security/senators-demand-military -lock-american-citizens-battlefield-they-define-being, both accessed December 11, 2011.

89. National Defense Authorization Act for Fiscal Year 2012 (Senate, November 30, 2011), 40–45, http://www.lawfareblog.com/wp-content/uploads/2011/12/Senate-NDAA -Debate-Nov-30-2011.pdf, accessed December 11, 2011.

90. National Defense Authorization Act, NDAA Senate Debate: Detainee Provisions, December 1, 2011, 50–51, http://www.lawfareblog.com/wp-content/uploads /2011/12/Senate-NDAA-Debate-Dec-1-2011.pdf, accessed December 11, 2011.

91. Library of Congress, Thomas, Bill Summary & Status, 112th Congress (2011–

2012) S.AMDT.1068, http://thomas.loc.gov/cgi-bin/bdquery/z?d112:sp1068; National Religious Campaign against Torture, "Urgent: Call Your Senators Today on Torture Amendment," November 29, 2011, http://www.maryknollogc.org/peace/torture _amendment.html; Human Rights First, "Retired Military Leaders Decry Torture Provisions in Defense Authorization Act," November 28, 2011, http://www.human rightsfirst.org/2011/11/28/retired-military-leaders-decry-torture-provisions-in-defense -authorization-act/, all accessed December 11, 2011.

92. Cole, "Gitmo Forever?"; ACLU, "Senators Demand the Military Lock Up of American Citizens in a 'Battlefield' They Define as Being Right Outside Your Window."

93. *New York Times*, December 8, December 15, December 16, 2011, February 29, 2012; "Obama Supports Defense Bill after Changes to Detainee Provisions," *ABC News*, December 14, 2011, http://abcnews.go.com/blogs/politics/2011/12/obama-supports -defense-bill-after-changes-to-detainee-provisions/, accessed December 15, 2011.

94. David Luban, "Liberalism, Torture, and the Ticking Bomb," *Virginia Law Review* 91, no. 6 (October 2005): 1425–61; A. T. H. Smith, "Disavowing Torture in the House of Lords," *Cambridge Law Journal* 65, no. 2 (July 2006): 251–54; Thomas A. Bass, "Counterinsurgency and Torture," *American Quarterly* 60, no. 2 (June 2008): 233–40; Winfried Brugger, "May Government Ever Use Torture? Two Responses from German Law," *American Journal of Comparative Law* 48, no. 4 (Autumn 2000): 661– 78; Kenneth Roth, "Review Essay: Getting Away with Torture," *Global Governance* 11, No. 3 (July–September 2005): 389–406.

95. *New York Times*, May 1, 2009.

96. Ibid.; *Washington Post*, June 1, 2011; Hap Ernstein, "Durang's 'Torture' Loses Sting to Silliness," *Palm Beach Arts Paper*, November 28, 2009, http://www.palm beachartspaper.com/Theater/Durangs-Torture-loses-satiric-sting-to-silliness.html; T. D. Mobley-Martinez, "Durang's 'Torture' Takes a Poke at Post-9/11 Paranoia," *The Gazette* (Colorado Springs), June 2, 2011, http://www.gazette.com/articles/durang -10830-colsprings-star-bar.html; Toby Zinman, "Durang's 'Torture,' at Advanced Age of 2," *The Inquirer* (Philadelphia), December 13, 2011, http://articles.philly.com/2011 -12-13/news/30512024_1_felicity-hildegarde-opening-night, all accessed January 18, 2012.

97. Sontag, "Regarding the Torture of Others," 25–29, 42.

Chapter 6. The Outcast of Camp Echo

Portions of this chapter were previously published in an essay titled "The Outcast of Camp Echo: The Punishment of David Hicks," *The Monthly* (Melbourne, June 2006).

1. Leigh Sales, *Detainee 002: The Case of David Hicks* (Melbourne: Melbourne University Press, 2007), 12–21.

2. Gerry J. Gilmore, "Rumsfeld Visits, Thanks U.S. Troops at Camp X-Ray in Cuba," *Armed Forces Press Services*, January 27, 2002, http://www.defense.gov/news /newsarticle.aspx?id=43817, accessed June 20, 2011; *New York Times*, January 4, 2002.

3. Debbie Whitmont, "The Case of David Hicks: Transcript," *Four Corners, Australian Broadcasting Corporation*, October 31, 2005, http://www.abc.net.au/4corners/content/2005/s1494795.htm, accessed June 13, 2011.

4. Grant Holloway, "Pressure Grows over Australian al Qaeda," *CNN World*, January 16, 2002, http://articles.cnn.com/2002-01-16/world/australia.hicks_1_australian-al-qaeda-australian-government-attorney-general-daryl-williams/2?_s=PM:asiapcf, accessed June 20, 2011; David Hicks, *Guantanamo: My Journey* (Sydney: William Heinemann, 2010), 304.

5. Shafiq Rasul et al., Petition for Writ of Habeas Corpus, U.S. District Court for the District of Columbia, February 19, 2002, Counsel for the Petitioners, Joseph Margulies et al., http://www.haguejusticeportal.net/Docs/NLP/US/Rasul_DC_District_Court_Habeas_Corpus_19-2-2002.pdf, accessed June 13, 2011.

6. Michael Ratner and Ellen Ray, *Guantanamo: What the World Should Know* (White River Junction: Chelsea Green, 2004), 8; Michael Ratner, University of California–Davis, "Conversation About Guantanamo," May 5, 2006.

7. Lex Lasry, QC, "United States v. David Matthew Hicks: Report of the Independent Legal Observer for the Law Council of Australia," July 2005, http://www.lawcouncil.asn.au/shadomx/apps/fms/fmsdownload.cfm?file_uuid=CE02C8B1-1E4F-17FA-D223-7DF89CC63161&siteName=lca, accessed June 13, 2011.

8. *New York Times*, February 13, 2005.

9. *Washington Post*, December 17, 2004; Mamdouh Habib, *My Story: The Tale of a Terrorist Who Wasn't* (Melbourne: Scribe, 2008), 178.

10. Ratner and Ray, *Guantanamo*, 7–9.

11. Hicks, *Guantanamo*, 342.

12. Richard Norton-Taylor, "Guantánamo Is Gulag of Our Time, Says Amnesty," *The Guardian*, May 26, 2005, http://www.guardian.co.uk/world/2005/may/26/usa.guantanamo, accessed June 13, 2011.

13. Dick Marty, *Alleged Secret Detentions and Unlawful Inter-State Transfers Involving Council of Europe Member States* (Parliamentary Assembly, Council of Europe, Report 10957, June 12, 2006), 9–23, 47–52, http://assembly.coe.int/main.asp?link=/documents/workingdocs/doc06/edoc10957.htm, accessed September 27, 2006; *New York Times*, May 1, 2005; Amnesty International, *Below the Radar: Secret Flight to Torture and "Disappearance"* (AMR 51/051/2006, April 5, 2006), 22–28, http://www.amnesty.org/en/library/info/AMR51/051/2006, accessed June 13, 2011.

14. Sales, *Detainee 002*, 36–37, 42–43.

15. U.S. Department of Justice, Office of Legal Counsel, Memorandum for William J. Haynes II, General Counsel, Department of Defense, December 28, 2001, From: Patrick F. Philbin, Deputy Assistant Attorney General, and John C. Yoo, Deputy Assistant Attorney General, in Karen J. Greenberg and Joshua L. Dratel, eds., *The Torture Papers: The Road to Abu Ghraib* (New York: Cambridge University Press, 2005), 29, 37.

16. Telephone interview with Joshua Dratel, Madison, WI, to New York, NY, May 17, 2006.

17. Major Michael Mori, "Why David Hicks Will Not Receive a Fair Trial Come His Day in Court," Melbourne University Law School, Annual Alumni Lecture, April 6, 2006, http://www.law.unimelb.edu.au/go/alumni, accessed May 12, 2006.

18. *New York Times*, January 12, 2002.

19. Mark Denbeaux, "Report on Guantánamo Detainees: A Profile of 517 Detainees through Analysis of Department of Defense Data," *Seton Hall Law School* (February 8, 2006), 1, 23m, http://law.shu.edu/publications/guantanamoReports /guantanamo_report_final_2_08_06.pdf, accessed December 9, 2011; Corine Hegland, "Who Is at Guantánamo Bay," *National Journal*, February 3, 2006, http://www .informationclearinghouse.info/article11825.htm, accessed February 21, 2006.

20. Suzanne Goldenberg, "Former Guantánamo Chief Clashed with Army Interrogators," *The Guardian*, May 19, 2004, http://www.guardian.co.uk/world/2004 /may/19/iraq.guantanamo, accessed June 13, 2011.

21. *Washington Post*, October 16, December 26, 2002; *New York Times*, November 23, 2002, March 9, 2003, June 21, June 22, June 23, 2004, January 1, May 30, 2005; M. Gregg Bloche and Jonathan H. Marks, "Doctors and Interrogators at Guantanamo Bay," *New England Journal of Medicine* 353, no. 1 (July 7, 2005): 7; John Barry, et al., "The Roots of Torture," *Newsweek*, May 24, 2004, 31–33; Bryan Bender and Charlie Savage, "Memos Detail Debate on Prisoners: Rumsfeld Reversed OK of Severe Interrogations," *Boston Globe*, June 23, 2004; Charlie Savage and Bryan Bender, "Pentagon, Lawyers Clashed," *Boston Globe*, June 24, 2004, https://secure.pqarchiver.com/boston /advancedsearch.html, accessed May 12, 2006; Goldenberg, "Former Guantánamo Chief Clashed with Army Interrogators"; William J. Haynes II, General Counsel, Department of Defense, For: Secretary of Defense, Subject: Counter-Resistance Techniques, November 27, 2002, http://www.washingtonpost.com/wp-srv/nation /documents/dodmemos.pdf, accessed June 28, 2004; U.S. Department of Defense, Special Defense Department Briefing, July 7, 2005, http://www.defenselink.mil /transcripts/2005/tr20050707–3301.html, accessed July 11, 2005.

22. U.S. Senate, Committee on Armed Services, 110th Congress, 2d Session, *Inquiry into the Treatment of Detainees in U.S. Custody* (Washington, DC: Government Printing Office, 2008), xviii–xix, xxviii.

23. *New York Times*, June 21, 2005; Adam Zagorin and Michael Duffy, "Inside the Interrogation of Detainee 063," *Time*, June 20, 2005, 26–33.

24. *New York Times*, September 17, 2006; The Federalist Society for Law and Public Policy Studies, "About Us," http://www.fed-soc.org/aboutus/, accessed August 4, 2011.

25. *Washington Post*, December 26, 2002; *New York Times*, November 23, 2002, March 9, 2003, June 21, June, 22, June 23, 2004, January 1, 2005; Michael Hirsh, "A Tortured Debate," *Newsweek*, June 21, 2004, 50; Savage and Bender, "Pentagon, Lawyers Clashed"; Jane Mayer, "The Experiment," *The New Yorker* (July 11–18, 2005), 70.

26. *Washington Post*, December 26, 2002; *New York Times*, November 23, 2002, March 9, 2003, June, 22, June 23, 2004, January 1, July 28, July 30, 2005; Barry, "The Roots of Torture"; Hirsh, "A Tortured Debate," 50; Savage and Bender, "Pentagon, Lawyers Clashed"; Mayer, "The Experiment," 70–71.

27. Major General Jack L. Rives, Memorandum for SAF/GC, February 6, 2003, U.S. Senate, 109th Congress, 1st Session, *Congressional Record*, vol. 151, no. 102 (July 25, 2005), S8794–95; Major General Jack L. Rives, Memorandum for SAF/GC, February 5, 2003, U.S. Senate, *Congressional Record* (July 25, 2005), S8796–97.

28. *Washington Post*, December 26, 2002; *New York Times*, November 23, 2002, March 9, 2003, June, 22, June 23, 2004, January 1, July 28, July 30, 2005; Barry, "The Roots of Torture," 32–33; Hirsh, "A Tortured Debate," 50; Savage and Bender, "Pentagon, Lawyers Clashed"; Mayer, "The Experiment," 70–71; Department of Defense, "Working Group Report on Detainee Interrogations in the Global War on Terrorism: Assessment of Legal, Historical, Policy, and Operational Considerations," March 6, 2003, www.torturingdemocracy.org/documents/20030404.pdf, accessed August 4, 2011; Donald Rumsfeld, Memorandum for the Commander, U.S. Southern Command, April 16, 2003, http://www.washingtonpost.com/wp-srv/nation/documents/041603rumsfeld.pdf, accessed June 28, 2004.

29. *New York Times*, June 8, 2004; Seymour M. Hersh, "The Gray Zone: How a Secret Pentagon Program Came to Abu Ghraib," *The New Yorker*, May 24, 2004, 42; Scott Horton, "Betr: Strafanzeige gegen den US-Verteidigungsminister Donald Rumsfeld, u.a.," An den: Herrn Generalbundesanwalt, Beim Bundesgerichtshof, Karlsruhe, January 29, 2005, para. 4, http://www.rav.de/StAR_290105_Horton.htm, accessed April 14, 2005.

30. Special Immigration Appeals Commission, CO/60/2006, between David Hicks, Appellant, and The Secretary of State for the Home Department, Respondent. First Statement of David Hicks, http://humanrights.ucdavis.edu/projects/the-guantanamo-testimonials-project/testimonies/prisoner-testimonies/first-statement-of-david-hicks, accessed June 13, 2011; Tom Allard, "Prisoner of Political Fortune Set Free," *Sydney Morning Herald*, December 28, 2007, http://www.smh.com.au/news/national/prisoner-of-political-fortune-set-free/2007/12/28/1198778703367.html, accessed June 13, 2011; Hicks, *Guantanamo*, 198–212.

31. Sales, *Detainee 002*, 152–53; Special Immigration Appeals Commission, CO/60/2006, First Statement of David Hicks.

32. Center for Constitutional Rights, "Detention in Afghanistan and Guantanamo Bay: Statement of Shafiq Rasul, Asif Iqbal and Rhuhel Ahmed," July 26, 2004, http://ccrjustice.org/v2/legal/september_11th/docs/Guantanamo_composite_statement_FINAL.pdf, accessed June 13, 2011; "Govt Position Used against Hicks: Ex-Detainees," *ABC News*, February 15, 2006, http://www.abc.net.au/news/newsitems/200602/s1570502.htm, accessed June 13, 2011.

33. Special Immigration Appeals Commission, CO/60/2006, First Statement of David Hicks.

34. Hicks, *Guantanamo*, 224–25, 227–28, 277–84.

35. Plea Agreement, *United States v. John Lindh*, U.S. District Court for the Eastern District of Virginia, Alexandria Division, http://www.justice.gov/ag/pleaagreement.htm, accessed June 13, 2011; Jim Garamone, "Lindh Plea Bargains, to Cooperate with

U.S. Officials," American Forces Press Service, July 15, 2002, http://www.defense.gov/news/newsarticle.aspx?id=43660, accessed June 13, 2011.

36. Telephone interview with Major Michael Dante Mori, Madison, WI, to Washington, DC, May 12, 2006; Sales, *Detainee 002*, 96–97, 109, 154, 250; Hicks, *Guantanamo*, 1–2, Illustration "Camp Echo Cell," 232–33; Habib, *My Story*, 178.

37. Special Immigration Appeals Commission, CO/60/2006, First Statement of David Hicks; interview with James Yee, University of California–Davis campus, May 5, 2006.

38. Human Rights First, "David Hicks' Father Speaks; Day Three," August 25, 2004, http://www.humanrightsfirst.org/2004/08/25/david-hicks'-father-speaks/, accessed June 13, 2011; Hicks, *Guantanamo*, 2, 309.

39. Hicks, *Guantanamo*, 289–91, 307, 333–34.

40. Interview with Dratel; Hicks, *Guantanamo*, 342–45.

41. Telephone interview with Michael Ratner, Madison, WI, to New York, NY, May 17, 2006.

42. Michael Winterbottom, *The Road to Guantanamo* (Revolution Films, 2006); Center for Constitutional Rights, "Detention in Afghanistan and Guantanamo Bay: Statement of Shafiq Rasul, Asif Iqbal and Rhuhel Ahmed," http://ccrjustice.org/v2/legal/september_11th/docs/Guantanamo_composite_statement_FINAL.pdf, accessed June 13, 2011.

43. Peter Walker and James Sturcke, "Q&A: Guantanamo Bay," *The Guardian*, December 8, 2008, http://www.guardian.co.uk/world/2007/jan/10/guantanamo.alqaida, accessed June 13, 2011.

44. Letter from T. J. Harrington, Deputy Assistant Director, Counterterrorism Division, Federal Bureau of Investigation, to Major General Donald J. Ryder, Criminal Investigation Command, Department of the Army, July 14, 2004, http://www.aclu.org/torturefoia/released/FBI_4622–2624.pdf, accessed March 8, 2005; *New York Times*, December 21, 2004.

45. *New York Times*, November 30, 2004.

46. U.S. District Court for the District of Columbia, *Shafiq Rasul v. George Walker Bush*, No. CV: 02-0299 (CKK), First Amended Petition for Writ of Habeas Corpus, February 2002, http://guantanamobile.org/pdf/2002motiontodismiss.pdf, accessed June 13, 2011; interview with Ratner, May 17, 2006.

47. Lex Lasry, QC, "United States v. David Matthew Hicks: First Report of the Independent Legal Observer for the Law Council of Australia—September 2004," http://www.lawcouncil.asn.au/shadomx/apps/fms/fmsdownload.cfm?file_uuid=CDFC66F7-1E4F-17FA-D23C-3E002478C5D6&siteName=lca, accessed June 13, 2011; Sales, *Detainee 002*, 187.

48. Deborah Pearlstein, "Military Commission Trial Observation, Day 5: August 27, 2004," Human Rights First, http://www.humanrightsfirst.org/us_law/detainees/military_commission_diary.htm#day1, accessed May 16, 2006.

49. Interview with Dratel, May 17, 2006.

50. Ibid.

51. Sales, *Detainee 002*, 115.

52. "Sacked Lawyer Vows to Fight for Hicks's Freedom," *ABC News* (Australia), February 9, 2005, http://www.abc.net.au/news/newsitems/200502/s1298950.htm, accessed June 13, 2011; Curtis Levy and Bentley Dean, *The President versus David Hicks* (Ronin Films, 2004); Sales, *Detainee 002*, 194–95.

53. U.S. Supreme Court, *Rasul v. Bush*, No. 03-334, June 28, 2004, http://caselaw .lp.findlaw.com/scripts/printer_friendly.pl?page=us/000/03-334.html, accessed December 10, 2011.

54. Lasry, "United States v. David Matthew Hicks: Report of the Independent Legal Observer for the Law Council of Australia" (July 2005).

55. Human Rights First, "David Hicks' Father Speaks; Day Three."

56. *New York Times*, August 26, 2004; Human Rights First, "David Hicks' Father Speaks; Day Three."

57. Sales, *Detainee 002*, 82, 258–60.

58. Deborah Pearlstein, "Military Commission Trial Observation: Good People, Flawed System," August 24, 2004, Human Rights First, http://www.humanrightsfirst .org/our-work/law-and-security/military-commissions/gitmo-diary/, accessed May 16, 2006.

59. Human Rights First, "Military Commission Trial Observation: Setting the Stage for Justice," November 1–2, 2004, http://www.humanrightsfirst.org/our-work /law-and-security/military-commissions/gitmo-diary/, accessed May 18, 2006.

60. Lasry, "United States v. David Matthew Hicks: Report of the Independent Legal Observer for the Law Council of Australia" (July 2005).

61. Human Rights First, "Military Commission Trial Observation: Setting the Stage for Justice," November 1–2, 2004; "Military Commission Trial Observation: Transient Life at Guantanamo," November 2, 2004, http://www.humanrightsfirst .org/our-work/law-and-security/military-commissions/gitmo-diary/, accessed May 18, 2006.

62. Human Rights First, "Military Commission Trial Observation: Enter the Federal Court," November 8, 2004, http://www.humanrightsfirst.org/our-work/law-and -security/military-commissions/gitmo-diary/, accessed May 18, 2006.

63. Jonathan Mahler, "The Bush Administration vs. Salim Hamdan," *New York Times Magazine*, January 8, 2006, 44–51; *New York Times*, November 8, November 16, 2005; U.S. Supreme Court, *Rasul v. Bush*, No. 03-334, June 28, 2004, http://caselaw .lp.findlaw.com/scripts/printer_friendly.pl?page=us/000/03–334.html, accessed July 16, 2006.

64. *Washington Post*, February 1, 2005.

65. *In Re Guantanamo Detainee Cases, 355 F.Supp.2d 443 (2005)*, Memorandum Opinion Denying in Part and Granting in Part Respondents' Motion to Dismiss or for Judgment as of Law, Joyce Hens Green, District Judge, U.S. District Court, District of Columbia, January 31, 2005, http://www.leagle.com/xmlResult.aspx?xmldoc=2005 798355FSupp2d443_1752.xml&docbase=CSLWAR2-1986-2006, accessed June 15, 2011.

66. *Washington Post*, January 6, January 29, 2005.

67. *New York Times*, May 30, July 15, July 16, 2005.

68. *New York Times*, May 27, 2005.

69. *New York Times*, June 16, June 18, 2005; Panel II of a Hearing of the Senate Judiciary Committee, Subject: Detainees, Chaired by: Senator Arlen Specter (R-PA), June 15, 2005, http://www.access.gpo.gov/congress/senate/pdf/109hrg/24332.pdf, accessed June 21, 2005.

70. Interview with Leigh Sales, former Washington correspondent, *Australian Broadcasting Corporation*, Sydney, August 15, 2006; Sales, *Detainee 002*, 165.

71. *New York Times*, August 1, 2005; Sales, *Detainee 002*, 160–64.

72. Dan Ephron, "Gitmo Grievances," *Newsweek*, May 17, 2008, http://www.newsweek.com/2008/05/17/gitmo-grievances.html, accessed June 14, 2011.

73. Prime Minister Howard Doorstop Interview, the Willard Intercontinental Hotel, Washington, DC, Interview Transcript, July 16, 2005, Subject: Washington Visit, David Hicks, ASIO Head, Indonesian Ambassador, Embassy of the United States, Canberra, http://usrsaustralia.state.gov/us-oz/2005/07/16/pm1.html, accessed June 14, 2011.

74. Robert Verkaik, "Guantanamo Treatment Is 'Monstrous,' Says Law Lord," *The Independent* (London), November 26, 2003, http://www.independent.co.uk/news/uk/crime/guantanamo-treatment-is-monstrous-says-law-lord-736984.html, accessed June 14, 2011.

75. "Guantanamo Detainee to Get British Citizenship," *The Times* (London), December 13, 2005, http://www.timesonline.co.uk/tol/news/uk/article762250.ece, accessed June 14, 2011; Sales, *Detainee 002*, 223–24; Hicks, *Guantanamo*, 359.

76. *New York Times*, January 4, 2006; "Guantanamo Detainee to Get British Citizenship," *The Times*.

77. *New York Times*, January 10, January 13, January 15, 2006; U.S. Supreme Court, *Salim Ahmed Hamdan v. Donald H. Rumsfeld*, No. 05-184, Respondents' Motion to Dismiss for Lack of Jurisdiction, January 2006, http://www.usdoj.gov/osg/briefs/2005/3mer/2mer/2005-0184.resp.pdf, accessed January 24, 2005; U.S. Supreme Court, *Salim Ahmed Hamdan v. Donald H. Rumsfeld*, No. 05-184, Oral Argument, March 28, 2006, 42, 49–49, http://www.supremecourtus.gov/oral_arguments/arugment_transcripts/05–184pdf, accessed July 7, 2006.

78. United Nations, Economic and Social Council, Commission on Human Rights, "Situation of Detainees at Guantánamo Bay" (E/CN.4/2006/120, February 15, 2006), 21–26, http://news.bbc.co.uk/1/shared/bsp/hi/pdfs/16_02_06_UN_Guantánamo.pdfs, accessed February 20, 2006; *New York Times*, February 17, 2006; United Nations, "Secretary-General Kofi Annan's Remarks at Press Encounter Following Monthly Luncheon with Security Council Members," February 16, 2006, http://www.un.org/apps/sg/printoffthecuff.asp?.nid=834, accessed February 21, 2006.

79. Speech, Council on Foreign Relations, as Delivered by Secretary of Defense Donald H. Rumsfeld, Harold Pratt House, New York, New York, Friday, February 17, 2006, http://www.defenselink.mil/speeches/2006/sp20060217-12574.html, accessed May 20, 2005.

80. *New York Times*, May 11, 2006.

81. European Parliament, Joint Motion for a Resolution . . . on Guantánamo (RC/602712EN.doc, February 15, 2006); U.S. Department of State, "Second Periodic Report of the United States of America to the Committee against Torture," May 6, 2006, 46–49, http://www.state.gov/g/drl/rls/45738.htm, accessed February 21, 2006; Amnesty International, "Memorandum to the U.S. Government on the Report of the UN Committee against Torture and the Question of Closing Guantánamo" (AMR 51/093/2006, June 23, 2006), 2, http://www.amnesty.org/en/library/info /AMR51/093/2006/en, accessed June 14, 2011; *New York Times*, May 6, May 9, May 20, June 4, 2006.

82. U.S. Supreme Court, *Salim Ahmed Hamdan v. Donald H. Rumsfeld*, No. 05-184, Opinion of Stevens, J., June 29, 2006, 6, 69–73; *New York Times*, March 27, June 30, 2006.

83. Harold Hongju Koh, Dean Yale Law School, Statement before the Senate Committee on the Judiciary regarding *Hamdan v. Rumsfeld*: Establishing a Constitutional Process, July 11, 2006, http://www.law.yale.edu/documents/pdf/Deans_Office /KOH__Hamdan_TESTIMONY.pdf, accessed June 15, 2011.

84. Interview with Mori, May 12, 2006; Hicks, *Guantanamo*, 354–58, 370–71.

85. Habib, *My Story*, 154.

86. The Honorable Alexander Downer, MP, and the Honorable Philip Ruddock, MP, "Government Finalises Transfer of Prisoner Arrangement with United States," Joint Media Release, May 9, 2006, http://www.foreignminister.gov.au/releases/2006 /joint_ruddock_prisoner_tranf_100506.html, accessed June 14, 2011.

87. Interview with Dratel, May 17, 2006.

88. Edmund Tadros, "Mori Wins Praise of Lawyer Fans," *Sydney Morning Herald*, August 16, 2006, http://www.smh.com.au/news/national/mori-wins-praise-of-lawyer -fans/2006/08/15/1155407814396.html, accessed June 14, 2011.

89. A. Fraser, "Don't Be Fooled Again by U.S.: Hicks Lawyer," *Canberra Times*, August 18, 2006; A. Fraser, "Leading the Charge to Bring Hicks Home," *Canberra Times*, August 19, 2006.

90. A. Mather, "Long Fight for Hicks Justice Comes to Town," *The Mercury*, August 19, 2006.

91. "Thousands Back Return of Hicks," *The Advertiser*, August 24, 2006.

92. "Executive Director of GetUp, Brett Solomon Gives a Speech to 2000 People Who Turned up in Adelaide, South Australia," August 23, 2006, www.youtube.com /watch?v=fzPryNc4tOw, accessed January 14, 2011.

93. "Bring David Hicks Home," http://www.getup.org.au/campaigns/bring-david -hicks-home, accessed June 14, 2011.

94. Sales, *Detainee 002*, 9, 212.

95. Richard Baker, "Plea from Churches for Hicks," *The Age*, October 10, 2006, http://www.theage.com.au/news/national/plea-from-churches-for-hicks/2006 /10/09/1160246071521.html, accessed June 16, 2011.

96. "Ruddock Dismisses Criticism of Govt Gandling of Hicks," *ABC News*,

July 3, 2006, http://www.abc.net.au/news/newsitems/200607/s1676921.htm, accessed June 20, 2011.

97. Law Council of Australia, "Bring Home David Hicks: It's a 'No-Brainer,'" Media Release, November 1, 2006, https://www.lawcouncil.asn.au/media/news-article .cfm?article=B55FE54D-1E4F-17FA-D274-BE9CFF8D9BC6, accessed June 15, 2011.

98. David Harrison, "Attorneys-General Call for Hicks Action," *Lateline, Australian Broadcasting Corporation*, November 10, 2006, http://www.abc.net.au/lateline /content/2006/s1786157.htm, access June 15, 2011.

99. Philip Ruddock, "The Insiders," *Australian Broadcasting Corporation*, October 1, 2006, http://parlinfo.aph.gov.au/parlInfo/search/display/display.w3p;query= (Id:media/tvprog/5f116);rec=0, accessed June 15, 2011.

100. Transcript of the Prime Minister the Honorable John Howard MP Interview with David Bevan, ABC Radio, Adelaide, October 5, 2006, http://parlinfo.aph.gov.au /parlInfo/search/display/display.w3p;query=(Id:media/radioprm/2k216);rec=0, accessed June 15, 2011.

101. "Guantanamo Prosecutions," *The Diane Rehm Show*, Radio WAMU 88.5, July 22, 2008, http://thedianerehmshow.org/shows/2008-07-22/guantanamo-prosecutions, accessed June 2, 2011; Sales, *Detainee 002*, 216; Hicks, *Guantanamo*, 367.

102. *Washington Post*, June 25, 2007, http://blog.washingtonpost.com/cheney /chapters/pushing_the_envelope_on_presi/, accessed June 2, 2011; Scott Horton, "The Great Guantánamo Puppet Theater," *Harper's*, February 2008, http://www.harpers.org /archive/2008/02/hbc-90002460, accessed June 14, 2011; Sales, *Detainee 002*, 224–25.

103. Sales, *Detainee 002*, 214–15, 218, 271–76.

104. *Washington Post*, April 1, 2007.

105. "Exit Poll Predicts Labor Win," *Australian Broadcasting Corporation*, November 24, 2007, http://www.abc.net.au/news/stories/2007/11/24/2100160.htm?site= elections/federal/2007, accessed June 15, 2011.

106. "Bring David Hicks Home," http://www.getup.org.au/campaigns/bring -david-hicks-home, accessed June 14, 2011.

107. Jano Gibson, "1.8m x 2.4m: Living like Hicks," *Sydney Morning Herald*, March 19, 2007, http://www.smh.com.au/news/national/18m-x-18m-living-like-hicks /2007/03/19/1174152949136.html, accessed June 15, 2011.

108. Australia Electoral Commission, Virtual Tally Room, NSW Division, Bennelong, Two Candidate Preferred Preference Flow, 12/11/2007, http://results.aec.gov .au/13745/website/HouseDivisionTcpFlow-13745–105.htm, accessed June 15, 2011.

109. Chris Johnston, "For the First Time, David Hicks Tells," *Sydney Morning Herald*, October 16, 2010, http://www.smh.com.au/entertainment/books/for-the -first-time-david-hicks-tells-20101015–16nkl.html; "Hicks' Plane Touches Down in Adelaide," *ABC News*, May 20, 2007, http://www.abc.net.au/news/newsitems/200705 /s1927776.htm, accessed June 15, 2011; Hicks, *Guantanamo*, 391–92.

110. Jane Holroyd, "David Hicks Freed from Jail," *Sydney Morning Herald*, December 29, 2007, http://www.smh.com.au/news/national/i-wont-let-you-down/2007 /12/29/1198778741695.html, accessed June 15, 2011.

111. "David Hicks Marries in Sydney," *Sydney Morning Herald*, August 3, 2009, http://www.smh.com.au/national/david-hicks-marries-in-sydney-20090802-e5y1 .html, accessed November 14, 2011; "Patrick Soars of Native Landscapes Gives David Hicks a Fair Go," *Manly Daily*, July 19, 2010, http://manly-daily.whereilive.com.au /news/story/patrick-soars-of-native-landscapes-gives-david-hicks-a-fair-go/, accessed June 15, 2011.

112. Jodie Minus, "Assange Could Share My Fate, Says Hicks," *The Australian*, May 23, 2011, http://www.theaustralian.com.au/in-depth/wikileaks/assange-could -share-my-fate-says-hicks/story-fn775xjq-1226060683664, accessed June 15, 2011; Johnston, "For the First Time, David Hicks Tells"; Hicks, *Guantanamo*, 405–8.

113. Amnesty International, *USA: Trials in Error* (July 16, 2009), fn. 46, http://www .amnesty.org/en/library/info/AMR51/083/2009, accessed June 30, 2011; *New York Times*, July 8, 2010, May 5, 2012; *BBC News*, "Guantanamo Inmate to Be Released," July 30, 2009, http://news.bbc.co.uk/2/hi/americas/8175644.stm, accessed June 30, 2011.

114. Gina Cavallaro, "Lawyer: Defending Detainee Slowed Promotion," *Marine Corps Times*, September 18, 2010, http://www.marinecorpstimes.com/news/2010/09 /marine-promotion-denied-for-defending-terrorism-suspect-091810w/; *Washington Post*, October 8, 2006.

Chapter 7. Psychological Torture and Public Forgetting

1. *New York Times*, August 6, August 7, August 9, August 12, August 14, August 15, August 16, August 17, August 20, August 29, September 26, September 27, September 28, September 30, October 1, November 8, 1969, April 4, 1971; James Olsfen, ed., *Dictionary of the Vietnam War* (New York: Peter Bedrick Books, 1987), 389–90.

2. *New York Times*, February 18, 1970.

3. *New York Times*, July 20, August 2, 1971; Victor Marchetti and John D. Marks, *The CIA and the Cult of Intelligence* (New York: Alfred A. Knopf, 1974), 246.

4. Mark Moyar, *Phoenix and the Birds of Prey: The CIA's Secret Campaign to Destroy the Viet Cong* (Annapolis: Naval Institute Press, 1997), 89–99; U.S. Senate, 93d Congress, 1st Session, Committee on Armed Services, Hearings on July 2, 20, 25, 1973, *Nomination of William E. Colby to be Head of Central Intelligence* (Washington, DC: Government Printing Office, 1973), 116–17.

5. "The Tiger Cages of Con Son," *Life*, July 17, 1970; Don Luce, "The Tiger Cages of Viet Nam," *Historians against the War*, http://www.historiansagainstwar.org/resources /torture/luce.html, accessed July 12, 2011; "Viet Nam: The Cages of Con Son Island," *Time*, July 20, 1970, http://www.time.com/time/magazine/article/0,9171,877079,00 .html, accessed July 12, 2011.

6. John Ranelagh, *The Agency: The Rise and Decline of the CIA* (New York: Simon and Schuster, 1986), 571–77, 585, 589.

7. Ibid., 571–76, 584–99.

8. Alexander Cockburn and Jeffrey St. Clair, *Whiteout: The CIA, Drugs and the Press* (New York: Verso, 1998), 210–11.

9. *New York Times*, June 11, 1979.

10. *New York Times*, August 2, 1977.

11. Frank Snepp, *Decent Interval: The American Debacle in Vietnam and the Fall of Saigon* (London: Allen Lane, 1980), 42–49; Merle L. Pribbenow, "The Man in the Snow White Cell: The Limits of Interrogation," Central Intelligence Agency, https://www.cia.gov/library/center-for-the-study-of-intelligence/csi-publications/csi-studies/studies/vol48no1/article06.html, accessed September 14, 2011.

12. *New York Times*, November 18, November 19, November 20, November 23, December 4, December 20, 1977.

13. Pribbenow, "The Man in the Snow White Cell."

14. *New York Times*, August 1, August 11, 1970.

15. *New York Times*, August 16, 1970; A. J. Langguth, *Hidden Terrors* (New York: Pantheon, 1978), 252–54, 285–88.

16. *New York Times*, August 5, 1978; Manuel Hevia Cosculluela, *Pasaporte 11333: Ocho Años con la CIA* (Havana: Editorial de Ciencias Sociales, 1978), 121–24, 279–87.

17. U.S. Senate, 92d Congress, 1st Session, Committee on Foreign Relations, Subcommittee on Western Hemisphere Affairs, *United States Policies and Programs in Brazil* (Washington, DC: Government Printing Office, 1971), 17–20, 39–40.

18. Langguth, *Hidden Terrors*, 299–301.

19. Ibid., 301; U.S. Senate, 93d Congress, 2d Session, Committee on Foreign Relations, *Foreign Assistance Act of 1974: Report of the Committee on Foreign Relations United States Senate on S. 3394 to Amend the Foreign Assistance Act of 1961, and For Other Purposes* (Washington, DC: Government Printing Office, 1974), 42.

20. Thomas David Lobe, "U.S. Police Assistance for the Third World" (Ph.D. dissertation, University of Michigan, 1975), 415, 421.

21. *New York Times*, October 20, 1984, January 29, 1997.

22. Central Intelligence Agency, Inspector General, "Special Review: Counterterrorism Detention and Interrogation Activities (September 2001–October 2003)" (May 7, 2004), 10, http://www.aclu.org/torturefoia/released/052708/052708_Special_Review.pdf, accessed October 5, 2011; James LeMoyne, "Testifying to Torture," *New York Times Magazine,* June 5, 1988, 47, 62.

23. LeMoyne, "Testifying to Torture," 45–47, 62–65.

24. U.S. Senate, Select Committee on Intelligence, "Transcript of Proceedings before the Select Committee on Intelligence: Honduran Interrogation Manual Hearing," June 16, 1988, Box 1, CIA Training Manuals, Folder: Interrogation Manual Hearing, National Security Archive [hereafter, NSA], 3–5.

25. Ibid., 14.

26. Ibid., 5, 15, 21–22.

27. Ibid., 24, 30; *New York Times*, October 20, 1984, January 29, 1997.

28. U.S. Senate, "Transcript of Proceedings before the Select Committee on Intelligence," 25–27.

29. Ibid., 28–29.

30. Ibid., 33–35.

31. Congressional Fact Sheet, 8 June 1988, Introduction to Central Intelligence Agency, *Human Resources Exploitation Training Manual—1983*, Box 1, CIA Training Manuals, NSA.

32. *New York Times*, July 9, 1996; Ole Vedel Rasmussen, "Medical Aspects of Torture," *Danish Medical Bulletin* 37, no. 1 (1990): 3, 30–31; William Rees-Mogg, "The Torture Industry," in Rehabilitation and Research Centre for Torture Victims, *Annual Report 1995* (Copenhagen: Rehabilitation and Research Centre for Torture Victims, 1996), 5–6; Inge Genefke, "Some Steps towards a World with Less Torture," in Rehabilitation and Research Centre, *Annual Report 1995*, 15–16; Rehabilitation and Research Centre, *Annual Report 1995*, 21–23, 32–34; Keith Carmichael et al., "The Need for REDRESS: Why Seek a Remedy? Reparations as Rehabilitation," *Torture* 6, no. 1 (1996): 7; Helena Cook, "The Role of Amnesty International in the Fight against Torture," in Antonio Cassese, ed., *The International Fight against Torture* (Baden Baden: Nomos Verlagsgesellschaft, 1991), 172–86.

33. Erik Holst, "International Efforts on the Rehabilitation of Torture Victims," in June C. Pagaduan Lopez and Elizabeth Protacio Marcelino, eds., *Torture Survivors and Caregivers: Proceedings of the International Workshop on Therapy and Research Issues* (Quezon City: University of the Philippines Press, 1995), 8–14, 190–91, 291–316, 356–57; United Nations, *Convention against Torture and Other Cruel, Inhuman or Degrading Treatment or Punishment*, http://www.hrweb.org/legal/cat.html, accessed September 20, 2011.

34. U.S. Senate, 100th Congress, 2d Session, Treaty Doc. 100-20, *Message from the President of the United States Transmitting the Convention against Torture and Other Cruel, Inhuman or Degrading Treatment or Punishment* (Washington, DC: Government Printing Office, 1988), iii–iv; Ahcene Boulesbaa, *The U.N. Convention on Torture and the Prospects for Enforcement* (The Hague: Martinus Nijhoff, 1999), 19.

35. The act can be found under U.S.C Title 28, Pt. IV, Ch. 85, § 1350. U.S. Senate, 102d Congress, 1st Session, Report 102-249, Committee on the Judiciary, *The Torture Victims Protection Act* (U.S. Senate, Calendar No. 382, November 26, 1991), 6–7; United States, *Congressional Record: Proceedings and Debates of the 102d Congress, First Session,. Volume 137—Part 23* (Washington, DC: Government Printing Office, 1991), November 25, 1991, 34785; United States, *Congressional Record: Proceedings and Debates of the 102d Congress, Second Session, Volume 138—Part 3* (Washington, DC: Government Printing Office, 1992), March 3, 1992, 4176–78.

36. *New York Times*, June 13, 1993.

37. Office of the United Nations High Commissioner for Human Rights, "Convention against Torture and Other Cruel, Inhuman or Degrading Treatment or Punishment," http://www2.ohchr.org/english/law/cat.htm, accessed July 14, 2009.

38. U.S. Senate, 101st Congress, 2d Session, Committee on Foreign Relations, *Convention against Torture: Hearing before the Committee on Foreign Relations* (Washington, DC: Government Printing Office, 1990), 1, 12–18, 34, 35, 40–43, 66–69, 70–71.

39. United Nations, *Convention against Torture and Other Cruel Inhuman or Degrading Treatment or Punishment, Reservation Made by the United States of America,* http://www.unhchr.ch/tbs/doc.nsf/0/5d7ce66547377b1f802567fd0056b533?Open Document, accessed September 18, 2011.

40. Ibid.

41. United States, *Congressional Record: Proceedings and Debates of the 103d Congress, Second Session, Volume 140—Part 1* (Washington, DC: Government Printing Office, 1994), February 2, 1994, 827; Foreign Relations Authorization Act, PL 103-236, Title V, Sec. 506, 108 Stat. 463 (1994), 18 USC§ 2340-2340A.

42. United States, *Weekly Compilation of Presidential Documents* 32, no. 34 (Washington, DC: Government Printing Office, 1996), 1482; U.S. House of Representatives, 104th Congress, 2d Session, *Congressional Record: Volume 142—Part 14* (Washington, DC: Government Printing Office, 1996), 19562–63. The text of the War Crimes Act can be found at http://www.law.cornell.edu/uscode/usc_sec_18_00002441-000-.html (accessed, September 18, 2011.)

43. Daniel Levin, Acting Assistant Attorney General, Office of Legal Counsel, "Legal Standards Applicable under 18 U.S.C. §§ 2340-2340A," December 30, 2004, http://www.justice.gov/olc/18usc23402340a2.htm, accessed September 19, 2011.

44. U.S. Code, Title 18, Part I, Chapter 113C, § 2340. http://www.law.cornell.edu/uscode/uscode18/usc_sec_18_00002340-000-.html, accessed July 21, 2009.

45. Department of the Army, Headquarters, *FM 34–52: Intelligence Interrogation* (Washington, DC: Department of the Army, September 28, 1992), iv, 1–8.

46. Ibid., iv–v, 1–7, 1–8.

47. Michael T. Klare, *War without End: American Planning for the Next Vietnams* (New York: Alfred A. Knopf, 1972), 300–304; *New York Times*, June 24, 2001.

48. James Hodge and Linda Cooper, *Disturbing the Peace: The Story of Father Roy Bourgeois and the Movement to Close the School of the Americas* (Maryknoll: Orbis Books, 2004), 1–4, 148–208.

49. Ibid., 157–66.

50. Gary Cohn, Ginger Thompson, and Mark Matthews, "Torture Was Taught by CIA," *Baltimore Sun*, January 27, 1997, http://articles.baltimoresun.com/1997-01-27/news/1997027049_1_training-manual-torture-methods-counterintelligence-interrogation, accessed July 21, 2011.

51. *Washington Post*, September 21, 1996.

52. *New York Times*, September 22, 1996.

53. Cohn, Thompson, and Matthews, "Torture Was Taught by CIA"; *Washington Post*, January 28, 1997; *New York Times*, January 29, 1997.

54. Cohn, Thompson, and Matthews, "Torture Was Taught by CIA."

55. *New York Times*, January 29, 1997.

56. *Washington Post*, March 14, 2004.

57. *New York Times*, September 17, 2006.

58. U.S. Senate, Committee on Armed Services, 110th Congress, 2d Session, *Inquiry into the Treatment of Detainees in U.S. Custody* (Washington, DC: Government

Printing Office, 2008), xiii, http://armed-services.senate.gov/Publications/Detainee%20Report%20Final_April%2022%202009.pdf, accessed July, 21, 2009; George W. Bush, The White House, Washington, For: The Vice President, "Subject: Humane Treatment of Taliban and al Qaeda Detainees," February 7, 2002, http://www.pegc.us/archive/White_House/bush_memo_20020207_ed.pdf, accessed July 27, 2009.

59. Stephen Grey, *Ghost Plane: The True Story of the CIA Torture Program* (New York: St. Martin's Press, 2006), 87, 181, 227, 269–308; *New York Times*, May 31, November 9, 2005.

60. Jane Mayer, "The Black Sites," *The New Yorker*, July 21, 2009, http://www.newyorker.com/reporting/2007/08/13/070813fa_fact_mayer, accessed July 20, 2009; U.S. Senate, *Inquiry into the Treatment of Detainees in U.S. Custody*, xiii.

61. Jay Bybee, Office of the Assistant Attorney General, "Memorandum for Alberto R. Gonzales, Counsel to the President, Re: Standards of Conduct for Interrogation under 18 U.S.C. §§ 2340-2340A," August 1, 2002, 1, www.washingtonpost.com/wp-srv/ . . . /torture_memo_aug2002.pdf, accessed July 19, 2009; U.S. Senate, *Inquiry into the Treatment of Detainees in U.S. Custody*, xv–xvi, xxi.

62. Jay S. Bybee, Office of the Assistant Attorney General, "Memorandum for John Rizzo, Acting General Counsel of the Central Intelligence Agency. Interrogation of al Qaeda Operative," August 1, 2002, p. 11, http://www.globalsecurity.org/intell/library/policy/national/olc_020801_bybee.htm, accessed October 4, 2011.

63. U.S. Senate, Committee on Armed Services, 110th Congress, 2d Session, *Hearing to Receive Testimony on the Origins of Aggressive Interrogation Techniques: Part I of the Committee's Inquiry into the Treatment of Detainees in U.S. Custody (A.M. Session)* (Washington, DC: Government Printing Office, June 17, 2008), 9.

64. Steven G. Bradbury, Office of Legal Counsel, "Memorandum for John A. Rizzo Senior Deputy General Counsel, Central Intelligence Agency, Re: Application of 18 U.S.C. §§ 2340-2340A to the Combined Use of Certain Techniques in the Interrogation of High Value al Qaeda Detainees," May 10, 2005, 60, http://www.hsdl.org/?view&did=37512, accessed June 29, 2011.

65. Steven G. Bradbury, Office of the Principal Deputy Assistant Attorney General, Office of Legal Counsel, "Memorandum for John A. Rizzo Senior Deputy Counsel, Central Intelligence Agency: Re: Application of United States Obligations under Article 16 of the Convention against Torture to Certain Techniques That May Be Used in the Interrogation of High Value al Qaeda Detainees," May 30, 2005, 38, http://media.luxmedia.com/aclu/olc_05102005_bradbury46pg.pdf, accessed June 29, 2011.

66. *New York Times*, March 2, 2009.

67. Bradbury, "Memorandum for John A. Rizzo Senior Deputy Counsel, Central Intelligence Agency," May 30, 2005, 37.

68. "Top Bush Advisors Approved 'Enhanced Interrogation,'" *ABC News*, April 9, 2008, accessed December 24, 2008; CIA, "Special Review," 5, 24, 45, 101.

69. U.S. Senate, *Inquiry into the Treatment of Detainees in U.S. Custody*, xix; William J. Haynes II, General Counsel, Department of Defense, "For: Secretary of Defense, Subject: Counter-Resistance Techniques," November 27, 2002, http://www

.gwu.edu/~nsarchiv/NSAEBB/NSAEBB127/02.12.02.pdf, accessed November 30, 2011; *New York Times*, June 18, 2008.

70. M. Gregg Bloche and Jonathan H. Marks, "Doctors and Interrogators at Guantanamo Bay," *New England Journal of Medicine* 353, no. 1 (July 7, 2005): 7; Jonathan H. Marks, "The Silence of the Doctors," *The Nation*, December 7, 2005, http://www.thenation.com/doc/20051226/marks, accessed July 19, 2009.

71. Ricardo S. Sanchez, "Memorandum for: C2, Combined Joint Task Force Seven, Baghdad, Iraq 09335, Subject: CJTF-7 Interrogation and Counter-Resistance Policy," September 14, 2003; Ricardo S. Sanchez, "Memorandum for: C2, Combined Joint Task Force Seven, Baghdad, Iraq 09335, Subject: CJTF-7 Interrogation and Counter-Resistance Policy," October 12, 2003, http://www.aclu.org/SafeandFree/Safe andFree.cfm?ID=17851&c=206, both accessed March 30, 2005.

72. U.S. Senate, *Inquiry into the Treatment of Detainees*, xix; Haynes, "For: Secretary of Defense, Subject: Counter-Resistance Techniques," November 27, 2002; *New York Times*, June 18, 2008.

73. *New York Times*, May 1, 2004; Seymour M. Hersh, "Torture at Abu Ghraib," *The New Yorker*, May 10, 2004, 42–47; *New York Times*, June 18, 2004; *Washington Post*, April 13, 2005; Leon Worden, "SCV Newsmaker of the Week: Brig. Gen. Janis Karpinski," *Signal Newspaper* (Santa Clarita, CA), July 4, 2004; "Abuse of Iraqi POWs by GIs Probed," *CBS News*, April 28, 2004, http://www.cbsnews.com /stories/2004/04/27/60II/printable614063.shtlm, accessed March 29, 2005.

74. CIA, "Special Review," 42–44, 69–79, 102–3.

75. Supreme Court of the United States, Oral Arguments, *Donald H. Rumsfeld v. Jose Padilla*, No. 03-1027, http://www.supremecourtus.gov/oral_arguments/argument_ transcripts/03–1027.pdf, accessed July 5, 2004.

76. U.S. Supreme Court, Oral Arguments, *Donald H. Rumsfeld v. Jose Padilla*, No. 03-1027; *New York Times*, July 4, 2004.

77. *NewsHour with Jim Lehrer*, PBS, May 4, 2004, http://www.pbs.org/newshour /bb/military/jan-june 04/abuse1_05_04.html, accessed June 14, 2004; *New York Times*, May 11, May 15, May 25, 2004; United Nations, Commission on Human Rights, 61st Session, *Report of the United Nations High Commissioner for Human Rights and Follow Up to the World Conference on Human Rights*, (Geneva: Commission on Human Rights, E/CN.4/2005/4, Advance Edited Edition, June 9, 2004), 18; "President Outlines Steps to Help Iraq Achieve Democracy and Freedom," May 24, 2004, http:// www.whitehouse.gov/news/release/2004/05/print/20040424-10.html, accessed June 14, 2004; *Washington Post*, May 13, June 22, 2004; *New York Times*, May 8, May 12, 2004.

78. *New York Times*, July 24, August 1, 2005; James Gerstenzang, "GOP Pressure Over Detainee Policy Leads to Defense Bill Delay," *Los Angeles Times*, July 27, 2005, http://pqasb.pqarchiver.com/latimes/advancedsearch.html, accessed September 19, 2009; Statement of Senator John McCain, Amendment on Army Field Manual, Arizona, News Center, July 25, 2005, http://mccain.senate.gov/index .cfm?fuseaction=Newscenter4.ViewPressRelease&Content id=1595, accessed July 29,

2005; U.S. Senate, 109th Congress, 1st Session, *Congressional Record*, vol. 151, no. 102 (July 25, 2005), S8789–90, 8798–99.

79. *New York Times*, July 24, August 1, 2005; "11 Retired Military Leaders Endorse McCain Amendments to Pending Defense Bill That Would Reform U.S. Interrogation Policy," U.S. Newswire, Washington, July 24, 2005, http://newswire.vlex.com /source/us-newswire-4246/issue/2005/7/24, accessed July 29, 2005; letter to Senator McCain from General Joseph Hoar (Ret. USMC) et al., July 25, 2005, http://www .humanrightsfirst.org/us_law/etn/pdf/mccain-072205.pdf, accessed August 2, 2005; Dick Cheney, *In My Time: A Personal and Political Memoir* (New York: Threshold Editions, 2011), 359–60; "Dick Cheney's Wars," *Wall Street Journal*, August 30, 2011, http://online.wsj.com/article/SB10001424053111904199404576538481141793772.html, accessed September 7, 2011.

80. Human Rights Watch, "News Release: Landmark Torture Ban Undercut," December 15, 2005, http://www.hrw.org/en/news/2005/12/15/us-landmark-torture-ban -undercut, accessed September 2, 2009; Supreme Court of the United States, *Rasul v. Bush*, No. 03-334, http://www.law.cornell.edu/supct/html/03-334.ZS.html, accessed September 19, 2009.

81. Cheney, *In My Time*, 360.

82. "Bush Accepts Sen. McCain's Torture Policy," Associated Press, December 15, 2005, http://www.msnbc.msn.com/id/10480690/ns/politics/t/bush-accepts-sen -mccains-torture-policy/#.T7K1J47-LiY, accessed September 19, 2009.

83. President's Statement on Signing of H.R. 2863, "Department of Defense, Emergency Supplemental Appropriations to Address Hurricanes in the Gulf of Mexico, and Pandemic Influenza Act, 2006," December 30, 2005, http://georgewbush-whitehouse .archives.gov/news/releases/2005/12/print/20051230–8.html, accessed September 2, 2009.

84. *New York Times*, January 15, 2006. See Alfred W. McCoy, "Invisible in Plain Sight," *Amnesty International Magazine*, http://www.amnestyusa.org/amnesty-magazine /amnesty-magazine/page.do?id=1105051, accessed September 14, 2009.

85. Cheney, *In My Time*, 360.

86. U.S. Supreme Court, *Salim Ahmed Hamdan v. Donald H. Rumsfeld*, No. 05-184, Opinion of Stevens, J., June 29, 2006, 6, 69–73; *New York Times*, March 27, June 30, 2006.

87. *New York Times*, September 7, September 8, 2006. The White House, Office of the Press Secretary, "President Discusses Creation of Military Commissions to Try Suspected Terrorists," September 6, 2006, http://www.whitehouse.gov/news /releases/2006/09/print/20060906-3.html, accessed September 8, 2006. See also Alfred W. McCoy, "The Myth of the Ticking Time Bomb," *The Progressive*, October 2006, 20–24.

88. House Armed Services Committee, Press Release, "Chairman Hunter Opening Statement, Hearing on Military Commissions and Standards Utilized in Trying Detainees," September 7, 2006, http://www.globalsecurity.org/security/library /congress/2006_h/060907-hunteropeningstatement.pdf, accessed September 18, 2006;

National Public Radio, *All Things Considered*, September 7, 2006, http://www.npr.org
/templates/story/story.php?storyID=5783523, accessed September 22, 2006; *Washington
Post*, September 8, 2006.

89. *New York Times*, September 15, September 16, 2006; The White House, Office
of the Press Secretary, "Setting the Record Straight: JAG Leaders Say Common Article
3 Provisions Would Be 'Helpful,'" http://www.whitehouse.gov/news/releases/2006/09
/print/20060915.html, accessed February 3, 2006. See also Alfred W. McCoy, *A Question of Torture: CIA Interrogation, from the Cold War to the War on Terror* (New York:
Metropolitan Books, 2006), 222.

90. *New York Times*, September 16, 2006; *Washington Post*, September 19, 2006.

91. Letter to Chairman Warner, From: General Joseph Hoar, USMC (ret.) et al.,
September 12, 2006, http://graphics8.nytimes.com/packages/pdf/politics/jagletter.pdf,
accessed September 22, 2006.

92. *New York Times*, September 22, September 23, September 26, September 27,
September 28, September 29, September 30, 2006; U.S. House of Representatives,
109th Congress, 2d Session, *H.R. 6166: A Bill to Amend Title 10, United States Code, to
Authorize Trial by Military Commission for Violations of the Law of War and for Other
Purposes*, September 25, 2006, http://www.gpo.gov/fdsys/pkg/BILLS-109hr6166rfs
/pdf/BILLS-109hr6166rfs.pdf, accessed February 12, 2012.

93. Bybee, "Memorandum for Alberto R. Gonzales Counsel to the President," August 1, 2002, 1; U.S. House of Representatives, *H.R. 6166: A Bill to Amend Title 10,
United States Code*, 29, 35.

94. U.S. House of Representatives, *H.R. 6166: A Bill to Amend Title 10, United
States Code*, 28.

95. *New York Times*, July 21, 2007; *Washington Post*, July 21, 2007.

96. U.S. Senate, *Inquiry into the Treatment of Detainees in U.S. Custody*, xii.

97. Ibid., xiii, 6–11.

98. Ibid., xiii, xvii; John Ley, "Memorandum for Legal Counsel to Chairman, Joint
Chiefs of Staff," Undated, Tab 12, Extracts, U.S. Senate, Committee on Armed Services, *Inquiry into the Treatment of Detainees in U.S. Custody*.

99. *New York Times*, August 12, 2009.

100. *New York Times*, January 23, 2009.

101. *New York Times*, December 14, 2009.

102. *New York Times*, December 20, 2008.

103. *Washington Post*, May 13, 2009.

104. *Los Angeles Times*, May 23, 2009.

105. The White House, Press Office, "Statement of President Barack Obama,"
April 16, 2009, http://www.whitehouse.gov/the_press_office/Statement-of-President
-Barack-Obama-on-Release-of-OLC-Memos/, accessed July 21, 2009.

106. *New York Times*, April 21, 2009; *Washington Post*, April 24, 2009, http://voices
.washingtonpost.com/44/2009/04/23/a_commission_on_enhanced_inter.html, accessed December 24, 2011.

107. *New York Times*, May 9, 2009; Jane Mayer, "Outsourcing Torture: The Se-

cret History of America's 'Extraordinary Rendition' Program," *The New Yorker*, February 14, 2005, http://www.newyorker.com/archive/2005/02/14/050214fa_fact6, accessed July 20, 2009.

108. United States, *Congressional Record: Proceedings and Debates of the 111th Congress, First Session*, May 11, 2009, 5305–07, http://frwebgate.access.gpo.gov/cgi-bin/getpage.cgi?position=all&page=S5305&dbname=2009_record, accessed February 27, 2011.

109. *New York Times*, May 9, 2009.

110. Cheney, *In My Time*, 521–22.

111. "Remarks by the President on National Security," Office of the Press Secretary, The White House, May 21, 2009, http://www.whitehouse.gov/the_press_office/Remarks-by-the-President-On-National-Security-5-21-09/; "Obama Heightens National Security Debate," *ABC News*, May 21, 2009, http://abcnews.go.com/video/playerIndex?id=7644689, both accessed September 9, 2011.

112. Jake Tapper, Jon Karl, and Karen Travers, "President Obama, Dick Cheney Face Off on National Security Issues," *ABC News*, May 21, 2009, http://abcnews.go.com/Politics/story?id=7643032&page=1, accessed November 14, 2010.

113. Steve Benen, "Political Animal: Nepotism Reigns," *The Washington Monthly*, May 22, 2009, http://www.washingtonmonthly.com/archives/monthly/2009_05.php, accessed, January 25, 2010; *Anderson Cooper 360 Degrees*, *CNN.com*, May 21, 2009, Transcript, http://transcripts.cnn.com/TRANSCRIPTS/0905/21/acd.01.html, accessed January 23, 2010.

114. *Washington Post*, August 25, 2009.

115. *New York Times*, May 9, August 26, August 31, 2009; Associated Press, "Ex-CIA Chiefs Ask Obama to Halt Probe," September 19, 2009, http://news.aol.com/article/ex-cia-directors-ask-obama-to-halt/637010, accessed September 19, 2009.

116. Statement by Liz Cheney in Response to President Obama's National Security Remarks, Keep America Safe, January 6, 2010, http://www.facebook.com/note.php?note_id=243193612065, accessed January 23, 2010.

117. "Dick Cheney: Waterboarding Should Have Been Option with Underwear Bomber," *ABC News, Good Morning America*, February 14, 2010, http://blogs.abc news.com/thenote/2010/02/cheney-waterboarding-should-have-been-option-with-underwear-bomber.html, accessed March 8, 2010.

118. *New York Times*, February 20, 2010; Associated Press, "DOJ Finds No Misconduct by Memo Authors," *New York Times*, February 20, 2010, http://www.nytimes.com/aponline/2010/02/20/us/politics/AP-US-Interrogation-Memos.html, accessed February 20, 2010.

119. American Civil Liberties Union, "Justice Department Wrong to Let Torture Lawyers Off the Hook, Says ACLU," April 14, 2011, http://www.aclu.org/national-security/justice-department-wrong-let-torture-lawyers-hook-says-aclu, accessed June 29, 2011.

120. "Keep America Safe: Who Are the Al Qaeda Seven?" http://www.youtube.com/watch?v=ZIxg7LmlEQg&feature=player_embedded#, accessed March 8, 2010; Ben Smith, "Cheney Group Questions Loyalty of Justice Department Lawyers," *Po-*

litico, March 2, 2010, http://www.politico.com/blogs/bensmith/0310/Cheney_group_questions_loyalty_of_Justice_lawyers.html?showall, accessed March 8, 2010; *New York Times*, March 8, 2010.

121. *New York Times*, March 10, March 12, April 10, 2010.

122. Haroon Siddique, "Waterboarding Is Torture, Downing Street Confirms," *The Guardian*, November 9, 2010, http://www.guardian.co.uk/world/2010/nov/09/george-bush-memoirs-waterboarding, accessed July 12, 2011; "Bush Waterboarding Claim Challenged," *Daily Express*, November 11, 2010, http://www.dailyexpress.co.uk/posts/view/210911/Bush-waterboarding-claim-challenged/, accessed November 14, 2010.

123. *New York Times*, February 17, September 22, September 23, December 14, 2009, January 4, January 21, 2010, May 29, 2012; Peter Baker, "Obama's War over Terror," *New York Times Magazine*, January 17, 2010, 36–37; "America's Secret Afghan Prisons," *Democracy Now*, February 2, 2010, http://www.democracynow.org/2010/2/2/americas_secret_afghan_prisons_investigation_unearths, accessed April 20, 2010.

124. *New York Times*, January 22, February 18, May 24, July 22, August 25, 2009; Eli Lake, "Panetta Backs Rendition but Not Torture," *Washington Times*, February 6, 2009, http://www.washingtontimes.com/news/2009/feb/06/panetta-supports-rendition-but-not-torture/, accessed July 12, 2011.

125. Jeremy Scahill, "The CIA's Secret Sites in Somalia," *The Nation*, July 12, 2011, http://www.thenation.com/print/article/161936/cias-secret-sites-somalia, accessed July 28, 2011.

126. *New York Times*, September 9, 2010, May 22, 2011.

127. Office of the Press Secretary, The White House, "Executive Order—Periodic Review of Individuals Detained at Guantánamo Bay Naval Station Pursuant to the Authorization for Use of Military Force," March 7, 2011, http://www.whitehouse.gov/the-press-office/2011/03/07/executive-order-periodic-review-individuals-detained-guant-namo-bay-nava, accessed June 29, 2011.

128. "At Guantanamo, Detainees Are Presumed Guilty," NACDL NewsRelease, National Association of Criminal Defense Lawyers, April 4, 2011, http://www.nacdl.org/public.nsf/NewsReleases/2011mn10?OpenDocument, accessed July 5, 2011.

129. *New York Times*, March 8, March 9, 2011.

130. *New York Times*, March 15, 2011; "Wikileaks Bradley Manning Faces 22 New Charges," *CBS News*, March 2, 2011, http://www.cbsnews.com/stories/2011/03/02/national/main20038464.shtml?tag=breakingnews, accessed July 12, 2011.

131. Ewan MacAskill, "Bradley Manning Case Sparks UN Criticism of US Government," *The Guardian*, April 11, 2011, http://www.guardian.co.uk/world/2011/apr/11/bradley-manning-juan-mendez-torture, accessed July 12, 2011; *Washington Post*, March 12, 2011.

132. Bruce Ackerman and Yochai Benkler, "Private Manning's Humiliation," *New York Review of Books*, April 28, 2011, http://www.nybooks.com/articles/archives/2011/apr/28/private-mannings-humiliation/, accessed July 12, 2011.

133. "Wikileaks Suspect Transferred to Fort Leavenworth," Associated Press, April 21, 2011, http://abcnews.go.com/US/wireStory?id=13421925, accessed July 12, 2011.

134. *New York Times*, January 24, January 25, 2012.

135. *New York Times*, June 22, 2008, January 24, January 25, 2012. U.S. District Court, Eastern District of Virginia, *United States of America v. John Kiriakou*, Case Number 1:12MJ33, "Criminal Complaint"; U.S. District Court, Eastern District of Virginia, *United States of America v. John Kiriakou*, Case Number 1:12MJ33, Joseph Capitano, "Affidavit in Support of Criminal Complaint and Arrest Warrant," January 23, 2012, http://www.justice.gov/opa/documents/kiriakou-complaint.pdf, both accessed January 27, 2012.

136. NRO Symposium, "Bin Laden, No More," *National Review Online*, May 2, 2011, http://www.nationalreview.com/articles/266271/bin-laden-no-more-nro-symposium ?page=6, accessed May 6, 2011.

137. *New York Times*, May 3, 2011.

138. John Yoo, "From Guantanamo to Abbottabad," *Wall Street Journal*, May 4, 2011, http://online.wsj.com/article/SB10001424052748703834804576301032595527372 .html, accessed July 12, 2011.

139. "Ex-CIA Counterterrorism Chief: 'Enhanced Interrogation' Led U.S. to bin Laden," *Time Swampland*, May 4, 2011, http://swampland.time.com/2011/05/04/did -torture-get-the-us-osama-bin-laden/, accessed May 6, 2011.

140. "Rumsfeld Flip-Flops in Harsh Interrogation of Detainees," *YouTube*, May 4, 2011, transcribed by Brett Reilly, http://www.youtube.com/watch?feature=player_ embedded&v=t5oatNXQBHk, accessed May 7, 2011.

141. Catherine Herridge, "Bush-Era Interrogations Provided Key Details on Bin Laden's Location," *FoxNews.com*, May 3, 2011, http://www.foxnews.com/politics /2011/05/02/bush-era-interrogations-provided-key-details-bin-ladens-location/, accessed June 26, 2011.

142. "Cheney: Justice Probe of CIA Interrogators an 'Outrage,'" *Fox News.com*, May 8, 2011, http://www.foxnews.com/politics/2011/05/08/cheney-justice-probe-cia -interrogators-outrage/, accessed May 8, 2011.

143. Michael B. Mukasey, "The Waterboarding Trail to Bin Laden," *Wall Street Journal*, May 6, 2011, http://online.wsj.com/article/SB10001424052748703859304576 05023876506348.html, accessed June 26, 2011.

144. "After Bin Laden Are We Safer?" *ABC News, This Week,* May 8, 2011, transcribed by Brett Reilly, http://abcnews.go.com/thisweek/video/memoriam-2011 –13555874&tab=9482930&section=1206874&playlist=13555957, accessed May 8, 2011.

145. "Ex-CIA Counterterrorism Chief: 'Enhanced Interrogation' Led U.S. to bin Laden," *Time Swampland*, May 4, 2011.

146. John McCain, "Bin Laden's Death and the Debate over Torture," *Washington Post*, May 11, 2011, http://www.washingtonpost.com/opinions/bin-ladens-death-and -the-debate-over-torture/2011/05/11/AFdimdsG_story.html, accessed June 27, 2011.

147. Office of Public Affairs, Department of Justice, "Statement of the Attorney General Regarding Investigation into the Interrogation of Certain Detainees," June 30, 2011, http://www.justice.gov/opa/pr/2011/June/11-ag-861.html, accessed July 4, 2011.

148. *New York Times*, July 1, 2011.

149. Cheney, *In My Time*, 357–59; "Dick Cheney's Wars," *Wall Street Journal.*

150. *New York Times*, August 26, 2011; U.S. Senate, Committee on the Judiciary, *What Went Wrong: Torture and the Office of Legal Counsel in the Bush Administration*, Testimony of Ali Soufan, May 13, 2009, http://judiciary.senate.gov/hearings/, accessed August 29, 2011; "The Interrogator," *Frontline*, PBS, September 13, 2011, http://www.pbs.org/wgbh/pages/frontline/iraq-war-on-terror/the-interrogator/transcript-7/, accessed September 13, 2011; Ali H. Soufan, *The Black Banners: The Inside Story of 9/11 and the War against al-Qaeda* (New York: W. W. Norton, 2011), 416–33.

151. *New York Times*, August 26, 2011; "The Interrogator," *Frontline*, September 13, 2011; Hard Measures, https://sites.google.com/site/hardmeasures/, accessed September 14, 2011; "Hard Measures: Ex-CIA Head Defends Post-9/11 Tactics," *CBS News, 60 Minutes* (Lesley Stahl, correspondent, Richard Bonin, producer), April 29, 2012, http://www.cbsnews.com/8301-18560_162-57423533/hard-measures-ex-cia-head-defends-post-9-11-tactics/?pageNum=5&tag=contentMain;contentBody, accessed May 5, 2012.

152. Embtel 242, Embassy Berlin to State, 06 February 2007, Secret/Noforn, Subject: Al-Masri Case-Chancellery Aware of USG Concerns, *WikiLeaks Cablegate Archive*, Reference ID: 07BERLIN242, http://wikileaks.org/cable/2007/02/07BERLIN242.html, accessed September 14, 2011.

153. Embtel 392, Embassy Madrid to State, 17 April 2009, Confidential, Subject: Spain: Attorney General Recommends Court Not Pursue GTMO Criminal Case vs. Former USG Officials, *WikiLeaks Cablegate Archive*, Reference ID: 09MADRID392, http://wikileaks.org/cable/2009/04/09MADRID392.html#, accessed September 14, 2011.

154. Embtel 440, Embassy Madrid to State, 05 May 2009, Official Use Only, SUBJECT: Garzon Opens Second Investigation into Alleged U.S. Torture of Terrorism Detainees. REF: A. MADRID 392, B. MADRID 393, C. 08 MADRID 1280, *Wikileaks Cablegate Archive*, Reference ID: 09MADRID440, http://www.wikileaks.ch/cable/2009/05/09MADRID440.html, accessed September 14, 2011.

155. Human Rights Watch, Appendix: Foreign State Proceedings Regarding U.S. Detainee Mistreatment, *Getting Away with Torture* (July 12, 2011), http://www.hrw.org/node/100262/section/7, accessed July 28, 2011.

156. Matthew Cole, "Convicted Spy Says 'We Broke the Law,'" *ABC News*, November 4, 2009, http://abcnews.go.com/Blotter/exclusive-convicted-cia-spy-broke-law/story?id=8995107, accessed July 28, 2011.

157. Amnesty International, "European Governments Must Provide Justice for Victims of CIA Porgrammes," November 15, 2010, http://www.amnesty.org/en/news-and-updates/report/european-governments-must-provide-justice-victims-cia-programmes-2010-11-15; Amnesty International, *Open Secret: Mounting Evidence of Europe's Complicity in Rendition and Secret Detention* (November 2010), Executive Summary, http://www.amnesty.org/en/library/info/EUR01/024/2010/en, both accessed June 26, 2011.

158. Jennifer Buley, "Former Defence Minister to Be Questioned in Torture Trial," *Copenhagen Post*, January 2, 2012, http://www.cphpost.dk/news/international/former-defence-minister-be-questioned-torture-trial, accessed February 5, 2012; *New York Times*, March 28, 2012.

159. Catherine Philp, "George W. Bush Calls Off Europe Visit after Arrest Threat over Torture of Terror Suspects," *The Australian*, February 7, 2011, http://www.the australian.com.au/news/world/george-w-bush-calls-off-europe-visit-after-arrest -threat-over-torture-of-terror-suspects/story-e6frg6so-1226001389417, accessed November 23, 2011.

160. Press Release, "No Immunity for Former Presidents under Law," Center for Constitutional Rights, February 7, 2011, http://ccrjustice.org/newsroom/press-releases /human-rights-groups-announce-bush-indictment-convention-against-torture-sign, accessed March 7, 2011.

161. Duncan Gardham and Gordon Rayner, "MI5 'Knew Guantanamo Detainee Binyam Mohamed Was Being Tortured'," *The Telegraph*, February 10, 2010, http://www.telegraph.co.uk/news/uknews/terrorism-in-the-uk/7204741/MI5-knew -Guantanamo-detainee-Binyam-Mohamed-was-being-tortured.html; "Dealt a Setback in 'State Secrets' Case, Obama Administration Says US-UK Intelligence-Sharing Might Be Damaged," *ABC News*, February 10, 2010, http://abcnews.go.com/blogs /politics/2010/02/dealt-a-setback-in-state-secrets-case-obama-administration-says -usuk-intelligencesharing-might-be-da/, both accessed January 17, 2012.

162. *New York Times*, July 7, November 17, 2010.

163. *New York Times*, September 9, 2011; Sir William Gage, *The Baha Mousa Public Inquiry Report: Volume I* (London: The Stationery Office, HC 1452-I, 2011), 1–9, http:// www.bahamousainquiry.org/f_report/vol%20i/volume%20i.pdf, accessed September 21, 2011; Nina Lakhani, "Colonel Daoud Mousa: 'I'm Glad Troops Came to Iraq. But I Still Weep for the Son They Killed'," *The Independent*, September 16, 2011, http:// www.independent.co.uk/news/uk/crime/colonel-daoud-mousa-im-glad-troops-came -to-iraq-but-i-still-weep-for-the-son-they-killed-2355551.html, accessed September 21, 2011.

164. *New York Times*, January 13, 2012; "UK Inquiry into Rendition and Torture Complicity Scrapped," *BBC News*, January 18, 2012, http://www.bbc.co.uk/news /world-16614514, accessed January 20, 2012.

165. Human Rights Watch, "United States: Investigate Bush, Other Top Officials for Torture," July 11, 2011, http://www.hrw.org/en/node/100390, accessed July 17, 2011.

166. *New York Times*, May 17, 2010.

167. *New York Times*, August 12, 2009; U.S. Senate, Committee on Armed Services, *Inquiry into the Treatment of Detainees in U.S. Custody*, 6–11.

168. Jake Berry, "Lower Newspaper Staffing Affects Investigative Reporting," *Nashua Telegraph*, March 19, 2011, http://www.nashuatelegraph.com/news/912966 -196/lower-newspaper-staffing-affects-investigative-reporting.html, accessed September 15, 2011.

169. Paul Aussaresses, *The Battle of the Casbah: Terrorism and Counter-Terrorism in Algeria 1955–1957* (New York: Enigma, 2002), 126–28, 162–63; *New York Times*, May 29, 2012; Bill Roggio and Alexander Mayer, "Charting the Data for US Airstrikes in Pakistan, 2004–2012," *Long War Journal*, May 28, 2012, http://www.longwarjournal .org/pakistan-strikes.php, accessed May 30, 2012.

Bibliography

Articles

Ackerman, Bruce, and Yochai Benkler. "Private Manning's Humiliation." *New York Review of Books*, April 28, 2011. http://www.nybooks.com/articles/archives/2011/apr/28/private-mannings-humiliation/. Accessed July 12, 2011.

Almendral, Gemma Nemenzo. "The Fall of the Regime." In Aurora Javate-De Dios et al., eds. *Dictatorship and Revolution: Roots of People's Power*, 176–220. Manila: Conspectus, 1988.

Alter, Jonathan. "Time to Think about Torture." *Newsweek*, November 5, 2001, 45.

American Psychological Association. "Amending the Ethics Code." *Monitor on Psychology* 41, no. 4 (April 2010). http://www.apa.org/monitor/2010/04/ethics.aspx. Accessed June 2, 2011.

———. "Overview of APA's Ongoing Efforts to Implement the Petition Resolution." September 10, 2009. http://www.apa.org/news/press/statements/implementation-steps.pdf. Accessed June 2, 2011.

———. "Report of the American Psychological Association Presidential Task Force on Psychological Ethics and National Security." June 2005. htttp://www.apa.org/releases/PENSTaskForceReportFinal.pdf. Accessed July 7, 2005.

Andradé, Dale. "Pacification." In Stanley Kutler, ed., *Encyclopedia of the Vietnam War*, 417–23. New York: Charles Scribner's Sons, 1996.

Bachman, Gideon. "Pasolini and the Marquis de Sade." *Sight and Sound* 45, no. 1 (Winter 1976): 50–54.

Baker, Peter. "Obama's War over Terror." *New York Times Magazine*, January 17, 2010, 30–42.

Baker, Richard. "Plea from Churches for Hicks." *The Age*, October 10, 2006. http://www.theage.com.au/news/national/plea-from-churches-for-hicks/2006/10/09/1160246071521.html. Accessed June 16, 2011.

Barry, John, et al. "The Roots of Torture." *Newsweek*, May 24, 2004, 26–34.

Basoglu, Metin. "A Multivariate Contextual Analysis of Torture and Cruel, Inhuman, and Degrading Treatments: Implications for an Evidence-Based Definition of Torture." *American Journal of Orthopsychiatry* 79, no. 2 (2009): 135–45.

Basoglu, Metin, et al. "Psychological Effects of Torture: A Comparison of Tortured with Nontortured Political Activists in Turkey." *American Journal of Psychiatry* 151, no. 1 (1994): 76–81.

Basoglu, Metin, Maria Livanou, and Cvetana Crnobaric. "Torture vs. Other Cruel, Inhuman, and Degrading Treatment: Is the Distinction Real or Apparent?" *Archives of General Psychiatry* 64, no. 3 (2007): 277–85.

Bass, Thomas A. "Counterinsurgency and Torture." *American Quarterly* 60, no. 2 (June 2008): 233–40.

Beecher, Henry K. "Ethics and Clinical Research." *New England Journal of Medicine* 274, no. 24 (June 16, 1966): 1354–60.

———. "Experimental Pharmacology and Measurement of the Subjective Response." *Science* 116, no. 3007 (August 15, 1952): 157–58.

———. "Experimentation in Man." *Journal of the American Medical Association* 169, no. 5 (January 31, 1959): 461–78.

———. Letter to *Science* 117, no. 3033 (February 13, 1953): 166–67.

———. "Response to the Ingersoll Lecture by a Physician." *Harvard Theological Review* 62, no. 1 (1969): 21–26.

Benen, Steve. "Political Animal: Nepotism Reigns." *Washington Monthly*, May 22, 2009. http://www.washingtonmonthly.com/archives/monthly/2009_05.php. Accessed January 25, 2010.

Benjamin, Mark. "Salon Exclusive: The Abu Ghraib Files." *Salon.com*, February 16, 2006. http://www.salon.com/news/feature/2006/02/16/abu_ghraib/. Accessed February 22, 2010.

Biderman, Albert D. "Communist Attempts to Elicit False Confessions from Air Force Prisoners of War." *Bulletin of the New York Academy of Medicine* 33, no. 9 (1957): 616–25.

Biderman, Albert D., and Herbert Zimmer. "Introduction." In Albert D. Biderman and Herbert Zimmer, eds., *The Manipulation of Human Behavior*, 1–18. New York: John Wiley, 1961.

Bloche, M. Gregg, and Jonathan H. Marks. "Doctors and Interrogators at Guantanamo Bay." *New England Journal of Medicine* 353, no. 1 (July 7, 2005): 6–8.

———. "When Doctors Go to War." *New England Journal of Medicine* 352 (January 6, 2005): 1497–99.

Bowden, Mark. "The Dark Art of Interrogation: A Survey of the Landscape of Persuasion." *Atlantic Monthly*, October 2003. http://www.theatlantic.com/magazine/archive/2003/10/the-dark-art-of-interrogation/2791/. Accessed January 22, 2012.

Brown, Richard E. "Alfred McCoy, Hebb, the CIA and Torture." *Journal of the History of the Behavioral Sciences* 43, no. 2 (2007): 205–13.

Brown, Richard E., and P. M. Milner. "The Legacy of Donald O. Hebb: More Than the Hebb Synapse." *Nature Reviews/Neuroscience* 4 (2003): 1013–19.

Brugger, Winfried. "May Government Ever Use Torture? Two Responses from German Law." *American Journal of Comparative Law* 48, no. 4 (Autumn 2000): 661–78.

Brzezinski, Matthew. "Bust and Boom." *Washington Post Magazine*, December 30, 2001. http://www.prisonplanet.com/bust_and_boom.html. Accessed June 17, 2011.

Budiansky, Stephen. "Intelligence: Truth Extraction." *Atlantic Monthly*, June 2005, 32–35.

Cameron, D. Ewan, et al. "The Depatterning Treatment of Schizophrenia." *Comprehensive Psychiatry* 3, no. 3 (1962): 65–76.

Canadian Society for Brain, Behaviour, and Cognitive Science. "The Donald O. Hebb Distinguished Contribution Award." http://www.csbbcs.org/hebbrec11.html. Accessed July 8, 2011.

Carmichael, Keith, et al. "The Need for REDRESS." *Torture* 6, no. 1 (1996): 7.

Carroll, James. "The Bush Crusade." *The Nation*, September 20, 2004, 14–22.

Center for Constitutional Rights. "No Immunity for Former Presidents under Law." February 7, 2011. http://ccrjustice.org/newsroom/press-releases/human-rights-groups-announce-bush-indictment-convention-against-torture-sign. Accessed March 7, 2011.

C.E.W. "Henry K. Beecher, M.D." *New England Journal of Medicine* 295, no. 13 (September 23, 11976): 730.

Cole, David. "Gitmo Forever? Congress's Dangerous New Bill." *New York Review of Books*, December 8, 2011. http://www.nybooks.com/blogs/nyrblog/2011/dec/08/gitmo-forever-dangerous-new-bill/. Accessed December 10, 2011.

Cook, Helena. "The Role of Amnesty International in the Fight against Torture." In Antonio Cassese, ed., *The International Fight against Torture*, 172–86. Baden-Baden: Nomos Verlagsgesellschaft, 1991.

Coronel, Sheila. "RAM: From Reform to Revolution." In Philippine Center for Investigative Journalism, *Kudeta: The Challenge to Philippine Democracy*, 51–85. Manila: Philippine Center for Investigative Journalism, 1990.

Coste, Philippine. "Cette prison ou l'Amerique recyclait des savants Nazis." *L'Express*, no. 2898 (January 18, 2007): 60–65.

Denbeaux, Mark. "Report on Guantánamo Detainees: A Profile of 517 Detainees through Analysis of Department of Defense Data." *Seton Hall Law School* (February 8, 2006). http://law.shu.edu/publications/guantanamoReports/guantanamo_report_final_2_08_06.pdf. Accessed December 9, 2011.

Dershowitz, Alan M. "Tortured Reasoning." In Sanford Levinson, ed., *Torture: A Collection*, 257–80. New York: Oxford University Press, 2004.

Diokno, Maria Serena I. "Peace and Human Rights: The Past Lives On." In Lorna Kalaw-Tirol, ed., *Duet for EDSA: 1996 Looking Back, Looking Forward*, 91–106. Manila: Foundation for Worldwide People Power, 1995.

———. "Unity and Struggle." In Aurora Javate-De Dios et al., eds., *Dictatorship and Revolution: Roots of People's Power*, 132–75. Manila: Conspectus, 1988.

Doerr-Zegers, Otto, Lawrence Hartmann, Elizabeth Lira, and Eugenia Weinstein.

"Torture: Psychiatric Sequeli and Phenomenology." *Psychiatry* 55, no. 2 (May 1992): 177–84.

Edelman, Lucila, and Diana Kordon. "Incidence of Social Belonging, Personal Identity, and Historical Memory in Different Approaches to Psychological Therapy." *Torture* 6, no. 1 (1996): 4–5.

Ephron, Dan. "Gitmo Grievances." *Newsweek*, May 17, 2008. http://www.newsweek.com/2008/05/17/gitmo-grievances.html. Accessed June 14, 2011.

Genefke, Inge. "Some Steps towards a World with Less Torture." In Rehabilitation and Research Centre, *Annual Report 1995*, 15–16. Copenhagen: Rehabilitation and Research Centre for Torture Victims, 1996.

Glasser, A. J. "Torture in Video Games." *Kotaku*, September 10, 2009. http://kotaku.com/5353873/torture-in-video-games?utm_source=feedburner&utm_medium=feed&utm_campaign=Feed%3A+kotaku%2Ffull+%28Kotaku%29. Accessed March 2, 2010.

Glenn, David. "A Policy on Torture Roils Psychologists Annual Meeting." *Chronicle of Higher Education*, September 7, 2007, A14–17.

Glickman, Stephen E. "Hebb, Donald Olding." In Alan E. Kazdin, ed., *Encyclopedia of Psychology*, 105–6. New York: Oxford University Press, 2000.

Greene, Nicholas M. "Henry Knowles Beecher, 1904–1976." *Anesthesiology* 45, no. 4 (October 1976): 377–78.

Greenfield, Patricia. "CIA's Behavior Caper." *APA Monitor* (December 1977). http://www.cia-on-campus.org/social/behavior.html. Accessed August 8, 2011.

Harkness, Jon, Susan E. Lederer, and Daniel Wikler. "Laying Ethical Foundations for Clinical Research." *Bulletin of the World Health Organization* 79, no. 4 (2001): 365–72.

Hartmann, Lawrence, et al. "Psychopathology of Torture Victims." *Torture* 3, no. 2 (1993): 36–38.

Hebb, D. O. "Drives and the C.N.S. (Conceptual Nervous System)." *Psychological Review* 62, no. 4 (1955): 243–54.

———. "This Is How It Was." Canadian Psychological Association, ca. 1980.

Hegland, Corine. "Who Is at Guantánamo Bay." *National Journal*, February 3, 2006. http://www.informationclearinghouse.info/article11825.htm. Accessed February 21, 2006.

Heitzman, Janusz, and Krzysztof Ruthkowski. "Mental Disorders in Persecuted and Tortured Victims of the Totalitarian System in Poland." *Torture* 6, no. 1 (1996): 19–22.

Heron, Woodburn. "The Pathology of Boredom." *Scientific American* 196 (January 1957): 52–56.

Heron, Woodburn, and D. O. Hebb. "Cognitive and Physiological Effect of Perceptual Isolation." In Philip Solomon, et al., eds., *Sensory Deprivation: A Symposium Held at Harvard Medical School*, 239–57. Cambridge, MA: Harvard University Press, 1961.

Hersh, Seymour M. "The Gray Zone: How a Secret Pentagon Program Came to

Abu Ghraib." *New Yorker,* May 24, 2004. http://www.newyorker.com/archive /2004/05/24/040524fa_fact. Accessed June 11, 2011.

———. "Torture at Abu Ghraib." *New Yorker,* May 10, 2004, 42–47.

Hinkle, Lawrence E., Jr. "The Physiological State of the Interrogation Subject as It Affects Brain Function." In Albert D. Biderman and Herbert Zimmer, eds., *The Manipulation of Human Behavior,* 19–50. New York: John Wiley, 1961.

Hinkle, Lawrence E., Jr., and Harold G. Wolff. "Communist Interrogation and Indoctrination of 'Enemies of the States': Analysis of Methods Used by the Communist State Police (A Special Report)." *Archives of Neurology and Psychiatry* 76, no. 2 (1956): 115–74.

Hirsh, Michael. "A Tortured Debate." *Newsweek,* June 21, 2004, 50.

Holcomb, Jesse. "Tortured Logic: Do Shows Like *24* Help Make Torture Acceptable?" *Sojourners Magazine* 36, no. 6 (June 1, 2007). http://www.sojo.net/index .cfm?action=magazine.article&issue=soj0706&article=07064b. Accessed February 15, 2010.

Holst, Erik. "International Efforts on the Rehabilitation of Torture Victims." In June C. Pagaduan Lopez and Elisabeth Protacio Marcelino, eds., *Torture Survivors and Caregivers: Proceedings of the International Workshop on Therapy and Research Issues,* 8–14. Quezon City: University of the Philippines Press, 1995.

Horton, Scott. "Betr: Strafanzeige gegen den US-Verteidigungsminister Donald Rumsfeld, u.a." An den: Herrn Generalbundesanwalt, Beim Bundesgerichtshof, Karlsruhe, January 29, 2005. http://www.rav.de/StAR_290105_Horton.htm. Accessed April 14, 2005.

———. "The Great Guantánamo Puppet Theater." *Harper's,* February 2008. http:// www.harpers.org/archive/2008/02/hbc-90002460. Accessed June 14, 2011.

Ignatieff, Michael. "Mirage in the Desert." *New York Times Magazine,* June 27, 2004. http://199.239.137.245/2004/06/27/magazine/27WWLN.html?pagewanted=1. Accessed December 12, 2011.

———. "What Did the C.I.A. Do to His Father?" *New York Times Magazine,* April 1, 2001, 56–61.

Jones, R. V. "Tizard's Task in the 'War Years' 1935–1952." In *Biographical Memoirs of the Fellows of the Royal Society,* 7:338–41. London: Royal Society, 1961.

Kangleon, Fr. Edgardo. "A Moment of Uncertainty." Manuscript. December 8, 1982.

Katz, Jay. "'Ethics and Clinical Research' Revisited: A Tribute to Henry K. Beecher." *Hastings Center Report* 23, no. 5 (1993): 31–39.

Kaye, Jeffrey. "Iraqi Torture Scandal Touches Highest Levels of NATO." *Truthout,* January 5, 2012. http://www.truth-out.org/iraqi-torture-scandal-touches-highest -levels-nato/1325794053. Accessed February 5, 2012.

Kleinhans, Chuck. "Imagining Torture." *Jump Cut: A Review of Contemporary Media* 51 (Spring 2009). http://www.ejumpcut.org/currentissue/. Accessed September 4, 2009.

Kopp, Vincent J. "Henry K. Beecher, M.D.: Contrarian (1904–1976)." *ASA Newsletter* 63, no. 9 (September 1999). http://www.asahq.org/Newsletters/1999/09_99 /beecher0999.html. Accessed June 5, 2007.

Kordon, Diana R., and Lucila I. Edelman. "Psychological Effects of Political Repression-II." In Diana R. Kordon, Lucila I. Edelman, et al., eds., *Psychological Effects of Political Repression*. Buenos Aires: Sudamericana/Planeta, 1988.

———. "Violation of Human Rights: Text or Context in Couple and Family Analysis." In Diana R. Kordon, Lucila I. Edelman, et al., eds., *Psychological Effects of Political Repression*. Buenos Aires: Sudamericana/Planeta, 1988.

Kordon, Diana R., and Lucila Edelman, et al. "Torture in Argentina." In Metin Basoglu, ed., *Torture and Its Consequences: Current Treatment Approaches*, 433–51. Cambridge: Cambridge University Press, 1992.

Krulak, Charles C., and Joseph P. Hoar. "It's Our Cage, Too: Torture Betrays Us and Breeds New Enemies." *Washington Post*, May 17, 2007. http://www.washington post.com/wp-dyn/content/article/2007/05/16/AR2007051602395.html. Accessed November 21, 2011.

Lambino, Antonio B., S.J. "Theological Reflection on the Filipino Exodus." In Pedro S. de Achutegui, S.J., ed., *The "Miracle" of the Philippine Revolution: Interdisciplinary Reflections*, 14–15. Manila: Loyola School of Theology, Ateneo de Manila University, 1986.

Langbein, John H. "The Legal History of Torture." In Sanford Levinson, ed., *Torture: A Collection*, 93–100. New York: Oxford University Press, 2004.

Lelyveld, Joseph. "Interrogating Ourselves." *New York Times Magazine*, June 12, 2005, 43. http://www.nytimes.com/2005/06/12/magazine/12TORTURE.html? pagewanted=all. Accessed June 17, 2011.

LeMoyne, James. "Testifying to Torture." *New York Times Magazine*, June 5, 1988. http://www.nytimes.com/1988/06/05/magazine/testifying-to-torture.html?page wanted=all&src=pm. Accessed June 17, 2011.

Levine, Arthur. "Collective Unconscionable." *Washington Monthly*, January–February 2007. http://www.washingtonmonthly.com/features/2007/0701.levine.html. Accessed May 28, 2007.

London, Leslie, M.D. "Conference Review. The VII International Symposium. 'Caring for Survivors of Torture: Challenges for the Medical and Health Professions.'" *Torture* 6, no. 3 (1996): 69.

Lopez, June Pagaduan, M.D. "Mainstreaming Is Prevention." *PST Quarterly* 1, no. 1 (April–June 1996): 2.

Luban, David. "Liberalism, Torture, and the Ticking Bomb." *Virginia Law Review* 91, no. 6 (October 2005): 1425–61.

Luce, Don. "The Tiger Cages of Viet Nam." *Historians against the War*. http://www.historiansagainstwar.org/resources/torture/luce.html. Accessed July 12, 2011.

Madariaga, Carlos. "Torture Prevention as a Public Health Problem." *Torture* 6, no. 4 (1996): 86–89.

Mahler, Jonathan. "The Bush Administration vs. Salim Hamdan." *New York Times Magazine*, January 8, 2006, 44–51.

Marcelino, Elisabeth. "The Philippine Experience: Rehabilitation of Survivors of Torture and Political Violence under a Continuing Stress Situation." *Torture* 2, no. 1 (1992): 19–21.

Maresco, Peter A. "Mel Gibson's *The Passion of the Christ*: Market Segmentation, Mass Marketing and Promotion, and the Internet." *Journal of Religion and Popular Culture* 8 (Fall 2004). http://www.usask.ca/relst/jrpc/art8-melgibsonmarketing.html. Accessed February 20, 2010.

Marks, Jonathan H. "The Silence of the Doctors." *The Nation*, December 7, 2005. http://www.thenation.com/article/silence-doctors. Accessed November 30, 2011.

Mayer, Jane. "The Black Sites." *New Yorker*, July 21, 2009. http://www.newyorker.com/reporting/2007/08/13/070813fa_fact_mayer. Accessed July 20, 2009.

———. "Outsourcing Torture: The Secret History of America's 'Extraordinary Rendition' Program." *New Yorker*, February 14, 2005, 106–16.

McCoy, Alfred W. "Invisible in Plain Sight." *Amnesty International Magazine*. http://www.amnestyusa.org/amnesty-magazine/amnesty-magazine/page.do?id=1105051. Accessed September 14, 2009.

———. "The Myth of the Ticking Time Bomb." *The Progressive*, October 2006, 20–24.

Michigan Sea Grant. "40 Years of Great Lakes Research, Education, and Outreach." *Upwellings Online Edition* (December 2009). http://www.miseagrant.umich.edu/upwellings/issues/09dec/09dec-article1-1.html. Accessed April 6, 2011.

Milgram, Stanley. "Group Pressure and Action against a Person." *Journal of Abnormal and Social Psychology* 9, no. 2 (1964): 137–43.

National Association of Criminal Defense Lawyers. "At Guantanamo, Detainees Are Presumed Guilty." NACDL NewsRelease, April 4, 2011. http://www.nacdl.org/public.nsf/NewsReleases/2011mn10?OpenDocument. Accessed July 5, 2011.

National Religious Campaign against Torture. "Urgent: Call Your Senators Today on Torture Amendment." November 29, 2011. http://www.maryknollogc.org/peace/torture_amendment.html. Accessed December 11, 2011.

Nemiroff, Martin J. "Near Drowning." *Respiratory Care* 37, no. 6 (June 1992): 600–608.

Nemiroff, Martin J., G. R. Saltz, and J. G. Weg. "Survival after Cold-Water Near-Drowning: The Protective Effect of the Diving Reflex." *American Review of Respiratory Disease* 115, no. 5 (1977): 145.

Ocampo, Satur C. "Leaving the Pain Behind." *PST Quarterly* 1, no. 2 (July–September 1996): 13.

Oldroyd, Rachel. "The Biggest Document Leak in History Exposes Real War." *Iraqi War Logs*, Bureau of Investigative Journalism, October 1, 2010. http://www.iraqwarlogs.com/2010/10/21/the-leaked-us-files-and-what-they-mean/. Accessed July 13, 2011.

Pagaduan Lopez, June C. "The History of the Study of Psycho-Social Trauma (PST)." In June C. Pagaduan Lopez and Protacio Marcelino, *Torture Survivors and Caregivers: Proceedings of the International Workshop on Therapy and Research Issues,*

77–83. Manila: Subprogram on Psychosocial Trauma, Center for Integrative and Development Studies, University of the Philippines, 1995.

Page, H. E. "The Role of Psychology in ONR." *American Psychologist* 9, no. 10 (1954): 621–22.

Perley, Sharon, et al. "The Nuremberg Code: An International Overview." In George J. Annas and Michael A. Grodin, eds., *The Nazi Doctors and the Nuremberg Code: Human Rights in Human Experimentation*, 149–68. New York: Oxford University Press, 1992.

Porter, Gareth. "Torture Orders Were Part of U.S. Sectarian War Strategy." *Antiwar. com*, November 2, 2010. http://original.antiwar.com/porter/2010/11/01/torture -orders-were-part-of/. Accessed July 28, 2011.

Press, Eyal. "In Torture We Trust?" *The Nation*, March 31, 2003, 11–15.

Pribbenow, Merle L. "The Man in the Snow White Cell: The Limits of Interrogation." Central Intelligence Agency. https://www.cia.gov/library/center-for-the-study -of-intelligence/csi-publications/csi-studies/studies/vol48no1/article06.html. Accessed September 14, 2011.

Price, David H. "Buying a Piece of Anthropology, Part II: The CIA and Our Tortured Past." *Anthropology Today* 23, no. 5, (2007). http://homepages.stmartin.edu/ fac_staff/dprice/Price-AT-HEF2.pdf. Accessed August 5, 2011.

Randall, Steve. "Pro-Pain Pundits." *Extra!* January–February 2002. http://fair.org/ extra/0201/pro-pain.html. Accessed December 22, 2002.

Rasmussen, Ole Vedel. "Medical Aspects of Torture." *Danish Medical Bulletin* 37, no. 1 (1990): 3, 30–31.

Rauh, Joseph L., Jr., and James C. Turner. "Anatomy of a Public Interest Case against the CIA." *Hamline Journal of Public Law and Policy* 11, no. 2 (1990): 307–63.

Rees-Mogg, William. "The Torture Industry." In Rehabilitation and Research Centre for Torture Victims, *Annual Report 1995*, 5–6. Copenhagen: Rehabilitation and Research Centre for Torture Victims, 1996.

Rehabilitation and Research Centre for Torture Victims. "Impunity." In *Annual Report 1995*, 6. Copenhagen: Rehabilitation and Research Centre for Torture Victims, 1996.

Ricchiardi, Sherry. "Missed Signals." *American Journalism Review* (August–September 2004). http://www.ajr.org/Article.asp?id=3716. Accessed February 21, 2010.

Rivera, Temario C. "Details of Torture Inflicted on Temario C. Rivera." Manuscript, August 1996.

Roggio, Bill, and Alexander Mayer. "Charting the Data for US Airstrikes in Pakistan, 2004–2012." *Long War Journal*, May 28, 2012. http://www.longwarjournal.org /pakistan-strikes.php. Accessed May 30, 2012.

Rosner, Cecil. "Isolation: A Canadian Professor's Research into Sensory Deprivation and Its Connection to Disturbing New Methods of Interrogation." *Canada's History* (August–September 2010): 29–37.

Roth, Kenneth. "Review Essay: Getting Away with Torture." *Global Governance* 11, no. 3 (July–September 2005): 389–406.

Sample, Mark L. "Virtual Torture: Video Games and the War on Terror." *Game Studies* 8, no. 2 (December 2008). http://74.125.95.132/search?q=cache:MsjUcyujRsEJ:

gamestudies.org/o8o2/articles/sample+video+games+%22torture%22&hl=en&gl =us&strip=1. Accessed March 1, 2010.

Sanford, Fillmore N. "Summary Report of the 1954 Annual Meeting." *American Psychologist* 9, no. 11 (1954): 708.

Sarantidis, Dimocritos, et al. "Long-Term Effects of Torture of Victims during the Period of Dictatorship in Greece." *Torture* 6, no. 1 (1996): 16–18.

Scahill, Jeremy. "The CIA's Secret Sites in Somalia." *The Nation*, July 12, 2011. http://www .thenation.com/print/article/161936/cias-secret-sites-somalia. Accessed July 28, 2011.

Schein, Edgar H. "Patterns of Reactions to Severe Chronic Stress in American Army Prisoners of War of the Chinese." In *Symposium No. 4. Methods of Forceful Indoctrination: Observations and Interviews*, 253–69. New York: Group for the Advancement of Psychiatry, 1957.

Sherwood, Ellen. "The Power Relationship between Captor and Captive." *Psychiatric Annals* 16, no. 11 (November 1986): 653–55.

Shotland, Michael, and Richard Yeo. "Introduction." In *Telling Lives in Science: Essays on Scientific Biography*, 1–44. Cambridge: Cambridge University Press, 1996.

Silver, Arnold M. "Questions, Questions, Questions: Memories of Oberursel." *Intelligence and National Security* 8, no. 2 (1993): 199–213.

Singer, Maxine F. "Foreword." In James D. Ebert, ed., *This Our Golden Age: Selected Annual Essays of Caryl P. Haskins, President, Carnegie Institution of Washington 1956–1971*, i–x. Washington, DC: Carnegie Institution of Washington, 1996.

Smith, A. T. H. "Disavowing Torture in the House of Lords." *Cambridge Law Journal* 65, no. 2 (July 2006): 251–54.

Söderqvist, Thomas. "Existential Projects and Existential Choice in Science: Science Biography as an Edifying Genre." In Michael Shotland and Richard Yeo, *Telling Lives in Science: Essays on Scientific Biography*, 45–84. Cambridge: Cambridge University Press, 1996.

Soldz, Stephen. "The Seven Paragraphs: Released Binyan Mohamed Abuse Evidence Poses Problems for Both British and US Governments." http://www.opednews .com/articles/The-Seven-Paragraphs-Rele-by-Stephen-Soldz-100210-56.html. Accessed February 10, 2010.

Somnier, Finn, Peter Vesti, Marianne Kastrup, and Inge Kemp Genefke. "Psycho-Social Consequences of Torture: Current Knowledge and Evidence." In Metin Basoglu, ed., *Torture and Its Consequences: Current Treatment Approaches*, 56–71. Cambridge: Cambridge University Press, 1992.

Sontag, Susan. "Regarding the Torture of Others." *New York Times Magazine*, May 23, 2004, 25–29, 42.

Stickler, Angus, and Chris Woods. "US Troops Ordered Not to Investigate Iraqi Torture." *Iraqi War Logs*, Bureau of Investigative Journalism, October 22, 2010. http://www.iraqwarlogs.com/2010/10/22/us-troops-ordered-not-to-investigate -iraqi-torture/. Accessed July 13, 2011.

Suarez-Orozco, Marcelo. "A Grammar of Terror: Pyschocultural Responses to State Terrorism in Dirty War and Post-Dirty War Argentina." In Carolyn Nordstrom and JoAnn Martin, eds., *The Paths to Domination, Resistance, and Terror*, 219–59. Berkeley: University of California Press, 1992.

Taylor, Telford. "Opening Statement for the Prosecution December 9, 1946." In George J. Annas and Michael A. Grodin, eds., *The Nazi Doctors and the Nuremberg Code: Human Rights in Human Experimentation*, 67–93. New York: Oxford University Press, 1992.

Thompson, Clive. "Why We Need More Torture in Videogames." *Wired*, December 15, 2008. http://www.wired.com/gaming/virtualworlds/commentary/games/2008/12/gamesfrontiers_1215. Accessed March 1, 2010.

Tiglao, Rigoberto D. "The Consolidation of the Dictatorship." In Aurora Javate-De Dios et al., eds., *Dictatorship and Revolution: Roots of People's Power*, 26–69. Manila: Conspectus, 1988.

Vest, Jason. "Pray and Tell." *American Prospect* 16, no. 7 (July 2005). http://prospect.org/article/pray-and-tell. Accessed June 12, 2011.

von Felsinger, J. M., L. Lasagna, and H. K. Beecher. "Drug-Induced Mood Changes in Man: 2. Personality and Reactions to Drugs." *Journal of the American Medical Association* 157, no. 13 (March 26, 1955): 1113–19.

———. "The Response of Normal Men to Lysergic Acid Derivatives (Di- and Mono-Ethyl Amides)." *Journal of Clinical and Experimental Psychopathology and Quarterly Review of Psychiatry and Neurology* 17, no. 4 (1956): 414–28.

Walzer, Michael. "Political Action: The Problem of Dirty Hands." *Philosophy and Public Affairs* 2, no. 2 (1973): 160–80.

Weisberg, Richard H. "Loose Professionalism, or Why Lawyers Take the Lead on Torture." In Sanford Levinson, ed., *Torture: A Collection*, 299–305. New York: Oxford University Press, 2004.

Weiss Fagen, Patricia. "Repression and State Security." In Juan E. Corradi, Patricia Weiss Fagen and Manuel Antonio Garretón, eds., *Fear at the Edge: State Terror and Resistance in Latin America*, 39–71. Berkeley: University of California Press, 1992.

West, Louis J. "United States Air Force Prisoners of the Chinese Communists." In *Symposium No. 4. Methods of Forceful Indoctrination: Observations and Interviews*, 270–84. New York: Group of the Advancement of Psychiatry, 1957.

Wexler, Donald, Jack Mendelson, Herbert Leiderman, and Philip Solomon. "Sensory Deprivation: A Technique for Studying Psychiatric Aspects of Stress." *A.M.A. Archives of Neurology and Psychiatry* 79, no. 1 (1958): 225–33.

Wheeler, Mary. "The 13 People Who Made Torture Possible." *Salon.com*, May 18, 2009. http://www.salon.com/news/feature/2009/05/18/torture/print.html. Accessed July 6, 2011.

Wilkerson, Colonel Lawrence B. "The Truth About Richard Bruce Cheney." *Washington Note*, May 13, 2009. http://www.thewashingtonnote.com/archives/2009/05/the_truth_about/. Accessed July 28, 2011.

Zagorin, Adam, and Michael Duffy. "Inside the Interrogation of Detainee 063." *Time*, June 20, 2005, 26–33.

Zimbardo, Philip. "When Good People Do Evil." *Yale Alumni Magazine* 70, no. 3

(January/February 2007). http://www.yalealumnimagazine.com/issues/2007_01 /milgram.html. Accessed June 15, 2011.

Books

Abat, Fortunato U. *The Day We Nearly Lost Mindanao: The CEMCOM Story.* San Juan: FCA, 1993.

Anderson, Martin Edward. *Dossier Secreto: Argentina's Desaparecidos and the Myth of the "Dirty War".* Boulder: Westview Press, 1993.

Aruiza, Arturo C. *Ferdinand E. Marcos: Malacañang to Makiki.* Quezon City: ACAruiza Enterprises, 1991.

Association of Major Religious Superiors in the Philippines. *Political Detainees in the Philippines Book Two.* Manila: Association of Major Religious Superiors in the Philippines, 1977.

Ayap, Jose G. *The 1971 Sword.* Baguio City: Cadet Corps Armed Forces of the Philippines, 1971.

Baer, Ron. *See No Evil: The True Story of a Ground Soldier in the CIA's War on Terrorism.* New York: Three Rivers Press, 2002.

Beecher, Henry K. *Measurement of Subjective Responses: Quantitative Effects of Drugs.* New York: Oxford University Press, 1959.

Blass, Thomas. *The Man Who Shocked the World: The Life and Legacy of Stanley Milgram.* New York: Basic Books, 2004.

Boulesbaa, Ahcene. *The U.N. Convention on Torture and the Prospects for Enforcement.* The Hague: Martinus Nijhoff, 1999.

Bowart, Walter. *Operation Mind Control.* New York: Dell Publishing, 1978.

Bower, Tom. *The Paperclip Conspiracy: The Hunt for Nazi Scientists.* Boston: Little, Brown, 1987.

Browning, Christopher R. *Ordinary Men: Reserve Police Battalion 101 and the Final Solution in Poland.* New York: HarperCollins, 1998.

Cheney, Dick. *In My Time: A Personal and Political Memoir.* New York: Threshold Editions, 2011.

Clark, Ronald W. *Tizard.* London: Methuen, 1965.

Clarke, Richard A. *Against All Enemies: Inside America's War on Terror.* New York: Free Press, 2004.

Cockburn, Alexander, and Jeffrey St. Clair. *Whiteout: The CIA, Drugs, and the Press.* New York: Verso, 1998.

Cosculluela, Manuel Hevia. *Pasaporte 11333: Ocho Años con la CIA.* Havana: Editorial de Ciencias Sociales, 1978.

Danner, Mark. *Torture and Truth: America, Abu Ghraib, and the War on Terror.* New York: New York Review of Books, 2004.

Dassin, Joan, ed. *Torture in Brazil.* New York: Vintage Books, 1986.

DeForest, Orrin, and David Chanoff. *Slow Burn: The Rise and Bitter Fall of American Intelligence in Vietnam.* New York: Simon and Schuster, 1990.

Dershowitz, Alan M. *Why Terrorism Works: Understanding the Threat, Responding to the Challenge.* New Haven: Yale University Press, 2002.

Duque, Colonel Sinforoso L. *Soldier Heroes: A Handbook on the Winners of the Major Medals Awarded by the Philippine Constabulary and Armed Forces since 1902.* Manila: National Media Production Center, 1981.

Eisenman, Stephen F. *The Abu Ghraib Effect.* London: Reaktion Books, 2007.

Feitlowitz, Marguerite. *A Lexicon of Terror: Argentina and the Legacies of Torture.* New York: Oxford University Press, 1998.

Foucault, Michel. *Discipline and Punish: The Birth of the Prison.* New York: Vintage, 1979.

Gay, Peter. *Voltaire's Politics: The Poet as Realist.* New York: Vintage, 1965.

Goliszek, Andrew. *In the Name of Science: A History of Secret Programs, Medical Research, and Human Experimentation.* New York: St. Martin's Press, 2003.

Graziano, Frank. *Divine Violence: Spectacle, Psychosexuality, and Radical Christianity in the Argentine "Dirty War."* Boulder: Westview Press, 1992.

Grey, Stephen. *Ghost Plane: The True Story of the CIA Torture Program.* New York: St. Martin's Press, 2006.

Gudjonsson, Gisli H. *The Psychology of Interrogations, Confessions, and Testimony.* New York: John Wiley and Sons, 1996.

Habib, Mamdouh. *My Story: The Tale of a Terrorist Who Wasn't.* Melbourne: Scribe, 2008.

Hebb, D. O. *Essay on Mind.* Hillsdale: Lawrence Erlbaum Associates, 1980.

———. *The Organization of Behavior: A Neuropsychological Theory.* New York: John Wiley and Sons, 1949.

Hellman, Hal. *Great Feuds in Science: Ten of the Liveliest Disputes Ever.* New York: John Wiley and Sons, 1998.

Hersh, Seymour M. *Chain of Command: The Road from 9/11 to Abu Ghraib.* New York: HarperCollins, 2004.

Hicks, David. *Guantanamo: My Journey.* Sydney: William Heinemann, 2010.

Hodge, James, and Linda Cooper, *Disturbing the Peace: The Story of Father Roy Bourgeois and the Movement to Close the School of the Americas.* Maryknoll: Orbis Books, 2004.

Hunt, Linda. *Secret Agenda: The United States Government, Nazi Scientists, and Project Paperclip, 1945 to 1990.* New York: St. Martin's Press, 1991.

Isikoff, Michael, and David Corn. *Hubris: The Inside Story of Spin, Scandal, and the Selling of the Iraq War.* New York: Crown, 2006.

Janis, Irving L. *Are the Cominform Countries Using Hypnotic Techniques to Elicit Confessions in Public Trials?* Santa Monica: Rand Corporation, U.S. Air Force Project Rand Research Memorandum, RM-161, April 25, 1949.

Klare, Michael T. *War Without End: American Planning for the Next Vietnams.* New York: Alfred A. Knopf, 1972.

Koch, Egmont R., and Michael Wech. *Deckname Artischocke.* Munich: Random House, 2003.

Komer, R. W. *Organization and Management of the "New Model" Pacification Program—1966–1969*. Santa Monica: Rand Corporation, 1970.

Krepinevich, Andrew F., Jr. *The Army and Vietnam*. Baltimore: Johns Hopkins University Press, 1986.

Kritz, Neil J., ed. *Transitional Justice: How Emerging Democracies Reckon with Former Regimes*. Volume 3, *Laws, Rulings, and Reports*. Washington, DC: U.S. Institute for Peace, 1995.

Langbein, John. *Torture and the Law of Proof: Europe and England in the Ancien Regime*. Chicago: University of Chicago Press, 1977.

Langguth, A. J. *Hidden Terrors*. New York: Pantheon, 1978.

Lawyers Committee for International Human Rights. *The Philippines: A Country in Crisis*. New York: Lawyers Committee, 1983.

Lee, Martin A., and Bruce Shlain. *Acid Dreams: The Complete Social History of LSD: The CIA, the Sixties, and Beyond*. New York: Grove Press, 1985.

Lifton, Robert Jay. *The Nazi Doctors: Medical Killing and the Psychology of Genocide*. New York: Basic Books, 1986.

Loftus, John. *The Belarus Secret*. New York: Knopf, 1982.

Maestro, Marcello. *Voltaire and Beccaria as Reformers of Criminal Law*. New York: Columbia University Press, 1942.

Maglipon, Jo-Ann Q. *Primed: Selected Stories, 1972–1992*. Manila: Anvil, 1993.

Marchetti, Victor, and John D. Marks. *The CIA and the Cult of Intelligence*. New York: Alfred A. Knopf, 1974.

Marcos, Ferdinand E. *Notes on the New Society of the Philippines*. Manila: Marcos Foundation, 1973.

Marguilies, Joseph. *Guantanamo and the Abuse of Presidential Power*. New York: Simon and Schuster, 2006.

Marks, John. *The Search for the "Manchurian Candidate": The CIA and Mind Control*. New York: Times Books, 1979.

Masterman, J.C. *The Double-Cross System: The Incredible True Story of How Nazi Spies Were Turned into Double Agents*. New York: Lyons Press, 2000.

Mayer, Jane. *The Dark Side*. New York: Anchor Books, 2009.

McCoy, Alfred W. *A Question of Torture: CIA Interrogation, from the Cold War to the War on Terror*. New York: Metropolitan Books, 2006.

———. *Priests on Trial*. Melbourne: Penguin Books, 1984.

McGehee, Ralph W. *Deadly Deceits: My 25 Years in the CIA*. New York: Sheridan Square Publications, 1983.

McNeill, Ian. *The Team: Australian Army Advisers in Vietnam, 1962–1972*. St. Lucia: University of Queensland Press, 1984.

Mellor, Alec. *La Torture: Son histoire, son abolition, sa réapparition au XXe siecle*. Paris: Horizons Litteraires, 1949.

Merback, Mitchell B. *The Thief, the Cross and the Wheel: Pain and the Spectacle of Punishment in Medieval and Renaissance Europe*. Chicago: University of Chicago Press, 1999.

Mercade, Rev. La Verne D., and Sister Mariani Dimaranan. *Philippines: Testimonies on Human Rights Violations*. Manila: World Council of Churches, 1986.

Milgram, Stanley. *Obedience to Authority: An Experimental View*. New York: Harper and Row, 1974.

Millacus, Joannes. *Praxis Criminis Persequendi*. Paris: Prostant and Simonem Colinacum, 1541.

Miller, Arthur G. *The Obedience Experiments: A Case Study of Controversy in Social Science*. New York: Praeger Publishers, 1986.

Miranda, Felipe. *The Politicization of the Military*. Quezon City: University of the Philippines Press, 1992.

Moreno, Jonathan D. *Undue Risk: Secret State Experiments on Humans*. New York: W. H. Freeman, 2000.

Moyar, Mark. *Phoenix and the Birds of Prey: The CIA's Secret Campaign to Destroy the Viet Cong*. Annapolis: Naval Institute Press, 1997.

The New Oxford Annotated Bible. New York: Oxford University Press, 1994.

Olsfen, James, ed. *Dictionary of the Vietnam War*. New York: Peter Bedrick Books, 1987.

Oshinsky, David M. *Polio: An American Story*. New York: Oxford University Press, 2005.

Pagaduan Lopez, June C., Lan Mercado Carreon, et al. *Human Rights Violations: What Perpetuates the Perpetrator*. Quezon City: Psychosocial Trauma Program, Center for Integrative and Development Studies, University of the Philippines, 1995.

Para Sa Bansa Gringo Honasan Sa Senado. Quezon City: Benny J. Brizuela, 1995.

Parry, Robert. *Lost History: Contras, Cocaine, and Other Crimes*. Arlington: Media Consortium 1997.

Peters, Edward. *Torture*. Philadelphia: University of Pennsylvania Press, 1996.

Promotion of Church People's Rights. *That We May Remember*. Quezon City: PCPR, May 1989.

Ranelagh, John. *The Agency: The Rise and Decline of the CIA*. New York: Simon and Schuster, 1986.

Ratner, Michael, and Ellen Ray. *Guantanamo: What the World Should Know*. White River Junction: Chelsea Green, 2004.

Rothman, Daniel J. *Strangers at the Bedside: A History of How Law and Bioethics Transformed Medical Decision Making*. New York: Basic Books, 1991.

Ruthven, Malise. *Torture: The Grand Conspiracy*. London: Weidenfeld and Nicolson, 1979.

Sales, Leigh. *Detainee 002: The Case of David Hicks*. Melbourne: Melbourne University Press, 2007.

Sallah, Michael D., and Mitch Weiss. *Tiger Force: A True Story of Men and War*. New York: Little, Brown, 2006.

Sands, Philippe. *Torture Team: Rumsfeld's Memo and the Betrayal of American Values*. New York: Macmillan, 2009.

Santiago, Angela Stuart. *Duet for EDSA: 1986 Chronology of a Revolution.* Manila: Foundation for Worldwide People Power, 1995.

Scarry, Elaine. *The Body in Pain: The Making and Unmaking of the World.* New York: Oxford University Press, 1985.

Schmidt, Ulf. *Justice at Nuremberg: Leo Alexander and the Nazi Doctors' Trial.* New York: Palgrave Macmillan, 2004.

Schultz, Richard H., Jr., *The Secret War against Hanoi: Kennedy's and Johnson's Use of Spies, Saboteurs, and Covert Warriors in North Vietnam.* New York: HarperCollins, 1999.

Scott, Peter Dale. *Listening to the Candle: A Poem on Impulse.* Toronto: McClelland and Stewart, 1992.

Simons, Lewis M. *Worth Dying For.* New York: William Morrow, 1987.

Simpson, Christopher. *Science of Coercion: Communication Research and Psychological Warfare, 1945–1960.* New York: Oxford University Press, 1994.

Slotten, Ross A. *The Heretic in Darwin's Court: The Life of Alfred Russel Wallace.* New York: Columbia University Press, 2004.

Snepp, Frank. *Decent Interval: The American Debacle in Vietnam and the Fall of Saigon.* London: Allen Lane, 1980.

Solomon, Philip, et al., eds., *Sensory Deprivation: A Symposium Held at Harvard Medical School.* Cambridge, MA: Harvard University Press, 1961.

Soufan, Ali H. *The Black Banners: The Inside Story of 9/11 and the War against al-Qaeda.* New York: W. W. Norton, 2011.

Task Force Detainees. *Pumipiglas: Political Detention and Military Atrocities in the Philippines.* Manila: Task Force Detainees of the Philippines, Association of Major Religious Superiors in the Philippines, 1980.

———. *Pumipiglas: Political Detention and Military Atrocities in the Philippines, 1981–1982.* Manila: Task Force Detainees of the Philippines, Association of Major Religious Superiors in the Philippines, 1986.

Taussig, Michael. *Shamanism, Colonialism, and the Wild Man: A Study in Terror and Healing.* Chicago: University of Chicago Press, 1987.

Thomas, Gordon. *Journey into Madness: Medical Torture and the Mind Controllers.* London: Bantam Press, 1988.

Valentine, Douglas. *The Phoenix Program.* New York: William Morrow, 1990.

Vrij, Aldert. *Detecting Lies and Deceit: The Psychology of Lying and the Implications for Professional Practice.* New York: John Wiley and Sons, 2000.

Vitug, Marites Dañguilan, and Glenda M. Gloria. *Under the Crescent Moon: Rebellion in Mindanao.* Quezon City: Ateneo Center for Social Policy and Public Affairs, 2000.

Weiner, Tim. *Legacy of Ashes: The History of the CIA.* New York: Random House, 2008.

Weinstein, Harvey M. *Psychiatry and the CIA: Victims of Mind Control.* Washington, DC: American Psychiatric Press, 1990.

Welsome, Eileen. *The Plutonium Files: America's Secret Medical Experiments in the Cold War.* New York: Delta, 1999.

Weschler, Lawrence. *A Miracle, a Universe: Settling Accounts with Torturers.* New York: Pantheon, 1990.

Wilson, Grove. *Great Men of Science: Their Lives and Discoveries.* New York: New Home Library, 1929.

Wohlstetter, Roberta. *Pearl Harbor: Warning and Decision.* Stanford: Stanford University Press, 1962.

Woodward, Bob. *The War Within: A Secret White House History, 2006–2008.* New York: Simon and Schuster, 2008.

Yabes, Criselda. *The Boys from the Barracks: The Philippine Military after EDSA.* Manila: Anvil, 1991.

Yoo, John. *War by Other Means: An Insider's Account of the War on Terror.* New York: Atlantic Monthly Press, 2006.

Zimmerman, David. *Top Secret Exchange: The Tizard Mission and the Scientific War.* Montreal: McGill-Queen's University Press, 1996.

U.S. Congressional Documents and Reports

92d Congress, 1st Session. Subcommittee of the Committee on Government Operations, Hearings on August 2, 1971, *U.S. Assistance Programs in Vietnam.* Washington, DC: Government Printing Office, 1971.

93d Congress, 1st Session. Committee on Armed Services, Hearings on July 2, 20, 25, 1973, *Nomination of William E. Colby To Be Head of Central Intelligence.* Washington, DC: Government Printing Office, 1973.

93d Congress, 2d Session. Committee on Foreign Relations, *Foreign Assistance Act of 1974: Report of the Committee on Foreign Relations United States Senate on S. 3394 to Amend the Foreign Assistance Act of 1961, and For Other Purposes.* Washington, DC: Government Printing Office, 1974.

94th Congress, 2d Session. *Final Report of the Select Committee to Study Governmental Operations with Respect to Intelligence Activities. Book I.* Washington, DC: Government Printing Office, 1976.

95th Congress, 1st Session. *Project MKUltra: The CIA's Program of Research in Behavioral Modification. Joint Hearing before the Select Committee on Intelligence and the Subcommittee on Health and Scientific Research of the Committee on Human Resources.* Washington, DC: Government Printing Office, 1977.

100th Congress, 2d Session. Treaty Doc. 100-20, *Message from the President of the United States Transmitting the Convention against Torture and Other Cruel, Inhuman or Degrading Treatment or Punishment.* Washington, DC: Government Printing Office, 1988.

100th Congress, 2d Session. Select Committee on Intelligence, "Transcript of Proceedings before the Select Committee on Intelligence: Honduran Interrogation Manual Hearing." June 16, 1988, Box 1, CIA Training Manuals, Folder: Interrogation Manual Hearings, National Security Archive.

101st Congress, 2d Session. Committee on Foreign Relations, *Convention against Tor-*

ture: Hearing before the Committee on Foreign Relations. Washington, DC: Government Printing Office, 1990.

102d Congress, 1st Session. Report 102-249, Committee on the Judiciary, *The Torture Victims Protection Act.* U.S. Senate, Calendar No. 382, November 26, 1991.

107th Congress, 2d Session. Cofer Black, Testimony to Senate Select Committee on Intelligence, Joint Inquiry into Intelligence Community Activities before and after the Terrorist Attacks of September 11, 2001, September 26, 2002. http://www.fas.org/irp/congress/2002_hr/092602black.html. Accessed May 22, 2011.

107th Congress, 2d Session. Committee on Armed Services. "Counter Resistance Strategy Minutes," October 2, 2002, TAB 7. "The origins of aggressive interrogation techniques; Part I of the Committee's inquiry into the treatment of detainees in U.S. custody." http://www.scribd.com/doc/33064573/Guantanamo-Source-2. Accessed August 2, 2011.

108th Congress, 2d Session. Senate and House Armed Services Committees, *Testimony of Secretary of Defense Donald H. Rumsfeld,* May 7, 2004. http://www.defenselink.mil/speeches/speech.aspx?speechid=118. Accessed August 25, 2009.

109th Congress, 1st Session. Armed Services Committee, *Hearing on Guantanamo Bay Detainee Treatment,* July 13, 2005. http://humanrights.ucdavis.edu/projects/the-guantanamo-testimonials-project/testimonies/testimonies-of-the-defense-department/senate-armed-services-committee-hearing-on-guantanamo-bay-detainee-treatment. Accessed October 4, 2011.

109th Congress, 1st Session. Panel II of a Hearing of the Senate Judiciary Committee, Subject: Detainees, Chaired by: Senator Arlen Specter (R-PA), June 15, 2005. http://www.access.gpo.gov/congress/senate/pdf/109hrg/24332.pdf. Accessed June 21, 2005.

109th Congress, 2d Session. *H.R. 6166: A Bill to Amend Title 10, United States Code, to Authorize Trial by Military Commission for Violations of the Law of War and for Other Purposes,* September 25, 2006. http://www.gpo.gov/fdsys/pkg/BILLS-109hr6166rfs/pdf/BILLS-109hr6166rfs.pdf. Accessed February 12, 2012.

109th Congress, 2d Session. *Report of the Select Committee on Intelligence on Postwar Findings About Iraq's WMD Programs and Links to Terrorism and How They Compare with Prewar Assessments.* Washington, DC: Government Printing Office, 2006.

110th Congress, 1st Session. House Committee on Foreign Affairs, Subcommittee on International Organizations, Human Rights, and Oversight, Subcommittee on Europe, *Extraordinary Rendition in U.S. Counter Terrorism Policy: The Impact on Transatlantic Relations.* Washington, DC: Government Printing Office, 2007.

110th Congress, 2d Session. Committee on Armed Services, *Hearing to Receive Testimony on the Origins of Aggressive Interrogation Techniques: Part I of the Committee's Inquiry into the Treatment of Detainees in U.S. Custody (A.M Session).* Washington, DC: Government Printing Office, June 17, 2008.

110th Congress, 2d Session. Committee on Armed Services, *Inquiry into the Treatment of Detainees in U.S. Custody.* Washington, DC: Government Printing Office,

2008. http://armed-services.senate.gov/Publications/Detainee%20Report%20 Final_April%2022%202009.pdf. Accessed July, 21, 2009.

111th Congress, 1st Session. Committee on the Judiciary, *What Went Wrong: Torture and the Office of Legal Counsel in the Bush Administration.* Testimony of Ali Soufan, May 13, 2009. http://judiciary.senate.gov/hearings/. Accessed August 29, 2011.

112th Congress, 1st Session. National Defense Authorization Act for Fiscal Year 2012 (Senate, November 30, 2011). http://www.lawfareblog.com/wp-content/uploads /2011/12/Senate-NDAA-Debate-Nov-30-2011.pdf. Accessed December 11, 2011.

112th Congress, 1st Session. National Defense Authorization Act, NDAA Senate Debate: Detainee Provisions, December 1, 2011. http://www.lawfareblog.com/wp -content/uploads/2011/12/Senate-NDAA-Debate-Dec-1-2011.pdf. Accessed December 11, 2011.

112th Congress, 1st Session. Select Committee on Intelligence, Nomination of General David Petraeus to Be Director of the Central Intelligence Agency, Questions for the Record, n.d. http://intelligence.senate.gov/110623/responses.pdf. Accessed November 21, 2011.

112th Congress, 1st Session. Select Intelligence Committee Holds Confirmation Hearing on the Nomination of General David H. Petraeus to Be CIA Director, June 23, 2011, *CQ Congressional Transcripts* (copy provided by office of Senator Dianne Feinstein, November 21, 2011).

U.S. Government Documents

The 9/11 Commission Report: Final Report of the National Commission on Terrorist Attacks upon the United States. New York: W. W. Norton, 2004.

Alberto R. Gonzales, Memorandum for the President, Subject: Decision re. Application of the Geneva Convention on Prisoners of War to the Conflict with Al Qaeda and the Taliban, January 25, 2002. http://news.lp.findlaw.com/hdocs/docs /torture/gnzls12502mem2gwb.html. Accessed February 6, 2012.

Allen Dulles to Undersecretary of State and Deputy Secretary of Defense, Memorandum, February 1953, Jackson, C. D.: Records, 1953–54, Box 2. "Brainwashing," Dwight D. Eisenhower Library.

Arthur M. Turner, M.D. to Dr. Henry K. Beecher, letter, February 7, 1947, Box 6, CIA Behavior Control Experiments Collection (John Marks Donation), National Security Archive.

Arthur M. Turner, M.D. to Dr. Henry K. Beecher, letter, March 24, 1947, Box 6, CIA Behavior Control Experiments Collection (John Marks Donation), National Security Archive.

BG Richard P. Formica. "Article 15–6 Investigation of CJSOTF-AP and 5th SF Group Detention Operations" (June 7, 2006). http://action.aclu.org/torturefoia /released/061906/FormicaReport.pdf. Accessed February 15, 2012.

Central Intelligence Agency. "Human Resource Exploitation Training Manual—1983."

http://www.gwu.edu/~nsarchiv/NSAEBB/NSAEBB27/02-06.htm. Accessed August 3, 2011, National Security Archive.

———. "Human Resource Exploitation Training Manual 1983." June 8, 1988, Box 1, CIA Training Manuals, Folder: Resources Exploitation Training Manual, National Security Archive.

———. Internal Security in South Vietnam—Phoenix, December 12, 1970. http://www.thememoryhole.org/phoenix/internal-security.pdf. Accessed May 8, 2006.

———. "KUBARK Counterintelligence Interrogation." July 1963. File: KUBARK, Box 1, CIA Training Manuals, National Security Archive.

———. "Memorandum for the Record, Subject: Project Artichoke." January 31, 1975. National Security Archive. http://www.gwu.edu/~nsarchiv/NSAEBB/NSAEBB54/st02.pdf. Accessed January 2, 2012.

———. Minutes of Meeting, June 6, 1951. File: Artichoke Docs. 59–155, Box 5, Central Intelligence Agency, Memorandum For: Assistant Director, SI, Subject: Progress on BLUEBIRD, July 9, 1951, File: Artichoke Docs. 59–155, Box 5, CIA Behavior Control Experiments Collection (John Marks Donation), National Security Archive.

———. Project NM 001 056.0, May 1, 1952, File: Naval Research, Box 8, CIA Behavior Control Experiments Collection (John Marks Donation), National Security Archive.

———. "Special Review: Counterterrorism Detention and Interrogation Activities (September 2001–October 2003)." May 7, 2004. http://www.aclu.org/torture foia/released/052708/052708_Special_Review.pdf. Accessed October 5, 2011.

———. Subject: Special Interrogation Program, March 19, 1951. CIA Behavior Control Experiments Collection (John Marks Donation), National Security Archive.

———. "Summary of Remarks by Mr. Allen W. Dulles at the National Alumni Conference of the Graduate Council of Princeton University, Hot Springs, VA." April 10, 1953. File: Artichoke Docs: 362–388, Box 5, CIA Behavior Control Experiments Collection, National Security Archive.

Charles E. Wilson to Allen Dulles, George Morgan (Acting Director of PSB), Mr. Nash, Letter, February 19, 1953, White House Office, National Security Council Staff: Papers, 1953–61, Psychological Strategy Board (PSB) Central Files Series, Box 29, "PSB 702.5 (1) Brainwashing during Korean War," Dwight D. Eisenhower Library.

Charles R. Norberg (Acting Deputy Assistant Director, Office of Coordination) to William Godel (Department of Defense), Memorandum, October 8, 1953, White House Office, National Security Council Staff: Papers, 1953–61, Psychological Strategy Board (PSB) Central Files Series, Box 26, "PSB 383.6 [Prisoners of War] (File #2) (2)," Dwight D. Eisenhower Library.

Charles R. Norberg (Acting Deputy Assistant Director, Office of Coordination). "Forced Confessions." Memorandum for the Record, May 8, 1953, White House Office, National Security Council Staff: Papers, 1953–61, Psychological Strategy Board (PSB) Central Files Series, Box 29, "PSB 702.5 (1) Brainwashing during Korean War," Dwight D. Eisenhower Library.

Chauncey D. Leake to Henry K. Beecher, letter, June 7, 1955, Box 6, CIA Behavior Control Experiments Collection (John Marks Donation), National Security Archive.

Congressional Fact Sheet, June 8, 1988, Introduction to Central Intelligence Agency, *Human Resources Exploitation Training Manual—1983*, Box 1, CIA Training Manuals, National Security Archive.

Daniel Levin, Acting Assistant Attorney General, Office of Legal Counsel. "Legal Standards Applicable under 18 U.S.C. §§ 2340–2340A," December 30, 2004. http://www.justice.gov/olc/18usc23402340a2.htm. Accessed September 19, 2011.

Department of the Army, Headquarters, *FM 34–52: Intelligence Interrogation*. Washington, DC: Department of the Army, September 28, 1992.

Donald Rumsfeld, Memorandum for the Commander, U.S. Southern Command, April 16, 2003. http://www.washingtonpost.com/wp-srv/nation/documents/041603rumsfeld.pdf. Accessed June 28, 2004.

Dwight D. Eisenhower. "Executive Order 10631—Code of Conduct for Members of the Armed Forces of the United States," August 17, 1955, American Presidency Project, University of California at Santa Barbara. http://www.presidency.ucsb.edu/ws/index.php?pid=59249#axzz1ZwwbuVnm. Accessed October 4, 2011.

Embtel 440, Embassy Madrid to State, 05 May 2009, Official Use Only, SUBJECT: Garzon Opens Second Investigation into Alleged U.S. Torture of Terrorism Detainees. Wikileaks Cablegate Archive, Reference ID: 09MADRID440. http://www.wikileaks.ch/cable/2009/05/09MADRID440.html. Accessed September 14, 2011.

Embtel 392, Embassy Madrid to State, 17 April 2009, Confidential, Subject: Spain: Attorney General Recommends Court Not Pursue GTMO Criminal Case vs. Former USG Officials, WikiLeaks Cablegate Archive, Reference ID: 09MADRID392. http://wikileaks.org/cable/2009/04/09MADRID392.html#. Accessed September 14, 2011.

Foreign Relations Authorization Act, PL 103–236, Title V, Sec. 506, 108 Stat. 463 (1994), 18 USC§ 2340–2340A.

General Joseph Hoar, USMC (ret.) et al., Letter to Chairman Warner, September 12, 2006. http://graphics8.nytimes.com/packages/pdf/politics/jagletter.pdf. Accessed September 22, 2006.

———. Letter to Senator McCain July 25, 2005. http://www.humanrightsfirst.org/us_law/etn/pdf/mccain-072205.pdf. Accessed August 2, 2005.

George W. Bush, The White House, Washington, For: The Vice President. "Subject: Humane Treatment of Taliban and al Qaeda Detainees," February 7, 2002. www.pegc.us/archive/White_House/bush_memo_20040207.doc. Accessed November 30, 2011.

Gordon E. Reckord, Memorandum to Dr. Craig, September 18, 1953, Psychological Strategy Board (PSB) Central Files Series, Box 29, PSB 702.5 (2), "Brainwashing during Korean War," Dwight D. Eisenhower Library.

Harold Hongju Koh, Dean Yale Law School, Statement before the Senate Committee on the Judiciary regarding *Hamdan v. Rumsfeld*: Establishing a Constitutional Process, July 11, 2006. http://www.law.yale.edu/documents/pdf/Deans_Office /KOH__Hamdan_TESTIMONY.pdf. Accessed June 15, 2011.

Henry K. Beecher to Colonel William S. Stone, letter, August 29, 1950, Box 6, CIA Behavior Control Experiments Collection (John Marks Donation), National Security Archive.

Henry K. Beecher to Colonel William S. Stone, June 15, 1950, Box 6, CIA Behavior Control Experiments Collection (John Marks Donation), National Security Archive.

Henry K. Beecher to Dr. E. Rothlin, August 4, 1952; letter from Henry K. Beecher to Colonel William S. Stone, August 29, 1950, Box 6, CIA Behavior Control Experiments Collection (John Marks Donation), National Security Archive.

———. Consultant, Subject: Information from Europe Related to the Ego-Depressants, 6 August to 29 August 1952, September 4, 1952, CIA Behavior Control Experiments Collection (John Marks Donation), National Security Archive.

Henry K. Beecher to the Surgeon General, letter, Department of the Army, October 21, 1951, Box 16, RG 319, U.S. National Archives and Research Administration (NARA), Project Title: Neuropsychiatry and Stress, Addendum. Beecher (MD 92), "Final Report, Response of Normal Men to Lysergic Acid Derivatives (Di- and Monoethylamide). Correlation of Personality and Drug Reactions," December 31, 1954, Box 6, CIA Behavior Control Experiments Collection (John Marks Donation), National Security Archive.

Henry P. Laughlin, M.D. "Brainwashing: A Supplemental Report." (Chairman, Public Information Committee, American Psychiatric Association), June 10, 1953, White House Office, National Security Council Staff: Papers, 1953–61, Psychological Strategy Board (PSB) Central Files Series, Box 29, "PSB 702.5 (1) Brainwashing during Korean War," Dwight D. Eisenhower Library.

House Armed Services Committee, Press Release. "Chairman Hunter Opening Statement, Hearing on Military Commissions and Standards Utilized in Trying Detainees," September 7, 2006. http://www.globalsecurity.org/security/library /congress/2006_h/060907-hunteropeningstatement.pdf. Accessed September 18, 2006.

ICEX Briefing, n.d. http://www.thememoryhole.org/phoenix/icex_briefing.pdf. Accessed May 8, 2006.

James R. Schlesinger et al. "Final Report of the Independent Panel to Review DoD Detention Operations," August 2004, 9, htttp://news.findlaw.com/cnn/docs/dod /abughraibrpt.pdf. Accessed August 26, 2004.

Jay S. Bybee. Office of the Assistant Attorney General. "Memorandum for Alberto R. Gonzales, Counsel to the President, Re.: Standards of Conduct for Interrogation under 18 U.S.C. §§ 2340–2340A," August 1, 2002. news.findlaw.com/wp/docs /doj/bybee80102mem.pdf. Accessed October 4, 2011.

———. Office of the Assistant Attorney General. "Memorandum for John Rizzo, Acting General Counsel of the Central Intelligence Agency. Interrogation of al Qaeda

Operative," August 1, 2002. http://www.globalsecurity.org/intell/library/policy /national/olc_020801_bybee.htm. Accessed October 4, 2011.

————. Assistant Attorney General, Office of Legal Counsel, U.S. Department of Justice. "Memorandum for Alberto R. Gonzales, Counsel to the President, and William J. Haynes II, General Counsel of the Department of Defense," January 22, 2002. http://www.washingtonpost.com/wp-srv/nation/documents/012202 bybee.pdf. Accessed June 28, 2004.

John Bruce Jessen. "Advances in Clinical Psychological Support of National Security Affairs, Operational Problems in the Behavioral Sciences Course." Symposium: Advances in Clinical Psychological Support of National Security Affairs" (n.d.), attached to Jason Leopold and Jeffrey Kaye. "CIA Psychologist's Notes Reveal True Purpose Behind Bush's Torture Program." *Truthout*, March 22, 2011. http:// www.truth-out.org/cia-psychologists-notes-reveal-bushs-torture-program68542. Accessed June 29, 2011.

John G. Lybrand, MACCORDS, Evaluation Report: Processing of Viet Cong Suspects, December 11, 1967. http://www.thememoryhole.org/phoenix/evaluation -report.pdf. Accessed May 8, 2006.

Joint Interrogation and Debriefing Center, Abu Ghurayb, Iraq. http://www.public integrity.org/docs/AbuGhraib/Tag29.pdf. Accessed March 29, 2005.

L. Wade Lathram, MACCORDS, Memorandum For: Ambassador R. W. Komer, Subject: Action Program for Attack on VC Infrastructure, 1967–1968, July 27, 1967. http://www.thememoryhole.org/phoenix/action_program.pdf. Accessed May 8, 2006.

Lawrence E. Hinkle, Jr. "A Consideration of the Circumstances Under Which Men May Be Interrogated, and the Effects That These May Have Upon the Function of the Brain" (n.d., ca. 1958), File: Hinkle, Box 7, CIA Behavior Control Experiments Collection (John Marks Donation), National Security Archive.

Library of Congress, Thomas, Bill Summary and Status, 112th Congress (2011–2012). http://thomas.loc.gov/cgi-bin/bdquery/z?d112:sp1068:. Accessed December 11, 2011.

Major Arthur R. Lund to Whom It May Concern, Letter, May 26, 1951; Project Title: Neuropsychiatry and Stress, December 31, 1954, Box 6, CIA Behavior Control Experiments Collection (John Marks Donation), National Security Archive.

Nelson H. Brickham, Memorandum For: Ambassador R. W. Komer, Subject: Personal Observations, May 26, 1967. http://www.thememoryhole.org/phoenix/. Accessed May 8, 2006.

Office of the President of the United States. *The Commission on the Intelligence Capabilities of the United States Regarding Weapons of Mass Destruction.* Washington, DC, March 31, 2005.

Office of the Press Secretary, The White House. "Executive Order—Periodic Review of Individuals Detained at Guantánamo Bay Naval Station Pursuant to the Authorization for Use of Military Force," March 7, 2011. http://www.whitehouse

.gov/the-press-office/2011/03/07/executive-order-periodic-review-individuals
-detained-guant-namo-bay-nava. Accessed June 29, 2011.

———. "Remarks by the President on National Security," May 21, 2009. http://
www.whitehouse.gov/the_press_office/Remarks-by-the-President-On-National
-Security-5-21-09/. Accessed September 9, 2011.

———. "President Discusses Creation of Military Commissions to Try Suspected Terrorists," September 6, 2006. http://www.whitehouse.gov/news/releases/2006/09
/print/20060906-3.html. Accessed September 8, 2006.

———. "Setting the Record Straight: JAG Leaders Say Common Article 3 Provisions Would Be 'Helpful'." http://www.whitehouse.gov/news/releases/2006/09
/print/20060915.html. Accessed February 3, 2006.

———. "Statement of President Barack Obama," April 16, 2009. http://www.white
house.gov/the_press_office/Statement-of-President-Barack-Obama-on-Release
-of-OLC-Memos/. Accessed July 21, 2009.

Office of Public Affairs, Department of Justice, "Statement of the Attorney General Regarding Investigation into the Interrogation of Certain Detainees," June 30, 2011.
http://www.justice.gov/opa/pr/2011/June/11-ag-861.html. Accessed July 4, 2011.

Paul E. Suplizio, Subj: Attack on VC Infrastructure, A Progress Report, To: CINCPAC,
November 1967. http://www.thememoryhole.org/phoenix/macv-dtg-06-09102
.pdf. Accessed May 8, 2006.

Press Release No. 1786. "Statement by the Honorable Charles W. Mayo." U.S. Delegation to the General Assembly, October 26, 1953, White House Office, National
Security Council Staff: Papers, 1953–61, Psychological Strategy Board (PSB) Central Files Series, Box 26, "PSB 383.6 [Prisoners of War] (File #2) (5)," Dwight D.
Eisenhower Library.

"Prisoner Abuse: Patterns From the Past. Electronic Briefing Book No. 122" Washington, May 12, 2004, National Security Archive. http://www.gwu.edu/%7Ensarchiv
/NSAEBB/NSAEBB122/index.htm#kubark. Accessed August 20, 2009.

Prof. Ernst Rothlin, Chief Pharmacologist, Sandoz Co., Basel, Switzerland. "d-Lysergic
Acid Diethylamide (LSD 25)," n.d., Box 6, CIA Behavior Control Experiments
Collection (John Marks Donation), National Security Archive.

"Project Title: Neuropsychiatry and Stress." Addendum. Beecher (MD 92). Final Report, "Response of Normal Men to Lysergic Acid Derivatives (Di- and Mono-
ethylamide). Correlation of Personality and Drug Reactions," December 31, 1954,
Box 6, CIA Behavior Control Experiments Collection (John Marks Donation),
National Security Archive.

Republic of Vietnam, Office of the Prime Minister, Directive of the Prime Minister on
the Neutralization of VCI, December 20, 1967. http://www.thememoryhole.org
/phoenix/directive-pm.pdf. Accessed May 8, 2006.

Ricardo S. Sanchez. "Memorandum for: C2, Combined Joint Task Force Seven,
Baghdad, Iraq 09335, Subject: CJTF-7 Interrogation and Counter-Resistance
Policy," September 14, 2003. http://www.aclu.org/SafeandFree/SafeandFree.cfm
?ID=17851&c=206. Accessed March 30, 2005.

Robert Komer, Memorandum to McGeorge Bundy and General Taylor. "Should Police Programs Be Transferred to the DOD?" Secret (Declassified), April 18, 1962. http://www.thememoryhole.org/phoenix/. Accessed May 8, 2006.

SA David A. England, Computer Crime Coordinator, 10th MP Bn (CID), 3d MP Group (CID), Baghdad, Iraq. "Agent's Investigation Report," January 2004.

Secretary of Defense C. E. Wilson, Memorandum for the Secretary of the Army, Secretary of the Navy, Secretary of the Air Force, Subject: Use of Human Volunteers in Experimental Research, February 26, 1953. http://www2.gwu.edu/~nsarchiv /radiation/dir/mstreet/commeet/meet8/brief8/tab_k/br8k1a.txt. Accessed April 6, 2011.

Secretary of Defense. "Memorandum for Chairman of the Joint Chiefs of Staff, Subject: Status of Taliban and Al Qaeda," January 19, 2002. In Karen J. Greenberg and Joshua L. Dratel, eds., *The Torture Papers: The Road to Abu Ghraib*. New York: Cambridge University Press, 2005, 80.

Speech, Council on Foreign Relations. as Delivered by Secretary of Defense Donald H. Rumsfeld, Harold Pratt House, New York, New York, Friday, February 17, 2006. http://www.defenselink.mil/speeches/2006/sp20060217-12574.html. Accessed May 20, 2005.

Statement of Senator John McCain, Amendment on Army Field Manual, Arizona, News Center, July 25, 2005. http://mccain.senate.gov/index.cfm?fuse action=Newscenter4.ViewPressRelease&Content id=1595. Accessed July 29, 2005.

Steven G. Bradbury, Office of the Principal Deputy Assistant Attorney General, Office of Legal Counsel. "Memorandum for John A. Rizzo Senior Deputy Counsel, Central Intelligence Agency: Re: Application of United States Obligations under Article 16 of the Convention against Torture to Certain Techniques That May be Used in the Interrogation of High Value al Qaeda Detainees," May 30, 2005. http://www.justice.gov/olc/docs/memo-bradbury2005.pdf. Accessed October 4, 2011.

———. Office of Legal Counsel. "Memorandum for John A. Rizzo Senior Deputy General Counsel, Central Intelligence Agency, Re: Application of 18 U.S.C. §§ 2340–2340A to the Combined Use of Certain Techniques in the Interrogation of High Value al Qaeda Detainees," May 10, 2005. http://www.hsdl .org/?view&did=37512. Accessed June 29, 2011.

———. "Memorandum for John A. Rizzo Senior Deputy Counsel, Central Intelligence Agency," May 30, 2005. http://media.luxmedia.com/aclu/olc_05302005_ bradbury.pdf. Accessed June 29, 2011.

Technical Report no. 3331-45. "German aviation medical research at the Dachau concentration camp," Oct. 1945, U.S. Naval Technical Mission to Europe, H MS c64, Box 11, Harvard Medical Library.

T. J. Harrington, Deputy Assistant Director, Counterterrorism Division, Federal Bureau of Investigation, Letter to Major General Donald J. Ryder, Criminal Investigation Command, Department of the Army, July 14, 2004. http://www.aclu.org /torturefoia/released/FBI_4622-2624.pdf. Accessed March 8, 2005.

United States, *Weekly Compilation of Presidential Documents* 32, no. 34. Washington, DC: Government Printing Office, 1996.

U.S. Army. "SCHREIBER, Dr. Walter P., December 15, 1949." In Egmont R. Koch and Michael Wech, *Deckname Artischocke*, 94. Munich: Random House, 2003.

U.S. Army Intelligence Center and School, Study Manual: Handling of Sources—1989 (Secret. Not Releasable to Foreign Nationals; Declassified by Authority of the Secretary of the Army, September 19, 1996), Box 2: Intelligence Training Course Manuals, Folder: Handling of Sources, National Security Archive.

U.S. Department of the Army, U.S. Army Intelligence Center and Fort Huachuca, Memorandum for Deputy Chief of Staff for Intelligence, Subject: History of Project X, [Sgd.] William J. Teeter, September 12, 1991, File: Project X, Consortium News, Arlington, Viriginia.

U.S. Department of Defense. "Army Regulation 15–6: Final Report: Investigation into FBI Allegation of Detainee Abuse at Guantanamo Bay, Cuba Detention Facility" (April 1, 2005; amended June 9, 2005). http://www.defenselink.mil/news/Jul2005 /d20050714report.pdf. Accessed July 18, 2005.

———. Assistant to the Secretary of Defense, Memorandum for Secretary of Defense, Subject: Interim Report on Improper Material in USSOUTHCOM Training Manuals (U)-Information Memorandum, October 4, 1991, File: Project X, Consortium News, Arlington, Virginia.

———. Office of the Assistant Secretary of Defense Command, Control, Communications and Intelligence, Memorandum for the Record, Subject: USSOUTHCOM CI Training-Supplemental Information (U), July 31, 1991, File: Project X, Consortium News, Arlington, Virginia.

———. Office of the Deputy Chief of Staff for Intelligence, Robert W. Singleton, Memorandum Thru the General Counsel, ATTN: PWC, Subject: History of Project X, November 4, 1991, File: Project X, Consortium News, Arlington, Virginia.

———. Office of the Assistant Secretary of Defense Command, Control, Communications and Intelligence, Point Paper Concerning USSOUTHCOM Proposed Counterintelligence (CI) Training to Foreign Governments, July 30, 1991, File: Project X, Consortium News, Arlington, Virginia.

———. Assistant to the Secretary of Defense, Report of Investigation: Improper Material in Spanish-Language Intelligence Training Manuals, March 10, 1992.

———. Special Defense Department Briefing, July 7, 2005. http://www.defenselink .mil/transcripts/2005/tr20050707-3301.html. Accessed July 11, 2005.

———. "Working Group Report on Detainee Interrogations in the Global War on Terrorism: Assessment of Legal, Historical, Policy, and Operational Considerations." March 6, 2003. www.torturingdemocracy.org/documents/20030404.pdf. Accessed August 4, 2011.

U.S. Department of Justice, Office of Legal Counsel. "Memorandum for William J. Haynes, II, General Counsel, Department of Defense," December 28, 2001,

From: Patrick F. Philbin, Deputy Assistant Attorney General, and John C. Yoo, Deputy Assistant Attorney General. In Karen J. Greenberg and Joshua L. Dratel, eds., *The Torture Papers: The Road to Abu Ghraib*. New York: Cambridge University Press, 2005, 29–37.

U.S. Department of State. "Second Periodic Report of the United States of America to the Committee against Torture," May 6, 2006. http://www.state.gov/g/drl/rls/45738.htm. Accessed February 21, 2006.

U.S. General Accounting Office. *Stopping U.S. Assistance to Foreign Police and Prisons.* Washington, DC: U.S. General Accounting Office, 1976.

U.S. National Security Council. "Memorandum of Discussion at the 229th Meeting of the National Security Council, Tuesday, December 21, 1954." U.S. Department of State, *Foreign Relations of the United States, 1952–1954. National Security Affairs* (Washington, DC: Government Printing Office, 1954), 832–44.

———. "Supplemental Progress Report on Actions Taken Pursuant to NSC Action 1290-d," September 6, 1956, U.S. State Department, *Foreign Relations of the United States, 1955–57, Volume X, Foreign Aid and Economic Defense Policy* (Washington, DC: Government Printing Office, 1956), 107–17.

Werner E. Michel, Assistant to the Secretary of Defense (Intelligence Oversight). "Subject: Improper Material in Spanish-Language Intelligence Training Manuals," March 10, 1992, Box 2, Intelligence Training Source Manuals, Folder: Untitled, National Security Archive.

White House, National Security Action Memorandum No 362, Subject: Responsibility for U.S. Role in Pacification (Revolutionary Development, May 9, 1967, Lyndon Baines Johnson Presidential Library. http://www.lbjlib.utexas.edu/johnson/archives.hom/nsams/nsam362.asp. Accessed December 19, 2011.

———. President Obama, News Conference, J.W. Marriott Ihilani Resort and Spa, Kapolei, Hawaii, The White House, November 13, 2011. http://www.whitehouse.gov/photos-and-video/video/2011/11/13/president-obama-holds-press-conference-apec-summit#transcript. Accessed November 20, 2011.

———. "President Outlines Steps to Help Iraq Achieve Democracy and Freedom," May 24, 2004. http://www.whitehouse.gov/news/release/2004/05/print/20040424-10.html. Accessed June 14, 2004.

———. President's Statement on Signing of H.R. 2863. "Department of Defense, Emergency Supplemental Appropriations to Address Hurricanes in the Gulf of Mexico, and Pandemic Influenza Act, 2006," December 30, 2005. http://georgewbush-whitehouse.archives.gov/news/releases/2005/12/print/20051230-8.html. Accessed September 2, 2009.

William J. Clinton, Memorandum for the Vice President, Subject: U.S. Policy on Counterterrorsim (U), June 21, 1992. http://www.fas.org/irp/offdocs/pdd39.htm. Accessed March 24, 2010.

William J. Haynes II, General Counsel, Department of Defense, For: Secretary of Defense. "Subject: Counter-Resistance Techniques," November 27, 2002. http://www.gwu.edu/~nsarchiv/NSAEBB/NSAEBB127/02.12.02.pdf. Accessed November 30, 2011.

U.S. Court and Legal Documents

Danilo P. Vizmanos, Proof of Claim Form for Torture Victims, *In Re. Estate of Ferdinand E. Marcos Human Rights Litigation*, MDL No. 840—Class Action. May 5, 1993.

In Re Guantanamo Detainee Cases, 355 F. Supp. 2d 443 (2005), Memorandum Opinion Denying in Part and Granting in Part Respondents' Motion to Dismiss or for Judgment as of Law, Joyce Hens Green, District Judge, U.S. District Court, District of Columbia, January 31, 2005. http://www.leagle.com/xmlResult.aspx?xmldoc=2005798355FSupp2d443_1752.xml&docbase=CSLWAR2–1986–2006. Accessed June 15, 2011.

New York Office of the Professions—Central Administration, Dr. Stephen Reisner, Licensing Complaint—John Francis Leso, NY License # 013492, Center for Justice and Accountability. http://www.cja.org/article.php?id=885. Accessed August 8, 2011.

Plea Agreement, *United States v. John Lindh*, U.S. District Court for the Eastern District of Virginia, Alexandria Division. http://www.justice.gov/ag/pleaagreement.htm. Accessed June 13, 2011.

Shafiq Rasul et al., Petition for Writ of Habeas Corpus, U.S. District Court for the District of Columbia, February 19, 2002, Counsel for the Petitioners, Joseph Margulies et al. http://www.haguejusticeportal.net/Docs/NLP/US/Rasul_DC_District_Court_Habeas_Corpus_19-2-2002.pdf. Accessed June 13, 2011.

U.S. Code, Title 18, Part I, Chapter 113C, § 2340. http://www.law.cornell.edu/uscode/uscode18/usc_sec_18_00002340–000-.html. Accessed July 21, 2009.

U.S. Code, Section 2340, 18 USC§ 2340–2340A. http://codes.lp.findlaw.com/uscode/18/I/113C/2340. Accessed September 20, 2011.

U.S. District Court for the District of Columbia, *Shafiq Rasul v. George Walker Bush*, No. CV: 02-0299 (CKK), First Amended Petition for Writ of Habeas Corpus, February 2002. http://guantanamobile.org/pdf/2002motiontodismiss.pdf. Accessed June 13, 2011.

U.S. District Court, Eastern District of Virginia, *United States of America v. John Kiriakou*, Case Number 1:12MJ33, "Criminal Complaint." http://www.justice.gov/opa/documents/kiriakou-complaint.pdf. Accessed January 27, 2012.

U.S. District Court, Eastern District of Virginia, *United States of America v. John Kiriakou*, Case Number 1:12MJ33, Joseph Capitano, "Affidavit in Support of Criminal Complaint and Arrest Warrant," January 23, 2012. http://www.justice.gov/opa/documents/kiriakou-complaint.pdf. Accessed January 27, 2012.

U.S. Supreme Court, Oral Arguments, *Donald H. Rumsfeld v. Jose Padilla*, No. 03-1027. http://www.supremecourtus.gov/oral_arguments/argument_transcripts/03-1027.pdf. Accessed July 5, 2004.

U.S. Supreme Court, *Rasul v. Bush*, No. 03-334, June 28, 2004. http://caselaw

.lp.findlaw.com/scripts/printer_friendly.pl?page=us/ooo/o3-334.html. Accessed December 10, 2011.

U.S. Supreme Court, *Salim Ahmed Hamdan v. Donald H. Rumsfeld*, No. 05-184, Opinion of Stevens, J., June 29, 2006. http://www.law.cornell.edu/supct/html/05-184 .ZO.html. Accessed April 6, 2011.

U.S. Supreme Court, *Salim Ahmed Hamdan v. Donald H. Rumsfeld*, No. 05-184, Oral Argument, March 28, 2006. http://www.supremecourtus.gov/oral_arguments /argument_transcripts/05-184pdf. Accessed July 7, 2006.

U.S. Supreme Court, *Salim Ahmed Hamdan v. Donald H. Rumsfeld*, No. 05-184, Respondents' Motion to Dismiss for Lack of Jurisdiction, January 2006. http:// www.usdoj.gov/osg/briefs/2005/3mer/2mer/2005-0184.resp.pdf. Accessed January 24, 2005.

United Nations Documents

United Nations. Commission on Human Rights, 61st Session, *Report of the United Nations High Commissioner for Human Rights and Follow Up to the World Conference on Human Rights*. Geneva: Commission on Human Rights, E/CN.4/2005/4, Advance Edited Edition, June 9, 2004.

———. *Convention against Torture and Other Cruel, Inhuman or Degrading Treatment or Punishment*. http://www.hrweb.org/legal/cat.html. Accessed September 20, 2011.

———. *Convention against Torture and Other Cruel Inhuman or Degrading Treatment or Punishment, Reservation Made by the United States of America*. http://www.unhchr. ch/tbs/doc.nsf/0/5d7ce66547377b1f802567fd0056b533?OpenDocument. Accessed September 18, 2011.

———. Economic and Social Council, Commission on Human Rights. "Situation of Detainees at Guantánamo Bay" (E/CN.4/2006/120, February 15, 2006). http://news.bbc.co.uk/1/shared/bsp/hi/pdfs/16_02_06_UN_Guantánamo.pdfs. Accessed February 20, 2006.

———. "Secretary-General Kofi Annan's Remarks at Press Encounter Following Monthly Luncheon with Security Council Members," February 16, 2006. http://www.un.org/apps/sg/printoffthecuff.asp?.nid=834. Accessed February 21, 2006.

United Nations Assistance Mission in Afghanistan, UN Office of the High Commissioner for Human Rights. "Treatment of Conflict Related Detainees in Afghan Custody" (Kabul, October 2011). http://unama.unmissions.org/Portals /UNAMA/Documents/October10_%202011_UNAMA_Detention_Full-Report _ENG.pdf. Accessed October 17, 2011.

Office of the United Nations High Commissioner for Human Rights. "Convention against Torture and Other Cruel, Inhuman or Degrading Treatment or Punishment." http://www2.ohchr.org/english/law/cat.htm. Accessed July 14, 2009.

Foreign Government and NGO Documents

American Civil Liberties Union. "Justice Department Wrong to Let Torture Lawyers Off the Hook, Says ACLU." April 14, 2011. http://www.aclu.org/national -security/justice-department-wrong-let-torture-lawyers-hook-says-aclu. Accessed June 29, 2011.

———. "Senators Demand the Military Lock Up of American Citizens in a 'Battlefield' They Define as Being Right Outside Your Window." http://www.aclu .org/blog/national-security/senators-demand-military-lock-american-citizens -battlefield-they-define-being. Accessed December 11, 2011.

Amnesty International. *Below the Radar: Secret Flight to Torture and "Disappearance."* AMR 51/051/2006, April 5, 2006. http://www.amnesty.org/en/library/info /AMR51/051/2006. Accessed June 13, 2011.

———. "European Governments Must Provide Justice for Victims of CIA Porgrammes." November 15, 2010. http://www.amnesty.org/en/news-and-updates /report/european-governments-must-provide-justice-victims-cia-programmes -2010-11-15. Accessed June 26, 2011.

———. *Human Rights Violations in the Philippines.* New York: Amnesty International USA, 1982.

———. "Memorandum to the U.S. Government on the Report of the UN Committee against Torture and the Question of Closing Guantánamo." AMR 51/093/2006, June 23, 2006. http://www.amnesty.org/en/library/info/AMR51/093/2006/en. Accessed June 14, 2011.

———. *Open Secret: Mounting Evidence of Europe's Complicity in Rendition and Secret Detention.* November 2010, Executive Summary. http://www.amnesty.org/en /library/info/EUR01/024/2010/en. Accessed June 26, 2011.

———. *Philippines: The Killing Goes On.* New York: Amnesty International, 1992.

———. *Philippines: Unlawful Killings by Military and Paramilitary Forces.* New York: Amnesty International, 1988.

———. *Report of an Amnesty International Mission to the Republic of the Philippines 11–28 November 1981.* London: Amnesty International, 1982.

———. *Report on Torture.* London: Duckworth, 1975.

———. *Torture in Greece: The First Torturers' Trial 1975.* London: Amnesty International, 1977.

———. *Torture in the Eighties.* London: Martin Robinson, 1984.

———. *USA: Trials in Error.* July 16, 2009. http://www.amnesty.org/en/library/info /AMR51/083/2009. Accessed June 30, 2011.

Australian Electoral Commission. Virtual Tally Room, NSW Division, Bennelong, Two Candidate Preferred Preference Flow, 12/11/2007. http://results.aec.gov .au/13745/website/HouseDivisionTcpFlow-13745-105.htm. Accessed June 15, 2011.

Brigadier General Isidoro de Guzman, Subject: Command Actions during the Crisis, To: Chief of Staff, NAFP [New Armed Forces of the Philippines], February 28, 1986.

"Bring David Hicks Home." http://www.getup.org.au/campaigns/bring-david-hicks -home. Accessed June 14, 2011.

Center for Constitutional Rights. "Detention in Afghanistan and Guantanamo Bay: Statement of Shafiq Rasul, Asif Iqbal and Rhuhel Ahmed," July 26, 2004. http:// ccrjustice.org/v2/legal/september_11th/docs/Guantanamo_composite_statement _FINAL.pdf. Accessed June 13, 2011.

Council of Europe, Secretary General. "Report by the Secretary General under Article 52 ECHR on the question of the secret detention and transport of detainees suspected of terrorist acts, notably by or at the instigation of foreign agencies." SG/Inf [2006], February 28, 2006.

Davis, Reg, and Harry James. *The Public Safety Story: An Informal Recollection of Events and Individuals Leading to the Formation of the A.I.D. Office of Public Safety*. Santee: The Public Safety Newsletter, 2001. http://pdf.usaid.gov/pdf_docs /PCAAB135.pdf. Accessed November 2, 2011.

Downer, Alexander, and Philip Ruddock. "Government Finalises Transfer of Prisoner Arrangement with United States." Joint Media Release, May 9, 2006. http://www .foreignminister.gov.au/releases/2006/joint_ruddock_prisoner_tranf_100506 .html. Accessed June 14, 2011.

Gage, Sir William. *The Baha Mousa Public Inquiry Report: Volume I*. London: The Stationery Office, HC 1452-I, 2011. http://www.bahamousainquiry.org/f_report /vol%20i/volume%20i.pdf. Accessed September 21, 2011.

Human Rights First. "David Hicks' Father Speaks; Day Three." August 25, 2004. http://www.humanrightsfirst.org/2004/08/25/david-hicks'-father-speaks/. Accessed June 13, 2011.

———. "Military Commission Trial Observation: Enter the Federal Court." November 8, 2004. http://www.humanrightsfirst.org/our-work/law-and-security /military-commissions/gitmo-diary/. Accessed May 18, 2006.

———. "Military Commission Trial Observation: Setting the Stage for Justice." November 1–2, 2004. http://www.humanrightsfirst.org/our-work/law-and-security /military-commissions/gitmo-diary/. Accessed May 18, 2006.

———. "Retired Military Leaders Decry Torture Provisions in Defense Authorization Act." November 28, 2011. http://www.humanrightsfirst.org/2011/11/28/retired -military-leaders-decry-torture-provisions-in-defense-authorization-act/. Accessed December 11, 2011.

Human Rights Watch. *Getting Away with Torture*. July 12, 2011. http://www.hrw.org /node/100262/section/7. Accessed July 28, 2011.

———. "News Release: Landmark Torture Ban Undercut." December 15, 2005. http:// www.hrw.org/en/news/2005/12/15/us-landmark-torture-ban-undercut. Accessed September 2, 2009.

———. *The Road to Abu Ghraib*. June 8, 2004. http://www.hrw.org/en/reports /2004/06/08/road-abu-ghraib. Accessed July, 21, 2009.

———. "United States: Investigate Bush, Other Top Officials for Torture." July 11, 2011. http://www.hrw.org/en/node/100390. Accessed July 17, 2011.

"Ireland v. The United Kingdom." No. 5310/17, European Court of Human Rights, January 18, 1978, Separate Opinion of Judge Evrigenis." http://cmiskp.echr.coe .int/tkp197/view.asp?item=1&portal=hbkm&action=html&highlight=5310/71& sessionid=26859787&skin=hudoc-en. Accessed July 19, 2009.

Lasry, Lex. "United States v. David Matthew Hicks: First Report of the Independent Legal Observer for the Law Council of Australia—September 2004." http://www .lawcouncil.asn.au/shadomx/apps/fms/fmsdownload.cfm?file_uuid=CDFC66F7 -1E4F-17FA-D23C-3E002478C5D6&siteName=lca. Accessed June 13, 2011.

———."United States v. David Matthew Hicks: Report of the Independent Legal Observer for the Law Council of Australia." July 2005. http://www.lawcouncil .asn.au/shadomx/apps/fms/fmsdownload.cfm?file_uuid=CE02C8B1-1E4F-17FA -D223-7DF89CC63161&siteName=lca. Accessed June 13, 2011.

Law Council of Australia. "Bring Home David Hicks: It's a 'No-Brainer.'" Media Release, November 1, 2006. https://www.lawcouncil.asn.au/media/news-article.cfm ?article=B55FE54D-1E4F-17FA-D274-BE9CFF8D9BC6. Accessed June 15, 2011.

Lord Parker of Waddington. *Report of the Committee of Privy Counsellors Appointed to Consider Authorised Procedures for the Interrogation of Persons Suspected of Terrorism*. London: Stationery Office, Cmnd. 4901, 1972.

Marty, Dick. *Alleged Secret Detentions and Unlawful Inter-State Transfers Involving Council of Europe Member States*. Parliamentary Assembly, Council of Europe, Report 10957, June 12, 2006. http://assembly.coe.int/main.asp?link=/documents /workingdocs/doc06/edoc10957.htm. Accessed September 27, 2006.

Nunca Mas: The Report of the Argentine National Commission on the Disappeared. New York: Farrar, Straus and Giroux, 1986.

Olivas, General Prospero. "Narration of Activities of CG PCM/DIR, MPF, 22–28 Feb 86."

Opinion of George Cooper, Q.C., Regarding Canadian Government Funding of the Allan Memorial Institute in the 1950's and 1960's. Ottawa: Minister of Supply and Services Canada, Cat. No. J2-63, 1986.

Pearlstein, Deborah. "Military Commission Trial Observation, Day 5: August 27, 2004." Human Rights First. http://www.humanrightsfirst.org/us_law/detainees /military_commission_diary.htm#day1. Accessed May 16, 2006.

Prime Minister Howard Doorstop Interview, the Willard Intercontinental Hotel, Washington, DC, Interview Transcript, July 16, 2005, Subject: Washington Visit, David Hicks, ASIO Head, Indonesian Ambassador, Embassy of the United States, Canberra. http://usrsaustralia.state.gov/us-oz/2005/07/16/pm1.html. Accessed June 14, 2011.

Report of the International Committee of the Red Cross (ICRC) on the Treatment by the Coalition Forces of Prisoners of War and Other Protected Persons by the Geneva Conventions in Iraq during Arrest, Internment and Interrogation. February 2004. http://www.redress.btinternet.co.uk/icrc_iraq.pdf.

Republic of the Philippines. *The Final Report of the Fact-Finding Commission (pursuant to R.A. No. 6832)*. Manila: Bookmark, 1990.

———. National Unification Commission. "Principles for Characterization of Offenses for Confidence-Building and Amnesty." March 11, 1993.

———. Office of the President, Executive Order No. 19, Fidel V. Ramos, September 1, 1992.

Tellez, Eliseo C., Jr. Proof of Claim Form for Torture Victims, December 8, 1992, Samahan ng mga Ex-Detainee Laban sa Detensyon at para sa Amnestia, Manila.

Newspapers and Mass Media

ABC News
ABC Radio (Australia)
The Advertiser
Armed Forces Press Services
Associated Press
The Australian
Australian Broadcasting Corporation
Baguio Midland Courier
Baltimore Sun
Bangkok Post
BBC News
BBC News US and Canada
BBC Radio 4
Boston Globe
Bulletin Today
Bureau of Investigative Journalism
Canberra Times
CBC News
CBS News
Chicago Daily Tribune
Chicago Sun-Times
Christian Science Monitor
Clarkson Integrator (Potsdam, NY)
CNET News
CNN
CNN World
Copenhagen Post
Daily Cardinal (Madison, WI)
Daily Express (London)
Daily Globe (Manila)
Daily News (New York)
Denver Post
Le Devoir (Montreal)
FOX News

The Gazette (Colorado Springs)
The Gazette (Montreal)
Globe and Mail (Toronto)
The Guardian (London)
Honolulu Star-Bulletin
The Independent (London)
The Inquirer (Philadelphia)
Los Angeles Times
Malaya (Manila)
Manila Bulletin
Manila Chronicle
Manly Daily (Australia)
Marine Corps Times
McGill Tribune
Meet the Press
Mr. & Ms. (Manila)
MSNBC
Nashua Telegraph
National Public Radio
National Review Online
NBC News
New York Times
Newsday (New York)
Newswire
The Observer (London)
Palm Beach Arts Paper
PBS
PC Journal (Manila)
Philippine Daily Inquirer
Philippine Free Press
Philippine Star
Politico
Signal Newspaper (Santa Clara, CA)
The Star-Ledger (Newark, NJ)
Stars and Stripes (European Edition)
Sydney Morning Herald
Tanod (Manila)
Time
The Times (London)
Times of India
Toledo Blade
Toronto Star
USA Today

Washington Post
Washington Times
Wisconsin State Journal

Motion Pictures and Documentary Films

Casino Royale. Directed by Martin Campbell. Columbia Pictures, 2006.
The Passion of the Christ. Directed by Mel Gibson. Newmarket Films, 2004.
The President versus David Hicks. Directed by Curtis Levy and Bentley Dean. Ronin Films, 2004.
The Road to Guantanamo. Directed by Michael Winterbottom. Revolution Films, 2006.
Salò or the 120 Days of Sodom. Directed by Pier Paolo Pasolini. Criterion Collection, DVD, No. 17d, 2008.

Conferences and Presentations

Co, Leoncio. University of the Philippines, Interdisciplinary Forum on Political Detainees, April 16, 1986.
Mori, Major Michael. "Why David Hicks Will Not Receive a Fair Trial Come His Day in Court." Melbourne University Law School, Annual Alumni Lecture, April 6, 2006. http://www.law.unimelb.edu.au/go/alumni. Accessed May 12, 2006.
Ratner, Michael. University of California–Davis. "Conversation About Guantanamo," May 5, 2006.

Theses and Dissertations

Hernandez, Carolina G. "The Extent of Civilian Control of the Military in the Philippines: 1946–1976." Doctoral dissertation, State University of New York at Buffalo, 1979.
Lobe, Thomas David. "U.S. Police Assistance for the Third World." Doctoral dissertation, University of Michigan, 1975.
Maynard, Harold W. "A Comparison of Military Elite Role Perceptions in Indonesia and the Philippines." Doctoral dissertation, American University, 1976.
Selochan, Viberto. "Professionalization and Politicization of the Armed Forces of the Philippines." Doctoral dissertation, Australian National University, 1990.

Interviews and Personal Communications

Ang, Maria Elena. Interview. Sydney. May 9, 1989.
Balbas, Colonel Braulio. Interview. Fort Bonifacio, Manila, Philippines. July 25, 1986.
Dratel, Joshua. Telephone interview. Madison, WI, to New York, NY. May 17, 2006.
Echanis, Randall. Interview. University of the Philippines, Manila. April 16, 1986.

Honasan, Colonel Gregorio "Gringo." Interview. Manila, Philippines. July 24, 1986.

Jalandoni, Luis. Telephone interview. Sydney, Australia, to Utrecht, Netherlands. February 18, 1988.

Kapunan, Colonel Eduardo "Red." Interview. Manila, Philippines. July 6, 1986.

Koch, Egmont. Email. March 13, May 29, 2007.

Komer, Robert. Interview II, August 18, 1970, Oral History Interviews, Lyndon Baines Johnson Presidential Library, Austin, TX.

Malajacan, Lieutenant Colonel Marcelino "Jake." Interview. Manila, Philippines. August 29, 1986.

Mori, Major Michael Dante. Telephone interview. Madison, WI, to Washington, DC. May 12, 2006.

Ocampo, Satur. Interview. Quezon City, Philippines. August 27, 1996.

Ratner, Michael. Telephone interview. Madison, WI, to New York, NY. May 17, 2006.

Retired medical doctors and McGill medical school graduates. Telephone interviews from Madison, WI. March 13, 2006, September 30, October 1, 2007.

Robles, Rex. Interview. Manila, Philippines. July 25, 1986.

Sales, Leigh. Interview. Sydney, Australia. August 15, 2006.

Scott, Peter Dale. Personal communication. Melbourne, Australia. August 10, 2006.

Sin, Jaime Cardinal. Interview. Manila, Philippines. July 21, 1986.

Tadiar, General Artemio. Interview. Fort Bonifacio, Manila, Philippines. August 31, 1986.

Yee, James. Interview. University of California–Davis. May 5, 2006.

Index

Critical Human Rights

Court of Remorse: Inside the International Criminal Tribunal for Rwanda
Thierry Cruvellier; translated by Chari Voss

Torture and Impunity: The U.S. Doctrine of Coercive Interrogation
Alfred W. McCoy

Remaking Rwanda: State Building and Human Rights after Mass Violence
Edited by Scott Straus and Lars Waldorf

Beyond Displacement: Campesinos, Refugees, and Collective Action in the Salvadoran Civil War
Molly Todd

The Politics of Necessity: Community Organizing and Democracy in South Africa
Elke Zuern